Best Jobs for the 21st Century™ for College Graduates

REFERENCE

J. Michael Farr and LaVerne L. Ludden, Ed.D.
with database work by Paul Mangin

jist *Publishing*

Best Jobs for the 21st Century for College Graduates
© 2000 JIST Publishing, Inc.

Published by JIST Works, an imprint of JIST Publishing, Inc.
8902 Otis Avenue
Indianapolis, IN 46216-1033
Phone: 800-648-JIST
E-mail: editorial@jist.com

Fax: 800-JIST-FAX
Web site: www.jist.com

Also in the *Best Jobs* series:
Best Jobs for the 21ˢᵗ Century, Second Edition

Quantity discounts are available for JIST books. Please call our sales department at 1-800-648-5478 for a free catalog and more information.

Printed in the United States of America
05 04 03 02 01   9 8 7 6 5 4 3 2

Library of Congress Cataloging-in-Publication Data
Farr, J. Michael.
    Best jobs for the 21st century for college graduates / J. Michael Farr and LaVerne L. Ludden.
        p. cm.
    Includes bibliographical references.
    ISBN 1-56370-608-3
        1. Vocational guidance. 2. College graduates—Employment. 3.
Occupations—Forecasting. I. Ludden, LaVerne, 1949-

HF5381 .F4563 2000
331.7'0235—dc21

00-023825

ISBN 1-56370-608-3

Credits and Acknowledgments

The occupational information used in this book is based on data obtained from both the U.S. Department of Labor and the U.S. Department of Commerce. These sources provide the most authoritative source of occupational information available. The job descriptions in Section 2 are based on information obtained from the Occupational Information Network (O*NET). The O*NET database of occupational information was developed by a team of researchers and developers working under the direction of the U.S. Department of Labor. They, in turn, were assisted by thousands of employers who provided details on the nature of work provided in the many thousands of job samplings that were used in the development of this database.

The O*NET database is based on the substantial work done on an earlier occupational database that was used to develop the *Dictionary of Occupational Titles* and other information sources. That database was first used in the 1939 edition of the *Dictionary of Occupational Titles* and has been continuously updated since. All of this work, over many years, has formed the basis for much of the occupational information used by employers, job seekers, career counselors, education and training institutions, researchers, policy makers, and many others. We have used Release 1.0, the most recent version of the O*NET database, which was released in December 1998. We appreciate and thank the U.S. Department of Labor for their efforts and expertise in providing such a rich source of data.

Please consider that the occupational information in this book has its limitations. It should not be used in legal settings as a basis for occupational injuries or other matters. This is because occupational information contained in this book reflects jobs as they have been found to occur in general, but they may not coincide in every respect with the content of jobs as performed in particular establishments or at certain localities. Users of this information demanding specific job requirements should supplement this data with local information detailing jobs within their community.

About This Book

We've written this book for:

- High school students thinking about going to college
- Adults considering a college degree
- College students thinking about changing their major
- College graduates who have just completed a college degree and want to find the best job
- College graduates who have a job but want to find a better one

The "best" job for you is a personal decision that only you can make. But there are objective criteria that can be used to identify jobs that are, for example, better paying than other jobs with similar duties. And that is what we have done in this book—we have sorted through the data for ALL jobs that typically require an associate, bachelor's, master's, professional, or doctor's degree.

There were 281 jobs that met these criteria, and descriptions for all of them are included in Section 2 of this book. We are not suggesting that all of these jobs are good ones for you to consider—they are not. But we present such a wide range of jobs to consider that you are likely to find one or more that will stand out—and these are the jobs you should consider most in your future career planning.

We've arranged the jobs into a variety of useful lists in Section 1. For example, you can find lists there for the best paying jobs, fastest growing jobs, and jobs with the most annual openings. We have also arranged the jobs in groupings based on interests, age, and gender, and in other ways that are very useful for career planning.

We encourage you to use this book to explore your career options. The lists in Section 1 are interesting and you can simply start there (who can resist knowing the fastest growing or highest paying jobs, for example). You can also use the Table of Contents to identify jobs that interest you. Then look up, in Section 2, the descriptions for jobs that interest you most.

Using this book is that easy. Unfortunately, making good career and educational decisions is more complex, but we hope that this book will help.

We hope you find this book as interesting to browse as we did in putting it together. We have tried to make it easy to use and as interesting as occupational information can be.

We wish you well in your career and in your life.

Contents at a Glance

Summary of Major Sections

Introduction

Good information on how to use the book for exploring career options, where the information came from, and other details.

Section 1: The Best Jobs Lists

The entire section consists of a series of lists presenting occupations sorted in different ways. It provides an effective way of identifying jobs with high pay, fast growth, or the most openings—or a combination of all three—as well as other useful criteria. Each of the listed jobs is described in Section 2. The Best Jobs lists are organized into major categories including: by age group, level of education, interests, and occupational types; for part-timers, self-employed, men, and women; and, of course, by best overall jobs.

Section 2: The Best Jobs Directory

Useful descriptions for the 281 jobs that typically require a two- or four-year college degree or more. The descriptions include details on what a person does in the job, average earnings, training and education required, key skills, similar jobs, training time, related college majors, and courses required. Arranged in alphabetic order.

Skills Appendix

A detailed explanation of each of the skills listed in Section 2, as required by specific jobs.

Jobs Described in Section 2

Accountants and auditors
Actuaries
Administrative services managers
Aerospace engineers
Agricultural and food scientists
Animal breeders and trainers
Architects
Artists and commercial artists
Atmospheric and Space Scientists
Biological scientists
Budget analysts
Cardiology technologists
Chemical engineers
Chemists
Chiropractors
Civil engineers
Clergy
Clinical laboratory technologists
College and university faculty
Communication, transportation, and
    utilities managers
Computer engineers
Computer programmers
Computer scientists
Construction managers
Counselors
Credit analysts
Curators, archivists, museum technicians,
    and restorers
Dental hygienists
Dentists
Designers
Dietitians and nutritionists
Director of Religious Education and
    Activities
Economists
Education administrators

Table of Contents

Table of Contents

Table of Contents

Table of Contents

Table of Contents

Introduction

This introduction is designed to help you better understand and use the rest of the book. We've kept it short and nontechnical in hopes that this will encourage you to actually read it.

Jobs are becoming increasingly complex. The use of computers, telecommunications devices, and specialized medical equipment are just some examples of technology that have made jobs more complicated. The need to understand advances in economic projections, systems theory, genetics, and molecular structures are other examples of greater job complexity. High skilled jobs demand high skilled workers.

The more skills you have the more valuable you become to an employer. A college education develops many skills that employers want in today's labor market. Some college majors—such as accounting, counseling, teaching, engineering, and nursing—prepare you with specific skills needed for a specific occupation. But a college education provides you with many general skills and experiences that will help you in the job market, such as researching, problem solving, reading, writing, speaking, critical thinking, meeting deadlines, and time management.

Employers value the skills most college graduates gain as a result of their education. As a result, college graduates often have higher earnings and experience lower rates of unemployment than those with less education. Look at the following table to see just how valuable education can be.

VALUE OF EDUCATION

Level of Education	Average Annual Earnings	Unemployment Rate
Professional degree	$71,700	1.3%
Doctorate	$62,400	1.4%
Master's Degrees	$50,000	1.6%
Bachelor's Degree	$40,100	1.9%
Associate Degree	$31,700	2.5%
Some College But No Degree	$30,400	3.2%
High School Graduate	$26,000	4.0%
High School Drop Out	$19,700	7.1%

As you can see, education pays off. Someone with a two-year associate degree will earn during his or her worklife an average of $228,000 more than someone with a high school diploma—and those with a four-year college degree will earn about $564,000 more.

All of the jobs we've included in our lists met our criteria for fast growth, high pay, or high number of job openings. All jobs listed typically require a four-year college degree.

We think this book will help anyone who either has a college degree, is considering getting one, or who is trying to decide on a college major. We hope you find our approach interesting and we hope that it encourages you to uncover possibilities for the future that you may not have previously considered.

How We Selected the Occupations

We gave a bit of information in the "About This Book" statement at the beginning of this book but here are a few more details about the occupations we selected to include in this book:

1. We started with the jobs included in the new O*NET database. The O*NET is a new database of occupational information developed by the U.S. Department of Labor. It includes information on about 1,200 occupations. The O*NET is now the primary source of detailed information on occupations, replacing the earlier *Dictionary of Occupational Titles* database. We used the O*NET as a basis for this book because the information is the newest and most reliable available from any source.

2. Because we wanted to include earnings, growth, and other data not included in the O*NET, we cross-referenced information on earnings developed by the U.S. Bureau of Labor Statistics (BLS) and U.S. Census Bureau. This information is the most reliable information we could obtain, but the BLS and Census Bureau earnings data use a different system of job titles than the O*NET. We were able to link the two systems and tie BLS data to many of the O*NET job titles we used to develop this book.

    Without going into the technical details, we'd like to provide a little warning about this data. The Bureau of Labor Statistics and Census Bureau use two methods to calculate data about occupations. One method may result in different data for the same occupation than another produces. We've tried to use the data that we think is most up-to-date and accurate. Sometimes it came from one source known as the Occupation and Employment Statistics and at other times from the Current Population Survey. As you look at the data, keep in mind that they are estimates. They give you a general idea about the number of workers employed, annual earnings, rate of job growth, and annual job openings. While the information comes from reliable sources, we suggest you use the data with care and common sense.

3. We then went through the resulting list of occupations and included those that require a either a two-year associate degree or a four-year college degree or higher. This yielded 115 BLS jobs that linked to 281 O*NET jobs. These 281 O*NET occupations, then, are the ones we included in this book.

Section 1: The Best Jobs Lists Sorted by a Variety of Criteria

Section 1 consists of a series of lists consisting of jobs sorted in a variety of ways. We had some fun in putting together lists we think are most likely to interest you. Doing so took a lot of database sorting but, hey, it's what we do.

All of the lists are easy to understand and you can simply browse the ones that interest you. We added notes to most of the lists where they appear in Section 1 to help you understand how we developed them or to provide you with tips on using them to best effect.

The lists are arranged in groupings that made sense to us. In reviewing the lists, keep in mind that the primary measures for selection as a "Best" job on any list is one or a combination of measures of high pay, high growth, and high number of job openings.

Introduction

The Table of Contents includes all of the lists provided in Section 1 along with the page number for each. We've included the title of each list here, along with comments for some of them.

Lists of the Best Overall Jobs for College Graduates for the 21st Century

These are among the most important lists in Section 1 since they use criteria most people consider important in selecting a "best" job—high pay, high growth, and large numbers of job openings. The names of the lists are

- The Best of the Best: Jobs with the Highest Pay, Fastest Growth, and Largest Number of Openings. This is a list that uses a score for jobs with the highest ratings for the combination of pay, projected increase in people employed, and the number of openings per year.

- Best Paying Jobs. Lists the jobs with the highest average earnings per year.

- Fastest Growing Jobs. Lists the jobs with the highest percentage growth rates projected through the year 2006.

- Jobs with the Most Openings. Lists the jobs expected to have the greatest number of openings per year.

Lists of Best Jobs for College Graduates Based on a Variety of Interesting Criteria

We thought it would be interesting to organize the 281 jobs that require a college degree into more specific subgroupings. We were limited to criteria available from the various databases we used. The data included some information on the people who worked in them, allowing us to create lists within these groupings:

- Lists of Best Jobs for College Graduates Aged 20–29

- Lists of Best Jobs with High Percentages of College Graduates Aged 55 and Older

- Lists of Best Jobs with High Percentages of Part-time College Graduates

- Lists of Best Jobs with High Percentages of Women College Graduates (Please review our criteria notes for including this before you form an opinion...)

- Lists of Best Jobs with High Percentages of Men College Graduates

- Lists of Best Jobs with High Percentages of Self-employed College Graduates

We then created five lists for each of the above groups, with each list using only those 281 jobs requiring a two- or four-year college degree. The lists include:

1. A list sorted by percentage of people meeting the criteria (age, gender, and self-employment

2. A list sorted in order of the highest combined ratings for pay, growth, and number of openings

3. A list sorted by highest pay

4. A list sorted by fastest growth

5. A list sorted by most annual openings

For example, there is a list in Section 1 that lists, from highest on down, the annual pay for jobs with high percentages of college graduates aged 20 to 29 years old.

We also created a series of lists using various secret database cross-referencing methods (at least that is what our database guy told us) based on level of education, interests, and occupational categories. Here are a few comments on each of these listing groups.

Best Jobs for People with Different Levels of Education, Training, and Experience

This is the one group of lists that includes jobs that do not require a college degree. We used the same categories for training and education the U.S. Department of Labor assigns as typically required for each occupation. These lists will help you identify jobs that pay more or that are more interesting to you at your current level of education—or can help you identify occupations on the level of education a person has or is willing to pursue. The lists include

- Best Jobs Requiring an Associate Degree. For those with a two-year college degree.

- Best Jobs Requiring a Bachelor's Degree. For those with a four-year college degree.

- Best Jobs Requiring a Degree Plus Work Experience. These jobs typically require a four-year college degree plus experience in a related job.

- Best Jobs Requiring a Graduate or Professional Degree. For those with a four-year college degree plus a master's, professional, or doctor's degree.

Lists of College Degreed Jobs Based on Interests

There is a good deal of research (as well as your own common sense) that tells us our interests can guide us in our career selection. For example, if you LOVE performing on stage, that just might give you a hint of the sorts of careers or leisure activities to consider. That's obvious enough, but constructing a list of major jobs by interest areas was a more complex task. Fortunately, our good friends at the U.S. Department of Labor developed the *Guide for Occupational Exploration,* or GOE, to assist in career exploration based on interests. Our clever database sorting allowed us to organize the 281 occupations requiring college degrees into groups of jobs based on interests. The lists by interest will help you explore career options you may not have previously considered. You will find lists of jobs in Section 1 organized into these groupings:

- Artistic Jobs

- Scientific Jobs

- Plant and Animal Jobs

Introduction

- Mechanical Jobs
- Industrial Jobs
- Business Detail Jobs
- Selling Jobs
- Accommodating/Personal Service Jobs
- Humanitarian/Helping Others Jobs
- Leading and Influencing Jobs
- Physical Performing and Sports Jobs

Lists of College Degreed Jobs Based on Occupational Types

John Holland has developed a model of personality types and work environments used in a popular career interest test titled "The Self Directed Search" (SDS) published by Psychological Assessment Resources, Inc. A basic concept of this model is that each personality type is attracted to one of six related work environments or combination of work environments. Some occupational systems cross-reference the SDS types and we've sorted the 281 jobs requiring college degrees into them. The groupings are very similar to some used by the GOE and you can use them in similar ways to identify jobs based on interests, even if you never use the SDS test itself. The SDS types include:

- Artistic Jobs
- Conventional Jobs
- Enterprising Jobs
- Investigative Jobs
- Realistic Jobs
- Social Jobs

These are the lists we include in Section 1 of this book. We hope you find them useful.

Section 2: The Best Jobs Directory
Descriptions of the 281 Best Jobs

The second section of this book provides job descriptions for the 281 occupations (of the 1,122 jobs in O*NET database) requiring an associate, bachelor's, master's, or doctor's degree.

The descriptions in Section 2 are listed in alphabetical order. We think this will help you quickly find a job from one of the lists we include in Section 1. Note that the descriptions are arranged under 115 more general job titles used by the Bureau of Labor Statistics—we did this so that we could include earnings and other data.

The information in each description comes from the O*NET database. As mentioned earlier, this data was developed by the U.S. Department of Labor and is the most recent and reliable data available.

We've included a sample description later in this section for your information and encourage you to refer to it as needed. Each description is packed with useful information and includes the following elements:

- **Job Title.** This is the title most often used to describe the occupation.

- **Average Yearly Earnings.** The average yearly pay received by all full-time workers in this occupation. This data is as collected by the U.S. Census Bureau.

- **Education.** The amount of education typically required for entry into this occupation.

- **Projected Growth.** The percentage increase in the number of people employed in the occupation in the ten years ending in the year 2006. This is the most recent data available at the time of this writing and gives you some measure of future demand for the job.

- **Annual Job Openings.** The estimated number of job openings projected per year. This gives you some measure of the ease of finding a job opening for this job.

- **Self-employed.** The percentage of self-employed workers in the occupation gives you a measure of self-employment as an option for this job.

- **Employed Part-time.** The percentage of part-time workers employed in the occupation gives you data on part-time opportunities that may be desirable to you.

- **O*NET Title.** This is the job title the U.S. Department of Labor uses in the O*NET database. There may be more than one O*NET related to a BLS job title.

- **Summary Description and Tasks.** Begins with a one-sentence summary description of the jobs. This is followed by a listing of tasks that are generally performed by people who work in the job.

- **Occupational Type.** A description used in the Self-Directed Search (a popular career interest test) that best describes the occupation. Sometimes called the "Holland Code," it allows you to cross-reference other systems using this description.

- **Skills Required.** The O*NET provides data on 10 basic skills that assist in learning new things and an additional 36 functional (or "transferable") skills that help you in a variety of job settings. We include only those skills, from among the 46, that are rated as the most important for that occupation.

- **College Majors.** This information will provide you guidance on what majors best prepare you for entry into the job. Some occupations have very specific entry requirements, like chemical engineering, and you're not likely to get a job in this field without that major. Other occupations, like paralegals, have less specific requirements allowing some people to enter this occupation with majors as divergent as anthropology to zoology. However, a person with a major in Paralegal or Legal

Assistant studies is more likely to get a job as a paralegal. The distinction about how critical a specific major is to entry into an occupation isn't indicated in the O*NET database, requiring you to research this yourself.

- **Supporting Courses.** Every job requires knowledge about fields of study outside a college major. We've identified those areas where the highest amount of knowledge is typically needed. Specific courses aren't noted but rather the general field or what often might be the department or school within a college or university. For example, English, Biology, and Education courses are more important for doing well as a Dietician than some other areas of knowledge. Art courses, on the other hand, are not considered important for a Dietician, so are no listed.

Job Title

Helpful Data

ACCOUNTANTS AND AUDITORS

	Education	Bachelor's degree
	Average Yearly Earnings	$38,168
	Projected Growth	12%
	Annual Job Openings	118,376
	Self-employed	10%
	Employed Part-time	8%

Related Job — ## Accountants

Job Description and Tasks

Analyze financial information and prepare financial reports to determine or maintain record of assets, liabilities, profit and loss, tax liability, or other financial activities within an organization. Exclude auditors. Analyzes operations, trends, costs, revenues, financial commitments, and obligations incurred, to project future revenues and expenses, using computer. Develops, maintains, and analyzes budgets, and prepares periodic reports comparing budgeted costs to actual costs. Analyzes records of financial transactions to determine accuracy and completeness of entries, using computer. Prepares balance sheet, profit and loss statement, amortization and depreciation schedules, and other financial reports, using calculator or computer.

Occupational Type

Type of Work

Conventional occupations frequently involve following set procedures and routines. These occupations can include working with data and details more than with ideas. Usually there is a clear line of authority to follow.

Skills required of Accountants

Reading Comprehension, Active Listening, Writing, Speaking, Mathematics, Critical Thinking, Active Learning.

Skills (see appendix for detailed explanation)

College Majors

Accounting. An instructional program that prepares individuals to practice the profession of accounting, and to perform related business functions. Includes instruction in accounting principles and theory, financial accounting, managerial accounting, cost accounting budget control, tax accounting, legal aspects of accounting, auditing, reporting procedures, statement analysis, planning and consulting, business information systems, accounting research methods, professional standards and ethics, and applications to specific for profit, public, and non-profit organizations.

Specific Degree Area and Description

Supporting Courses

Administration and Management: Knowledge of principles and processes involved in business and organizational planning, coordination, and execution. This includes strategic planning, resource allocation, manpower modeling, leadership techniques, and production methods. **Clerical:** Knowledge of administrative and clerical procedures and systems such as word processing systems, filing and records management systems, stenography and transcription, forms design principles, and other office procedures and terminology. **Economics and Accounting:** Knowledge of economic and accounting principles and practices, the financial markets, banking, and the analysis and reporting of financial data.

Useful Supporting Courses Recommended

Caveat Datum (or, Loosely Translated, Beware of Data)

One of the problems with data is that it is true on the average. But just as there is no precisely average person, there is no such thing as a statistically average example of a job as a biologist—or any other particular job. We say this because data, while helpful, can also be misleading.

Take, for example, the "Average Earnings" information we include in this book. It tells us the average annual pay received by people in various job titles. The average earnings may sound great, except that you have to realize that about half of all people in that occupation earned less than that number, and half more. For example, people just entering the occupation or with a few years of work experience will often earn much less than average. People who work in rural areas typically earn less than those who do similar work in cities (where the cost of living is higher). People who work with small employers tend to earn less than those working for large employers. And people living in certain areas of the country earn less than those in others. In some jobs, such as Adult Education Instructors, a large percentage of the workforce is part-time (in this case, a whopping 43 percent) and the lower annual pay of these part-timers lowers the "average" pay for this occupation, even though full-time Adult Education Instructors earn much more.

So, in reviewing the information in Section 2, please understand the limitations of data. You still need to use your own good common sense in career decision-making as in most other things in life. Even so, we hope that you find the information helpful and interest.

Thanks for reading the Introduction. You are surely a more thorough person than those who jumped into the rest of the book without doing so. The truth is, at least one of the authors of this book is the type of person who never reads documentation before trying to use software. That same type of person turns to a book's good parts and skips the Introduction, which is, now that I think of it, the point we were making so awkwardly earlier: Each of us is different but there is somewhere good for each of us.

Section I

The Best Jobs Lists

Introduction

We've tried to make the lists in this section both fun to use and informative. Use the table of contents to find the lists that most interest you or simply browse the lists that follow. Most, such as the list of jobs with the highest pay, are very easy to understand and require little explanation. We provide comments as needed on the lists to inform you of the selection criteria or other details we think you may want to know.

As you review the lists, one or more of the occupations may appeal to you enough to seek additional information. As this happens, bookmark that occupation (or write it on a separate sheet of paper) so that you can look up its description later in Section 2.

Most of the lists emphasize occupations with high pay, high growth, or large numbers of openings because many consider one or more of these factors important in selecting a desirable job. These measures are also easily quantified and are, therefore, often presented in lists of best jobs you read about in the newspapers and other media.

While earnings, growth and openings are important, there are other factors to consider. For example, location, liking the people you work with, having an opportunity to serve others, and enjoying your work are just a few of the many factors that define the ideal job for you. These measures are difficult or impossible to objectively quantify based on the data we have available and, so, are not used in this book. You will need to consider the importance of these issues yourself. Having said this, the lists do include those measures that are easily quantified, can be easily sorted, and can be put into list form.

The earnings figures are based on the average annual pay received by full-time workers in 1997—the most recent data we had available. Since some occupations have high percentages of part-time workers, those workers would receive, of course, relatively less pay on a weekly basis. The earnings also represent the national averages and actual pay rates can vary greatly by location, amount of previous work experience, and other factors.

The future growth of an occupation is based on the projected number of new jobs that will be created between the years 1996 to 2006. Again, these were the most recent projections available to us. A change in the economy can result in higher or lower numbers of job openings but previous predictions have been quite accurate.

The number of job openings for each occupation is the third factor we used in rating the occupations included in this section. This number comes from data collected in 1996. The projected number of openings provides a measure of how difficult it may be to obtain employment in that occupation. Typically, the more openings there are, the easier it is to find employment. Occupations employing large numbers of people will typically have large numbers of openings as well, and these larger occupations are given more weight in our ratings.

If it occurs to you that the data we use is old, try to appreciate that the U.S. Department of Labor takes about two to three years to collect, analyze, and disseminate the data we use. We use the most recent data available and there simply is no more reliable source, so this is what we use. The good news is that occupational trends are pretty stable, so a fast growing or high paying job is highly likely to remain so for some time. This makes the data we use pretty darn useful.

Lists of the Best Overall Jobs for College Graduates for the 21st Century

We've created four lists of occupations in this grouping. Three list jobs with the highest earnings, growth, and job openings and a fourth combines scores from the other three lists to create a listing of occupations with the highest combined rankings.

The Best of the Best: Jobs with the Highest Pay, Fastest Growth, and Largest Number of Openings

This is our premier list—the list that most people will want to know about. It contains all jobs for college graduates ranked from the highest to lowest total scores for pay, growth, and number of openings. The top 20 jobs are dominated by technology, business, and health related occupations. On the other hand the bottom 20 occupations have only two technology, two health, and no business related occupations.

To obtain this list, we sorted the jobs requiring college degrees into three lists in order of highest pay, fastest growth, and largest number of openings. The occupation with the highest pay was given a score of 1, the one with the next highest pay was given a score of 2. This scoring process was continued for each occupation on each of the three lists, resulting in a total score for each occupation. Then a new list was created based on the total score given to each occupation based on its ranking on all three measures. Engineering, mathematical, and natural science managers was the occupation with the lowest combined score—just like in golf having the lowest score is best—and it is on the top of the list that follows. The other occupations follow, in descending order based on their total scores.

Scores range from 46 at the low end to 322 at the upper end. Sometimes there were ties in the score but we've decided not to complicate the lists by using some special method for noting these. Just keep in mind that there may be small or no differences between scores of jobs that are near each other on a list. For example, only six points separate the first four jobs on the list.

THE BEST OF THE BEST JOBS

Rank	Jobs	Annual Earnings	Percent Growth	Annual Openings
1	Engineering, mathematical, and natural science managers	$68,620	45	37,494
2	Marketing, advertising, and public relations managers	$57,100	29	54,601
3	Computer engineers	$56,590	109	34,884
4	Systems analysts	$51,360	103	87,318
5	Physicians	$100,920	21	29,681
6	Lawyers	$72,840	19	45,929
7	Physical therapists	$56,060	71	19,122
8	Service managers	$51,410	21	171,229
9	General managers and top executives	$60,960	15	288,825
10	Financial managers	$57,060	18	74,296
11	Computer scientists	$47,570	118	26,733
12	Electrical and electronics engineers	$56,820	29	19,098
13	Computer programmers	$50,490	23	58,990
14	Management analysts	$52,110	21	46,026
15	Special education teachers	$39,200	59	49,029
16	Management support workers	$39,680	26	154,129
17	College and university faculty	$48,917	19	126,583
18	Registered nurses	$41,400	21	165,362
19	Dental hygienists	$44,840	48	18,372
20	Occupational therapists	$50,610	66	9,543
21	Secondary school teachers	$39,010	22	168,392
22	Management support specialists	$40,630	20	124,342
23	Speech-language pathologists and audiologists	$44,370	51	12,203
24	Chiropractors	$68,000	27	2,594
25	Education administrators	$55,900	12	39,332

continued

THE BEST OF THE BEST JOBS

Rank	Jobs	Annual Earnings	Percent Growth	Annual Openings
26	Loan officers and counselors	$39,430	28	29,989
27	Social workers	$31,680	32	75,553
28	Artists and commercial artists	$34,360	28	46,893
29	Civil engineers	$52,750	18	15,978
30	Production engineers	$57,070	14	19,706
31	Economists	$52,370	19	11,343
32	Personnel, training, and labor relations managers	$50,080	18	20,995
33	Paralegals	$33,300	68	21,705
34	Medical scientists	$56,430	25	3,333
35	Construction managers	$49,280	18	22,043
36	Physician assistants	$44,980	47	5,089
37	Pharmacists	$57,990	13	13,827
38	Mechanical engineers	$52,210	16	14,290
39	Physical scientists	$50,040	28	4,131
40	Writers and editors	$36,940	21	41,449
41	Designers	$32,480	26	42,479
42	Veterinarians and veterinary inspectors	$55,430	23	2,381
43	Architects	$50,170	20	10,404
44	Residential counselors	$19,910	41	38,515
45	Healthcare support specialists	$30,800	24	45,720
46	Biological scientists	$47,550	25	7,111
47	Accountants and auditors	$40,550	12	118,376
48	Personnel, training, and labor relations specialists	$39,570	18	36,049
49	Public relations specialists and publicity writers	$36,260	27	17,954
50	Counselors	$39,060	19	27,181
51	Communication, transportation, and utilities managers	$51,790	15	10,840
52	Preschool and kindergarten teachers	$26,525	20	77,151
53	Insurance claims examiners	$42,310	22	7,281
54	Dentists	$91,280	8	5,072
55	Administrative services managers	$47,030	11	24,604
56	Chemists	$47,200	18	10,572
57	Elementary teachers	$37,310	10	164,163
58	Radiologic technologists	$32,840	29	12,865
59	Respiratory therapists	$34,110	46	9,452
60	Medical records technicians	$21,220	51	13,258
61	Chemical engineers	$58,400	15	1,434
62	Tutors and instructors	$30,650	15	149,065

Rank	Jobs	Annual Earnings	Percent Growth	Annual Openings
63	Recreation workers	$18,570	22	29,880
64	Electrical and electronic technicians	$36,120	15	31,145
65	Property and real estate managers	$34,680	16	29,483
66	Optometrists	$65,170	12	1,630
67	Aerospace engineers	$63,130	8	3,771
68	Clinical laboratory technologists	$38,350	15	23,944
69	Geologists, geophysicists, and oceanographers	$55,600	15	1,688
70	Industrial production managers	$54,860	-3	14,917
71	Therapeutic services and administration	$31,590	67	4,767
72	Director of Religious Education and Activities	$25,650	36	10,780
73	Industrial engineers	$52,350	14	3,555
74	Interior designers	$32,120	28	9,238
75	Podiatrists	$83,040	10	617
76	Psychologists	$49,460	8	10,913
77	Agricultural and food scientists	$43,200	20	2,016
78	Judges and magistrates	$62,160	2	3,558
79	Engineering technicians	$35,147	7	44,475
80	Budget analysts	$46,350	12	8,204
81	Operations research analysts	$50,740	8	5,316
82	General purchasing agents	$40,030	6	21,175
83	Cardiology technologists	$33,720	35	1,686
84	Landscape architects	$39,970	21	1,593
85	Foresters and conservation scientists	$42,230	17	3,200
86	Science and mathematics technicians	$32,760	13	23,271
87	Purchasing managers	$44,400	8	10,746
88	Credit analysts	$38,960	16	5,454
89	Nuclear engineers	$64,380	5	714
90	Physicists and astronomers	$68,060	-2	1,073
91	Actuaries	$64,160	0	1,165
92	Employment interviewers	$34,590	16	10,430
93	Underwriters	$40,460	6	10,918
94	Materials engineers	$54,930	7	933
95	Petroleum engineers	$68,300	-14	549
96	Librarians	$38,400	5	16,810
97	Wholesale and retail buyers	$34,780	0	22,432
98	Dietitians and nutritionists	$34,120	18	4,079
99	Clergy	$30,480	13	14,515
100	Atmospheric and Space Scientists	$51,730	8	421
101	Recreational therapists	$27,920	21	3,414

continued

THE BEST OF THE BEST JOBS

Rank	Jobs	Annual Earnings	Percent Growth	Annual Openings
102	Urban and regional planners	$43,670	5	3,856
103	Social scientists	$41,880	5	4,907
104	Psychiatric technicians	$22,020	9	14,819
105	Mining engineers	$53,650	-13	130
106	Mathematicians	$42,150	9	960
107	Statisticians	$49,830	1	936
108	Nuclear medicine technologists	$39,670	13	865
109	Curators, archivists, museum technicians, and restorers	$33,130	15	2,367
110	Law clerks	$28,360	12	8,181
111	Tax examiners and revenue agents	$39,540	2	3,637
112	Life scientists	$44,510	-3	53
113	Farm and home management advisors	$37,350	-38	3,078
114	Reporters and correspondents	$29,660	-3	6,294
115	Animal breeders and trainers	$24,620	0	1,327

The Best Paying Jobs for College Graduates

We know that many people will turn to this list first. Like most people, you probably consider the amount of money you can earn at a job to be important in selecting a career. That is one of the reasons we provide the *Best Paying Jobs* list. Keep in mind that the earnings reflect the national average earnings for all workers in the occupation. This is an important consideration because starting pay in the job is usually a lot less than what can be earned with several years of experience. Earnings also vary significantly by region of the country, so actual pay in your area could be substantially different.

The highest paying job on this list is physicians, with average annual earnings of $100,920. All of the top 10 jobs have average annual earnings greater than $64,000. The national average annual earnings for all workers at all levels of education is slightly more than $26,000 so the top 25 jobs on this list earn more than double the national average.

This list illustrates the direct relationship between education and earnings. Seven of the top ten best paying jobs require a doctor's degree, which normally requires three or more years of education beyond a bachelor's degree. Workers with doctor's degrees have average lifetime earnings four times greater than those of high school graduates.

Other lists later in this section present highpaying jobs at all levels of education. While it is clear that higher levels of education and training are often required for jobs with high earnings, there remain opportunities for higher-than-average pay at all levels of education.

BEST PAYING JOBS FOR COLLEGE GRADUATES

Rank	Best Paying Jobs	Average Annual Earnings
1	Physicians	$100,920
2	Dentists	$91,280
3	Podiatrists	$83,040
4	Lawyers	$72,840
5	Engineering, mathematical, and natural science managers	$68,620
6	Petroleum engineers	$68,300
7	Physicists and astronomers	$68,060
8	Chiropractors	$68,000
9	Optometrists	$65,170
10	Nuclear engineers	$64,380
11	Actuaries	$64,160
12	Aerospace engineers	$63,130
13	Judges and magistrates	$62,160
14	General managers and top executives	$60,960
15	Chemical engineers	$58,400
16	Pharmacists	$57,990
17	Marketing, advertising, and public relations managers	$57,100
18	Production engineers	$57,070
19	Financial managers	$57,060
20	Electrical and electronics engineers	$56,820
21	Computer engineers	$56,590
22	Medical scientists	$56,430
23	Physical therapists	$56,060
24	Education administrators	$55,900
25	Geologists, geophysicists, and oceanographers	$55,600

The Fastest Growing Jobs for College Graduates

This is a list of occupations that are projected to have the highest percentage increase in the numbers of people employed in these occupations through the year 2006. Fast growing jobs excite our imaginations because they reflect changes occurring in our society.

The fastest growing jobs are computer scientists, computer engineers, and systems analysts. These jobs are all expected to more than double the number of people they employ by the year 2006. It is not surprising to find that computer and technology-related jobs lead this list—just like computers are leading the advances in this information age. Health-related professions also dominate the list, which is consistent with the increasing health needs of the aging baby boom generation. Ten (or 40 percent) of the top twenty-five fastest growing jobs are in health-related occupations. Both computer-related and health related jobs will provide many opportunities for college students to find employment in the 21st century. But, as this list demonstrates, these jobs are not the only ones with potential for strong growth.

FASTEST GROWING JOBS FOR COLLEGE GRADUATES

Rank	Fastest Growing Jobs to the Year 2006	Percent of Growth
1	Computer scientists	118
2	Computer engineers	109
3	Systems analysts	103
4	Physical therapists	71
5	Paralegals	68
6	Therapeutic services and administration	67
7	Occupational therapists	66
8	Special education teachers	59
9	Speech-language pathologists and audiologists	51
10	Medical records technicians	51
11	Dental hygienists	48
12	Physician assistants	47
13	Respiratory therapists	46
14	Engineering, mathematical, and natural science managers	45
15	Residential counselors	41
16	Director of Religious Education and Activities	36
17	Cardiology technologists	35
18	Social workers	32
19	Marketing, advertising, and public relations managers	29
20	Electrical and electronics engineers	29
21	Radiologic technologists	29
22	Physical scientists	28
23	Loan officers and counselors	28
24	Artists and commercial artists	28
25	Interior designers	28

Jobs with the Most Openings for College Graduates

Occupations with the most annual openings often provide easier entry for new workers and the ability to move from one job to another with relative ease. Such jobs are also attractive to people reentering the labor market, part-time job seekers, and workers who want to move from one employer to another.

The education and business fields dominate jobs with the most openings. There are seven education jobs and eight business jobs on this list.

JOBS WITH THE MOST OPENINGS FOR COLLEGE GRADUATES

Rank	Jobs with the Most Annual Openings	Number of Openings
1	General managers and top executives	288,825
2	Service managers	171,229
3	Secondary school teachers	168,392
4	Registered nurses	165,362
5	Elementary teachers	164,163
6	Management support workers	154,129
7	Tutors and instructors	149,065
8	College and university faculty	126,583
9	Management support specialists	124,342
10	Accountants and auditors	118,376
11	Systems analysts	87,318
12	Preschool and kindergarten teachers	77,151
13	Social workers	75,553
14	Financial managers	74,296
15	Computer programmers	58,990
16	Marketing, advertising, and public relations managers	54,601
17	Special education teachers	49,029
18	Artists and commercial artists	46,893
19	Management analysts	46,026
20	Lawyers	45,929
21	Healthcare support specialists	45,720
22	Engineering technicians	44,475
23	Designers	42,479
24	Writers and editors	41,449
25	Education administrators	39,332

Lists of Best Jobs for College Graduates Based on a Variety of Interesting Criteria

These lists examine the best jobs for younger workers, older workers, part-time workers, self-employed workers, and jobs dominated by men and women.

There are actually five lists for each of the categories we included in this list group. For example, the best jobs lists for younger workers includes

- Jobs with the Highest Percentage of Younger Workers Ages 20–29
- Best Jobs for Younger Workers Ages 20–29
- Best Paying Jobs for Younger Worker Ages 20–29

- Fastest Growing Jobs for Younger Workers Ages 20–29
- Jobs with the Most Annual Openings for Younger Workers Ages 20–29

As in the previous groupings, the Best Jobs for Younger Workers Ages 20–29 list—and the lists that are similarly named—are based on a combined score for pay, growth, and number of openings.

The Potential Controversy

We considered excluding the best jobs list for women to avoid upsetting some readers. But we know that people can handle the facts. So we asked our computer to tell us which jobs employed the highest percentages of men and women.

The computer told us that most Preschool and Kindergarten Teachers are women and most Mechanical Engineers are men and made other similar revelations. Many of these facts should not come as a surprise to anyone who lives in the real world. We also found that more than one-third of all Insurance Claims Examiners are young and one-third of all clergy are older—facts not so readily apparent. Some findings will make sense while others are simply interesting.

We think you can learn some interesting information from these lists, perhaps something you can use to plan your career. As needed, we provide additional comments prior to each list.

Lists of Jobs with High Percentages of College Graduates Aged 20–29

There were two major decisions that we had to make to compile these lists. First, we had to decide what ages defined younger workers. Second, we had to decide what percentage of workers had to be younger in order to be included in the list.

We decided to define younger workers as those workers 20 to 29 years of age. We selected this age range because the majority of college students graduate and begin their careers during this time of life. For example, a person graduating from high school at 18 and taking two years to complete an associate degree in electrical engineering technology would get that degree at 20 years of age. At the other extreme, students that take four years to complete a biology or pre-med degree, followed by three years for medical school, plus a one 1 year internship and a 3 year residency, would be 29 by the time they completed their education to become physicians. Thus, it makes sense that younger workers for jobs requiring college degrees be 20 to 29 years old.

We also decided that an occupation had to have 20 percent or more younger workers to be included in the list. Our reasoning is based on two facts. About 23 percent of all workers in the labor force are in the 20 to 29 year age range. However, for the jobs requiring college degrees only 17 percent of workers are in this age range. Twenty percent is midway between these two percentages.

It is interesting to note that the percent of workers in the 30–39 year range nearly doubles at 33 percent. This might be a result of a delayed entry into the workforce for college graduates. This idea is reinforced when you consider the jobs with the lowest percentage of younger workers.

The twenty jobs with the highest percentage of younger workers are ones that provide quicker entry into a career requiring a college degree. However, a quick start isn't always the best in the long run when it comes to earnings. These top 20 jobs have average earnings of $36,800 versus $47,100 for all workers with a college degree. In fact, the bottom 10 jobs in this list contain physicians, chiropractors, optometrists, dentists, podiatrists, and veterinarians. All of these jobs require at least three years of education beyond a bachelor's degree but are among those jobs with the highest pay for college graduates.

We have noticed some interesting facts about jobs for younger workers. For example, healthcareers seem to provide excellent opportunities for younger workers. Almost half of the best jobs for younger workers are in the health industry and this is also true for the fastest growing jobs for younger workers. Science jobs account for almost half of all the best paying jobs for younger workers.

The first list contains all occupations requiring a college degree, so that you can compare the percentage of younger workers for all jobs requiring a college degree. The other lists focus on the 43 jobs that met our criteria of employing 20 percent or more younger workers.

JOBS WITH HIGHEST PERCENTAGE OF COLLEGE GRADUATES AGED 20–29

Rank	Job	Percent Ages 20–29	Annual Earnings	Growth	Openings
1	Insurance claims examiners	35.7	$42,310	22	7,281
2	Paralegals	33.9	$33,300	68	21,705
3	Science and mathematics technicians	32.1	$32,760	13	23,271
4	Preschool and kindergarten teachers	28.9	$26,525	20	77,151
5	Wholesale and retail buyers	28.4	$34,780	0	22,432
6	Reporters and correspondents	26.7	$29,660	-3	6,294
7	Occupational therapists	26.3	$50,610	66	9,543
8	Physical therapists	26.3	$56,060	71	19,122
9	Recreational therapists	26.3	$27,920	21	3,414
10	Respiratory therapists	26.3	$34,110	46	9,452
11	Speech-language pathologists and audiologists	26.3	$44,370	51	12,203
12	Therapeutic services and administration	26.3	$31,590	67	4,767
13	Accountants and auditors	25.9	$40,550	12	118,376
14	Psychiatric technicians	25.5	$22,020	9	14,819
15	Cardiology technologists	25.4	$33,720	35	1,686
16	Dental hygienists	25.4	$44,840	48	18,372

continued

JOBS WITH HIGHEST PERCENTAGE OF COLLEGE GRADUATES AGED 20–29

Rank	Job	Percent Ages 20–29	Annual Earnings	Growth	Openings
17	Medical records technicians	25.4	$21,220	51	13,258
18	Management support workers	24.1	$39,680	26	154,129
19	Social workers	23.9	$31,680	32	75,553
20	Nuclear medicine technologists	23.9	$39,670	13	865
21	Radiologic technologists	23.9	$32,840	29	12,865
22	Public relations specialists and publicity writers	23.6	$36,260	27	17,954
23	Healthcare support specialists	23.6	$30,800	24	45,720
24	Computer programmers	23.3	$50,490	23	58,990
25	Farm and home management advisors	23	$37,350	-38	3,078
26	Clinical laboratory technologists	22.9	$38,350	15	23,944
27	Artists and commercial artists	22.5	$34,360	28	46,893
28	Law clerks	22.5	$28,360	12	8,181
29	Engineering technicians	22.1	$35,147	7	44,475
30	Production engineers	21.7	$57,070	14	19,706
31	Tutors and instructors	21.7	$30,650	15	149,065
32	Underwriters	20.7	$40,460	6	10,918
33	Agricultural and food scientists	20.4	$43,200	20	2,016
34	Biological scientists	20.4	$47,550	25	7,111
35	Foresters and conservation scientists	20.4	$42,230	17	3,200
36	Medical scientists	20.4	$56,430	25	3,333
37	Life scientists	20.4	$44,510	-3	53
38	Chemists	20.4	$47,200	18	10,572
39	Geologists, geophysicists, and oceanographers	20.4	$55,600	15	1,688
40	Atmospheric and Space Scientists	20.4	$51,730	8	421
41	Physicists and astronomers	20.4	$68,060	-2	1,073
42	Physical scientists	20.4	$50,040	28	4,131
43	Writers and editors	20.3	$36,940	21	41,449
44	Economists	19.9	$52,370	19	11,343
45	Designers	19.9	$32,480	26	42,479
46	Interior designers	19.9	$32,120	28	9,238
47	Management support specialists	19.6	$40,630	20	124,342
48	Computer engineers	19.4	$56,590	109	34,884
49	Systems analysts	19.4	$51,360	103	87,318
50	Director of Religious Education and Activities	19.4	$25,650	36	10,780
51	Recreation workers	19.4	$18,570	22	29,880

Rank	Job	Percent Ages 20–29	Annual Earnings	Growth	Openings
52	Residential counselors	19.4	$19,910	41	38,515
53	Counselors	19.4	$39,060	19	27,181
54	Actuaries	19.1	$64,160	0	1,165
55	Statisticians	19.1	$49,830	1	936
56	Mathematicians	19.1	$42,150	9	960
57	Budget analysts	19	$46,350	12	8,204
58	Credit analysts	19	$38,960	16	5,454
59	Loan officers and counselors	19	$39,430	28	29,989
60	Employment interviewers	18.5	$34,590	16	10,430
61	Personnel, training, and labor relations specialists	18.5	$39,570	18	36,049
62	Computer scientists	18.4	$47,570	118	26,733
63	Industrial engineers	17.9	$52,350	14	3,555
64	Electrical and electronic technicians	17.8	$36,120	15	31,145
65	Elementary teachers	17.7	$37,310	10	164,163
66	College and university faculty	17.6	$48,917	19	126,583
67	Mechanical engineers	17.5	$52,210	16	14,290
68	Pharmacists	17.1	$57,990	13	13,827
69	Physician assistants	17.1	$44,980	47	5,089
70	Aerospace engineers	16.8	$63,130	8	3,771
71	Chemical engineers	16.8	$58,400	15	1,434
72	Materials engineers	16.8	$54,930	7	933
73	Mining engineers	16.8	$53,650	-13	130
74	Nuclear engineers	16.8	$64,380	5	714
75	Petroleum engineers	16.8	$68,300	-14	549
76	Operations research analysts	16.8	$50,740	8	5,316
77	Civil engineers	16.7	$52,750	18	15,978
78	Financial managers	16.5	$57,060	18	74,296
79	Special education teachers	16.4	$39,200	59	49,029
80	Dietitians and nutritionists	16.4	$34,120	18	4,079
81	Property and real estate managers	15.8	$34,680	16	29,483
82	Marketing, advertising, and public relations managers	15.4	$57,100	29	54,601
83	Urban and regional planners	15.2	$43,670	5	3,856
84	Social scientists	15.2	$41,880	5	4,907
85	General purchasing agents	15.1	$40,030	6	21,175
86	Electrical and electronics engineers	15.1	$56,820	29	19,098
87	Registered nurses	14.7	$41,400	21	165,362
88	Purchasing managers	13.6	$44,400	8	10,746

continued

JOBS WITH HIGHEST PERCENTAGE OF COLLEGE GRADUATES AGED 20–29

Rank	Job	Percent Ages 20–29	Annual Earnings	Growth	Openings
89	Secondary school teachers	13.6	$39,010	22	168,392
90	Curators, archivists, museum technicians, and restorers	13.1	$33,130	15	2,367
91	Service managers	12.8	$51,410	21	171,229
92	Architects	12.4	$50,170	20	10,404
93	Landscape architects	12.4	$39,970	21	1,593
94	Personnel, training, and labor relations managers	12.3	$50,080	18	20,995
95	Psychologists	12.3	$49,460	8	10,913
96	Animal breeders and trainers	12.3	$24,620	0	1,327
97	Lawyers	12.1	$72,840	19	45,929
98	Judges and magistrates	11.6	$62,160	2	3,558
99	Librarians	11.4	$38,400	5	16,810
100	Administrative services managers	11.0	$47,030	11	24,604
101	Communication, transportation, and utilities managers	11.0	$51,790	15	10,840
102	Construction managers	11.0	$49,280	18	22,043
103	Engineering, mathematical, and natural science managers	11.0	$68,620	45	37,494
104	General managers and top executives	11.0	$60,960	15	288,825
105	Industrial production managers	11.0	$54,860	-3	14,917
106	Physicians	10.0	$100,920	21	29,681
107	Education administrators	9.3	$55,900	12	39,332
108	Chiropractors	8.8	$68,000	27	2,594
109	Dentists	8.8	$91,280	8	5,072
110	Optometrists	8.8	$65,170	12	1,630
111	Podiatrists	8.8	$83,040	10	617
112	Veterinarians and veterinary inspectors	8.8	$55,430	23	2,381
113	Tax examiners and revenue agents	8.4	$39,540	2	3,637
114	Management analysts	8.3	$52,110	21	46,026
115	Clergy	6.2	$30,480	13	14,515

Jobs with the Best Combination of Pay, Growth, and Number of Openings for College Graduates Aged 20–29

Rank	Job	Percent Ages 20–29	Annual Earnings	Growth	Openings
1	Paralegals	33.9	$33,300	68	21,705
2	Physical therapists	26.3	$56,060	71	19,122
3	Preschool and kindergarten teachers	28.9	$26,525	20	77,151
4	Management support workers	24.1	$39,680	26	154,129
5	Social workers	23.9	$31,680	32	75,553
6	Occupational therapists	26.3	$50,610	66	9,543
7	Speech-language pathologists and audiologists	26.3	$44,370	51	12,203
8	Dental hygienists	25.4	$44,840	48	18,372
9	Medical records technicians	25.4	$21,220	51	13,258
10	Respiratory therapists	26.3	$34,110	46	9,452
11	Artists and commercial artists	22.5	$34,360	28	46,893
12	Science and mathematics technicians	32.1	$32,760	13	23,271
13	Therapeutic services and administration	26.3	$31,590	67	4,767
14	Computer programmers	23.3	$50,490	23	58,990
15	Insurance claims examiners	35.7	$42,310	22	7,281
16	Accountants and auditors	25.9	$40,550	12	118,376
17	Healthcare support specialists	23.6	$30,800	24	45,720
18	Radiologic technologists	23.9	$32,840	29	12,865
19	Public relations specialists and publicity writers	23.6	$36,260	27	17,954
20	Wholesale and retail buyers	28.4	$34,780	0	22,432

BEST PAYING JOBS FOR COLLEGE GRADUATES AGED 20–29

Rank	Job	Percent Ages 20–29	Annual Earnings
1	Physicists and astronomers	20.4	$68,060
2	Production engineers	21.7	$57,070
3	Medical scientists	20.4	$56,430
4	Physical therapists	26.3	$56,060
5	Geologists, geophysicists, and oceanographers	20.4	$55,600
6	Atmospheric and Space Scientists	20.4	$51,730
7	Occupational therapists	26.3	$50,610
8	Computer programmers	23.3	$50,490
9	Physical scientists	20.4	$50,040
10	Biological scientists	20.4	$47,550
11	Chemists	20.4	$47,200
12	Dental hygienists	25.4	$44,840
13	Life scientists	20.4	$44,510
14	Speech-language pathologists and audiologists	26.3	$44,370
15	Agricultural and food scientists	20.4	$43,200
16	Insurance claims examiners	35.7	$42,310
17	Foresters and conservation scientists	20.4	$42,230
18	Accountants and auditors	25.9	$40,550
19	Underwriters	20.7	$40,460
20	Management support workers	24.1	$39,680

FASTEST GROWING JOBS FOR COLLEGE GRADUATES AGED 20–29

Rank	Job	Percent Age 20–29	Percent Growth
1	Physical therapists	26.3	71
2	Paralegals	33.9	68
3	Therapeutic services and administration	26.3	67
4	Occupational therapists	26.3	66
5	Speech-language pathologists and audiologists	26.3	51
6	Medical records technicians	25.4	51
7	Dental hygienists	25.4	48
8	Respiratory therapists	26.3	46
9	Cardiology technologists	25.4	35
10	Social workers	23.9	32
11	Radiologic technologists	23.9	29
12	Physical scientists	20.4	28
13	Artists and commercial artists	22.5	28
14	Public relations specialists and publicity writers	23.6	27
15	Management support workers	24.1	26
16	Medical scientists	20.4	25
17	Biological scientists	20.4	25
18	Healthcare support specialists	23.6	24
19	Computer programmers	23.3	23
20	Insurance claims examiners	35.7	22

JOBS WITH MOST ANNUAL OPENINGS FOR COLLEGE GRADUATES AGED 20–29

Rank	Job	Percent Ages 20–29	Annual Openings
1	Management support workers	24.1	154,129
2	Tutors and instructors	21.7	149,065
3	Accountants and auditors	25.9	118,376
4	Preschool and kindergarten teachers	28.9	77,151
5	Social workers	23.9	75,553
6	Computer programmers	23.3	58,990
7	Artists and commercial artists	22.5	46,893
8	Healthcare support specialists	23.6	45,720
9	Engineering technicians	22.1	44,475
10	Writers and editors	20.3	41,449
11	Clinical laboratory technologists	22.9	23,944
12	Science and mathematics technicians	32.1	23,271
13	Wholesale and retail buyers	28.4	22,432
14	Paralegals	33.9	21,705
15	Production engineers	21.7	19,706
16	Physical therapists	26.3	19,122
17	Dental hygienists	25.4	18,372
18	Public relations specialists and publicity writers	23.6	17,954
19	Psychiatric technicians	25.5	14,819
20	Medical records technicians	25.4	13,258

Lists of Best Jobs with High Percentages of College Graduates Aged 55 and Over

As you will soon see, older college graduates have different types of jobs than younger ones. Workers 55 and older account for 12.5 percent of the workforce, and lower percentages of them work than is the case for younger workers. This makes sense, since people begin to retire as they pass 55 years of age. In addition, many in this age range were affected by layoffs during the 1980s and 1990s and some never went back to full-time employment.

The percent of self-employed workers in this age group is almost four times greater than the percentage for all other college graduates. This is partly due to the difficulty some older workers have in finding jobs and, in other cases, a result of older workers wanting more freedom or higher pay than available from conventional employment. Other occupations on the list, like clergy and physicians, take many years of training and experience. Once people are established in these careers, they often work in that occupation until retirement.

The first list shows the percentage of older workers for all occupations requiring a college degree. All but the first list then exclude jobs that had fewer than 13 percent of their workers aged 55 or older. Just 35 jobs met these criteria and these are the ones used in the all but the first list.

One use of these lists is to help identify careers that might interest you if you want to change careers as you approach retirement. For example, some occupations are on the lists because they provide more flexibility in a work schedule—an attractive element to many older workers.

JOBS WITH HIGHEST PERCENTAGE OF COLLEGE GRADUATES AGED 55 AND OVER

Rank	Job	Percent 55 & Over	Average Earnings	Annual Growth	Openings
1	Clergy	31.2	$30,480	13	4,515
2	Animal breeders and trainers	29.3	$24,620	0	1,327
3	Property and real estate managers	27.0	$34,680	16	29,483
4	Management analysts	22.3	$52,110	21	46,026
5	Librarians	20.7	$38,400	5	16,810
6	Curators, archivists, museum technicians, and restorers	20.1	$33,130	15	2,367
7	College and university faculty	19.0	$48,917	19	126,583
8	Physicians	18.0	$100,920	21	29,681
9	Civil engineers	17.3	$52,750	18	15,978
10	Director of Religious Education and Activities	17.3	$25,650	36	10,780
11	Recreation workers	17.3	$18,570	22	29,880
12	Chiropractors	17.3	$68,000	27	2,594
13	Dentists	17.3	$91,280	8	5,072
14	Optometrists	17.3	$65,170	12	1,630
15	Podiatrists	17.3	$83,040	10	617
16	Veterinarians and veterinary inspectors	17.3	$55,430	23	2,381
17	Tax examiners and revenue agents	16.8	$39,540	2	3,637
18	Education administrators	15.3	$55,900	12	39,332
19	Dietitians and nutritionists	15.3	$34,120	18	4,079
20	Tutors and instructors	15.0	$30,650	15	149,065
21	Administrative services managers	14.7	$47,030	11	24,604
22	Communication, transportation, and utilities managers	14.7	$51,790	15	10,840
23	Construction managers	14.7	$49,280	18	22,043
24	Engineering, mathematical, and natural science managers	14.7	$68,620	45	37,494
25	General managers and top executives	14.7	$60,960	15	288,825
26	Industrial production managers	14.7	$54,860	-3	14,917
27	Service managers	14.6	$51,410	21	171,229
28	Mechanical engineers	14.4	$52,210	16	14,290

continued

Jobs with Highest Percentage of College Graduates Aged 55 and Over

Rank	Job	Percent 55 & Over	Average Earnings	Annual Growth	Openings
29	Judges and magistrates	13.8	$62,160	2	3,558
30	Farm and home management advisors	13.7	$37,350	-38	3,078
31	Writers and editors	13.6	$36,940	21	41,449
32	Psychiatric technicians	13.5	$22,020	9	14,819
33	Designers	13.2	$32,480	26	42,479
34	Interior designers	13.2	$32,120	28	9,238
35	Artists and commercial artists	13.1	$34,360	28	46,893
36	Public relations specialists and publicity writers	12.9	$36,260	27	17,954
37	Residential counselors	12.8	$19,910	41	38,515
38	Counselors	12.8	$39,060	19	27,181
39	Lawyers	12.6	$72,840	19	45,929
40	Industrial engineers	12.5	$52,350	14	3,555
41	Management support specialists	12.1	$40,630	20	124,342
42	Aerospace engineers	12.1	$63,130	8	3,771
43	Chemical engineers	12.1	$58,400	15	1,434
44	Materials engineers	12.1	$54,930	7	933
45	Mining engineers	12.1	$53,650	-13	130
46	Nuclear engineers	12.1	$64,380	5	714
47	Petroleum engineers	12.1	$68,300	-14	549
48	Personnel, training, and labor relations managers	12.0	$50,080	18	20,995
49	General purchasing agents	12.0	$40,030	6	21,175
50	Underwriters	12.0	$40,460	6	10,918
51	Budget analysts	11.9	$46,350	12	8,204
52	Credit analysts	11.9	$38,960	16	5,454
53	Loan officers and counselors	11.9	$39,430	28	29,989
54	Reporters and correspondents	11.8	$29,660	-3	6,294
55	Employment interviewers	10.9	$34,590	16	10,430
56	Personnel, training, and labor relations specialists	10.9	$39,570	18	36,049
57	Management support workers	10.8	$39,680	26	154,129
58	Psychologists	10.6	$49,460	8	10,913
59	Accountants and auditors	10.5	$40,550	12	118,376
60	Architects	10.4	$50,170	20	10,404
61	Landscape architects	10.4	$39,970	21	1,593
62	Elementary teachers	10.3	$37,310	10	164,163
63	Secondary school teachers	10.2	$39,010	22	168,392
64	Wholesale and retail buyers	10.0	$34,780	0	22,432

Rank	Job	Percent 55 & Over	Average Earnings	Annual Growth	Openings
65	Urban and regional planners	9.9	$43,670	5	3,856
66	Social scientists	9.9	$41,880	5	4,907
67	Registered nurses	9.8	$41,400	21	165,362
68	Production engineers	9.6	$57,070	14	19,706
69	Social workers	9.4	$31,680	32	75,553
70	Electrical and electronics engineers	9.2	$56,820	29	19,098
71	Pharmacists	9.2	$57,990	13	13,827
72	Physician assistants	9.2	$44,980	47	5,089
73	Law clerks	9.1	$28,360	12	8,181
74	Agricultural and food scientists	9.0	$43,200	20	2,016
75	Biological scientists	9.0	$47,550	25	7,111
76	Foresters and conservation scientists	9.0	$42,230	17	3,200
77	Medical scientists	9.0	$56,430	25	3,333
78	Life scientists	9.0	$44,510	-3	53
79	Chemists	9.0	$47,200	18	10,572
80	Geologists, geophysicists, and oceanographers	9.0	$55,600	15	1,688
81	Atmospheric and Space Scientists	9.0	$51,730	8	421
82	Physicists and astronomers	9.0	$68,060	-2	1,073
83	Physical scientists	9.0	$50,040	28	4,131
84	Special education teachers	8.9	$39,200	59	49,029
85	Purchasing managers	8.6	$44,400	8	10,746
86	Healthcare support specialists	8.2	$30,800	24	45,720
87	Financial managers	8.0	$57,060	18	74,296
88	Preschool and kindergarten teachers	7.9	$26,525	20	77,151
89	Operations research analysts	7.8	$50,740	8	5,316
90	Nuclear medicine technologists	7.8	$39,670	13	865
91	Radiologic technologists	7.8	$32,840	29	12,865
92	Marketing, advertising, and public relations managers	7.7	$57,100	29	54,601
93	Clinical laboratory technologists	7.4	$38,350	15	23,944
94	Insurance claims examiners	7.1	$42,310	22	7,281
95	Engineering technicians	7.0	$35,147	7	44,475
96	Cardiology technologists	6.9	$33,720	35	1,686
97	Dental hygienists	6.9	$44,840	48	18,372
98	Medical records technicians	6.9	$21,220	51	13,258
99	Electrical and electronic technicians	6.3	$36,120	15	31,145
100	Science and mathematics technicians	6.1	$32,760	13	23,271
101	Economists	5.4	$52,370	19	11,343
102	Computer scientists	5.3	$47,570	118	26,733

continued

JOBS WITH HIGHEST PERCENTAGE OF COLLEGE GRADUATES AGED 55 AND OVER

Rank	Job	Percent 55 & Over	Average Earnings	Annual Growth	Openings
103	Paralegals	5.3	$33,300	68	21,705
104	Actuaries	5.0	$64,160	0	1,165
105	Statisticians	5.0	$49,830	1	936
106	Mathematicians	5.0	$42,150	9	960
107	Computer programmers	4.4	$50,490	23	58,990
108	Computer engineers	4.0	$56,590	109	34,884
109	Systems analysts	4.0	$51,360	103	87,318
110	Occupational therapists	4.0	$50,610	66	9,543
111	Physical therapists	4.0	$56,060	71	19,122
112	Recreational therapists	4.0	$27,920	21	3,414
113	Respiratory therapists	4.0	$34,110	46	9,452
114	Speech-language pathologists and audiologists	4.0	$44,370	51	12,203
115	Therapeutic services and administration	4.0	$31,590	67	4,767

JOBS WITH THE BEST COMBINATION OF PAY, GROWTH, AND NUMBER OF OPENINGS FOR COLLEGE GRADUATES AGED 55 AND OVER

Rank	Job	Percent 55 & Over	Annual Earnings	Growth	Openings
1	Engineering, mathematical, and natural science managers	14.7	$68,620	45	37,494
2	Physicians	18.0	$100,920	21	29,681
3	General managers and top executives	14.7	$60,960	15	288,825
4	Service managers	14.6	$51,410	21	171,229
5	Management analysts	22.3	$52,110	21	46,026
6	Artists and commercial artists	13.1	$34,360	28	46,893
7	College and university faculty	19.0	$48,917	19	126,583
8	Chiropractors	17.3	$68,000	27	2,594
9	Designers	13.2	$32,480	26	42,479
10	Education administrators	15.3	$55,900	12	39,332
11	Civil engineers	17.3	$52,750	18	15,978
12	Writers and editors	13.6	$36,940	21	41,449
13	Construction managers	14.7	$49,280	18	22,043
14	Veterinarians and veterinary inspectors	17.3	$55,430	23	2,381
15	Mechanical engineers	14.4	$52,210	16	14,290
16	Recreation workers	17.3	$18,570	22	29,880
17	Property and real estate managers	27.0	$34,680	16	29,483
18	Tutors and instructors	15.0	$30,650	15	149,065
19	Dentists	17.3	$91,280	8	5,072
20	Communication, transportation, and utilities managers	14.7	$51,790	15	10,840

BEST PAYING JOBS FOR COLLEGE GRADUATES AGED 55 AND OVER

Rank	Job	Percent 55 & Over	Annual Earnings
1	Physicians	18.0	$100,920
2	Dentists	17.3	$91,280
3	Podiatrists	17.3	$83,040
4	Engineering, mathematical, and natural science managers	14.7	$68,620
5	Chiropractors	17.3	$68,000
6	Optometrists	17.3	$65,170
7	Judges and magistrates	13.8	$62,160
8	General managers and top executives	14.7	$60,960
9	Education administrators	15.3	$55,900
10	Veterinarians and veterinary inspectors	17.3	$55,430
11	Industrial production managers	14.7	$54,860
12	Civil engineers	17.3	$52,750
13	Mechanical engineers	14.4	$52,210
14	Management analysts	22.3	$52,110
15	Communication, transportation, and utilities managers	14.7	$51,790
16	Service managers	14.6	$51,410
17	Construction managers	14.7	$49,280
18	College and university faculty	19.0	$48,917
19	Administrative services managers	14.7	$47,030
20	Tax examiners and revenue agents	16.8	$39,540

FASTEST GROWING JOBS FOR COLLEGE GRADUATES AGED 55 AND OVER

Rank	Job	Percent 55 & Over	Percent Growth
1	Engineering, mathematical, and natural science managers	14.7	45
2	Director of Religious Education and Activities	17.3	36
3	Artists and commercial artists	13.1	28
4	Interior designers	13.2	28
5	Chiropractors	17.3	27
6	Designers	13.2	26
7	Veterinarians and veterinary inspectors	17.3	23
8	Recreation workers	17.3	22
9	Physicians	18.0	21
10	Management analysts	22.3	21
11	Service managers	14.6	21
12	Writers and editors	13.6	21
13	College and university faculty	19.0	19
14	Civil engineers	17.3	18
15	Construction managers	14.7	18
16	Dietitians and nutritionists	15.3	18
17	Mechanical engineers	14.4	16
18	Property and real estate managers	27.0	16
19	General managers and top executives	14.7	15
20	Communication, transportation, and utilities managers	14.7	15

JOBS WITH THE MOST ANNUAL OPENINGS FOR COLLEGE GRADUATES AGED 55 AND OVER

Rank	Job	Percent 55 & Over	Growth
1	General managers and top executives	14.7	288,825
2	Service managers	14.6	171,229
3	Tutors and instructors	15.0	149,065
4	College and university faculty	19.0	126,583
5	Artists and commercial artists	13.1	46,893
6	Management analysts	22.3	46,026
7	Designers	13.2	42,479
8	Writers and editors	13.6	41,449
9	Education administrators	15.3	39,332
10	Engineering, mathematical, and natural science managers	14.7	37,494
11	Recreation workers	17.3	29,880
12	Physicians	18.0	29,681
13	Property and real estate managers	27.0	29,483
14	Administrative services managers	14.7	24,604
15	Construction managers	14.7	22,043
16	Librarians	20.7	16,810
17	Civil engineers	17.3	15,978
18	Industrial production managers	14.7	14,917
19	Psychiatric technicians	13.5	14,819
20	Clergy	31.2	14,515

Lists of Best Jobs with High Percentages of Part-time College Graduates

Many people prefer to work less than full-time. For example, people who are attending school or who have young children may prefer part-time work so that they can attend classes or spend more time with their family. There are also money-related reasons, such as working a second job to supplement income or working two or more part-time jobs because one desirable full-time job was not available. If you want to work part-time, these lists will be helpful in identifying where most others are finding opportunities for this kind of work.

About 12 percent of all workers in jobs requiring a college degree are employed part-time. We decided to include all jobs in our lists that had 16 percent or more workers employed part-time. It is interesting to note that half of the top 20 jobs ranked by percent of part-time workers are in health related areas and almost a third are education-related.

The first list contains all major occupations requiring a college degree arranged by percent employed part-time. The other lists are limited to the 40 occupations employing

16 percent or more part-time workers. Note that these are the only lists where earnings are reported as hourly earnings—we thought this made sense for evaluating these jobs, many of which are not highly compensated.

JOBS WITH HIGHEST PERCENTAGE OF PART-TIME COLLEGE GRADUATES

Rank	Job	Percent Part-time	Hourly Earnings	Growth	Openings
1	Farm and home management advisors	42.5	17.96	-38	3,078
2	Tutors and instructors	39.7	14.74	15	149,065
3	Preschool and kindergarten teachers	32.4	12.75	20	77,151
4	College and university faculty	32.3	23.52	19	126,583
5	Dietitians and nutritionists	29.1	16.40	18	4,079
6	Psychiatric technicians	26.4	10.59	9	14,819
7	Registered nurses	26.3	19.90	21	165,362
8	Public relations specialists and publicity writers	25.3	17.43	27	17,954
9	Pharmacists	24.6	27.88	13	13,827
10	Physician assistants	24.6	21.63	47	5,089
11	Artists and commercial artists	24.0	16.52	28	46,893
12	Psychologists	23.4	23.78	8	10,913
13	Dental hygienists	22.9	21.56	48	18,372
14	Cardiology technologists	22.9	16.21	35	1,686
15	Medical records technicians	22.9	10.20	51	13,258
16	Librarians	22.4	18.46	5	16,810
17	Healthcare support specialists	22.3	14.81	24	45,720
18	Property and real estate managers	21.9	16.67	16	29,483
19	Curators, archivists, museum technicians, and restorers	21.9	15.93	15	2,367
20	Animal breeders and trainers	21.9	11.84	0	1,327
21	Physical therapists	20.8	26.95	71	19,122
22	Occupational therapists	20.8	24.33	66	9,543
23	Speech-language pathologists and audiologists	20.8	21.33	51	12,203
24	Respiratory therapists	20.8	16.40	46	9,452
25	Therapeutic services and administration	20.8	15.19	67	4,767
26	Recreational therapists	20.8	13.42	21	3,414
27	Dentists	20.6	43.88	8	5,072
28	Management support workers	20.6	19.08	26	154,129
29	Designers	20.0	15.62	26	42,479
30	Interior designers	20.0	15.44	28	9,238
31	Management analysts	19.5	25.05	21	46,026
32	Clinical laboratory technologists	19.5	18.44	15	23,944

Rank	Job	Percent Part-time	Hourly Earnings	Growth	Openings
33	Writers and editors	18.5	17.76	21	41,449
34	Urban and regional planners	18.1	21.00	5	3,856
35	Social scientists	18.1	20.13	5	4,907
36	Counselors	18.0	18.78	19	27,181
37	Residential counselors	18.0	9.57	41	38,515
38	Nuclear medicine technologists	17.5	19.07	13	865
39	Radiologic technologists	17.5	15.79	29	12,865
40	Wholesale and retail buyers	16.5	16.72	0	22,432
41	Reporters and correspondents	14.6	14.26	-3	6,294
42	Director of Religious Education and Activities	14.0	12.33	36	10,780
43	Recreation workers	14.0	8.93	22	29,880
44	Special education teachers	12.9	18.85	59	49,029
45	Paralegals	12.5	16.01	68	21,705
46	Social workers	11.9	15.23	32	75,553
47	Elementary teachers	11.7	17.94	10	164,163
48	Science and mathematics technicians	11.7	15.75	13	23,271
49	Clergy	10.8	14.65	13	14,515
50	Secondary school teachers	10.6	18.75	22	168,392
51	Podiatrists	10.5	39.92	10	617
52	Chiropractors	10.5	32.69	27	2,594
53	Optometrists	10.5	31.33	12	1,630
54	Veterinarians and veterinary inspectors	10.5	26.65	23	2,381
55	Education administrators	9.8	26.88	12	39,332
56	Law clerks	9.6	13.63	12	8,181
57	Economists	8.8	25.18	19	11,343
58	Underwriters	8.4	19.45	6	10,918
59	Architects	8.0	24.12	20	10,404
60	Landscape architects	8.0	19.22	21	1,593
61	Judges and magistrates	7.8	29.88	2	3,558
62	Accountants and auditors	7.8	19.50	12	118,376
63	Management support specialists	7.7	19.53	20	124,342
64	Engineering technicians	7.4	16.90	7	44,475
65	Computer programmers	7.3	24.27	23	58,990
66	Insurance claims examiners	7.3	20.34	22	7,281
67	Physicians	7.2	48.52	21	29,681
68	Service managers	7.2	24.72	21	171,229
69	Budget analysts	7.2	22.28	12	8,204
70	Loan officers and counselors	7.2	18.96	28	29,989
71	Credit analysts	7.2	18.73	16	5,454

continued

JOBS WITH HIGHEST PERCENTAGE OF PART-TIME COLLEGE GRADUATES

Rank	Job	Percent Part-time	Hourly Earnings	Growth	Openings
72	Lawyers	7.0	35.02	19	45,929
73	Personnel, training, and labor relations specialists	6.9	19.02	18	36,049
74	Employment interviewers	6.9	16.63	16	10,430
75	Physicists and astronomers	6.6	32.72	-2	1,073
76	Medical scientists	6.6	27.13	25	3,333
77	Atmospheric and Space Scientists	6.6	24.87	8	421
78	Physical scientists	6.6	24.06	28	4,131
79	Biological scientists	6.6	22.86	25	7,111
80	Life scientists	6.6	21.40	-3	53
81	Agricultural and food scientists	6.6	20.77	20	2,016
82	Foresters and conservation scientists	6.6	20.30	17	3,200
83	Geologists, geophysicists, and oceanographers	6.3	26.73	15	1,688
84	Engineering, mathematical, and natural science managers	6.1	32.99	45	37,494
85	General managers and top executives	6.1	29.31	15	288,825
86	Industrial production managers	6.1	26.38	-3	14,917
87	Communication, transportation, and utilities managers	6.1	24.90	15	10,840
88	Construction managers	6.1	23.69	18	22,043
89	Administrative services managers	6.1	22.61	11	24,604
90	Computer engineers	5.7	27.21	109	34,884
91	Systems analysts	5.7	24.69	103	87,318
92	Computer scientists	5.7	22.87	118	26,733
93	Civil engineers	5.4	25.36	18	15,978
94	Actuaries	5.2	30.85	0	1,165
95	Statisticians	5.2	23.96	1	936
96	Mathematicians	5.2	20.26	9	960
97	Production engineers	4.5	27.44	14	19,706
98	Tax examiners and revenue agents	4.2	19.01	2	3,637
99	Personnel, training, and labor relations managers	3.6	24.08	18	20,995
100	Chemists	3.3	22.69	18	10,572
101	Petroleum engineers	3.1	32.84	-14	549
102	Nuclear engineers	3.1	30.95	5	714
103	Materials engineers	3.1	26.41	7	933
104	Mining engineers	3.1	25.79	-13	130
105	Electrical and electronic technicians	3.1	17.37	15	31,145

Rank	Job	Percent Part-time	Hourly Earnings	Growth	Openings
106	Purchasing managers	2.9	21.35	8	10,746
107	Operations research analysts	2.8	24.39	8	5,316
108	Marketing, advertising, and public relations managers	2.6	27.45	29	54,601
109	Financial managers	2.6	27.43	18	74,296
110	Electrical and electronics engineers	2.6	27.32	29	19,098
111	Industrial engineers	2.4	25.17	14	3,555
112	General purchasing agents	2.3	19.25	6	21,175
113	Mechanical engineers	2.1	25.10	16	14,290
114	Aerospace engineers	1.6	30.35	8	3,771
115	Chemical engineers	1.6	28.08	15	1,434

JOBS WITH THE BEST COMBINATION OF PAY, GROWTH, AND NUMBER OF OPENINGS FOR PART-TIME COLLEGE GRADUATES

Rank	Job	Percent Part-time	Hourly Earnings	Annual Growth	Openings
1	Physical therapists	20.8	$26.95	71	19,122
2	Management analysts	19.5	$25.05	21	46,026
3	Management support workers	20.6	$19.08	26	154,129
4	Dental hygienists	22.9	$21.56	48	18,372
5	Registered nurses	26.3	$19.90	21	165,362
6	College and university faculty	32.3	$23.52	19	126,583
7	Occupational therapists	20.8	$24.33	66	9,543
8	Speech-language pathologists and audiologists	20.8	$21.33	51	12,203
9	Artists and commercial artists	24.0	$16.52	28	46,893
10	Physician assistants	24.6	$21.63	47	5,089
11	Writers and editors	18.5	$17.76	21	41,449
12	Public relations specialists and publicity writers	25.3	$17.43	27	17,954
13	Pharmacists	24.6	$27.88	13	13,827
14	Counselors	18.0	$18.78	19	27,181
15	Designers	20.0	$15.62	26	42,479
16	Healthcare support specialists	22.3	$14.81	24	45,720
17	Clinical laboratory technologists	19.5	$18.44	15	23,944
18	Residential counselors	18.0	$9.57	41	38,515
19	Property and real estate managers	21.9	$16.67	16	29,483
20	Respiratory therapists	20.8	$16.40	46	9,452

BEST PAYING JOBS FOR PART-TIME COLLEGE GRADUATES

Rank	Job	Percent Part-time	Hourly Earnings
1	Dentists	20.6	$43.88
2	Pharmacists	24.6	$27.88
3	Physical therapists	20.8	$26.95
4	Management analysts	19.5	$25.05
5	Occupational therapists	20.8	$24.33
6	Psychologists	23.4	$23.78
7	College and university faculty	32.3	$23.52
8	Physician assistants	24.6	$21.63
9	Dental hygienists	22.9	$21.56
10	Speech-language pathologists and audiologists	20.8	$21.33
11	Urban and regional planners	18.1	$21.00
12	Social scientists	18.1	$20.13
13	Registered nurses	26.3	$19.90
14	Management support workers	20.6	$19.08
15	Nuclear medicine technologists	17.5	$19.07
16	Counselors	18.0	$18.78
17	Librarians	22.4	$18.46
18	Clinical laboratory technologists	19.5	$18.44
19	Farm and home management advisors	42.5	$17.96
20	Writers and editors	18.5	$17.76

FASTEST GROWING JOBS FOR PART-TIME COLLEGE GRADUATES

Rank	Job	Percent Part-time	Percent Growth
1	Physical therapists	20.8	71
2	Therapeutic services and administration	20.8	67
3	Occupational therapists	20.8	66
4	Speech-language pathologists and audiologists	20.8	51
5	Medical records technicians	22.9	51
6	Dental hygienists	22.9	48
7	Physician assistants	24.6	47
8	Respiratory therapists	20.8	46
9	Residential counselors	18.0	41
10	Cardiology technologists	22.9	35
11	Radiologic technologists	17.5	29
12	Artists and commercial artists	24.0	28
13	Interior designers	20.0	28
14	Public relations specialists and publicity writers	25.3	27
15	Management support workers	20.6	26
16	Designers	20.0	26
17	Healthcare support specialists	22.3	24
18	Management analysts	19.5	21
19	Registered nurses	26.3	21
20	Writers and editors	18.5	21

JOBS WITH THE MOST OPENINGS FOR PART-TIME COLLEGE GRADUATES

Rank	Job	Percent Part-time	Annual Openings
1	Registered nurses	26.3	165,362
2	Management support workers	20.6	154,129
3	Tutors and instructors	39.7	149,065
4	College and university faculty	32.3	126,583
5	Preschool and kindergarten teachers	32.4	77,151
6	Artists and commercial artists	24.0	46,893
7	Management analysts	19.5	46,026
8	Healthcare support specialists	22.3	45,720
9	Designers	20.0	42,479
10	Writers and editors	18.5	41,449
11	Residential counselors	18.0	38,515
12	Property and real estate managers	21.9	29,483
13	Counselors	18.0	27,181
14	Clinical laboratory technologists	19.5	23,944
15	Wholesale and retail buyers	16.5	22,432
16	Physical therapists	20.8	19,122
17	Dental hygienists	22.9	18,372
18	Public relations specialists and publicity writers	25.3	17,954
19	Librarians	22.4	16,810
20	Psychiatric technicians	26.4	14,819

Lists of Best Jobs with High Percentages of Self-employed College Graduates

About 11 percent of all working people are self-employed or own their own business. This is a substantial part of our workforce, yet they get little mention in most career books. That is one reason we have included these lists.

Many occupations in these lists, such as Artists or Writers and editors, are held by people who operate one- or two-person businesses and who may also do this work part-time. Others develop small businesses and have dozens of employees working for them.

While the lists do not show it, older workers and women make up a rapidly growing part of the self-employed. Following the large-scale layoffs of the 1980s and 1990s, many highly experienced older workers had difficulty finding employment and set up consulting and other small businesses as a result. Large numbers of women are now forming small businesses or creating self-employment opportunities as an alternative to traditional employment.

Some occupations, such as Physicians and Lawyers, have a high percentage of self-employment but they have set up business structures where they technically work for a corporation rather than themselves. These workers are not included in the percent of self-employed used in these lists.

About 6 percent of all people working in jobs typically requiring a college degree are self-employed or own their own business. We sorted our database of occupations and included those jobs where more than 11 percent of the workers are self-employed. Nearly 50 percent of the top 20 occupations with the highest percent of self-employment require a master's or doctor's degree. This is quite high since less than 20 percent of all jobs requiring a college degree specify this level of education.

There are only 67 jobs included in the first list ranking all jobs because the remainder have virtually no self-employed workers. The remaining lists are based on the 24 occupations that met our criteria of 11 percent or more self-employed workers.

JOBS WITH HIGHEST PERCENTAGE OF SELF-EMPLOYED COLLEGE GRADUATES

Rank	Job	Percent Self-employed	Annual Earnings	Percent Growth	Annual Openings
1	Artists and commercial artists	60.9	$34,360	28	46,893
2	Chiropractors	57.7	$68,000	27	2,594
3	Service managers	49.4	$51,410	21	171,229
4	Dentists	48.6	$91,280	8	5,072
5	Podiatrists	46.6	$83,040	10	617
6	Management analysts	46.4	$52,110	21	46,026
7	Interior designers	46.3	$32,120	28	9,238
8	Psychologists	43.7	$49,460	8	10,913
9	Property and real estate managers	40.2	$34,680	16	29,483
10	Veterinarians and veterinary inspectors	39.6	$55,430	23	2,381
11	Optometrists	37.5	$65,170	12	1,630
12	Lawyers	36.0	$72,840	19	45,929
13	Designers	31.9	$32,480	26	42,479
14	Writers and editors	31.2	$36,940	21	41,449
15	Architects	30.8	$50,170	20	10,404
16	Landscape architects	21.6	$39,970	21	1,593
17	Physicians	20.4	$100,920	21	29,681
18	Economists	18.9	$52,370	19	11,343
19	Agricultural and food scientists	15.5	$43,200	20	2,016
20	Geologists, geophysicists, and oceanographers	15.1	$55,600	15	1,688
21	Education administrators	13.8	$55,900	12	39,332
22	Dietitians and nutritionists	13.2	$34,120	18	4,079
23	Reporters and correspondents	11.9	$29,660	-3	6,294
24	Actuaries	11.6	$64,160	0	1,165
25	Accountants and auditors	10.6	$40,550	12	118,376

continued

JOBS WITH HIGHEST PERCENTAGE OF SELF-EMPLOYED COLLEGE GRADUATES

Rank	Job	Percent Self-employed	Annual Earnings	Percent Growth	Annual Openings
26	Wholesale and retail buyers	10.5	$34,780	0	22,432
27	Speech-language pathologists and audiologists	10.5	$44,370	51	12,203
28	Recreational therapists	9.8	$27,920	21	3,414
29	Therapeutic services and administration	8.4	$31,590	67	4,767
30	Systems analysts	7.7	$51,360	103	87,318
31	Physical scientists	7.6	$50,040	28	4,131
32	Physical therapists	5.9	$56,060	71	19,122
33	Occupational therapists	5.6	$50,610	66	9,543
34	Public relations specialists and publicity writers	5.6	$36,260	27	17,954
35	Management support specialists	5.4	$40,630	20	124,342
36	Materials engineers	5.4	$54,930	7	933
37	Social scientists	5.2	$41,880	5	4,907
38	Physicists and astronomers	5.0	$68,060	-2	1,073
39	Civil engineers	4.9	$52,750	18	15,978
40	Biological scientists	4.9	$47,550	25	7,111
41	Computer programmers	4.8	$50,490	23	58,990
42	Pharmacists	4.2	$57,990	13	13,827
43	Computer engineers	4.1	$56,590	109	34,884
44	Healthcare support specialists	4.0	$30,800	24	45,720
45	Tutors and instructors	3.9	$30,650	15	149,065
46	Mechanical engineers	3.5	$52,210	16	14,290
47	Urban and regional planners	3.5	$43,670	5	3,856
48	Social workers	3.1	$31,680	32	75,553
49	Electrical and electronics engineers	2.9	$56,820	29	19,098
50	Medical scientists	2.8	$56,430	25	3,333
51	Production engineers	2.7	$57,070	14	19,706
52	Computer scientists	2.7	$47,570	118	26,733
53	Personnel, training, and labor relations specialists	2.6	$39,570	18	36,049
54	Law clerks	2.5	$28,360	12	8,181
55	Marketing, advertising, and public relations managers	2.4	$57,100	29	54,601
56	Foresters and conservation scientists	2.4	$42,230	17	3,200
57	Management support workers	2.4	$39,680	26	154,129
58	Electrical and electronic technicians	2.2	$36,120	15	31,145

Rank	Job	Percent Self-employed	Annual Earnings	Percent Growth	Annual Openings
59	Chemical engineers	2.0	$58,400	15	1,434
60	Engineering technicians	1.9	$35,147	7	44,475
61	Aerospace engineers	1.8	$63,130	8	3,771
62	Dental hygienists	1.6	$44,840	48	18,372
63	Preschool and kindergarten teachers	1.5	$26,525	20	77,151
64	Financial managers	1.4	$57,060	18	74,296
65	Director of Religious Education and Activities	1.2	$25,650	36	10,780
66	Construction managers	1.0	$49,280	18	22,043
67	Chemists	1.0	$47,200	18	10,572

JOBS WITH THE BEST COMBINATION OF PAY, GROWTH, AND NUMBER OF OPENINGS FOR SELF-EMPLOYED COLLEGE GRADUATES

Rank	Job	Percent Self-employed	Annual Earnings	Percent Growth	Openings
1	Physicians	20.4	$100,920	21	29,681
2	Lawyers	36.0	$72,840	19	45,929
3	Management analysts	46.4	$52,110	21	46,026
4	Service managers	49.4	$51,410	21	171,229
5	Artists and commercial artists	60.9	$34,360	28	46,893
6	Chiropractors	57.7	$68,000	27	2,594
7	Designers	31.9	$32,480	26	42,479
8	Veterinarians and veterinary inspectors	39.6	$55,430	23	2,381
9	Education administrators	13.8	$55,900	12	39,332
10	Writers and editors	31.2	$36,940	21	41,449
11	Economists	18.9	$52,370	19	11,343
12	Architects	30.8	$50,170	20	10,404
13	Dentists	48.6	$91,280	8	5,072
14	Interior designers	46.3	$32,120	28	9,238
15	Property and real estate managers	40.2	$34,680	16	29,483
16	Optometrists	37.5	$65,170	12	1,630
17	Geologists, geophysicists, and oceanographers	15.1	$55,600	15	1,688
18	Podiatrists	46.6	$83,040	10	617
19	Agricultural and food scientists	15.5	$43,200	20	2,016
20	Psychologists	43.7	$49,460	8	10,913

BEST PAYING JOBS FOR SELF-EMPLOYED COLLEGE GRADUATES

Rank	Job	Percent Self-employed	Annual Earnings
1	Physicians	20.4	$100,920
2	Dentists	48.6	$91,280
3	Podiatrists	46.6	$83,040
4	Lawyers	36.0	$72,840
5	Chiropractors	57.7	$68,000
6	Optometrists	37.5	$65,170
7	Actuaries	11.6	$64,160
8	Education administrators	13.8	$55,900
9	Geologists, geophysicists, and oceanographers	15.1	$55,600
10	Veterinarians and veterinary inspectors	39.6	$55,430
11	Economists	18.9	$52,370
12	Management analysts	46.4	$52,110
13	Service managers	49.4	$51,410
14	Architects	30.8	$50,170
15	Psychologists	43.7	$49,460
16	Agricultural and food scientists	15.5	$43,200
17	Landscape architects	21.6	$39,970
18	Writers and editors	31.2	$36,940
19	Property and real estate managers	40.2	$34,680
20	Artists and commercial artists	60.9	$34,360

FASTEST GROWING JOBS FOR SELF-EMPLOYED COLLEGE GRADUATES

Rank	Job	Percent Self-employed	Percent Growth
1	Artists and commercial artists	60.9	28
2	Interior designers	46.3	28
3	Chiropractors	57.7	27
4	Designers	31.9	26
5	Veterinarians and veterinary inspectors	39.6	23
6	Physicians	20.4	21
7	Management analysts	46.4	21
8	Service managers	49.4	21
9	Landscape architects	21.6	21
10	Writers and editors	31.2	21
11	Architects	30.8	20
12	Agricultural and food scientists	15.5	20
13	Lawyers	36.0	19
14	Economists	18.9	19
15	Dietitians and nutritionists	13.2	18
16	Property and real estate managers	40.2	16
17	Geologists, geophysicists, and oceanographers	15.1	15
18	Optometrists	37.5	12
19	Education administrators	13.8	12
20	Podiatrists	46.6	10

JOBS WITH THE MOST OPENINGS FOR SELF-EMPLOYED COLLEGE GRADUATES

Rank	Job	Percent Self-employed	Growth
1	Service managers	49.4	171,229
2	Artists and commercial artists	60.9	46,893
3	Management analysts	46.4	46,026
4	Lawyers	36.0	45,929
5	Designers	31.9	42,479
6	Writers and editors	31.2	41,449
7	Education administrators	13.8	39,332
8	Physicians	20.4	29,681
9	Property and real estate managers	40.2	29,483
10	Economists	18.9	11,343
11	Psychologists	43.7	10,913
12	Architects	30.8	10,404
13	Interior designers	46.3	9,238
14	Reporters and correspondents	11.9	6,294
15	Dentists	48.6	5,072
16	Dietitians and nutritionists	13.2	4,079
17	Chiropractors	57.7	2,594
18	Veterinarians and veterinary inspectors	39.6	2,381
19	Agricultural and food scientists	15.5	2,016
20	Geologists, geophysicists, and oceanographers	15.1	1,688

Lists of Best Jobs with High Percentages of Women College Graduates

We suggest you read the introductory material to "Lists of Best Jobs for College Graduates Based on a Variety of Interesting Criteria" and "Lists of Jobs with High Percentages of Men College Graduates" to better understand the purpose for our creating the following lists. These lists are not meant to restrict women from considering job options. Our reason for including these lists is exactly the opposite. We hope that the lists help people see possibilities that they might not otherwise have considered. For example, we suggest that women also browse the lists that employ high percentages of men. Many of these occupations pay quite well and could be handled by women who want to do them—and who get the necessary education and training.

As with most other lists in this book, we started these lists with all occupations typically requiring a two or four year college degree or more. We then included jobs where 60 percent or more of the workers were women. We then excluded any occupations with a growth rate of zero or lower. That left 32 jobs for women that met our criteria.

In comparing these lists to those with a high percentage of men, it struck us that there were distinct differences beyond the obvious. For example, jobs employing high percentages of women are growing much faster than the similar lists for men. The average job growth for the top 20 jobs for women is 34 percent while it is less than half that rate for men—15 percent. The number of annual job openings shows a similar pattern. Occupations with the highest percentage of men average 11,000 openings per year while there were triple the number of openings—34,000—for women.

This might explain why men have had more problems than women in adapting to an economy dominated by service and information-based jobs. Many women may simply be better prepared, with more appropriate skills for the jobs that are now growing rapidly and that have the most job openings. Economists have long noticed that men over 50 who are laid off find it very difficult to locate new jobs. Looking over our lists based on gender, you can see how this might be so. This trend is likely to continue as more women than men pursue a college degree—significantly more than of all college students are now women.

Perhaps you can come to other conclusions, but there is a variety of evidence that women equipped with a good education are doing quite well in the labor market. And it is increasingly true that either gender, without these skills, is less likely to find the best jobs.

JOBS WITH HIGHEST PERCENTAGE OF WOMEN COLLEGE GRADUATES

Rank	Job	Percent Women	Annual Earnings	Percent Annual Growth	Openings
1	Preschool and kindergarten teachers	98.0	$26,525	20	77,151
2	Registered nurses	93.8	$41,400	21	165,362
3	Dietitians and nutritionists	91.9	$34,120	18	4,079
4	Psychiatric technicians	88.9	$22,020	9	14,819
5	Pharmacists	86.1	$57,990	13	13,827
6	Physician assistants	86.1	$44,980	47	5,089
7	Elementary teachers	85.5	$37,310	10	164,163
8	Special education teachers	83.7	$39,200	59	49,029
9	Librarians	83.7	$38,400	5	16,810
10	Cardiology technologists	81.5	$33,720	35	1,686
11	Dental hygienists	81.5	$44,840	48	18,372
12	Medical records technicians	81.5	$21,220	51	13,258
13	Curators, archivists, museum technicians, and restorers	81.0	$33,130	15	2,367
14	Paralegals	79.8	$33,300	68	21,705
15	Healthcare support specialists	77.7	$30,800	24	45,720
16	Clinical laboratory technologists	76.8	$38,350	15	23,944
17	Insurance claims examiners	74.8	$42,310	22	7,281
18	Occupational therapists	74.2	$50,610	66	9,543
19	Physical therapists	74.2	$56,060	71	19,122
20	Recreational therapists	74.2	$27,920	21	3,414
21	Respiratory therapists	74.2	$34,110	46	9,452
22	Speech-language pathologists and audioloists	74.2	$44,370	51	12,203

continued

JOBS WITH HIGHEST PERCENTAGE OF WOMEN COLLEGE GRADUATES

Rank	Job	Percent Women	Annual Earnings	Percent Annual Growth	Openings
23	Therapeutic services and administration	74.2	$31,590	67	4,767
24	Nuclear medicine technologists	74.0	$39,670	13	865
25	Radiologic technologists	74.0	$32,840	29	12,865
26	Social workers	69.3	$31,680	32	75,553
27	Residential counselors	67.8	$19,910	41	38,515
28	Counselors	67.8	$39,060	19	27,181
29	Employment interviewers	64.9	$34,590	16	10,430
30	Personnel, training, and labor relations specialists	64.9	$39,570	18	36,049
31	Education administrators	62.0	$55,900	12	39,332
32	Personnel, training, and labor relations managers	61.9	$50,080	18	20,995

JOBS WITH THE BEST COMBINATION OF PAY, GROWTH, AND NUMBER OF OPENINGS THAT EMPLOY 60 PERCENT OR MORE OF WOMEN COLLEGE GRADUATES

Rank	Job	Percent Women	Annual Earnings	Percent Growth	Openings
1	Physical therapists	74.2	$56,060	71	19,122
2	Special education teachers	83.7	$39,200	59	49,029
3	Registered nurses	93.8	$41,400	21	165,362
4	Dental hygienists	81.5	$44,840	48	18,372
5	Occupational therapists	74.2	$50,610	66	9,543
6	Speech-language pathologists and audiologists	74.2	$44,370	51	12,203
7	Paralegals	79.8	$33,300	68	21,705
8	Education administrators	62.0	$55,900	12	39,332
9	Personnel, training, and labor relations managers	61.9	$50,080	18	20,995
10	Physician assistants	86.1	$44,980	47	5,089
11	Personnel, training, and labor relations specialists	64.9	$39,570	18	36,049
12	Social workers	69.3	$31,680	32	75,553
13	Counselors	67.8	$39,060	19	27,181
14	Pharmacists	86.1	$57,990	13	13,827
15	Healthcare support specialists	77.7	$30,800	24	45,720
16	Insurance claims examiners	74.8	$42,310	22	7,281
17	Elementary teachers	85.5	$37,310	10	164,163
18	Clinical laboratory technologists	76.8	$38,350	15	23,944
19	Preschool and kindergarten teachers	98.0	$26,525	20	77,151
20	Residential counselors	67.8	$19,910	41	38,515

BEST PAYING JOBS EMPLOYING 60 PERCENT OR MORE OF WOMEN COLLEGE GRADUATES

Rank	Job	Percent Women	Annual Earnings
1	Pharmacists	86.1	$57,990
2	Physical therapists	74.2	$56,060
3	Education administrators	62.0	$55,900
4	Occupational therapists	74.2	$50,610
5	Personnel, training, and labor relations managers	61.9	$50,080
6	Physician assistants	86.1	$44,980
7	Dental hygienists	81.5	$44,840
8	Speech-language pathologists and audiologists	74.2	$44,370
9	Insurance claims examiners	74.8	$42,310
10	Registered nurses	93.8	$41,400
11	Nuclear medicine technologists	74.0	$39,670
12	Personnel, training, and labor relations specialists	64.9	$39,570
13	Special education teachers	83.7	$39,200
14	Counselors	67.8	$39,060
15	Librarians	83.7	$38,400
16	Clinical laboratory technologists	76.8	$38,350
17	Farm and home management advisors	62.8	$37,350
18	Elementary teachers	85.5	$37,310
19	Employment interviewers	64.9	$34,590
20	Dietitians and nutritionists	91.9	$34,120

FASTEST GROWING JOBS EMPLOYING 60 PERCENT OR MORE OF WOMEN COLLEGE GRADUATES

Rank	Job	Percent Women	Percent Growth
1	Physical therapists	74.2	71
2	Paralegals	79.8	68
3	Therapeutic services and administration	74.2	67
4	Occupational therapists	74.2	66
5	Special education teachers	83.7	59
6	Speech-language pathologists and audiologists	74.2	51
7	Medical records technicians	81.5	51
8	Dental hygienists	81.5	48
9	Physician assistants	86.1	47
10	Respiratory therapists	74.2	46
11	Residential counselors	67.8	41
12	Cardiology technologists	81.5	35
13	Social workers	69.3	32
14	Radiologic technologists	74.0	29
15	Healthcare support specialists	77.7	24
16	Insurance claims examiners	74.8	22
17	Registered nurses	93.8	21
18	Recreational therapists	74.2	21
19	Preschool and kindergarten teachers	98.0	20
20	Counselors	67.8	19

JOBS WITH THE MOST OPENINGS EMPLOYING 60 PERCENT
OR MORE OF WOMEN COLLEGE GRADUATES

Rank	Job	Percent Women	Annual Openings
1	Registered nurses	93.8	165,362
2	Elementary teachers	85.5	164,163
3	Preschool and kindergarten teachers	98.0	77,151
4	Social workers	69.3	75,553
5	Special education teachers	83.7	49,029
6	Healthcare support specialists	77.7	45,720
7	Education administrators	62.0	39,332
8	Residential counselors	67.8	38,515
9	Personnel, training, and labor relations specialists	64.9	36,049
10	Counselors	67.8	27,181
11	Clinical laboratory technologists	76.8	23,944
12	Paralegals	79.8	21,705
13	Personnel, training, and labor relations managers	61.9	20,995
14	Physical therapists	74.2	19,122
15	Dental hygienists	81.5	18,372
16	Librarians	83.7	16,810
17	Psychiatric technicians	88.9	14,819
18	Pharmacists	86.1	13,827
19	Medical records technicians	81.5	13,258
20	Radiologic technologists	74.0	12,865

Lists of Jobs with High Percentages of Men College Graduates

We suggest you read the introductory material to "The Best Jobs Lists for Different Types of Workers" and "Lists of Best Jobs with High Percentages of Women College Graduates" to better understand why we included the following lists. As stated earlier, we are not suggesting that the best jobs lists for men include the only jobs that men should consider.

For example, male nurses and elementary school teachers are in short supply, and the few available are highly recruited and often find jobs quickly. Just as women should consider careers typically held by men, many men should consider career opportunities usually held by women. This is particularly true now, since occupations with high percentages of women workers are growing more rapidly than our similar lists for men.

Note that 11 of the best jobs for men are in the engineering or science fields while 13 of the best jobs for women are in the health and education fields. This confirms the concern of many educators, counselors, and social advocates have about gender stereotyping of occupations. In many cases, both men and women would be well advised to consider occupations typically held by the opposite gender.

Another thing we noticed is that the 20 best-paying jobs for men have earnings significantly higher than the women's best-paying jobs. You have to go to the 16th position on the men's list before finding a job that earns less than the highest-paying job for women. Nine of the highest paying jobs for women are in the health field and none are in engineering. Eight of the highest paying jobs for men are in the engineering field and five are in the health field. However, the health-related jobs for men are physicians and dentists compared with the health-related jobs for women of physician assistants and dental hygienists. This indicates that women interested in improving their earnings might want to seriously consider jobs traditionally dominated by men.

We used similar criteria for selecting the jobs for men as we did with women. In both cases, we included only those jobs where 60 percent or more were of the appropriate gender, and excluded jobs with zero or negative growth rates. For men, this meant that 48 jobs met our criteria for the lists that follow.

JOBS WITH HIGHEST PERCENTAGE OF MEN COLLEGE GRADUATES

Rank	Job	Percent Men	Annual Earnings	Percent Annual Growth	Openings
1	Mechanical engineers	94.8	$52,210	16	14,290
2	Electrical and electronics engineers	93.5	$56,820	29	19,098
3	Civil engineers	91.9	$52,750	18	15,978
4	Aerospace engineers	91.7	$63,130	8	3,771
5	Chemical engineers	91.7	$58,400	15	1,434
6	Materials engineers	91.7	$54,930	7	933
7	Nuclear engineers	91.7	$64,380	5	714
8	Production engineers	89.6	$57,070	14	19,706
9	Clergy	88.6	$30,480	13	14,515
10	Electrical and electronic technicians	85.0	$36,120	15	31,145
11	Industrial engineers	84.8	$52,350	14	3,555
12	Architects	83.5	$50,170	20	10,404
13	Landscape architects	83.5	$39,970	21	1,593
14	Chiropractors	78.5	$68,000	27	2,594
15	Dentists	78.5	$91,280	8	5,072
16	Optometrists	78.5	$65,170	12	1,630
17	Podiatrists	78.5	$83,040	10	617
18	Veterinarians and veterinary inspectors	78.5	$55,430	23	2,381

Rank	Job	Percent Men	Annual Earnings	Percent Annual Growth	Openings
19	Physicians	77.8	$100,920	21	29,681
20	Engineering technicians	76.5	$35,147	7	44,475
21	Lawyers	75.4	$72,840	19	45,929
22	Judges and magistrates	75.3	$62,160	2	3,558
23	Administrative services managers	71.8	$47,030	11	24,604
24	Communication, transportation, and utilities managers	71.8	$51,790	15	10,840
25	Construction managers	71.8	$49,280	18	22,043
26	Engineering, mathematical, and natural science managers	71.8	$68,620	45	37,494
27	General managers and top executives	71.8	$60,960	15	288,825
28	Computer programmers	70.9	$50,490	23	58,990
29	Animal breeders and trainers	69.8	$24,620	0	1,327
30	Agricultural and food scientists	69.1	$43,200	20	2,016
31	Biological scientists	69.1	$47,550	25	7,111
32	Foresters and conservation scientists	69.1	$42,230	17	3,200
33	Medical scientists	69.1	$56,430	25	3,333
34	Computer scientists	69.1	$47,570	118	26,733
35	Chemists	69.1	$47,200	18	10,572
36	Geologists, geophysicists, and oceanographers	69.1	$55,600	15	1,688
37	Atmospheric and Space Scientists	69.1	$51,730	8	421
38	Physical scientists	69.1	$50,040	28	4,131
39	Computer engineers	68.7	$56,590	109	34,884
40	Systems analysts	68.7	$51,360	103	87,318
41	Actuaries	66.4	$64,160	0	1,165
42	Statisticians	66.4	$49,830	1	936
43	Mathematicians	66.4	$42,150	9	960
44	Management analysts	66.1	$52,110	21	46,026
45	Marketing, advertising, and public relations managers	65.6	$57,100	29	54,601
46	Service managers	64.1	$51,410	21	171,229
47	Purchasing managers	63.7	$44,400	8	10,746
48	Science and mathematics technicians	63.1	$32,760	13	23,271

JOBS WITH THE BEST COMBINATION OF PAY, GROWTH, AND NUMBER OF OPENINGS THAT EMPLOY 60 PERCENT OR MORE OF MEN COLLEGE GRADUATES

Rank	Job	Percent Men	Annual Earnings	Percent Annual Growth	Openings
1	Engineering, mathematical, and natural science managers	71.8	$68,620	45	37,494
2	Physicians	77.8	$100,920	21	29,681
3	Marketing, advertising, and public relations managers	65.6	$57,100	29	54,601
4	Lawyers	75.4	$72,840	19	45,929
5	Computer engineers	68.7	$56,590	109	34,884
6	Systems analysts	68.7	$51,360	103	87,318
7	General managers and top executives	71.8	$60,960	15	288,825
8	Electrical and electronics engineers	93.5	$56,820	29	19,098
9	Management analysts	66.1	$52,110	21	46,026
10	Service managers	64.1	$51,410	21	171,229
11	Computer programmers	70.9	$50,490	23	58,990
12	Chiropractors	78.5	$68,000	27	2,594
13	Computer scientists	69.1	$47,570	118	26,733
14	Medical scientists	69.1	$56,430	25	3,333
15	Production engineers	89.6	$57,070	14	19,706
16	Civil engineers	91.9	$52,750	18	15,978
17	Dentists	78.5	$91,280	8	5,072
18	Veterinarians and veterinary inspectors	78.5	$55,430	23	2,381
19	Physical scientists	69.1	$50,040	28	4,131
20	Mechanical engineers	94.8	$52,210	16	14,290

BEST PAYING JOBS EMPLOYING 60 PERCENT
OR MORE OF MEN COLLEGE GRADUATES

Rank	Job	Percent Men	Annual Earnings
1	Physicians	77.8	$100,920
2	Dentists	78.5	$91,280
3	Podiatrists	78.5	$83,040
4	Lawyers	75.4	$72,840
5	Engineering, mathematical, and natural science managers	71.8	$68,620
6	Petroleum engineers	91.7	$68,300
7	Physicists and astronomers	69.1	$68,060
8	Chiropractors	78.5	$68,000
9	Optometrists	78.5	$65,170
10	Nuclear engineers	91.7	$64,380
11	Actuaries	66.4	$64,160
12	Aerospace engineers	91.7	$63,130
13	Judges and magistrates	75.3	$62,160
14	General managers and top executives	71.8	$60,960
15	Chemical engineers	91.7	$58,400
16	Marketing, advertising, and public relations managers	65.6	$57,100
17	Production engineers	89.6	$57,070
18	Electrical and electronics engineers	93.5	$56,820
19	Computer engineers	68.7	$56,590
20	Medical scientists	69.1	$56,430

FASTEST GROWING JOBS EMPLOYING 60 PERCENT
OR MORE OF MEN COLLEGE GRADUATES

Rank	Job	Percent Men	Growth
1	Computer scientists	69.1	118
2	Computer engineers	68.7	109
3	Systems analysts	68.7	103
4	Engineering, mathematical, and natural science managers	71.8	45
5	Marketing, advertising, and public relations managers	65.6	29
6	Electrical and electronics engineers	93.5	29
7	Physical scientists	69.1	28
8	Chiropractors	78.5	27
9	Medical scientists	69.1	25
10	Biological scientists	69.1	25
11	Veterinarians and veterinary inspectors	78.5	23
12	Computer programmers	70.9	23
13	Physicians	77.8	21
14	Management analysts	66.1	21
15	Service managers	64.1	21
16	Landscape architects	83.5	21
17	Architects	83.5	20
18	Agricultural and food scientists	69.1	20
19	Lawyers	75.4	19
20	Civil engineers	91.9	18

JOBS WITH THE MOST ANNUAL OPENINGS EMPLOYING 60 PERCENT OR MORE OF MEN COLLEGE GRADUATES

Rank	Job	Percent Men	Annual Growth
1	General managers and top executives	71.8	288,825
2	Service managers	64.1	171,229
3	Systems analysts	68.7	87,318
4	Computer programmers	70.9	58,990
5	Marketing, advertising, and public relations managers	65.6	54,601
6	Management analysts	66.1	46,026
7	Lawyers	75.4	45,929
8	Engineering technicians	76.5	44,475
9	Engineering, mathematical, and natural science managers	71.8	37,494
10	Computer engineers	68.7	34,884
11	Electrical and electronic technicians	85.0	31,145
12	Physicians	77.8	29,681
13	Computer scientists	69.1	26,733
14	Administrative services managers	71.8	24,604
15	Science and mathematics technicians	63.1	23,271
16	Construction managers	71.8	22,043
17	Production engineers	89.6	19,706
18	Electrical and electronics engineers	93.5	19,098
19	Civil engineers	91.9	15,978
20	Industrial production managers	71.8	14,917

Lists of Best Jobs Based on Levels of Education: Those with the Best Combination of Pay, Growth, and Number of Openings

A very clear relationship exists between education and earnings—the more education you have, the more you are likely to earn. The chart contained in the Introduction to this book vividly illustrates this fact. The lists that follow arrange all major jobs by level of education typically required for a new entrant to begin work in the occupation. Once again, our lists use the same categories now used by the U.S. Department of Labor for entry into various occupations.

Unlike many of the other lists, we did not include separate lists for highest pay, growth, or number of openings. Instead, we included on one list all the occupations in our database that fit into each of the education levels. They are ranked by the score combining best pay, growth, and job openings.

Section I: The Best Jobs Lists

Use the Lists to Locate Better Job Opportunities

You can use these lists to identify a job with higher potential but with a similar level of education to the job you now hold. For example, statisticians and economists develop and use many of the same skills. Both jobs require extensive math skills and the ability to deal with complex problems. A look at the list for jobs requiring a bachelor's degree reveals that economists are better paid, new jobs are being created at a reasonable rate, and there are 10 times the annual number of job openings than for statisticians. Knowing this can be very helpful since it will tell you how to leverage your present skills and experience into jobs that might be better for you.

You can also use these lists to figure out the possibilities if you were to get additional training, education, or work experience. For example, high school or college students can use these lists to identify occupations that offer high potential. College graduates can use the lists to identify graduate degrees that could improve their employment options.

The lists of jobs by education should also help you when planning your education. For example, you might be thinking about a major in nuclear engineering because the pay is very good. However, computer, civil, and production engineers offer a much greater potential for the same general educational requirements.

Caveat Datum Revisited

We warned you in the Introduction to beware the data, and we want to do it again here. The occupational data we used in this book is the most accurate available anywhere, but it has its limitations. For example, a four-year degree in accounting, finance, or a related area is typically required for entry into the accounting profession. But some people working as accountants don't have such a degree, and others have much more education than the "minimum" required for entry.

In a similar way, people with a graduate degree will typically earn considerably more than someone with a bachelor's degree. However, many people with a bachelor's degree earn considerably more than the highest paying occupations listed in this book. On the other hand, some people with a bachelor's degree earn much less than the average shown in this book—this is particularly true early in a person's career.

So as you browse the lists that follow, please use them as a way to be encouraged rather than discouraged. Education and training are very important for success in the labor market of the future, but so is ability, drive, initiative, and, yes, luck.

Having said this, we encourage you to get as much education and training as you can. It used to be that you got your schooling and never went back, but this is not a good attitude to have now. You will probably need to continue learning new things throughout your working life. This can be done by going to school, and this is a good thing for many people to do. But there are also many other ways to learn such as workshops, adult education programs, certification programs, employer training, professional conferences, Internet training, reading related books and magazines, and many others. Upgrading your computer and other technical skills is particularly important in our rapidly changing workplace, and you avoid doing so at your peril.

As one of our grandfathers used to say, "The harder you work, the luckier you get." It is just as true now as it was then.

Explanation of Education Levels

College degrees have no universal standards. Each college or university determines the number of credit hours and courses that are required for a specific degree. For example, we compared requirements for an anthropology degree at three universities and found that the major required anywhere from 27 to 36 semester hours—and total credits to get a bachelor's degree ranged from 120 to 126 hours. Also, there can be a wide difference in degree requirements depending on the type of major. An example is one university where a Bachelor of Architecture degree requires 160 semester hours while a Bachelor of Arts in History requires 126 hours. Thus, when a job indicates that a bachelor's degree is required, additional research is needed to determine exactly what investment in years and courses is required for the specific occupation.

There are however, general guidelines that can help you understand what is generally meant by a specific degree. The following definitions should be useful as you examine the lists of jobs by education level.

Associate Degree   The associate degree usually requires about 60 to 63 semester hours to complete. A normal course load for a full-time student each semester is 15 hours. This means that it typically takes two years to complete an associate degree.

Bachelor's Degree   A bachelor's degree usually requires about 120 to 130 semester hours to complete. This will usually take four to five years for a full-time student to complete—depending on the complexity of courses. Traditionally people have thought of the bachelor's degree as a four-year degree. There are some bachelor's degrees—like the Bachelor of Architecture degree we previously mentioned—that are considered a first professional degree and take a full five or more years to complete.

Master's Degree   This degree is usually 33 to 60 semester hours beyond the bachelor's degree. The academic master's degrees—like a Master of Arts in political science—usually require 33 to 36 hours. A first professional degree at the master's level—like a Master of Social Work—requires almost two years of full-time work.

First Professional Degree   Some professional degrees require three or more years of full-time academic study beyond the bachelor's degree. A professional degree prepares you for a specific profession. It uses theory and research to teach practical applications in a professional occupation. Examples of this type of degree are Doctor of Medicine (M.D.) for physicians, Doctor of Ministry (D.Min.) for clergy, and Juris Doctor (J.D.) for attorneys.

Doctor's Degree The Doctor's degree prepares students for careers that consist primarily of theory development, research, and/or college teaching. This type of degree is typically the Doctor of Philosophy (Ph.D.) and Doctor of Education (Ed.D.). Normally, a requirement for a doctor's degree is the completion of a master's degree plus an additional two to three years of full-time coursework and a one-to-two-semester research paper called the dissertation. It usually takes 4 to 5 years beyond the bachelor's degree to complete a doctor's degree.

We've organized all major jobs into four lists by educational level. They are associate, bachelor's, graduate degree, and bachelor's degree plus work experience. We've combined jobs requiring a master's degree, first professional degree, or doctor's degree in the graduate degree list. We did this because of the small number of jobs in each particular category. However, the job descriptions in Section 2 contain the specific type of graduate degree required. The list with jobs requiring a bachelor's degree plus work experience also contains two jobs that frequently require a graduate degree plus work experience.

BEST JOBS REQUIRING AN ASSOCIATE DEGREE

Rank	Job	Annual Earnings	Percent Growth	Annual Openings
1	Registered nurses	$41,400	21	165,362
2	Dental hygienists	$44,840	48	18,372
3	Paralegals	$33,300	68	21,705
4	Electrical and electronic technicians	$36,120	15	31,145
5	Healthcare support specialists	$30,800	24	45,720
6	Engineering technicians	$35,147	7	44,475
7	Respiratory therapists	$34,110	46	9,452
8	Cardiology technologists	$33,720	35	1,686
9	Medical records technicians	$21,220	51	13,258
10	Radiologic technologists	$32,840	29	12,865
11	Nuclear medicine technologists	$39,670	13	865
12	Science and mathematics technicians	$32,760	13	23,271
13	Psychiatric technicians	$22,020	9	14,819

BEST JOBS REQUIRING A BACHELOR'S DEGREE

Rank	Job	Annual Earnings	Percent Growth	Annual Openings
1	Computer engineers	$56,590	109	34,884
2	Systems analysts	$51,360	103	87,318
3	Physical therapists	$56,060	71	19,122
4	Electrical and electronics engineers	$56,820	29	19,098
5	Computer scientists	$47,570	118	26,733
6	Computer programmers	$50,490	23	58,990

Rank	Job	Annual Earnings	Percent Growth	Annual Openings
7	Management support workers	$39,680	26	154,129
8	Special education teachers	$39,200	59	49,029
9	Occupational therapists	$50,610	66	9,543
10	Secondary school teachers	$39,010	22	168,392
11	Management support specialists	$40,630	20	124,342
12	Loan officers and counselors	$39,430	28	29,989
13	Civil engineers	$52,750	18	15,978
14	Production engineers	$57,070	14	19,706
15	Social workers	$31,680	32	75,553
16	Economists	$52,370	19	11,343
17	Construction managers	$49,280	18	22,043
18	Physician assistants	$44,980	47	5,089
19	Pharmacists	$57,990	13	13,827
20	Physical scientists	$50,040	28	4,131
21	Designers	$32,480	26	42,479
22	Mechanical engineers	$52,210	16	14,290
23	Writers and editors	$36,940	21	41,449
24	Architects	$50,170	20	10,404
25	Personnel, training, and labor relations specialists	$39,570	18	36,049
26	Residential counselors	$19,910	41	38,515
27	Accountants and auditors	$40,550	12	118,376
28	Public relations specialists and publicity writers	$36,260	27	17,954
29	Insurance claims examiners	$42,310	22	7,281
30	Chemists	$47,200	18	10,572
31	Preschool and kindergarten teachers	$26,525	20	77,151
32	Elementary teachers	$37,310	10	164,163
33	Chemical engineers	$58,400	15	1,434
34	Aerospace engineers	$63,130	8	3,771
35	Industrial production managers	$54,860	-3	14,917
36	Tutors and instructors	$30,650	15	149,065
37	Recreation workers	$18,570	22	29,880
38	Director of Religious Education and Activities	$25,650	36	10,780
39	Geologists, geophysicists, and oceanographers	$55,600	15	1,688
40	Clinical laboratory technologists	$38,350	15	23,944
41	Property and real estate managers	$34,680	16	29,483
42	Therapeutic services and administration	$31,590	67	4,767
43	Interior designers	$32,120	28	9,238
44	Agricultural and food scientists	$43,200	20	2,016
45	Industrial engineers	$52,350	14	3,555
46	General purchasing agents	$40,030	6	21,175

continued

BEST JOBS REQUIRING A BACHELOR'S DEGREE

Rank	Job	Annual Earnings	Percent Growth	Annual Openings
47	Budget analysts	$46,350	12	8,204
48	Landscape architects	$39,970	21	1,593
49	Nuclear engineers	$64,380	5	714
50	Foresters and conservation scientists	$42,230	17	3,200
51	Actuaries	$64,160	0	1,165
52	Underwriters	$40,460	6	10,918
53	Credit analysts	$38,960	16	5,454
54	Materials engineers	$54,930	7	933
55	Employment interviewers	$34,590	16	10,430
56	Petroleum engineers	$68,300	-14	549
57	Wholesale and retail buyers	$34,780	0	22,432
58	Atmospheric and Space Scientists	$51,730	8	421
59	Dietitians and nutritionists	$34,120	18	4,079
60	Recreational therapists	$27,920	21	3,414
61	Mining engineers	$53,650	-13	130
62	Statisticians	$49,830	1	936
63	Tax examiners and revenue agents	$39,540	2	3,637
64	Law clerks	$28,360	12	8,181
65	Reporters and correspondents	$29,660	-3	6,294
66	Farm and home management advisors	$37,350	-38	3,078
67	Animal breeders and trainers	$24,620	0	1,327

BEST JOBS REQUIRING A BACHELOR'S DEGREE PLUS WORK EXPERIENCE

Rank	Job	Annual Earnings	Percent Growth	Annual Openings
1	Engineering, mathematical, and natural science managers	$68,620	45	37,494
2	Marketing, advertising, and public relations managers	$57,100	29	54,601
3	General managers and top executives	$60,960	15	288,825
4	Financial managers	$57,060	18	74,296
5	Service managers	$51,410	21	171,229
6	Artists and commercial artists	$34,360	28	46,893
7	Education administrators	$55,900	12	39,332
8	Personnel, training, and labor relations managers	$50,080	18	20,995
9	Communication, transportation, and utilities managers	$51,790	15	10,840
10	Judges and magistrates	$62,160	2	3,558
11	Administrative services managers	$47,030	11	24,604
12	Purchasing managers	$44,400	8	10,746

BEST JOBS REQUIRING A GRADUATE OR PROFESSIONAL DEGREE

Rank	Job	Annual Earnings	Percent Growth	Annual Openings
1	Physicians	$100,920	21	29,681
2	Lawyers	$72,840	19	45,929
3	Management analysts	$52,110	21	46,026
4	College and university faculty	$48,917	19	126,583
5	Chiropractors	$68,000	27	2,594
6	Speech-language pathologists and audiologists	$44,370	51	12,203
7	Medical scientists	$56,430	25	3,333
8	Biological scientists	$47,550	25	7,111
9	Dentists	$91,280	8	5,072
10	Veterinarians and veterinary inspectors	$55,430	23	2,381
11	Counselors	$39,060	19	27,181
12	Podiatrists	$83,040	10	617
13	Optometrists	$65,170	12	1,630
14	Operations research analysts	$50,740	8	5,316
15	Psychologists	$49,460	8	10,913
16	Clergy	$30,480	13	14,515
17	Physicists and astronomers	$68,060	-2	1,073
18	Librarians	$38,400	5	16,810
19	Urban and regional planners	$43,670	5	3,856
20	Curators, archivists, museum technicians, and restorers	$33,130	15	2,367
21	Social scientists	$41,880	5	4,907
22	Mathematicians	$42,150	9	960
23	Life scientists	$44,510	-3	53

Lists of College Degreed Jobs Based on Interests

These lists organize occupations into groupings based on interests. The system using these interest areas was developed by the U.S. Department of Labor as an intuitive system to assist in career exploration. The system is called the *Guide for Occupational Exploration*, or GOE. The GOE is a very helpful system for exploring career alternatives, as it organizes all jobs (over 12,000 titles) within 12 interest areas and then into increasingly specific subgroups. You can obtain additional information on the GOE from books titled *The Guide for Occupational Exploration* or *The Enhanced Guide for Occupational Exploration*.

Within each GOE interest grouping, occupations are arranged in order of their total scores based on earnings, pay, and number of openings. All jobs that are described in Section 2 are included in these lists. The lists provide a useful way to identify jobs that are related to ones you have had in the past or that require similar skills to those you want to use in the future.

Section 1: The Best Jobs Lists

There are 12 interest groups in the GOE but three interest groups—Protective, Industrial, and Physical Performing—didn't have any jobs requiring a college degree and are not included in the lists.

Artistic Jobs

Involve an interest in the creative expression of feelings or ideas.

Rank	Job	Annual Earnings	Percent Growth	Annual Openings
1	Artists and commercial artists	$34,360	28	46,893
2	Designers	$32,480	26	42,479
3	Writers and editors	$36,940	21	41,449
4	Interior designers	$32,120	28	9,238

Scientific Jobs

Involve an interest in discovering, collecting, and analyzing information about the natural world, and in applying scientific research findings to problems in medicine, the life sciences, and the natural sciences.

Rank	Job	Annual Earnings	Percent Growth	Annual Openings
1	Physicians	$100,920	21	29,681
2	Chiropractors	$68,000	27	2,594
3	Speech-language pathologists and audiologists	$44,370	51	12,203
4	Medical scientists	$56,430	25	3,333
5	Physical scientists	$50,040	28	4,131
6	Pharmacists	$57,990	13	13,827
7	Biological scientists	$47,550	25	7,111
8	Dentists	$91,280	8	5,072
9	Chemists	$47,200	18	10,572
10	Veterinarians and veterinary inspectors	$55,430	23	2,381
11	Clinical laboratory technologists	$38,350	15	23,944
12	Geologists, geophysicists, and oceanographers	$55,600	15	1,688
13	Optometrists	$65,170	12	1,630
14	Science and mathematics technicians	$32,760	13	23,271
15	Foresters and conservation scientists	$42,230	17	3,200
16	Agricultural and food scientists	$43,200	20	2,016
17	Podiatrists	$83,040	10	617
18	Physicists and astronomers	$68,060	-2	1,073
19	Atmospheric and Space Scientists	$51,730	8	421
20	Nuclear medicine technologists	$39,670	13	865
21	Life scientists	$44,510	-3	53

Plants and Animals Jobs

Involve an interest in working with plants and animals, usually outdoors.

Rank	Job	Annual Earnings	Percent Growth	Annual Openings
1	Animal breeders and trainers	$24,620	0	1,327

Mechanical Jobs

Involved an interest in applying mechanical principles to practical situations by use of machines or hand tools.

Rank	Job	Annual Earnings	Percent Growth	Annual Openings
1	Engineering, mathematical, and natural science managers	$68,620	45	37,494
2	Computer engineers	$56,590	109	34,884
3	Electrical and electronics engineers	$56,820	29	19,098
4	Production engineers	$57,070	14	19,706
5	Civil engineers	$52,750	18	15,978
6	Construction managers	$49,280	18	22,043
7	Aerospace engineers	$63,130	8	3,771
8	Chemical engineers	$58,400	15	1,434
9	Architects	$50,170	20	10,404
10	Mechanical engineers	$52,210	16	14,290
11	Electrical and electronic technicians	$36,120	15	31,145
12	Landscape architects	$39,970	21	1,593
13	Engineering technicians	$35,147	7	44,475
14	Nuclear engineers	$64,380	5	714
15	Industrial production managers	$54,860	-3	14,917
16	Industrial engineers	$52,350	14	3,555
17	Petroleum engineers	$68,300	-14	549
18	Materials engineers	$54,930	7	933
19	Mining engineers	$53,650	-13	130

Business Detail Jobs

Involve an interest in organized, clearly defined activities requiring accuracy and attention to details, primarily in an office setting.

Rank	Job	Annual Earnings	Percent Growth	Annual Openings
1	Medical records technicians	$21,220	51	13,258
2	Insurance claims examiners	$42,310	22	7,281
3	Law clerks	$28,360	12	8,181

Selling Jobs

Involve an interest in bringing others to a particular point of view by personal persuasion, using sales and promotional techniques.

Rank	Job	Annual Earnings	Percent Growth	Annual Openings
1	Wholesale and retail buyers	$34,780	0	22,432

Accommodating/Personal Service Jobs

Involve an interest in catering to the wishes and needs of others, usually on a one-to-one basis.

Rank	Job	Annual Earnings	Percent Growth	Annual Openings
1	Recreation workers	$ 18,570	22	29,880

Humanitarian/Helping People Jobs

Involve an interest in helping others with their mental, spiritual, social, physical, or vocational needs.

Rank	Job	Annual Earnings	Percent Growth	Annual Openings
1	Physical therapists	$56,060	71	19,122
2	Special education teachers	$39,200	59	49,029
3	Dental hygienists	$44,840	48	18,372
4	Occupational therapists	$50,610	66	9,543
5	Registered nurses	$41,400	21	165,362
6	Social workers	$31,680	32	75,553
7	Physician assistants	$44,980	47	5,089
8	Respiratory therapists	$34,110	46	9,452
9	Therapeutic services and administration	$31,590	67	4,767
10	Healthcare support specialists	$30,800	24	45,720
11	Radiologic technologists	$32,840	29	12,865
12	Preschool and kindergarten teachers	$26,525	20	77,151
13	Cardiology technologists	$33,720	35	1,686
14	Director of Religious Education and Activities	$25,650	36	10,780
15	Clergy	$30,480	13	14,515
16	Psychiatric technicians	$22,020	9	14,819
17	Recreational therapists	$27,920	21	3,414

Leading and Influencing Jobs

Involve an interest in leading and influencing others by using high-level verbal or numerical abilities.

Rank	Job	Annual Earnings	Percent Growth	Annual Openings
1	Systems analysts	$48,360	103	87,318
2	Marketing, advertising, and public relations managers	$57,100	29	54,601
3	Systems analysts	$51,360	103	87,318
4	Service managers	$51,410	21	171,229
5	Lawyers	$72,840	19	45,929
6	General managers and top executives	$60,960	15	288,825
7	Management analysts	$52,110	21	46,026
8	Financial managers	$57,060	18	74,296
9	Computer programmers	$50,490	23	58,990
10	College and university faculty	$48,917	19	126,583
11	Computer scientists	$47,570	118	26,733
12	Management support workers	$39,680	26	154,129
13	Management support specialists	$40,630	20	124,342
14	Secondary school teachers	$39,010	22	168,392
15	Education administrators	$55,900	12	39,332
16	Economists	$52,370	19	11,343
17	Loan officers and counselors	$39,430	28	29,989
18	Personnel, training, and labor relations managers	$50,080	18	20,995
19	Accountants and auditors	$40,550	12	118,376
20	Communication, transportation, and utilities managers	$51,790	15	10,840
21	Personnel, training, and labor relations specialists	$39,570	18	36,049
22	Residential counselors	$19,910	41	38,515
23	Paralegals	$33,300	68	21,705
24	Counselors	$39,060	19	27,181
25	Public relations specialists and publicity writers	$36,260	27	17,954
26	Administrative services managers	$47,030	11	24,604
27	Elementary teachers	$37,310	10	164,163
28	Tutors and instructors	$30,650	15	149,065
29	Psychologists	$49,460	8	10,913
30	Property and real estate managers	$34,680	16	29,483
31	Operations research analysts	$50,740	8	5,316
32	Budget analysts	$46,350	12	8,204
33	Judges and magistrates	$62,160	2	3,558

continued

Rank	Job	Annual Earnings	Percent Growth	Annual Openings
34	Purchasing managers	$44,400	8	10,746
35	General purchasing agents	$40,030	6	21,175
36	Actuaries	$64,160	0	1,165
37	Credit analysts	$38,960	16	5,454
38	Underwriters	$40,460	6	10,918
39	Employment interviewers	$34,590	16	10,430
40	Urban and regional planners	$43,670	5	3,856
41	Dietitians and nutritionists	$34,120	18	4,079
42	Mathematicians	$42,150	9	960
43	Social scientists	$41,880	5	4,907
44	Librarians	$38,400	5	16,810
45	Statisticians	$49,830	1	936
46	Curators, archivists, museum technicians, and restorers	$33,130	15	2,367
47	Tax examiners and revenue agents	$39,540	2	3,637
48	Farm and home management advisors	$37,350	-38	3,078
49	Reporters and correspondents	$29,660	-3	6,294

Lists of College Degreed Jobs Based on Six Occupational Types

One of the most popular career theories is John L. Holland's concept of six personality types and their relationship to careers. The six interest categories used to describe occupations are **Realistic, Investigative, Artistic, Social, Enterprising,** and **Conventional.** The Self-Directed Search (SDS), published by Psychological Assessment Resources, Inc., was developed as a practical tool for determining type and matching this to specific occupations. This instrument is used by many counselors and educators and so you may have taken the SDS at some time. If so, you might recall your type and can use that information in identifying jobs that match your type. It is also possible to use this section even though you haven't taken the SDS. Simply read each of the six type descriptions and determine the one that most closely describes yourself. We've ranked the jobs in each of the six SDS areas by earnings, growth, and annual job openings.

Artistic Jobs

Artistic occupations frequently involve working with forms, designs, and patterns. They often require self-expression and the work can be done without following a clear set of rules.

Rank	Job	Annual Earnings	Percent Growth	Annual Openings
1	Artists and commercial artists	$34,360	28	46,893
2	Architects	$50,170	20	10,404
3	Designers	$32,480	26	42,479
4	Writers and editors	$36,940	21	41,449
5	Landscape architects	$39,970	21	1,593
6	Librarians	$38,400	5	16,810
7	Interior designers	$32,120	28	9,238
8	Curators, archivists, museum technicians, and restorers	$33,130	15	2,367
9	Reporters and correspondents	$29,660	-3	6,294

Conventional Jobs

Conventional occupations frequently involve following set procedures and routines. These occupations can include working with data and details more than with ideas. Usually there is a clear line of authority to follow.

Rank	Job	Annual Earnings	Percent Growth	Annual Openings
1	Management analysts	$52,110	21	46,026
2	Management support specialists	$40,630	20	124,342
3	Accountants and auditors	$40,550	12	118,376
4	Budget analysts	$46,350	12	8,204
5	Medical records technicians	$21,220	51	13,258
6	Underwriters	$40,460	6	10,918
7	Actuaries	$64,160	0	1,165
8	Credit analysts	$38,960	16	5,454
9	Tax examiners and revenue agents	$39,540	2	3,637

Enterprising Jobs

Enterprising occupations frequently involve starting up and carrying out projects. These occupations can involve leading people and making many decisions. Sometimes they require risk taking and often deal with business.

Rank	Job	Annual Earnings	Percent Growth	Annual Openings
1	Engineering, mathematical, and natural science managers	$68,620	45	37,494
2	Marketing, advertising, and public relations managers	$57,100	29	54,601

continued

Rank	Job	Annual Earnings	Percent Growth	Annual Openings
3	Lawyers	$72,840	19	45,929
4	Financial managers	$57,060	18	74,296
5	General managers and top executives	$60,960	15	288,825
6	Service managers	$51,410	21	171,229
7	Education administrators	$55,900	12	39,332
8	Loan officers and counselors	$39,430	28	29,989
9	Construction managers	$49,280	18	22,043
10	Paralegals	$33,300	68	21,705
11	Personnel, training, and labor relations managers	$50,080	18	20,995
12	Public relations specialists and publicity writers	$36,260	27	17,954
13	Administrative services managers	$47,030	11	24,604
14	Communication, transportation, and utilities managers	$51,790	15	10,840
15	Property and real estate managers	$34,680	16	29,483
16	Insurance claims examiners	$42,310	22	7,281
17	Judges and magistrates	$62,160	2	3,558
18	Industrial production managers	$54,860	-3	14,917
19	General purchasing agents	$40,030	6	21,175
20	Purchasing managers	$44,400	8	10,746
21	Wholesale and retail buyers	$34,780	0	22,432
22	Law clerks	$28,360	12	8,181

Investigative Jobs

Investigative occupations frequently involve working with ideas and require an extensive amount of thinking. These occupations can involve searching for facts and figuring out problems mentally.

Rank	Job	Annual Earnings	Percent Growth	Annual Openings
1	Computer engineers	$56,590	109	34,884
2	Physicians	$100,920	21	29,681
3	Electrical and electronics engineers	$56,820	29	19,098
4	Systems analysts	$51,360	103	87,318
5	Computer scientists	$47,570	118	26,733
6	Computer programmers	$50,490	23	58,990
7	Chiropractors	$68,000	27	2,594
8	Production engineers	$57,070	14	19,706
9	Civil engineers	$52,750	18	15,978
10	Pharmacists	$57,990	13	13,827
11	Economists	$52,370	19	11,343

Rank	Job	Annual Earnings	Percent Growth	Annual Openings
12	Medical scientists	$56,430	25	3,333
13	Dentists	$91,280	8	5,072
14	Mechanical engineers	$52,210	16	14,290
15	Physician assistants	$44,980	47	5,089
16	Physical scientists	$50,040	28	4,131
17	Veterinarians and veterinary inspectors	$55,430	23	2,381
18	Biological scientists	$47,550	25	7,111
19	Respiratory therapists	$34,110	46	9,452
20	Radiologic technologists	$32,840	29	12,865
21	Chemists	$47,200	18	10,572
22	Aerospace engineers	$63,130	8	3,771
23	Chemical engineers	$58,400	15	1,434
24	Optometrists	$65,170	12	1,630
25	Geologists, geophysicists, and oceanographers	$55,600	15	1,688
26	Clinical laboratory technologists	$38,350	15	23,944
27	Industrial engineers	$52,350	14	3,555
28	Podiatrists	$83,040	10	617
29	Operations research analysts	$50,740	8	5,316
30	Psychologists	$49,460	8	10,913
31	Agricultural and food scientists	$43,200	20	2,016
32	Cardiology technologists	$33,720	35	1,686
33	Physicists and astronomers	$68,060	-2	1,073
34	Dietitians and nutritionists	$34,120	18	4,079
35	Foresters and conservation scientists	$42,230	17	3,200
36	Nuclear engineers	$64,380	5	714
37	Petroleum engineers	$68,300	-14	549
38	Materials engineers	$54,930	7	933
39	Urban and regional planners	$43,670	5	3,856
40	Social scientists	$41,880	5	4,907
41	Atmospheric and Space Scientists	$51,730	8	421
42	Mathematicians	$42,150	9	960
43	Mining engineers	$53,650	-13	130
44	Statisticians	$49,830	1	936
45	Nuclear medicine technologists	$39,670	13	865
46	Life scientists	$44,510	-3	53

Realistic Jobs

Realistic occupations frequently involve work activities that include practical, hands-on problems and solutions. They often deal with plants, animals, and real-world materials like wood, tools, and machinery. Many of the occupations require working outside, and do not involve a lot of paperwork or working closely with others.

Rank	Job	Annual Earnings	Percent Growth	Annual Openings
1	Electrical and electronic technicians	$36,120	15	31,145
2	Engineering technicians	$35,147	7	44,475
3	Science and mathematics technicians	$32,760	13	23,271
4	Animal breeders and trainers	$24,620	0	1,327

Social Jobs

Social occupations frequently involve working with, communicating with, and teaching people. These occupations often involve helping or providing service to others.

Rank	Job	Annual Earnings	Percent Growth	Annual Openings
1	Physical therapists	$56,060	71	19,122
2	Special education teachers	$39,200	59	49,029
3	Registered nurses	$41,400	21	165,362
4	Secondary school teachers	$39,010	22	168,392
5	Dental hygienists	$44,840	48	18,372
6	Occupational therapists	$50,610	66	9,543
7	Speech-language pathologists and audiologists	$44,370	51	12,203
8	Social workers	$31,680	32	75,553
9	Healthcare support specialists	$30,800	24	45,720
10	Personnel, training, and labor relations specialists	$39,570	18	36,049
11	Elementary school teachers	$37,310	10	164,163
12	Counselors	$39,060	19	27,181
13	Therapeutic services and administration	$31,590	67	4,767
14	Residential counselors	$19,910	41	38,515
15	Tutors and instructors	$30,650	15	149,065
16	Preschool and kindergarten teachers	$26,525	20	77,151
17	Recreation workers	$18,570	22	29,880
18	Director of Religious Education and Activities	$25,650	36	10,780
19	Employment interviewers	$34,590	16	10,430
20	Clergy	$30,480	13	14,515
21	Recreational therapists	$27,920	21	3,414
22	Farm and home management advisors	$37,350	-38	3,078
23	Psychiatric technicians	$22,020	9	14,819

Section 2

The Best Jobs Directory Descriptions of the 281 Best Jobs

This section of the book provides useful information for a large number of occupations that typically require a two or four year college degree. Among them are the jobs with the highest pay, fastest growth, and largest number of openings.

The occupations are arranged in alphabetic order. You can find a complete list of them in the Table of Contents. If you have not already read the Introduction to this book, please consider doing so because it provides important information on the selection criteria used for the descriptions included this directory. It also provides details on the descriptions themselves that will help you better understand them. If you refuse to read the Introduction, we ask you to at least feel a bit guilty for not doing so, though we do understand.

ACCOUNTANTS AND AUDITORS

Education	Bachelor's degree
Average Yearly Earnings	$38,168
Projected Growth	12%
Annual Job Openings	118,376
Self-employed	10%
Employed Part-time	8%

Accountants

Analyze financial information and prepare financial reports to determine or maintain record of assets, liabilities, profit and loss, tax liability, or other financial activities within an organization. (Excludes auditors.) Analyzes operations, trends, costs, revenues, financial commitments, and obligations incurred, to project future revenues and expenses, using computer. Develops, maintains, and analyzes budgets, and prepares periodic reports comparing budgeted costs to actual costs. Analyzes records of financial transactions to determine accuracy and completeness of entries, using computer. Prepares balance sheet, profit and loss statement, amortization and depreciation schedules, and other financial reports, using calculator or computer. Reports finances of establishment to management, and advises management about resource utilization, tax strategies, and assumptions underlying budget forecasts. Develops, implements, modifies, and documents budgeting, cost, general, property, and tax accounting systems. Predicts revenues and expenditures, and submits reports to management. Computes taxes owed; ensures compliance with tax payment, reporting, and other tax requirements; and represents establishment before taxing authority. Surveys establishment operations to ascertain accounting needs. Establishes table of accounts, and assigns entries to proper accounts. Audits contracts and prepares reports to substantiate transactions prior to settlement. Prepares forms and manuals for workers performing accounting and bookkeeping tasks. Appraises, evaluates, and inventories real property and equipment, and records description, value, location, and other information. Adapts accounting and recordkeeping functions to current technology of computerized accounting systems. Directs activities of workers performing accounting and bookkeeping tasks.

Occupational Type

Conventional occupations frequently involve following set procedures and routines. These occupations can include working with data and details more than with ideas. Usually there is a clear line of authority to follow.

Skills required of Accountants

Reading Comprehension, Active Listening, Writing, Speaking, Mathematics, Critical Thinking, Active Learning, Learning Strategies, Monitoring, Persuasion, Negotiation, Instructing, Problem Identification, Information Gathering, Information Organization, Synthesis/Reorganization, Idea Generation, Idea Evaluation, Implementation Planning, Operations Analysis, Equipment Selection, Product Inspection, Visioning, Systems Perception, Identifying Downstream Consequences, Identification of Key Causes, Judgment and Decision Making, Systems Evaluation, Time Management, Management of Financial Resources, Management of Material Resources, Management of Personnel Resources

College Majors

Accounting: An instructional program that prepares individuals to practice the profession of accounting, and to perform related business functions. Includes instruction in accounting principles and theory, financial accounting, managerial accounting, cost accounting, budget control, tax accounting, legal aspects of accounting, auditing, reporting procedures, statement analysis, planning and consulting, business information systems, accounting research methods, professional standards and ethics, and applications to specific for-profit, public, and non-profit organizations.

Supporting Courses

Administration and Management: Knowledge of principles and processes involved in business and organizational planning, coordination, and execution. This includes strategic planning, resource allocation, manpower modeling, leadership techniques, and production methods. **Clerical:** Knowledge of administrative and clerical procedures and systems such as word processing systems, filing and records management systems, stenography and transcription, forms design principles, and other office procedures and terminology.

Economics and Accounting: Knowledge of economic and accounting principles and practices, the financial markets, banking, and the analysis and reporting of financial data. **Personnel and Human Resources:** Knowledge of policies and practices involved in personnel/ human resource functions. This includes recruitment, selection, training, and promotion regulations and procedures; compensation and benefits packages; labor relations and negotiation strategies; and personnel information systems. **Computers and Electronics:** Knowledge of electric circuit boards, processors, chips, and computer hardware and software, including applications and programming. **Mathematics:** Knowledge of numbers, their operations, and interrelationships including arithmetic, algebra, geometry, calculus, statistics, and their applications. **Sociology and Anthropology:** Knowledge of group behavior and dynamics, societal trends and influences, cultures, their history, migrations, ethnicity, and origins. **Education and Training:** Knowledge of instructional methods and training techniques including curriculum design principles, learning theory, group and individual teaching techniques, design of individual development plans, and test design principles. **English Language:** Knowledge of the structure and content of the English language including the meaning and spelling of words, rules of composition, and grammar. **Philosophy and Theology:** Knowledge of different philosophical systems and religions, including their basic principles, values, ethics, ways of thinking, customs, and practices, and their impact on human culture. **Law, Government, and Jurisprudence:** Knowledge of laws, legal codes, court procedures, precedents, government regulations, executive orders, agency rules, and the democratic political process.

Auditors

Examine and analyze accounting records to determine financial status of establishment and prepare financial reports concerning operating procedures. Reviews data about material assets, net worth, liabilities, capital stock, surplus, income, and expenditures. Analyzes annual reports, financial statements, and other records, using accepted accounting and statistical procedures, to determine financial condition. Evaluates reports from commission regarding solvency and profitability of company. Inspects account books and system for efficiency, effectiveness, and use of accepted accounting procedures to record transactions. Inspects cash on hand, notes receivable and payable, negotiable securities, and canceled checks. Reports to management about asset utilization and audit results, and recommends changes in operations and financial activities. Reviews taxpayer accounts, and conducts audits on-site, by correspondence, or by summoning taxpayer to office. Analyzes data for deficient controls, duplicated effort, extravagance, fraud, or noncompliance with laws, regulations, and management policies. Audits records to determine unemployment insurance premiums, liabilities, and compliance with tax laws. Examines payroll and personnel records to determine worker's compensation coverage. Examines records, tax returns, and related documents pertaining to settlement of decedent's estate. Verifies journal and ledger entries by examining inventory. Studies costs and revenue requirements, and designs new rate structure. Confers with company officials about financial and regulatory matters. Evaluates taxpayer finances to determine tax liability, notifies taxpayer of liability, and advises taxpayer of appeal rights. Examines records and interviews workers to ensure recording of transactions and compliance with laws and regulations. Supervises auditing of establishments, and determines scope of investigation required. Prepares and presents testimony to regulatory commission hearings. Directs activities of personnel engaged in filing, recording, compiling, and transmitting financial records.

Occupational Type

Conventional occupations frequently involve following set procedures and routines. These occupations can include working with data and details more than with ideas. Usually there is a clear line of authority to follow.

Skills required of Auditors

Reading Comprehension, Active Listening, Writing, Speaking, Mathematics, Critical Thinking, Active Learning, Monitoring, Problem Identification, Information Gathering, Information Organization, Synthesis/Reorganization, Idea Generation, Idea Evaluation, Implementation Planning, Visioning, Systems Perception, Identifying Downstream Consequences, Identification of Key Causes, Judgment and Decision Making, Systems Evaluation, Time Management, Management of Financial Resources, Management of Personnel Resources

College Majors

Accounting: An instructional program that prepares individuals to practice the profession of accounting, and to perform related business functions. Includes instruction in accounting principles and theory, financial accounting, managerial accounting, cost accounting, budget control, tax accounting, legal aspects of accounting, auditing, reporting procedures, statement analysis, planning and consulting, business information systems, accounting research methods, professional standards and ethics, and applications to specific for-profit, public, and non-profit organizations.

Supporting Courses

Administration and Management: Knowledge of principles and processes involved in business and organizational planning, coordination, and execution. This includes strategic planning, resource allocation, manpower modeling, leadership techniques, and production methods. **Clerical:** Knowledge of administrative and clerical procedures and systems such as word processing systems, filing and records management systems, stenography and transcription, forms design principles, and other office procedures and terminology. **Economics and Accounting:** Knowledge of economic and accounting principles and practices, the financial markets, banking, and the analysis and reporting of financial data. **Computers and Electronics:** Knowledge of electric circuit boards, processors, chips, and computer hardware and software, including applications and programming. **Mathematics:** Knowledge of numbers, their operations, and interrelationships including arithmetic, algebra, geometry, calculus, statistics, and their applications. **English Language:** Knowledge of the structure and content of the English language including the meaning and spelling of words, rules of composition, and grammar. **Philosophy and Theology:** Knowledge of different philosophical systems and religions, including their basic principles, values, ethics, ways of thinking, customs, and practices, and their impact on human culture. **Law, Government, and Jurisprudence:** Knowledge of laws, legal codes, court procedures, precedents, government regulations, executive orders, agency rules, and the democratic political process.

Data Processing Auditors

Plan and conduct audits of data processing systems and applications to safeguard assets, ensure accuracy of data, and promote operational efficiency. Gathers data by interviewing workers, examining records, and using computer. Analyzes data to evaluate effectiveness of controls, accuracy of reports, and efficiency and security of operations. Establishes objectives and plan for audit, following general audit plan and previous audit reports. Writes audit report and recommendations, using computer. Devises, writes, and tests computer program to obtain information needed for audit. Devises controls for new or modified computer application, for error detection, and to prevent inaccuracy and data loss.

Occupational Type

Conventional occupations frequently involve following set procedures and routines. These occupations can include working with data and details more than with ideas. Usually there is a clear line of authority to follow.

Skills required of Data Processing Auditors

Reading Comprehension, Active Listening, Writing, Speaking, Critical Thinking, Active Learning, Learning Strategies, Monitoring, Problem Identification, Information Gathering, Information Organization, Synthesis/Reorganization, Idea Generation, Idea Evaluation, Implementation Planning, Operations Analysis, Technology Design, Equipment Selection, Programming, Testing, Product Inspection, Visioning, Systems Perception, Identifying Downstream Consequences, Identification of Key Causes, Judgment and Decision Making, Systems Evaluation

College Majors

Computer Programming: An instructional program that prepares individuals to apply methods and procedures used in designing and writing computer programs to developing solutions to specific operational problems and use requirements, including testing and troubleshooting prototype software packages.

Supporting Courses

Administration and Management: Knowledge of principles and processes involved in business and organizational planning, coordination, and execution. This includes strategic planning, resource allocation, manpower modeling, leadership techniques, and production methods. **Clerical:** Knowledge of administrative and clerical procedures and systems such as word processing systems, filing and records management systems, stenography and transcription, forms design principles, and other office procedures and terminology. **Economics and Accounting:** Knowledge of economic and accounting principles and practices, the financial markets, banking, and the analysis and reporting of financial data.

Computers and Electronics: Knowledge of electric circuit boards, processors, chips, and computer hardware and software, including applications and programming. **Mathematics:** Knowledge of numbers, their operations, and interrelationships including arithmetic, algebra, geometry, calculus, statistics, and their applications. **Philosophy and Theology:** Knowledge of different philosophical systems and religions, including their basic principles, values, ethics, ways of thinking, customs, and practices, and their impact on human culture. **Telecommunications:** Knowledge of transmission, broadcasting, switching, control, and operation of telecommunications systems.

ACTUARIES

Actuaries

	Education	Bachelor's degree
	Average Yearly Earnings	$66,352
	Projected Growth	0%
	Annual Job Openings	1,165
	Self-employed	0%
	Employed Part-time	5%

Apply knowledge of mathematics, probability, statistics, and principles of finance and business to problems in life, health, social, and casualty insurance, annuities, and pensions. Determines mortality, accident, sickness, disability, and retirement rates. Constructs probability tables regarding fire, natural disasters, and unemployment, based on analysis of statistical data and other pertinent information. Designs or reviews insurance and pension plans and calculates premiums. Determines equitable basis for distributing surplus earnings under participating insurance and annuity contracts in mutual companies. Ascertains premium rates required and cash reserves and liabilities necessary to ensure payment of future benefits.

Occupational Type

Conventional occupations frequently involve following set procedures and routines. These occupations can include working with data and details more than with ideas. Usually there is a clear line of authority to follow.

Skills required of Actuaries

Reading Comprehension, Writing, Mathematics, Critical Thinking, Active Learning, Monitoring, Information Gathering, Information Organization, Synthesis/Reorganization, Idea Generation, Idea Evaluation, Implementation Planning, Programming, Visioning, Systems Perception, Identifying Downstream Consequences, Identification of Key Causes, Judgment and Decision Making, Systems Evaluation, Management of Financial Resources

College Majors

Finance, General: An instructional program that generally prepares individuals to plan, manage, and analyze the financial and monetary aspects and performance of business enterprises, banking institutions, or other organizations. Includes instruction in principles of accounting; financial instruments; capital planning; funds acquisition; asset and debt management; budgeting; financial analysis; and investments and portfolio management.

 Supporting Courses

Clerical: Knowledge of administrative and clerical procedures and systems such as word processing systems, filing and records management systems, stenography and transcription, forms design principles, and other office procedures and terminology. **Economics and Accounting:** Knowledge of economic and accounting principles and practices, the financial markets, banking, and the analysis and reporting of financial data. **Mathematics:** Knowledge of numbers, their operations, and interrelationships including arithmetic, algebra, geometry, calculus, statistics, and their applications. **Sociology and Anthropology:** Knowledge of group behavior and dynamics, societal trends and influences, cultures, their history, migrations, ethnicity, and origins. **History and Archeology:** Knowledge of past historical events and their causes, indicators, and impact on particular civilizations and cultures. **Philosophy and Theology:** Knowledge of different philosophical systems and religions, including their basic principles, values, ethics, ways of thinking, customs, and practices, and their impact on human culture. **Law, Government, and Jurisprudence:** Knowledge of laws, legal codes, court procedures, precedents, government regulations, executive orders, agency rules, and the democratic political process.

ADMINISTRATIVE SERVICES MANAGERS

Property Officers and Contract Administrators

Education	Work experience, plus degree
Average Yearly Earnings	$44,200
Projected Growth	11%
Annual Job Openings	24,604
Self-employed	0%
Employed Part-time	6%

Coordinate property procurement and disposition activities of a business, agency, or other organization. Administer contracts for purchase or sale of equipment, materials, products, or services. Directs activities concerned with unclaimed property, and contracts for purchase of equipment, materials, products, or services. Authorizes obtaining and purchase of materials, supplies and equipment, and equipment maintenance. Prepares plans for selling and maintaining materials and property. Prepares, reviews, and negotiates bids and estimates with firms, bidders, and customers. Recommends disposal of materials and property. Examines performance requirements, property-related data, delivery schedules, and estimates of costs of material, equipment, and production. Advises company departments concerning contractual rights and obligations. Inspects inventory and transfers or fills material and equipment requests. Examines and evaluates materials and property to ensure conformance to company standards. Coordinates work of sales department.

Occupational Type

Enterprising occupations frequently involve starting up and carrying out projects. These occupations can involve leading people and making many decisions. Sometimes they involve risk taking and often deal with business.

Skills required of Property Officers and Contract Administrators

Reading Comprehension, Writing, Speaking, Coordination, Negotiation, Implementation Planning, Judgment and Decision Making, Time Management, Management of Financial Resources, Management of Material Resources, Management of Personnel Resources

College Majors

Public Administration: An instructional program that prepares individuals to serve as managers in the executive arm of local, state, and Federal government; and that describes the systematic study of executive organization and management. Includes instruction in the roles, development, and principles of public administration; the management of public policy; executive-legislative relations; public budgetary processes and financial management; administrative law; public personnel management; professional ethics; and research methods.

Supporting Courses

Administration and Management: Knowledge of principles and processes involved in business and organizational planning, coordination, and execution. This includes strategic planning, resource allocation, manpower modeling, leadership techniques, and production methods. **Economics and Accounting:** Knowledge of economic and accounting principles and practices, the financial markets, banking, and the analysis and reporting of financial data. **Sales and Marketing:** Knowledge of principles and methods involved in showing, promoting, and selling products or services. This includes marketing strategies and tactics, product demonstration and sales techniques, and sales control systems. **Law, Government, and Jurisprudence:** Knowledge of laws, legal codes, court procedures, precedents, government regulations, executive orders, agency rules, and the democratic political process. **Transportation:** Knowledge of principles and methods for moving people or goods by air, rail, sea, or road, including their relative costs, advantages, and limitations.

Administrative Services Managers

Plan, direct, and coordinate supportive services of an organization, such as recordkeeping, mail distribution, telephone reception, and other office support services. May oversee facilities planning and maintenance and custodial operations. Include facilities managers. (Excludes procurement managers.) Coordinates activities of clerical and administrative personnel in establishment or organization. Analyzes and organizes office operations, procedures, and production to improve efficiency. Recommends cost-saving methods, such as supply changes and disposal of records to improve efficiency of department. Prepares and reviews reports and schedules to ensure accuracy and efficiency. Formulates budgetary reports. Hires and terminates clerical and administrative personnel. Conducts classes to teach procedures to staff.

Occupational Type

Enterprising occupations frequently involve starting up and carrying out projects. These occupations can involve leading people and making many decisions. Sometimes they involve risk taking and often deal with business.

Skills required of Administrative Services Managers

Reading Comprehension, Writing, Speaking, Learning Strategies, Monitoring, Social Perceptiveness, Coordination, Persuasion, Instructing, Idea Generation, Idea Evaluation, Visioning, Identification of Key Causes, Judgment and Decision Making, Systems Evaluation, Time Management, Management of Financial Resources, Management of Material Resources, Management of Personnel Resources

College Majors

Health Systems/Health Services Administration: An instructional program that prepares physicians and other professionals to develop, plan, and manage healthcare systems and service networks. Includes instruction in planning and coordination, business and financial management, fundraising and marketing, public relations, human resources management, technical operations of healthcare systems, resource allocation, health law, and applications to specific health service situations.

Supporting Courses

Administration and Management: Knowledge of principles and processes involved in business and organizational planning, coordination, and execution. This includes strategic planning, resource allocation, manpower modeling, leadership techniques, and production methods. **Clerical:** Knowledge of administrative and clerical procedures and systems such as word processing systems, filing and records management systems, stenography and transcription, forms design principles, and other office procedures and terminology. **Economics and Accounting:** Knowledge of economic and accounting principles and practices, the financial markets, banking, and the analysis and reporting of financial data. **Personnel and Human Resources:** Knowledge of policies and practices involved in personnel/human resource functions. This includes recruitment, selection, training, and promotion regulations and procedures; compensation and benefits packages; labor relations and negotiation strategies; and personnel information systems. **Mathematics:** Knowledge of numbers, their operations, and interrelationships including arithmetic, algebra, geometry, calculus, statistics, and their applications. **Psychology:** Knowledge of human behavior and performance, mental processes, psychological research methods, and the assessment and treatment of behavioral and affective disorders. **Education and Training:** Knowledge of instructional methods and training techniques including curriculum design principles, learning theory, group and individual teaching techniques, design of individual development plans, and test design principles. **English Language:** Knowledge of the structure and content of the English language including the meaning and spelling of words, rules of composition, and grammar.

AEROSPACE ENGINEERS

Education		Bachelor's degree
Average Yearly Earnings		$59,634
Projected Growth		8%
Annual Job Openings		3,771
Self-employed		0%
Employed Part-time		2%

Aerospace Engineers

Perform a variety of engineering work in designing, constructing, and testing aircraft, missiles, and spacecraft. May conduct basic and applied research to evaluate adaptability of materials and equipment to aircraft design and manufacture. May recommend improvements in testing equipment and techniques. Include aeronautical and astronautical engineers. Develops design criteria for aeronautical or aerospace products or systems, including testing methods, production costs, quality standards, and completion dates. Analyzes project requests and proposals and engineering data to determine feasibility, producibility, cost, and production time of aerospace or aeronautical product. Formulates conceptual design of aeronautical or aerospace products or systems to meet customer requirements. Formulates mathematical models or other methods of computer analysis to develop, evaluate, or modify design according to customer engineering requirements. Plans and conducts experimental, environmental, operational, and stress tests on models and prototypes of aircraft and aerospace systems and equipment. Evaluates product data and design from inspections and reports for conformance to engineering principles, customer requirements, and quality standards. Directs and coordinates activities of engineering or technical personnel designing, fabricating, modifying, or testing aircraft or aerospace products. Directs research and development programs to improve production methods, parts, and equipment technology and to reduce costs. Reviews performance reports and documentation from customers and field engineers, and inspects malfunctioning or damaged products to determine problem. Plans and coordinates activities concerned with investigating and resolving customers reports of technical problems with aircraft or aerospace vehicles. Writes technical reports and other documentation, such as handbooks and bulletins, for use by engineering staff, management, and customers. Maintains records of performance reports for future reference. Evaluates and approves selection of vendors by study of past performance and new advertisements.

Occupational Type

Investigative occupations frequently involve working with ideas, and require an extensive amount of thinking. These occupations can involve searching for facts and figuring out problems mentally.

Skills required of Aerospace Engineers

Reading Comprehension, Active Listening, Writing, Speaking, Mathematics, Science, Critical Thinking, Active Learning, Learning Strategies, Monitoring, Coordination, Instructing, Problem Identification, Information Gathering, Information Organization, Synthesis/ Reorganization, Idea Generation, Idea Evaluation, Implementation Planning, Operations Analysis, Technology Design, Equipment Selection, Installation, Programming, Testing, Operation Monitoring, Operation and Control, Product Inspection, Troubleshooting, Repairing, Visioning, Systems Perception, Identifying Downstream Consequences, Identification of Key Causes, Judgment and Decision Making, Systems Evaluation, Time Management, Management of Financial Resources, Management of Material Resources, Management of Personnel Resources

College Majors

Aerospace, Aeronautical and Astronautical Engineering: An instructional program that prepares individuals to apply mathematical and scientific principles to the design, development and operational evaluation of aircraft, space vehicles, and their systems; applied research on flight characteristics; and the development of systems and procedures for the launching, guidance, and control of air and space vehicles.

Supporting Courses

Administration and Management: Knowledge of principles and processes involved in business and organizational planning, coordination, and execution. This includes strategic planning, resource allocation, manpower modeling, leadership techniques, and production methods. **Economics and Accounting:** Knowledge of economic and accounting principles and practices, the financial markets, banking, and the analysis and reporting of financial data. **Customer and Personal Service:** Knowledge of principles and processes for providing customer and personal services including needs assessment techniques, quality service standards, alternative delivery systems, and customer satisfaction evaluation techniques. **Personnel and Human Resources:** Knowledge of policies and practices involved in personnel/human resource functions. This includes recruitment, selection, training, and promotion regulations and procedures; compensation and benefits packages; labor relations and negotiation strategies; and personnel information systems. **Production and Processing:** Knowledge of inputs, outputs, raw materials, waste, quality control, costs, and techniques for maximizing the manufacture and distribution of goods. **Computers and Electronics:** Knowledge of electric circuit boards, processors, chips, and computer hardware and software, including applications and programming. **Engineering and Technology:** Knowledge of equipment, tools, mechanical devices, and their uses to produce motion, light, power, technology, and other applications. **Design:** Knowledge of design techniques, principles, tools and instruments involved in the production and use of precision technical plans, blueprints, drawings, and models. **Building and Construction:** Knowledge of materials, methods, and the appropriate tools to construct objects, structures, and buildings.

Mechanical: Knowledge of machines and tools, including their designs, uses, benefits, repair, and maintenance. **Mathematics:** Knowledge of numbers, their operations, and interrelationships including arithmetic, algebra, geometry, calculus, statistics, and their applications. **Physics:** Knowledge and prediction of physical principles, laws, and applications including air, water, material dynamics, light, atomic principles, heat, electric theory, earth formations, and meteorological and related natural phenomena. **English Language:** Knowledge of the structure and content of the English language including the meaning and spelling of words, rules of composition, and grammar. **Telecommunications:** Knowledge of transmission, broadcasting, switching, control, and operation of telecommunications systems. **Communications and Media:** Knowledge of media production, communication, and dissemination techniques and methods including alternative ways to inform and entertain via written, oral, and visual media.

AGRICULTURAL AND FOOD SCIENTISTS

Animal Scientists

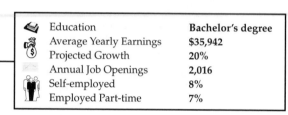

Education	Bachelor's degree
Average Yearly Earnings	$35,942
Projected Growth	20%
Annual Job Openings	2,016
Self-employed	8%
Employed Part-time	7%

Research or study selection, breeding, feeding, management, and marketing of livestock, pets, or other economically important animals. Studies nutritional requirements of animals and nutritive value of feed materials for animals and poultry. Studies effects of management practices, processing methods, feed, and environmental conditions on quality and quantity of animal products, such as eggs and milk. Researches and controls selection and breeding practices to increase efficiency of production and improve quality of animals. Develops improved practices in incubation, brooding, and artificial insemination. Develops improved practices in feeding, housing, sanitation, and parasite and disease control of animals and poultry. Determines generic composition of animal population and heritability of traits, utilizing principles of genetics. Crossbreeds animals with existing strains, or crosses strains to obtain new combinations of desirable characteristics.

Occupational Type

Investigative occupations frequently involve working with ideas, and require an extensive amount of thinking. These occupations can involve searching for facts and figuring out problems mentally.

Skills required of Animal Scientists

Reading Comprehension, Writing, Mathematics, Science, Critical Thinking, Active Learning, Monitoring, Problem Identification, Information Gathering, Information Organization, Synthesis/Reorganization, Idea Generation, Idea Evaluation, Implementation Planning,

Operations Analysis, Technology Design, Equipment Selection, Programming, Testing, Product Inspection, Visioning, Systems Perception, Identifying Downstream Consequences, Identification of Key Causes, Judgment and Decision Making, Systems Evaluation

College Majors

Agriculture/Agricultural Sciences, General: An instructional program that generally describes the principles and practices of agricultural research and production, and may prepare individuals to apply such knowledge and skills to the solution of practical agricultural problems. Includes instruction in basic animal, plant, and soil science; animal husbandry and plant cultivation; and soil conservation.

Supporting Courses

Food Production: Knowledge of techniques and equipment for planting, growing, and harvesting of food for consumption including crop rotation methods, animal husbandry, and food storage/handling techniques. **Chemistry:** Knowledge of the composition, structure, and properties of substances and of the chemical processes and transformations that they undergo. This includes uses of chemicals and their interactions, danger signs, production techniques, and disposal methods. **Biology:** Knowledge of plant and animal living tissue, cells, organisms, and entities, including their functions, interdependencies, and interactions with each other and the environment. **Medicine and Dentistry:** Knowledge of the information and techniques needed to diagnose and treat injuries, diseases, and deformities. This includes symptoms, treatment alternatives, drug properties and interactions, and preventive healthcare measures. **History and Archeology:** Knowledge of past historical events and their causes, indicators, and impact on particular civilizations and cultures.

Plant Scientists

Conduct research in breeding, production, and yield of plants or crops, and control of pests. Conducts research to determine best methods of planting, spraying, cultivating, and harvesting horticultural products. Experiments to develop new or improved varieties of products having specific features, such as higher yield, resistance to disease, size, or maturity. Studies crop production to discover effects of various climatic and soil conditions on crops. Develops methods for control of noxious weeds, crop diseases, and insect pests. Conducts experiments and investigations to determine methods of storing, processing, and transporting horticultural products. Studies insect distribution and habitat, and recommends methods to prevent importation and spread of injurious species. Aids in control and elimination of agricultural, structural, and forest pests by developing new and improved pesticides. Conducts experiments regarding causes of bee diseases and factors affecting yields of nectar pollen on various plants visited by bees. Identifies and classifies species of insects and allied forms, such as mites and spiders. Prepares articles and gives lectures on horticultural subjects. Improves bee strains, utilizing selective breeding by artificial insemination.

Occupational Type

Investigative occupations frequently involve working with ideas, and require an extensive amount of thinking. These occupations can involve searching for facts and figuring out problems mentally.

Skills required of Plant Scientists

Reading Comprehension, Writing, Speaking, Mathematics, Science, Critical Thinking, Active Learning, Problem Identification, Information Gathering, Information Organization, Synthesis/Reorganization, Idea Generation, Idea Evaluation, Implementation Planning, Operations Analysis, Testing, Product Inspection, Visioning, Identifying Downstream Consequences, Judgment and Decision Making, Time Management

College Majors

Agriculture/Agricultural Sciences, General: An instructional program that generally describes the principles and practices of agricultural research and production, and may prepare individuals to apply such knowledge and skills to the solution of practical agricultural problems. Includes instruction in basic animal, plant, and soil science; animal husbandry and plant cultivation; and soil conservation.

Supporting Courses

Food Production: Knowledge of techniques and equipment for planting, growing, and harvesting of food for consumption including crop rotation methods, animal husbandry, and food storage/handling techniques. **Chemistry:** Knowledge of the composition, structure, and properties of substances and of the chemical processes and transformations that they undergo. This includes uses of chemicals and their interactions, danger signs, production techniques, and disposal methods. **Biology:** Knowledge of plant and animal living tissue, cells, organisms, and entities, including their functions, interdependencies, and interactions with each other and the environment. **Geography:** Knowledge of various methods for describing the location and distribution of land, sea, and air masses including their physical locations, relationships, and characteristics. **Education and Training:** Knowledge of instructional methods and training techniques including curriculum design principles, learning theory, group and individual teaching techniques, design of individual development plans, and test design principles. **English Language:** Knowledge of the structure and content of the English language including the meaning and spelling of words, rules of composition, and grammar. **History and Archeology:** Knowledge of past historical events and their causes, indicators, and impact on particular civilizations and cultures. **Communications and Media:** Knowledge of media production, communication, and dissemination techniques and methods including alternative ways to inform and entertain via written, oral, and visual media.

Food Scientists

Apply scientific and engineering principles in research, development, production, packaging, and processing of foods. Conducts research on new products and development of foods, applying scientific and engineering principles. Develops new and improved methods and systems for food processing, production, quality control, packaging, and distribution. Studies methods to improve quality of foods, such as flavor, color, texture, nutritional value, and convenience. Studies methods to improve physical, chemical, and microbiological composition of foods. Develops food standards, safety and sanitary regulations, and waste management and water supply specifications. Confers with process engineers, flavor experts, and packaging and marketing specialists to resolve problems in product development. Tests new products in test kitchen.

 ## Occupational Type

Investigative occupations frequently involve working with ideas, and require an extensive amount of thinking. These occupations can involve searching for facts and figuring out problems mentally.

 ## Skills required of Food Scientists

Reading Comprehension, Mathematics, Science, Critical Thinking, Active Learning, Information Gathering, Synthesis/Reorganization, Idea Generation, Idea Evaluation, Implementation Planning, Operations Analysis, Technology Design, Equipment Selection, Programming, Testing, Product Inspection, Visioning, Identifying Downstream Consequences, Identification of Key Causes, Judgment and Decision Making

 ## College Majors

Agriculture/Agricultural Sciences, General: An instructional program that generally describes the principles and practices of agricultural research and production, and may prepare individuals to apply such knowledge and skills to the solution of practical agricultural problems. Includes instruction in basic animal, plant, and soil science; animal husbandry and plant cultivation; and soil conservation.

 ## Supporting Courses

Production and Processing: Knowledge of inputs, outputs, raw materials, waste, quality control, costs, and techniques for maximizing the manufacture and distribution of goods. **Food Production:** Knowledge of techniques and equipment for planting, growing, and harvesting of food for consumption including crop rotation methods, animal husbandry, and food storage/handling techniques. **Chemistry:** Knowledge of the composition, structure, and properties of substances and of the chemical processes and transformations that they undergo. This includes uses of chemicals and their interactions, danger signs, production techniques, and disposal methods. **Biology:** Knowledge of plant and animal living tissue, cells, organisms, and entities, including their functions, interdependencies, and interactions with each other and the environment. **Law, Government, and Jurisprudence:** Knowledge of laws, legal codes, court procedures, precedents, government regulations, executive orders, agency rules, and the democratic political process.

Soil Scientists

Research or study soil characteristics, map soil types, and investigate responses of soils to known management practices to determine use capabilities of soils and effects of alternative practices on soil productivity. Studies soil characteristics and classifies soils according to standard types. Investigates responses of specific soil types to soil management practices, such as fertilization, crop rotation, and industrial waste control. Conducts experiments on farms or experimental stations to determine best soil types for different plants. Performs chemical analysis on microorganism content of soil to determine microbial reactions and chemical mineralogical relationship to plant growth. Provides advice on rural or urban land use.

Occupational Type

Investigative occupations frequently involve working with ideas, and require an extensive amount of thinking. These occupations can involve searching for facts and figuring out problems mentally.

Skills required of Soil Scientists

Reading Comprehension, Writing, Speaking, Mathematics, Science, Critical Thinking, Active Learning, Information Gathering, Information Organization, Idea Generation, Idea Evaluation, Operations Analysis, Programming, Testing, Identification of Key Causes

College Majors

Soil Sciences: An instructional program that describes the scientific classification and study of soils and soil properties. Includes instruction in soil chemistry, soil physics, soil biology, soil fertility, morphogenesis, mineralogy and hydrology, and soil conservation and management.

Supporting Courses

Food Production: Knowledge of techniques and equipment for planting, growing, and harvesting of food for consumption including crop rotation methods, animal husbandry, and food storage/handling techniques. **Chemistry:** Knowledge of the composition, structure, and properties of substances and of the chemical processes and transformations that they undergo. This includes uses of chemicals and their interactions, danger signs, production techniques, and disposal methods. **Biology:** Knowledge of plant and animal living tissue, cells, organisms, and entities, including their functions, interdependencies, and interactions with each other and the environment. **Geography:** Knowledge of various methods for describing the location and distribution of land, sea, and air masses including their physical locations, relationships, and characteristics.

ANIMAL BREEDERS AND TRAINERS

Education	Bachelor's degree
Average Yearly Earnings	$23,130
Projected Growth	0%
Annual Job Openings	1,327
Self-employed	0%
Employed Part-time	22%

Animal Breeders

Breed livestock or pets, such as cattle, goats, horses, sheep, swine, dogs, and cats. Breed animals for purposes such as riding, working, or show; and for products such as milk, wool, meat, and hair. Select and breed animals according to knowledge of animals' genealogy, characteristics, and offspring. Selects animals to be bred, according to knowledge of animals' genealogy, traits, and offspring desired. Examines animals to detect symptoms of illness or injury. Records weight, diet, and other breeding data. Feeds and waters animals, and cleans pens, cages, yards, and hutches. Brands, tags, dehorns, tattoos, or castrates animals. Treats minor injuries and ailments and engages veterinarian to treat animals with serious illnesses or injuries. Milks cows and goats. Clips or shears hair on animals. Adjusts controls to maintain specific temperature in building. Arranges for sale of animals to hospitals, research centers, pet shops, and food processing plants. Builds and maintains hutches, pens, and fenced yards. Exhibits animals at shows. Kills animals, removes their pelts, and arranges for sale of pelts.

Occupational Type

Realistic occupations frequently involve work activities that include practical, hands-on problems and solutions. They often deal with plants, animals, and real-world materials like wood, tools, and machinery. Many of the occupations require working outside, and do not involve a lot of paperwork or working closely with others.

Skills required of Animal Breeders

Information on specific skills required is not available.

College Majors

Agricultural Production Workers and Managers, General: An instructional program that generally prepares individuals to plan and economically use facilities, natural resources, labor and capital in the production of plant and animal products.

Supporting Courses

Sales and Marketing: Knowledge of principles and methods involved in showing, promoting, and selling products or services. This includes marketing strategies and tactics, product demonstration and sales techniques, and sales control systems. **Food Production:**

Knowledge of techniques and equipment for planting, growing, and harvesting of food for consumption including crop rotation methods, animal husbandry, and food storage/ handling techniques. **Biology:** Knowledge of plant and animal living tissue, cells, organisms, and entities, including their functions, interdependencies, and interactions with each other and the environment. **Medicine and Dentistry:** Knowledge of the information and techniques needed to diagnose and treat injuries, diseases, and deformities. This includes symptoms, treatment alternatives, drug properties and interactions, and preventive healthcare measures.

Animal Trainers

Train animals for riding, harness, security, or obedience. Accustom animals to human voice and contact, and condition animals to respond to oral, hand, spur, and reign commands. Train animals according to prescribed standards for show or competition. May train animals to carry pack loads or work as part of pack team. Trains animals to obey commands, compete in shows, or perform tricks to entertain audience. Conducts training program to develop desired behavior. Trains horses for riding, show, work, or racing. Rehearses animal according to script for motion picture, television film, stage, or circus program. Evaluates animal to determine temperament, ability, and aptitude for training. Cues or signals animal during performance. Trains guard dog to protect property, and teaches guide dog and its master to function as team. Trains horses as independent operator, and advises owners regarding purchase of horses. Observes animal's physical condition to detect illness or unhealthy condition requiring medical care. Organizes format show. Feeds, exercises, and gives general care to animal. Arranges for mating of stallions and mares, and assists mares during foaling.

Occupational Type

Social occupations frequently involve working with, communicating with, and teaching people. These occupations often involve helping or providing service to others.

Skills required of Animal Trainers

Learning Strategies, Monitoring, Persuasion, Instructing

College Majors

Animal Trainer: An instructional program that prepares individuals to teach animals to obey commands perform services; perform in sports and leisure activities; provide security; assist in law enforcement; assist in search and rescue operations or perform entertainment tricks.

Supporting Courses

Sales and Marketing: Knowledge of principles and methods involved in showing, promoting, and selling products or services. This includes marketing strategies and tactics, product demonstration and sales techniques, and sales control systems. **Customer and**

Personal Service: Knowledge of principles and processes for providing customer and personal services including needs assessment techniques, quality service standards, alternative delivery systems, and customer satisfaction evaluation techniques. **Biology:** Knowledge of plant and animal living tissue, cells, organisms, and entities, including their functions, interdependencies, and interactions with each other and the environment. **Therapy and Counseling:** Knowledge of information and techniques needed to rehabilitate physical and mental ailments and to provide career guidance including alternative treatments, rehabilitation equipment and its proper use, and methods to evaluate treatment effects. **Education and Training:** Knowledge of instructional methods and training techniques including curriculum design principles, learning theory, group and individual teaching techniques, design of individual development plans, and test design principles.

ARCHITECTS

Architects, Except Landscape and Marine

Education		**Bachelor's degree**
Average Yearly Earnings		**$46,883**
Projected Growth		20%
Annual Job Openings		10,404
Self-employed		28%
Employed Part-time		8%

Plan and design structures, such as
private residences, office buildings, theaters, factories, and other structural property. Prepares information regarding design, structure specifications, materials, color, equipment, estimated costs, and construction time. Plans layout of project. Integrates engineering element into unified design. Prepares scale drawings. Consults with client to determine functional and spatial requirements of structure. Estimates costs and construction time. Conducts periodic onsite observation of work during construction to monitor compliance with plans. Directs activities of workers engaged in preparing drawings and specification documents. Prepares contract documents for building contractors. Represents client in obtaining bids and awarding construction contracts. Administers construction contracts. Prepares operating and maintenance manuals, studies, and reports.

 ## Occupational Type

Artistic occupations frequently involve working with forms, designs, and patterns. They often require self-expression and the work can be done without following a clear set of rules.

 ## Skills required of Architects, Except Landscape and Marine

Reading Comprehension, Active Listening, Writing, Speaking, Mathematics, Monitoring, Coordination, Negotiation, Service Orientation, Problem Identification, Information Gathering, Information Organization, Synthesis/Reorganization, Idea Generation, Idea Evaluation, Implementation Planning, Operations Analysis, Technology Design, Equipment Selection, Product Inspection, Visioning, Systems Perception, Identification of Key Causes,

Judgment and Decision Making, Time Management, Management of Financial Resources, Management of Material Resources, Management of Personnel Resources

College Majors

Architecture: An instructional program that prepares individuals for the independent professional practice of architecture. Includes instruction in architectural design; architectural history and theory; building structures and environmental systems; site planning; construction; professional responsibilities and standards; and the cultural, social, economic and environmental issues relating to architectural practice.

Supporting Courses

Administration and Management: Knowledge of principles and processes involved in business and organizational planning, coordination, and execution. This includes strategic planning, resource allocation, manpower modeling, leadership techniques, and production methods. **Economics and Accounting:** Knowledge of economic and accounting principles and practices, the financial markets, banking, and the analysis and reporting of financial data. **Sales and Marketing:** Knowledge of principles and methods involved in showing, promoting, and selling products or services. This includes marketing strategies and tactics, product demonstration and sales techniques, and sales control systems. **Customer and Personal Service:** Knowledge of principles and processes for providing customer and personal services including needs assessment techniques, quality service standards, alternative delivery systems, and customer satisfaction evaluation techniques. **Personnel and Human Resources:** Knowledge of policies and practices involved in personnel/human resource functions. This includes recruitment, selection, training, and promotion regulations and procedures; compensation and benefits packages; labor relations and negotiation strategies; and personnel information systems. **Engineering and Technology:** Knowledge of equipment, tools, mechanical devices, and their uses to produce motion, light, power, technology, and other applications. **Design:** Knowledge of design techniques, principles, tools and instruments involved in the production and use of precision technical plans, blueprints, drawings, and models. **Building and Construction:** Knowledge of materials, methods, and the appropriate tools to construct objects, structures, and buildings. **Mathematics:** Knowledge of numbers, their operations, and interrelationships including arithmetic, algebra, geometry, calculus, statistics, and their applications. **Physics:** Knowledge and prediction of physical principles, laws, and applications including air, water, material dynamics, light, atomic principles, heat, electric theory, earth formations, and meteorological and related natural phenomena. **Geography:** Knowledge of various methods for describing the location and distribution of land, sea, and air masses including their physical locations, relationships, and characteristics. **English Language:** Knowledge of the structure and content of the English language including the meaning and spelling of words, rules of composition, and grammar. **Fine Arts:** Knowledge of theory and techniques required to produce, compose, and perform works of music, dance, visual arts, drama, and sculpture. **History and Archeology:** Knowledge of past historical events and their causes, indicators, and impact on particular civilizations and cultures. **Public Safety**

and Security: Knowledge of weaponry, public safety, and security operations, rules, regulations, precautions, prevention, and the protection of people, data, and property. **Law, Government, and Jurisprudence:** Knowledge of laws, legal codes, court procedures, precedents, government regulations, executive orders, agency rules, and the democratic political process. **Communications and Media:** Knowledge of media production, communication, and dissemination techniques and methods including alternative ways to inform and entertain via written, oral, and visual media.

Artists and Commercial Artists

Education	Work experience, plus degree	
Average Yearly Earnings	$33,114	
Projected Growth	28%	
Annual Job Openings	46,893	
Self-employed	57%	
Employed Part-time	24%	

Painters and Illustrators

Paint or draw subject material to produce original artwork or provide illustrations to explain or adorn written or spoken word, using watercolors, oils, acrylics, tempera, or other paint mediums. Renders drawings, illustrations, and sketches of buildings, manufactured products, or models, working from sketches, blueprints, memory, or reference materials. Paints scenic backgrounds, murals, and portraiture for motion picture and television production sets, glass artworks, and exhibits. Etches, carves, paints, or draws artwork on material, such as stone, glass, canvas, wood, and linoleum. Develops drawings, paintings, diagrams, and models of medical or biological subjects for use in publications, exhibits, consultations, research, and teaching. Integrates and develops visual elements, such as line, space, mass, color, and perspective, to produce desired effect. Brushes or sprays protective or decorative finish on completed background panels, informational legends, exhibit accessories, or finished painting. Confers with professional personnel or client to discuss objectives of museum exhibits, develop illustration ideas, and theme to be portrayed. Selects colored glass, cuts glass, and arranges pieces in design pattern for painting. Integrates knowledge of glass cutting, stresses, portraiture, symbolism, heraldry, ornamental and historical styles, and related factors with functional requirements to conceptualize idea. Photographs person, artifacts, scenes, plants, or other objects, and develops negatives to obtain prints to be used in exhibits. Studies style, techniques, colors, textures, and materials used by artist to maintain consistency in reconstruction or retouching procedures. Cuts, carves, scrapes, molds, or otherwise shapes material to fashion exhibit accessories from clay, plastic, wood, fiberglass, and papier-mâché. Performs tests to determine factors, such as age, structure, pigment stability, and probable reaction to various cleaning agents and solvents. Removes painting from frame or paint layer from canvas to restore artwork, following specified technique and equipment. Applies select solvents and cleaning agents to clean surface of painting and remove accretions, discolorations, and deteriorated varnish. Examines surfaces of paintings and proofs of artwork, using magnifying device, to determine method of restoration or needed corrections. Assembles, leads, and solders finished glass to fabricate stained glass article. Installs finished stained glass in window or doorframe.

Occupational Type

Artistic occupations frequently involve working with forms, designs, and patterns. They often require self-expression and the work can be done without following a clear set of rules.

 Skills required of Painters and Illustrators

Idea Generation, Operations Analysis

 College Majors

Graphic Design, Commercial Art, and Illustration: An instructional program in the applied visual arts that prepares individuals to use artistic techniques to effectively communicate ideas and information to business and consumer audiences via illustrations and other forms of printed media. Includes instruction in concept design, layout, paste-up, and techniques such as engraving, etching, silkscreen, lithography, offset, drawing and cartooning, painting, collage, and computer graphics.

 Supporting Courses

Design: Knowledge of design techniques, principles, tools and instruments involved in the production and use of precision technical plans, blueprints, drawings, and models. **Chemistry:** Knowledge of the composition, structure, and properties of substances and of the chemical processes and transformations that they undergo. This includes uses of chemicals and their interactions, danger signs, production techniques, and disposal methods. **Fine Arts:** Knowledge of theory and techniques required to produce, compose, and perform works of music, dance, visual arts, drama, and sculpture. **History and Archeology:** Knowledge of past historical events and their causes, indicators, and impact on particular civilizations and cultures.

Sketch Artists

Sketch likenesses of subjects according to observation or descriptions either to assist law enforcement agencies in identifying suspects or for entertainment purposes of patrons, using mediums such as pencil, charcoal, and pastels. Draws sketch, profile, or likeness of posed subject or photograph, using pencil, charcoal, pastels, or other medium. Assembles and arranges outlines of features to form composite image, according to information provided by witness or victim. Alters copy of composite image until witness or victim is satisfied that composite is best possible representation of suspect. Interviews crime victims and witnesses to obtain descriptive information concerning physical build, sex, nationality, and facial features of unidentified suspect. Prepares series of simple line drawings conforming to description of suspect and presents drawings to informant for selection of sketch. Poses subject to accentuate most pleasing features or profile. Classifies and codes components of image, using established system, to help identify suspect. Measures distances and develops sketches of crime scene from photograph and measurements. Adjusts strong lights to cast subject's shadow on backdrop to aid in viewing subject's profile. Cuts profile from photograph or cuts freehand outline of profile from paper. Glues silhouette on paper of contrasting color or mounts silhouette in frame or folder. Operates photocopy or similar machine to reproduce composite image. Searches police photograph records, using classification and coding system, to determine if existing photograph of suspect is available.

Occupational Type

Artistic occupations frequently involve working with forms, designs, and patterns. They often require self-expression and the work can be done without following a clear set of rules.

Skills required of Sketch Artists

Active Listening, Information Organization

College Majors

Forensic Technology/Technician: An instructional program that prepares individuals to conduct crime scene and laboratory analyses and evaluations of evidentiary materials, including human remains, under the supervision of a pathologist, forensic administrator or other law enforcement personnel. Includes instruction in principles of pathology, laboratory technology and procedures, dusting and fingerprinting, reconstructive analysis and related skills.

Supporting Courses

Design: Knowledge of design techniques, principles, tools and instruments involved in the production and use of precision technical plans, blueprints, drawings, and models. **Fine Arts:** Knowledge of theory and techniques required to produce, compose, and perform works of music, dance, visual arts, drama, and sculpture.

Graphic Designers

Design art and copy layouts for material to be presented by visual communications media, such as books, magazines, newspapers, television, and packaging. Draws sample of finished layout and presents sample to art director for approval. Draws and prints charts, graphs, illustrations, and other artwork, using computer. Arranges layout based upon available space, knowledge of layout principles, and aesthetic design concepts. Marks up, pastes, and assembles final layouts to prepare layouts for printer. Keys information into computer equipment to create layouts for client or supervisor. Determines size and arrangement of illustrative material and copy, and selects style and size of type. Prepares illustrations or rough sketches of material according to instructions of client or supervisor. Produces still and animated graphic formats for on-air and taped portions of television news broadcasts, using electronic video equipment. Studies illustrations and photographs to plan presentation of material, product, or service. Reviews final layout and suggests improvements as needed. Prepares series of drawings to illustrate sequence and timing of story development for television production. Confers with client regarding layout design. Photographs layouts, using camera, to make layout prints for supervisor or client. Prepares notes and instructions for workers who assemble and prepare final layouts for printing. Develops negatives and prints, using negative and print developing equipment and tools and work aids, to produce layout photographs.

Occupational Type

Artistic occupations frequently involve working with forms, designs, and patterns. They often require self-expression and the work can be done without following a clear set of rules.

Skills required of Graphic Designers

Idea Generation, Programming

College Majors

Graphic Design, Commercial Art, and Illustration: An instructional program in the applied visual arts that prepares individuals to use artistic techniques to effectively communicate ideas and information to business and consumer audiences via illustrations and other forms of printed media. Includes instruction in concept design, layout, paste-up, and techniques such as engraving, etching, silkscreen, lithography, offset, drawing and cartooning, painting, collage, and computer graphics.

Supporting Courses

Computers and Electronics: Knowledge of electric circuit boards, processors, chips, and computer hardware and software, including applications and programming. **Design:** Knowledge of design techniques, principles, tools and instruments involved in the production and use of precision technical plans, blueprints, drawings, and models. **Fine Arts:** Knowledge of theory and techniques required to produce, compose, and perform works of music, dance, visual arts, drama, and sculpture. **Telecommunications:** Knowledge of transmission, broadcasting, switching, control, and operation of telecommunications systems. **Communications and Media:** Knowledge of media production, communication, and dissemination techniques and methods including alternative ways to inform and entertain via written, oral, and visual media.

Cartoonists and Animators

Draw cartoons or other animated images by hand for publication, motion pictures, or television. May specialize in creating storyboards, laying out scenes, painting, in-betweening, developing characters, or cleanup. Sketches and submits cartoon or animation for approval. Renders sequential drawings of characters or other subject material which, when photographed and projected at specific speed, becomes animated. Creates and prepares sketches and model drawings of characters, providing details from memory, live models, manufactured products, or reference material. Develops personal ideas for cartoons, comic strips, or animations, or reads written material to develop ideas. Makes changes and corrections to cartoon, comic strip, or animation as necessary. Develops color patterns and moods and paints background layouts to dramatize action for animated cartoon scenes. Labels each section with designated colors when colors are used. Discusses ideas for cartoons, comic strips, or animations with editor or publisher's representative.

 ## Occupational Type

Artistic occupations frequently involve working with forms, designs, and patterns. They often require self-expression and the work can be done without following a clear set of rules.

 ## Skills required of Cartoonists and Animators

Idea Generation

 ## College Majors

Crafts, Folk Art, and Artisanry: An instructional program that describes the aesthetics, techniques, and creative processes for designing and fashioning objects in one or more of the handcraft or folk art traditions, and that prepares individuals to create in any of these media.

 ## Supporting Courses

Sales and Marketing: Knowledge of principles and methods involved in showing, promoting, and selling products or services. This includes marketing strategies and tactics, product demonstration and sales techniques, and sales control systems. **Fine Arts:** Knowledge of theory and techniques required to produce, compose, and perform works of music, dance, visual arts, drama, and sculpture. **Communications and Media:** Knowledge of media production, communication, and dissemination techniques and methods including alternative ways to inform and entertain via written, oral, and visual media.

Sculptors

Design and construct three-dimensional artworks, using materials such as stone, wood, plaster, and metal and employing various manual and tool techniques. Carves objects from stone, concrete, plaster, wood, or other material, using abrasives and tools such as chisels, gouges, and mall. Constructs artistic forms from metal or stone, using metalworking, welding, or masonry tools and equipment. Cuts, bends, laminates, arranges, and fastens individual or mixed raw and manufactured materials and products to form works of art. Models substances, such as clay or wax, using fingers and small hand tools to form objects.

 ## Occupational Type

Artistic occupations frequently involve working with forms, designs, and patterns. They often require self-expression and the work can be done without following a clear set of rules.

Skills required of Sculptors

Information on specific skills required not available.

 College Majors

Art, General: An instructional program that generally describes art, including its development and practice. Includes instruction in art appreciation, a basic knowledge of art history, fundamental principles of design and color, and an introduction to various media and studio techniques.

 Supporting Courses

Design: Knowledge of design techniques, principles, tools and instruments involved in the production and use of precision technical plans, blueprints, drawings, and models. **Fine Arts:** Knowledge of theory and techniques required to produce, compose, and perform works of music, dance, visual arts, drama, and sculpture.

Glass Blowers, Molders, Benders, and Finishers

Shape molten glass according to patterns. Shapes, bends, or joins sections of glass, using paddles, pressing and flattening hand tools, or cork. Blows tubing into specified shape, using compressed air or own breath. Places glass into die or mold of press and controls press to form products, such as, glassware components or optical blanks. Dips end of blowpipe into molten glass to collect gob on pipe head or cuts gob from molten glass, using sheers. Preheats or melts glass pieces or anneals or cools glass products and components, using ovens and refractory powder. Heats glass to pliable stage, using gas flame or oven. Cuts length of tubing to specified size, using file or cutting wheel. Inspects and measures product to verify conformance to specifications, using instruments, such as micrometers, calipers, magnifier, and ruler. Examines gob of molten glass for imperfections, utilizing knowledge of molten glass characteristics. Strikes neck of finished article to separate article from blowpipe. Determines type and quantity of glass required to fabricate product. Adjusts press stroke length and pressure, and regulates oven temperatures according to glass type processed. Develops sketch of glass product into blueprint specifications, applying knowledge of glass technology and glass blowing.

 Occupational Type

Realistic occupations frequently involve work activities that include practical, hands-on problems and solutions. They often deal with plants, animals, and real-world materials like wood, tools, and machinery. Many of the occupations require working outside, and do not involve a lot of paperwork or working closely with others.

 Skills required of Glass Blowers, Molders, Benders, and Finishers

Information on specific skills required not available.

College Majors

Laser and Optical Technology/Technician: An instructional program that prepares individuals to apply basic engineering principles and technical skills in support of engineers and other professionals engaged in developing and using lasers and other optical for commercial or research purposes. Includes instruction in laser and optical principles, testing and maintenance procedures, safety precautions, specific applications to various tasks, and report preparation.

 Supporting Courses

Production and Processing: Knowledge of inputs, outputs, raw materials, waste, quality control, costs, and techniques for maximizing the manufacture and distribution of goods.

Throwers

Mold clay into ware as clay revolves on potter's wheel. Raises and shapes clay into ware, such as vases, saggers, and pitchers, on revolving wheel, using hands, fingers, and thumbs. Smoothes surfaces of finished piece, using rubber scrapers and wet sponge. Adjusts speed of wheel according to feel of changing firmness of clay. Positions ball of clay in center of potters wheel. Starts motor, or pumps treadle with foot to revolve wheel. Pulls wire through base of article and wheel to separate finished piece. Verifies size and form, using calipers and templates. Moves piece from wheel to dry.

 Occupational Type

Realistic occupations frequently involve work activities that include practical, hands-on problems and solutions. They often deal with plants, animals, and real-world materials like wood, tools, and machinery. Many of the occupations require working outside, and do not involve a lot of paperwork or working closely with others.

 Skills required of Throwers

Information on specific skills required is not available.

 College Majors

Art, General: An instructional program that generally describes art, including its development and practice. Includes instruction in art appreciation, a basic knowledge of art history, fundamental principles of design and color, and an introduction to various media and studio techniques.

 Supporting Courses

Fine Arts: Knowledge of theory and techniques required to produce, compose, and perform works of music, dance, visual arts, drama, and sculpture.

Model and Mold Makers

Construct molds or models, using fiberglass, plaster, or clay. Shapes sculptured clay surfaces to form details of mold or model, using various sculptor's tools, hands, and scrapers. Pours plaster or compound over model and spreads evenly over surface, using brush or spatula. Builds layers of material, such as fiberglass, resin, or rubber paint around model to form mold or cast, and shield around cast. Cuts and removes sections of hardened mold or cast, using hand or power tools. Reassembles sections of shield and cast to form complete mold, using shellac or concrete. Mixes water and powder or catalytic compound, and clay, according to specifications, to form plaster or other compound. Punches holes in surface of model to assure plaster will adhere. Smoothes surface of cast to remove excess materials, using electric grinder, polishing wheel, file, or sandpaper. Cuts templates of model according to blueprints or layout drawings. Constructs frame to support figure while modeling. Verifies uniformity and smoothness of curved surfaces. Brushes liquid soap or wax onto model or frame to prevent adhesion of plaster or fiberglass. Duplicates completed model half to make measurements of unfinished half symmetrical. Covers specified portions of model with aluminum foil or transparent media trim to identify or detail. Repairs molds using carpenter tools.

 Occupational Type

Realistic occupations frequently involve work activities that include practical, hands-on problems and solutions. They often deal with plants, animals, and real-world materials like wood, tools, and machinery. Many of the occupations require working outside, and do not involve a lot of paperwork or working closely with others.

 Skills required of Model and Mold Makers

Information on specific skills required is not available.

 College Majors

Plastics Technology/Technician: An instructional program that prepares individuals to apply basic engineering principles and technical skills in support of engineers and other professionals engaged in developing and using industrial polymers. Includes instruction in the principles of macromolecular chemistry, polymerization and plastic manufacturing processes and equipment, design and operational testing procedures, equipment maintenance and repair procedures, safety procedures, applications to specific products, and report preparation.

 Supporting Courses

Building and Construction: Knowledge of materials, methods, and the appropriate tools to construct objects, structures, and buildings. **Fine Arts:** Knowledge of theory and techniques required to produce, compose, and perform works of music, dance, visual arts, drama, and sculpture.

Precision Painters

Paint decorative freehand designs on objects, such as pottery, cigarette cases, and lampshades, using hand brushes. Applies paint or metallic leaf to workpiece, using handbrush, airbrush, or roller. Sketches or traces design or lettering onto workpiece or pattern material to prepare pattern or stencil, using measuring and drawing instruments. Designs pattern or lettering to paint workpieces, such as signs, glassware, pottery, or zinc plates, using measuring and drawing instruments. Removes excess paint, using brush or cotton swab. Mixes paint according to established formulas to obtain specified color and desired consistency. Examines workpiece to compare with pattern and to detect imperfections. Applies preservative coating to workpiece. Reads work order to determine work procedures and materials required. Positions and aligns workpiece on work area. Uses wheel equipment to hold and revolve workpiece while applying paint. Cuts out letters or designs using hand or powered cutting tools. Hangs workpieces on rack to dry or places workpieces on conveyor. Maintains daily production records.

 ## Occupational Type

Artistic occupations frequently involve working with forms, designs, and patterns. They often require self-expression and the work can be done without following a clear set of rules.

 ## Skills required of Precision Painters

Information on specific skills required is not available.

 ## College Majors

Graphic Design, Commercial Art, and Illustration: An instructional program in the applied visual arts that prepares individuals to use artistic techniques to effectively communicate ideas and information to business and consumer audiences via illustrations and other forms of printed media. Includes instruction in concept design, layout, paste-up, and techniques such as engraving, etching, silkscreen, lithography, offset, drawing and cartooning, painting, collage, and computer graphics.

Supporting Courses

Design: Knowledge of design techniques, principles, tools and instruments involved in the production and use of precision technical plans, blueprints, drawings, and models. **Fine Arts:** Knowledge of theory and techniques required to produce, compose, and perform works of music, dance, visual arts, drama, and sculpture.

Silk Screen Process Decorators

Apply lettering, designs, or coloring to products, using silk screen process. Applies ink or glaze to screen or pattern over drawing or plate and prints design. Positions mask or applies protective coating over parts not to be shaded. Selects and prepares color glaze or ink. Cleans ink, glaze, or protective coating from parts of drawing not to be shaded. Cuts stencil by hand, using cutting tools, or photographs design on film. Reads job order and examines drawing or design to determine method of making stencil. Catalogs and stores screens for future orders.

Occupational Type

Realistic occupations frequently involve work activities that include practical, hands-on problems and solutions. They often deal with plants, animals, and real-world materials like wood, tools, and machinery. Many of the occupations require working outside, and do not involve a lot of paperwork or working closely with others.

Skills required of Silk Screen Process Decorators

Information on specific skills required is not available.

College Majors

Graphic Design, Commercial Art, and Illustration: An instructional program in the applied visual arts that prepares individuals to use artistic techniques to effectively communicate ideas and information to business and consumer audiences via illustrations and other forms of printed media. Includes instruction in concept design, layout, paste-up, and techniques such as engraving, etching, silkscreen, lithography, offset, drawing and cartooning, painting, collage, and computer graphics.

Supporting Courses

Production and Processing: Knowledge of inputs, outputs, raw materials, waste, quality control, costs, and techniques for maximizing the manufacture and distribution of goods. **Fine Arts:** Knowledge of theory and techniques required to produce, compose, and perform works of music, dance, visual arts, drama, and sculpture.

Engravers/Carvers

Engrave or carve designs or lettering onto objects, using handheld power tools. Holds workpiece against outer edge of wheel and twists and turns workpiece to grind glass according to marked design. Carves design on workpiece, using electric hand tool. Cuts outline of impression with graver and removes excess material with knife. Traces, sketches, or presses design or facsimile signature on workpiece by hand, or by using artist equipment. Selects and mounts wheel and miter on lathe, and equips lathe with water to cool wheel and prevent dust. Polishes engravings using felt and cork wheels. Prepares workpiece to be engraved or carved, such as glassware, rubber, or plastic product. Attaches engraved workpiece to mount, using cement. Dresses and shapes cutting wheels by holding dressing stone against rotating wheel. Suggests original designs to customer or management.

Occupational Type

Realistic occupations frequently involve work activities that include practical, hands-on problems and solutions. They often deal with plants, animals, and real-world materials like wood, tools, and machinery. Many of the occupations require working outside, and do not involve a lot of paperwork or working closely with others.

 Skills required of Engravers/Carvers

Information on specific skills required is not available.

 College Majors

Crafts, Folk Art, and Artisanry: An instructional program that describes the aesthetics, techniques, and creative processes for designing and fashioning objects in one or more of the handcraft or folk art traditions, and that prepares individuals to create in any of these media.

 Supporting Courses

Production and Processing: Knowledge of inputs, outputs, raw materials, waste, quality control, costs, and techniques for maximizing the manufacture and distribution of goods. **Fine Arts:** Knowledge of theory and techniques required to produce, compose, and perform works of music, dance, visual arts, drama, and sculpture.

Etchers

Etch or cut artistic designs in glass articles, using acid solutions, sandblasting equipment, and design patterns. Immerses waxed ware in hydrofluoric acid to etch design on glass surface. Sandblasts exposed area of glass, using spray gun, to cut design in surface. Places template against glassware surface and sprays with sand to cut design in surface. Positions pattern against waxed or taped ware and sprays ink through pattern to transfer design to wax or tape. Removes wax or tape, using stylus or knife, to expose glassware surface to be etched. Coats glass in molten wax or masks glassware with tape. Immerses ware in hot water to remove wax or peels off tape.

 Occupational Type

Realistic occupations frequently involve work activities that include practical, hands-on problems and solutions. They often deal with plants, animals, and real-world materials like wood, tools, and machinery. Many of the occupations require working outside, and do not involve a lot of paperwork or working closely with others.

 Skills required of Etchers

Information on specific skills required is not available.

College Majors

Art, General: An instructional program that generally describes art, including its development and practice. Includes instruction in art appreciation, a basic knowledge of art history, fundamental principles of design and color, and an introduction to various media and studio techniques.

 Supporting Courses

Production and Processing: Knowledge of inputs, outputs, raw materials, waste, quality control, costs, and techniques for maximizing the manufacture and distribution of goods. **Chemistry:** Knowledge of the composition, structure, and properties of substances and of the chemical processes and transformations that they undergo. This includes uses of chemicals and their interactions, danger signs, production techniques, and disposal methods. **Fine Arts:** Knowledge of theory and techniques required to produce, compose, and perform works of music, dance, visual arts, drama, and sculpture.

Tracers and Letterers

Lay out and trace lettering and designs on various surfaces, using stylus or writing instruments and master copies. Draws designs, letters, and lines by hand, according to specifications, using artist and drafting tools. Traces lettering or designs on workpiece, using light box, opaque projector, and artist and drafting equipment. Designs letters, borders, scrollwork, characters, or script, according to specifications. Positions design on workpiece and lays out reference points on design, using measuring instruments. Reads work order or manuscript to determine words and symbols needed. Measures width, thickness, and spacing of characters and design, using optical or measuring instruments. Cuts out letters or designs, using cutting tools. Applies colors to patterns, using stylus, pen, brush, sponge, opaque, India ink, and paints. Applies coatings to workpiece, such as metallic leaf, shellac, oil, glue, or lacquer, using brush, spray, roller, or hand tools. Positions and secures work piece. Rubs metallic leaf with burnishing agate, cotton pad, or gloved hand to polish leaf or simulate worn metal finish. Assembles composite design to determine accuracy for final approved form. Corrects errors in design to make ready for printing. Determines availability of characters specified on order. Reproduces reference copies, using automatic film developer or duplication equipment. Types lines and characters, such as letters, musical notations, Braille symbols, using typewriter or computer. Maintains detailed records of jobs and reference sources.

 Occupational Type

Realistic occupations frequently involve work activities that include practical, hands-on problems and solutions. They often deal with plants, animals, and real-world materials like wood, tools, and machinery. Many of the occupations require working outside, and do not involve a lot of paperwork or working closely with others.

Skills required of Tracers and Letterers

Information on specific skills required not available.

 College Majors

Graphic and Printing Equipment Operator, General: An instructional program that generally prepares individuals to apply technical knowledge and skills to plan, prepare and execute commercial and industrial visual image and print products using mechanical, electronic, and digital graphic and printing equipment.

 Supporting Courses

Production and Processing: Knowledge of inputs, outputs, raw materials, waste, quality control, costs, and techniques for maximizing the manufacture and distribution of goods. **Design:** Knowledge of design techniques, principles, tools and instruments involved in the production and use of precision technical plans, blueprints, drawings, and models. **Fine Arts:** Knowledge of theory and techniques required to produce, compose, and perform works of music, dance, visual arts, drama, and sculpture.

Gilders

Cover surfaces of items, such as books, furniture, and signs, with metal leaf, using hand tools. Picks up leaf with brush or felt-edged tool and lays leaf over sizing. Smoothes leaf over surface and removes excess, using brush. Presses sheets or ribbons of leaf onto sizing by hand. Brushes sizing (thin glue) on sections of items to be covered with leaf, according to design. Rubs leaf with polished burnishing agent or cotton pad to polish leaf or simulate worn metal finish. Transfers leaf from supply book onto pallet.

 Occupational Type

Realistic occupations frequently involve work activities that include practical, hands-on problems and solutions. They often deal with plants, animals, and real-world materials like wood, tools, and machinery. Many of the occupations require working outside, and do not involve a lot of paperwork or working closely with others.

 Skills required of Gilders

Information on specific skills required is not available.

 College Majors

Graphic Design, Commercial Art, and Illustration: An instructional program in the applied visual arts that prepares individuals to use artistic techniques to effectively communicate ideas and information to business and consumer audiences via illustrations and other

---

forms of printed media. Includes instruction in concept design, layout, paste-up, and techniques such as engraving, etching, silkscreen, lithography, offset, drawing and cartooning, painting, collage, and computer graphics.

Supporting Courses

Fine Arts: Knowledge of theory and techniques required to produce, compose, and perform works of music, dance, visual arts, drama, and sculpture.

ATMOSPHERIC AND SPACE SCIENTISTS

Education		Bachelor's degree
Average Yearly Earnings		$47,674
Projected Growth		8%
Annual Job Openings		421
Self-employed		0%
Employed Part-time		7%

Atmospheric and Space Scientists

Investigate atmospheric phenomena and interpret meteorological data gathered by surface and air stations, satellites, and radar, to prepare reports and forecasts for public and other uses. Include weather analysts and forecasters who work for radio and TV stations and whose functions require the detailed knowledge of a meteorologist. Analyzes and interprets meteorological data gathered by surface and upper air stations, satellites, and radar, to prepare reports and forecasts. Studies and interprets synoptic reports, maps, photographs, and prognostic charts to predict long- and short-range weather conditions. Prepares special forecasts and briefings for air and sea transportation, agriculture, fire prevention, air-pollution control, and school groups. Operates computer graphic equipment to produce weather reports and maps for analysis, distribution, or use in televised weather broadcast. Conducts basic or applied research in meteorology. Issues hurricane and other severe weather warnings. Broadcasts weather forecasts over television or radio. Directs forecasting services at weather station or at radio or television broadcasting facility. Establishes and staffs weather observation stations.

Occupational Type

Investigative occupations frequently involve working with ideas, and require an extensive amount of thinking. These occupations can involve searching for facts and figuring out problems mentally.

Skills required of Atmospheric and Space Scientists

Reading Comprehension, Writing, Speaking, Mathematics, Science, Critical Thinking, Active Learning, Learning Strategies, Monitoring, Instructing, Information Gathering, Information Organization, Synthesis/Reorganization, Idea Generation, Idea Evaluation, Implementation Planning, Operations Analysis, Equipment Selection, Visioning, Systems Perception, Identifying Downstream Consequences, Judgment and Decision Making,

Systems Evaluation, Time Management, Management of Material Resources, Management of Personnel Resources

College Majors

Atmospheric Sciences and Meteorology: An instructional program that describes the scientific study of the composition and behavior of the atmospheric envelopes surrounding the earth and other planets, the effect of earth's atmosphere on terrestrial weather, and related problems of environment and climate. Includes instruction in atmospheric chemistry and physics, atmospheric dynamics, climatology and climate change, weather simulation, weather forecasting, climate modelling and mathematical theory; and studies of specific phenomena such as clouds, weather systems, storms, and precipitation patterns.

Supporting Courses

Administration and Management: Knowledge of principles and processes involved in business and organizational planning, coordination, and execution. This includes strategic planning, resource allocation, manpower modeling, leadership techniques, and production methods. **Clerical:** Knowledge of administrative and clerical procedures and systems such as word processing systems, filing and records management systems, stenography and transcription, forms design principles, and other office procedures and terminology. **Personnel and Human Resources:** Knowledge of policies and practices involved in personnel/human resource functions. This includes recruitment, selection, training, and promotion regulations and procedures; compensation and benefits packages; labor relations and negotiation strategies; and personnel information systems. **Computers and Electronics:** Knowledge of electric circuit boards, processors, chips, and computer hardware and software, including applications and programming. **Mathematics:** Knowledge of numbers, their operations, and interrelationships including arithmetic, algebra, geometry, calculus, statistics, and their applications. **Physics:** Knowledge and prediction of physical principles, laws, and applications including air, water, material dynamics, light, atomic principles, heat, electric theory, earth formations, and meteorological and related natural phenomena. **Sociology and Anthropology:** Knowledge of group behavior and dynamics, societal trends and influences, cultures, their history, migrations, ethnicity, and origins. **Geography:** Knowledge of various methods for describing the location and distribution of land, sea, and air masses including their physical locations, relationships, and characteristics. **Education and Training:** Knowledge of instructional methods and training techniques including curriculum design principles, learning theory, group and individual teaching techniques, design of individual development plans, and test design principles. **English Language:** Knowledge of the structure and content of the English language including the meaning and spelling of words, rules of composition, and grammar. **Foreign Language:** Knowledge of the structure and content of a foreign (non-English) language including the meaning and spelling of words, rules of composition and grammar, and pronunciation. **Telecommunications:** Knowledge of transmission, broadcasting, switching, control, and operation of telecommunications systems. **Communications and Media:** Knowledge of media production, communication, and dissemination techniques and methods including alternative ways to inform and entertain via written, oral, and visual media.

BIOLOGICAL SCIENTISTS

	Education	Doctor's degree
	Average Yearly Earnings	$41,829
	Projected Growth	25%
	Annual Job Openings	7,111
	Self-employed	4%
	Employed Part-time	7%

Biochemists

Research or study chemical composition and processes of living organisms that affect vital processes such as growth and aging, to determine chemical actions and effects on organisms, such as the action of foods, drugs, or other substances on body functions and tissues. Studies chemistry of living processes, such as cell development, breathing, and digestion, and living energy changes, such as growth, aging, and death. Researches methods of transferring characteristics, such as resistance to disease, from one organism to another. Researches and determines chemical action of substances, such as drugs, serums, hormones, and food, on tissues and vital processes. Examines chemical aspects of formation of antibodies, and researches chemistry of cells and blood corpuscles. Isolates, analyzes, and identifies hormones, vitamins, allergens, minerals, and enzymes, and determines their effects on body functions. Develops and executes tests to detect disease, genetic disorders, or other abnormalities. Develops methods to process, store, and use food, drugs, and chemical compounds. Develops and tests new drugs and medications used for commercial distribution. Prepares reports and recommendations based upon research outcomes. Designs and builds laboratory equipment needed for special research projects. Cleans, purifies, refines, and otherwise prepares pharmaceutical compounds for commercial distribution. Analyzes foods to determine nutritional value and effects of cooking, canning, and processing on this value.

Occupational Type

Investigative occupations frequently involve working with ideas, and require an extensive amount of thinking. These occupations can involve searching for facts and figuring out problems mentally.

Skills required of Biochemists

Reading Comprehension, Writing, Mathematics, Science, Critical Thinking, Active Learning, Problem Identification, Information Gathering, Information Organization, Synthesis/Reorganization, Idea Generation, Idea Evaluation, Operations Analysis, Equipment Selection, Programming, Testing, Visioning, Systems Perception, Identifying Downstream Consequences, Identification of Key Causes

College Majors

Biochemistry: An instructional program that describes the chemical processes of living organisms. Includes instruction in the chemical mechanisms of genetic information storage and transmission; the chemistry of cell components; blood chemistry; the chemistry of biological systems and biological products; and the chemistry of life processes such as respiration, digestion, and reproduction.

Supporting Courses

Building and Construction: Knowledge of materials, methods, and the appropriate tools to construct objects, structures, and buildings. **Mathematics:** Knowledge of numbers, their operations, and interrelationships including arithmetic, algebra, geometry, calculus, statistics, and their applications. **Chemistry:** Knowledge of the composition, structure, and properties of substances and of the chemical processes and transformations that they undergo. This includes uses of chemicals and their interactions, danger signs, production techniques, and disposal methods. **Biology:** Knowledge of plant and animal living tissue, cells, organisms, and entities, including their functions, interdependencies, and interactions with each other and the environment.

Biologists

Study the relationship among organisms and between organisms and their environment. Studies basic principles of plant and animal life, such as origin, relationship, development, anatomy, and functions. Studies aquatic plants and animals and environmental conditions affecting them, such as radioactivity or pollution. Collects and analyzes biological data about relationship among and between organisms and their environment. Studies reactions of plants, animals, and marine species to parasites. Identifies, classifies, and studies structure, behavior, ecology, physiology, nutrition, culture, and distribution of plant and animal species. Measures salinity, acidity, light, oxygen content, and other physical conditions of water to determine their relationship to aquatic life. Studies and manages wild animal populations. Develops methods and apparatus for securing representative plant, animal, aquatic, or soil samples. Investigates and develops pest management and control measures. Communicates test results to state and Federal representatives and general public. Prepares environmental impact reports for industry, government, or publication. Cultivates, breeds, and grows aquatic life, such as lobsters, clams, or fish farming. Plans and administers biological research programs for government, research firms, medical industries, or manufacturing firms. Researches environmental effects of present and potential uses of land and water areas, and determines methods of improving environment or crop yields. Develops methods of extracting drugs from aquatic plants and animals.

 ## Occupational Type

Investigative occupations frequently involve working with ideas, and require an extensive amount of thinking. These occupations can involve searching for facts and figuring out problems mentally.

 ## Skills required of Biologists

Reading Comprehension, Writing, Mathematics, Science, Critical Thinking, Active Learning, Learning Strategies, Problem Identification, Information Gathering, Information Organization, Synthesis/Reorganization, Idea Generation, Idea Evaluation, Implementation Planning, Programming, Systems Perception, Identification of Key Causes

College Majors

Marine/Aquatic Biology: An instructional program that describes the scientific study of marine organisms and their environments. Includes instruction in freshwater and salt-water organisms, physiological and anatomical marine adaptations, ocean and freshwater ecologies, marine microbiology, marine mammalogy, ichthyology, marine botany, and bio-chemical products of marine life used by humans.

 Supporting Courses

Food Production: Knowledge of techniques and equipment for planting, growing, and harvesting of food for consumption including crop rotation methods, animal husbandry, and food storage/handling techniques. **Mathematics:** Knowledge of numbers, their operations, and interrelationships including arithmetic, algebra, geometry, calculus, statistics, and their applications. **Physics:** Knowledge and prediction of physical principles, laws, and applications including air, water, material dynamics, light, atomic principles, heat, electric theory, earth formations, and meteorological and related natural phenomena. **Chemistry:** Knowledge of the composition, structure, and properties of substances and of the chemical processes and transformations that they undergo. This includes uses of chemicals and their interactions, danger signs, production techniques, and disposal methods. **Biology:** Knowledge of plant and animal living tissue, cells, organisms, and entities, including their functions, interdependencies, and interactions with each other and the environment. **English Language:** Knowledge of the structure and content of the English language including the meaning and spelling of words, rules of composition, and grammar.

Biophysicists

Research or study physical principles of living cells and organisms, their electrical and mechanical energy, and related phenomena. Studies physical principles of living cells and organisms and their electrical and mechanical energy. Researches manner in which characteristics of plants and animals are carried through successive generations. Researches transformation of substances in cells, using atomic isotopes. Investigates damage to cells and tissues caused by X-rays and nuclear particles. Studies spatial configuration of submicroscopic molecules, such as proteins, using X-ray and electron microscope. Investigates transmission of electrical impulses along nerves and muscles. Investigates dynamics of seeing and hearing. Analyzes functions of electronic and human brains, such as learning, thinking, and memory. Researches cancer treatment, using radiation and nuclear particles. Studies absorption of light by chlorophyll in photosynthesis or by pigments of eye involved in vision.

 Occupational Type

Investigative occupations frequently involve working with ideas, and require an extensive amount of thinking. These occupations can involve searching for facts and figuring out problems mentally.

Skills required of Biophysicists

Reading Comprehension, Writing, Mathematics, Science, Critical Thinking, Active Learning, Information Gathering, Information Organization, Idea Generation, Idea Evaluation, Programming

 College Majors

Biochemistry: An instructional program that describes the chemical processes of living organisms. Includes instruction in the chemical mechanisms of genetic information storage and transmission; the chemistry of cell components; blood chemistry; the chemistry of biological systems and biological products; and the chemistry of life processes such as respiration, digestion, and reproduction.

Supporting Courses

Mathematics: Knowledge of numbers, their operations, and interrelationships including arithmetic, algebra, geometry, calculus, statistics, and their applications. **Physics:** Knowledge and prediction of physical principles, laws, and applications including air, water, material dynamics, light, atomic principles, heat, electric theory, earth formations, and meteorological and related natural phenomena. **Chemistry:** Knowledge of the composition, structure, and properties of substances and of the chemical processes and transformations that they undergo. This includes uses of chemicals and their interactions, danger signs, production techniques, and disposal methods. **Biology:** Knowledge of plant and animal living tissue, cells, organisms, and entities, including their functions, interdependencies, and interactions with each other and the environment.

Botanists

Research or study development of life processes, physiology, heredity, environment, distribution, morphology, and economic value of plants for application in such fields as agronomy, forestry, horticulture, and pharmacology. Studies development, life processes, and economic value of plants and fungi for application in such fields as horticulture and pharmacology. Studies behavior, internal and external structure, mechanics, and biochemistry of plant or fungi cells, using microscope and scientific equipment. Investigates effect of rainfall, deforestation, pollution, acid rain, temperature, climate, soil, and elevation on plant or fungi growth. Studies and compares healthy and diseased plants to determine agents responsible for diseased conditions. Investigates comparative susceptibility of different varieties of plants to disease, and develops plant varieties immune to disease. Studies rates of spread and intensity of plant diseases under different environmental conditions, and predicts disease outbreaks. Inspects flower and vegetable seed stocks and flowering bulbs, to determine presence of diseases, infections, and insect infestation. Identifies and classifies plants or fungi based on study and research. Tests disease control measures under laboratory and field conditions for comparative effectiveness, practicality, and economy. Plans and administers environmental research programs for government, research firms, medical industries, or manufacturing firms. Devises methods of destroying or controlling disease-causing agents. Prepares reports and recommendations based upon research outcomes. Develops drugs, medicines, molds, yeasts, or foods from plants or fungi, or develops new types of plants. Develops practices to prevent or reduce deterioration of perishable plant products in transit or storage. Develops improved methods of propagating and growing edible fungi.

Occupational Type

Investigative occupations frequently involve working with ideas, and require an extensive amount of thinking. These occupations can involve searching for facts and figuring out problems mentally.

Skills required of Botanists

Reading Comprehension, Writing, Mathematics, Science, Critical Thinking, Active Learning, Information Gathering, Information Organization, Synthesis/Reorganization, Idea Generation, Programming, Identifying Downstream Consequences, Identification of Key Causes

College Majors

Plant Sciences, General: An instructional program that generally describes the scientific theories and principles involved in the production and management of plants for food, feed, fiber, and soil conservation.

Supporting Courses

Chemistry: Knowledge of the composition, structure, and properties of substances and of the chemical processes and transformations that they undergo. This includes uses of chemicals and their interactions, danger signs, production techniques, and disposal methods. **Biology:** Knowledge of plant and animal living tissue, cells, organisms, and entities, including their functions, interdependencies, and interactions with each other and the environment.

Microbiologists

Research or study growth, structure, development, and general characteristics of bacteria and other microorganisms. Studies growth, structure, development, and general characteristics of bacteria and other microorganisms. Examines physiological, morphological, and cultural characteristics, using microscope, to identify microorganisms. Studies growth structure and development of viruses and rickettsiae. Observes action of microorganisms upon living tissues of plants, higher animals, and other microorganisms, and on dead organic matter. Isolates and makes cultures of bacteria or other microorganisms in prescribed media, controlling moisture, aeration, temperature, and nutrition. Conducts chemical analyses of substances, such as acids, alcohols, and enzymes. Researches use of bacteria and microorganisms to develop vitamins, antibiotics, amino acids, grain alcohol, sugars, and polymers. Prepares technical reports and recommendations based upon research outcomes. Plans and administers biological research program for government, private research centers, or medical industry.

Occupational Type

Investigative occupations frequently involve working with ideas, and require an extensive amount of thinking. These occupations can involve searching for facts and figuring out problems mentally.

Skills required of Microbiologists

Reading Comprehension, Writing, Mathematics, Science, Active Learning, Problem Identification, Information Gathering, Synthesis/Reorganization, Idea Evaluation, Equipment Selection, Programming

College Majors

Biochemistry: An instructional program that describes the chemical processes of living organisms. Includes instruction in the chemical mechanisms of genetic information storage and transmission; the chemistry of cell components; blood chemistry; the chemistry of biological systems and biological products; and the chemistry of life processes such as respiration, digestion, and reproduction.

Supporting Courses

Mathematics: Knowledge of numbers, their operations, and interrelationships including arithmetic, algebra, geometry, calculus, statistics, and their applications. **Chemistry:** Knowledge of the composition, structure, and properties of substances and of the chemical processes and transformations that they undergo. This includes uses of chemicals and their interactions, danger signs, production techniques, and disposal methods. **Biology:** Knowledge of plant and animal living tissue, cells, organisms, and entities, including their functions, interdependencies, and interactions with each other and the environment. **English Language:** Knowledge of the structure and content of the English language including the meaning and spelling of words, rules of composition, and grammar.

Geneticists

Research or study inheritance and variation of characteristics on forms of life to determine laws, mechanisms, and environmental factors in origin, transmission, and development of inherited traits. Conducts experiments to determine laws, mechanisms, and environmental factors in origin, transmission, and development of inherited traits. Analyses determinants responsible for specific inherited traits, such as color differences, size, and disease resistance. Studies genetic determinants to understand relationship of heredity to maturity, fertility, or other factors. Devises methods for altering or producing new traits, using chemicals, heat, light, or other means. Prepares technical reports and recommendations based upon research outcomes. Counsels clients in human and medical genetics. Plans and administers genetic research program for government, private research centers, or medical industry.

Occupational Type

Investigative occupations frequently involve working with ideas, and require an extensive amount of thinking. These occupations can involve searching for facts and figuring out problems mentally.

Skills required of Geneticists

Reading Comprehension, Active Listening, Writing, Speaking, Mathematics, Science, Critical Thinking, Active Learning, Learning Strategies, Persuasion, Instructing, Problem Identification, Information Gathering, Information Organization, Synthesis/Reorganization, Idea Generation, Idea Evaluation, Equipment Selection, Programming, Visioning, Systems Perception, Management of Financial Resources, Management of Personnel Resources

College Majors

Biochemistry: An instructional program that describes the chemical processes of living organisms. Includes instruction in the chemical mechanisms of genetic information storage and transmission; the chemistry of cell components; blood chemistry; the chemistry of biological systems and biological products; and the chemistry of life processes such as respiration, digestion, and reproduction.

Supporting Courses

Administration and Management: Knowledge of principles and processes involved in business and organizational planning, coordination, and execution. This includes strategic planning, resource allocation, manpower modeling, leadership techniques, and production methods. **Mathematics:** Knowledge of numbers, their operations, and interrelationships including arithmetic, algebra, geometry, calculus, statistics, and their applications. **Chemistry:** Knowledge of the composition, structure, and properties of substances and of the chemical processes and transformations that they undergo. This includes uses of chemicals and their interactions, danger signs, production techniques, and disposal methods. **Biology:** Knowledge of plant and animal living tissue, cells, organisms, and entities, including their functions, interdependencies, and interactions with each other and the environment. **Medicine and Dentistry:** Knowledge of the information and techniques needed to diagnose and treat injuries, diseases, and deformities. This includes symptoms, treatment alternatives, drug properties and interactions, and preventive healthcare measures. **Therapy and Counseling:** Knowledge of information and techniques needed to rehabilitate physical and mental ailments and to provide career guidance including alternative treatments, rehabilitation equipment and its proper use, and methods to evaluate treatment effects. **Foreign Language:** Knowledge of the structure and content of a foreign (non-English) language including the meaning and spelling of words, rules of composition and grammar, and pronunciation.

Physiologists and Cytologists

Research or study cellular structure and functions, or organ-system functions, of plants and animals. Studies cells, cellular structure, cell division, and organ-system functions of plants and animals. Studies functions of plants and animals, such as growth, respiration, movement, and reproduction, under normal and abnormal conditions. Conducts experiments to determine effects of internal and external environmental factors on life processes and functions. Studies physiology of plants, animals, or particular human body area, function, organ, or system. Utilizes microscope, X-ray equipment, spectroscope, and other equipment to study cell structure and function and to perform experiments. Studies glands and their relationship to bodily functions. Analyzes reproductive cells and methods by which chromosomes divide or unite. Studies formation of sperm and eggs in animal sex glands, and studies origin of blood and tissue cells. Researches physiology of unicellular organisms, such as protozoa, to ascertain physical and chemical factors of growth. Studies influence of physical and chemical factors on malignant and normal cells. Assesses and evaluates hormonal status and presence of atypical or malignant changes in exfoliated, aspirated, or abraded cells. Selects and sections minute particles of animal or plant tissue for microscopic study, using microtome and other equipment. Stains tissue sample to make cell structures visible or to differentiate parts. Prepares technical reports and recommendations based upon research outcomes. Plans and administers biological research programs for government, private research centers, or medical industry.

Occupational Type

Investigative occupations frequently involve working with ideas, and require an extensive amount of thinking. These occupations can involve searching for facts and figuring out problems mentally.

Skills required of Physiologists and Cytologists

Reading Comprehension, Writing, Mathematics, Science, Critical Thinking, Active Learning, Problem Identification, Information Gathering, Information Organization, Synthesis/Reorganization, Idea Generation, Idea Evaluation, Implementation Planning, Equipment Selection, Programming, Operation Monitoring, Operation and Control, Visioning, Identifying Downstream Consequences, Identification of Key Causes

College Majors

Plant Sciences, General: An instructional program that generally describes the scientific theories and principles involved in the production and management of plants for food, feed, fiber, and soil conservation.

Supporting Courses

Administration and Management: Knowledge of principles and processes involved in business and organizational planning, coordination, and execution. This includes strategic

planning, resource allocation, manpower modeling, leadership techniques, and production methods. **Chemistry:** Knowledge of the composition, structure, and properties of substances and of the chemical processes and transformations that they undergo. This includes uses of chemicals and their interactions, danger signs, production techniques, and disposal methods. **Biology:** Knowledge of plant and animal living tissue, cells, organisms, and entities, including their functions, interdependencies, and interactions with each other and the environment.

Zoologists

Research or study origins, interrelationships, classification, habits, life histories, life processes, diseases, relation to environment, growth, development, genetics, and distribution of animals. Studies origins, interrelationships, classification, life histories, diseases, development, genetics, and distribution of animals. Analyzes characteristics of animals to identify and classify animals. Studies animals in their natural habitats, and assesses effects of environment on animals. Collects and dissects animal specimens and examines specimens under microscope. Prepares collections of preserved specimens or microscopic slides for species identification and study of species development or animal disease. Conducts experimental studies, using chemicals and various types of scientific equipment. Raises specimens for study and observation or for use in experiments.

 ## Occupational Type

Investigative occupations frequently involve working with ideas, and require an extensive amount of thinking. These occupations can involve searching for facts and figuring out problems mentally.

 ## Skills required of Zoologists

Reading Comprehension, Writing, Mathematics, Science, Critical Thinking, Active Learning, Learning Strategies, Problem Identification, Information Gathering, Information Organization, Synthesis/Reorganization, Idea Generation, Idea Evaluation, Equipment Selection, Identifying Downstream Consequences

College Majors

Zoology, General: An instructional program that generally describes the scientific study of animals, including their structure, reproduction, growth, heredity, evolution, behavior, and distribution.

 ## Supporting Courses

Chemistry: Knowledge of the composition, structure, and properties of substances and of the chemical processes and transformations that they undergo. This includes uses of chemicals and their interactions, danger signs, production techniques, and disposal methods. **Biology:** Knowledge of plant and animal living tissue, cells, organisms, and entities, including their functions, interdependencies, and interactions with each other and the environment.

Toxicologists

Research or study the effects of toxic substances on physiological functions of humans, animals, and plants. Researches effects of toxic substances on physiological functions of humans, animals, and plants for consumer protection and industrial safety programs. Designs and conducts studies to determine physiological effects of various substances on laboratory animals, plants, and human tissue. Interprets results of studies in terms of toxicological properties of substances and hazards associated with their misuse. Collects and prepares samples of toxic materials for analysis or examination. Dissects dead animals, using surgical instruments, and examines organs for toxic substances. Applies cosmetic or ingredient onto skin, or injects substance into animal, and observes animal for abnormalities, inflammation, or irritation. Analyzes samples of toxic materials to identify compound and develop treatment. Tests and analyzes blood samples for presence of toxic conditions, using microscope and laboratory test equipment. Reviews toxicological data for accuracy, and suggests clarifications or corrections to data. Writes and maintains records and reports of studies and tests for use as toxicological resource material. Informs regulatory agency personnel and industrial firms concerning toxicological properties of products and materials. Advises governmental and industrial personnel on degree of hazard of toxic materials and on precautionary labeling. Testifies as expert witness on toxicology in hearings and court proceedings.

Occupational Type

Investigative occupations frequently involve working with ideas, and require an extensive amount of thinking. These occupations can involve searching for facts and figuring out problems mentally.

Skills required of Toxicologists

Reading Comprehension, Writing, Mathematics, Science, Critical Thinking, Active Learning, Learning Strategies, Problem Identification, Information Gathering, Idea Evaluation, Equipment Selection, Programming, Testing, Identification of Key Causes

College Majors

Biochemistry: An instructional program that describes the chemical processes of living organisms. Includes instruction in the chemical mechanisms of genetic information storage and transmission; the chemistry of cell components; blood chemistry; the chemistry of biological systems and biological products; and the chemistry of life processes such as respiration, digestion, and reproduction.

Supporting Courses

Mathematics: Knowledge of numbers, their operations, and interrelationships including arithmetic, algebra, geometry, calculus, statistics, and their applications. **Chemistry:** Knowledge of the composition, structure, and properties of substances and of the chemical processes and transformations that they undergo. This includes uses of chemicals and their interactions, danger signs, production techniques, and disposal methods. **Biology:** Knowledge of plant and animal living tissue, cells, organisms, and entities, including their functions, interdependencies, and interactions with each other and the environment. **English Language:** Knowledge of the structure and content of the English language including the meaning and spelling of words, rules of composition, and grammar.

BUDGET ANALYSTS

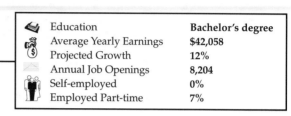

Education		Bachelor's degree
Average Yearly Earnings		$42,058
Projected Growth		12%
Annual Job Openings		8,204
Self-employed		0%
Employed Part-time		7%

Budget Analysts

Examine budget estimates for completeness, accuracy, and conformance with procedures and regulations. Examine requests for budget revisions, recommend approval or denial, and draft correspondence. Analyze monthly department budgeting and accounting reports for the purpose of maintaining expenditure controls. Provide technical assistance to officials in the preparation of budgets. Analyzes accounting records to determine financial resources required to implement program, and submits recommendations for budget allocations. Reviews operating budgets periodically to analyze trends affecting budget needs. Analyzes costs in relation to services performed during previous fiscal years to prepare comparative analyses of operating programs. Recommends approval or disapproval of requests for funds. Advises staff on cost analysis and fiscal allocations. Correlates appropriations for specific programs with appropriations for divisional programs, and includes items for emergency funds. Directs preparation of regular and special budget reports to interpret budget directives and to establish policies for carrying out directives. Consults with unit heads to ensure adjustments are made in accordance with program changes to facilitate long-term planning. Directs compilation of data based on statistical studies and analyses of past and current years to prepare budgets. Testifies regarding proposed budgets before examining and fund-granting authorities to clarify reports and gain support for estimated budget needs. Administers personnel functions of budget department, such as training, work scheduling, promotions, transfers, and performance ratings.

Occupational Type

Conventional occupations frequently involve following set procedures and routines. These occupations can include working with data and details more than with ideas. Usually there is a clear line of authority to follow.

Skills required of Budget Analysts

Reading Comprehension, Active Listening, Writing, Speaking, Mathematics, Critical Thinking, Active Learning, Learning Strategies, Monitoring, Coordination, Persuasion,

---

Negotiation, Instructing, Problem Identification, Information Gathering, Information Organization, Synthesis/Reorganization, Idea Generation, Idea Evaluation, Implementation Planning, Visioning, Systems Perception, Identifying Downstream Consequences, Identification of Key Causes, Judgment and Decision Making, Systems Evaluation, Time Management, Management of Financial Resources, Management of Material Resources, Management of Personnel Resources

 ## College Majors

Public Administration: An instructional program that prepares individuals to serve as managers in the executive arm of local, state, and Federal government; and that describes the systematic study of executive organization and management. Includes instruction in the roles, development, and principles of public administration; the management of public policy; executive-legislative relations; public budgetary processes and financial management; administrative law; public personnel management; professional ethics; and research methods.

Supporting Courses

Administration and Management: Knowledge of principles and processes involved in business and organizational planning, coordination, and execution. This includes strategic planning, resource allocation, manpower modeling, leadership techniques, and production methods. **Economics and Accounting:** Knowledge of economic and accounting principles and practices, the financial markets, banking, and the analysis and reporting of financial data. **Personnel and Human Resources:** Knowledge of policies and practices involved in personnel/human resource functions. This includes recruitment, selection, training, and promotion regulations and procedures; compensation and benefits packages; labor relations and negotiation strategies; and personnel information systems. **Computers and Electronics:** Knowledge of electric circuit boards, processors, chips, and computer hardware and software, including applications and programming. **Mathematics:** Knowledge of numbers, their operations, and interrelationships including arithmetic, algebra, geometry, calculus, statistics, and their applications. **Education and Training:** Knowledge of instructional methods and training techniques including curriculum design principles, learning theory, group and individual teaching techniques, design of individual development plans, and test design principles.

CARDIOLOGY
TECHNOLOGISTS

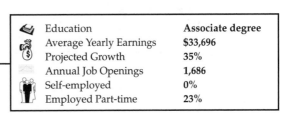

Education		Associate degree
Average Yearly Earnings		$33,696
Projected Growth		35%
Annual Job Openings		1,686
Self-employed		0%
Employed Part-time		23%

CHEMICAL ENGINEERS

	Education	Bachelor's degree
	Average Yearly Earnings	$55,765
	Projected Growth	15%
	Annual Job Openings	1,434
	Self-employed	2%
	Employed Part-time	2%

Chemical Engineers

Design chemical plant equipment and devise processes for manufacturing chemicals and products such as gasoline, synthetic rubber, plastics, detergents, cement, paper, and pulp by applying principles and technology of chemistry, physics, and engineering. Devise processes to separate components of liquids or gases, using absorbent such as fuller's earth or carbons. Conducts research to develop new and improved chemical manufacturing processes. Designs and plans layout, and oversees workers engaged in constructing and improving equipment to implement chemical processes on commercial scale. Designs measurement and control systems for chemical plants based on data collected in laboratory experiments and in pilot plant operations. Develops electrochemical processes to generate electric currents, using controlled chemical reactions, or to produce chemical changes, using electric currents. Determines most effective arrangement of operations, such as mixing, crushing, heat transfer, distillation, and drying. Performs laboratory studies of steps in manufacture of new product, and tests proposed process in small-scale operation (pilot plant). Performs tests throughout stages of production to determine degree of control over variables, including temperature, density, specific gravity, and pressure. Develops safety procedures to be employed by workers operating equipment or working in close proximity to ongoing chemical reactions. Prepares estimate of production costs and production progress reports for management. Directs activities of workers who operate equipment such as absorption and evaporation towers and electromagnets to effect required chemical reaction. Directs workers using absorption method to remove soluble constituent or vapor by dissolving in a liquid.

Occupational Type

Investigative occupations frequently involve working with ideas, and require an extensive amount of thinking. These occupations can involve searching for facts and figuring out problems mentally.

Skills required of Chemical Engineers

Reading Comprehension, Writing, Speaking, Mathematics, Science, Critical Thinking, Active Learning, Learning Strategies, Monitoring, Coordination, Instructing, Problem Identification, Information Gathering, Information Organization, Synthesis/Reorganization, Idea Generation, Idea Evaluation, Implementation Planning, Operations Analysis, Technology Design, Equipment Selection, Installation, Programming, Testing, Operation Monitoring, Product Inspection, Troubleshooting, Visioning, Systems Perception, Identifying Downstream Consequences, Identification of Key Causes, Judgment and Decision Making,

Systems Evaluation, Time Management, Management of Financial Resources, Management of Material Resources, Management of Personnel Resources

College Majors

Chemical Engineering: An instructional program that prepares individuals to apply mathematical and scientific principles to the design, development and operational evaluation of systems employing chemical processes, such as chemical reactors, kinetic systems, electrochemical systems, energy conservation processes, heat and mass transfer systems, and separation processes; and the applied analysis of chemical problems such as corrosion, particle abrasion, energy loss, pollution, and fluid mechanics.

Supporting Courses

Administration and Management: Knowledge of principles and processes involved in business and organizational planning, coordination, and execution. This includes strategic planning, resource allocation, manpower modeling, leadership techniques, and production methods. **Economics and Accounting:** Knowledge of economic and accounting principles and practices, the financial markets, banking, and the analysis and reporting of financial data. **Production and Processing:** Knowledge of inputs, outputs, raw materials, waste, quality control, costs, and techniques for maximizing the manufacture and distribution of goods. **Computers and Electronics:** Knowledge of electric circuit boards, processors, chips, and computer hardware and software, including applications and programming. **Engineering and Technology:** Knowledge of equipment, tools, mechanical devices, and their uses to produce motion, light, power, technology, and other applications. **Design:** Knowledge of design techniques, principles, tools and instruments involved in the production and use of precision technical plans, blueprints, drawings, and models. **Mechanical:** Knowledge of machines and tools, including their designs, uses, benefits, repair, and maintenance. **Mathematics:** Knowledge of numbers, their operations, and interrelationships including arithmetic, algebra, geometry, calculus, statistics, and their applications. **Physics:** Knowledge and prediction of physical principles, laws, and applications including air, water, material dynamics, light, atomic principles, heat, electric theory, earth formations, and meteorological and related natural phenomena. **Chemistry:** Knowledge of the composition, structure, and properties of substances and of the chemical processes and transformations that they undergo. This includes uses of chemicals and their interactions, danger signs, production techniques, and disposal methods. **Biology:** Knowledge of plant and animal living tissue, cells, organisms, and entities, including their functions, interdependencies, and interactions with each other and the environment. **English Language:** Knowledge of the structure and content of the English language including the meaning and spelling of words, rules of composition, and grammar. **Public Safety and Security:** Knowledge of weaponry, public safety, and security operations, rules, regulations, precautions, prevention, and the protection of people, data, and property. **Law, Government, and Jurisprudence:** Knowledge of laws, legal codes, court procedures, precedents, government regulations, executive orders, agency rules, and the democratic political process.

Chemists

✍	Education	Bachelor's degree
💰	Average Yearly Earnings	$43,306
	Projected Growth	18%
	Annual Job Openings	10,572
	Self-employed	0%
	Employed Part-time	3%

Chemists, Except Biochemists

Conduct qualitative and quantitative chemical analyses or chemical experiments in laboratories for quality or process control or to develop new products or knowledge. Analyzes organic and inorganic compounds to determine chemical and physical properties, composition, structure, relationships, and reactions, utilizing chromatography, spectroscopy, and spectrophotometry techniques. Induces changes in composition of substances by introducing heat, light, energy, and chemical catalysts for quantitative and qualitative analysis. Develops, improves, and customizes products, equipment, formulas, processes, and analytical methods. Compiles and analyzes test information to determine process or equipment operating efficiency and to diagnose malfunctions. Studies effects of various methods of processing, preserving, and packaging on composition and properties of foods. Prepares test solutions, compounds, and reagents for laboratory personnel to conduct test. Confers with scientists and engineers to conduct analyses of research projects, interpret test results, or develop nonstandard tests. Writes technical papers and reports and prepares standards and specifications for processes, facilities, products, and tests. Directs, coordinates, and advises personnel in test procedures for analyzing components and physical properties of materials. Tests, or supervises workers in testing, food and beverage samples to ensure compliance with applicable laws and quality and purity standards.

Occupational Type

Investigative occupations frequently involve working with ideas, and require an extensive amount of thinking. These occupations can involve searching for facts and figuring out problems mentally.

Skills required of Chemists, Except Biochemists

Reading Comprehension, Active Listening, Writing, Speaking, Mathematics, Science, Critical Thinking, Active Learning, Learning Strategies, Monitoring, Coordination, Instructing, Problem Identification, Information Gathering, Information Organization, Synthesis/Reorganization, Idea Generation, Idea Evaluation, Implementation Planning, Operations Analysis, Technology Design, Equipment Selection, Programming, Testing, Operation Monitoring, Product Inspection, Systems Perception, Identifying Downstream Consequences, Identification of Key Causes, Judgment and Decision Making, Systems Evaluation, Time Management, Management of Personnel Resources

College Majors

Chemistry, General: A group of instructional programs that generally describes the scientific study of the composition and behavior of matter, including its micro- and macro-structure, the processes of chemical change, and the theoretical description and laboratory simulation of these phenomena.

Supporting Courses

Administration and Management: Knowledge of principles and processes involved in business and organizational planning, coordination, and execution. This includes strategic planning, resource allocation, manpower modeling, leadership techniques, and production methods. **Production and Processing:** Knowledge of inputs, outputs, raw materials, waste, quality control, costs, and techniques for maximizing the manufacture and distribution of goods. **Computers and Electronics:** Knowledge of electric circuit boards, processors, chips, and computer hardware and software, including applications and programming. **Engineering and Technology:** Knowledge of equipment, tools, mechanical devices, and their uses to produce motion, light, power, technology, and other applications. **Mathematics:** Knowledge of numbers, their operations, and interrelationships including arithmetic, algebra, geometry, calculus, statistics, and their applications. **Physics:** Knowledge and prediction of physical principles, laws, and applications including air, water, material dynamics, light, atomic principles, heat, electric theory, earth formations, and meteorological and related natural phenomena. **Chemistry:** Knowledge of the composition, structure, and properties of substances and of the chemical processes and transformations that they undergo. This includes uses of chemicals and their interactions, danger signs, production techniques, and disposal methods. **Biology:** Knowledge of plant and animal living tissue, cells, organisms, and entities, including their functions, interdependencies, and interactions with each other and the environment. **English Language:** Knowledge of the structure and content of the English language including the meaning and spelling of words, rules of composition, and grammar.

CHIROPRACTORS

Chiropractors

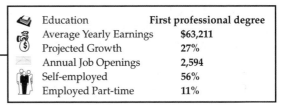

Education	First professional degree
Average Yearly Earnings	$63,211
Projected Growth	27%
Annual Job Openings	2,594
Self-employed	56%
Employed Part-time	11%

Adjust spinal column and other articulations of the body to prevent disease and correct abnormalities of the human body believed to be caused by interference with the nervous system. Examine patient to determine nature and extent of disorder. Manipulate spine or other involved area. May utilize supplementary measures such as exercise, rest, water, light, heat, and nutritional therapy. Examines patient to determine nature and extent of disorder. Manipulates spinal column and other extremities to adjust, align, or correct abnormalities caused by neurologic and kinetic articular dysfunction. Utilizes supplementary measures, such as exercise, rest, water, light, heat, and nutritional therapy. Performs diagnostic procedures, including physical, neurologic, and orthopedic examinations, and laboratory tests, using instruments and equipment such as X-ray machine and electrocardiograph.

 Occupational Type

Investigative occupations frequently involve working with ideas, and require an extensive amount of thinking. These occupations can involve searching for facts and figuring out problems mentally.

Skills required of Chiropractors

Reading Comprehension, Active Listening, Speaking, Science, Critical Thinking, Active Learning, Learning Strategies, Monitoring, Social Perceptiveness, Persuasion, Instructing, Service Orientation, Problem Identification, Information Gathering, Information Organization, Synthesis/Reorganization, Idea Generation, Idea Evaluation, Implementation Planning, Equipment Selection, Visioning, Systems Perception, Identifying Downstream Consequences, Identification of Key Causes, Judgment and Decision Making, Systems Evaluation, Time Management

College Majors

Chiropractic (D.C., D.C.M.): An instructional program that prepares individuals to be independent professional practitioners of chiropractic, either straight or progressive. Includes instruction in chiropractic theory, spinal mechanics, spinal manipulation therapy, and radiologic diagnosis; and may also include principles of neurologic health, nutrition, hydrotherapy, diet and exercise therapy, clinic and practice management, applicable regulations, and patient counseling.

Supporting Courses

Customer and Personal Service: Knowledge of principles and processes for providing customer and personal services including needs assessment techniques, quality service standards, alternative delivery systems, and customer satisfaction evaluation techniques. **Physics:** Knowledge and prediction of physical principles, laws, and applications including air, water, material dynamics, light, atomic principles, heat, electric theory, earth formations, and meteorological and related natural phenomena. **Chemistry:** Knowledge of the composition, structure, and properties of substances and of the chemical processes and transformations that they undergo. This includes uses of chemicals and their interactions, danger signs, production techniques, and disposal methods. **Biology:** Knowledge of plant and animal living tissue, cells, organisms, and entities, including their functions, interdependencies, and interactions with each other and the environment. **Psychology:** Knowledge of human behavior and performance, mental processes, psychological research methods, and the assessment and treatment of behavioral and affective disorders. **Sociology and Anthropology:** Knowledge of group behavior and dynamics, societal trends and influences, cultures, their history, migrations, ethnicity, and origins. **Medicine and Dentistry:** Knowledge of the information and techniques needed to diagnose and treat injuries, diseases, and deformities. This includes symptoms, treatment alternatives, drug properties and interactions, and preventive healthcare measures. **Therapy and Counseling:** Knowledge of information and techniques needed to rehabilitate physical and mental ailments and to provide career guidance including alternative treatments, rehabilitation equipment and its proper use, and methods to evaluate treatment effects. **English Language:** Knowledge of the structure and content of the English language including the meaning and spelling of words, rules of composition, and grammar. **Philosophy and Theology:** Knowledge of different philosophical systems and religions, including their basic principles, values, ethics, ways of thinking, customs, and practices, and their impact on human culture.

CIVIL ENGINEERS

	Education	Bachelor's degree
	Average Yearly Earnings	$49,920
	Projected Growth	18%
	Annual Job Openings	15,978
	Self-employed	6%
	Employed Part-time	5%

Civil Engineers, Including Traffic

Perform engineering duties in planning, designing, and overseeing construction and maintenance of structures and facilities such as roads, railroads, airports, bridges, harbors, channels, dams, irrigation projects, pipelines, power plants, water and sewage systems, and waste disposal units. Include traffic engineers who specialize in studying vehicular and pedestrian traffic conditions. Analyzes survey reports, maps, drawings, blueprints, aerial photography, and other topographical or geologic data to plan projects. Plans and designs transportation or hydraulic systems and structures, following construction and government standards, using design software and drawing tools. Estimates quantities and cost of materials, equipment, or labor to determine project feasibility. Directs construction, operations, and maintenance activities at project site. Computes load and grade requirements, water flow rates, and material stress factors to determine design specifications. Directs or participates in surveying to lay out installations and establish reference points, grades, and elevations to guide construction. Inspects project sites to monitor progress and ensure conformance to design specifications and safety or sanitation standards. Conducts studies of traffic patterns or environmental conditions to identify engineering problems and assess the potential impact of projects. Tests soils and materials to determine the adequacy and strength of foundations, concrete, asphalt, or steel. Provides technical advice regarding design, construction, or program modifications and structural repairs to industrial and managerial personnel. Prepares or presents public reports, such as bid proposals, deeds, environmental impact statements, and property and right-of-way descriptions.

Occupational Type

Realistic occupations frequently involve work activities that include practical, hands-on problems and solutions. They often deal with plants, animals, and real-world materials like wood, tools, and machinery. Many of the occupations require working outside, and do not involve a lot of paperwork or working closely with others.

Skills required of Civil Engineers, Including Traffic

Reading Comprehension, Active Listening, Writing, Speaking, Mathematics, Science, Critical Thinking, Active Learning, Monitoring, Coordination, Persuasion, Problem Identification, Information Gathering, Synthesis/Reorganization, Idea Generation, Idea Evaluation, Implementation Planning, Operations Analysis, Technology Design, Equipment Selection, Installation, Programming, Testing, Product Inspection, Troubleshooting, Visioning, Systems Perception, Identifying Downstream Consequences, Identification of Key Causes, Judgment and Decision Making, Systems Evaluation, Management of Financial Resources, Management of Material Resources, Management of Personnel Resources

College Majors

Agricultural Mechanization, General: An instructional program that prepares individuals in a general way to sell, select and service agriculture or agribusiness technical equipment and facilities, including computers, specialized software, power units, machinery, equipment, structures and utilities. Includes instruction in agricultural power units; the planning and selection of materials for the construction of agricultural facilities; the mechanical practices associated with irrigation and water conservation; erosion control; and data processing systems.

Supporting Courses

Administration and Management: Knowledge of principles and processes involved in business and organizational planning, coordination, and execution. This includes strategic planning, resource allocation, manpower modeling, leadership techniques, and production methods. **Economics and Accounting:** Knowledge of economic and accounting principles and practices, the financial markets, banking, and the analysis and reporting of financial data. **Computers and Electronics:** Knowledge of electric circuit boards, processors, chips, and computer hardware and software, including applications and programming. **Engineering and Technology:** Knowledge of equipment, tools, mechanical devices, and their uses to produce motion, light, power, technology, and other applications. **Design:** Knowledge of design techniques, principles, tools and instruments involved in the production and use of precision technical plans, blueprints, drawings, and models. **Building and Construction:** Knowledge of materials, methods, and the appropriate tools to construct objects, structures, and buildings. **Mathematics:** Knowledge of numbers, their operations, and interrelationships including arithmetic, algebra, geometry, calculus, statistics, and their applications. **Physics:** Knowledge and prediction of physical principles, laws, and applications including air, water, material dynamics, light, atomic principles, heat, electric theory, earth formations, and meteorological and related natural phenomena. **Geography:** Knowledge of various methods for describing the location and distribution of land, sea, and air masses including their physical locations, relationships, and characteristics. **English Language:** Knowledge of the structure and content of the English language including the meaning and spelling of words, rules of composition, and grammar. **Public Safety and Security:** Knowledge of weaponry, public safety, and security operations, rules, regulations, precautions, prevention, and the protection of people, data, and property. **Law, Government, and Jurisprudence:** Knowledge of laws, legal codes, court procedures, precedents, government regulations, executive orders, agency rules, and the democratic political process. **Transportation:** Knowledge of principles and methods for moving people or goods by air, rail, sea, or road, including their relative costs, advantages, and limitations.

CLERGY

Clergy

Education	**First professional degree**	
Average Yearly Earnings	$28,870	
Projected Growth	13%	
Annual Job Openings	14,515	
Self-employed	0%	
Employed Part-time	11%	

Conduct religious worship and perform other spiritual functions associated with beliefs and practices of religious faith or denomination, as delegated by ordinance, license, or other authorization. Provide spiritual and moral guidance and assistance to members. Leads congregation in worship services. Conducts wedding and funeral services. Administers religious rites or ordinances. Counsels those in spiritual need. Interprets doctrine of religion. Instructs people who seek conversion to faith. Prepares and delivers sermons and other talks. Visits sick and shut-ins, and helps poor. Engages in inter-faith, community, civic, educational, and recreational activities sponsored by or related to interest of denomination. Writes articles for publication. Teaches in seminaries and universities.

Occupational Type

Social occupations frequently involve working with, communicating with, and teaching people. These occupations often involve helping or providing service to others.

Skills required of Clergy

Reading Comprehension, Active Listening, Writing, Speaking, Active Learning, Learning Strategies, Monitoring, Social Perceptiveness, Persuasion, Negotiation, Instructing, Service Orientation, Idea Generation, Implementation Planning, Visioning

College Majors

Bible/Biblical Studies: An instructional program that describes the study of the Bible and its component books from the standpoint of the Christian or Jewish faiths, with an emphasis on understanding and interpreting the theological, doctrinal, and ethical messages contained within it. May include preparation for applying these studies in various church-related vocations.

Supporting Courses

Psychology: Knowledge of human behavior and performance, mental processes, psychological research methods, and the assessment and treatment of behavioral and affective disorders. **Sociology and Anthropology:** Knowledge of group behavior and dynamics, societal trends and influences, cultures, their history, migrations, ethnicity, and origins. **Therapy and Counseling:** Knowledge of information and techniques needed to rehabilitate physical and mental ailments and to provide career guidance including alternative treatments, rehabilitation equipment and its proper use, and methods to evaluate treatment effects. **Education and Training:** Knowledge of instructional methods and training techniques including curriculum design principles, learning theory, group and individual teaching techniques, design of individual development plans, and test design principles. **English Language:** Knowledge of the structure and content of the English language including the meaning and spelling of words, rules of composition, and grammar. **History and Archeology:** Knowledge of past historical events and their causes, indicators, and impact on particular civilizations and cultures. **Philosophy and Theology:** Knowledge of different philosophical systems and religions, including their basic principles, values, ethics, ways of thinking, customs, and practices, and their impact on human culture. **Communications and Media:** Knowledge of media production, communication, and dissemination techniques and methods including alternative ways to inform and entertain via written, oral, and visual media.

CLINICAL LABORATORY TECHNOLOGISTS

Medical and Clinical Laboratory Technologists

	Education	Bachelor's degree
	Average Yearly Earnings	$30,805
	Projected Growth	15%
	Annual Job Openings	23,944
	Self-employed	1%
	Employed Part-time	20%

Perform a wide range of complex procedures in the general area of the clinical laboratory, or perform specialized procedures in such areas as cytology, histology, and microbiology. Duties may include supervising and coordinating activities of workers engaged in laboratory testing. Include workers who teach medical technology when teaching is not their primary activity. Cuts, stains, and mounts biological material on slides for microscopic study and diagnosis, following standard laboratory procedures. Examines slides under microscope to detect deviations from norm and to report abnormalities for further study. Analyzes samples of biological material for chemical content or reaction. Selects and prepares specimen and media for cell culture, using aseptic technique and knowledge of medium components and cell requirements. Harvests cell culture at optimum time sequence based on knowledge of cell cycle differences and culture conditions. Prepares slide of cell culture to identify chromosomes, views and photographs slide under photomicroscope, and prints picture. Cultivates, isolates, and assists in identifying microbial organisms, and performs various tests on these microorganisms. Examines and tests human, animal, or other materials for microbial organisms. Conducts chemical analysis of body fluids, including blood, urine, and spinal fluid, to determine presence of normal and abnormal components. Performs tests to determine blood group, type, and compatibility for transfusion purposes. Studies blood cells, number of blood cells, and morphology, using microscopic technique. Cuts images of chromosomes from photograph and identifies and arranges them in numbered pairs on karyotype chart, using standard practices. Conducts research under direction of microbiologist or biochemist. Communicates with physicians, family members, and researchers requesting technical information regarding test results. Calibrates and maintains equipment used in quantitative and qualitative analysis, such as spectrophotometers, calorimeters, flame photometers, and computer-controlled analyzers. Enters analysis of medical tests and clinical results into computer for storage. Sets up, cleans, and maintains laboratory equipment.

 ## Occupational Type

Investigative occupations frequently involve working with ideas, and require an extensive amount of thinking. These occupations can involve searching for facts and figuring out problems mentally.

 ## Skills required of Medical and Clinical Laboratory Technologists

Reading Comprehension, Active Listening, Writing, Speaking, Science, Critical Thinking, Active Learning, Learning Strategies, Monitoring, Instructing, Problem Identification,

Information Gathering, Information Organization, Synthesis/Reorganization, Equipment Selection, Systems Evaluation, Time Management, Management of Financial Resources, Management of Material Resources, Management of Personnel Resources

College Majors

Cytotechnologist: An instructional program that prepares individuals to perform oncological and related pathological analyses of human tissue samples, under the supervision of a pathologist. Includes instruction in pathology laboratory procedures; equipment operation and maintenance; conducting Pap and other test procedures for cancer diagnosis; analytical procedures for other cell abnormalities; slide and tissue sample preparation; and recordkeeping.

Supporting Courses

Clerical: Knowledge of administrative and clerical procedures and systems such as word processing systems, filing and records management systems, stenography and transcription, forms design principles, and other office procedures and terminology. **Personnel and Human Resources:** Knowledge of policies and practices involved in personnel/human resource functions. This includes recruitment, selection, training, and promotion regulations and procedures; compensation and benefits packages; labor relations and negotiation strategies; and personnel information systems. **Chemistry:** Knowledge of the composition, structure, and properties of substances and of the chemical processes and transformations that they undergo. This includes uses of chemicals and their interactions, danger signs, production techniques, and disposal methods. **Biology:** Knowledge of plant and animal living tissue, cells, organisms, and entities, including their functions, interdependencies, and interactions with each other and the environment. **Psychology:** Knowledge of human behavior and performance, mental processes, psychological research methods, and the assessment and treatment of behavioral and affective disorders. **Medicine and Dentistry:** Knowledge of the information and techniques needed to diagnose and treat injuries, diseases, and deformities. This includes symptoms, treatment alternatives, drug properties and interactions, and preventive healthcare measures. **Therapy and Counseling:** Knowledge of information and techniques needed to rehabilitate physical and mental ailments and to provide career guidance including alternative treatments, rehabilitation equipment and its proper use, and methods to evaluate treatment effects. **Education and Training:** Knowledge of instructional methods and training techniques including curriculum design principles, learning theory, group and individual teaching techniques, design of individual development plans, and test design principles. **English Language:** Knowledge of the structure and content of the English language including the meaning and spelling of words, rules of composition, and grammar. **Philosophy and Theology:** Knowledge of different philosophical systems and religions, including their basic principles, values, ethics, ways of thinking, customs, and practices, and their impact on human culture. **Communications and Media:** Knowledge of media production, communication, and dissemination techniques and methods including alternative ways to inform and entertain via written, oral, and visual media.

Medical and Clinical Laboratory Technicians

Perform routine tests in medical laboratory for use in treatment and diagnosis of disease. Prepare vaccines, biologicals, and serums for prevention of disease. Prepare tissue samples for pathologists, take blood samples, and execute such laboratory tests as urinalysis and blood counts. May work under the general supervision of a medical laboratory technologist. Conducts quantitative and qualitative chemical analyses of body fluids, such as blood, urine, and spinal fluid. Performs blood counts, using microscope. Incubates bacteria for specified period and prepares vaccines and serums by standard laboratory methods. Conducts blood tests for transfusion purposes. Inoculates fertilized eggs, broths, or other bacteriological media with organisms. Tests vaccines for sterility and virus inactivity. Prepares standard volumetric solutions and reagents used in testing. Draws blood from patient, observing principles of asepsis to obtain blood sample.

 ## Occupational Type

Realistic occupations frequently involve work activities that include practical, hands-on problems and solutions. They often deal with plants, animals, and real-world materials like wood, tools, and machinery. Many of the occupations require working outside, and do not involve a lot of paperwork or working closely with others.

 ## Skills required of Medical and Clinical Laboratory Technicians

Science, Testing

 ## College Majors

Hematology Technology/Technician: An instructional program that prepares individuals to perform tests and analyses of patients' blood samples under the supervision of a hospital laboratory director or physician. Includes instruction in laboratory procedures; laboratory hematology; conducting quantitative, qualitative, and coagulation tests on cellular and plasma blood components; equipment operation and maintenance, and recordkeeping.

 ## Supporting Courses

Mathematics: Knowledge of numbers, their operations, and interrelationships including arithmetic, algebra, geometry, calculus, statistics, and their applications. **Chemistry:** Knowledge of the composition, structure, and properties of substances and of the chemical processes and transformations that they undergo. This includes uses of chemicals and their interactions, danger signs, production techniques, and disposal methods. **Biology:** Knowledge of plant and animal living tissue, cells, organisms, and entities, including their functions, interdependencies, and interactions with each other and the environment. **Medicine and Dentistry:** Knowledge of the information and techniques needed to diagnose and treat injuries, diseases, and deformities. This includes symptoms, treatment alternatives, drug properties and interactions, and preventive healthcare measures. **Philosophy and Theology:** Knowledge of different philosophical systems and religions, including their basic principles, values, ethics, ways of thinking, customs, and practices, and their impact on human culture.

COLLEGE AND UNIVERSITY FACULTY

Education		Doctor's degree
Average Yearly Earnings		$44,800
Projected Growth		19%
Annual Job Openings		126,583
Self-employed		0%
Employed Part-time		32%

Nursing Instructors: Postsecondary

Demonstrate and teach patient care in classroom and clinical units to nursing students. Instruct students in principles and application of physical, biological, and psychological subjects related to nursing. Conduct and supervise laboratory experiments. Issue assignments, direct seminars, etc. Participate in planning curriculum with medical and nursing personnel and in evaluating and improving teaching and nursing practices. May specialize in specific subjects, such as anatomy or chemistry, or in a type of nursing activity, such as nursing of surgical patients. Instructs and lectures nursing students in principles and application of physical, biological, and psychological subjects related to nursing. Conducts and supervises laboratory work. Issues assignments to students. Participates in planning curriculum, teaching schedule, and course outline with medical and nursing personnel. Directs seminars and panels. Supervises student nurses and demonstrates patient care in clinical units of hospital. Cooperates with medical and nursing personnel in evaluating and improving teaching and nursing practices. Prepares and administers examinations to nursing students. Evaluates student progress and maintains records of student classroom and clinical experience. Conducts classes for patients in health practices and procedures.

Occupational Type

Social occupations frequently involve working with, communicating with, and teaching people. These occupations often involve helping or providing service to others.

Skills required of Nursing Instructors: Postsecondary

Reading Comprehension, Active Listening, Writing, Speaking, Science, Critical Thinking, Active Learning, Learning Strategies, Monitoring, Social Perceptiveness, Coordination, Persuasion, Instructing, Service Orientation, Information Organization, Idea Generation, Idea Evaluation, Implementation Planning, Testing, Visioning, Systems Perception, Identification of Key Causes, Judgment and Decision Making, Time Management, Management of Personnel Resources

College Majors

Nursing (R.N. Training): An instructional program that generally prepares individuals in the knowledge, techniques and procedures for promoting health, providing care for sick, disabled, informed, or other individuals or groups. Includes instruction in the administration of medication and treatments, assisting a physician during treatments and examinations, referring patients to physicians and other healthcare specialists, and planning education for health maintenance.

Supporting Courses

Administration and Management: Knowledge of principles and processes involved in business and organizational planning, coordination, and execution. This includes strategic planning, resource allocation, manpower modeling, leadership techniques, and production methods. **Customer and Personal Service:** Knowledge of principles and processes for providing customer and personal services including needs assessment techniques, quality service standards, alternative delivery systems, and customer satisfaction evaluation techniques. **Personnel and Human Resources:** Knowledge of policies and practices involved in personnel/human resource functions. This includes recruitment, selection, training, and promotion regulations and procedures; compensation and benefits packages; labor relations and negotiation strategies; and personnel information systems. **Chemistry:** Knowledge of the composition, structure, and properties of substances and of the chemical processes and transformations that they undergo. This includes uses of chemicals and their interactions, danger signs, production techniques, and disposal methods. **Biology:** Knowledge of plant and animal living tissue, cells, organisms, and entities, including their functions, interdependencies, and interactions with each other and the environment. **Psychology:** Knowledge of human behavior and performance, mental processes, psychological research methods, and the assessment and treatment of behavioral and affective disorders. **Sociology and Anthropology:** Knowledge of group behavior and dynamics, societal trends and influences, cultures, their history, migrations, ethnicity, and origins. **Medicine and Dentistry:** Knowledge of the information and techniques needed to diagnose and treat injuries, diseases, and deformities. This includes symptoms, treatment alternatives, drug properties and interactions, and preventive heathcare measures. **Therapy and Counseling:** Knowledge of information and techniques needed to rehabilitate physical and mental ailments and to provide career guidance including alternative treatments, rehabilitation equipment and its proper use, and methods to evaluate treatment effects. **Education and Training:** Knowledge of instructional methods and training techniques including curriculum design principles, learning theory, group and individual teaching techniques, design of individual development plans, and test design principles. **English Language:** Knowledge of the structure and content of the English language including the meaning and spelling of words, rules of composition, and grammar. **Philosophy and Theology:** Knowledge of different philosophical systems and religions, including their basic principles, values, ethics, ways of thinking, customs, and practices, and their impact on human culture. **Public Safety and Security:** Knowledge of weaponry, public safety, and security operations, rules, regulations, precautions, prevention, and the protection of people, data, and property. **Law, Government, and Jurisprudence:** Knowledge of laws, legal codes, court procedures, precedents, government regulations, executive orders, agency rules, and the democratic political process.

Life Sciences Teachers: Postsecondary

Teach courses pertaining to living organisms, such as biological sciences, agricultural sciences, and medical sciences. Include teachers of subjects such as botany, zoology, agronomy, biochemistry, biophysics, soil conservation, forestry, psychiatry, surgery, and obstetrics. Prepares and delivers lectures to students. Stimulates class discussions. Compiles bibliographies of specialized materials for outside reading assignments. Compiles, administers, and grades examinations, or assigns this work to others. Advises students on academic and vocational curricula. Directs research of other teachers or graduate students working for advanced academic degrees. Conducts research in particular field of knowledge and publishes findings in professional journals. Acts as adviser to student organizations. Serves on faculty committee providing professional consulting services to government and industry.

Occupational Type

Investigative occupations frequently involve working with ideas, and require an extensive amount of thinking. These occupations can involve searching for facts and figuring out problems mentally.

Skills required of Life Sciences Teachers: Postsecondary

Reading Comprehension, Active Listening, Writing, Speaking, Mathematics, Science, Critical Thinking, Active Learning, Learning Strategies, Monitoring, Social Perceptiveness, Instructing, Problem Identification, Information Gathering, Information Organization, Synthesis/Reorganization, Idea Generation, Idea Evaluation, Implementation Planning, Programming, Visioning, Systems Perception, Identification of Key Causes, Judgment and Decision Making, Time Management, Management of Financial Resources

College Majors

Agriculture/Agricultural Sciences, General: An instructional program that generally describes the principles and practices of agricultural research and production, and may prepare individuals to apply such knowledge and skills to the solution of practical agricultural problems. Includes instruction in basic animal, plant, and soil science; animal husbandry and plant cultivation; and soil conservation.

Supporting Courses

Administration and Management: Knowledge of principles and processes involved in business and organizational planning, coordination, and execution. This includes strategic planning, resource allocation, manpower modeling, leadership techniques, and production methods. **Clerical:** Knowledge of administrative and clerical procedures and systems such as word processing systems, filing and records management systems, stenography and transcription, forms design principles, and other office procedures and terminology. **Food Production:** Knowledge of techniques and equipment for planting, growing, and harvesting of food for consumption including crop rotation methods, animal husbandry, and food storage/handling techniques. **Computers and Electronics:** Knowledge of electric circuit boards, processors, chips, and computer hardware and software, including applications and programming. **Mathematics:** Knowledge of numbers, their operations, and interrelationships including arithmetic, algebra, geometry, calculus, statistics, and their applications. **Physics:** Knowledge and prediction of physical principles, laws, and applications including air, water, material dynamics, light, atomic principles, heat, electric theory, earth formations, and meteorological and related natural phenomena. **Chemistry:** Knowledge of the composition, structure, and properties of substances and of the chemical processes and transformations that they undergo. This includes uses of chemicals and their interactions, danger signs, production techniques, and disposal methods. **Biology:** Knowledge of plant and animal living tissue, cells, organisms, and entities, including their functions, interdependencies, and interactions with each other and the environment. **Psychology:** Knowledge of human behavior and performance, mental processes, psychological research methods, and the assessment and treatment of behavioral and affective disorders. **Medicine and Dentistry:** Knowledge of the information and techniques needed to diagnose and treat injuries, diseases, and deformities. This includes symptoms, treatment alternatives, drug properties and interactions, and preventive heathcare measures. **Therapy and Counseling:** Knowledge of information and techniques needed to rehabilitate physical and mental ailments and to provide career guidance including alternative treatments, rehabilitation equipment and its proper use, and methods to evaluate treatment effects. **Education and Training:** Knowledge of instructional methods and training techniques including curriculum design principles, learning theory, group and individual teaching techniques, design of individual development plans, and test design principles. **English Language:** Knowledge of the structure and content of the English language including the meaning and spelling of words, rules of composition, and grammar. **Communications and Media:** Knowledge of media production, communication, and dissemination techniques and methods including alternative ways to inform and entertain via written, oral, and visual media.

Chemistry Teachers: Postsecondary

Teach courses pertaining to the chemical and physical properties and compositional changes of substances. Work may include instruction in the methods of qualitative and quantitative chemical analysis. Prepares and delivers lectures to students. Stimulates class discussions. Compiles, administers, and grades examinations, or assigns this work to others. Compiles bibliographies of specialized materials for outside reading assignments. Directs research of other teachers or graduate students working for advanced academic degrees. Advises students on academic and vocational curricula. Conducts research in particular field of knowledge and publishes findings in professional journals. Acts as adviser to student organizations. Serves on faculty committee providing professional consulting services to government and industry.

Occupational Type

Investigative occupations frequently involve working with ideas, and require an extensive amount of thinking. These occupations can involve searching for facts and figuring out problems mentally.

Skills required of Chemistry Teachers: Postsecondary

Reading Comprehension, Active Listening, Writing, Speaking, Mathematics, Science, Critical Thinking, Active Learning, Learning Strategies, Monitoring, Social Perceptiveness, Coordination, Negotiation, Instructing, Information Gathering, Information Organization,

Synthesis/Reorganization, Idea Generation, Idea Evaluation, Implementation Planning, Equipment Selection, Visioning, Identification of Key Causes, Judgment and Decision Making, Time Management, Management of Personnel Resources

College Majors

Physical Sciences, General: An instructional program that generally describes the major topics, concepts, processes, and interrelationships of physical phenomena as studied in any combination of physical science disciplines.

Supporting Courses

Administration and Management: Knowledge of principles and processes involved in business and organizational planning, coordination, and execution. This includes strategic planning, resource allocation, manpower modeling, leadership techniques, and production methods. **Computers and Electronics:** Knowledge of electric circuit boards, processors, chips, and computer hardware and software, including applications and programming. **Engineering and Technology:** Knowledge of equipment, tools, mechanical devices, and their uses to produce motion, light, power, technology, and other applications. **Mathematics:** Knowledge of numbers, their operations, and interrelationships including arithmetic, algebra, geometry, calculus, statistics, and their applications. **Physics:** Knowledge and prediction of physical principles, laws, and applications including air, water, material dynamics, light, atomic principles, heat, electric theory, earth formations, and meteorological and related natural phenomena. **Chemistry:** Knowledge of the composition, structure, and properties of substances and of the chemical processes and transformations that they undergo. This includes uses of chemicals and their interactions, danger signs, production techniques, and disposal methods. **Biology:** Knowledge of plant and animal living tissue, cells, organisms, and entities, including their functions, interdependencies, and interactions with each other and the environment. **Psychology:** Knowledge of human behavior and performance, mental processes, psychological research methods, and the assessment and treatment of behavioral and affective disorders. **Sociology and Anthropology:** Knowledge of group behavior and dynamics, societal trends and influences, cultures, their history, migrations, ethnicity, and origins. **Education and Training:** Knowledge of instructional methods and training techniques including curriculum design principles, learning theory, group and individual teaching techniques, design of individual development plans, and test design principles. **English Language:** Knowledge of the structure and content of the English language including the meaning and spelling of words, rules of composition, and grammar. **Foreign Language:** Knowledge of the structure and content of a foreign (non-English) language including the meaning and spelling of words, rules of composition and grammar, and pronunciation.

Physics Teachers: Postsecondary

Teach courses pertaining to the laws of matter and energy. Prepares and delivers lectures to students. Stimulates class discussions. Compiles, administers, and grades examinations, or assigns this work to others. Compiles bibliographies of specialized materials for outside reading assignments. Advises students on academic and vocational curricula. Directs research of other teachers or graduate students working for advanced academic degrees. Conducts research in particular field of knowledge and publishes findings in professional journals. Serves on faculty committee providing professional consulting services to government and industry. Acts as adviser to student organizations.

Occupational Type

Investigative occupations frequently involve working with ideas, and require an extensive amount of thinking. These occupations can involve searching for facts and figuring out problems mentally.

Skills required of Physics Teachers: Postsecondary

Reading Comprehension, Active Listening, Writing, Speaking, Mathematics, Science, Critical Thinking, Active Learning, Learning Strategies, Monitoring, Social Perceptiveness, Coordination, Instructing, Information Gathering, Information Organization, Synthesis/Reorganization, Idea Generation, Idea Evaluation, Implementation Planning, Testing, Visioning, Identifying Downstream Consequences, Identification of Key Causes, Judgment and Decision Making, Time Management, Management of Personnel Resources

College Majors

Biological and Physical Sciences: An instructional program that describes either a general synthesis of one or more of the biological and physical sciences, or a specialization which draws from the biological and physical sciences.

Supporting Courses

Administration and Management: Knowledge of principles and processes involved in business and organizational planning, coordination, and execution. This includes strategic planning, resource allocation, manpower modeling, leadership techniques, and production methods. **Engineering and Technology:** Knowledge of equipment, tools, mechanical devices, and their uses to produce motion, light, power, technology, and other applications. **Mathematics:** Knowledge of numbers, their operations, and interrelationships including arithmetic, algebra, geometry, calculus, statistics, and their applications. **Physics:** Knowledge and prediction of physical principles, laws, and applications including air, water, material dynamics, light, atomic principles, heat, electric theory, earth formations, and meteorological and related natural phenomena. **Chemistry:** Knowledge of the composition, structure, and properties of substances and of the chemical processes and transformations that they undergo. This includes uses of chemicals and their interactions, danger signs, production techniques, and disposal methods. **Psychology:** Knowledge of human behavior and performance, mental processes, psychological research methods, and the assessment and treatment of behavioral and affective disorders. **Sociology and Anthropology:** Knowledge of group behavior and dynamics, societal trends and influences, cultures, their history, migrations, ethnicity, and origins. **Therapy and Counseling:** Knowledge of information and techniques needed to rehabilitate physical and mental ailments and to provide career guidance including alternative treatments, rehabilitation equipment and its proper use, and methods to evaluate treatment effects. **Education and Training:** Knowledge of instructional methods and training techniques including curriculum design principles, learning theory, group and individual teaching techniques, design of individual development plans, and test design principles. **English Language:** Knowledge of the structure and content of the English language including the meaning and spelling of words, rules of composition, and grammar. **Foreign Language:** Knowledge of the structure and content of a foreign (non-English) language including the meaning and spelling of words, rules of composition and grammar, and pronunciation. **History and Archeology:** Knowledge of past historical events and their causes, indicators, and impact on particular civilizations and cultures. **Philosophy and Theology:** Knowledge of different philosophical systems and religions, including their basic principles, values, ethics, ways of thinking, customs, and practices, and their impact on human culture.

All Other Physical Science Teachers: Postsecondary

Teach courses in the physical sciences, except chemistry and physics. Include teachers of subjects such as astronomy, atmospheric and space sciences, geology, and geography.

 ### Occupational Type

Specific information not available.

 ### Skills required of All Other Physical Science Teachers: Postsecondary

Information on specific skills required is not available.

College Majors

Physical Sciences, General: An instructional program that generally describes the major topics, concepts, processes, and interrelationships of physical phenomena as studied in any combination of physical science disciplines.

 ### Supporting Courses

No specific courses for this occupation.

Social Science Teachers: Postsecondary

Teach courses pertaining to human society and its characteristic elements, with economic and social relations and with scientific data relating to human behavior and mental processes. Include teachers of subjects such as psychology, economics, history, political science, and sociology. Prepares and delivers lectures to students. Stimulates class discussions. Compiles, administers, and grades examinations, or assigns this work to others. Compiles bibliographies of specialized materials for outside reading assignments. Advises students on academic and vocational curricula. Directs research of other teachers or graduate students working for advanced academic degrees. Conducts research in particular field of knowledge and publishes findings in professional journals. Serves on faculty committee providing professional consulting services to government and industry. Acts as adviser to student organizations.

Occupational Type

Social occupations frequently involve working with, communicating with, and teaching people. These occupations often involve helping or providing service to others.

Skills required of Social Science Teachers: Postsecondary

Reading Comprehension, Active Listening, Writing, Speaking, Mathematics, Science, Critical Thinking, Active Learning, Learning Strategies, Monitoring, Social Perceptiveness, Persuasion, Negotiation, Instructing, Service Orientation, Problem Identification, Information Gathering, Information Organization, Synthesis/Reorganization, Idea Generation, Idea Evaluation, Implementation Planning, Programming, Visioning, Identification of Key Causes, Time Management, Management of Financial Resources

College Majors

Agricultural Business and Management, General: An instructional program that generally prepares individuals to apply modern economic and business principles involved in the organization, operation and management of farm and agricultural businesses.

Supporting Courses

Administration and Management: Knowledge of principles and processes involved in business and organizational planning, coordination, and execution. This includes strategic planning, resource allocation, manpower modeling, leadership techniques, and production methods. **Clerical:** Knowledge of administrative and clerical procedures and systems such as word processing systems, filing and records management systems, stenography and transcription, forms design principles, and other office procedures and terminology. **Economics and Accounting:** Knowledge of economic and accounting principles and practices, the financial markets, banking, and the analysis and reporting of financial data. **Personnel and Human Resources:** Knowledge of policies and practices involved in personnel/human resource functions. This includes recruitment, selection, training, and promotion regulations and procedures; compensation and benefits packages; labor relations and negotiation strategies; and personnel information systems. **Computers and Electronics:** Knowledge of electric circuit boards, processors, chips, and computer hardware and software, including applications and programming. **Mathematics:** Knowledge of numbers, their operations, and interrelationships including arithmetic, algebra, geometry, calculus, statistics, and their applications. **Psychology:** Knowledge of human behavior and performance, mental processes, psychological research methods, and the assessment and treatment of behavioral and affective disorders. **Sociology and Anthropology:** Knowledge of group behavior and dynamics, societal trends and influences, cultures, their history, migrations, ethnicity, and origins. **Geography:** Knowledge of various methods for describing the location and distribution of land, sea, and air masses including their physical locations, relationships, and characteristics. **Therapy and Counseling:** Knowledge of information and techniques needed to rehabilitate physical and mental ailments and to provide career guidance including alternative treatments, rehabilitation equipment and its proper use, and methods to evaluate treatment effects. **Education and Training:** Knowledge of instructional methods and training techniques including curriculum design principles, learning theory, group and individual teaching techniques, design of individual development plans, and test design principles. **English Language:** Knowledge of the structure and content of the English language including the meaning and spelling of words, rules of composition, and grammar. **History and Archeology:** Knowledge of past historical events and their causes, indicators, and impact on particular civilizations and cultures. **Philosophy and Theology:** Knowledge of different philosophical systems and religions, including their basic principles, values, ethics, ways of thinking, customs, and practices, and their impact on human culture. **Law, Government, and Jurisprudence:** Knowledge of laws, legal codes, court procedures, precedents, government regulations, executive orders, agency rules, and the democratic political process. **Communications and Media:** Knowledge of media production, communication, and dissemination techniques and methods including alternative ways to inform and entertain via written, oral, and visual media.

Health Specialties Teachers: Postsecondary

Teach courses in health specialties such as veterinary medicine, dentistry, pharmacy, therapy, laboratory technology, and public health. (Excludes nursing instructors and medical sciences teachers.) Prepares and delivers lectures to students. Compiles bibliographies of specialized materials for outside reading assignments. Stimulates class discussions. Compiles, administers, and grades examinations, or assigns this work to others. Advises students on academic and vocational curricula. Directs research of other teachers or graduate students working for advanced academic degrees. Conducts research in particular field of knowledge and publishes findings in professional journals. Acts as adviser to student organizations. Serves on faculty committee providing professional consulting services to government and industry.

Occupational Type

Investigative occupations frequently involve working with ideas, and require an extensive amount of thinking. These occupations can involve searching for facts and figuring out problems mentally.

Skills required of Health Specialties Teachers: Postsecondary

Reading Comprehension, Active Listening, Writing, Speaking, Mathematics, Science, Critical Thinking, Active Learning, Learning Strategies, Monitoring, Social Perceptiveness, Coordination, Persuasion, Negotiation, Instructing, Service Orientation, Problem Identification, Information Gathering, Information Organization, Synthesis/Reorganization, Idea Generation, Idea Evaluation, Implementation Planning, Operations Analysis, Equipment

Selection, Visioning, Systems Perception, Identifying Downstream Consequences, Identification of Key Causes, Time Management, Management of Financial Resources, Management of Personnel Resources

College Majors

Gerontology: An instructional program that describes the study of the human aging process and aged human populations, using the knowledge and methodologies of the social sciences, psychology and the biological and health sciences.

Supporting Courses

Administration and Management: Knowledge of principles and processes involved in business and organizational planning, coordination, and execution. This includes strategic planning, resource allocation, manpower modeling, leadership techniques, and production methods. **Clerical:** Knowledge of administrative and clerical procedures and systems such as word processing systems, filing and records management systems, stenography and transcription, forms design principles, and other office procedures and terminology. **Computers and Electronics:** Knowledge of electric circuit boards, processors, chips, and computer hardware and software, including applications and programming. **Mathematics:** Knowledge of numbers, their operations, and interrelationships including arithmetic, algebra, geometry, calculus, statistics, and their applications. **Chemistry:** Knowledge of the composition, structure, and properties of substances and of the chemical processes and transformations that they undergo. This includes uses of chemicals and their interactions, danger signs, production techniques, and disposal methods. **Biology:** Knowledge of plant and animal living tissue, cells, organisms, and entities, including their functions, interdependencies, and interactions with each other and the environment. **Psychology:** Knowledge of human behavior and performance, mental processes, psychological research methods, and the assessment and treatment of behavioral and affective disorders. **Sociology and Anthropology:** Knowledge of group behavior and dynamics, societal trends and influences, cultures, their history, migrations, ethnicity, and origins. **Medicine and Dentistry:** Knowledge of the information and techniques needed to diagnose and treat injuries, diseases, and deformities. This includes symptoms, treatment alternatives, drug properties and interactions, and preventive heathcare measures. **Therapy and Counseling:** Knowledge of information and techniques needed to rehabilitate physical and mental ailments and to provide career guidance including alternative treatments, rehabilitation equipment and its proper use, and methods to evaluate treatment effects. **Education and Training:** Knowledge of instructional methods and training techniques including curriculum design principles, learning theory, group and individual teaching techniques, design of individual development plans, and test design principles. **English Language:** Knowledge of the structure and content of the English language including the meaning and spelling of words, rules of composition, and grammar. **Philosophy and Theology:** Knowledge of different philosophical systems and religions, including their basic principles, values, ethics, ways of thinking, customs, and practices, and their impact on human culture. **Law, Government, and Jurisprudence:** Knowledge of laws, legal codes, court procedures, precedents, government regulations, executive orders, agency rules, and the democratic political process.

Communications and Media: Knowledge of media production, communication, and dissemination techniques and methods including alternative ways to inform and entertain via written, oral, and visual media.

English and Foreign Language Teachers: Postsecondary

Teach courses in English language and literature or in foreign languages and literature. Include teachers of subjects such as journalism, classics, and linguistics. Prepares and delivers lectures to students. Compiles, administers, and grades examinations, or assigns this work to others. Compiles bibliographies of specialized materials for outside reading assignments. Stimulates class discussions. Advises students on academic and vocational curricula. Directs research of other teachers or graduate students working for advanced academic degrees. Conducts research in particular field of knowledge and publishes findings in professional journals. Acts as adviser to student organizations. Serves on faculty committee providing professional consulting services to government and industry.

 ## Occupational Type

Artistic occupations frequently involve working with forms, designs, and patterns. They often require self-expression and the work can be done without following a clear set of rules.

 ## Skills required of English and Foreign Language Teachers: Postsecondary

Reading Comprehension, Active Listening, Writing, Speaking, Critical Thinking, Active Learning, Learning Strategies, Monitoring, Social Perceptiveness, Persuasion, Negotiation, Instructing, Service Orientation, Information Gathering, Information Organization, Synthesis/Reorganization, Idea Generation, Idea Evaluation, Implementation Planning, Visioning, Systems Perception, Identifying Downstream Consequences, Identification of Key Causes, Systems Evaluation, Time Management, Management of Financial Resources, Management of Personnel Resources

 ## College Majors

Journalism: An instructional program that describes the methods and techniques for gathering, processing and delivering news, and that prepares individuals to be professional print journalists. Includes instruction in news writing and editing, reporting, journalism law and policy, professional standards and ethics, and journalism history and research.

 ## Supporting Courses

Clerical: Knowledge of administrative and clerical procedures and systems such as word processing systems, filing and records management systems, stenography and transcription, forms design principles, and other office procedures and terminology. **Computers and Electronics:** Knowledge of electric circuit boards, processors, chips, and computer hardware and software, including applications and programming. **Sociology and**

Anthropology: Knowledge of group behavior and dynamics, societal trends and influences, cultures, their history, migrations, ethnicity, and origins. **Therapy and Counseling:** Knowledge of information and techniques needed to rehabilitate physical and mental ailments and to provide career guidance including alternative treatments, rehabilitation equipment and its proper use, and methods to evaluate treatment effects. **Education and Training:** Knowledge of instructional methods and training techniques including curriculum design principles, learning theory, group and individual teaching techniques, design of individual development plans, and test design principles. **English Language:** Knowledge of the structure and content of the English language including the meaning and spelling of words, rules of composition, and grammar. **Foreign Language:** Knowledge of the structure and content of a foreign (non-English) language including the meaning and spelling of words, rules of composition and grammar, and pronunciation. **History and Archeology:** Knowledge of past historical events and their causes, indicators, and impact on particular civilizations and cultures. **Philosophy and Theology:** Knowledge of different philosophical systems and religions, including their basic principles, values, ethics, ways of thinking, customs, and practices, and their impact on human culture. **Communications and Media:** Knowledge of media production, communication, and dissemination techniques and methods including alternative ways to inform and entertain via written, oral, and visual media.

Art, Drama, and Music Teachers: Postsecondary

Teach courses in art, drama, and music, including painting and sculpture. Prepares and delivers lectures to students. Stimulates class discussions. Compiles bibliographies of specialized materials for outside reading assignments. Compiles, administers, and grades examinations, or assigns this work to others. Advises students on academic and vocational curricula. Directs research of other teachers or graduate students working for advanced academic degrees. Conducts research in particular field of knowledge and publishes findings in professional journals. Serves on faculty committee providing professional consulting services to government and industry. Acts as adviser to student organizations.

Occupational Type

Artistic occupations frequently involve working with forms, designs, and patterns. They often require self-expression and the work can be done without following a clear set of rules.

Skills required of Art, Drama, and Music Teachers: Postsecondary

Reading Comprehension, Active Listening, Writing, Speaking, Critical Thinking, Active Learning, Learning Strategies, Monitoring, Social Perceptiveness, Persuasion, Negotiation, Instructing, Service Orientation, Information Gathering, Information Organization, Synthesis/Reorganization, Idea Generation, Idea Evaluation, Implementation Planning, Programming, Visioning, Identification of Key Causes, Time Management, Management of Personnel Resources

College Majors

Crafts, Folk Art, and Artisanry: An instructional program that describes the aesthetics, techniques, and creative processes for designing and fashioning objects in one or more of the handcraft or folk art traditions, and that prepares individuals to create in any of these media.

Supporting Courses

Administration and Management: Knowledge of principles and processes involved in business and organizational planning, coordination, and execution. This includes strategic planning, resource allocation, manpower modeling, leadership techniques, and production methods. **Clerical:** Knowledge of administrative and clerical procedures and systems such as word processing systems, filing and records management systems, stenography and transcription, forms design principles, and other office procedures and terminology. **Sociology and Anthropology:** Knowledge of group behavior and dynamics, societal trends and influences, cultures, their history, migrations, ethnicity, and origins. **Therapy and Counseling:** Knowledge of information and techniques needed to rehabilitate physical and mental ailments and to provide career guidance including alternative treatments, rehabilitation equipment and its proper use, and methods to evaluate treatment effects. **Education and Training:** Knowledge of instructional methods and training techniques including curriculum design principles, learning theory, group and individual teaching techniques, design of individual development plans, and test design principles. **English Language:** Knowledge of the structure and content of the English language including the meaning and spelling of words, rules of composition, and grammar. **Fine Arts:** Knowledge of theory and techniques required to produce, compose, and perform works of music, dance, visual arts, drama, and sculpture. **History and Archeology:** Knowledge of past historical events and their causes, indicators, and impact on particular civilizations and cultures. **Philosophy and Theology:** Knowledge of different philosophical systems and religions, including their basic principles, values, ethics, ways of thinking, customs, and practices, and their impact on human culture. **Communications and Media:** Knowledge of media production, communication, and dissemination techniques and methods including alternative ways to inform and entertain via written, oral, and visual media.

Engineering Teachers: Postsecondary

Teach courses pertaining to the application of physical laws and principles of engineering for the development of machines, materials, instruments, processes, and services. Include teachers of subjects such as chemical, civil, electrical, industrial, mechanical, mineral, and petroleum engineering. Prepares and delivers lectures to students. Stimulates class discussions. Compiles bibliographies of specialized materials for outside reading assignments. Compiles, administers, and grades examinations, or assigns this work to others. Advises students on academic and vocational curricula. Directs research of other teachers or graduate students working for advanced academic degrees. Conducts research in particular field of knowledge and publishes findings in professional journals. Serves on faculty committee providing professional consulting services to government and industry. Acts as adviser to student organizations.

Occupational Type

Investigative occupations frequently involve working with ideas, and require an extensive amount of thinking. These occupations can involve searching for facts and figuring out problems mentally.

Skills required of Engineering Teachers: Postsecondary

Reading Comprehension, Active Listening, Writing, Speaking, Mathematics, Science, Critical Thinking, Active Learning, Learning Strategies, Monitoring, Social Perceptiveness, Instructing, Problem Identification, Information Gathering, Information Organization, Synthesis/Reorganization, Idea Generation, Idea Evaluation, Implementation Planning, Operations Analysis, Technology Design, Equipment Selection, Programming, Troubleshooting, Visioning, Systems Perception, Identifying Downstream Consequences, Identification of Key Causes, Judgment and Decision Making, Systems Evaluation, Time Management, Management of Financial Resources, Management of Material Resources

College Majors

Engineering, General: An instructional program that generally prepares individuals to apply mathematical and scientific principles to solve a wide variety of practical problems in industry, social organization, public works, and commerce.

Supporting Courses

Administration and Management: Knowledge of principles and processes involved in business and organizational planning, coordination, and execution. This includes strategic planning, resource allocation, manpower modeling, leadership techniques, and production methods. **Clerical:** Knowledge of administrative and clerical procedures and systems such as word processing systems, filing and records management systems, stenography and transcription, forms design principles, and other office procedures and terminology. **Computers and Electronics:** Knowledge of electric circuit boards, processors, chips, and computer hardware and software, including applications and programming. **Engineering and Technology:** Knowledge of equipment, tools, mechanical devices, and their uses to produce motion, light, power, technology, and other applications. **Design:** Knowledge of design techniques, principles, tools and instruments involved in the production and use of precision technical plans, blueprints, drawings, and models. **Building and Construction:** Knowledge of materials, methods, and the appropriate tools to construct objects, structures, and buildings. **Mathematics:** Knowledge of numbers, their operations, and interrelationships including arithmetic, algebra, geometry, calculus, statistics, and their applications. **Physics:** Knowledge and prediction of physical principles, laws, and applications including air, water, material dynamics, light, atomic principles, heat, electric theory, earth formations, and meteorological and related natural phenomena. **Chemistry:** Knowledge of the composition, structure, and properties of substances and of the chemical processes and transformations that they undergo.

This includes uses of chemicals and their interactions, danger signs, production techniques, and disposal methods. **Therapy and Counseling:** Knowledge of information and techniques needed to rehabilitate physical and mental ailments and to provide career guidance including alternative treatments, rehabilitation equipment and its proper use, and methods to evaluate treatment effects. **Education and Training:** Knowledge of instructional methods and training techniques including curriculum design principles, learning theory, group and individual teaching techniques, design of individual development plans, and test design principles. **English Language:** Knowledge of the structure and content of the English language including the meaning and spelling of words, rules of composition, and grammar. **Telecommunications:** Knowledge of transmission, broadcasting, switching, control, and operation of telecommunications systems. **Communications and Media:** Knowledge of media production, communication, and dissemination techniques and methods including alternative ways to inform and entertain via written, oral, and visual media.

Mathematical Sciences Teachers: Postsecondary

Teach courses pertaining to mathematical concepts, statistics, and actuarial science and to the application of original and standardized mathematical techniques in solving specific problems and situations. Prepares and delivers lectures to students. Compiles, administers, and grades examinations, or assigns this work to others. Stimulates class discussions. Directs research of other teachers or graduate students working for advanced academic degrees. Compiles bibliographies of specialized materials for outside reading assignments. Conducts research in particular field of knowledge and publishes findings in professional journals. Advises students on academic and vocational curricula. Acts as adviser to student organizations. Serves on faculty committee providing professional consulting services to government and industry.

 ### Occupational Type

Investigative occupations frequently involve working with ideas, and require an extensive amount of thinking. These occupations can involve searching for facts and figuring out problems mentally.

 ### Skills required of Mathematical Sciences Teachers: Postsecondary

Reading Comprehension, Active Listening, Writing, Speaking, Mathematics, Science, Critical Thinking, Active Learning, Learning Strategies, Monitoring, Instructing, Problem Identification, Information Gathering, Information Organization, Synthesis/Reorganization, Idea Generation, Idea Evaluation, Implementation Planning, Operations Analysis, Programming, Identifying Downstream Consequences, Judgment and Decision Making, Systems Evaluation, Time Management

College Majors

Biostatistics: An instructional program that describes the application of statistical methods and techniques to the study of living organisms and biological systems. Includes instruction in experimental design and data analysis, projection methods, descriptive statistics, and specific applications to biological subdisciplines.

Supporting Courses

Administration and Management: Knowledge of principles and processes involved in business and organizational planning, coordination, and execution. This includes strategic planning, resource allocation, manpower modeling, leadership techniques, and production methods. **Clerical:** Knowledge of administrative and clerical procedures and systems such as word processing systems, filing and records management systems, stenography and transcription, forms design principles, and other office procedures and terminology. **Computers and Electronics:** Knowledge of electric circuit boards, processors, chips, and computer hardware and software, including applications and programming. **Mathematics:** Knowledge of numbers, their operations, and interrelationships including arithmetic, algebra, geometry, calculus, statistics, and their applications. **Education and Training:** Knowledge of instructional methods and training techniques including curriculum design principles, learning theory, group and individual teaching techniques, design of individual development plans, and test design principles. **English Language:** Knowledge of the structure and content of the English language including the meaning and spelling of words, rules of composition, and grammar. **Philosophy and Theology:** Knowledge of different philosophical systems and religions, including their basic principles, values, ethics, ways of thinking, customs, and practices, and their impact on human culture. **Communications and Media:** Knowledge of media production, communication, and dissemination techniques and methods including alternative ways to inform and entertain via written, oral, and visual media.

Computer Science Teachers: Postsecondary

Teach courses in computer science. May specialize in a field of computer science, such as the design and function of computers or operations and research analysis. Prepares and delivers lectures to students. Stimulates class discussions. Compiles bibliographies of specialized materials for outside reading assignments. Compiles, administers, and grades examinations, or assigns this work to others. Directs research of other teachers or graduate students working for advanced academic degrees. Conducts research in particular field of knowledge and publishes findings in professional journals. Advises students on academic and vocational curricula. Acts as adviser to student organizations. Serves on faculty committee providing professional consulting services to government and industry.

Occupational Type

Investigative occupations frequently involve working with ideas, and require an extensive amount of thinking. These occupations can involve searching for facts and figuring out problems mentally.

Skills required of Computer Science Teachers: Postsecondary

Reading Comprehension, Active Listening, Writing, Speaking, Mathematics, Science, Critical Thinking, Active Learning, Learning Strategies, Monitoring, Social Perceptiveness,

Coordination, Persuasion, Instructing, Service Orientation, Problem Identification, Information Gathering, Information Organization, Synthesis/Reorganization, Idea Generation, Idea Evaluation, Implementation Planning, Operations Analysis, Technology Design, Equipment Selection, Programming, Testing, Troubleshooting, Visioning, Systems Perception, Identifying Downstream Consequences, Identification of Key Causes, Judgment and Decision Making, Time Management, Management of Material Resources, Management of Personnel Resources

 College Majors

Computer and Information Sciences, General: An instructional program that generally describes the study of data and information storage and processing systems, including hardware, software, basic design principles, user requirements analysis, and related economic and policy issues.

Supporting Courses

Administration and Management: Knowledge of principles and processes involved in business and organizational planning, coordination, and execution. This includes strategic planning, resource allocation, manpower modeling, leadership techniques, and production methods. **Clerical:** Knowledge of administrative and clerical procedures and systems such as word processing systems, filing and records management systems, stenography and transcription, forms design principles, and other office procedures and terminology. **Computers and Electronics:** Knowledge of electric circuit boards, processors, chips, and computer hardware and software, including applications and programming. **Engineering and Technology:** Knowledge of equipment, tools, mechanical devices, and their uses to produce motion, light, power, technology, and other applications. **Design:** Knowledge of design techniques, principles, tools and instruments involved in the production and use of precision technical plans, blueprints, drawings, and models. **Mathematics:** Knowledge of numbers, their operations, and interrelationships including arithmetic, algebra, geometry, calculus, statistics, and their applications. **Physics:** Knowledge and prediction of physical principles, laws, and applications including air, water, material dynamics, light, atomic principles, heat, electric theory, earth formations, and meteorological and related natural phenomena. **Psychology:** Knowledge of human behavior and performance, mental processes, psychological research methods, and the assessment and treatment of behavioral and affective disorders. **Sociology and Anthropology:** Knowledge of group behavior and dynamics, societal trends and influences, cultures, their history, migrations, ethnicity, and origins. **Therapy and Counseling:** Knowledge of information and techniques needed to rehabilitate physical and mental ailments and to provide career guidance including alternative treatments, rehabilitation equipment and its proper use, and methods to evaluate treatment effects. **Education and Training:** Knowledge of instructional methods and training techniques including curriculum design principles, learning theory, group and individual teaching techniques, design of individual development plans, and test design principles. **English Language:** Knowledge of the structure and content of the English language including the meaning and spelling of words, rules of composition, and grammar. **Philosophy and Theology:** Knowledge of different philosophical systems and religions, including their basic principles, values, ethics, ways of thinking, customs, and practices, and their impact on human culture. **Telecommunications:** Knowledge of transmission, broadcasting, switching, control, and operation of telecommunications systems. **Communications and Media:** Knowledge of media production, communication, and dissemination techniques and methods including alternative ways to inform and entertain via written, oral, and visual media.

All Other Postsecondary Teachers

All other postsecondary teachers not elsewhere classified. Include teachers of subjects such as business, physical education, education, theology, law, and home economics.

 ### Occupational Type

Specific information not available.

 ### Skills required of All Other Postsecondary Teachers

Information on specific skills required is not available.

 ### College Majors

Agricultural Business and Management, General: An instructional program that generally prepares individuals to apply modern economic and business principles involved in the organization, operation and management of farm and agricultural businesses.

 ### Supporting Courses

No specific courses for this occupation.

COMMUNICATION, TRANSPORTATION, AND UTILITIES MANAGERS

Education	Work experience, plus degree	
Average Yearly Earnings	$48,818	
Projected Growth	15%	
Annual Job Openings	10,840	
Self-employed	0%	
Employed Part-time	6%	

Transportation Managers

Plan, direct, and coordinate the transportation operations within an organization, or the activities of organizations that provide transportation services. Directs and coordinates, through subordinates, activities of operations department to obtain use of equipment, facilities, and human resources. Confers and cooperates with management and other in formulating and implementing administrative, operational, and customer relations policies and procedures. Analyzes expenditures and other financial reports to develop plans, policies, and budgets for increasing profits and improving services. Enforces compliance of operations personnel with administrative policies, procedures, safety rules, and government regulations. Reviews transportation schedules, worker assignments, and routes to ensure compliance with standards for personnel selection, safety, and union contract terms. Conducts investigations in cooperation with government agencies to determine causes of transportation accidents and to improve safety procedures. Oversees activities relating to dispatching, routing, and tracking transportation vehicles, such as aircraft and railroad cars. Prepares management recommendations, such as need for increasing fares, tariffs, or expansion or changes to existing schedules. Recommends or authorizes capital expenditures for acquisition of new equipment or property to increase efficiency and services of operations department. Oversees process of investigation and response to customer or shipper complaints relating to operations department. Oversees workers assigning tariff classifications and preparing billing according to mode of transportation and destination of shipment. Acts as organization representative before commissions or regulatory bodies during hearings, such as to increase rates and change routes and schedules. Inspects or oversees repairs and maintenance to equipment, vehicles, and facilities to enforce standards for safety, efficiency, cleanliness, and appearance. Oversees procurement process, including research and testing of equipment, vendor contacts, and approval of requisitions. Negotiates and authorizes contracts with equipment and materials suppliers. Participates in union contract negotiations and settlement of grievances.

Occupational Type

Enterprising occupations frequently involve starting up and carrying out projects. These occupations can involve leading people and making many decisions. Sometimes they involve risk taking and often deal with business.

Skills required of Transportation Managers

Reading Comprehension, Monitoring, Coordination, Persuasion, Negotiation, Idea Generation, Idea Evaluation, Implementation Planning, Operations Analysis, Equipment Selection, Visioning, Systems Perception, Identifying Downstream Consequences, Identification of Key Causes, Judgment and Decision Making, Systems Evaluation, Time Management, Management of Financial Resources, Management of Material Resources, Management of Personnel Resources

College Majors

Agricultural Production Workers and Managers, General: An instructional program that generally prepares individuals to plan and economically use facilities, natural resources, labor and capital in the production of plant and animal products.

Supporting Courses

Administration and Management: Knowledge of principles and processes involved in business and organizational planning, coordination, and execution. This includes strategic planning, resource allocation, manpower modeling, leadership techniques, and production methods. **Economics and Accounting:** Knowledge of economic and accounting principles and practices, the financial markets, banking, and the analysis and reporting of financial data. **Sales and Marketing:** Knowledge of principles and methods involved in showing, promoting, and selling products or services. This includes marketing strategies and tactics, product demonstration and sales techniques, and sales control systems. **Personnel and Human Resources:** Knowledge of policies and practices involved in personnel/human resource functions. This includes recruitment, selection, training, and promotion regulations and procedures; compensation and benefits packages; labor relations and negotiation strategies; and personnel information systems. **Mathematics:** Knowledge of numbers, their operations, and interrelationships including arithmetic, algebra, geometry, calculus, statistics, and their applications. **Geography:** Knowledge of various methods for describing the location and distribution of land, sea, and air masses including their physical locations, relationships, and characteristics. **Public Safety and Security:** Knowledge of weaponry, public safety, and security operations, rules, regulations, precautions, prevention, and the protection of people, data, and property. **Law, Government, and Jurisprudence:** Knowledge of laws, legal codes, court procedures, precedents, government regulations, executive orders, agency rules, and the democratic political process. **Transportation:** Knowledge of principles and methods for moving people or goods by air, rail, sea, or road, including their relative costs, advantages, and limitations.

Communications Managers

Plan, direct, and coordinate the communication operations within an organization, or the activities of organizations that provide communication services, such as radio and TV broadcasting or telecommunications. Supervises personnel directly or through subordinates, and coordinates worker or departmental activities. Directs investigation of rates, services, activities, or station operations to ensure compliance with government regulations. Prepares or directs preparation of plans, proposals, reports, or other documents. Develops operating procedures and policies and interprets for personnel. Analyzes reports, data, studies, or governmental rulings to determine status, appropriate response, or effect on operations or profitability. Confers with officials, administrators, management, or others to discuss programs, services, production, or procedures. Directs, coordinates, and inspects equipment installations to ensure compliance with regulations, standards, and deadlines. Plans work activities and prepares schedules. Directs testing and inspection of equipment for operational performance. Makes recommendations or advises personnel regarding procedures, acquisitions, complaints, or business activities. Negotiates settlements, contractual agreements, or services with company representatives or owners. Reviews and authorizes or approves recommendations, contracts, plans, or requisitions for equipment and supplies. Prepares budget for department, station, or program, and monitors expenses. Determines workforce requirement, hires and discharges workers, and assigns work. Conducts studies to determine effectiveness and adequacy of equipment, workload, or estimated equipment and maintenance costs. Reviews accounts and records and verifies accuracy of cash balances.

Occupational Type

Enterprising occupations frequently involve starting up and carrying out projects. These occupations can involve leading people and making many decisions. Sometimes they involve risk taking and often deal with business.

Skills required of Communications Managers

Active Listening, Writing, Speaking, Monitoring, Social Perceptiveness, Coordination, Persuasion, Negotiation, Instructing, Information Gathering, Idea Generation, Idea Evaluation, Implementation Planning, Operations Analysis, Product Inspection, Visioning, Systems Perception, Identifying Downstream Consequences, Identification of Key Causes, Judgment and Decision Making, Systems Evaluation, Time Management, Management of Financial Resources, Management of Material Resources, Management of Personnel Resources

College Majors

Business Administration and Management, General: An instructional program that generally prepares individuals to plan, organize, direct, and control the functions and processes of a firm or organization. Includes instruction in management theory, human resources management and behavior, accounting and other quantitative methods, purchasing and logistics, organization and production, marketing, and business decision-making.

Supporting Courses

Administration and Management: Knowledge of principles and processes involved in business and organizational planning, coordination, and execution. This includes strategic planning, resource allocation, manpower modeling, leadership techniques, and production methods. **Economics and Accounting:** Knowledge of economic and accounting principles and practices, the financial markets, banking, and the analysis and reporting of financial data. **Personnel and Human Resources:** Knowledge of policies and practices involved in personnel/human resource functions. This includes recruitment, selection, training, and promotion regulations and procedures; compensation and benefits packages; labor relations and negotiation strategies; and personnel information systems. **Computers and Electronics:** Knowledge of electric circuit boards, processors, chips, and computer hardware and software, including applications and programming. **Engineering and Technology:** Knowledge of equipment, tools, mechanical devices, and their uses to produce motion, light, power, technology, and other applications. **Mathematics:** Knowledge of numbers, their operations, and interrelationships including arithmetic, algebra, geometry, calculus, statistics, and their applications. **Psychology:** Knowledge of human behavior and performance, mental processes, psychological research methods, and the assessment and treatment of behavioral and affective disorders. **English Language:** Knowledge of the structure and content of the English language including the meaning and spelling of words, rules of composition, and grammar. **Telecommunications:** Knowledge of transmission, broadcasting, switching, control, and operation of telecommunications systems. **Communications and Media:** Knowledge of media production, communication, and dissemination techniques and methods including alternative ways to inform and entertain via written, oral, and visual media.

Utilities Managers

Plan, direct, and coordinate the activities or operations of organizations that provide utility services, such as electricity, natural gas, sanitation, and water. Schedules and coordinates activities such as processing and distribution of services, patrolling and inspection of facilities, and maintenance activities. Formulates, implements, and interprets policies and procedures. Develops plans to meet expanded needs, such as increasing capacity or facilities or modifying equipment. Plans methods and sequence of operations to obtain optimum utilization of facilities and land or to facilitate system modifications. Authorizes repair, movement, installation, or construction of equipment, supplies, or facilities. Hires, discharges, supervises, and coordinates activities of workers directly or through subordinates. Confers with management, personnel, customers, and other to solve technical or administrative problems, discuss matters, and coordinate activities. Analyzes data, trends, reports, consumption, or test results to determine adequacy of facilities, system performance, or development areas. Develops test procedures, directs and schedules testing activities, and analyzes results. Investigates and evaluates new developments in materials, tools, or equipment. Forecasts consumption of utilities to meet demands or to determine construction, equipment, or maintenance requirements. Inspects project, operations, or site to determine progress, need for repair, or compliance with specifications and regulations. Prepares budget estimates based on anticipated material, equipment, and personnel needs. Determines action to be taken in event of emergencies, such as machine, equipment, or power failure. Prepares reports, directives, records, work orders, specifications for work methods, and other documents.

Occupational Type

Enterprising occupations frequently involve starting up and carrying out projects. These occupations can involve leading people and making many decisions. Sometimes they involve risk taking and often deal with business.

Skills required of Utilities Managers

Active Listening, Writing, Speaking, Mathematics, Critical Thinking, Active Learning, Monitoring, Social Perceptiveness, Coordination, Negotiation, Problem Identification, Information Gathering, Information Organization, Synthesis/Reorganization, Idea Generation, Idea Evaluation, Implementation Planning, Operations Analysis, Equipment Selection, Visioning, Systems Perception, Identifying Downstream Consequences, Identification of Key Causes, Judgment and Decision Making, Systems Evaluation, Time Management, Management of Financial Resources, Management of Material Resources, Management of Personnel Resources

College Majors

Agricultural Business and Management, General: An instructional program that generally prepares individuals to apply modern economic and business principles involved in the organization, operation and management of farm and agricultural businesses.

 Supporting Courses

Administration and Management: Knowledge of principles and processes involved in business and organizational planning, coordination, and execution. This includes strategic planning, resource allocation, manpower modeling, leadership techniques, and production methods. **Economics and Accounting:** Knowledge of economic and accounting principles and practices, the financial markets, banking, and the analysis and reporting of financial data. **Sales and Marketing:** Knowledge of principles and methods involved in showing, promoting, and selling products or services. This includes marketing strategies and tactics, product demonstration and sales techniques, and sales control systems. **Personnel and Human Resources:** Knowledge of policies and practices involved in personnel/human resource functions. This includes recruitment, selection, training, and promotion regulations and procedures; compensation and benefits packages; labor relations and negotiation strategies; and personnel information systems. **Engineering and Technology:** Knowledge of equipment, tools, mechanical devices, and their uses to produce motion, light, power, technology, and other applications. **Design:** Knowledge of design techniques, principles, tools and instruments involved in the production and use of precision technical plans, blueprints, drawings, and models. **Building and Construction:** Knowledge of materials, methods, and the appropriate tools to construct objects, structures, and buildings. **Mathematics:** Knowledge of numbers, their operations, and interrelationships including arithmetic, algebra, geometry, calculus, statistics, and their applications. **Physics:** Knowledge and prediction of physical principles, laws, and applications including air, water, material dynamics, light, atomic principles, heat, electric theory, earth formations, and meteorological and related natural phenomena. **Psychology:** Knowledge of human behavior and performance, mental processes, psychological research methods, and the assessment and treatment of behavioral and affective disorders.

Storage and Distribution Managers

Plan, direct, and coordinate the storage and distribution operations within an organization, or the activities of organizations that are engaged in storing and distributing materials and products. Establishes standard and emergency operating procedures for receiving, handling, storing, shipping, or salvaging products or materials. Confers with department heads to coordinate warehouse activities, such as production, sales, records control, and purchasing. Plans, develops, and implements warehouse safety and security programs and activities. Reviews invoices, work orders, consumption reports, and demand forecasts to estimate peak delivery periods and issue work assignments. Supervises the activities of workers engaged in receiving, storing, testing, and shipping products or materials. Inspects physical condition of warehouse and equipment and prepares work orders for testing, maintenance, or repair. Negotiates contracts, settlements, and freight-handling agreements to resolve problems between foreign and domestic shippers. Develops and implements plans for facility modification or expansion, such as equipment purchase or changes in space allocation or structural design. Examines invoices and shipping manifests for conformity to tariff and customs regulations, and contacts customs officials to effect release of shipments. Interviews, selects, and trains warehouse and supervisory personnel. Schedules air or surface pickup, delivery, or distribution of products or materials. Prepares or directs preparation of correspondence, reports, and operations, maintenance, and safety manuals. Interact with customers or shippers to solicit new business, answer questions about services offered or required, and investigate complaints. Examines products or materials to estimate quantities or weight and type of container required for storage or transport.

Occupational Type

Enterprising occupations frequently involve starting up and carrying out projects. These occupations can involve leading people and making many decisions. Sometimes they involve risk taking and often deal with business.

Skills required of Storage and Distribution Managers

Learning Strategies, Coordination, Negotiation, Instructing, Problem Identification, Implementation Planning, Operations Analysis, Product Inspection, Visioning, Systems Perception, Identifying Downstream Consequences, Systems Evaluation, Time Management, Management of Material Resources, Management of Personnel Resources

College Majors

General Distribution Operations: An instructional program that prepares individuals to perform marketing tasks specifically applicable to storing and shipping commodities, either for businesses or retail consumers.

Supporting Courses

Administration and Management: Knowledge of principles and processes involved in business and organizational planning, coordination, and execution. This includes strategic planning, resource allocation, manpower modeling, leadership techniques, and production methods. **Economics and Accounting:** Knowledge of economic and accounting principles and practices, the financial markets, banking, and the analysis and reporting of financial data. **Sales and Marketing:** Knowledge of principles and methods involved in showing, promoting, and selling products or services. This includes marketing strategies and tactics, product demonstration and sales techniques, and sales control systems. **Personnel and Human Resources:** Knowledge of policies and practices involved in personnel/human resource functions. This includes recruitment, selection, training, and promotion regulations and procedures; compensation and benefits packages; labor relations and negotiation strategies; and personnel information systems. **Production and Processing:** Knowledge of inputs, outputs, raw materials, waste, quality control, costs, and techniques for maximizing the manufacture and distribution of goods. **Design:** Knowledge of design techniques, principles, tools and instruments involved in the production and use of precision technical plans, blueprints, drawings, and models. **Mathematics:** Knowledge of numbers, their operations, and interrelationships including arithmetic, algebra, geometry, calculus, statistics, and their applications. **Psychology:** Knowledge of human behavior and performance, mental processes, psychological research methods, and the assessment and treatment of behavioral and affective disorders. **Education and Training:** Knowledge of instructional methods and training techniques including curriculum design principles, learning theory, group and individual teaching techniques, design of individual development plans, and test design principles. **Public Safety and Security:** Knowledge of weaponry, public safety, and security operations, rules, regulations, precautions, prevention, and the protection of people, data, and property. **Law, Government, and Jurisprudence:** Knowledge of laws, legal codes, court procedures, precedents, government regulations, executive orders, agency rules, and the democratic political process. **Communications and Media:** Knowledge of media production, communication, and dissemination techniques and methods including alternative ways to inform and entertain via written, oral, and visual media. **Transportation:** Knowledge of principles and methods for moving people or goods by air, rail, sea, or road, including their relative costs, advantages, and limitations.

COMPUTER ENGINEERS

Computer Engineers

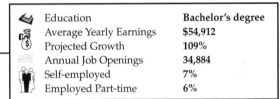

Education	Bachelor's degree
Average Yearly Earnings	$54,912
Projected Growth	109%
Annual Job Openings	34,884
Self-employed	7%
Employed Part-time	6%

Analyze data processing requirements to plan EDP system to provide system capabilities required for projected workloads. Plan layout and installation of new system or modification of existing system. May set up and control analog or hybrid computer systems to solve scientific and engineering problems. Analyzes software requirements to determine feasibility of design within time and cost constraints. Analyzes information to determine, recommend, and plan layout for type of computers and peripheral equipment modifications to existing systems. Consults with engineering staff to evaluate interface between hardware and software and operational and performance requirements of overall system. Evaluates factors such as reporting formats required, cost constraints, and need for security restrictions to determine hardware configuration. Formulates and designs software system, using scientific analysis and mathematical models to predict and measure outcome and consequences of design. Confers with data processing and project managers to obtain information on limitations and capabilities for data processing projects. Develops and directs software system testing procedures, programming, and documentation. Coordinates installation of software system. Monitors functioning of equipment to ensure system operates in conformance with specifications. Consults with customer concerning maintenance of software system. Specifies power supply requirements and configuration. Enters data into computer terminal to store, retrieve, and manipulate data for analysis of system capabilities and requirements. Recommends purchase of equipment to control dust, temperature, and humidity in area of system installation. Trains users to use new or modified equipment.

Occupational Type

Investigative occupations frequently involve working with ideas, and require an extensive amount of thinking. These occupations can involve searching for facts and figuring out problems mentally.

Skills required of Computer Engineers

Reading Comprehension, Active Listening, Writing, Speaking, Mathematics, Science, Critical Thinking, Active Learning, Learning Strategies, Monitoring, Coordination, Persuasion, Instructing, Problem Identification, Information Gathering, Information Organization, Synthesis/Reorganization, Idea Generation, Idea Evaluation, Implementation Planning, Operations Analysis, Technology Design, Equipment Selection, Installation, Programming, Testing, Operation Monitoring, Operation and Control, Product Inspection, Troubleshooting, Visioning, Systems Perception, Identifying Downstream Consequences, Identification of Key Causes, Judgment and Decision Making, Systems Evaluation, Management of Financial Resources, Management of Material Resources, Management of Personnel Resources

 ## College Majors

Information Sciences and Systems: An instructional program that describes the scientific study and development of electronic systems for transmitting information via signalling networks, and the study of information transmission from the point of generation to reception and human interpretation. Includes instruction in information systems planning and design, user needs analysis, and provider capacity and requirements analysis.

 ## Supporting Courses

Administration and Management: Knowledge of principles and processes involved in business and organizational planning, coordination, and execution. This includes strategic planning, resource allocation, manpower modeling, leadership techniques, and production methods. **Clerical:** Knowledge of administrative and clerical procedures and systems such as word processing systems, filing and records management systems, stenography and transcription, forms design principles, and other office procedures and terminology. **Economics and Accounting:** Knowledge of economic and accounting principles and practices, the financial markets, banking, and the analysis and reporting of financial data. **Customer and Personal Service:** Knowledge of principles and processes for providing customer and personal services including needs assessment techniques, quality service standards, alternative delivery systems, and customer satisfaction evaluation techniques. **Computers and Electronics:** Knowledge of electric circuit boards, processors, chips, and computer hardware and software, including applications and programming. **Engineering and Technology:** Knowledge of equipment, tools, mechanical devices, and their uses to produce motion, light, power, technology, and other applications. **Design:** Knowledge of design techniques, principles, tools and instruments involved in the production and use of precision technical plans, blueprints, drawings, and models. **Mathematics:** Knowledge of numbers, their operations, and interrelationships including arithmetic, algebra, geometry, calculus, statistics, and their applications. **Education and Training:** Knowledge of instructional methods and training techniques including curriculum design principles, learning theory, group and individual teaching techniques, design of individual development plans, and test design principles. **English Language:** Knowledge of the structure and content of the English language including the meaning and spelling of words, rules of composition, and grammar. **Telecommunications:** Knowledge of transmission, broadcasting, switching, control, and operation of telecommunications systems. **Communications and Media:** Knowledge of media production, communication, and dissemination techniques and methods, including alternative ways to inform and entertain via written, oral, and visual media.

COMPUTER PROGRAMMERS

Computer Support Specialists

Education	Bachelor's degree
Average Yearly Earnings	$48,360
Projected Growth	23%
Annual Job Openings	58,990
Self-employed	3%
Employed Part-time	7%

Provide technical assistance and training to system users. Investigate and resolve computer software and hardware problems of users. Answer clients' inquiries in person and via telephone concerning the use of computer hardware and software, including printing, word processing, programming languages, electronic mail, and operating systems. Installs and performs minor repairs to hardware, software, and peripheral equipment, following design or installation specifications. Confers with staff, users, and management to determine requirements for new systems or modifications. Reads technical manuals, confers with users, and conducts computer diagnostics to determine nature of problems and provide technical assistance. Develops training materials and procedures, and conducts training programs. Enters commands and observes system functioning to verify correct operations and detect errors. Tests and monitors software, hardware, and peripheral equipment to evaluate use, effectiveness, and adequacy of product for user. Prepares evaluations of software and hardware, and submits recommendations to management for review. Refers major hardware or software problems or defective products to vendors or technicians for service. Maintains record of daily data communication transactions, problems and remedial action taken, and installation activities. Conducts office automation feasibility studies, including workflow analysis, space design, and cost comparison analysis. Reads trade magazines and technical manuals, and attends conferences and seminars to maintain knowledge of hardware and software. Supervises and coordinates workers engaged in problem-solving, monitoring, and installing data communication equipment and software. Inspects equipment and reads order sheets to prepare for delivery to users.

Occupational Type

Investigative occupations frequently involve working with ideas, and require an extensive amount of thinking. These occupations can involve searching for facts and figuring out problems mentally.

Skills required of Computer Support Specialists

Reading Comprehension, Active Listening, Writing, Speaking, Mathematics, Science, Critical Thinking, Active Learning, Learning Strategies, Monitoring, Social Perceptiveness, Coordination, Persuasion, Negotiation, Instructing, Service Orientation, Problem Identification, Information Gathering, Information Organization, Idea Generation, Idea

Evaluation, Implementation Planning, Operations Analysis, Technology Design, Equipment Selection, Installation, Programming, Testing, Troubleshooting, Visioning, Systems Perception, Identifying Downstream Consequences, Identification of Key Causes, Judgment and Decision Making, Systems Evaluation, Time Management, Management of Financial Resources, Management of Material Resources, Management of Personnel Resources

College Majors

Information Sciences and Systems: An instructional program that describes the scientific study and development of electronic systems for transmitting information via signalling networks, and the study of information transmission from the point of generation to reception and human interpretation. Includes instruction in information systems planning and design, user needs analysis, and provider capacity and requirements analysis.

Supporting Courses

Administration and Management: Knowledge of principles and processes involved in business and organizational planning, coordination, and execution. This includes strategic planning, resource allocation, manpower modeling, leadership techniques, and production methods. **Economics and Accounting:** Knowledge of economic and accounting principles and practices, the financial markets, banking, and the analysis and reporting of financial data. **Sales and Marketing:** Knowledge of principles and methods involved in showing, promoting, and selling products or services. This includes marketing strategies and tactics, product demonstration and sales techniques, and sales control systems. **Customer and Personal Service:** Knowledge of principles and processes for providing customer and personal services including needs assessment techniques, quality service standards, alternative delivery systems, and customer satisfaction evaluation techniques. **Computers and Electronics:** Knowledge of electric circuit boards, processors, chips, and computer hardware and software, including applications and programming. **Mathematics:** Knowledge of numbers, their operations, and interrelationships including arithmetic, algebra, geometry, calculus, statistics, and their applications. **Education and Training:** Knowledge of instructional methods and training techniques including curriculum design principles, learning theory, group and individual teaching techniques, design of individual development plans, and test design principles. **Telecommunications:** Knowledge of transmission, broadcasting, switching, control, and operation of telecommunications systems.

Computer Programmers

Convert project specifications and statements of problems and procedures to detailed logical flowcharts for coding into computer language. Develop and write computer programs to store, locate, and retrieve specific documents, data, and information. Analyzes, reviews, and rewrites programs, using workflow chart and diagram, applying knowledge of computer capabilities, subject matter, and symbolic logic. Converts detailed logical flowchart to language processable by computer. Resolves symbolic formulations, prepares flowcharts and block diagrams, and encodes resultant equations for processing. Develops programs from workflow charts or diagrams, considering computer storage capacity, speed, and intended use of output data. Prepares or receives detailed workflow chart and diagram to illustrate sequence of steps to describe input, output, and logical operation. Compiles and writes documentation of program development and subsequent revisions. Revises or directs revision of existing programs to increase operating efficiency or adapt to new requirements. Consults with managerial and engineering and technical personnel to clarify program intent, identify problems, and suggest changes. Enters program and test data into computer, using keyboard. Writes instructions to guide operating personnel during production runs. Observes computer monitor screen to interpret program operating codes. Prepares records and reports. Collaborates with computer manufacturers and other users to develop new programming methods. Assists computer operators or system analysts to resolve problems in running computer program. Assigns, coordinates, and reviews work of programming personnel. Trains subordinates in programming and program coding. Directs and coordinates activities of computer programmers working as part of project team.

Occupational Type

Investigative occupations frequently involve working with ideas, and require an extensive amount of thinking. These occupations can involve searching for facts and figuring out problems mentally.

Skills required of Computer Programmers

Reading Comprehension, Active Listening, Writing, Speaking, Mathematics, Critical Thinking, Active Learning, Learning Strategies, Monitoring, Coordination, Instructing, Problem Identification, Information Organization, Synthesis/Reorganization, Idea Generation, Idea Evaluation, Implementation Planning, Operations Analysis, Technology Design, Equipment Selection, Programming, Testing, Product Inspection, Troubleshooting, Visioning, Systems Perception, Identifying Downstream Consequences, Identification of Key Causes, Systems Evaluation, Time Management, Management of Personnel Resources

College Majors

Computer Programming: An instructional program that prepares individuals to apply methods and procedures used in designing and writing computer programs to developing solutions to specific operational problems and use requirements, including testing and troubleshooting prototype software packages.

Supporting Courses

Administration and Management: Knowledge of principles and processes involved in business and organizational planning, coordination, and execution. This includes strategic planning, resource allocation, manpower modeling, leadership techniques, and production methods. **Clerical:** Knowledge of administrative and clerical procedures and systems such as word processing systems, filing and records management systems, stenography and transcription, forms design principles, and other office procedures and terminology. **Personnel and Human Resources:** Knowledge of policies and practices involved in personnel/human resource functions. This includes recruitment, selection, training, and promotion regulations and procedures; compensation and benefits packages; labor relations and negotiation strategies; and personnel information systems. **Computers and Electronics:** Knowledge of electric circuit boards, processors, chips, and computer hardware and software, including applications and programming. **Design:** Knowledge of design techniques, principles, tools and instruments involved in the production and use of precision technical plans, blueprints, drawings, and models. **Mathematics:** Knowledge of numbers, their operations, and interrelationships including arithmetic, algebra, geometry, calculus, statistics, and their applications. **Education and Training:** Knowledge of instructional methods and training techniques including curriculum design principles, learning theory, group and individual teaching techniques, design of individual development plans, and test design principles. **English Language:** Knowledge of the structure and content of the English language including the meaning and spelling of words, rules of composition, and grammar. **Communications and Media:** Knowledge of media production, communication, and dissemination techniques and methods including alternative ways to inform and entertain via written, oral, and visual media.

COMPUTER SCIENTISTS

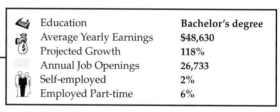

Education	Bachelor's degree
Average Yearly Earnings	$48,630
Projected Growth	118%
Annual Job Openings	26,733
Self-employed	2%
Employed Part-time	6%

Database Administrators

Coordinate changes to computer databases; test and implement the database, applying knowledge of database management systems. May plan, coordinate, and implement security measures to safeguard computer databases. Writes logical and physical database descriptions, including location, space, access method, and security. Establishes and calculates optimum values for database parameters, using manuals and calculator. Develops data model describing data elements and how they are used, following procedures using pen, template, or computer software. Codes database descriptions and specifies identifiers of database to management system, or directs others in coding descriptions. Tests, corrects errors, and modifies changes to programs or to database. Reviews project request describing database user needs, estimating time and cost required to accomplish project. Selects and enters codes to monitor database performance and to create production database. Directs programmers and analysts to make changes to database management system. Reviews workflow charts developed by programmer analyst to understand tasks computer will perform, such as updating records. Reviews procedures in database management system manuals for making changes to database. Confers with coworkers to determine scope and limitations of project. Revises company definition of data as defined in data dictionary. Specifies user and user access levels for each segment of database. Trains users and answers questions.

 Occupational Type

Investigative occupations frequently involve working with ideas, and require an extensive amount of thinking. These occupations can involve searching for facts and figuring out problems mentally.

Skills required of Database Administrators

Mathematics, Critical Thinking, Monitoring, Instructing, Information Organization, SynthesisReorganization, Idea Generation, Operations Analysis, Technology Design Installation, Programming, Testing, Troubleshooting, Visioning, Systems Perception Identifying Downstream Consequences, Identification of Key Causes, Systems Evaluation, Management of Personnel Resources

 College Majors

Computer and Information Sciences, General: An instructional program that generally describes the study of data and information storage and processing systems, including hardware, software, basic design principles, user requirements analysis, and related economic and policy issues.

 Supporting Courses

Administration and Management: Knowledge of principles and processes involved in business and organizational planning, coordination, and execution. This includes strategic planning, resource allocation, manpower modeling, leadership techniques, and production methods. **Computers and Electronics:** Knowledge of electric circuit boards, processors, chips, and computer hardware and software, including applications and programming. **Mathematics:** Knowledge of numbers, their operations, and interrelationships including arithmetic, algebra, geometry, calculus, statistics, and their applications. **Education and Training:** Knowledge of instructional methods and training techniques including curriculum design principles, learning theory, group and individual teaching techniques, design of individual development plans, and test design principles.

CONSTRUCTION MANAGERS

Landscaping Managers

	Education	Bachelor's degree
	Average Yearly Earnings	$46,301
	Projected Growth	18%
	Annual Job Openings	22,043
	Self-employed	16%
	Employed Part-time	6%

Plan and direct landscaping functions and sequences of work to landscape grounds of private residences, public areas, or commercial and industrial properties, according to landscape design and clients' specifications. Confers with prospective client and studies landscape designs, drawings, and bills of materials to ascertain scope of landscaping work required. Formulates and submits estimate and contract for client or bid to industrial concern or governmental agency. Calculates labor, equipment, material, and overhead costs to determine minimum estimate or bid which will provide for margin of profit. Plans landscaping functions and sequences of work at various sites to obtain optimum utilization of workforce and equipment. Inspects work at sites for compliance with terms and specifications of contract. Inspects grounds or area to determine equipment requirements for grading, tilling, or replacing top soil, and labor requirements. Directs and coordinates activities of workers engaged in performing landscaping functions in contractual agreement. Purchases and ensures that materials are on-site as needed.

Occupational Type

Enterprising occupations frequently involve starting up and carrying out projects. These occupations can involve leading people and making many decisions. Sometimes they involve risk taking and often deal with business.

Skills required of Landscaping Managers

Mathematics, Coordination, Negotiation, Implementation Planning, Operations Analysis, Equipment Selection, Product Inspection, Visioning, Systems Perception, Identifying Downstream Consequences, Identification of Key Causes, Systems Evaluation, Time Management, Management of Financial Resources, Management of Material Resources, Management of Personnel Resources

College Majors

Horticulture Services Operations and Management, General: An instructional program that generally prepares individuals to produce, process and market plants, shrubs and trees used principally for ornamental, recreational and aesthetic purposes and to establish, maintain, and manage horticultural enterprises.

Supporting Courses

Administration and Management: Knowledge of principles and processes involved in business and organizational planning, coordination, and execution. This includes strategic planning, resource allocation, manpower modeling, leadership techniques, and production methods. **Economics and Accounting:** Knowledge of economic and accounting principles and practices, the financial markets, banking, and the analysis and reporting of financial data. **Sales and Marketing:** Knowledge of principles and methods involved in showing, promoting, and selling products or services. This includes marketing strategies and tactics, product demonstration and sales techniques, and sales control systems. **Customer and Personal Service:** Knowledge of principles and processes for providing customer and personal services including needs assessment techniques, quality service standards, alternative delivery systems, and customer satisfaction evaluation techniques. **Personnel and Human Resources:** Knowledge of policies and practices involved in personnel/human resource functions. This includes recruitment, selection, training, and promotion regulations and procedures; compensation and benefits packages; labor relations and negotiation strategies; and personnel information systems. **Design:** Knowledge of design techniques, principles, tools and instruments involved in the production and use of precision technical plans, blueprints, drawings, and models. **Chemistry:** Knowledge of the composition, structure, and properties of substances and of the chemical processes and transformations that they undergo. This includes uses of chemicals and their interactions, danger signs, production techniques, and disposal methods. **Biology:** Knowledge of plant and animal living tissue, cells, organisms, and entities, including their functions, inter-dependencies, and interactions with each other and the environment.

Construction Managers

Plan, direct, coordinate, and budget, usually through subordinate supervisory personnel, activities concerned with the construction and maintenance of structures, facilities, and systems. Participate in the conceptual development of a construction project and oversee its organization, scheduling, and implementation. Include specialized construction fields such as carpentry or plumbing. Include general superintendents, project managers, and constructors who manage, coordinate, and supervise the construction process. Plans, organizes, and directs activities concerned with construction and maintenance of structures, facilities, and systems. Confers with supervisory personnel to discuss such matters as work procedures, complaints, and construction problems. Inspects and reviews construction work, repair projects, and reports to ensure work conforms to specifications. Studies job specifications to plan and approve construction of project. Directs and supervises workers on construction site to ensure project meets specifications. Contracts workers to perform construction work in accordance with specifications. Requisitions supplies and materials to complete construction project. Interprets and explains plans and contract terms to administrative staff, workers, and clients. Formulates reports concerning such areas as work progress, costs, and scheduling. Dispatches workers to construction sites to work on specified projects. Investigates reports of damage at construction sites to ensure proper procedures are being carried out.

 ## Occupational Type

Enterprising occupations frequently involve starting up and carrying out projects. These occupations can involve leading people and making many decisions. Sometimes they involve risk taking and often deal with business.

 ## Skills required of Construction Managers

Active Listening, Writing, Speaking, Mathematics, Critical Thinking, Active Learning, Monitoring, Coordination, Persuasion, Negotiation, Problem Identification, Idea Generation, Idea Evaluation, Implementation Planning, Operations Analysis, Equipment Selection, Product Inspection, Visioning, Identifying Downstream Consequences, Identification of Key Causes, Judgment and Decision Making, Systems Evaluation, Time Management, Management of Financial Resources, Management of Material Resources, Management of Personnel Resources

 ## College Majors

Various. Many bachelor studies contribute to expertise in this field.

 ## Supporting Courses

Administration and Management: Knowledge of principles and processes involved in business and organizational planning, coordination, and execution. This includes strategic

planning, resource allocation, manpower modeling, leadership techniques, and production methods. **Personnel and Human Resources:** Knowledge of policies and practices involved in personnel/human resource functions. This includes recruitment, selection, training, and promotion regulations and procedures; compensation and benefits packages; labor relations and negotiation strategies; and personnel information systems. **Design:** Knowledge of design techniques, principles, tools and instruments involved in the production and use of precision technical plans, blueprints, drawings, and models. **Building and Construction:** Knowledge of materials, methods, and the appropriate tools to construct objects, structures, and buildings. **Public Safety and Security:** Knowledge of weaponry, public safety, and security operations, rules, regulations, precautions, prevention, and the protection of people, data, and property. **Law, Government, and Jurisprudence:** Knowledge of laws, legal codes, court procedures, precedents, government regulations, executive orders, agency rules, and the democratic political process.

COUNSELORS

Vocational and Educational Counselors

Education		Master's degree
Average Yearly Earnings		$36,566
Projected Growth		19%
Annual Job Openings		27,181
Self-employed		2%
Employed Part-time		18%

Counsel individuals and provide group educational and vocational guidance services. Advises counselees to assist them in developing their educational and vocational objectives. Advises counselees to assist them in understanding and overcoming personal and social problems. Collects and evaluates information about counselees' abilities, interests, and personality characteristics, using records, tests, and interviews. Compiles and studies occupational, educational, and economic information to assist counselees in making and carrying out vocational and educational objectives. Interprets program regulations or benefit requirements and assists counselees in obtaining needed supportive services. Refers qualified counselees to employer or employment service for placement. Conducts follow-up interviews with counselees and maintains case records. Establishes and maintains relationships with employers and personnel from supportive service agencies to develop opportunities for counselees. Plans and conducts orientation programs and group conferences to promote adjustment of individuals to new life experiences. Teaches vocational and educational guidance classes. Addresses community groups and faculty members to explain counseling services.

 Occupational Type

Social occupations frequently involve working with, communicating with, and teaching people. These occupations often involve helping or providing service to others.

 Skills required of Vocational and Educational Counselors

Reading Comprehension, Active Listening, Writing, Speaking, Critical Thinking, Active Learning, Learning Strategies, Monitoring, Social Perceptiveness, Coordination,

Persuasion, Negotiation, Instructing, Service Orientation, Problem Identification, Information Gathering, Information Organization, Synthesis/Reorganization, Idea Generation, Idea Evaluation, Implementation Planning, Visioning, Identification of Key Causes, Judgment and Decision Making, Systems Evaluation

College Majors

Bilingual/Bicultural Education: An instructional program that describes the design and provision of teaching and other educational services to bilingual/bicultural children or adults, and/or the design and implementation of educational programs having the goal of producing bilingual/bicultural individuals. Includes preparation to serve as teachers and administrators in bilingual/bicultural education programs.

Supporting Courses

Personnel and Human Resources: Knowledge of policies and practices involved in personnel/human resource functions. This includes recruitment, selection, training, and promotion regulations and procedures; compensation and benefits packages; labor relations and negotiation strategies; and personnel information systems. **Psychology:** Knowledge of human behavior and performance, mental processes, psychological research methods, and the assessment and treatment of behavioral and affective disorders. **Sociology and Anthropology:** Knowledge of group behavior and dynamics, societal trends and influences, cultures, their history, migrations, ethnicity, and origins. **Therapy and Counseling:** Knowledge of information and techniques needed to rehabilitate physical and mental ailments and to provide career guidance including alternative treatments, rehabilitation equipment and its proper use, and methods to evaluate treatment effects. **Education and Training:** Knowledge of instructional methods and training techniques including curriculum design principles, learning theory, group and individual teaching techniques, design of individual development plans, and test design principles. **English Language:** Knowledge of the structure and content of the English language including the meaning and spelling of words, rules of composition, and grammar.

Vocational Rehabilitation Coordinators

Develop and coordinate implementation of vocational rehabilitation programs. Develops proposals for rehabilitation programs to provide needed services, utilizing knowledge of program funding sources and government regulations. Consults with community groups and personnel from rehabilitation agencies to identify need for new or modified vocational rehabilitation programs. Collects and analyzes data to define and resolve rehabilitation problems, utilizing knowledge of vocational rehabilitation theory and practice. Monitors program operations and recommends additional measures to ensure that programs meet defined needs. Negotiates contracts for rehabilitation program equipment and supplies. Plans and provides training for vocational rehabilitation staff.

Occupational Type

Social occupations frequently involve working with, communicating with, and teaching people. These occupations often involve helping or providing service to others.

Skills required of Vocational Rehabilitation Coordinators

Reading Comprehension, Active Listening, Writing, Speaking, Mathematics, Critical Thinking, Active Learning, Monitoring, Coordination, Negotiation, Instructing, Service Orientation, Problem Identification, Information Gathering, Information Organization, Idea Generation, Idea Evaluation, Implementation Planning, Operations Analysis, Visioning, Systems Perception, Identifying Downstream Consequences, Identification of Key Causes, Judgment and Decision Making, Systems Evaluation, Time Management, Management of Financial Resources, Management of Material Resources, Management of Personnel Resources

 ## College Majors

Education Administration and Supervision, General: An instructional program that generally describes the study of the principles and techniques of administering a wide variety of schools and other educational organizations and facilities, supervising educational personnel at the school or staff level, and that may prepare individuals as general administrators and supervisors.

 ## Supporting Courses

Administration and Management: Knowledge of principles and processes involved in business and organizational planning, coordination, and execution. This includes strategic planning, resource allocation, manpower modeling, leadership techniques, and production methods. **Personnel and Human Resources:** Knowledge of policies and practices involved in personnel/human resource functions. This includes recruitment, selection, training, and promotion regulations and procedures; compensation and benefits packages; labor relations and negotiation strategies; and personnel information systems. **Psychology:** Knowledge of human behavior and performance, mental processes, psychological research methods, and the assessment and treatment of behavioral and affective disorders. **Sociology and Anthropology:** Knowledge of group behavior and dynamics, societal trends and influences, cultures, their history, migrations, ethnicity, and origins. **Therapy and Counseling:** Knowledge of information and techniques needed to rehabilitate physical and mental ailments and to provide career guidance including alternative treatments, rehabilitation equipment and its proper use, and methods to evaluate treatment effects. **Education and Training:** Knowledge of instructional methods and training techniques including curriculum design principles, learning theory, group and individual teaching techniques, design of individual development plans, and test design principles. **English Language:** Knowledge of the structure and content of the English language including the meaning and spelling of words, rules of composition, and grammar. **Philosophy and Theology:** Knowledge of different philosophical systems and religions, including their basic principles, values, ethics, ways of thinking, customs, and practices, and their impact on human culture. **Law, Government, and Jurisprudence:** Knowledge of laws, legal codes, court procedures, precedents, government regulations, executive orders, agency rules, and the democratic political process.

CREDIT ANALYSTS

	Education	Bachelor's degree
	Average Yearly Earnings	$36,962
	Projected Growth	16%
	Annual Job Openings	5,454
	Self-employed	0%
	Employed Part-time	7%

Credit Analysts

Analyze current credit data and financial statements of individuals or firms to determine the degree of risk involved in extending credit or lending money. Prepare reports with this credit information for use in decision making. Analyzes credit data and financial statements to determine degree of risk involved in extending credit or lending money. Generates financial ratios, using computer program, to evaluate customer's financial status. Analyzes financial data, such as income growth, quality of management, and market share, to determine profitability of loan. Compares liquidity, profitability, and credit history with similar establishments of same industry and geographic location. Evaluates customer records and recommends payment plan based on earnings, savings data, payment history, and purchase activity. Completes loan application, including credit analysis and summary of loan request, and submits to loan committee for approval. Confers with credit association and other business representatives to exchange credit information. Reviews individual or commercial customer files to identify and select delinquent accounts for collection. Consults with customers to resolve complaints and verify financial and credit transactions, and adjusts accounts as needed.

Occupational Type

Conventional occupations frequently involve following set procedures and routines. These occupations can include working with data and details more than with ideas. Usually there is a clear line of authority to follow.

Skills required of Credit Analysts

Active Listening, Speaking, Mathematics, Critical Thinking, Active Learning, Monitoring, Negotiation, Service Orientation, Problem Identification, Information Gathering, Information Organization, Idea Evaluation, Programming, Systems Perception, Identifying Downstream Consequences, Identification of Key Causes, Judgment and Decision Making, Systems Evaluation, Management of Financial Resources

College Majors

Finance, General: An instructional program that generally prepares individuals to plan, manage, and analyze the financial and monetary aspects and performance of business enterprises, banking institutions, or other organizations. Includes instruction in principles of accounting; financial instruments; capital planning; funds acquisition; asset and debt management; budgeting; financial analysis; and investments and portfolio management.

Supporting Courses

Economics and Accounting: Knowledge of economic and accounting principles and practices, the financial markets, banking, and the analysis and reporting of financial data. **Personnel and Human Resources:** Knowledge of policies and practices involved in personnel/human resource functions. This includes recruitment, selection, training, and promotion regulations and procedures; compensation and benefits packages; labor relations and negotiation strategies; and personnel information systems. **Computers and Electronics:** Knowledge of electric circuit boards, processors, chips, and computer hardware and software, including applications and programming. **Mathematics:** Knowledge of numbers, their operations, and interrelationships including arithmetic, algebra, geometry, calculus, statistics, and their applications. **Geography:** Knowledge of various methods for describing the location and distribution of land, sea, and air masses including their physical locations, relationships, and characteristics. **History and Archeology:** Knowledge of past historical events and their causes, indicators, and impact on particular civilizations and cultures. **Philosophy and Theology:** Knowledge of different philosophical systems and religions, including their basic principles, values, ethics, ways of thinking, customs, and practices, and their impact on human culture. **Law, Government, and Jurisprudence:** Knowledge of laws, legal codes, court procedures, precedents, government regulations, executive orders, agency rules, and the democratic political process.

CURATORS, ARCHIVISTS, MUSEUM TECHNICIANS, AND RESTORERS

Education		Master's degree
Average Yearly Earnings		$30,035
Projected Growth		15%
Annual Job Openings		2,367
Self-employed		0%
Employed Part-time		22%

Curators

Plan, direct, and coordinate activities of exhibiting institution, such as museum, art gallery, botanical garden, zoo, or historic site. Direct instructional, acquisition, exhibitory, safekeeping, research, and public service activities of institution. Plans and organizes acquisition, storage, and exhibition of collections and related educational materials. Develops and maintains institution's registration, cataloging, and basic recordkeeping systems. Studies, examines, and tests acquisitions to authenticate their origin, composition, history, and current value. Negotiates and authorizes purchase, sale, exchange, or loan of collections. Directs and coordinates activities of curatorial, personnel, fiscal, technical, research, and clerical staff. Confers with institution's board of directors to formulate and interpret policies, determine budget requirements, and plan overall operations. Arranges insurance coverage for objects on loan or special exhibits, and recommends changes in coverage for entire collection. Plans and conducts special research projects. Writes and reviews grant proposals, journal articles, institutional reports, and publicity materials. Attends meetings, conventions, and civic events to promote use of institution's services, seek financing, and maintain community alliances. Conducts or organizes tours, workshops, and instructional sessions to acquaint individuals with use of institution's facilities and materials. Reserves facilities for group tours and social events and collects admission fees. Inspects premises for evidence of deterioration and need for repair. Schedules special events at facility and organizes details such as refreshment, entertainment, and decorations.

 ## Occupational Type

Artistic occupations frequently involve working with forms, designs, and patterns. They often require self-expression and the work can be done without following a clear set of rules.

 ## Skills required of Curators

Reading Comprehension, Active Listening, Writing, Speaking, Critical Thinking, Active Learning, Learning Strategies, Monitoring, Social Perceptiveness, Coordination, Persuasion, Negotiation, Instructing, Service Orientation, Problem Identification, Information Gathering, Information Organization, Synthesis/Reorganization, Idea Generation, Idea Evaluation, Implementation Planning, Operations Analysis, Product Inspection, Visioning, Systems Perception, Identifying Downstream Consequences, Identification of Key Causes, Judgment and Decision Making, Systems Evaluation, Time Management, Management of Financial Resources, Management of Material Resources, Management of Personnel Resources

 ## College Majors

Education, General: An instructional program that generally describes the theory and practice of learning and teaching; the basic principles of educational psychology; the art of teaching; the planning and administration of educational activities; and the social foundations of education.

 ## Supporting Courses

Administration and Management: Knowledge of principles and processes involved in business and organizational planning, coordination, and execution. This includes strategic planning, resource allocation, manpower modeling, leadership techniques, and production methods. **Clerical:** Knowledge of administrative and clerical procedures and systems such as word processing systems, filing and records management systems, stenography and transcription, forms design principles, and other office procedures and terminology. **Economics and Accounting:** Knowledge of economic and accounting principles and practices, the financial markets, banking, and the analysis and reporting of financial data. **Sales and Marketing:** Knowledge of principles and methods involved in showing, promoting, and selling products or services. This includes marketing strategies and tactics, product demonstration and sales techniques, and sales control systems. **Sociology and Anthropology:** Knowledge of group behavior and dynamics, societal trends and influences, cultures, their history, migrations, ethnicity, and origins. **Geography:** Knowledge of various methods for describing the location and distribution of land, sea, and air masses including their physical locations, relationships, and characteristics. **English Language:** Knowledge of the structure and content of the English language including the meaning and spelling of words, rules of composition, and grammar. **Foreign Language:** Knowledge of the structure and content of a foreign (non-English) language including the meaning and spelling of words, rules of composition and grammar, and pronunciation. **Fine Arts:** Knowledge of theory and techniques required to produce, compose, and perform works of music, dance, visual arts, drama, and sculpture. **History and Archeology:** Knowledge of past historical events and their causes, indicators, and impact on particular civilizations and cultures. **Philosophy and Theology:** Knowledge of different philosophical systems and religions, including their basic principles, values, ethics, ways of thinking, customs, and practices, and their impact on human culture. **Communications and Media:** Knowledge of media production, communication, and dissemination techniques and methods including alternative ways to inform and entertain via written, oral, and visual media.

Archivists

Appraise, edit, and direct safekeeping of permanent records and historically valuable documents. Participate in research activities based on archival materials. Directs activities of workers engaged in cataloging and safekeeping of valuable materials and disposition of worthless materials. Directs filing and cross-indexing of selected documents in alphabetical and chronological order. Prepares document descriptions and reference aids for use of archives, such as accession lists, bibliographies, abstracts, and microfilmed documents. Directs acquisition and physical arrangement of new materials. Analyzes documents by ascertaining date of writing, author, or original recipient of letter to appraise value to posterity. Establishes policy guidelines concerning public access and use of materials. Selects and edits documents for publication and display, according to knowledge of subject, literary expression, and techniques for presentation and display. Requests or recommends pertinent materials available in libraries, private collections, or other archives. Advises government agencies, scholars, journalists, and others conducting research by supplying available materials and information.

 Occupational Type

Investigative occupations frequently involve working with ideas, and require an extensive amount of thinking. These occupations can involve searching for facts and figuring out problems mentally.

 Skills required of Archivists

Reading Comprehension, Active Listening, Writing, Speaking, Coordination, Service Orientation, Information Gathering, Information Organization, Synthesis/Reorganization, Implementation Planning, Operations Analysis, Product Inspection, Identification of Key Causes, Judgment and Decision Making, Time Management, Management of Material Resources, Management of Personnel Resources

College Majors

Museology/Museum Studies: An instructional program that describes the attitudes, knowledge, and skills required to develop, prepare, organize, administer, conserve, store and retrieve artifacts, exhibits and entire collections in museums and galleries, and that prepares individuals to assume curatorial, technical and managerial positions in museums. Includes instruction in institutional management, acquisition, exhibit design, conservation, packing techniques, and public relations.

 Supporting Courses

Administration and Management: Knowledge of principles and processes involved in business and organizational planning, coordination, and execution. This includes strategic planning, resource allocation, manpower modeling, leadership techniques, and production methods. **Clerical:** Knowledge of administrative and clerical procedures and systems such as word processing systems, filing and records management systems, stenography and transcription, forms design principles, and other office procedures and terminology. **Sociology and Anthropology:** Knowledge of group behavior and dynamics, societal trends and influences, cultures, their history, migrations, ethnicity, and origins. **English Language:** Knowledge of the structure and content of the English language including the meaning and spelling of words, rules of composition, and grammar. **History and Archeology:** Knowledge of past historical events and their causes, indicators, and impact on particular civilizations and cultures. **Philosophy and Theology:** Knowledge of different philosophical systems and religions, including their basic principles, values, ethics, ways of thinking, customs, and practices, and their impact on human culture. **Communications and Media:** Knowledge of media production, communication, and dissemination techniques and methods including alternative ways to inform and entertain via written, oral, and visual media.

Museum Research Workers

Plan, organize, and conduct research in scientific, historical, cultural, or artistic fields to document or support exhibits in museums and museum publications. Conducts research on historic monuments, buildings, and scenes to construct exhibits. Develops plans for project or studies guidelines for project prepared by professional staff member to outline research procedures. Plans schedule according to variety of methods to be used, availability and quantity of resources, and number of personnel assigned. Conducts research, utilizing institution library, archives, and collections, and other sources of information, to collect, record, analyze, and evaluate facts. Discusses findings with other personnel to evaluate validity of findings. Prepares reports of completed projects for publication, for presentation to agency requesting project, or for use in other research activities. Monitors construction of exhibits to ensure authenticity of proportion, color, and costumes.

 Occupational Type

Investigative occupations frequently involve working with ideas, and require an extensive amount of thinking. These occupations can involve searching for facts and figuring out problems mentally.

 Skills required of Museum Research Workers

Reading Comprehension, Active Listening, Writing, Speaking, Mathematics, Science, Critical Thinking, Active Learning, Learning Strategies, Monitoring, Problem Identification,

Information Gathering, Information Organization, Synthesis/Reorganization, Idea Generation, Idea Evaluation, Implementation Planning, Operations Analysis, Programming, Visioning, Systems Perception, Identifying Downstream Consequences, Identification of Key Causes, Judgment and Decision Making, Systems Evaluation, Time Management, Management of Personnel Resources

College Majors

Museology/Museum Studies: An instructional program that describes the attitudes, knowledge, and skills required to develop, prepare, organize, administer, conserve, store and retrieve artifacts, exhibits and entire collections in museums and galleries, and that prepares individuals to assume curatorial, technical and managerial positions in museums. Includes instruction in institutional management, acquisition, exhibit design, conservation, packing techniques, and public relations.

Supporting Courses

Administration and Management: Knowledge of principles and processes involved in business and organizational planning, coordination, and execution. This includes strategic planning, resource allocation, manpower modeling, leadership techniques, and production methods. **Computers and Electronics:** Knowledge of electric circuit boards, processors, chips, and computer hardware and software, including applications and programming. **Mathematics:** Knowledge of numbers, their operations, and interrelationships including arithmetic, algebra, geometry, calculus, statistics, and their applications. **Psychology:** Knowledge of human behavior and performance, mental processes, psychological research methods, and the assessment and treatment of behavioral and affective disorders. **Sociology and Anthropology:** Knowledge of group behavior and dynamics, societal trends and influences, cultures, their history, migrations, ethnicity, and origins. **Geography:** Knowledge of various methods for describing the location and distribution of land, sea, and air masses including their physical locations, relationships, and characteristics. **English Language:** Knowledge of the structure and content of the English language including the meaning and spelling of words, rules of composition, and grammar. **Foreign Language:** Knowledge of the structure and content of a foreign (non-English) language including the meaning and spelling of words, rules of composition and grammar, and pronunciation. **Fine Arts:** Knowledge of theory and techniques required to produce, compose, and perform works of music, dance, visual arts, drama, and sculpture. **History and Archeology:** Knowledge of past historical events and their causes, indicators, and impact on particular civilizations and cultures. **Philosophy and Theology:** Knowledge of different philosophical systems and religions, including their basic principles, values, ethics, ways of thinking, customs, and practices, and their impact on human culture. **Telecommunications:** Knowledge of transmission, broadcasting, switching, control, and operation of telecommunications systems. **Communications and Media:** Knowledge of media production, communication, and dissemination techniques and methods including alternative ways to inform and entertain via written, oral, and visual media.

Museum Technicians and Conservators

Prepare specimens, such as fossils, skeletal parts, and textiles, for museum collection and exhibits. May restore documents or install, arrange, and exhibit materials. Preserves or directs preservation of objects, using plaster, resin, sealants, hardeners, and shellac. Repairs and restores surfaces of artifacts to original appearance and to prevent deterioration, according to accepted procedures. Evaluates need for repair and determines safest and most effective method of treating surface of object. Cleans objects, such as paper, textiles, wood, metal, glass, rock, pottery, and furniture, using cleansers, solvents, soap solutions, and polishes. Constructs skeletal mounts of fossils, replicas of archeological artifacts, or duplicate specimens, using variety of materials and hand tools. Repairs or reassembles broken objects, using glue, solder, hand tools, power tools, and small machines. Studies descriptive information on object or conducts standard chemical and physical tests to determine age, composition, and original appearance. Designs and fabricates missing or broken parts. Cuts and welds metal sections in reconstruction or renovation of exterior structural sections and accessories of exhibits. Recommends preservation measures, such as control of temperature, humidity, and exposure to light, to curatorial and building maintenance staff. Installs, arranges, assembles, and prepares artifacts for exhibition. Plans and conducts research to develop and improve methods of restoring and preserving specimens. Records methods and treatment taken to repair, preserve, and restore each artifact, and maintains museum files. Prepares reports of activities. Notifies superior when restoration of artifact requires outside experts. Directs curatorial and technical staff in handling, mounting, care, and storage of art objects. Estimates cost of restoration work. Builds, repairs, and installs wooden steps, scaffolds, and walkways to gain access to or permit improved view of exhibited equipment.

Occupational Type

Artistic occupations frequently involve working with forms, designs, and patterns. They often require self-expression and the work can be done without following a clear set of rules.

Skills required of Museum Technicians and Conservators

Writing, Information Organization, Operations Analysis, Equipment Selection, Installation, Product Inspection, Repairing, Management of Material Resources, Management of Personnel Resources

College Majors

Museology/Museum Studies: An instructional program that describes the attitudes, knowledge, and skills required to develop, prepare, organize, administer, conserve, store and retrieve artifacts, exhibits and entire collections in museums and galleries, and that prepares individuals to assume curatorial, technical and managerial positions in museums. Includes instruction in institutional management, acquisition, exhibit design, conservation, packing techniques, and public relations.

Supporting Courses

Building and Construction: Knowledge of materials, methods, and the appropriate tools to construct objects, structures, and buildings. **Chemistry:** Knowledge of the composition, structure, and properties of substances and of the chemical processes and transformations that they undergo. This includes uses of chemicals and their interactions, danger signs, production techniques, and disposal methods. **Sociology and Anthropology:** Knowledge of group behavior and dynamics, societal trends and influences, cultures, their history, migrations, ethnicity, and origins. **Fine Arts:** Knowledge of theory and techniques required to produce, compose, and perform works of music, dance, visual arts, drama, and sculpture. **History and Archeology:** Knowledge of past historical events and their causes, indicators, and impact on particular civilizations and cultures. **Philosophy and Theology:** Knowledge of different philosophical systems and religions, including their basic principles, values, ethics, ways of thinking, customs, and practices, and their impact on human culture.

Craft Demonstrators

Demonstrate and explain techniques and purposes of historic crafts. Engages in activities such as molding candles, shoeing horses, operating looms, or working in appropriate period setting to demonstrate craft. Describes craft techniques and explains the relationship of craft to traditional lifestyle of time and area. Practices techniques involved in handicraft to ensure accurate and skillful demonstrations. Answers visitor questions, or refers visitors to other sources for information. Studies historical and technical literature to acquire information about time period and lifestyle depicted in display and craft techniques. Drafts outline of talk, assisted by research personnel, to acquaint visitors with customs and crafts associated with folk life depicted.

 Occupational Type

Social occupations frequently involve working with, communicating with, and teaching people. These occupations often involve helping or providing service to others.

 Skills required of Craft Demonstrators

Instructing, Service Orientation

 College Majors

Crafts, Folk Art, and Artisanry: An instructional program that describes the aesthetics, techniques, and creative processes for designing and fashioning objects in one or more of the handcraft or folk art traditions, and that prepares individuals to create in any of these media.

 Supporting Courses

Sociology and Anthropology: Knowledge of group behavior and dynamics, societal trends and influences, cultures, their history, migrations, ethnicity, and origins. **Geography:**

Knowledge of various methods for describing the location and distribution of land, sea, and air masses including their physical locations, relationships, and characteristics. **Fine Arts:** Knowledge of theory and techniques required to produce, compose, and perform works of music, dance, visual arts, drama, and sculpture. **History and Archeology:** Knowledge of past historical events and their causes, indicators, and impact on particular civilizations and cultures. **Philosophy and Theology:** Knowledge of different philosophical systems and religions, including their basic principles, values, ethics, ways of thinking, customs, and practices, and their impact on human culture.

Dental hygienists

	Education	Associate degree
	Average Yearly Earnings	$42,432
	Projected Growth	48%
	Annual Job Openings	18,372
	Self-employed	0%
	Employed Part-time	23%

Dentists

	Education	First professional degree
	Average Yearly Earnings	$85,509
	Projected Growth	8%
	Annual Job Openings	5,072
	Self-employed	44%
	Employed Part-time	21%

Oral Pathologists

Research or study nature, cause, effects, and development of diseases associated with mouth. Examines oral tissue specimen to determine pathological conditions, such as tumors and lesions, using microscope and other laboratory equipment. Determines nature and cause of oral condition. Evaluates previous and future development of oral condition. Examines patient's mouth, jaw, face, and associated areas. Obtains oral tissue specimen from patient, using medical instruments. Discusses diagnosis with patient and referring practitioner.

 Occupational Type

Investigative occupations frequently involve working with ideas, and require an extensive amount of thinking. These occupations can involve searching for facts and figuring out problems mentally.

 Skills required of Oral Pathologists

Reading Comprehension, Active Listening, Writing, Speaking, Mathematics, Science, Critical Thinking, Active Learning, Learning Strategies, Monitoring, Persuasion, Service Orientation, Problem Identification, Information Gathering, Information Organization,

Synthesis/Reorganization, Idea Generation, Idea Evaluation, Implementation Planning, Equipment Selection, Identification of Key Causes, Judgment and Decision Making

 College Majors

Oral Pathology Specialty: A residency training program that prepares dentists in the functional and structural changes that affect the oral cavity, including diagnosis of diseases, abnormalities and tumors.

Supporting Courses

Chemistry: Knowledge of the composition, structure, and properties of substances and of the chemical processes and transformations that they undergo. This includes uses of chemicals and their interactions, danger signs, production techniques, and disposal methods. **Biology:** Knowledge of plant and animal living tissue, cells, organisms, and entities, including their functions, interdependencies, and interactions with each other and the environment. **Psychology:** Knowledge of human behavior and performance, mental processes, psychological research methods, and the assessment and treatment of behavioral and affective disorders. **Medicine and Dentistry:** Knowledge of the information and techniques needed to diagnose and treat injuries, diseases, and deformities. This includes symptoms, treatment alternatives, drug properties and interactions, and preventive heathcare measures. **Therapy and Counseling:** Knowledge of information and techniques needed to rehabilitate physical and mental ailments and to provide career guidance including alternative treatments, rehabilitation equipment and its proper use, and methods to evaluate treatment effects. **English Language:** Knowledge of the structure and content of the English language including the meaning and spelling of words, rules of composition, and grammar.

Dentists

Diagnose, prevent, and treat problems of the teeth and tissue of the mouth. (Excludes orthodontists; prosthodontists; oral and maxillofacial surgeons; and oral pathologists.) Fills, extracts, and replaces teeth, using rotary and hand instruments, dental appliances, medications, and surgical implements. Applies fluoride and sealants to teeth. Treats exposure of pulp by pulp capping, removal of pulp from pulp chamber, or root canal, using dental instruments. Treats infected root canal and related tissues. Fills pulp chamber and canal with endodontic materials. Eliminates irritating margins of fillings and corrects occlusions, using dental instruments. Examines teeth, gums, and related tissues to determine condition, using dental instruments, X-ray, and other diagnostic equipment. Formulates plan of treatment for patient's teeth and mouth tissue. Removes pathologic tissue or diseased tissue using surgical instruments. Restores natural color of teeth by bleaching, cleaning, and polishing. Analyzes and evaluates dental needs to determine changes and trends in patterns of dental disease. Counsels and advises patients about growth and development of dental problems and preventive oral healthcare services. Fabricates prosthodontic appliances, such as space maintainers, bridges, dentures, and obturating appliances. Fits and adjusts prosthodontic appliances in patient's mouth. Produces and evaluates dental health educational materials. Plans, organizes, and maintains dental health programs.

Occupational Type

Investigative occupations frequently involve working with ideas, and require an extensive amount of thinking. These occupations can involve searching for facts and figuring out problems mentally.

Skills required of Dentists

Reading Comprehension, Science, Critical Thinking, Active Learning, Learning Strategies, Monitoring, Service Orientation, Problem Identification, Idea Generation, Idea Evaluation, Implementation Planning, Judgment and Decision Making, Management of Financial Resources

College Majors

Dentistry (D.D.S., D.M.D.): An instructional program that prepares individuals for the independent professional practice of dentistry. Includes instruction in the prevention, diagnosis, and treatment of diseases and abnormalities of the teeth and gums and related parts of the oral cavity; related anatomical and physiological principles; professional ethics and standards; and supervised clinical practice. **Dental Clinical Sciences/Graduate Dentistry (M.S., Ph.D.):** An instructional program that generally describes advanced study or research, by dentists or other medical doctors, in dental practice specialties and related sciences such as oral biology, endodontics, oral/maxillofacial surgery, orthodontics, pediatric dentistry, periodontics, dental materials, dental diagnostics, prosthodontics, dental nutrition, dental immunology, and dental pathology.

Supporting Courses

Chemistry: Knowledge of the composition, structure, and properties of substances and of the chemical processes and transformations that they undergo. This includes uses of chemicals and their interactions, danger signs, production techniques, and disposal methods. **Biology:** Knowledge of plant and animal living tissue, cells, organisms, and entities, including their functions, interdependencies, and interactions with each other and the environment. **Medicine and Dentistry:** Knowledge of the information and techniques needed to diagnose and treat injuries, diseases, and deformities. This includes symptoms, treatment alternatives, drug properties and interactions, and preventive heathcare measures. **English Language:** Knowledge of the structure and content of the English language including the meaning and spelling of words, rules of composition, and grammar.

Orthodontists

Examine, diagnose, and treat dental malocclusions and oral cavity anomalies. Design and fabricate appliances to realign teeth and jaws to produce and maintain normal function and to improve appearance. Diagnoses teeth and jaw or other dental-facial abnormalities. Plans treatment, using cephalometric, height, and weight records, dental X-rays and front and lateral dental photographs. Examines patient's mouth to determine position of teeth and jaw development. Fits dental appliances in patient's mouth to alter position and relationship of teeth and jaws and to realign teeth. Adjusts dental appliances periodically to produce and maintain normal function. Designs and fabricates appliances, such as space maintainers, retainers, and labial and lingual arch wires.

Occupational Type

Investigative occupations frequently involve working with ideas, and require an extensive amount of thinking. These occupations can involve searching for facts and figuring out problems mentally.

Skills required of Orthodontists

Reading Comprehension, Active Listening, Science, Critical Thinking, Active Learning, Learning Strategies, Monitoring, Service Orientation, Problem Identification, Synthesis/ Reorganization, Idea Generation, Idea Evaluation, Implementation Planning, Operations Analysis, Technology Design, Equipment Selection, Installation, Identification of Key Causes, Judgment and Decision Making, Management of Financial Resources

College Majors

Orthodontics Specialty: A residency training program that prepares dentists in the principles and techniques involved in the prevention and correction of dental malocclusions and oral cavity anomalies.

Supporting Courses

Customer and Personal Service: Knowledge of principles and processes for providing customer and personal services including needs assessment techniques, quality service standards, alternative delivery systems, and customer satisfaction evaluation techniques. **Chemistry:** Knowledge of the composition, structure, and properties of substances and of the chemical processes and transformations that they undergo. This includes uses of chemicals and their interactions, danger signs, production techniques, and disposal methods. **Biology:** Knowledge of plant and animal living tissue, cells, organisms, and entities, including their functions, interdependencies, and interactions with each other and the environment. **Medicine and Dentistry:** Knowledge of the information and techniques needed to diagnose and treat injuries, diseases, and deformities. This includes symptoms, treatment alternatives, drug properties and interactions, and preventive heathcare measures. **Therapy and Counseling:** Knowledge of information and techniques needed to rehabilitate physical and mental ailments and to provide career guidance including alternative treatments, rehabilitation equipment and its proper use, and methods to evaluate treatment effects.

Prosthodontists

Construct oral prostheses to replace missing teeth and other oral structures; to correct natural and acquired deformation of mouth and jaws; to restore and maintain oral function, such as chewing and speaking; and to improve appearance. Designs and fabricates dental prostheses. Corrects natural and acquired deformation of mouth and jaws through use of prosthetic appliances. Records physiologic position of jaws to determine shape and size of dental prostheses, using face bows, dental articulators, and recording devices. Adjusts prostheses to fit patient. Replaces missing teeth and associated oral structures with artificial teeth to improve chewing, speech, and appearance.

Occupational Type

Investigative occupations frequently involve working with ideas, and require an extensive amount of thinking. These occupations can involve searching for facts and figuring out problems mentally.

Skills required of Prosthodontists

Reading Comprehension, Mathematics, Science, Critical Thinking, Active Learning, Learning Strategies, Service Orientation, Problem Identification, Synthesis/Reorganization, Operations Analysis, Technology Design, Equipment Selection, Product Inspection, Judgment and Decision Making

College Majors

Prosthodontics Specialty: A residency training program that prepares dentists in the principles and techniques of constructing oral prostheses, and the restoration and maintenance of oral function by the replacement of missing teeth and other oral structures with such artificial devices.

Supporting Courses

Chemistry: Knowledge of the composition, structure, and properties of substances and of the chemical processes and transformations that they undergo. This includes uses of chemicals and their interactions, danger signs, production techniques, and disposal methods. **Biology:** Knowledge of plant and animal living tissue, cells, organisms, and entities, including their functions, interdependencies, and interactions with each other and the environment. **Medicine and Dentistry:** Knowledge of the information and techniques needed to diagnose and treat injuries, diseases, and deformities. This includes symptoms, treatment alternatives, drug properties and interactions, and preventive heathcare measures.

Oral and Maxillofacial Surgeons

Perform surgery on mouth, jaws, and related head and neck structure to execute difficult and multiple extractions of teeth, to remove tumors and other abnormal growths; to correct abnormal jaw relations by mandibular or maxillary revision; to prepare mouth for insertion of dental prosthesis; or to treat fractured jaws. Executes difficult and multiple extraction of teeth. Removes tumors and other abnormal growths, using surgical instruments. Performs preprosthetic surgery to prepare mouth for insertion of dental prosthesis. Corrects abnormal jaw relations by mandibular or maxillary revision. Treats fractures of jaws. Administers general and local anesthetics.

Occupational Type

Investigative occupations frequently involve working with ideas, and require an extensive amount of thinking. These occupations can involve searching for facts and figuring out problems mentally.

Skills required of Oral and Maxillofacial Surgeons

Reading Comprehension, Active Listening, Writing, Speaking, Mathematics, Science, Critical Thinking, Active Learning, Learning Strategies, Monitoring, Service Orientation, Problem Identification, Idea Generation, Idea Evaluation, Implementation Planning, Visioning, Identification of Key Causes, Judgment and Decision Making

College Majors

Dental/Oral Surgery Specialty: A residency training program that prepares dentists and medical surgeons in advanced clinical training and practice in the surgery of the oral cavity and jaws, including the removal of cancerous and other diseased tissue, removal of teeth, and reconstruction of the jaw and related facial structure.

Supporting Courses

Chemistry: Knowledge of the composition, structure, and properties of substances and of the chemical processes and transformations that they undergo. This includes uses of chemicals and their interactions, danger signs, production techniques, and disposal methods. **Biology:** Knowledge of plant and animal living tissue, cells, organisms, and entities, including their functions, interdependencies, and interactions with each other and the environment. **Psychology:** Knowledge of human behavior and performance, mental processes, psychological research methods, and the assessment and treatment of behavioral and affective disorders. **Medicine and Dentistry:** Knowledge of the information and techniques needed to diagnose and treat injuries, diseases, and deformities. This includes symptoms, treatment alternatives, drug properties and interactions, and preventive heathcare measures. **Therapy and Counseling:** Knowledge of information and techniques needed to rehabilitate physical and mental ailments and to provide career guidance including alternative treatments, rehabilitation equipment and its proper use, and methods to evaluate treatment effects. **English Language:** Knowledge of the structure and content of the English language including the meaning and spelling of words, rules of composition, and grammar.

DESIGNERS

Fashion Designers

Education	Bachelor's degree
Average Yearly Earnings	$30,867
Projected Growth	26%
Annual Job Openings	42,479
Self-employed	36%
Employed Part-time	20%

Design clothing and accessories. Create original garments or design garments that follow well-established fashion trends. May develop the line of color and

---

kinds of materials. Designs custom garments for clients. Integrates findings of analysis and discussion, and personal tastes and knowledge of design, to originate design ideas. Sketches rough and detailed drawings of apparel or accessories, and writes specifications, such as color scheme, construction, or material type. Draws pattern for article designed, cuts pattern, and cuts material according to pattern, using measuring and drawing instruments, and scissors. Examines sample garment on and off model, and modifies design to achieve desired effect. Attends fashion shows and reviews garment magazines and manuals to analyze fashion trends, predictions, and consumer preferences. Confers with sales and management executives or with clients regarding design ideas. Sews together sections to form mockup or sample of garment or article, using sewing equipment. Arranges for showing of sample garments at sales meetings or fashion shows. Directs and coordinates workers who draw and cut patterns, and constructs sample or finished garment.

Occupational Type

Artistic occupations frequently involve working with forms, designs, and patterns. They often require self-expression and the work can be done without following a clear set of rules.

Skills required of Fashion Designers

Active Learning, Social Perceptiveness, Coordination, Persuasion, Negotiation, Service Orientation, Synthesis/Reorganization, Idea Generation, Idea Evaluation, Operations Analysis, Product Inspection, Systems Perception, Identifying Downstream Consequences, Identification of Key Causes, Judgment and Decision Making, Systems Evaluation, Time Management, Management of Financial Resources, Management of Material Resources, Management of Personnel Resources

College Majors

Clothing, Apparel and Textile Workers and Managers, General: An instructional program that generally prepares individuals for occupations concerned with the entire spectrum of clothing, apparel, and textiles management, production, and services, including but not limited to construction; fabric and fabric care; pattern design; principles in clothing construction and selection; fitting and alterations of ready-to-wear garments; custom tailoring; clothing maintenance; and textiles testing.

Supporting Courses

Sales and Marketing: Knowledge of principles and methods involved in showing, promoting, and selling products or services. This includes marketing strategies and tactics, product demonstration and sales techniques, and sales control systems. **Customer and Personal Service:** Knowledge of principles and processes for providing customer and personal services including needs assessment techniques, quality service standards, alternative delivery systems, and customer satisfaction evaluation techniques. **Production and Processing:** Knowledge of inputs, outputs, raw materials, waste, quality control, costs, and techniques for maximizing the manufacture and distribution of goods. **Design:**

Knowledge of design techniques, principles, tools and instruments involved in the production and use of precision technical plans, blueprints, drawings, and models. **Education and Training:** Knowledge of instructional methods and training techniques including curriculum design principles, learning theory, group and individual teaching techniques, design of individual development plans, and test design principles. **Fine Arts:** Knowledge of theory and techniques required to produce, compose, and perform works of music, dance, visual arts, drama, and sculpture.

Commercial and Industrial Designers

Develop and design manufactured products, such as cars, home appliances, and children's toys. Combine artistic talent with research on product use, marketing, and materials, to create the most functional and appealing product design. Confers with engineering, marketing, production, or sales department, or with customer, to establish design concepts for manufactured products. Integrates findings and concepts and sketches design ideas. Prepares detailed drawings, illustrations, artwork, or blueprints, using drawing instruments or paints and brushes. Designs packaging and containers for products, such as foods, beverages, toiletries, or medicines. Evaluates design ideas for feasibility based on factors such as appearance, function, serviceability, budget, production costs/methods, and market characteristics. Creates and designs graphic material for use as ornamentation, illustration, or advertising on manufactured materials and packaging. Presents design to customer or design committee for approval and discusses need for modification. Modifies design to conform with customer specifications, production limitations, or changes in design trends. Reads publications, attends showings, and studies traditional, period, and contemporary design styles and motifs to obtain perspective and design concepts. Directs and coordinates preparation of detailed drawings from sketches or fabrication of models or samples. Fabricates model or sample in paper, wood, glass, fabric, plastic, or metal, using hand and power tools. Prepares itemized production requirements to produce item.

Occupational Type

Artistic occupations frequently involve working with forms, designs, and patterns. They often require self-expression and the work can be done without following a clear set of rules.

Skills required of Commercial and Industrial Designers

Reading Comprehension, Active Listening, Speaking, Critical Thinking, Active Learning, Monitoring, Social Perceptiveness, Coordination, Persuasion, Negotiation, Instructing, Service Orientation, Information Organization, Synthesis/Reorganization, Idea Generation, Idea Evaluation, Implementation Planning, Operations Analysis, Technology Design, Equipment Selection, Programming, Visioning, Identifying Downstream Consequences, Identification of Key Causes, Judgment and Decision Making, Systems Evaluation, Time Management, Management of Financial Resources

College Majors

Home Furnishings and Equipment Installers and Consultants: An instructional program that generally prepares individuals to assist in the entire spectrum of home furnishings and decorations. Includes instruction in selecting, purchasing, designing, and decorating; home furnishings and equipment; floral design; accessory construction; textiles; and upholstery.

Supporting Courses

Sales and Marketing: Knowledge of principles and methods involved in showing, promoting, and selling products or services. This includes marketing strategies and tactics, product demonstration and sales techniques, and sales control systems. **Production and Processing:** Knowledge of inputs, outputs, raw materials, waste, quality control, costs, and techniques for maximizing the manufacture and distribution of goods. **Design:** Knowledge of design techniques, principles, tools and instruments involved in the production and use of precision technical plans, blueprints, drawings, and models. **Education and Training:** Knowledge of instructional methods and training techniques including curriculum design principles, learning theory, group and individual teaching techniques, design of individual development plans, and test design principles. **Fine Arts:** Knowledge of theory and techniques required to produce, compose, and perform works of music, dance, visual arts, drama, and sculpture. **History and Archeology:** Knowledge of past historical events and their causes, indicators, and impact on particular civilizations and cultures.

Set Designers

Design sets for theatrical, motion picture, and television productions. Integrates requirements including script, research, budget, and available locations to develop design. Prepares rough draft and scale working drawings of sets, including floor plans, scenery, and properties to be constructed. Presents drawings for approval and makes changes and corrections as directed. Designs and builds scale models of set design or miniature sets used in filming backgrounds or special effects. Selects furniture, draperies, pictures, lamps, and rugs for decorative quality and appearance. Researches and consults experts to determine architectural and furnishing styles to depict given periods or locations. Confers with heads of production and direction to establish budget and schedules, and to discuss design ideas. Estimates costs of design materials and construction, or rental of location or props. Directs and coordinates set construction, erection, or decoration activities to ensure conformance to design, budget, and schedule requirements. Reads script to determine location, set, or decoration requirements. Examines dressed set to ensure props and scenery do not interfere with movements of cast or view of camera. Assigns staff to complete design ideas and prepare sketches, illustrations, and detailed drawings of sets, or graphics and animation.

Occupational Type

Artistic occupations frequently involve working with forms, designs, and patterns. They often require self-expression and the work can be done without following a clear set of rules.

Skills required of Set Designers

Active Listening, Speaking, Critical Thinking, Active Learning, Monitoring, Social Perceptiveness, Coordination, Persuasion, Negotiation, Information Gathering, Synthesis/

Reorganization, Idea Generation, Implementation Planning, Operations Analysis, Technology Design, Equipment Selection, Product Inspection, Visioning, Identification of Key Causes, Systems Evaluation, Time Management, Management of Financial Resources, Management of Material Resources, Management of Personnel Resources

College Majors

Interior Design: An instructional program in the applied visual arts that prepares individuals to apply artistic principles and techniques to the professional planning, designing, equipping, and furnishing residential and commercial interior spaces. Includes instruction in drafting and graphic techniques; principles of interior lighting, acoustics, systems integration, and color coordination; furniture and furnishings; textiles and their finishing; the history of interior design and period styles; basic structural design; building codes and inspection regulations; and applications to office, hotel, factory, restaurant and housing design.

Supporting Courses

Design: Knowledge of design techniques, principles, tools and instruments involved in the production and use of precision technical plans, blueprints, drawings, and models. **Building and Construction:** Knowledge of materials, methods, and the appropriate tools to construct objects, structures, and buildings. **Geography:** Knowledge of various methods for describing the location and distribution of land, sea, and air masses including their physical locations, relationships, and characteristics. **Fine Arts:** Knowledge of theory and techniques required to produce, compose, and perform works of music, dance, visual arts, drama, and sculpture. **History and Archeology:** Knowledge of past historical events and their causes, indicators, and impact on particular civilizations and cultures. **Communications and Media:** Knowledge of media production, communication, and dissemination techniques and methods including alternative ways to inform and entertain via written, oral, and visual media.

Exhibit Designers

Plan, design, and oversee construction and installation of permanent and temporary exhibits and displays. Prepares preliminary drawings of proposed exhibit, including detailed construction, layout, material specifications, or special effects diagrams. Designs display to decorate streets, fairgrounds, buildings, or other places for celebrations, using paper, cloth, plastic, or other materials. Designs, draws, paints, or sketches backgrounds and fixtures for use in windows or interior displays. Oversees preparation of artwork, construction of exhibit components, and placement of collection to ensure intended interpretation of concepts and conformance to specifications. Confers with client or staff regarding theme, interpretative or informational purpose, planned location, budget, materials, or promotion. Submits plans for approval, and adapts plan to serve intended purpose or to conform to budget or fabrication restrictions. Arranges for acquisition of specimens or graphics, or building of exhibit structures by outside contractors to complete exhibit. Inspects installed exhibit for conformance to specifications and satisfactory operation of special effects components.

Occupational Type

Artistic occupations frequently involve working with forms, designs, and patterns. They often require self-expression and the work can be done without following a clear set of rules.

 Skills required of Exhibit Designers

Social Perceptiveness, Coordination, Persuasion, Negotiation, Service Orientation, Information Organization, Synthesis/Reorganization, Idea Evaluation, Implementation Planning, Operations Analysis, Installation, Visioning, Identification of Key Causes, Systems Evaluation, Time Management, Management of Financial Resources, Management of Material Resources, Management of Personnel Resources

 College Majors

Home Furnishings and Equipment Installers and Consultants: An instructional program that generally prepares individuals to assist in the entire spectrum of home furnishings and decorations. Includes instruction in selecting, purchasing, designing, and decorating; home furnishings and equipment; floral design; accessory construction; textiles; and upholstery.

Supporting Courses

Sales and Marketing: Knowledge of principles and methods involved in showing, promoting, and selling products or services. This includes marketing strategies and tactics, product demonstration and sales techniques, and sales control systems. **Customer and Personal Service:** Knowledge of principles and processes for providing customer and personal services including needs assessment techniques, quality service standards, alternative delivery systems, and customer satisfaction evaluation techniques. **Computers and Electronics:** Knowledge of electric circuit boards, processors, chips, and computer hardware and software, including applications and programming. **Design:** Knowledge of design techniques, principles, tools and instruments involved in the production and use of precision technical plans, blueprints, drawings, and models. **Building and Construction:** Knowledge of materials, methods, and the appropriate tools to construct objects, structures, and buildings. **Fine Arts:** Knowledge of theory and techniques required to produce, compose, and perform works of music, dance, visual arts, drama, and sculpture.

Art Directors

Formulate design concepts and presentation approaches, and direct workers engaged in artwork, layout design, and copy writing for visual communications media, such as magazines, books, newspapers, and packaging. Assigns and directs staff members to develop design concepts into art layouts or prepare layouts for printing. Formulates basic layout design or presentation approach, and conceives material details, such as style and size of type, photographs, graphics, and arrangement. Reviews and approves art and copy materials developed by staff, and proofs of printed copy. Reviews illustrative material and confers with client concerning objectives, budget, background information, and presentation approaches, styles, and techniques. Confers with creative, art, copy writing, or production department heads to discuss client requirements, outline presentation concepts, and coordinate creative activities. Presents final layouts to client for approval. Prepares detailed storyboard showing sequence and timing of story development for television production. Writes typography instructions, such as margin widths and type sizes, and submits for typesetting or printing. Marks up, pastes, and completes layouts to prepare for printing. Draws custom illustrations for project.

Occupational Type

Artistic occupations frequently involve working with forms, designs, and patterns. They often require self-expression and the work can be done without following a clear set of rules.

Skills required of Art Directors

Active Listening, Speaking, Critical Thinking, Active Learning, Learning Strategies, Monitoring, Social Perceptiveness, Coordination, Persuasion, Negotiation, Service Orientation, Information Organization, Synthesis/Reorganization, Idea Generation, Idea Evaluation, Implementation Planning, Operations Analysis, Equipment Selection, Visioning, Systems Perception, Identifying Downstream Consequences, Identification of Key Causes, Systems Evaluation, Time Management, Management of Financial Resources, Management of Material Resources, Management of Personnel Resources

College Majors

Advertising: An instructional program that describes the creation, execution, transmission, and evaluation of commercial messages concerned with the promotion and sale of products and services, and that prepares individuals to function as advertising assistants, technicians, managers and executives. Includes instruction in advertising theory; marketing strategy; advertising copy/art, layout and production methods; and media relations.

Supporting Courses

Administration and Management: Knowledge of principles and processes involved in business and organizational planning, coordination, and execution. This includes strategic planning, resource allocation, manpower modeling, leadership techniques, and production methods. **Sales and Marketing:** Knowledge of principles and methods involved in showing, promoting, and selling products or services. This includes marketing strategies and tactics, product demonstration and sales techniques, and sales control systems. **Production and Processing:** Knowledge of inputs, outputs, raw materials, waste, quality control, costs, and techniques for maximizing the manufacture and distribution of goods. **Design:** Knowledge of design techniques, principles, tools and instruments involved in the production and use of precision technical plans, blueprints, drawings, and models. **Psychology:** Knowledge of human behavior and performance, mental processes, psychological research methods, and the assessment and treatment of behavioral and affective disorders. **Fine Arts:**

Knowledge of theory and techniques required to produce, compose, and perform works of music, dance, visual arts, drama, and sculpture. **Communications and Media:** Knowledge of media production, communication, and dissemination techniques and methods including alternative ways to inform and entertain via written, oral, and visual media.

Floral Designers

Design and fashion live, cut, dried, and artificial floral and foliar arrangements for events, such as holidays, anniversaries, weddings, balls, and funerals. Plans arrangement according to client's requirements, utilizing knowledge of design and properties of materials, or selects appropriate standard design pattern. Selects flora and foliage for arrangement. Trims material and arranges bouquets, wreaths, terrariums, and other items using trimmers, shapers, wire, pin, floral tape, foam, and other materials. Confers with client regarding price and type of arrangement desired. Decorates buildings, halls, churches, or other facilities where events are planned. Packs and wraps completed arrangements. Estimates costs and prices arrangements. Conducts classes, demonstrations, or trains other workers.

 ### Occupational Type

Artistic occupations frequently involve working with forms, designs, and patterns. They often require self-expression and the work can be done without following a clear set of rules.

 ### Skills required of Floral Designers

Negotiation, Service Orientation, Management of Financial Resources, Management of Material Resources

 ### College Majors

Floristry Marketing Operations: An instructional program that prepares individual to perform marketing tasks specifically applicable to the floristry industry.

 ### Supporting Courses

Customer and Personal Service: Knowledge of principles and processes for providing customer and personal services including needs assessment techniques, quality service standards, alternative delivery systems, and customer satisfaction evaluation techniques. **Fine Arts:** Knowledge of theory and techniques required to produce, compose, and perform works of music, dance, visual arts, drama, and sculpture.

Merchandise Displayers and Window Trimmers

Plan and erect commercial displays, such as those in windows and interiors of retail stores and at trade exhibitions. Constructs or assembles prefabricated display properties from fabric, glass, paper, and plastic, using hand tools and woodworking power tools, according to specifications. Originates ideas for merchandise display or window decoration. Develops layout and selects theme, lighting, colors, and props to be used. Prepares sketches or floor plans of proposed displays. Installs booths, exhibits, displays, carpets, and drapes, as guided by floor plan of building and specifications. Consults with advertising and sales staff to determine type of merchandise to be featured and time and place for each display. Cuts out designs on cardboard, hardboard, and plywood, according to motif of event. Arranges properties, furniture, merchandise, backdrop, and other accessories, as shown in prepared sketch. Installs decorations, such as flags, banners, festive lights, and bunting, on or in building, street, exhibit hall, or booth. Places price and descriptive signs on backdrop, fixtures, merchandise, or floor. Dresses mannequins for use in displays.

Occupational Type

Artistic occupations frequently involve working with forms, designs, and patterns. They often require self-expression and the work can be done without following a clear set of rules.

Skills required of Merchandise Displayers and Window Trimmers

Idea Generation, Idea Evaluation, Installation

College Majors

Home Furnishings and Equipment Installers and Consultants: An instructional program that generally prepares individuals to assist in the entire spectrum of home furnishings and decorations. Includes instruction in selecting, purchasing, designing, and decorating; home furnishings and equipment; floral design; accessory construction; textiles; and upholstery.

Supporting Courses

Sales and Marketing: Knowledge of principles and methods involved in showing, promoting, and selling products or services. This includes marketing strategies and tactics, product demonstration and sales techniques, and sales control systems. **Design:** Knowledge of design techniques, principles, tools and instruments involved in the production and use of precision technical plans, blueprints, drawings, and models. **Sociology and Anthropology:** Knowledge of group behavior and dynamics, societal trends and influences, cultures, their history, migrations, ethnicity, and origins. **Fine Arts:** Knowledge of theory and techniques required to produce, compose, and perform works of music, dance, visual arts, drama, and sculpture. **Communications and Media:** Knowledge of media production, communication, and dissemination techniques and methods including alternative ways to inform and entertain via written, oral, and visual media.

DIETITIANS AND NUTRITIONISTS

Dietitians and Nutritionists

Education		Bachelor's degree
Average Yearly Earnings		$32,406
Projected Growth		18%
Annual Job Openings		4,079
Self-employed		16%
Employed Part-time		29%

Organize, plan, and conduct food service or nutritional programs to assist in promotion of health and control of disease. May administer activities of department providing quantity food service. May plan, organize, and conduct programs in nutritional research. Develops and implements dietary-care plans based on assessments of nutritional needs, diet restrictions, and other current health plans. Consults with physicians and healthcare personnel to determine nutritional needs and diet restrictions of patients or clients. Instructs patients and their families in nutritional principles, dietary plans, and food selection and preparation. Monitors food service operations and ensures conformance to nutritional and quality standards. Plans, organizes, and conducts training programs in dietetics, nutrition, and institutional management and administration for medical students and hospital personnel. Supervises activities of workers engaged in planning, preparing, and serving meals. Evaluates nutritional care plans and provides follow-up on continuity of care. Plans, conducts, and evaluates dietary, nutritional, and epidemiological research, and analyzes findings for practical applications. Inspects meals served for conformance to prescribed diets and standards of palatability and appearance. Develops curriculum and prepares manuals, visual aids, course outlines, and other materials used in teaching. Writes research reports and other publications to document and communicate research findings. Plans and prepares grant proposals to request program funding. Confers with design, building, and equipment personnel to plan for construction and remodeling of food service units.

 ## Occupational Type

Investigative occupations frequently involve working with ideas, and require an extensive amount of thinking. These occupations can involve searching for facts and figuring out problems mentally.

 ## Skills required of Dietitians and Nutritionists

Reading Comprehension, Active Listening, Writing, Speaking, Science, Critical Thinking, Active Learning, Learning Strategies, Monitoring, Social Perceptiveness, Coordination, Persuasion, Negotiation, Instructing, Service Orientation, Problem Identification, Information Gathering, Information Organization, Synthesis/Reorganization, Idea Generation, Idea Evaluation, Implementation Planning, Operations Analysis, Programming, Visioning, Systems Perception, Identifying Downstream Consequences, Identification of Key Causes, Judgment and Decision Making, Systems Evaluation, Time Management, Management of Financial Resources, Management of Material Resources, Management of Personnel Resources

 ## College Majors

Foods and Nutrition Studies, General: An instructional program that generally describes the study of the role of food and nutrition in individual and family health and wellness, and in the study of food production, preparation and service operations. Includes instruction in food product consumption, nutritional care and education, and the organization and administration of food systems.

 ## Supporting Courses

Food Production: Knowledge of techniques and equipment for planting, growing, and harvesting of food for consumption including crop rotation methods, animal husbandry, and food storage/handling techniques. **Computers and Electronics:** Knowledge of electric

circuit boards, processors, chips, and computer hardware and software, including applications and programming. **Chemistry:** Knowledge of the composition, structure, and properties of substances and of the chemical processes and transformations that they undergo. This includes uses of chemicals and their interactions, danger signs, production techniques, and disposal methods. **Biology:** Knowledge of plant and animal living tissue, cells, organisms, and entities, including their functions, interdependencies, and interactions with each other and the environment. **Psychology:** Knowledge of human behavior and performance, mental processes, psychological research methods, and the assessment and treatment of behavioral and affective disorders. **Medicine and Dentistry:** Knowledge of the information and techniques needed to diagnose and treat injuries, diseases, and deformities. This includes symptoms, treatment alternatives, drug properties and interactions, and preventive healthcare measures. **Education and Training:** Knowledge of instructional methods and training techniques including curriculum design principles, learning theory, group and individual teaching techniques, design of individual development plans, and test design principles. **English Language:** Knowledge of the structure and content of the English language including the meaning and spelling of words, rules of composition, and grammar. **History and Archeology:** Knowledge of past historical events and their causes, indicators, and impact on particular civilizations and cultures.

DIRECTOR OF RELIGIOUS EDUCATION AND ACTIVITIES

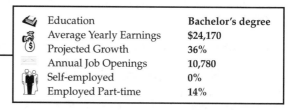

Education		Bachelor's degree
Average Yearly Earnings		$24,170
Projected Growth		36%
Annual Job Openings		10,780
Self-employed		0%
Employed Part-time		14%

Directors, Religious Activities and Education

Direct and coordinate activities of a denominational group to meet religious needs of students. Plan, organize, and direct church school programs designed to promote religious education among church membership. Provide counseling and guidance relative to marital, health, financial, and religious problems. Coordinates activities with religious advisers, councils, and university officials to meet religious needs of students. Counsels individuals regarding marital, health, financial, and religious problems. Plans congregational activities and projects to encourage participation in religious education programs. Develops, organizes, and directs study courses and religious education programs within congregation. Supervises instructional staff in religious education program. Promotes student participation in extracurricular congregational activities. Assists and advises groups in promoting interfaith understanding. Plans and conducts conferences dealing with interpretation of religious ideas and convictions. Solicits support, participation, and interest in religious education programs from congregation members, organizations, officials, and clergy. Analyzes member participation and changes in congregation emphasis to determine needs for religious education. Interprets policies of university to community religious workers. Interprets religious education to public through speaking, leading discussions, and writing articles for local and national publications. Analyzes revenue and program cost data to determine budget priorities. Orders and distributes school supplies.

Occupational Type

Social occupations frequently involve working with, communicating with, and teaching people. These occupations often involve helping or providing service to others.

Skills required of Directors, Religious Activities and Education

Reading Comprehension, Active Listening, Writing, Speaking, Critical Thinking, Learning Strategies, Monitoring, Social Perceptiveness, Coordination, Persuasion, Instructing, Service Orientation, Idea Evaluation, Implementation Planning, Visioning, Systems Perception, Identifying Downstream Consequences, Identification of Key Causes, Judgment and Decision Making, Systems Evaluation, Time Management, Management of Financial Resources, Management of Material Resources, Management of Personnel Resources

College Majors

Bible/Biblical Studies: An instructional program that describes the study of the Bible and its component books from the standpoint of the Christian or Jewish faiths, with an emphasis on understanding and interpreting the theological, doctrinal, and ethical messages contained within it. May include preparation for applying these studies in various church-related vocations.

Supporting Courses

Administration and Management: Knowledge of principles and processes involved in business and organizational planning, coordination, and execution. This includes strategic planning, resource allocation, manpower modeling, leadership techniques, and production methods. **Economics and Accounting:** Knowledge of economic and accounting principles and practices, the financial markets, banking, and the analysis and reporting of financial data. **Psychology:** Knowledge of human behavior and performance, mental processes, psychological research methods, and the assessment and treatment of behavioral and affective disorders. **Sociology and Anthropology:** Knowledge of group behavior and dynamics, societal trends and influences, cultures, their history, migrations, ethnicity, and origins. **Therapy and Counseling:** Knowledge of information and techniques needed to rehabilitate physical and mental ailments and to provide career guidance including alternative treatments, rehabilitation equipment and its proper use, and methods to evaluate treatment effects. **Education and Training:** Knowledge of instructional methods and training techniques including curriculum design principles, learning theory, group and individual teaching techniques, design of individual development plans, and test design principles. **English Language:** Knowledge of the structure and content of the English language including the meaning and spelling of words, rules of composition, and grammar. **Philosophy and Theology:** Knowledge of different philosophical systems and religions, including their basic principles, values, ethics, ways of thinking, customs, and practices, and their impact on human culture. **Communications and Media:** Knowledge of media production, communication, and dissemination techniques and methods including alternative ways to inform and entertain via written, oral, and visual media.

All Other Religious Workers

All other religious workers not classified separately above.

 ## Occupational Type

Specific information is not available.

 ## Skills required of All Other Religious Workers

Information on specific skills required is not available.

 ## College Majors

Religious Education: An instructional program that describes the theory and practice of providing educational services to members of faith communities, within the context of a particular religion, and that prepares individuals to serve as religious educators. Includes instruction in planning and teaching lessons; organizing and supervising instructional activities; designing and developing instructional materials; and administering religious education programs and facilities.

 ## Supporting Courses

No specific courses for this occupation.

ECONOMISTS

Economists

Education	Bachelor's degree
Average Yearly Earnings	$50,544
Projected Growth	19%
Annual Job Openings	11,343
Self-employed	21%
Employed Part-time	9%

Conduct research, prepare reports, or formulate plans to aid in solution of economic problems arising from production and distribution of goods and services. May collect and process economic and statistical data using econometric and sampling techniques. (Excludes market research analysts.) Studies economic and statistical data in area of specialization, such as finance, labor, or agriculture. Reviews and analyzes data to prepare reports, to forecast future marketing trends, and to stay abreast of economic changes. Organizes research data into report format, including graphic illustrations of research findings. Compiles data relating to research area, such as employment, productivity, and wages and hours. Formulates recommendations, policies, or plans to interpret markets or solve economic problems. Devises methods and procedures for collecting and processing data, using various econometric and sampling techniques. Develops economic guidelines and standards in preparing points of view used in forecasting trends and formulating economic policy. Supervises research projects and students' study projects. Provides advice and consultation to business and public and private agencies. Testifies at regulatory or legislative hearings to present recommendations. Teaches theories, principles, and methods of economics. Assigns work to staff.

Occupational Type

Investigative occupations frequently involve working with ideas, and require an extensive amount of thinking. These occupations can involve searching for facts and figuring out problems mentally.

Skills required of Economists

Reading Comprehension, Active Listening, Writing, Speaking, Mathematics, Science, Critical Thinking, Active Learning, Learning Strategies, Monitoring, Social Perceptiveness, Coordination, Persuasion, Negotiation, Instructing, Service Orientation, Problem Identification, Information Gathering, Information Organization, Synthesis/Reorganization, Idea Generation, Idea Evaluation, Implementation Planning, Operations Analysis, Programming, Visioning, Systems Perception, Identifying Downstream Consequences, Identification of Key Causes, Judgment and Decision Making, Systems Evaluation, Time Management, Management of Financial Resources, Management of Material Resources, Management of Personnel Resources

College Majors

Agricultural Business and Management, General: An instructional program that generally prepares individuals to apply modern economic and business principles involved in the organization, operation, and management of farm and agricultural businesses.

Supporting Courses

Economics and Accounting: Knowledge of economic and accounting principles and practices, the financial markets, banking, and the analysis and reporting of financial data. **Personnel and Human Resources:** Knowledge of policies and practices involved in personnel/human resource functions. This includes recruitment, selection, training, and promotion regulations and procedures; compensation and benefits packages; labor relations and negotiation strategies; and personnel information systems. **Production and Processing:** Knowledge of inputs, outputs, raw materials, waste, quality control, costs, and techniques for maximizing the manufacture and distribution of goods. **Food Production:** Knowledge of techniques and equipment for planting, growing, and harvesting of food for consumption including crop rotation methods, animal husbandry, and food storage/handling techniques. **Computers and Electronics:** Knowledge of electric circuit boards, processors, chips, and computer hardware and software, including applications and programming. **Mathematics:** Knowledge of numbers, their operations, and interrelationships including arithmetic, algebra, geometry, calculus, statistics, and their applications. **Geography:** Knowledge of various methods for describing the location and distribution of land, sea, and air masses including their physical locations, relationships, and characteristics. **Education and Training:** Knowledge of instructional methods and training techniques including curriculum design principles, learning theory, group and individual teaching techniques, design of individual development plans, and test design principles. **History and Archeology:** Knowledge of past historical events and their causes, indicators, and impact on particular civilizations and cultures. **Philosophy and Theology:** Knowledge of different philosophical systems and religions, including their basic principles, values, ethics, ways of thinking, customs, and practices, and their impact on human culture. **Law, Government, and Jurisprudence:** Knowledge of laws, legal codes, court procedures, precedents, government regulations, executive orders, agency rules, and the democratic political process.

Market Research Analysts

Research market conditions in local, regional, or national areas to determine potential sales of a product or service. May gather information on competitors, prices, sales, and methods of marketing and distribution. May use survey results to create a marketing campaign based on regional preferences and buying habits. Examines and analyzes statistical data to forecast future marketing trends and to identify potential markets. Gathers data on competitors, and analyzes prices, sales, and method of marketing and distribution. Establishes research methodology and designs format for data gathering, such as surveys, opinion polls, or questionnaires. Collects data on customer preferences and buying habits. Checks consumer reaction to new or improved products or services. Prepares reports and graphic illustrations of findings. Attends staff conferences to submit findings and proposals to management for consideration. Translates complex numerical data into nontechnical, written text.

 ## Occupational Type

Investigative occupations frequently involve working with ideas, and require an extensive amount of thinking. These occupations can involve searching for facts and figuring out problems mentally.

 ## Skills required of Market Research Analysts

Reading Comprehension, Active Listening, Writing, Speaking, Mathematics, Critical Thinking, Active Learning, Learning Strategies, Monitoring, Social Perceptiveness, Persuasion, Information Gathering, Information Organization, Synthesis/Reorganization, Idea Generation, Idea Evaluation, Implementation Planning, Operations Analysis, Programming, Visioning, Systems Perception, Identifying Downstream Consequences, Identification of Key Causes, Systems Evaluation, Management of Material Resources

College Majors

Economics, General: An instructional program that generally describes the systematic study of the production, conservation and allocation of resources in conditions of scarcity, together with the organizational frameworks related to these processes. Includes instruction in economic theory, micro- and macroeconomics, comparative economic systems, money and banking systems, international economics, quantitative analytical methods, and applications to specific industries and public policy issues.

 ## Supporting Courses

Economics and Accounting: Knowledge of economic and accounting principles and practices, the financial markets, banking, and the analysis and reporting of financial data. **Sales and Marketing:** Knowledge of principles and methods involved in showing, promoting, and selling products or services. This includes marketing strategies and tactics, product demonstration and sales techniques, and sales control systems. **Customer and Personal Service:** Knowledge of principles and processes for providing customer and personal services including needs assessment techniques, quality service standards, alternative delivery systems, and customer satisfaction evaluation techniques. **Food Production:** Knowledge of techniques and equipment for planting, growing, and harvesting of food for consumption including crop rotation methods, animal husbandry, and food storage/handling techniques. **Computers and Electronics:** Knowledge of electric circuit boards, processors, chips, and computer hardware and software, including applications and programming. **Mathematics:** Knowledge of numbers, their operations, and interrelationships including arithmetic, algebra, geometry, calculus, statistics, and their applications. **Psychology:** Knowledge of human behavior and performance, mental processes, psychological research methods, and the assessment and treatment of behavioral and affective disorders. **Geography:** Knowledge of various methods for describing the location and distribution of land, sea, and air masses including their physical locations, relationships, and characteristics. **Philosophy and Theology:** Knowledge of different philosophical systems and religions, including their basic principles, values, ethics, ways of thinking, customs, and practices, and their impact on human culture.

EDUCATION ADMINISTRATORS

College and University Administrators

Education	Work experience, plus degree	
Average Yearly Earnings	$52,437	
Projected Growth	12%	
Annual Job Openings	39,332	
Self-employed	7%	
Employed Part-time	10%	

Plan, direct, and coordinate research and instructional programs at postsecondary institutions, including universities, colleges, and junior and community colleges. (Excludes college presidents.) Establishes operational policies and procedures and develops academic objectives. Directs work activities of personnel engaged in administration of academic institutions, departments, and alumni organizations. Meets with academic and administrative personnel to disseminate information, identify problems, monitor progress reports, and ensure adherence to goals and objectives. Evaluates personnel and physical plant operations, student programs, and statistical and research data to implement procedures or modifications to administrative policies. Advises staff and students on problems relating to policies, program administration, and financial and personal matters, and recommends solutions. Estimates and allocates department funding based on financial success of previous courses and other pertinent factors. Completes and submits operating budget for approval, controls expenditures, and maintains financial reports and records. Consults with staff, students, alumni, and subject experts to determine needs/feasibility, and to formulate admission policies and educational programs. Represents college/university as liaison officer with accrediting agencies and to exchange information between academic institutions and in community. Determines course schedules and correlates room assignments to ensure optimum use of buildings and equipment. Confers with other academic staff to explain admission requirements and transfer credit policies, and compares course equivalencies to university/college curriculum. Negotiates with foundation and industry representatives to secure loans for university and identify costs and materials for building construction. Recruits, employs, trains, and terminates department personnel. Reviews student misconduct reports requiring disciplinary action and counsels students to ensure conformance to university policies. Coordinates alumni functions and encourages alumni endorsement of recruiting and fundraising activities. Plans and promotes athletic policies, sports events, ticket sales, and student participation in social, cultural, and recreational activities. Assists faculty and staff to conduct orientation programs, teach classes, issue student transcripts, and prepare commencement lists. Audits financial status of student organization and facility accounts, and certifies income reports from event ticket sales. Advises student organizations, sponsors faculty activities, and arranges for caterers, entertainers, and decorators at scheduled events. Selects and counsels candidates for financial aid, and coordinates issuing and collecting of student aid payments.

Occupational Type

Enterprising occupations frequently involve starting up and carrying out projects. These occupations can involve leading people and making many decisions. Sometimes they involve risk taking and often deal with business.

Skills required of College and University Administrators

Reading Comprehension, Active Listening, Writing, Speaking, Mathematics, Critical Thinking, Active Learning, Learning Strategies, Monitoring, Social Perceptiveness, Coordination, Persuasion, Negotiation, Instructing, Service Orientation, Problem Identification, Information Gathering, Information Organization, Synthesis/Reorganization, Idea Generation, Idea Evaluation, Implementation Planning, Operations Analysis, Product Inspection, Visioning, Systems Perception, Identifying Downstream Consequences, Identification of Key Causes, Judgment and Decision Making, Systems Evaluation, Time Management, Management of Financial Resources, Management of Material Resources, Management of Personnel Resources

College Majors

Education, General: An instructional program that generally describes the theory and practice of learning and teaching; the basic principles of educational psychology; the art of

---

teaching; the planning and administration of educational activities; and the social foundations of education.

 ## Supporting Courses

Administration and Management: Knowledge of principles and processes involved in business and organizational planning, coordination, and execution. This includes strategic planning, resource allocation, manpower modeling, leadership techniques, and production methods. **Economics and Accounting:** Knowledge of economic and accounting principles and practices, the financial markets, banking, and the analysis and reporting of financial data. **Sales and Marketing:** Knowledge of principles and methods involved in showing, promoting, and selling products or services. This includes marketing strategies and tactics, product demonstration and sales techniques, and sales control systems. **Customer and Personal Service:** Knowledge of principles and processes for providing customer and personal services including needs assessment techniques, quality service standards, alternative delivery systems, and customer satisfaction evaluation techniques. **Personnel and Human Resources:** Knowledge of policies and practices involved in personnel/human resource functions. This includes recruitment, selection, training, and promotion regulations and procedures; compensation and benefits packages; labor relations and negotiation strategies; and personnel information systems. **Mathematics:** Knowledge of numbers, their operations, and interrelationships including arithmetic, algebra, geometry, calculus, statistics, and their applications. **Psychology:** Knowledge of human behavior and performance, mental processes, psychological research methods, and the assessment and treatment of behavioral and affective disorders. **Sociology and Anthropology:** Knowledge of group behavior and dynamics, societal trends and influences, cultures, their history, migrations, ethnicity, and origins. **Therapy and Counseling:** Knowledge of information and techniques needed to rehabilitate physical and mental ailments and to provide career guidance including alternative treatments, rehabilitation equipment and its proper use, and methods to evaluate treatment effects. **Education and Training:** Knowledge of instructional methods and training techniques including curriculum design principles, learning theory, group and individual teaching techniques, design of individual development plans, and test design principles. **English Language:** Knowledge of the structure and content of the English language including the meaning and spelling of words, rules of composition, and grammar. **Foreign Language:** Knowledge of the structure and content of a foreign (non-English) language including the meaning and spelling of words, rules of composition and grammar, and pronunciation. **History and Archeology:** Knowledge of past historical events and their causes, indicators, and impact on particular civilizations and cultures. **Philosophy and Theology:** Knowledge of different philosophical systems and religions, including their basic principles, values, ethics, ways of thinking, customs, and practices, and their impact on human culture. **Public Safety and Security:** Knowledge of weaponry, public safety, and security operations, rules, regulations, precautions, prevention, and the protection of people, data, and property. **Law, Government, and Jurisprudence:** Knowledge of laws, legal codes, court procedures, precedents, government regulations, executive orders, agency rules, and the democratic political process. **Communications and Media:** Knowledge of media production, communication, and dissemination techniques and methods including alternative ways to inform and entertain via written, oral, and visual media.

Educational Program Directors

Plan, develop, and administer programs to provide educational opportunities for students. Establishes program philosophy, plans, policies, and academic codes of ethics to maintain educational standards for student screening, placement, and training. Plans, directs, and monitors instructional methods and content for educational, vocational, or student activity programs. Reviews and approves new programs or recommends modifications to existing programs. Evaluates programs to determine effectiveness, efficiency, and utilization, and to ensure activities comply with Federal, state, and local regulations. Prepares and submits budget requests, or grant proposals to solicit program funding. Determines scope of educational program offerings, and prepares drafts of course schedules and descriptions to estimate staffing and facility requirements. Coordinates outreach activities with businesses, communities, and other institutions or organizations to identify educational needs and establish and coordinate programs. Collects and analyzes survey data, regulatory information, and demographic and employment trends to forecast enrollment patterns and curriculum changes. Directs and coordinates activities of teachers or administrators at daycare centers, schools, public agencies, and institutions. Determines allocations of funds for staff, supplies, materials, and equipment, and authorizes purchases. Organizes and directs committees of specialists, volunteers, and staff to provide technical and advisory assistance for programs. Plans and coordinates consumer research and educational services to assist organizations in product development and marketing. Recruits, hires, trains, and evaluates primary and supplemental staff, and recommends personnel actions for programs and services. Contacts and addresses commercial, community, or political groups to promote educational programs and services or to lobby for legislative changes. Writes articles, manuals, and other publications and assists in the distribution of promotional literature. Confers with parents and staff to discuss educational activities, policies, and student behavioral or learning problems. Counsels and provides guidance to students regarding personal, academic, or behavioral problems. Reviews and interprets government codes and develops programs to ensure facility safety, security, and maintenance. Completes, maintains, or assigns preparation of attendance, activity, planning, or personnel reports and records for officials and agencies. Teaches classes or courses to students.

Occupational Type

Social occupations frequently involve working with, communicating with, and teaching people. These occupations often involve helping or providing service to others.

Skills required of Educational Program Directors

Reading Comprehension, Active Listening, Writing, Speaking, Critical Thinking, Active Learning, Learning Strategies, Monitoring, Social Perceptiveness, Coordination, Persuasion, Negotiation, Instructing, Service Orientation, Problem Identification, Information Gathering, Information Organization, Synthesis/Reorganization, Idea Generation, Idea Evaluation, Implementation Planning, Operations Analysis, Visioning, Systems Perception, Identifying Downstream Consequences, Identification of Key Causes, Judgment and Decision Making, Systems Evaluation, Time Management, Management of Financial Resources, Management of Material Resources, Management of Personnel Resources

College Majors

Agricultural Extension: An instructional program that prepares individuals to provide referral, consulting, assistance and educational services to farmers and ranchers via local, state or Federal government agencies. Includes instruction in agricultural sciences, agricultural business operations, agricultural law and administrative regulations, public relations, and communications skills.

Supporting Courses

Administration and Management: Knowledge of principles and processes involved in business and organizational planning, coordination, and execution. This includes strategic planning, resource allocation, manpower modeling, leadership techniques, and production methods. **Clerical:** Knowledge of administrative and clerical procedures and systems such as word processing systems, filing and records management systems, stenography and transcription, forms design principles, and other office procedures and terminology. **Economics and Accounting:** Knowledge of economic and accounting principles and practices, the financial markets, banking, and the analysis and reporting of financial data. **Sales and Marketing:** Knowledge of principles and methods involved in showing, promoting, and selling products or services. This includes marketing strategies and tactics, product demonstration and sales techniques, and sales control systems. **Customer and Personal Service:** Knowledge of principles and processes for providing customer and personal services including needs assessment techniques, quality service standards, alternative delivery systems, and customer satisfaction evaluation techniques. **Personnel and Human Resources:** Knowledge of policies and practices involved in personnel/human resource functions. This includes recruitment, selection, training, and promotion regulations and procedures; compensation and benefits packages; labor relations and negotiation strategies; and personnel information systems. **Food Production:** Knowledge of techniques and equipment for planting, growing, and harvesting of food for consumption including crop rotation methods, animal husbandry, and food storage/handling techniques. **Mathematics:** Knowledge of numbers, their operations, and interrelationships including arithmetic, algebra, geometry, calculus, statistics, and their applications. **Psychology:** Knowledge of human behavior and performance, mental processes, psychological research methods, and the assessment and treatment of behavioral and affective disorders. **Sociology and Anthropology:** Knowledge of group behavior and dynamics, societal trends and influences, cultures, their history, migrations, ethnicity, and origins. **Therapy and Counseling:** Knowledge of information and techniques needed to rehabilitate physical and mental ailments and to provide career guidance including alternative treatments, rehabilitation equipment and its proper use, and methods to evaluate treatment effects. **Education and Training:** Knowledge of instructional methods and training techniques including curriculum design principles, learning theory, group and individual teaching techniques, design of individual development plans, and test design principles. **English Language:** Knowledge of the structure and content of the English language including the meaning and spelling of words, rules of composition, and grammar. **History and Archeology:** Knowledge of past historical events and their causes, indicators, and impact on particular civilizations and cultures. **Philosophy and Theology:** Knowledge of different philosophical systems and religions, including their basic principles, values, ethics, ways of thinking, customs, and practices, and their impact on human culture. **Public Safety and Security:** Knowledge of weaponry, public safety, and security operations, rules, regulations, precautions, prevention, and the protection of people, data, and property. **Law, Government, and Jurisprudence:** Knowledge of laws, legal codes, court procedures, precedents, government regulations, executive orders, agency rules, and the democratic political process. **Telecommunications:** Knowledge of transmission, broadcasting, switching, control, and operation of telecommunications systems. **Communications and Media:** Knowledge of media production, communication, and dissemination techniques and methods including alternative ways to inform and entertain via written, oral, and visual media.

Instructional Coordinators

Develop instructional material, educational content, and instructional methods to provide guidelines to educators and instructors for developing curricula, conducting courses, and incorporating current technology. Researches, evaluates, and prepares recommendations on curricula, instructional methods, and materials for school system. Develops tests, questionnaires, and procedures to measure effectiveness of curriculum and to determine if program objectives are being met. Prepares or approves manuals, guidelines, and reports on state educational policies and practices for distribution to school districts. Orders or authorizes purchase of instructional materials, supplies, equipment, and visual aids designed to meet educational needs of students. Confers with school officials, teachers, and administrative staff to plan and develop curricula and establish guidelines for educational programs. Confers with educational committees and advisory groups to gather information on instructional methods and materials related to specific academic subjects. Advises teaching and administrative staff in assessment, curriculum development, management of student behavior, and use of materials and equipment. Observes, evaluates, and recommends changes in work of teaching staff to strengthen teaching skills in classroom. Plans, conducts, and evaluates training programs and conferences for teachers to study new classroom procedures, instructional materials, and teaching aids. Advises school officials on implementation of state and Federal programs and procedures. Conducts or participates in workshops, committees, and conferences designed to promote intellectual, social, and physical welfare of students. Coordinates activities of workers engaged in cataloging, distributing, and maintaining educational materials and equipment in curriculum library and laboratory. Interprets and enforces provisions of state education codes and rules and regulations of state board of education. Prepares or assists in preparation of grant proposals, budgets, and program policies and goals. Addresses public audiences to explain and elicit support for program objectives. Recruits, interviews, and recommends hiring of teachers. Reviews student files and confers with educators, parents, and other concerned parties to decide student placement and provision of services. Inspects and authorizes repair of instructional equipment, such as musical instruments.

Occupational Type

Social occupations frequently involve working with, communicating with, and teaching people. These occupations often involve helping or providing service to others.

Skills required of Instructional Coordinators

Reading Comprehension, Active Listening, Writing, Speaking, Critical Thinking, Active Learning, Learning Strategies, Monitoring, Social Perceptiveness, Coordination, Persuasion, Negotiation, Instructing, Information Gathering, Information Organization, Synthesis/Reorganization, Idea Generation, Idea Evaluation, Implementation Planning, Operations Analysis, Equipment Selection, Visioning, Systems Perception, Identifying Downstream Consequences, Identification of Key Causes, Judgment and Decision Making, Systems Evaluation, Time Management, Management of Financial Resources, Management of Material Resources, Management of Personnel Resources

College Majors

Education, General: An instructional program that generally describes the theory and practice of learning and teaching; the basic principles of educational psychology; the art of teaching; the planning and administration of educational activities; and the social foundations of education.

Supporting Courses

Administration and Management: Knowledge of principles and processes involved in business and organizational planning, coordination, and execution. This includes strategic planning, resource allocation, manpower modeling, leadership techniques, and production methods. **Economics and Accounting:** Knowledge of economic and accounting principles and practices, the financial markets, banking, and the analysis and reporting of financial data. **Sales and Marketing:** Knowledge of principles and methods involved in showing, promoting, and selling products or services. This includes marketing strategies and tactics, product demonstration and sales techniques, and sales control systems. **Personnel and Human Resources:** Knowledge of policies and practices involved in personnel/human resource functions. This includes recruitment, selection, training, and promotion regulations and procedures; compensation and benefits packages; labor relations and negotiation strategies; and personnel information systems. **Psychology:** Knowledge of human behavior and performance, mental processes, psychological research methods, and the assessment and treatment of behavioral and affective disorders. **Sociology and Anthropology:** Knowledge of group behavior and dynamics, societal trends and influences, cultures, their history, migrations, ethnicity, and origins. **Therapy and Counseling:** Knowledge of information and techniques needed to rehabilitate physical and mental ailments and to provide career guidance including alternative treatments, rehabilitation equipment and its proper use, and methods to evaluate treatment effects. **Education and Training:** Knowledge of instructional methods and training techniques including curriculum design principles, learning theory, group and individual teaching techniques, design of individual development plans, and test design principles. **English Language:** Knowledge of the structure and content of the English language including the meaning and spelling of words, rules of composition, and grammar. **Foreign Language:** Knowledge of the structure and content of a foreign (non-English) language including the meaning and spelling of words, rules of composition and grammar, and pronunciation. **Fine Arts:** Knowledge of theory and techniques required to produce, compose, and perform works of music, dance, visual arts, drama, and sculpture. **History and Archeology:** Knowledge of past historical events and their causes, indicators, and impact on particular civilizations and cultures. **Philosophy and Theology:** Knowledge of different philosophical systems and religions, including their basic principles, values, ethics, ways of thinking, customs, and practices, and their impact on human culture. **Law, Government, and Jurisprudence:** Knowledge of laws, legal codes, court procedures, precedents, government regulations, executive orders, agency rules, and the democratic political process. **Communications and Media:** Knowledge of media production, communication, and dissemination techniques and methods including alternative ways to inform and entertain via written, oral, and visual media.

ELECTRICAL AND ELECTRONIC TECHNICIANS

Education	Associate degree
Average Yearly Earnings	$33,800
Projected Growth	15%
Annual Job Openings	31,145
Self-employed	0%
Employed Part-time	3%

ELECTRICAL AND ELECTRONICS ENGINEERS

Education	Bachelor's degree
Average Yearly Earnings	$53,227
Projected Growth	29%
Annual Job Openings	19,098
Self-employed	3%
Employed Part-time	3%

Electrical Engineers

Design, develop, test, or supervise the manufacturing and installation of electrical equipment, components, or systems for commercial, industrial, military, or scientific use. (Excludes computer engineers.) Designs electrical instruments, equipment, facilities, components, products, and systems for commercial, industrial, and domestic purposes. Plans and implements research methodology and procedures to apply principles of electrical theory to engineering projects. Prepares and studies technical drawings, specifications of electrical systems, and topographical maps to ensure installation and operations conform to standards and customer requirements. Develops applications of controls, instruments, and systems for new commercial, domestic, and industrial uses. Directs operations and coordinates manufacturing, construction, installation, maintenance, and testing activities to ensure compliance with specifications, applicable codes, and customer requirements. Plans layout of electric power-generating plants and distribution lines and stations. Conducts field surveys and studies maps, graphs, diagrams, and other data to identify and correct power system problems. Performs detailed calculations to compute and establish manufacturing, construction, and installation standards and specifications. Confers with engineers, customers, and others to discuss existing or potential engineering projects and products. Inspects completed installations and observes operations for conformance to design and equipment specifications, and operational and safety standards. Evaluates and analyzes data regarding electric power systems and stations, and recommends changes to improve operating efficiency. Estimates labor, material, and construction costs, and prepares specifications for purchase of materials and equipment. Collects data relating to commercial and residential development, population, and power system interconnection to determine operating efficiency of electrical systems. Compiles data and writes reports regarding existing and potential engineering studies and projects. Operates computer-assisted engineering and design software and equipment to perform engineering tasks. Investigates customer or public complaints, determines nature and extent of problem, and recommends remedial measures.

Occupational Type

Investigative occupations frequently involve working with ideas, and require an extensive amount of thinking. These occupations can involve searching for facts and figuring out problems mentally.

Skills required of Electrical Engineers

Reading Comprehension, Active Listening, Writing, Speaking, Mathematics, Science, Critical Thinking, Active Learning, Learning Strategies, Problem Identification, Information Gathering, Information Organization, Synthesis/Reorganization, Idea Generation, Idea Evaluation, Implementation Planning, Operations Analysis, Technology Design, Equipment Selection, Programming, Testing, Operation Monitoring, Troubleshooting, Visioning, Systems Perception, Identifying Downstream Consequences, Identification of Key Causes, Judgment and Decision Making, Systems Evaluation, Management of Financial Resources, Management of Material Resources

College Majors

Electrical, Electronics, and Communications Engineering: An instructional program that prepares individuals to apply mathematical and scientific principles to the design, development and operational evaluation of electrical, electronic and related communications systems and their components, including electrical power generation systems; and the analysis of problems such as superconduction, wave propagation, energy storage and retrieval, and reception and amplification.

Supporting Courses

Administration and Management: Knowledge of principles and processes involved in business and organizational planning, coordination, and execution. This includes strategic planning, resource allocation, manpower modeling, leadership techniques, and production methods. **Economics and Accounting:** Knowledge of economic and accounting principles and practices, the financial markets, banking, and the analysis and reporting of financial data. **Production and Processing:** Knowledge of inputs, outputs, raw materials, waste, quality control, costs, and techniques for maximizing the manufacture and distribution of goods. **Computers and Electronics:** Knowledge of electric circuit boards, processors, chips, and computer hardware and software, including applications and programming.

Engineering and Technology: Knowledge of equipment, tools, mechanical devices, and their uses to produce motion, light, power, technology, and other applications. **Design:** Knowledge of design techniques, principles, tools and instruments involved in the production and use of precision technical plans, blueprints, drawings, and models. **Building and Construction:** Knowledge of materials, methods, and the appropriate tools to construct objects, structures, and buildings. **Mechanical:** Knowledge of machines and tools, including their designs, uses, benefits, repair, and maintenance. **Mathematics:** Knowledge of numbers, their operations, and interrelationships including arithmetic, algebra, geometry, calculus, statistics, and their applications. **Physics:** Knowledge and prediction of physical principles, laws, and applications including air, water, material dynamics, light, atomic principles, heat, electric theory, earth formations, and meteorological and related natural phenomena. **Public Safety and Security:** Knowledge of weaponry, public safety, and security operations, rules, regulations, precautions, prevention, and the protection of people, data, and property. **Telecommunications:** Knowledge of transmission, broadcasting, switching, control, and operation of telecommunications systems.

Electronics Engineers, Except Computer

Research, design, develop, and test electronic components and systems for commercial, industrial, military, or scientific use, utilizing knowledge of electronic theory and materials properties. Design electronic circuits and components for use in fields such as telecommunications, aerospace guidance and propulsion control, acoustics, or instruments and controls. (Excludes computer hardware engineers.) Designs electronic components, products, and systems for commercial, industrial, medical, military, and scientific applications. Develops operational, maintenance, and testing procedures for electronic products, components, equipment, and systems. Plans and develops applications and modifications for electronic properties used in components, products, and systems, to improve technical performance. Plans and implements research, methodology, and procedures to apply principles of electronic theory to engineering projects. Directs and coordinates activities concerned with manufacture, construction, installation, maintenance, operation, and modification of electronic equipment, products, and systems. Evaluates operational systems and recommends repair or design modifications based on factors such as environment, service, cost, and system capabilities. Analyzes system requirements, capacity, cost, and customer needs to determine feasibility of project and to develop system plan. Conducts studies to gather information regarding current services, equipment capacities, traffic data, and acquisition and installation costs. Inspects electronic equipment, instruments, products, and systems to ensure conformance to specifications, safety standards, and applicable codes and regulations. Prepares engineering sketches and specifications for construction, relocation, and installation of transmitting and receiving equipment, facilities, products, and systems. Confers with engineers, customers, and others to discuss existing and potential engineering projects or products. Operates computer-assisted engineering and design software and equipment to perform engineering tasks. Provides technical assistance to field and laboratory staff regarding equipment standards and problems, and applications of transmitting and receiving methods. Prepares, reviews, and maintains maintenance schedules and operational reports and charts. Reviews or prepares budget and cost estimates for equipment, construction, and installation projects, and controls expenditures. Determines material and equipment needs, and orders supplies. Investigates causes of personal injury resulting from contact with high-voltage communications equipment.

Occupational Type

Investigative occupations frequently involve working with ideas, and require an extensive amount of thinking. These occupations can involve searching for facts and figuring out problems mentally.

Skills required of Electronics Engineers, Except Computer

Reading Comprehension, Writing, Mathematics, Science, Critical Thinking, Active Learning, Problem Identification, Information Gathering, Idea Generation, Idea Evaluation, Operations Analysis, Technology Design, Equipment Selection, Programming, Operation Monitoring, Visioning, Systems Perception, Identifying Downstream Consequences, Identification of Key Causes, Judgment and Decision Making, Systems Evaluation, Management of Financial Resources, Management of Material Resources

College Majors

Computer Engineering: An instructional program that prepares individuals to apply mathematical and scientific principles to the design, development and operational evaluation of computer hardware and software systems and related equipment and facilities; and the analysis of specific problems of computer applications to various tasks.

Supporting Courses

Administration and Management: Knowledge of principles and processes involved in business and organizational planning, coordination, and execution. This includes strategic planning, resource allocation, manpower modeling, leadership techniques, and production methods. **Economics and Accounting:** Knowledge of economic and accounting principles and practices, the financial markets, banking, and the analysis and reporting of financial data. **Customer and Personal Service:** Knowledge of principles and processes for providing customer and personal services including needs assessment techniques, quality service standards, alternative delivery systems, and customer satisfaction evaluation techniques. **Production and Processing:** Knowledge of inputs, outputs, raw materials, waste, quality control, costs, and techniques for maximizing the manufacture and distribution of goods. **Computers and Electronics:** Knowledge of electric circuit boards, processors, chips, and computer hardware and software, including applications and programming. **Engineering and Technology:** Knowledge of equipment, tools, mechanical devices, and their uses to produce motion, light, power, technology, and other applications. **Design:** Knowledge of design techniques, principles, tools and instruments involved in the production and use of precision technical plans, blueprints, drawings, and models. **Building and Construction:** Knowledge of materials, methods, and the appropriate tools to construct objects, structures, and buildings. **Mechanical:** Knowledge of machines and tools, including their designs, uses, benefits, repair, and maintenance. **Mathematics:** Knowledge of numbers, their operations, and interrelationships including arithmetic, algebra, geometry, calculus, statistics, and their applications. **Physics:** Knowledge and prediction of physical principles, laws, and applications including air, water, material dynamics, light, atomic principles, heat, electric theory, earth formations, and meteorological and related natural phenomena. **English Language:** Knowledge of the structure and content of the English language including the meaning and spelling of words, rules of composition, and grammar. **Telecommunications:** Knowledge of transmission, broadcasting, switching, control, and operation of telecommunications systems. **Communications and Media:** Knowledge of media production, communication, and dissemination techniques and methods including alternative ways to inform and entertain via written, oral, and visual media.

ELEMENTARY SCHOOL TEACHERS

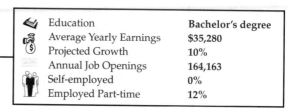

	Education	Bachelor's degree
	Average Yearly Earnings	$35,280
	Projected Growth	10%
	Annual Job Openings	164,163
	Self-employed	0%
	Employed Part-time	12%

Teachers: Elementary School

Teach elementary pupils in public or private schools basic academic, social, and other formulative skills. (Excludes special education teachers of the handicapped.) Lectures, demonstrates, and uses audiovisual aids and computers to present academic, social, and motor skill subject matter to class. Teaches subjects such as math, science, or social studies. Prepares course objectives and outline for course of study, following curriculum guidelines or requirements of state and school. Prepares, administers, and corrects tests, and records results. Assigns lessons, corrects papers, and hears oral presentations. Teaches rules of conduct and maintains discipline and suitable learning environment in classroom and on playground. Evaluates student performance and discusses pupil academic and behavioral attitudes and achievements with parents. Keeps attendance and grade records and prepares reports as required by school. Counsels pupils when adjustment and academic problems arise. Supervises outdoor and indoor play activities. Teaches combined grade classes. Attends staff meetings, serves on committees, and attends workshops or in-service training activities. Coordinates class field trips. Prepares bulletin boards.

Occupational Type

Social occupations frequently involve working with, communicating with, and teaching people. These occupations often involve helping or providing service to others.

Skills required of Teachers: Elementary School

Speaking, Active Learning, Learning Strategies, Monitoring, Social Perceptiveness, Coordination, Persuasion, Instructing, Service Orientation, Information Organization, Implementation Planning, Time Management

College Majors

Education, General: An instructional program that generally describes the theory and practice of learning and teaching; the basic principles of educational psychology; the art of teaching; the planning and administration of educational activities; and the social foundations of education.

 Supporting Courses

Administration and Management: Knowledge of principles and processes involved in business and organizational planning, coordination, and execution. This includes strategic planning, resource allocation, manpower modeling, leadership techniques, and production methods. **Clerical:** Knowledge of administrative and clerical procedures and systems such as word processing systems, filing and records management systems, stenography and transcription, forms design principles, and other office procedures and terminology. **Customer and Personal Service:** Knowledge of principles and processes for providing customer and personal services including needs assessment techniques, quality service standards, alternative delivery systems, and customer satisfaction evaluation techniques. **Mathematics:** Knowledge of numbers, their operations, and interrelationships including arithmetic, algebra, geometry, calculus, statistics, and their applications. **Chemistry:** Knowledge of the composition, structure, and properties of substances and of the chemical processes and transformations that they undergo. This includes uses of chemicals and their interactions, danger signs, production techniques, and disposal methods. **Biology:** Knowledge of plant and animal living tissue, cells, organisms, and entities, including their functions, interdependencies, and interactions with each other and the environment. **Psychology:** Knowledge of human behavior and performance, mental processes, psychological research methods, and the assessment and treatment of behavioral and affective disorders. **Sociology and Anthropology:** Knowledge of group behavior and dynamics, societal trends and influences, cultures, their history, migrations, ethnicity, and origins. **Geography:** Knowledge of various methods for describing the location and distribution of land, sea, and air masses including their physical locations, relationships, and characteristics. **Medicine and Dentistry:** Knowledge of the information and techniques needed to diagnose and treat injuries, diseases, and deformities. This includes symptoms, treatment alternatives, drug properties and interactions, and preventive healthcare measures. **Therapy and Counseling:** Knowledge of information and techniques needed to rehabilitate physical and mental ailments and to provide career guidance including alternative treatments, rehabilitation equipment and its proper use, and methods to evaluate treatment effects. **Education and Training:** Knowledge of instructional methods and training techniques including curriculum design principles, learning theory, group and individual teaching techniques, design of individual development plans, and test design principles. **English Language:** Knowledge of the structure and content of the English language including the meaning and spelling of words, rules of composition, and grammar. **Foreign Language:** Knowledge of the structure and content of a foreign (non-English) language including the meaning and spelling of words, rules of composition and grammar, and pronunciation. **Fine Arts:** Knowledge of theory and techniques required to produce, compose, and perform works of music, dance, visual arts, drama, and sculpture. **History and Archeology:** Knowledge of past historical events and their causes, indicators, and impact on particular civilizations and cultures. **Philosophy and Theology:** Knowledge of different philosophical systems and religions, including their basic principles, values, ethics, ways of thinking, customs, and practices, and their impact on human culture. **Law, Government, and Jurisprudence:** Knowledge of laws, legal codes, court procedures, precedents, government regulations, executive orders, agency rules, and the democratic political process. **Transportation:** Knowledge of principles and methods for moving people or goods by air, rail, sea, or road, including their relative costs, advantages, and limitations.

EMPLOYMENT INTERVIEWERS

	Education	Bachelor's degree
	Average Yearly Earnings	$35,090
	Projected Growth	16%
	Annual Job Openings	10,430
	Self-employed	0%
	Employed Part-time	7%

Employment Interviewers, Private or Public Employment Service

Interview job applicants in employment office and refer them to prospective employers for consideration. Search application files, notify selected applicants of job openings, and refer qualified applicants to prospective employers. Contact employers to verify referral results. Record and evaluate various pertinent data. Interviews job applicants to select people meeting employer qualifications. Refers selected applicants to person placing job order, according to policy of organization. Reviews employment applications and evaluates work history, education and training, job skills, compensation needs, and other qualifications of applicants. Records additional knowledge, skills, abilities, interests, test results, and other data pertinent to selection and referral of applicants. Reviews job orders and matches applicants with job requirements, utilizing manual or computerized file search. Informs applicants of job duties and responsibilities, compensation and benefits, work schedules, working conditions, promotional opportunities, and other related information. Keeps records of applicants not selected for employment. Searches for and recruits applicants for open positions. Conducts or arranges for skills, intelligence, or psychological testing of applicants. Performs reference and background checks on applicants. Evaluates selection and testing techniques by conducting research or follow-up activities and conferring with management and supervisory personnel. Contacts employers to solicit orders for job vacancies, and records information on forms to describe duties, hiring requirements, and related data. Refers applicants to vocational counseling services.

 Occupational Type

Social occupations frequently involve working with, communicating with, and teaching people. These occupations often involve helping or providing service to others.

Skills required of Employment Interviewers

Active Listening, Speaking, Social Perceptiveness, Service Orientation, Idea Generation, Management of Personnel Resources

 College Majors

Human Resources Management: An instructional program that prepares individuals to manage the development of human capital in organizations, and to provide related services to individuals and groups. Includes instruction in personnel and organization policy, human resource dynamics and flows, labor relations, sex roles, civil rights, human resources law and regulations, motivation and compensation systems, work systems, career management, employee testing and assessment, recruitment and selection, managing employee and job training programs, and the management of human resources programs and operations.

Supporting Courses

Administration and Management: Knowledge of principles and processes involved in business and organizational planning, coordination, and execution. This includes strategic planning, resource allocation, manpower modeling, leadership techniques, and production methods. **Clerical:** Knowledge of administrative and clerical procedures and systems such as word processing systems, filing and records management systems, stenography and transcription, forms design principles, and other office procedures and terminology. **Sales and Marketing:** Knowledge of principles and methods involved in showing, promoting, and selling products or services. This includes marketing strategies and tactics, product demonstration and sales techniques, and sales control systems. **Customer and Personal Service:** Knowledge of principles and processes for providing customer and personal services including needs assessment techniques, quality service standards, alternative delivery systems, and customer satisfaction evaluation techniques. **Personnel and Human Resources:** Knowledge of policies and practices involved in personnel/human resource functions. This includes recruitment, selection, training, and promotion regulations and procedures; compensation and benefits packages; labor relations and negotiation strategies; and personnel information systems. **Psychology:** Knowledge of human behavior and performance, mental processes, psychological research methods, and the assessment and treatment of behavioral and affective disorders. **Sociology and Anthropology:** Knowledge of group behavior and dynamics, societal trends and influences, cultures, their history, migrations, ethnicity, and origins. **Therapy and Counseling:** Knowledge of information and techniques needed to rehabilitate physical and mental ailments and to provide career guidance including alternative treatments, rehabilitation equipment and its proper use, and methods to evaluate treatment effects.

ENGINEERING TECHNICIANS

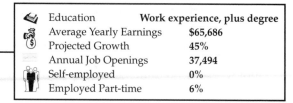	Education	**Associate degree**
	Average Yearly Earnings	**$34,237**
	Projected Growth	**7%**
	Annual Job Openings	**44,475**
	Self-employed	**0%**
	Employed Part-time	**7%**

ENGINEERING, MATHEMATICAL, AND NATURAL SCIENCE MANAGER

Engineering Managers

	Education	**Work experience, plus degree**
	Average Yearly Earnings	**$65,686**
	Projected Growth	**45%**
	Annual Job Openings	**37,494**
	Self-employed	**0%**
	Employed Part-time	**6%**

Plan, direct, and coordinate activities in such fields as architecture, engineering, and related research and development. These persons spend the greatest portion of their time in managerial work, for which a background consistent with that described for engineers is required. (Excludes natural science managers; mathematical managers; computer operations, information systems, computer programming, and data processing managers; as well as managers of computer-related occupations.) Establishes procedures and directs testing, operation, maintenance, and repair of transmitter equipment. Evaluates contract proposals, directs negotiation of research contracts, and prepares bids and contracts. Plans and directs installation, maintenance, testing, and repair of facilities and equipment. Directs, reviews, and approves product design and changes, and directs testing. Plans, coordinates, and directs engineering project, organizes and assigns staff, and directs integration of technical activities with products. Plans and directs oilfield development, gas and oil production, and geothermal drilling. Analyzes technology, resource needs, and market demand, and confers with management, production, and marketing staff to plan and assess feasibility of project. Plans, directs, and coordinates survey work with activities of other staff, certifies survey work, and writes land legal descriptions. Administers highway planning, construction, and maintenance, and reviews and recommends or approves contracts and cost estimates. Directs engineering of water control, treatment, and distribution projects. Confers with and prepares reports for officials, and speaks to public to solicit support.

 Occupational Type

Enterprising occupations frequently involve starting up and carrying out projects. These occupations can involve leading people and making many decisions. Sometimes they involve risk taking and often deal with business.

 Skills required of Engineering Managers

Reading Comprehension, Active Listening, Writing, Speaking, Mathematics, Science, Critical Thinking, Active Learning, Monitoring, Social Perceptiveness, Coordination,

---

Persuasion, Negotiation, Problem Identification, Information Gathering, Information Organization, Synthesis/Reorganization, Idea Generation, Idea Evaluation, Implementation Planning, Operations Analysis, Technology Design, Equipment Selection, Installation, Programming, Testing, Product Inspection, Equipment Maintenance, Troubleshooting, Repairing, Visioning, Systems Perception, Identifying Downstream Consequences, Identification of Key Causes, Judgment and Decision Making, Systems Evaluation, Time Management, Management of Financial Resources, Management of Material Resources, Management of Personnel Resources

 ## College Majors

Civil Engineering, General: An instructional program that generally prepares individuals to apply mathematical and scientific principles to the design, development and operational evaluation of structural, loadbearing, material moving, transportation, water resource, and material control systems; and related equipment and environmental safety measures.

Supporting Courses

Administration and Management: Knowledge of principles and processes involved in business and organizational planning, coordination, and execution. This includes strategic planning, resource allocation, manpower modeling, leadership techniques, and production methods. **Economics and Accounting:** Knowledge of economic and accounting principles and practices, the financial markets, banking, and the analysis and reporting of financial data. **Sales and Marketing:** Knowledge of principles and methods involved in showing, promoting, and selling products or services. This includes marketing strategies and tactics, product demonstration and sales techniques, and sales control systems. **Personnel and Human Resources:** Knowledge of policies and practices involved in personnel/human resource functions. This includes recruitment, selection, training, and promotion regulations and procedures; compensation and benefits packages; labor relations and negotiation strategies; and personnel information systems. **Engineering and Technology:** Knowledge of equipment, tools, mechanical devices, and their uses to produce motion, light, power, technology, and other applications. **Design:** Knowledge of design techniques, principles, tools and instruments involved in the production and use of precision technical plans, blueprints, drawings, and models. **Building and Construction:** Knowledge of materials, methods, and the appropriate tools to construct objects, structures, and buildings. **Mechanical:** Knowledge of machines and tools, including their designs, uses, benefits, repair, and maintenance. **Mathematics:** Knowledge of numbers, their operations, and interrelationships including arithmetic, algebra, geometry, calculus, statistics, and their applications. **Physics:** Knowledge and prediction of physical principles, laws, and applications including air, water, material dynamics, light, atomic principles, heat, electric theory, earth formations, and meteorological and related natural phenomena. **Chemistry:** Knowledge of the composition, structure, and properties of substances and of the chemical processes and transformations that they undergo. This includes uses of chemicals and their interactions, danger signs, production techniques, and disposal methods. **Psychology:** Knowledge of human behavior and performance, mental processes, psychological research methods, and the assessment and treatment of behavioral and affective disorders.

Geography: Knowledge of various methods for describing the location and distribution of land, sea, and air masses including their physical locations, relationships, and characteristics. **English Language:** Knowledge of the structure and content of the English language including the meaning and spelling of words, rules of composition, and grammar. **History and Archeology:** Knowledge of past historical events and their causes, indicators, and impact on particular civilizations and cultures. **Public Safety and Security:** Knowledge of weaponry, public safety, and security operations, rules, regulations, precautions, prevention, and the protection of people, data, and property. **Law, Government, and Jurisprudence:** Knowledge of laws, legal codes, court procedures, precedents, government regulations, executive orders, agency rules, and the democratic political process. **Telecommunications:** Knowledge of transmission, broadcasting, switching, control, and operation of telecommunications systems. **Communications and Media:** Knowledge of media production, communication, and dissemination techniques and methods including alternative ways to inform and entertain via written, oral, and visual media.

Natural Science Managers

Plan, direct, and coordinate activities in such fields as life sciences, physical sciences, mathematics, statistics, and related research and development. These persons spend the greatest portion of their time in managerial work, for which a background consistent with that described for mathematicians or natural scientists is required. (Excludes engineering managers; computer operations, information systems, computer programming, and data processing managers; as well as managers of computer-related occupations.) Schedules, directs, and assigns duties to engineers, technicians, researchers, and other staff. Plans and directs research, development, and production activities of chemical plant. Coordinates successive phases of problem analysis, solution proposals, and testing. Prepares and administers budget, approves and reviews expenditures, and prepares financial reports. Reviews project activities, and prepares and reviews research, testing, and operational reports. Confers with scientists, engineers, regulators, and others to plan and review projects and to provide technical assistance. Advises and assists in obtaining patents or other legal requirements. Provides technical assistance to agencies conducting environmental studies.

Occupational Type

Investigative occupations frequently involve working with ideas, and require an extensive amount of thinking. These occupations can involve searching for facts and figuring out problems mentally.

Skills required of Natural Science Managers

Reading Comprehension, Active Listening, Writing, Speaking, Mathematics, Science, Critical Thinking, Active Learning, Learning Strategies, Monitoring, Social Perceptiveness, Coordination, Persuasion, Negotiation, Instructing, Problem Identification, Information Gathering, Information Organization, Synthesis/Reorganization, Idea Generation, Idea Evaluation, Implementation Planning, Operations Analysis, Technology Design, Equipment Selection, Testing, Product Inspection, Troubleshooting, Visioning, Systems Perception,

Identifying Downstream Consequences, Identification of Key Causes, Judgment and Decision Making, Systems Evaluation, Time Management, Management of Financial Resources, Management of Material Resources, Management of Personnel Resources

College Majors

Natural Resources Conservation, General: An instructional program that generally describes activities involving the conservation and/or improvement of natural resources such as air, soil, water, land, fish, and wildlife for economic and recreation purposes.

Supporting Courses

Administration and Management: Knowledge of principles and processes involved in business and organizational planning, coordination, and execution. This includes strategic planning, resource allocation, manpower modeling, leadership techniques, and production methods. **Economics and Accounting:** Knowledge of economic and accounting principles and practices, the financial markets, banking, and the analysis and reporting of financial data. **Personnel and Human Resources:** Knowledge of policies and practices involved in personnel/human resource functions. This includes recruitment, selection, training, and promotion regulations and procedures; compensation and benefits packages; labor relations and negotiation strategies; and personnel information systems. **Production and Processing:** Knowledge of inputs, outputs, raw materials, waste, quality control, costs, and techniques for maximizing the manufacture and distribution of goods. **Engineering and Technology:** Knowledge of equipment, tools, mechanical devices, and their uses to produce motion, light, power, technology, and other applications. **Mathematics:** Knowledge of numbers, their operations, and interrelationships including arithmetic, algebra, geometry, calculus, statistics, and their applications. **Physics:** Knowledge and prediction of physical principles, laws, and applications including air, water, material dynamics, light, atomic principles, heat, electric theory, earth formations, and meteorological and related natural phenomena. **Chemistry:** Knowledge of the composition, structure, and properties of substances and of the chemical processes and transformations that they undergo. This includes uses of chemicals and their interactions, danger signs, production techniques, and disposal methods. **Biology:** Knowledge of plant and animal living tissue, cells, organisms, and entities, including their functions, interdependencies, and interactions with each other and the environment. **Psychology:** Knowledge of human behavior and performance, mental processes, psychological research methods, and the assessment and treatment of behavioral and affective disorders. **Geography:** Knowledge of various methods for describing the location and distribution of land, sea, and air masses including their physical locations, relationships, and characteristics. **Education and Training:** Knowledge of instructional methods and training techniques including curriculum design principles, learning theory, group and individual teaching techniques, design of individual development plans, and test design principles. **English Language:** Knowledge of the structure and content of the English language including the meaning and spelling of words, rules of composition, and grammar. **Foreign Language:** Knowledge of the structure and content of a foreign (non-English) language including the meaning and spelling of words, rules of composition and grammar, and pronunciation. **History and Archeology:** Knowledge of past historical events and their causes, indicators, and impact on particular civilizations and cultures. **Law, Government, and Jurisprudence:** Knowledge of laws, legal codes, court procedures, precedents, government regulations, executive orders, agency rules, and the democratic political process.

Computer and Information Systems Managers

Plan, direct, and coordinate activities in such fields as electronic data processing, information systems, systems analysis, and computer programming. These persons spend the greatest portion of their time in managerial work, for which a background consistent with that described for computer professionals, such as computer systems analysts, computer scientists, database administrators, computer programmers, and computer support specialists would be required. Evaluates data processing project proposals and assesses project feasibility. Directs department, prepares and reviews operational reports, adjusts schedule to meet priorities, and prepares progress reports. Establishes work standards, directs training, participates in staffing and promotion decisions, and disciplines workers. Consults with users, management, vendors, and technicians to determine computing needs and system requirements. Analyzes workflow; assigns, schedules, and reviews work; and directs and coordinates with other departments. Meets with department heads, managers, supervisors, vendors, and others to solicit cooperation and resolve problems. Approves, prepares, monitors, and adjusts operational budget. Develops and interprets organizational goals, policies, and procedures, and reviews project plans.

 Occupational Type

Enterprising occupations frequently involve starting up and carrying out projects. These occupations can involve leading people and making many decisions. Sometimes they involve risk taking and often deal with business.

 Skills required of Computer and Information Systems Managers

Reading Comprehension, Active Listening, Writing, Speaking, Mathematics, Active Learning, Learning Strategies, Monitoring, Social Perceptiveness, Coordination, Persuasion, Negotiation, Instructing, Service Orientation, Problem Identification, Information Gathering, Information Organization, Synthesis/Reorganization, Idea Generation, Idea Evaluation, Implementation Planning, Operations Analysis, Technology Design, Programming, Visioning, Systems Perception, Identifying Downstream Consequences, Identification of Key Causes, Judgment and Decision Making, Systems Evaluation, Time Management, Management of Financial Resources, Management of Material Resources, Management of Personnel Resources

 College Majors

Management Information Systems and Business Data Processing, General: An instructional program that generally prepares individuals to provide and manage data systems and related facilities for processing and retrieving internal business information; select systems and train personnel; and respond to external data requests. Includes instruction in cost and accounting information systems, management control systems, personnel information systems, data storage and security, business systems networking, report preparation, computer facilities and equipment operation and maintenance, operator supervision and training, and management information systems policy and planning.

 Supporting Courses

Administration and Management: Knowledge of principles and processes involved in business and organizational planning, coordination, and execution. This includes strategic planning, resource allocation, manpower modeling, leadership techniques, and production methods. **Clerical:** Knowledge of administrative and clerical procedures and systems such as word processing systems, filing and records management systems, stenography and transcription, forms design principles, and other office procedures and terminology. **Economics and Accounting:** Knowledge of economic and accounting principles and practices, the financial markets, banking, and the analysis and reporting of financial data. **Sales and Marketing:** Knowledge of principles and methods involved in showing, promoting, and selling products or services. This includes marketing strategies and tactics, product demonstration and sales techniques, and sales control systems. **Customer and Personal Service:** Knowledge of principles and processes for providing customer and personal services including needs assessment techniques, quality service standards, alternative delivery systems, and customer satisfaction evaluation techniques. **Personnel and Human Resources:** Knowledge of policies and practices involved in personnel/human resource functions. This includes recruitment, selection, training, and promotion regulations and procedures; compensation and benefits packages; labor relations and negotiation strategies; and personnel information systems. **Computers and Electronics:** Knowledge of electric circuit boards, processors, chips, and computer hardware and software, including applications and programming. **Mathematics:** Knowledge of numbers, their operations, and interrelationships including arithmetic, algebra, geometry, calculus, statistics, and their applications. **Psychology:** Knowledge of human behavior and performance, mental processes, psychological research methods, and the assessment and treatment of behavioral and affective disorders. **Education and Training:** Knowledge of instructional methods and training techniques including curriculum design principles, learning theory, group and individual teaching techniques, design of individual development plans, and test design principles. **English Language:** Knowledge of the structure and content of the English language including the meaning and spelling of words, rules of composition, and grammar. **Communications and Media:** Knowledge of media production, communication, and dissemination techniques and methods including alternative ways to inform and entertain via written, oral, and visual media.

Laboratory Managers

Coordinate activities of university science laboratory to assist faculty in teaching and research programs. Prepares and puts in place equipment scheduled for use during laboratory teaching sessions. Confers with teaching staff to evaluate new equipment and methods. Consults with laboratory coordinator to determine equipment purchase priorities based on budget allowances, condition of existing equipment, and scheduled activities. Demonstrates care and use of equipment to teaching assistants. Trains teaching staff and students in application and use of new equipment. Develops methods of laboratory experimentation, applying knowledge of scientific theory and computer capability. Builds prototype equipment, applying electromechanical knowledge and using hand tools and power tools. Diagnoses and repairs malfunctioning equipment, applying knowledge of shop mechanics and using gauges, meters, hand tools, and power tools. Teaches laboratory sessions in absence of teaching assistant.

Occupational Type

Investigative occupations frequently involve working with ideas, and require an extensive amount of thinking. These occupations can involve searching for facts and figuring out problems mentally.

Skills required of Laboratory Managers

Reading Comprehension, Active Listening, Speaking, Science, Active Learning, Learning Strategies, Coordination, Instructing, Service Orientation, Information Gathering, Idea Generation, Idea Evaluation, Implementation Planning, Operations Analysis, Technology Design, Equipment Selection, Installation, Programming, Testing, Equipment Maintenance, Troubleshooting, Repairing, Judgment and Decision Making, Time Management, Management of Financial Resources, Management of Material Resources, Management of Personnel Resources

College Majors

Various: Many bachelor studies contribute to expertise in this field.

Supporting Courses

Administration and Management: Knowledge of principles and processes involved in business and organizational planning, coordination, and execution. This includes strategic planning, resource allocation, manpower modeling, leadership techniques, and production methods. **Economics and Accounting:** Knowledge of economic and accounting principles and practices, the financial markets, banking, and the analysis and reporting of financial data. **Computers and Electronics:** Knowledge of electric circuit boards, processors, chips, and computer hardware and software, including applications and programming. **Engineering and Technology:** Knowledge of equipment, tools, mechanical devices, and their uses to produce motion, light, power, technology, and other applications. **Mathematics:** Knowledge of numbers, their operations, and interrelationships including arithmetic, algebra, geometry, calculus, statistics, and their applications. **Physics:** Knowledge and prediction of physical principles, laws, and applications including air, water, material dynamics, light, atomic principles, heat, electric theory, earth formations, and meteorological and related natural phenomena. **Chemistry:** Knowledge of the composition, structure, and properties of substances and of the chemical processes and transformations that they undergo. This includes uses of chemicals and their interactions, danger signs, production techniques, and disposal methods. **Biology:** Knowledge of plant and animal living tissue, cells, organisms, and entities, including their functions, interdependencies, and interactions with each other and the environment. **Education and Training:** Knowledge of instructional methods and training techniques including curriculum design principles, learning theory, group and individual teaching techniques, design of individual development plans, and test design principles. **English Language:** Knowledge of the structure and content of the English language including the meaning and spelling of words, rules of composition, and grammar.

FARM AND HOME MANAGEMENT ADVISORS

	Education	Bachelor's degree
	Average Yearly Earnings	$48,506
	Projected Growth	-38%
	Annual Job Openings	3,078
	Self-employed	9%
	Employed Part-time	43%

Farm and Home Management Advisors

Advise, instruct, and assist individuals and families engaged in agriculture, agricultural-related processes, or home economics activities. Demonstrate procedures and apply research findings to solve problems; instruct and train in product development, sales, and the utilization of machinery and equipment to promote general welfare. Include county agricultural agents, feed and farm management advisers, home economists, and extension service advisers. Advises farmers in matters such as feeding and health maintenance of livestock, cultivation, growing and harvesting practices, and budgeting. Advises individuals and families on home management practices, such as budget planning, meal preparation, energy conservation, clothing, and home furnishings. Conducts classes to educate others in subjects such as nutrition, home management, home furnishing, childcare, and farming techniques. Plans, develops, organizes, and evaluates training programs in subjects such as home management, horticulture, and consumer information. Collects and evaluates data to ascertain needs and develop programs beneficial to community. Delivers lectures to organizations or talks over radio and television to disseminate information and promote objectives of program. Organizes, advises, and participates in community activities and organizations, such as county and state fair events and 4-H clubs. Prepares leaflets, pamphlets, and other material, such as visual aids for educational and informational purposes.

Occupational Type

Social occupations frequently involve working with, communicating with, and teaching people. These occupations often involve helping or providing service to others.

Skills required of Farm and Home Management Advisors

Reading Comprehension, Active Listening, Writing, Speaking, Active Learning, Learning Strategies, Monitoring, Persuasion, Negotiation, Instructing, Service Orientation, Problem

Identification, Information Gathering, Idea Generation, Idea Evaluation, Implementation Planning, Operations Analysis, Programming, Visioning, Systems Perception, Identifying Downstream Consequences, Identification of Key Causes, Systems Evaluation, Management of Financial Resources

 ## College Majors

Agricultural Business and Management, General: An instructional program that generally prepares individuals to apply modern economic and business principles involved in the organization, operation and management of farm and agricultural businesses.

 ## Supporting Courses

Administration and Management: Knowledge of principles and processes involved in business and organizational planning, coordination, and execution. This includes strategic planning, resource allocation, manpower modeling, leadership techniques, and production methods. **Economics and Accounting:** Knowledge of economic and accounting principles and practices, the financial markets, banking, and the analysis and reporting of financial data. **Sales and Marketing:** Knowledge of principles and methods involved in showing, promoting, and selling products or services. This includes marketing strategies and tactics, product demonstration and sales techniques, and sales control systems. **Personnel and Human Resources:** Knowledge of policies and practices involved in personnel/human resource functions. This includes recruitment, selection, training, and promotion regulations and procedures; compensation and benefits packages; labor relations and negotiation strategies; and personnel information systems. **Food Production:** Knowledge of techniques and equipment for planting, growing, and harvesting of food for consumption including crop rotation methods, animal husbandry, and food storage/handling techniques. **Computers and Electronics:** Knowledge of electric circuit boards, processors, chips, and computer hardware and software, including applications and programming. **Mathematics:** Knowledge of numbers, their operations, and interrelationships including arithmetic, algebra, geometry, calculus, statistics, and their applications. **Chemistry:** Knowledge of the composition, structure, and properties of substances and of the chemical processes and transformations that they undergo. This includes uses of chemicals and their interactions, danger signs, production techniques, and disposal methods. **Biology:** Knowledge of plant and animal living tissue, cells, organisms, and entities, including their functions, interdependencies, and interactions with each other and the environment. **Education and Training:** Knowledge of instructional methods and training techniques including curriculum design principles, learning theory, group and individual teaching techniques, design of individual development plans, and test design principles. **Communications and Media:** Knowledge of media production, communication, and dissemination techniques and methods including alternative ways to inform and entertain via written, oral, and visual media. **Transportation:** Knowledge of principles and methods for moving people or goods by air, rail, sea, or road, including their relative costs, advantages, and limitations.

FINANCIAL MANAGERS

Treasurers, Controllers, and Chief Financial Officers

Education	**Work experience, plus degree**
Average Yearly Earnings	$54,392
Projected Growth	18%
Annual Job Openings	74,296
Self-employed	1%
Employed Part-time	3

Plan, direct, and coordinate the financial activities of an organization at the highest level of management. Include financial reserve officers. Directs financial planning, procurement, and investment of funds for organization. Directs preparation of budgets. Prepares reports or directs preparation of reports summarizing organization's current and forecasted financial position, business activity, and reports required by regulatory agencies. Prepares financial reports or directs preparation of reports. Recommends to management major economic objectives and policies. Delegates authority for receipt, disbursement, banking, protection, and custody of funds, securities, and financial instruments. Analyzes past, present, and expected operations. Plans and implements new operating procedures to improve efficiency and reduce costs. Ensures that institution reserves meet legal requirements. Coordinates activities of assigned program and interprets policies and practices. Arranges audits of company accounts. Advises management on investments and loans for short- and long-range financial plans. Manages accounting department. Evaluates need for procurement of funds and investment of surplus. Determines methods and procedures for carrying out assigned program. Develops policies and procedures for account collections and extension of credit to customers.

Occupational Type

Enterprising occupations frequently involve starting up and carrying out projects. These occupations can involve leading people and making many decisions. Sometimes they involve risk taking and often deal with business.

Skills required of Treasurers, Controllers, and Chief Financial Officers

Reading Comprehension, Writing, Speaking, Mathematics, Critical Thinking, Active Learning, Learning Strategies, Monitoring, Coordination, Persuasion, Negotiation, Problem Identification, Information Gathering, Information Organization, Synthesis/Reorganization, Idea Generation, Idea Evaluation, Implementation Planning, Operations Analysis, Visioning, Systems Perception, Identifying Downstream Consequences, Identification of Key Causes, Judgment and Decision Making, Systems Evaluation, Time Management, Management of Financial Resources, Management of Material Resources, Management of Personnel Resources

College Majors

Finance, General: An instructional program that generally prepares individuals to plan, manage, and analyze the financial and monetary aspects and performance of business enterprises, banking institutions, or other organizations. Includes instruction in principles of accounting; financial instruments; capital planning; funds acquisition; asset and debt management; budgeting; financial analysis; and investments and portfolio management.

Supporting Courses

Administration and Management: Knowledge of principles and processes involved in business and organizational planning, coordination, and execution. This includes strategic planning, resource allocation, manpower modeling, leadership techniques, and production methods. **Economics and Accounting:** Knowledge of economic and accounting principles and practices, the financial markets, banking, and the analysis and reporting of financial data. **Sales and Marketing:** Knowledge of principles and methods involved in showing, promoting, and selling products or services. This includes marketing strategies and tactics, product demonstration and sales techniques, and sales control systems. **Personnel and Human Resources:** Knowledge of policies and practices involved in personnel/human resource functions. This includes recruitment, selection, training, and promotion regulations and procedures; compensation and benefits packages; labor relations and negotiation strategies; and personnel information systems. **Mathematics:** Knowledge of numbers, their operations, and interrelationships including arithmetic, algebra, geometry, calculus, statistics, and their applications. **Psychology:** Knowledge of human behavior and performance, mental processes, psychological research methods, and the assessment and treatment of behavioral and affective disorders. **English Language:** Knowledge of the structure and content of the English language including the meaning and spelling of words, rules of composition, and grammar. **History and Archeology:** Knowledge of past historical events and their causes, indicators, and impact on particular civilizations and cultures. **Philosophy and Theology:** Knowledge of different philosophical systems and religions, including their basic principles, values, ethics, ways of thinking, customs, and practices, and their impact on human culture. **Law, Government, and Jurisprudence:** Knowledge of laws, legal codes, court procedures, precedents, government regulations, executive orders, agency rules, and the democratic political process. **Communications and Media:** Knowledge of media production, communication, and dissemination techniques and methods including alternative ways to inform and entertain via written, oral, and visual media.

Financial Managers, Branch or Department

Direct and coordinate financial activities of workers in a branch, office, or department of an establishment, such as branch bank, brokerage firm, risk and insurance department, or credit department. Directs and coordinates activities of workers engaged in conducting credit investigations and collecting delinquent accounts of customers. Plans, directs, and coordinates risk and insurance programs of establishment to control risks and losses. Manages branch or office of financial institution. Directs and coordinates activities to implement institution policies, procedures, and practices concerning granting or extending lines of credit and loans. Prepares financial and regulatory reports required by law, regulations, and board of directors. Analyzes and classifies risks as to frequency and financial impact of risk on company. Selects appropriate technique to minimize loss, such as avoidance and loss prevention and reduction. Prepares operational and risk reports for management analysis. Directs floor operations of brokerage firm engaged in buying and selling securities at exchange. Establishes procedures for custody and control of assets, records, loan collateral, and securities to ensure safekeeping. Evaluates effectiveness of current collection policies and procedures. Directs insurance negotiations, selects insurance brokers and carriers, and places insurance. Evaluates data pertaining to costs to plan budget. Reviews collection reports to ascertain status of collections and balances outstanding. Monitors order flow and transactions that brokerage firm executes on floor of exchange. Reviews reports of securities transactions and price lists to analyze market conditions. Establishes credit limitations on customer account. Examines, evaluates, and processes loan applications. Submits delinquent accounts to attorney or outside agency for collection.

Occupational Type

Enterprising occupations frequently involve starting up and carrying out projects. These occupations can involve leading people and making many decisions. Sometimes they involve risk taking and often deal with business.

Skills required of Financial Managers, Branch or Department

Reading Comprehension, Active Listening, Writing, Speaking, Mathematics, Critical Thinking, Active Learning, Learning Strategies, Monitoring, Social Perceptiveness, Coordination, Persuasion, Negotiation, Service Orientation, Problem Identification, Information Gathering, Information Organization, Synthesis/Reorganization, Idea Generation, Idea Evaluation, Implementation Planning, Operations Analysis, Visioning, Systems Perception, Identifying Downstream Consequences, Identification of Key Causes, Judgment and Decision Making, Systems Evaluation, Time Management, Management of Financial Resources, Management of Material Resources, Management of Personnel Resources

College Majors

Finance, General: An instructional program that generally prepares individuals to plan, manage, and analyze the financial and monetary aspects and performance of business enterprises, banking institutions, or other organizations. Includes instruction in principles of accounting; financial instruments; capital planning; funds acquisition; asset and debt management; budgeting; financial analysis; and investments and portfolio management.

Supporting Courses

Administration and Management: Knowledge of principles and processes involved in business and organizational planning, coordination, and execution. This includes strategic planning, resource allocation, manpower modeling, leadership techniques, and production methods. **Economics and Accounting:** Knowledge of economic and accounting principles and practices, the financial markets, banking, and the analysis and reporting of financial data. **Sales and Marketing:** Knowledge of principles and methods involved in showing, promoting, and selling products or services. This includes marketing strategies and tactics, product demonstration and sales techniques, and sales control systems. **Personnel and Human**

Resources: Knowledge of policies and practices involved in personnel/human resource functions. This includes recruitment, selection, training, and promotion regulations and procedures; compensation and benefits packages; labor relations and negotiation strategies; and personnel information systems. **Mathematics:** Knowledge of numbers, their operations, and interrelationships including arithmetic, algebra, geometry, calculus, statistics, and their applications. **Psychology:** Knowledge of human behavior and performance, mental processes, psychological research methods, and the assessment and treatment of behavioral and affective disorders. **English Language:** Knowledge of the structure and content of the English language including the meaning and spelling of words, rules of composition, and grammar. **History and Archeology:** Knowledge of past historical events and their causes, indicators, and impact on particular civilizations and cultures. **Law, Government, and Jurisprudence:** Knowledge of laws, legal codes, court procedures, precedents, government regulations, executive orders, agency rules, and the democratic political process.

FORESTERS AND CONSERVATION SCIENTISTS

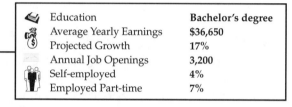

Education		Bachelor's degree
Average Yearly Earnings		$36,650
Projected Growth		17%
Annual Job Openings		3,200
Self-employed		4%
Employed Part-time		7%

Environmental Scientists

Conduct research to develop methods of abating, controlling, or remediating sources of environmental pollutants, utilizing knowledge of various scientific disciplines. Identify and analyze sources of pollution to determine their effects. Collect and synthesize data derived from pollution-emission measurements, atmospheric monitoring, meteorological and mineralogical information, or soil and water samples. (Excludes wildlife conservationists and natural resource scientists.) Plans and develops research models using knowledge of mathematical and statistical concepts. Collects, identifies, and analyzes data to assess sources of pollution, determine their effects, and establish standards. Determines data collection methods to be employed in research projects and surveys. Prepares graphs or charts from data samples, and advises enforcement personnel on proper standards and regulations.

Occupational Type

Investigative occupations frequently involve working with ideas, and require an extensive amount of thinking. These occupations can involve searching for facts and figuring out problems mentally.

Skills required of Environmental Scientists

Reading Comprehension, Writing, Mathematics, Science, Critical Thinking, Active Learning, Information Gathering, Information Organization, Synthesis/Reorganization, Idea Generation, Idea Evaluation, Operations Analysis, Visioning, Systems Perception, Identifying Downstream Consequences, Identification of Key Causes, Systems Evaluation

College Majors

Natural Resources Conservation, General: An instructional program that generally describes activities involving the conservation and/or improvement of natural resources such as air, soil, water, land, fish, and wildlife for economic and recreation purposes.

 Supporting Courses

Mathematics: Knowledge of numbers, their operations, and interrelationships including arithmetic, algebra, geometry, calculus, statistics, and their applications. **Physics:** Knowledge and prediction of physical principles, laws, and applications including air, water, material dynamics, light, atomic principles, heat, electric theory, earth formations, and meteorological and related natural phenomena. **Chemistry:** Knowledge of the composition, structure, and properties of substances and of the chemical processes and transformations that they undergo. This includes uses of chemicals and their interactions, danger signs, production techniques, and disposal methods. **Biology:** Knowledge of plant and animal living tissue, cells, organisms, and entities, including their functions, interdependencies, and interactions with each other and the environment.

Foresters

Plan, develop, and control environmental factors affecting forests and their resources for economic and recreation purposes. Plans and directs forestation and reforestation projects. Investigates adaptability of different tree species to new environmental conditions, such as soil type, climate, and altitude. Determines methods of cutting and removing timber with minimum waste and environmental damage. Plans cutting programs to assure continuous production or to assist timber companies to achieve production goals. Researches forest propagation and culture affecting tree growth rates, yield, and duration and seed production, growth viability, and germination of different species. Analyzes forest conditions to determine reason for prevalence of different variety of trees. Studies classification, life history, light and soil requirements, and resistance to disease and insects of different tree species. Maps forest areas and estimates standing timber and future growth. Manages tree nurseries and thins forest to encourage natural growth of sprouts or seedlings of desired varieties. Participates in environmental studies and prepares environmental reports. Assists in planning and implementing projects for control of floods, soil erosion, tree diseases, infestation, and forest fires. Plans and directs construction and maintenance of recreation facilities, fire towers, trails, roads, and fire breaks. Develops techniques for measuring and identifying trees. Patrols forests and enforces laws. Directs suppression of forest fires and fights forest fires. Advises landowners on forestry management techniques. Conducts public educational programs on forest care and conservation. Suggests methods of processing wood for various uses. Manages timber sales for government agency or landowner, and administers budgets. Supervises activities of other forestry workers.

 Occupational Type

Realistic occupations frequently involve work activities that include practical, hands-on problems and solutions. They often deal with plants, animals, and real-world materials like

---

wood, tools, and machinery. Many of the occupations require working outside, and do not involve a lot of paperwork or working closely with others.

Skills required of Foresters

Reading Comprehension, Active Listening, Writing, Speaking, Mathematics, Science, Critical Thinking, Active Learning, Learning Strategies, Monitoring, Social Perceptiveness, Coordination, Persuasion, Negotiation, Instructing, Problem Identification, Information Gathering, Information Organization, Synthesis/Reorganization, Idea Generation, Idea Evaluation, Implementation Planning, Operations Analysis, Visioning, Systems Perception, Identifying Downstream Consequences, Identification of Key Causes, Judgment and Decision Making, Systems Evaluation, Time Management, Management of Financial Resources, Management of Material Resources, Management of Personnel Resources

College Majors

Horticulture Services Operations and Management, General: An instructional program that generally prepares individuals to produce, process and market plants, shrubs, and trees used principally for ornamental, recreational and aesthetic purposes and to establish, maintain, and manage horticultural enterprises.

Supporting Courses

Administration and Management: Knowledge of principles and processes involved in business and organizational planning, coordination, and execution. This includes strategic planning, resource allocation, manpower modeling, leadership techniques, and production methods. **Economics and Accounting:** Knowledge of economic and accounting principles and practices, the financial markets, banking, and the analysis and reporting of financial data. **Sales and Marketing:** Knowledge of principles and methods involved in showing, promoting, and selling products or services. This includes marketing strategies and tactics, product demonstration and sales techniques, and sales control systems. **Personnel and Human Resources:** Knowledge of policies and practices involved in personnel/human resource functions. This includes recruitment, selection, training, and promotion regulations and procedures; compensation and benefits packages; labor relations and negotiation strategies; and personnel information systems. **Production and Processing:** Knowledge of inputs, outputs, raw materials, waste, quality control, costs, and techniques for maximizing the manufacture and distribution of goods. **Engineering and Technology:** Knowledge of equipment, tools, mechanical devices, and their uses to produce motion, light, power, technology, and other applications. **Design:** Knowledge of design techniques, principles, tools and instruments involved in the production and use of precision technical plans, blueprints, drawings, and models. **Building and Construction:** Knowledge of materials, methods, and the appropriate tools to construct objects, structures, and buildings. **Mathematics:** Knowledge of numbers, their operations, and interrelationships including arithmetic, algebra, geometry, calculus, statistics, and their applications. **Physics:** Knowledge and prediction of physical principles, laws, and applications including air, water, material dynamics, light, atomic principles, heat, electric theory, earth formations, and meteorological and related natural phenomena. **Chemistry:** Knowledge of the composition, structure, and properties of substances and of the chemical processes and transformations that they undergo. This includes uses of chemicals and their interactions, danger signs, production techniques, and disposal methods. **Biology:** Knowledge of plant and animal living tissue, cells, organisms, and entities, including their functions, interdependencies, and interactions with each other and the environment. **Sociology and Anthropology:** Knowledge of group behavior and dynamics, societal trends and influences, cultures, their history, migrations, ethnicity, and origins. **Geography:** Knowledge of various methods for describing the location and distribution of land, sea, and air masses including their physical locations, relationships, and characteristics. **Education and Training:** Knowledge of instructional methods and training techniques including curriculum design principles, learning theory, group and individual teaching techniques, design of individual development plans, and test design principles. **English Language:** Knowledge of the structure and content of the English language including the meaning and spelling of words, rules of composition, and grammar. **History and Archeology:** Knowledge of past historical events and their causes, indicators, and impact on particular civilizations and cultures. **Philosophy and Theology:** Knowledge of different philosophical systems and religions, including their basic principles, values, ethics, ways of thinking, customs, and practices, and their impact on human culture. **Public Safety and Security:** Knowledge of weaponry, public safety, and security operations, rules, regulations, precautions, prevention, and the protection of people, data, and property. **Law, Government, and Jurisprudence:** Knowledge of laws, legal codes, court procedures, precedents, government regulations, executive orders, agency rules, and the democratic political process. **Telecommunications:** Knowledge of transmission, broadcasting, switching, control, and operation of telecommunications systems. **Communications and Media:** Knowledge of media production, communication, and dissemination techniques and methods including alternative ways to inform and entertain via written, oral, and visual media. **Transportation:** Knowledge of principles and methods for moving people or goods by air, rail, sea, or road, including their relative costs, advantages, and limitations.

Soil Conservationists

Plan and develop coordinated practices for soil erosion control, soil and water conservation, and sound land use. Plans soil management practices, such as crop rotation, reforestation, permanent vegetation, contour plowing, or terracing, to maintain soil and conserve water. Develops plans for conservation, such as conservation cropping systems, woodlands management, pasture planning, and engineering systems. Analyzes results of investigations to determine measures needed to maintain or restore proper soil management. Conducts surveys and investigations of various land uses, such as rural or urban, agriculture, construction, forestry, or mining. Computes design specification for implementation of conservation practices, using survey and field information technical guides, engineering manuals, and calculator. Develops or participates in environmental studies. Monitors projects during and after construction to ensure projects conform to design specifications. Computes cost estimates of different conservation practices based on needs of land users, maintenance requirements, and life expectancy of practices. Surveys property to mark locations and measurements, using surveying instruments. Discusses conservation plans, problems, and alternative solutions with land users, applying knowledge of agronomy, soil science, forestry, or agricultural sciences. Revisits land users to view implemented land use practices and plans.

Occupational Type

Investigative occupations frequently involve working with ideas, and require an extensive amount of thinking. These occupations can involve searching for facts and figuring out problems mentally.

Skills required of Soil Conservationists

Reading Comprehension, Active Listening, Writing, Speaking, Mathematics, Science, Critical Thinking, Active Learning, Learning Strategies, Monitoring, Persuasion, Negotiation, Problem Identification, Information Gathering, Information Organization, Synthesis/Reorganization, Idea Generation, Idea Evaluation, Implementation Planning, Operations Analysis, Product Inspection, Visioning, Systems Perception, Identifying Downstream Consequences, Identification of Key Causes, Judgment and Decision Making, Systems Evaluation, Time Management

College Majors

Soil Sciences: An instructional program that describes the scientific classification and study of soils and soil properties. Includes instruction in soil chemistry, soil physics, soil biology, soil fertility, morphogenesis, mineralogy and hydrology, and soil conservation and management.

Supporting Courses

Administration and Management: Knowledge of principles and processes involved in business and organizational planning, coordination, and execution. This includes strategic planning, resource allocation, manpower modeling, leadership techniques, and production methods. **Economics and Accounting:** Knowledge of economic and accounting principles and practices, the financial markets, banking, and the analysis and reporting of financial data. **Food Production:** Knowledge of techniques and equipment for planting, growing, and harvesting of food for consumption including crop rotation methods, animal husbandry, and food storage/handling techniques. **Engineering and Technology:** Knowledge of equipment, tools, mechanical devices, and their uses to produce motion, light, power, technology, and other applications. **Design:** Knowledge of design techniques, principles, tools and instruments involved in the production and use of precision technical plans, blueprints, drawings, and models. **Building and Construction:** Knowledge of materials, methods, and the appropriate tools to construct objects, structures, and buildings. **Mathematics:** Knowledge of numbers, their operations, and interrelationships including arithmetic, algebra, geometry, calculus, statistics, and their applications. **Physics:** Knowledge and prediction of physical principles, laws, and applications including air, water, material dynamics, light, atomic principles, heat, electric theory, earth formations, and meteorological and related natural phenomena. **Chemistry:** Knowledge of the composition, structure, and properties of substances and of the chemical processes and transformations that they undergo. This includes uses of chemicals and their interactions, danger signs, production techniques, and disposal methods. **Biology:** Knowledge of plant and animal living tissue, cells, organisms, and entities, including their functions, interdependencies, and interactions with each other and the environment. **Geography:** Knowledge of various methods for describing the location and distribution of land, sea, and air masses including their physical locations, relationships, and characteristics. **Education and Training:** Knowledge of instructional methods and training techniques including curriculum design principles, learning theory, group and individual teaching techniques, design of individual development plans, and test design principles. **English Language:** Knowledge of the structure and content of the English language including the meaning and spelling of words, rules of composition, and grammar. **History and Archeology:** Knowledge of past historical events and their causes, indicators, and impact on particular civilizations and cultures. **Philosophy and Theology:** Knowledge of different philosophical systems and religions, including their basic principles, values, ethics, ways of thinking, customs, and practices, and their impact on human culture.

Wood Technologists

Conduct research to determine composition, properties, behavior, utilization, development, treatments, and processing methods of wood and wood products. Studies methods of curing wood to determine best and most economical procedure. Investigates processes for converting wood into commodities such as alcohol, veneer, plywood, wood plastics, and other uses. Investigates methods of turning waste wood materials into useful products. Analyzes physical, chemical, and biological properties of wood. Develops and improves methods of preserving and treating wood with substances to increase resistance to wear, fire, fungi, and infestation. Conducts test to determine stability, strength, hardness, and crystallinity of wood under variety of conditions. Determines best types of wood for specific applications. Conducts tests to determine ability of wood adhesives to withstand water, oil penetration, and temperature extremes. Evaluates and improves effectiveness of industrial equipment and production processes for wood.

 ## Occupational Type

Investigative occupations frequently involve working with ideas, and require an extensive amount of thinking. These occupations can involve searching for facts and figuring out problems mentally.

 ## Skills required of Wood Technologists

Reading Comprehension, Mathematics, Science, Critical Thinking, Active Learning, Learning Strategies, Problem Identification, Information Gathering, Information Organization, Synthesis/Reorganization, Idea Generation, Idea Evaluation, Implementation Planning, Operations Analysis, Technology Design, Equipment Selection, Testing, Product Inspection, Visioning, Systems Perception, Identifying Downstream Consequences, Identification of Key Causes, Judgment and Decision Making, Systems Evaluation

College Majors

Forest Products Technology/Technician: An instructional program that prepares individuals to assist a manager, engineer, chemist, or forest product scientist in the measurement, analysis of quality, testing, and processing of harvested forest raw materials, and the selection, grading and marketing of forest products to be used for specific purposes. Includes instruction in identifying, measuring, assessing quality, evaluating commercial value, and strength testing.

 Supporting Courses

Production and Processing: Knowledge of inputs, outputs, raw materials, waste, quality control, costs, and techniques for maximizing the manufacture and distribution of goods. **Engineering and Technology:** Knowledge of equipment, tools, mechanical devices, and their uses to produce motion, light, power, technology, and other applications. **Building and Construction:** Knowledge of materials, methods, and the appropriate tools to construct objects, structures, and buildings. **Mathematics:** Knowledge of numbers, their operations, and interrelationships including arithmetic, algebra, geometry, calculus, statistics, and their applications. **Physics:** Knowledge and prediction of physical principles, laws, and applications including air, water, material dynamics, light, atomic principles, heat, electric theory, earth formations, and meteorological and related natural phenomena. **Chemistry:** Knowledge of the composition, structure, and properties of substances and of the chemical processes and transformations that they undergo. This includes uses of chemicals and their interactions, danger signs, production techniques, and disposal methods. **Biology:** Knowledge of plant and animal living tissue, cells, organisms, and entities, including their functions, interdependencies, and interactions with each other and the environment. **Geography:** Knowledge of various methods for describing the location and distribution of land, sea, and air masses including their physical locations, relationships, and characteristics. **English Language:** Knowledge of the structure and content of the English language including the meaning and spelling of words, rules of composition, and grammar.

Range Managers

Research or study rangeland management practices to provide sustained production of forage, livestock, and wildlife. Studies rangelands to determine best grazing seasons. Studies rangelands to determine number and kind of livestock that can be most profitably grazed. Studies forage plants and their growth requirements to determine varieties best suited to particular range. Develops improved practices for range reseeding. Develops methods for controlling poisonous plants in rangelands. Develops methods for protecting range from fire and rodent damage. Plans and directs maintenance of range improvements. Plans and directs construction of range improvements, such as fencing, corrals, stock-watering reservoirs and soil-erosion control structures.

Occupational Type

Investigative occupations frequently involve working with ideas, and require an extensive amount of thinking. These occupations can involve searching for facts and figuring out problems mentally.

Skills required of Range Managers

Science, Critical Thinking, Active Learning, Problem Identification, Information Gathering, Synthesis/Reorganization, Idea Generation, Idea Evaluation, Implementation Planning, Operations Analysis, Technology Design, Equipment Selection, Visioning, Systems Perception, Identifying Downstream Consequences, Identification of Key Causes, Judgment and Decision Making, Systems Evaluation, Management of Material Resources, Management of Personnel Resources

College Majors

Plant Sciences, General: An instructional program that generally describes the scientific theories and principles involved in the production and management of plants for food, feed, and fiber and soil conservation.

Supporting Courses

Administration and Management: Knowledge of principles and processes involved in business and organizational planning, coordination, and execution. This includes strategic planning, resource allocation, manpower modeling, leadership techniques, and production methods. **Economics and Accounting:** Knowledge of economic and accounting principles and practices, the financial markets, banking, and the analysis and reporting of financial data. **Food Production:** Knowledge of techniques and equipment for planting, growing, and harvesting of food for consumption including crop rotation methods, animal husbandry, and food storage/handling techniques. **Building and Construction:** Knowledge of materials, methods, and the appropriate tools to construct objects, structures, and buildings. **Biology:** Knowledge of plant and animal living tissue, cells, organisms, and entities, including their functions, interdependencies, and interactions with each other and the environment. **Geography:** Knowledge of various methods for describing the location and distribution of land, sea, and air masses including their physical locations, relationships, and characteristics. **Law, Government, and Jurisprudence:** Knowledge of laws, legal codes, court procedures, precedents, government regulations, executive orders, agency rules, and the democratic political process.

Park Naturalists

Plan, develop, and conduct programs to inform public of historical, natural, and scientific features of national, state, or local park. Conducts field trips to point out scientific, historic, and natural features of park. Plans and develops audiovisual devices for public programs. Interviews specialists in desired fields to obtain and develop data for park information programs. Confers with park staff to determine subjects to be presented to public. Prepares and presents illustrated lectures of park features. Constructs historical, scientific, and nature visitor-center displays. Takes photographs and motion pictures to illustrate lectures and publications and to develop displays. Surveys park to determine forest conditions. Surveys park to determine distribution and abundance of fauna and flora. Plans and organizes activities of seasonal staff members. Maintains official park photographic and information files. Performs emergency duties to protect human life, government property, and natural features of park.

Occupational Type

Social occupations frequently involve working with, communicating with, and teaching people. These occupations often involve helping or providing service to others.

Skills required of Park Naturalists

Speaking, Service Orientation, Implementation Planning, Operations Analysis, Technology Design, Systems Perception, Identifying Downstream Consequences, Time Management, Management of Material Resources, Management of Personnel Resources

College Majors

Plant Sciences, General: An instructional program that generally describes the scientific theories and principles involved in the production and management of plants for food, feed, fiber, and soil conservation.

Supporting Courses

Administration and Management: Knowledge of principles and processes involved in business and organizational planning, coordination, and execution. This includes strategic planning, resource allocation, manpower modeling, leadership techniques, and production methods. **Biology:** Knowledge of plant and animal living tissue, cells, organisms, and entities, including their functions, interdependencies, and interactions with each other and the environment. **Geography:** Knowledge of various methods for describing the location and distribution of land, sea, and air masses including their physical locations, relationships, and characteristics. **Education and Training:** Knowledge of instructional methods and training techniques including curriculum design principles, learning theory, group and individual teaching techniques, design of individual development plans, and test design principles. **English Language:** Knowledge of the structure and content of the English language including the meaning and spelling of words, rules of composition, and grammar. **Fine Arts:** Knowledge of theory and techniques required to produce, compose, and perform works of music, dance, visual arts, drama, and sculpture. **History and Archeology:** Knowledge of past historical events and their causes, indicators, and impact on particular civilizations and cultures. **Communications and Media:** Knowledge of media production, communication, and dissemination techniques and methods including alternative ways to inform and entertain via written, oral, and visual media.

GENERAL MANAGERS AND TOP EXECUTIVES

Mining Superintendents and Supervisors

Education	Work experience, plus degree
Average Yearly Earnings	$58,344
Projected Growth	15%
Annual Job Openings	288,825
Self-employed	0%
Employed Part-time	6%

Plan, direct, and coordinate mining operations to extract mineral ore or aggregate from underground or surface mines, quarries, or pits. Confers with engineering, supervisory, and maintenance personnel to plan and coordinate mine development and operations. Directs opening or closing of mine sections, pits, or other work areas, and installation or removal of equipment. Studies land contours and rock formations to specify locations for mine shafts, pillars, and timbers and to determine equipment needs. Directs and coordinates enforcement of mining laws and safety regulations and reports violations. Studies maps and blueprints to determine prospective locations for mine haulage ways, access roads, rail tracks, and conveyor systems. Reviews, consolidates, and oversees updating of mine records, such as geological and survey reports, air quality, safety reports, and production logs. Inspects mine to detect production, equipment, safety, and personnel problems, and recommends steps to improve conditions and increase production. Calculates mining and quarrying operational costs and potential income, and determines activities to maximize income. Negotiates with workers, supervisors, union personnel, and other parties to resolve grievances or settle complaints.

Occupational Type

Enterprising occupations frequently involve starting up and carrying out projects. These occupations can involve leading people and making many decisions. Sometimes they involve risk taking and often deal with business.

Skills required of Mining Superintendents and Supervisors

Active Listening, Science, Active Learning, Monitoring, Coordination, Persuasion, Negotiation, Idea Evaluation, Implementation Planning, Management of Financial Resources, Management of Material Resources, Management of Personnel Resources

College Majors

Various: Many bachelor studies contribute to expertise in this field.

Supporting Courses

Administration and Management: Knowledge of principles and processes involved in business and organizational planning, coordination, and execution. This includes strategic planning, resource allocation, manpower modeling, leadership techniques, and production methods. **Economics and Accounting:** Knowledge of economic and accounting principles and practices, the financial markets, banking, and the analysis and reporting of financial data. **Personnel and Human Resources:** Knowledge of policies and practices involved in personnel/human resource functions. This includes recruitment, selection, training, and promotion regulations and procedures; compensation and benefits packages; labor relations and negotiation strategies; and personnel information systems. **Production and Processing:** Knowledge of inputs, outputs, raw materials, waste, quality control, costs, and techniques for maximizing the manufacture and distribution of goods. **Design:** Knowledge of design techniques, principles, tools and instruments involved in the production and use of precision technical plans, blueprints, drawings, and models. **Building and Construction:** Knowledge of materials, methods, and the appropriate tools to construct objects, structures, and buildings. **Geography:** Knowledge of various methods for describing the location and distribution of land, sea, and air masses including their physical locations, relationships, and characteristics. **Public Safety and Security:** Knowledge of weaponry, public safety, and security operations, rules, regulations, precautions, prevention, and the protection of people, data, and property.

Oil and Gas Drilling and Production Superintendents

Plan, direct, and coordinate activities required to erect, install, and maintain equipment for exploratory or production drilling of oil and gas. May direct technical processes and analyses to resolve drilling problems and to monitor and control operating costs and production efficiency. Plans and directs erection of drilling rigs and installation and maintenance of equipment, such as pumping units and compressor stations. Determines procedures to resolve drilling problems, service well equipment, clean wells, and dismantle and store derricks and drill equipment. Directs technical processes related to drilling, such as treatment of oil and gas, sediment analysis, well logging, and formation testing. Analyzes production reports and formulates drilling and production procedures to control well production in accordance with proration regulations. Directs petroleum exploration parties engaged in drilling for samples of subsurface stratigraphy and in seismic prospecting.

 ## Occupational Type

Enterprising occupations frequently involve starting up and carrying out projects. These occupations can involve leading people and making many decisions. Sometimes they involve risk taking and often deal with business.

 ## Skills required of Oil and Gas Drilling and Production Superintendents

Science, Critical Thinking, Coordination, Negotiation, Instructing, Problem Identification, Implementation Planning, Equipment Selection, Installation, Operation Monitoring, Operation and Control, Identifying Downstream Consequences, Identification of Key Causes, Time Management, Management of Material Resources, Management of Personnel Resources

 ## College Majors

Various: Many bachelor studies contribute to expertise in this field.

Supporting Courses

Administration and Management: Knowledge of principles and processes involved in business and organizational planning, coordination, and execution. This includes strategic planning, resource allocation, manpower modeling, leadership techniques, and production methods. **Production and Processing:** Knowledge of inputs, outputs, raw materials, waste, quality control, costs, and techniques for maximizing the manufacture and distribution of goods. **Engineering and Technology:** Knowledge of equipment, tools, mechanical devices, and their uses to produce motion, light, power, technology, and other applications. **Building and Construction:** Knowledge of materials, methods, and the appropriate tools to construct objects, structures, and buildings. **Physics:** Knowledge and prediction of physical principles, laws, and applications including air, water, material dynamics, light, atomic principles, heat, electric theory, earth formations, and meteorological and related natural phenomena.

Private Sector Executives

Determine and formulate policies and business strategies, and provide overall direction of private sector organizations. Plan, direct, and coordinate operational activities at the highest level of management, with the help of subordinate managers. Directs, plans, and implements policies and objectives of organization or business in accordance with charter and board of directors. Directs activities of organization to plan procedures, establish responsibilities, and coordinate functions among departments and sites. Confers with board members, organization officials, and staff members to establish policies and formulate plans. Analyzes operations to evaluate performance of company and staff and to determine areas of cost reduction and program improvement. Reviews financial statements and sales and activity reports to ensure that organization's objectives are achieved. Directs and coordinates organization's financial and budget activities to fund operations, maximize investments, and increase efficiency. Assigns or delegates responsibilities to subordinates. Directs and coordinates activities of business or department concerned with production, pricing, sales, and/or distribution of products. Directs and coordinates activities of business involved with buying and selling investment products and financial services. Directs nonmerchandising departments of business, such as advertising, purchasing, credit, and accounting. Establishes internal control procedures. Prepares reports and budgets. Presides over or serves on board of directors, management committees, or other governing boards. Negotiates or approves contracts with suppliers and distributors, and with maintenance, janitorial, and security providers. Promotes objectives of institution or business before associations, public, government agencies, or community groups. Screens, selects, hires, transfers, and discharges employees. Administers program for selection of sites, construction of buildings, and provision of equipment and supplies. Directs in-service training of staff.

 Occupational Type

Enterprising occupations frequently involve starting up and carrying out projects. These occupations can involve leading people and making many decisions. Sometimes they involve risk taking and often deal with business.

Skills required of Private Sector Executives

Reading Comprehension, Active Listening, Writing, Speaking, Mathematics, Critical Thinking, Active Learning, Learning Strategies, Monitoring, Social Perceptiveness, Coordination, Persuasion, Negotiation, Service Orientation, Problem Identification, Information Gathering, Information Organization, Synthesis/Reorganization, Idea Generation, Idea Evaluation, Implementation Planning, Operations Analysis, Visioning, Systems Perception, Identifying Downstream Consequences, Identification of Key Causes, Judgment and Decision Making, Systems Evaluation, Time Management, Management of Financial Resources, Management of Material Resources, Management of Personnel Resources

 ## College Majors

General Retailing Operations: An instructional program that prepares individuals to perform marketing tasks specifically applicable to retail operations in a wide variety of settings.

 ## Supporting Courses

Administration and Management: Knowledge of principles and processes involved in business and organizational planning, coordination, and execution. This includes strategic planning, resource allocation, manpower modeling, leadership techniques, and production methods. **Economics and Accounting:** Knowledge of economic and accounting principles and practices, the financial markets, banking, and the analysis and reporting of financial data. **Sales and Marketing:** Knowledge of principles and methods involved in showing, promoting, and selling products or services. This includes marketing strategies and tactics, product demonstration and sales techniques, and sales control systems. **Customer and Personal Service:** Knowledge of principles and processes for providing customer and personal services including needs assessment techniques, quality service standards, alternative delivery systems, and customer satisfaction evaluation techniques. **Personnel and Human Resources:** Knowledge of policies and practices involved in personnel/human resource functions. This includes recruitment, selection, training, and promotion regulations and procedures; compensation and benefits packages; labor relations and negotiation strategies; and personnel information systems. **Production and Processing:** Knowledge of inputs, outputs, raw materials, waste, quality control, costs, and techniques for maximizing the manufacture and distribution of goods. **Food Production:** Knowledge of techniques and equipment for planting, growing, and harvesting of food for consumption including crop rotation methods, animal husbandry, and food storage/handling techniques. **Engineering and Technology:** Knowledge of equipment, tools, mechanical devices, and their uses to produce motion, light, power, technology, and other applications. **Building and Construction:** Knowledge of materials, methods, and the appropriate tools to construct objects, structures, and buildings. **Mathematics:** Knowledge of numbers, their operations, and interrelationships including arithmetic, algebra, geometry, calculus, statistics, and their applications. **Psychology:** Knowledge of human behavior and performance, mental processes, psychological research methods, and the assessment and treatment of behavioral and affective disorders. **Sociology and Anthropology:** Knowledge of group behavior and dynamics, societal trends and influences, cultures, their history, migrations, ethnicity, and origins. **Geography:** Knowledge of various methods for describing the location and distribution of land, sea, and air masses including their physical locations, relationships, and characteristics. **Therapy and Counseling:** Knowledge of information and techniques needed to rehabilitate physical and mental ailments and to provide career guidance including alternative treatments, rehabilitation equipment and its proper use, and methods to evaluate treatment effects. **Education and Training:** Knowledge of instructional methods and training techniques including curriculum design principles, learning theory, group and individual teaching techniques, design of individual development plans, and test design principles. **English Language:** Knowledge of the structure and content of the English language including the meaning and spelling of words, rules of composition, and grammar. **Foreign Language:** Knowledge of the structure and content of a foreign (non-English) language including the meaning and spelling of words, rules of composition and grammar, and pronunciation. **History and Archeology:** Knowledge of past historical events and their causes, indicators, and impact on particular civilizations and cultures. **Philosophy and Theology:** Knowledge of different philosophical systems and religions, including their basic principles, values, ethics, ways of thinking, customs, and practices, and their impact on human culture. **Public Safety and Security:** Knowledge of weaponry, public safety, and security operations, rules, regulations, precautions, prevention, and the protection of people, data, and property. **Law, Government, and Jurisprudence:** Knowledge of laws, legal codes, court procedures, precedents, government regulations, executive orders, agency rules, and the democratic political process. **Communications and Media:** Knowledge of media production, communication, and dissemination techniques and methods including alternative ways to inform and entertain via written, oral, and visual media. **Transportation:** Knowledge of principles and methods for moving people or goods by air, rail, sea, or road, including their relative costs, advantages, and limitations.

GENERAL PURCHASING AGENTS

Education		Bachelor's degree
Average Yearly Earnings		$35,859
Projected Growth		6%
Annual Job Openings		21,175
Self-employed		1%
Employed Part-time		2%

Purchasing Agents and Contract Specialists

Coordinate activities involved with procuring goods and services from suppliers. May negotiate with suppliers to draw up procurement contracts and administer, terminate, or renegotiate contracts. (Excludes purchasing agents and buyers of farm products.) Negotiates or renegotiates and administers contracts with suppliers, vendors, and other representatives. Locates and arranges for purchase of goods and services necessary for efficient operation of organization. Formulates policies and procedures for bid proposals and procurement of goods and services. Analyzes price proposals, financial reports, and other data and information to determine reasonable prices. Prepares purchase orders, or bid proposals and reviews requisitions for goods and services. Directs and coordinates workers' activities involving bid proposals and procurement of goods and services. Evaluates and monitors contract performance to determine need for changes and to ensure compliance with contractual obligations. Arbitrates claims and resolves complaints generated during performance of contract. Maintains and reviews computerized or manual records of items purchased, costs, delivery, product performance, and inventories. Confers with personnel, users, and vendors to discuss defective or unacceptable goods or services, and determines corrective action.

Occupational Type

Enterprising occupations frequently involve starting up and carrying out projects. These occupations can involve leading people and making many decisions. Sometimes they involve risk taking and often deal with business.

Skills required of Purchasing Agents and Contract Specialists

Reading Comprehension, Active Listening, Writing, Speaking, Mathematics, Critical Thinking, Active Learning, Monitoring, Coordination, Persuasion, Negotiation, Problem Identification, Information Gathering, Synthesis/Reorganization, Idea Generation, Implementation Planning, Identifying Downstream Consequences, Identification of Key Causes, Judgment and Decision Making, Systems Evaluation, Management of Financial Resources, Management of Material Resources

College Majors

Agricultural Supplies Retailing and Wholesaling: An instructional program that generally prepares individuals to sell supplies for agricultural production, provide agricultural services and purchase and market agricultural products.

Supporting Courses

Administration and Management: Knowledge of principles and processes involved in business and organizational planning, coordination, and execution. This includes strategic planning, resource allocation, manpower modeling, leadership techniques, and production methods. **Clerical:** Knowledge of administrative and clerical procedures and systems such as word processing systems, filing and records management systems, stenography and transcription, forms design principles, and other office procedures and terminology. **Economics and Accounting:** Knowledge of economic and accounting principles and practices, the financial markets, banking, and the analysis and reporting of financial data. **Sales and Marketing:** Knowledge of principles and methods involved in showing, promoting, and selling products or services. This includes marketing strategies and tactics, product demonstration and sales techniques, and sales control systems. **Computers and Electronics:** Knowledge of electric circuit boards, processors, chips, and computer hardware and software, including applications and programming. **Law, Government, and Jurisprudence:** Knowledge of laws, legal codes, court procedures, precedents, government regulations, executive orders, agency rules, and the democratic political process. **Transportation:** Knowledge of principles and methods for moving people or goods by air, rail, sea, or road, including their relative costs, advantages, and limitations.

Procurement Engineers

Coordinate the development and use of engineering specifications and requirements to facilitate the procurement of parts, tools, equipment, or other products or materials. Develops and establishes specifications and performance test requirements for equipment to be purchased. Coordinates engineering, tool design, purchasing, and other activities to facilitate production and procurement of tooling. Coordinates procurement and production activities to expedite movement of tools between departments or vendors. Analyzes technical data, designs, preliminary specifications, and availability of parts and equipment. Evaluates tooling orders to determine whether tooling should be manufactured in-house or purchased from outside vendors. Calculates and records tool requirements, and maintains records of procurement, status, and disposition information. Prepares requisitions for tooling purchases, and processes requests for tool repairs. Investigates equipment makers and potential suppliers, and recommends those most desirable. Advises personnel, suppliers, and customers of nature and function of parts and equipment. Arranges conferences between suppliers, engineers, purchasers, inspectors, and other personnel to facilitate procurement process.

Occupational Type

Conventional occupations frequently involve following set procedures and routines. These occupations can include working with data and details more than with ideas. Usually there is a clear line of authority to follow.

Skills required of Procurement Engineers

Reading Comprehension, Active Listening, Writing, Mathematics, Science, Critical Thinking, Active Learning, Learning Strategies, Monitoring, Coordination, Persuasion, Negotiation, Problem Identification, Information Gathering, Synthesis/Reorganization, Idea Evaluation, Implementation Planning, Operations Analysis, Technology Design, Equipment Selection, Visioning, Identifying Downstream Consequences, Identification of Key Causes, Judgment and Decision Making, Systems Evaluation, Time Management, Management of Financial Resources, Management of Material Resources

College Majors

Aerospace, Aeronautical and Astronautical Engineering: An instructional program that prepares individuals to apply mathematical and scientific principles to the design, development and operational evaluation of aircraft, space vehicles, and their systems; applied research on flight characteristics; and the development of systems and procedures for the launching, guidance, and control of air and space vehicles.

Supporting Courses

Administration and Management: Knowledge of principles and processes involved in business and organizational planning, coordination, and execution. This includes strategic planning, resource allocation, manpower modeling, leadership techniques, and production methods. **Clerical:** Knowledge of administrative and clerical procedures and systems such as word processing systems, filing and records management systems, stenography and transcription, forms design principles, and other office procedures and terminology. **Economics and Accounting:** Knowledge of economic and accounting principles and practices, the financial markets, banking, and the analysis and reporting of financial data. **Sales and Marketing:** Knowledge of principles and methods involved in showing, promoting, and selling products or services. This includes marketing strategies and tactics, product demonstration and sales techniques, and sales control systems. **Production and Processing:** Knowledge of inputs, outputs, raw materials, waste, quality control, costs, and techniques for maximizing the manufacture and distribution of goods. **Engineering and Technology:** Knowledge of equipment, tools, mechanical devices, and their uses to produce motion, light, power, technology, and other applications. **Design:** Knowledge of design techniques, principles, tools and instruments involved in the production and use of precision technical plans, blueprints, drawings, and models. **Mathematics:** Knowledge of numbers, their operations, and interrelationships including arithmetic, algebra, geometry, calculus, statistics, and their applications. **Physics:** Knowledge and prediction of physical principles, laws, and applications including air, water, material dynamics, light, atomic principles, heat, electric theory, earth formations, and meteorological and related natural phenomena.

Price Analysts

Compile and analyze statistical data to determine feasibility of buying products and to establish price objectives for contract transactions. Compiles and analyzes statistical data to establish price objectives and to determine purchasing feasibility. Evaluates findings and makes recommendations regarding feasibility of manufacturing or purchasing needed products. Compiles information from periodicals, catalogs, and other sources to keep informed on price trends and manufacturing processes. Determines manufacturing costs within company divisions to obtain data for cost analysis studies. Confers with vendors and analyzes vendors' operations to determine factors that affect prices. Prepares reports, charts, and graphs to track statistical data, price information, and cost analysis findings.

Occupational Type

Conventional occupations frequently involve following set procedures and routines. These occupations can include working with data and details more than with ideas. Usually there is a clear line of authority to follow.

Skills required of Price Analysts

Reading Comprehension, Writing, Speaking, Mathematics, Critical Thinking, Active Learning, Persuasion, Problem Identification, Information Gathering, Information Organization, Synthesis/Reorganization, Idea Generation, Idea Evaluation, Operations Analysis, Programming, Visioning, Systems Perception, Identifying Downstream Consequences, Identification of Key Causes, Judgment and Decision Making, Systems Evaluation, Management of Financial Resources

College Majors

Business Administration and Management, General: An instructional program that generally prepares individuals to plan, organize, direct, and control the functions and processes of a firm or organization. Includes instruction in management theory, human resources management and behavior, accounting and other quantitative methods, purchasing and logistics, organization and production, marketing, and business decisionmaking.

Supporting Courses

Economics and Accounting: Knowledge of economic and accounting principles and practices, the financial markets, banking, and the analysis and reporting of financial data. **Mathematics:** Knowledge of numbers, their operations, and interrelationships including arithmetic, algebra, geometry, calculus, statistics, and their applications.

GEOLOGISTS, GEOPHYSICISTS, AND OCEANOGRAPHERS

Education	Bachelor's degree
Average Yearly Earnings	$52,083
Projected Growth	15%
Annual Job Openings	1,688
Self-employed	15%
Employed Part-time	6%

Geologists

Study composition, structure, and history of the earth's crust; examine rocks, minerals, and fossil remains to identify and determine the sequence of processes affecting the development of the earth; apply knowledge of chemistry, physics, biology, and mathematics to explain these phenomena and to help locate mineral and petroleum deposits and underground water resources; prepare geologic reports and maps; and interpret research data to recommend further action for study. Studies, examines, measures, and classifies composition, structure, and history of earth's crust, including rocks, minerals, fossils, soil, and ocean floor. Identifies and determines sequence of processes affecting development of earth. Locates and estimates probable gas and oil deposits, using aerial photographs, charts, and research and survey results. Prepares geological reports, maps, charts, and diagrams. Interprets research data, and recommends further study or action. Analyzes engineering problems at construction projects, such as dams, tunnels, and large buildings, applying geological knowledge. Tests industrial diamonds and abrasives, soil, or rocks to determine geological characteristics, using optical, X-ray, heat, acid, and precision instruments. Inspects proposed construction site and sets up test equipment and drilling machinery. Measures characteristics of earth, using seismograph, gravimeter, torsion balance, magnetometer, pendulum devices, and electrical resistivity apparatus. Directs field crews drilling exploratory wells and boreholes or collecting samples of rocks and soil. Recommends and prepares reports on foundation design, acquisition, retention, or release of property leases, or areas of further research. Develops instruments for geological work, such as diamond tools and dies, jeweled bearings, and grinding laps and wheels. Repairs diamond and abrasive tools.

Occupational Type

Investigative occupations frequently involve working with ideas, and require an extensive amount of thinking. These occupations can involve searching for facts and figuring out problems mentally.

Skills required of Geologists

Reading Comprehension, Writing, Mathematics, Science, Critical Thinking, Active Learning, Coordination, Problem Identification, Information Gathering, Information Organization, Synthesis/Reorganization, Idea Generation, Idea Evaluation, Implementation Planning, Operations Analysis, Technology Design, Equipment Selection, Installation, Programming, Testing, Product Inspection, Repairing, Visioning, Systems Perception, Identifying Downstream Consequences, Identification of Key Causes, Judgment and Decision Making, Systems Evaluation, Time Management, Management of Personnel Resources

College Majors

Mining Technology/Technician: An instructional program that prepares individuals to apply basic engineering principles and technical skills in support of engineers and other professionals engaged in the development and operation of mines and related mineral processing facilities. Includes instruction in principles of mineral extraction and related geology, mineral field mapping and site analysis, testing and sampling methods, instrument calibration, assay analysis, test equipment operation and maintenance, mine environment and safety monitoring procedures, mine inspection procedures, and report preparation.

Supporting Courses

Administration and Management: Knowledge of principles and processes involved in business and organizational planning, coordination, and execution. This includes strategic planning, resource allocation, manpower modeling, leadership techniques, and production methods. **Engineering and Technology:** Knowledge of equipment, tools, mechanical devices, and their uses to produce motion, light, power, technology, and other applications. **Design:** Knowledge of design techniques, principles, tools and instruments involved in the production and use of precision technical plans, blueprints, drawings, and models. **Mechanical:** Knowledge of machines and tools, including their designs, uses, benefits, repair, and maintenance. **Mathematics:** Knowledge of numbers, their operations, and interrelationships including arithmetic, algebra, geometry, calculus, statistics, and their applications. **Physics:** Knowledge and prediction of physical principles, laws, and applications including air, water, material dynamics, light, atomic principles, heat, electric theory, earth formations, and meteorological and related natural phenomena. **Chemistry:** Knowledge of the composition, structure, and properties of substances and of the chemical processes and transformations that they undergo. This includes uses of chemicals and their interactions, danger signs, production techniques, and disposal methods. **Biology:** Knowledge of plant and animal living tissue, cells, organisms, and entities, including their functions, interdependencies, and interactions with each other and the environment. **Psychology:** Knowledge of human behavior and performance, mental processes, psychological research methods, and the assessment and treatment of behavioral and affective disorders.

Sociology and Anthropology: Knowledge of group behavior and dynamics, societal trends and influences, cultures, their history, migrations, ethnicity, and origins. **Geography:** Knowledge of various methods for describing the location and distribution of land, sea, and air masses including their physical locations, relationships, and characteristics. **English Language:** Knowledge of the structure and content of the English language including the meaning and spelling of words, rules of composition, and grammar. **History and Archeology:** Knowledge of past historical events and their causes, indicators, and impact on particular civilizations and cultures. **Communications and Media:** Knowledge of media production, communication, and dissemination techniques and methods including alternative ways to inform and entertain via written, oral, and visual media.

Geophysicists

Study physical aspects of the earth, including the atmosphere and hydrosphere. Investigate and measure seismic, gravitational, electrical, thermal, and magnetic forces affecting the earth, utilizing principles of physics, mathematics, and chemistry. Studies and analyzes physical aspects of the earth, including atmosphere and hydrosphere, and interior structure. Studies, measures, and interprets seismic, gravitational, electrical, thermal, and magnetic forces and data affecting the earth. Studies, maps, and charts distribution, disposition, and development of waters of land areas, including form and intensity of precipitation. Studies waters of land areas to determine modes of return to ocean and atmosphere. Investigates origin and activity of glaciers, volcanoes, and earthquakes. Compiles and evaluates data to prepare navigational charts and maps, predict atmospheric conditions, and prepare environmental reports. Evaluates data in reference to project planning, such as flood and drought control, water power and supply, drainage, irrigation, and inland navigation. Prepares and issues maps and reports indicating areas of seismic risk to existing or proposed construction or development.

 ## Occupational Type

Investigative occupations frequently involve working with ideas, and require an extensive amount of thinking. These occupations can involve searching for facts and figuring out problems mentally.

 ## Skills required of Geophysicists

Reading Comprehension, Writing, Mathematics, Science, Critical Thinking, Active Learning, Problem Identification, Information Gathering, Information Organization, Synthesis/Reorganization, Idea Generation, Idea Evaluation, Implementation Planning, Operations Analysis, Programming, Visioning, Systems Perception, Identifying Downstream Consequences, Identification of Key Causes, Judgment and Decision Making

 ## College Majors

Geology: An instructional program that describes the scientific study of the earth; the forces acting upon it; and the behavior of the solids, liquids and gases comprising it. Includes instruction in historical geology, geomorphology, sedimentology, the chemistry of rocks and soils, stratigraphy, mineralogy, petrology, geostatistics, volcanology, glaciology, geophysical principles, and applications to research and industrial problems.

Supporting Courses

Mathematics: Knowledge of numbers, their operations, and interrelationships including arithmetic, algebra, geometry, calculus, statistics, and their applications. **Physics:** Knowledge and prediction of physical principles, laws, and applications including air, water, material dynamics, light, atomic principles, heat, electric theory, earth formations, and meteorological and related natural phenomena. **Chemistry:** Knowledge of the composition, structure, and properties of substances and of the chemical processes and transformations that they undergo. This includes uses of chemicals and their interactions, danger signs, production techniques, and disposal methods. **Geography:** Knowledge of various methods for describing the location and distribution of land, sea, and air masses including their physical locations, relationships, and characteristics. **English Language:** Knowledge of the structure and content of the English language including the meaning and spelling of words, rules of composition, and grammar. **History and Archeology:** Knowledge of past historical events and their causes, indicators, and impact on particular civilizations and cultures. **Communications and Media:** Knowledge of media production, communication, and dissemination techniques and methods including alternative ways to inform and entertain via written, oral, and visual media.

HEALTHCARE SUPPORT SPECIALISTS

All Other Health Diagnosing and Treating Practitioners

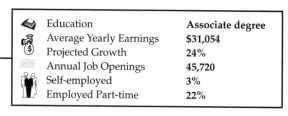

Education	Associate degree	
Average Yearly Earnings	$31,054	
Projected Growth	24%	
Annual Job Openings	45,720	
Self-employed	3%	
Employed Part-time	22%	

All other health diagnosing and treating practitioners not classified separately above.

Occupational Type

Specific information is not available.

Skills required of All Other Health Diagnosing and Treating Practitioners

Information on specific skills required is not available.

College Majors

Hypnotherapy: An instructional program that prepares individuals to employ hypnosis as a tool to assist patients in reducing physical pain, resolving emotional conflicts and enhancing communications with others. Includes instruction in trance inducement and its relation to other healing arts specialties.

Supporting Courses

Specific information is not available.

INDUSTRIAL ENGINEERS

	Education	**Bachelor's degree**
	Average Yearly Earnings	**$51,064**
	Projected Growth	**14%**
	Annual Job Openings	**3,555**
	Self-employed	**3%**
	Employed Part-time	**2%**

Industrial Engineers, Except Safety

Perform engineering duties in planning and overseeing the utilization of production facilities and personnel in department or other subdivision of industrial establishment. Plan equipment layout, work flow, and accident prevention measures to maintain efficient and safe utilization of plant facilities. Plan and oversee work, study, and training programs to promote efficient worker utilization. Develop and oversee quality control, inventory control, and production record systems. (Excludes industrial product safety engineers.) Analyzes statistical data and product specifications to determine standards and establish quality and reliability objectives of finished product. Develops manufacturing methods, labor utilization standards, and cost analysis systems to promote efficient staff and facility utilization. Drafts and designs layout of equipment, materials, and workspace to illustrate maximum efficiency, using drafting tools and computer. Plans and establishes sequence of operations to fabricate and assemble parts or products and to promote efficient utilization of resources. Reviews production schedules, engineering specifications, orders, and related information to obtain knowledge of manufacturing methods, procedures, and activities. Studies operations sequence, material flow, functional statements, organization charts, and project information to determine worker functions and responsibilities. Formulates sampling procedures and designs and develops forms and instructions for recording, evaluating, and reporting quality and reliability data. Applies statistical methods and performs mathematical calculations to determine manufacturing processes, staff requirements, and production standards. Coordinates quality control objectives and activities to resolve production problems, maximize product reliability, and minimize cost. Communicates with management and user personnel to develop production and design standards. Recommends methods for improving utilization of personnel, material, and utilities. Estimates production cost and effect of product design changes for management review, action, and control. Completes production reports, purchase orders, and material, tool, and equipment lists. Directs workers engaged in product measurement, inspection, and testing activities to ensure quality control and reliability. Records or oversees recording of information to ensure currency of engineering drawings and documentation of production problems. Regulates and alters work flow schedules, according to established manufacturing sequences and lead times, to expedite production operations. Implements methods and procedures for disposition of discrepant material and defective or damaged parts, and assesses cost and responsibility. Evaluates precision and accuracy of production and testing equipment and engineering drawings to formulate corrective action plan. Confers with vendors, staff, and management personnel regarding purchases, procedures, product specifications, manufacturing capabilities, and project status. Schedules deliveries based on production forecasts, material substitutions, storage and handling facilities, and maintenance requirements.

Occupational Type

Enterprising occupations frequently involve starting up and carrying out projects. These occupations can involve leading people and making many decisions. Sometimes they involve risk taking and often deal with business.

Skills required of Industrial Engineers, Except Safety

Reading Comprehension, Mathematics, Science, Critical Thinking, Active Learning, Problem Identification, Information Gathering, Idea Generation, Idea Evaluation, Implementation Planning, Operations Analysis, Technology Design, Product Inspection, Visioning, Identifying Downstream Consequences, Judgment and Decision Making, Systems Evaluation, Time Management, Management of Material Resources

College Majors

Industrial/Manufacturing Engineering: An instructional program that prepares individuals to apply mathematical and scientific principles to the design, development and operational evaluation of integrated systems for managing industrial production processes, including the optimization of human work factors, efficiency engineering, logistics and material flow, just-in-time manufacturing, industrial quality control, automation, cost analysis, and production coordination.

Supporting Courses

Administration and Management: Knowledge of principles and processes involved in business and organizational planning, coordination, and execution. This includes strategic planning, resource allocation, manpower modeling, leadership techniques, and production methods. **Clerical:** Knowledge of administrative and clerical procedures and systems such as word processing systems, filing and records management systems, stenography and transcription, forms design principles, and other office procedures and terminology. **Economics and Accounting:** Knowledge of economic and accounting principles and practices, the financial markets, banking, and the analysis and reporting of financial data. **Personnel and Human Resources:** Knowledge of policies and practices involved in personnel/human resource functions. This includes recruitment, selection, training, and promotion regulations and procedures; compensation and benefits packages; labor relations and negotiation strategies; and personnel information systems. **Production and Processing:** Knowledge of inputs, outputs, raw materials, waste, quality control, costs, and techniques for maximizing the manufacture and distribution of goods. **Engineering and Technology:** Knowledge of equipment, tools, mechanical devices, and their uses to produce motion, light, power, technology, and other applications. **Design:** Knowledge of design techniques, principles, tools and instruments involved in the production and use of precision technical plans, blueprints, drawings, and models. **Mathematics:** Knowledge of numbers, their operations, and interrelationships including arithmetic, algebra, geometry, calculus, statistics, and their applications. **Physics:** Knowledge and prediction of physical principles, laws, and applications including air, water, material dynamics, light, atomic principles, heat, electric theory, earth formations, and meteorological and related natural phenomena. **Psychology:** Knowledge of human behavior and performance, mental processes, psychological research methods, and the assessment and treatment of behavioral and affective disorders. **Education and Training:** Knowledge of instructional methods and training techniques including curriculum design principles, learning theory, group and individual teaching techniques, design of individual development plans, and test design principles. **Public Safety and Security:** Knowledge of weaponry, public safety, and security operations, rules, regulations, precautions, prevention, and the protection of people, data, and property.

INDUSTRIAL PRODUCTION MANAGERS

Industrial Production Managers

Education	Bachelor's degree
Average Yearly Earnings	$50,710
Projected Growth	-3%
Annual Job Openings	14,917
Self-employed	0%
Employed Part-time	6%

Plan, organize, direct, control, and co-ordinate the work activities and resources necessary for manufacturing products in accordance with cost, quality, and quantity specifications. Directs and coordinates production, processing, distribution, and marketing activities of industrial organization. Reviews processing schedules and production orders to determine staffing requirements, work procedures, and duty assignments. Reviews plans and confers with research and support staff to develop new products and processes or the quality of existing products. Initiates and coordinates inventory and cost control programs. Analyzes production, quality control, maintenance, and other operational reports to detect production problems. Reviews operations and confers with technical or administrative staff to resolve production or processing problems. Negotiates material prices with suppliers. Develops budgets and approves expenditures for supplies, materials, and human resources. Coordinates and recommends procedures for facility and equipment maintenance or modification. Examines samples of raw products or directs testing during processing to ensure finished products conform to prescribed quality standards. Prepares and maintains production reports and personnel records. Hires, trains, evaluates, and discharges staff. Resolves personnel grievances. Plans and develops sales or promotional programs for products in new and existing markets.

Occupational Type

Enterprising occupations frequently involve starting up and carrying out projects. These occupations can involve leading people and making many decisions. Sometimes they involve risk taking and often deal with business.

Skills required of Industrial Production Managers

Speaking, Critical Thinking, Active Learning, Monitoring, Social Perceptiveness, Coordination, Persuasion, Negotiation, Problem Identification, Information Gathering, Synthesis/Reorganization, Idea Generation, Idea Evaluation, Implementation Planning, Operations Analysis, Equipment Selection, Installation, Product Inspection, Equipment Maintenance, Troubleshooting, Visioning, Systems Perception, Identifying Downstream Consequences, Identification of Key Causes, Judgment and Decision Making, Systems Evaluation, Time Management, Management of Financial Resources, Management of Material Resources, Management of Personnel Resources

College Majors

Agricultural and Food Products Processing Operations and Management: An instructional program that prepares individuals to receive, inspect, store, and process agricultural food or products preparatory to marketing. Includes instruction in the characteristics and properties of agricultural products, and processing and storage techniques.

Supporting Courses

Administration and Management: Knowledge of principles and processes involved in business and organizational planning, coordination, and execution. This includes strategic planning, resource allocation, manpower modeling, leadership techniques, and production methods. **Economics and Accounting:** Knowledge of economic and accounting principles and practices, the financial markets, banking, and the analysis and reporting of financial data. **Sales and Marketing:** Knowledge of principles and methods involved in showing, promoting, and selling products or services. This includes marketing strategies and tactics, product demonstration and sales techniques, and sales control systems. **Customer and Personal Service:** Knowledge of principles and processes for providing customer and personal services including needs assessment techniques, quality service standards, alternative delivery systems, and customer satisfaction evaluation techniques. **Personnel and Human Resources:** Knowledge of policies and practices involved in personnel/human resource functions. This includes recruitment, selection, training, and promotion regulations and procedures; compensation and benefits packages; labor relations and negotiation strategies; and personnel information systems. **Production and Processing:** Knowledge of inputs, outputs, raw materials, waste, quality control, costs, and techniques for maximizing the manufacture and distribution of goods. **Food Production:** Knowledge of techniques and equipment for planting, growing, and harvesting of food for consumption including crop rotation methods, animal husbandry, and food storage/handling techniques. **Chemistry:** Knowledge of the composition, structure, and properties of substances and of the chemical processes and transformations that they undergo. This includes uses of chemicals and their interactions, danger signs, production techniques, and disposal methods. **Psychology:** Knowledge of human behavior and performance, mental processes, psychological research methods, and the assessment and treatment of behavioral and affective disorders. **Sociology and Anthropology:** Knowledge of group behavior and dynamics, societal trends and influences, cultures, their history, migrations, ethnicity, and origins. **Education and Training:** Knowledge of instructional methods and training techniques including curriculum design principles, learning theory, group and individual teaching techniques, design of individual development plans, and test design principles. **Law, Government, and Jurisprudence:** Knowledge of laws, legal codes, court procedures, precedents, government regulations, executive orders, agency rules, and the democratic political process. **Communications and Media:** Knowledge of media production, communication, and dissemination techniques and methods including alternative ways to inform and entertain via written, oral, and visual media. **Transportation:** Knowledge of principles and methods for moving people or goods by air, rail, sea, or road, including their relative costs, advantages, and limitations.

INSURANCE CLAIMS EXAMINERS

	Education	Bachelor's degree
	Average Yearly Earnings	$41,142
	Projected Growth	22%
	Annual Job Openings	7,281
	Self-employed	0%
	Employed Part-time	7%

Claims Examiners, Property and Casualty Insurance

Review settled insurance claims to determine that payments and settlements have been made in accordance with company practices and procedures, ensuring that adjusters have followed proper methods. Report overpayments, underpayments, and other irregularities. Confer with legal counsel on claims requiring litigation. Analyzes data used in settling claim to determine its validity in payment of claims. Reports overpayments, underpayments, and other irregularities. Confers with legal counsel on claims requiring litigation.

Occupational Type

Conventional occupations frequently involve following set procedures and routines. These occupations can include working with data and details more than with ideas. Usually there is a clear line of authority to follow.

Skills required of Claims Examiners, Property and Casualty Insurance

Reading Comprehension, Mathematics, Monitoring, Problem Identification, Information Gathering, Judgment and Decision Making, Systems Evaluation

College Majors

Finance, General: An instructional program that generally prepares individuals to plan, manage, and analyze the financial and monetary aspects and performance of business enterprises, banking institutions, or other organizations. Includes instruction in principles of accounting; financial instruments; capital planning; funds acquisition; asset and debt management; budgeting; financial analysis; and investments and portfolio management.

Supporting Courses

Law, Government, and Jurisprudence: Knowledge of laws, legal codes, court procedures, precedents, government regulations, executive orders, agency rules, and the democratic political process.

INTERIOR DESIGNERS

Education		Bachelor's degree
Average Yearly Earnings		$32,094
Projected Growth		28%
Annual Job Openings		9,238
Self-employed		41%
Employed Part-time		20%

Interior Designers

Plan, design, and furnish interiors of residential, commercial, or industrial buildings. Formulate design which is practical, aesthetic, and conducive to intended purposes, such as raising productivity, selling merchandise, or improving lifestyle. May specialize in a particular field, style, or phase of interior design. (Excludes merchandise display designers.) Formulates environmental plan to be practical, aesthetic, and conducive to intended purposes, such as raising productivity or selling merchandise. Selects or designs and purchases furnishings, artworks, and accessories. Confers with client to determine factors affecting planning interior environments, such as budget, architectural preferences, and purpose and function. Plans and designs interior environments for boats, planes, buses, trains, and other enclosed spaces. Advises client on interior design factors, such as space planning, layout, and utilization of furnishings and equipment, and color coordination. Renders design ideas in form of paste-ups or drawings. Estimates material requirements and costs, and presents design to client for approval. Subcontracts fabrication, installation, and arrangement of carpeting, fixtures, accessories, draperies, paint and wall coverings, artwork, furniture, and related items.

Occupational Type

Artistic occupations frequently involve working with forms, designs, and patterns. They often require self-expression and the work can be done without following a clear set of rules.

Skills required of Interior Designers

Active Listening, Speaking, Mathematics, Coordination, Persuasion, Negotiation, Service Orientation, Synthesis/Reorganization, Idea Generation, Idea Evaluation, Implementation Planning, Operations Analysis, Visioning, Identification of Key Causes, Time Management, Management of Financial Resources, Management of Material Resources

College Majors

Interior Architecture: An instructional program that prepares individuals for the independent professional practice of interior architecture, the processes and techniques of designing living, work and leisure indoor environments as integral components of a building system. Includes instruction in building design and structural systems, heating, and cooling systems, safety and health standards, and interior design principles and standards.

 ## Supporting Courses

Administration and Management: Knowledge of principles and processes involved in business and organizational planning, coordination, and execution. This includes strategic planning, resource allocation, manpower modeling, leadership techniques, and production methods. **Sales and Marketing:** Knowledge of principles and methods involved in showing, promoting, and selling products or services. This includes marketing strategies and tactics, product demonstration and sales techniques, and sales control systems. **Customer and Personal Service:** Knowledge of principles and processes for providing customer and personal services including needs assessment techniques, quality service standards, alternative delivery systems, and customer satisfaction evaluation techniques. **Design:** Knowledge of design techniques, principles, tools and instruments involved in the production and use of precision technical plans, blueprints, drawings, and models. **Fine Arts:** Knowledge of theory and techniques required to produce, compose, and perform works of music, dance, visual arts, drama, and sculpture.

JUDGES AND MAGISTRATES

Judges and Magistrates

	Education	Work experience, plus degree
	Average Yearly Earnings	$51,667
	Projected Growth	2%
	Annual Job Openings	3,558
	Self-employed	0%
	Employed Part-time	8%

Judges arbitrate, advise, and administer justice in a court of law. Sentence defendant in criminal cases according to statutes of state or Federal government. May determine liability of defendant in civil cases. Magistrates adjudicate criminal cases not involving penitentiary sentences and civil cases concerning damages below a sum specified by state law. May issue marriage licenses and perform wedding ceremonies. Listens to presentation of case, rules on admissibility of evidence and methods of conducting testimony, and settles disputes between opposing attorneys. Instructs jury on applicable law, and directs jury to deduce facts from evidence presented. Sentences defendant in criminal cases, on conviction by jury, according to statutes of state or Federal government. Adjudicates cases involving motor vehicle laws. Establishes rules of procedure on questions for which standard procedures have not been established by law or by superior court. Conducts preliminary hearings in felony cases to determine reasonable and probable cause to hold defendant for further proceedings or trial. Reads or listens to allegations made by plaintiff in civil suits to determine their sufficiency. Awards judicial relief to litigants in civil cases in relation to findings by jury or by court. Examines evidence in criminal cases to determine if evidence will support charges. Performs wedding ceremonies.

Occupational Type

Enterprising occupations frequently involve starting up and carrying out projects. These occupations can involve leading people and making many decisions. Sometimes they involve risk taking and often deal with business.

Skills required of Judges and Magistrates

Reading Comprehension, Active Listening, Writing, Speaking, Critical Thinking, Active Learning, Learning Strategies, Monitoring, Social Perceptiveness, Coordination, Persuasion, Negotiation, Problem Identification, Information Gathering, Information Organization, Synthesis/Reorganization, Idea Generation, Idea Evaluation, Implementation Planning, Visioning, Systems Perception, Identifying Downstream Consequences, Identification of Key Causes, Judgment and Decision Making, Systems Evaluation, Time Management

College Majors

Law (L.L.B., J.D.): An instructional program that prepares individuals for the independent professional practice of law and for advanced research in jurisprudence. Includes instruction in the theory and practice of the legal system, including the statutory, administrative, and judicial components of civil and criminal law.

Supporting Courses

Economics and Accounting: Knowledge of economic and accounting principles and practices, the financial markets, banking, and the analysis and reporting of financial data. **Personnel and Human Resources:** Knowledge of policies and practices involved in personnel/ human resource functions. This includes recruitment, selection, training, and promotion regulations and procedures; compensation and benefits packages; labor relations and negotiation strategies; and personnel information systems. **Psychology:** Knowledge of human behavior and performance, mental processes, psychological research methods, and the assessment and treatment of behavioral and affective disorders. **Sociology and Anthropology:** Knowledge of group behavior and dynamics, societal trends and influences, cultures, their history, migrations, ethnicity, and origins. **Geography:** Knowledge of various methods for describing the location and distribution of land, sea, and air masses including their physical locations, relationships, and characteristics. **English Language:** Knowledge of the structure and content of the English language including the meaning and spelling of words, rules of composition, and grammar. **History and Archeology:** Knowledge of past historical events and their causes, indicators, and impact on particular civilizations and cultures. **Philosophy and Theology:** Knowledge of different philosophical systems and religions, including their basic principles, values, ethics, ways of thinking, customs, and practices, and their impact on human culture. **Public Safety and Security:** Knowledge of weaponry, public safety, and security operations, rules, regulations, precautions, prevention, and the protection of people, data, and property. **Law, Government, and Jurisprudence:** Knowledge of laws, legal codes, court procedures, precedents, government regulations, executive orders, agency rules, and the democratic political process.

Communications and Media: Knowledge of media production, communication, and dissemination techniques and methods including alternative ways to inform and entertain via written, oral, and visual media.

Adjudicators, Hearings Officers, and Judicial Reviewers

Conduct hearings to review and decide claims filed by the government against individuals or organizations, or individual eligibility issues concerning social programs, disability, or unemployment benefits. Determine the existence and the amount of liability; recommend the acceptance or rejection of claims; or compromise settlements according to laws, regulations, policies, and precedent decisions. Confer with persons or organizations involved, and prepare written decisions. Arranges and conducts hearings to obtain information and evidence relative to disposition of claim. Determines existence and amount of liability, according to law, administrative and judicial precedents, and evidence. Counsels parties, and recommends acceptance or rejection of compromise settlement offers. Prepares written opinions and decisions. Analyzes evidence and applicable law, regulations, policy, and precedent decisions to determine conclusions. Interviews or corresponds with claimants or agents to elicit information. Questions witnesses to obtain information. Reviews and evaluates data on documents, such as claim applications, birth or death certificates, and physician or employer records. Rules on exceptions, motions, and admissibility of evidence. Researches laws, regulations, policies, and precedent decisions to prepare for hearings. Participates in court proceedings. Issues subpoenas and administers oaths to prepare for formal hearing. Obtains additional information to clarify evidence. Authorizes payment of valid claims. Notifies claimant of denied claim and appeal rights. Conducts studies of appeals procedures in field agencies to ensure adherence to legal requirements and to facilitate determination of cases.

Occupational Type

Enterprising occupations frequently involve starting up and carrying out projects. These occupations can involve leading people and making many decisions. Sometimes they involve risk taking and often deal with business.

Skills required of Adjudicators, Hearings Officers, and Judicial Reviewers

Reading Comprehension, Active Listening, Writing, Speaking, Critical Thinking, Active Learning, Social Perceptiveness, Negotiation, Information Gathering, Information Organization, Synthesis/Reorganization, Idea Generation, Idea Evaluation, Judgment and Decision Making

College Majors

Law (L.L.B., J.D.): An instructional program that prepares individuals for the independent professional practice of law and for advanced research in jurisprudence. Includes instruction in the theory and practice of the legal system, including the statutory, administrative, and judicial components of civil and criminal law.

Supporting Courses

Administration and Management: Knowledge of principles and processes involved in business and organizational planning, coordination, and execution. This includes strategic planning, resource allocation, manpower modeling, leadership techniques, and production methods. **Psychology:** Knowledge of human behavior and performance, mental processes, psychological research methods, and the assessment and treatment of behavioral and affective disorders. **Sociology and Anthropology:** Knowledge of group behavior and dynamics, societal trends and influences, cultures, their history, migrations, ethnicity, and origins. **Therapy and Counseling:** Knowledge of information and techniques needed to rehabilitate physical and mental ailments and to provide career guidance including alternative treatments, rehabilitation equipment and its proper use, and methods to evaluate treatment effects. **English Language:** Knowledge of the structure and content of the English language including the meaning and spelling of words, rules of composition, and grammar. **History and Archeology:** Knowledge of past historical events and their causes, indicators, and impact on particular civilizations and cultures. **Philosophy and Theology:** Knowledge of different philosophical systems and religions, including their basic principles, values, ethics, ways of thinking, customs, and practices, and their impact on human culture. **Law, Government, and Jurisprudence:** Knowledge of laws, legal codes, court procedures, precedents, government regulations, executive orders, agency rules, and the democratic political process.

LANDSCAPE ARCHITECTS

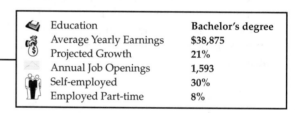

Education		Bachelor's degree
Average Yearly Earnings		$38,875
Projected Growth		21%
Annual Job Openings		1,593
Self-employed		30%
Employed Part-time		8%

Landscape Architects

Plan and design land areas for such projects as parks and other recreational facilities, airports, highways, hospitals, schools, land subdivisions, and commercial, industrial, and residential sites. Prepares site plans, specifications, and cost estimates for land development, coordinating arrangement of existing and proposed land features and structures. Compiles and analyzes data on conditions, such as location, drainage, and location of structures, for environmental reports and landscaping plans. Inspects landscape work to ensure compliance with specifications, approves quality of materials and work, and advises client and construction personnel. Confers with clients, engineering personnel, and architects on overall program.

Occupational Type

Artistic occupations frequently involve working with forms, designs, and patterns. They often require self-expression and the work can be done without following a clear set of rules.

Skills required of Landscape Architects

Reading Comprehension, Active Listening, Writing, Speaking, Mathematics, Critical Thinking, Active Learning, Learning Strategies, Monitoring, Coordination, Persuasion, Negotiation,

Problem Identification, Information Gathering, Information Organization, Synthesis Reorganization, Idea Generation, Idea Evaluation, Implementation Planning, Operations Analysis, Product Inspection, Visioning, Systems Perception, Identifying Downstream Consequences, Identification of Key Causes, Judgment and Decision Making, Systems Evaluation, Management of Financial Resources, Management of Material Resources

College Majors

Architectural Environmental Design: An instructional program that prepares individuals for the independent professional practice of environmental architecture, the processes and techniques of designing total environments and living systems for human populations, both indoor and outdoor. Includes instruction in relating the structural, aesthetic and social concerns affecting life and work to the needs of clients and the constraints of the site environment.

Supporting Courses

Administration and Management: Knowledge of principles and processes involved in business and organizational planning, coordination, and execution. This includes strategic planning, resource allocation, manpower modeling, leadership techniques, and production methods. **Economics and Accounting:** Knowledge of economic and accounting principles and practices, the financial markets, banking, and the analysis and reporting of financial data. **Customer and Personal Service:** Knowledge of principles and processes for providing customer and personal services including needs assessment techniques, quality service standards, alternative delivery systems, and customer satisfaction evaluation techniques. **Engineering and Technology:** Knowledge of equipment, tools, mechanical devices, and their uses to produce motion, light, power, technology, and other applications. **Design:** Knowledge of design techniques, principles, tools and instruments involved in the production and use of precision technical plans, blueprints, drawings, and models. **Building and Construction:** Knowledge of materials, methods, and the appropriate tools to construct objects, structures, and buildings. **Mathematics:** Knowledge of numbers, their operations, and interrelationships including arithmetic, algebra, geometry, calculus, statistics, and their applications. **Physics:** Knowledge and prediction of physical principles, laws, and applications including air, water, material dynamics, light, atomic principles, heat, electric theory, earth formations, and meteorological and related natural phenomena. **Biology:** Knowledge of plant and animal living tissue, cells, organisms, and entities, including their functions, interdependencies, and interactions with each other and the environment. **Geography:** Knowledge of various methods for describing the location and distribution of land, sea, and air masses including their physical locations, relationships, and characteristics. **English Language:** Knowledge of the structure and content of the English language including the meaning and spelling of words, rules of composition, and grammar. **Fine Arts:** Knowledge of theory and techniques required to produce, compose, and perform works of music, dance, visual arts, drama, and sculpture. **History and Archeology:** Knowledge of past historical events and their causes, indicators, and impact on particular civilizations and cultures. **Public Safety and Security:** Knowledge of weaponry, public safety, and security operations, rules, regulations, precautions, prevention, and the protection of people, data, and property. **Law, Government, and Jurisprudence:** Knowledge of laws, legal codes, court procedures, precedents, government regulations, executive orders, agency rules, and the democratic political process.

LAW CLERKS

Education	**Associate degree**	
Average Yearly Earnings	$26,749	
Projected Growth	12%	
Annual Job Openings	8,181	
Self-employed	2%	
Employed Part-time	10%	

LAWYERS

Education	**First professional degree**	
Average Yearly Earnings	$70,117	
Projected Growth	19%	
Annual Job Openings	45,929	
Self-employed	31%	
Employed Part-time	7%	

Lawyers

Conduct criminal and civil lawsuits, draw up legal documents, advise clients as to legal rights, and practice other phases of law. May represent client in court or before quasi-judicial or administrative agencies of government. May specialize in a single area of law, such as patent law, corporate law, or criminal law. Conducts case, examining and cross-examining witnesses, and summarizes case to judge or jury. Represents client in court or before government agency, or prosecutes or defends defendant in civil or criminal litigation. Advises client concerning business transactions, claim liability, advisability of prosecuting or defending lawsuits, or legal rights and obligations. Interviews client and witnesses to ascertain facts of case. Gathers evidence to formulate defense or to initiate legal actions. Examines legal data to determine advisability of defending or prosecuting lawsuit. Evaluates findings and develops strategy and arguments in preparation for presentation of case. Studies Constitution, statutes, decisions, regulations, and ordinances of quasi-judicial bodies. Confers with colleagues with specialty in area of legal issue to establish and verify basis for legal proceeding. Interprets laws, rulings, and regulations for individuals and business. Prepares and files legal briefs. Presents evidence to grand jury for indictment or release of accused. Prepares and drafts legal documents, such as wills, deeds, patent applications, mortgages, leases, and contracts. Prepares opinions on legal issues. Probates wills and represents and advises executors and administrators of estates. Acts as agent, trustee, guardian, or executor for business or individual. Searches for and examines public and other legal records to write opinions or establish ownership.

Occupational Type

Enterprising occupations frequently involve starting up and carrying out projects. These occupations can involve leading people and making many decisions. Sometimes they involve risk taking and often deal with business.

Skills required of Lawyers

Reading Comprehension, Active Listening, Writing, Speaking, Critical Thinking, Active Learning, Learning Strategies, Monitoring, Social Perceptiveness, Coordination, Persuasion, Negotiation, Instructing, Problem Identification, Information Gathering, Information

Organization, Synthesis/Reorganization, Idea Generation, Idea Evaluation, Implementation Planning, Visioning, Systems Perception, Identifying Downstream Consequences, Identification of Key Causes, Judgment and Decision Making, Systems Evaluation, Time Management, Management of Financial Resources

 College Majors

Law (L.L.B., J.D.): An instructional program that prepares individuals for the independent professional practice of law and for advanced research in jurisprudence. Includes instruction in the theory and practice of the legal system, including the statutory, administrative and judicial components of civil and criminal law.

Supporting Courses

Administration and Management: Knowledge of principles and processes involved in business and organizational planning, coordination, and execution. This includes strategic planning, resource allocation, manpower modeling, leadership techniques, and production methods. **Clerical:** Knowledge of administrative and clerical procedures and systems such as word processing systems, filing and records management systems, stenography and transcription, forms design principles, and other office procedures and terminology. **Computers and Electronics:** Knowledge of electric circuit boards, processors, chips, and computer hardware and software, including applications and programming. **Psychology:** Knowledge of human behavior and performance, mental processes, psychological research methods, and the assessment and treatment of behavioral and affective disorders. **Sociology and Anthropology:** Knowledge of group behavior and dynamics, societal trends and influences, cultures, their history, migrations, ethnicity, and origins. **Therapy and Counseling:** Knowledge of information and techniques needed to rehabilitate physical and mental ailments and to provide career guidance including alternative treatments, rehabilitation equipment and its proper use, and methods to evaluate treatment effects. **Education and Training:** Knowledge of instructional methods and training techniques including curriculum design principles, learning theory, group and individual teaching techniques, design of individual development plans, and test design principles. **English Language:** Knowledge of the structure and content of the English language including the meaning and spelling of words, rules of composition, and grammar. **Public Safety and Security:** Knowledge of weaponry, public safety, and security operations, rules, regulations, precautions, prevention, and the protection of people, data, and property. **Law, Government, and Jurisprudence:** Knowledge of laws, legal codes, court procedures, precedents, government regulations, executive orders, agency rules, and the democratic political process.

LIBRARIANS

Librarians

Administer library services; provide library patrons access to or instruction

	Education	**Master's degree**
	Average Yearly Earnings	**$36,629**
	Projected Growth	5%
	Annual Job Openings	16,810
	Self-employed	0%
	Employed Part-time	22%

in accessing library resources; and select, acquire, process, and organize library materials and collections for patron use. Organizes collections of books, publications, documents, audiovisual aids, and other reference materials for convenient access. Reviews and evaluates resource material to select and order books, periodicals, audiovisual aids, and other materials for acquisition. Assists patrons in selecting books and informational material and in research problems. Codes, classifies, and catalogs books, publications, films, audiovisual aids, and other library materials. Researches, retrieves, and disseminates information from books, periodicals, reference materials, or commercial databases in response to requests. Manages library resources stored in files, on film, or in computer data bases for research information. Reviews, compiles, and publishes listing of library materials, including bibliographies and book reviews, to notify users. Explains use of library facilities, resources, equipment, and services and provides information governing library use and policies. Manages library program for children and other special groups. Assembles and arranges display materials. Directs and trains library staff in duties, including receiving, shelving, researching, cataloging, and equipment use. Keys information into computer to store or search for selected material or databases. Compiles lists of overdue materials and notifies borrowers. Confers with teachers, parents, and community organizations to develop, plan, and conduct programs in reading, viewing, and communication skills.

Occupational Type

Artistic occupations frequently involve working with forms, designs, and patterns. They often require self-expression and the work can be done without following a clear set of rules.

Skills required of Librarians

Reading Comprehension, Active Listening, Speaking, Learning Strategies, Social Perceptiveness, Instructing, Service Orientation, Information Gathering, Information Organization, Synthesis/Reorganization, Implementation Planning, Time Management, Management of Material Resources, Management of Personnel Resources

College Majors

Educational/Instructional Media Design: An instructional program that describes the principles and techniques of creating instructional materials and related educational resources in various media or combinations, such as film, video, recording, text, art, software, and three-dimensional objects, and that prepares individuals to function as instructional media designers. Includes instruction in the techniques specific to creating in various media; the behavioral principles applicable to using various media in learning and teaching; the design, testing and production of instructional materials; and the management of educational/ instructional media facilities and programs.

Supporting Courses

Administration and Management: Knowledge of principles and processes involved in business and organizational planning, coordination, and execution. This includes strategic

planning, resource allocation, manpower modeling, leadership techniques, and production methods. **Clerical:** Knowledge of administrative and clerical procedures and systems such as word processing systems, filing and records management systems, stenography and transcription, forms design principles, and other office procedures and terminology. **Sales and Marketing:** Knowledge of principles and methods involved in showing, promoting, and selling products or services. This includes marketing strategies and tactics, product demonstration and sales techniques, and sales control systems. **Customer and Personal Service:** Knowledge of principles and processes for providing customer and personal services including needs assessment techniques, quality service standards, alternative delivery systems, and customer satisfaction evaluation techniques. **Personnel and Human Resources:** Knowledge of policies and practices involved in personnel/human resource functions. This includes recruitment, selection, training, and promotion regulations and procedures; compensation and benefits packages; labor relations and negotiation strategies; and personnel information systems. **Computers and Electronics:** Knowledge of electric circuit boards, processors, chips, and computer hardware and software, including applications and programming. **Psychology:** Knowledge of human behavior and performance, mental processes, psychological research methods, and the assessment and treatment of behavioral and affective disorders. **Sociology and Anthropology:** Knowledge of group behavior and dynamics, societal trends and influences, cultures, their history, migrations, ethnicity, and origins. **Geography:** Knowledge of various methods for describing the location and distribution of land, sea, and air masses including their physical locations, relationships, and characteristics. **Education and Training:** Knowledge of instructional methods and training techniques including curriculum design principles, learning theory, group and individual teaching techniques, design of individual development plans, and test design principles. **English Language:** Knowledge of the structure and content of the English language including the meaning and spelling of words, rules of composition, and grammar. **Foreign Language:** Knowledge of the structure and content of a foreign (non-English) language including the meaning and spelling of words, rules of composition and grammar, and pronunciation. **Fine Arts:** Knowledge of theory and techniques required to produce, compose, and perform works of music, dance, visual arts, drama, and sculpture. **History and Archeology:** Knowledge of past historical events and their causes, indicators, and impact on particular civilizations and cultures. **Philosophy and Theology:** Knowledge of different philosophical systems and religions, including their basic principles, values, ethics, ways of thinking, customs, and practices, and their impact on human culture. **Communications and Media:** Knowledge of media production, communication, and dissemination techniques and methods including alternative ways to inform and entertain via written, oral, and visual media.

Library Research Workers

Research specific subjects and make information available to library patrons on an individual basis. Researches and retrieves information on specified subjects in response to inquiries from library patrons. Compiles and analyzes information on specified subjects from books, periodicals, reference materials, or commercial databases. Prepares summary of research and analysis and transmits information to inquirers.

Occupational Type

Investigative occupations frequently involve working with ideas, and require an extensive amount of thinking. These occupations can involve searching for facts and figuring out problems mentally.

Skills required of Library Research Workers

Reading Comprehension, Writing, Active Learning, Information Gathering, Information Organization, Synthesis/Reorganization

College Majors

Library Assistant: An instructional program that prepares individuals to assist professional librarians. Includes instruction in principles, systems, processes, and procedures of library operation; library resources and services; processes of acquisition, cataloging, storage, and display systems; discovery and retrieval of requested materials; management of books, periodicals, and other documents.

Supporting Courses

Customer and Personal Service: Knowledge of principles and processes for providing customer and personal services including needs assessment techniques, quality service standards, alternative delivery systems, and customer satisfaction evaluation techniques. **English Language:** Knowledge of the structure and content of the English language including the meaning and spelling of words, rules of composition, and grammar. **Foreign Language:** Knowledge of the structure and content of a foreign (non-English) language including the meaning and spelling of words, rules of composition and grammar, and pronunciation. **Philosophy and Theology:** Knowledge of different philosophical systems and religions, including their basic principles, values, ethics, ways of thinking, customs, and practices, and their impact on human culture. **Communications and Media:** Knowledge of media production, communication, and dissemination techniques and methods including alternative ways to inform and entertain via written, oral, and visual media.

LIFE SCIENTISTS

Biochemists

Education	Doctor's degree
Average Yearly Earnings	$44,138
Projected Growth	3%
Annual Job Openings	53
Self-employed	0%
Employed Part-time	7%

Research or study chemical composition and processes of living organisms that affect vital processes such as growth and aging, to determine chemical actions and effects on organisms, such as the action of foods, drugs, or other substances on body functions and tissues. Studies chemistry of living processes, such as cell development, breathing, and digestion, and living energy changes, such as growth, aging, and death. Researches methods of transferring characteristics, such as resistance to disease, from one organism to another. Researches and determines chemical action of substances, such as drugs, serums, hormones, and food, on tissues and vital processes. Examines chemical aspects of formation of antibodies, and researches chemistry of cells and blood corpuscles. Isolates, analyzes, and identifies hormones, vitamins, allergens, minerals, and enzymes, and determines their effects on body functions. Develops and executes tests to detect disease, genetic disorders, or other abnormalities. Develops methods to process, store, and use food, drugs, and chemical compounds. Develops and tests new drugs and medications used for commercial distribution. Prepares reports and recommendations based upon research outcomes. Designs and builds laboratory equipment needed for special research projects. Cleans, purifies, refines, and otherwise prepares pharmaceutical compounds for commercial distribution. Analyzes foods to determine nutritional value and effects of cooking, canning, and processing on this value.

Occupational Type

Investigative occupations frequently involve working with ideas, and require an extensive amount of thinking. These occupations can involve searching for facts and figuring out problems mentally.

Skills required of Biochemists

Reading Comprehension, Writing, Mathematics, Science, Critical Thinking, Active Learning, Problem Identification, Information Gathering, Information Organization, Synthesis/ Reorganization, Idea Generation, Idea Evaluation, Operations Analysis, Equipment Selection, Programming, Testing, Visioning, Systems Perception, Identifying Downstream Consequences, Identification of Key Causes

College Majors

Biochemistry: An instructional program that describes the chemical processes of living organisms. Includes instruction in the chemical mechanisms of genetic information storage and transmission; the chemistry of cell components; blood chemistry; the chemistry of biological systems and biological products; and the chemistry of life processes such as respiration, digestion, and reproduction.

Supporting Courses

Building and Construction: Knowledge of materials, methods, and the appropriate tools to construct objects, structures, and buildings. **Mathematics:** Knowledge of numbers, their operations, and interrelationships including arithmetic, algebra, geometry, calculus, statistics, and their applications. **Chemistry:** Knowledge of the composition, structure, and properties of substances and of the chemical processes and transformations that they undergo. This includes uses of chemicals and their interactions, danger signs, production techniques, and disposal methods. **Biology:** Knowledge of plant and animal living tissue, cells, organisms, and entities, including their functions, interdependencies, and interactions with each other 'and the environment.

Biologists

Study the relationship among organisms and between organisms and their environment. Studies basic principles of plant and animal life, such as origin, relationship, development, anatomy, and functions. Studies aquatic plants and animals and environmental conditions affecting them, such as radioactivity or pollution. Collects and analyzes biological data about relationship among and between organisms and their environment. Studies reactions of plants, animals, and marine species to parasites. Identifies, classifies, and studies structure, behavior, ecology, physiology, nutrition, culture, and distribution of plant and animal species. Measures salinity, acidity, light, oxygen content, and other physical conditions of water to determine their relationship to aquatic life. Studies and manages wild animal populations. Develops methods and apparatus for securing representative plant, animal, aquatic, or soil samples. Investigates and develops pest management and control measures. Communicates test results to state and Federal representatives and general public. Prepares environmental impact reports for industry, government, or publication. Cultivates, breeds, and grows aquatic life, such as lobsters, clams, or fish farming. Plans and administers biological research programs for government, research firms, medical industries, or manufacturing firms. Researches environmental effects of present and potential uses of land and water areas, and determines methods of improving environment or crop yields. Develops methods of extracting drugs from aquatic plants and animals.

Occupational Type

Investigative occupations frequently involve working with ideas, and require an extensive amount of thinking. These occupations can involve searching for facts and figuring out problems mentally.

Skills required of Biologists

Reading Comprehension, Writing, Mathematics, Science, Critical Thinking, Active Learning, Learning Strategies, Problem Identification, Information Gathering, Information Organization, Synthesis/Reorganization, Idea Generation, Idea Evaluation, Implementation Planning, Programming, Systems Perception, Identification of Key Causes

College Majors

Marine/Aquatic Biology: An instructional program that describes the scientific study of marine organisms and their environments. Includes instruction in freshwater and saltwater organisms, physiological and anatomical marine adaptations, ocean and freshwater ecologies, marine microbiology, marine mammalogy, ichthyology, marine botany, and biochemical products of marine life used by humans.

Supporting Courses

Food Production: Knowledge of techniques and equipment for planting, growing, and harvesting of food for consumption including crop rotation methods, animal husbandry, and food storage/handling techniques. **Mathematics:** Knowledge of numbers, their operations, and interrelationships including arithmetic, algebra, geometry, calculus, statistics, and their applications. **Physics:** Knowledge and prediction of physical principles, laws, and applications including air, water, material dynamics, light, atomic principles, heat, electric theory, earth formations, and meteorological and related natural phenomena. **Chemistry:** Knowledge of the composition, structure, and properties of substances and of the chemical processes and transformations that they undergo. This includes uses of chemicals and their interactions, danger signs, production techniques, and disposal methods. **Biology:** Knowledge of plant and animal living tissue, cells, organisms, and entities, including their functions, interdependencies, and interactions with each other and the environment. **English Language:** Knowledge of the structure and content of the English language including the meaning and spelling of words, rules of composition, and grammar.

Biophysicists

Research or study physical principles of living cells and organisms, their electrical and mechanical energy, and related phenomena. Studies physical principles of living cells and organisms and their electrical and mechanical energy. Researches manner in which characteristics of plants and animals are carried through successive generations. Researches transformation of substances in cells, using atomic isotopes. Investigates damage to cells and tissues caused by X-rays and nuclear particles. Studies spatial configuration of submicroscopic molecules, such as proteins, using X-ray and electron microscope. Investigates transmission of electrical impulses along nerves and muscles. Investigates dynamics of seeing and hearing. Analyzes functions of electronic and human brains, such as learning, thinking, and memory. Researches cancer treatment, using radiation and nuclear particles. Studies absorption of light by chlorophyll in photosynthesis or by pigments of eye involved in vision.

Occupational Type

Investigative occupations frequently involve working with ideas, and require an extensive amount of thinking. These occupations can involve searching for facts and figuring out problems mentally.

Skills required of Biophysicists

Reading Comprehension, Writing, Mathematics, Science, Critical Thinking, Active Learning, Information Gathering, Information Organization, Idea Generation, Idea Evaluation, Programming

College Majors

Biochemistry: An instructional program that describes the chemical processes of living organisms. Includes instruction in the chemical mechanisms of genetic information storage and transmission; the chemistry of cell components; blood chemistry; the chemistry of biological systems and biological products; and the chemistry of life processes such as respiration, digestion, and reproduction.

Supporting Courses

Mathematics: Knowledge of numbers, their operations, and interrelationships including arithmetic, algebra, geometry, calculus, statistics, and their applications. **Physics:** Knowledge and prediction of physical principles, laws, and applications including air, water, material dynamics, light, atomic principles, heat, electric theory, earth formations, and meteorological and related natural phenomena. **Chemistry:** Knowledge of the composition, structure, and properties of substances and of the chemical processes and transformations that they undergo. This includes uses of chemicals and their interactions, danger signs, production techniques, and disposal methods. **Biology:** Knowledge of plant and animal living tissue, cells, organisms, and entities, including their functions, interdependencies, and interactions with each other and the environment.

Botanists

Research or study development of life processes, physiology, heredity, environment, distribution, morphology, and economic value of plants for application in such fields as agronomy, forestry, horticulture, and pharmacology. Studies development, life processes, and economic value of plants and fungi for application in such fields as horticulture and pharmacology. Studies behavior, internal and external structure, mechanics, and biochemistry of plant or fungi cells, using microscope and scientific equipment. Investigates effect of rainfall, deforestation, pollution, acid rain, temperature, climate, soil, and elevation on plant or fungi growth. Studies and compares healthy and diseased plants to determine agents responsible for diseased conditions. Investigates comparative susceptibility of different varieties of plants to disease, and develops plant varieties immune to disease. Studies rates of spread and intensity of plant diseases under different environmental conditions, and predicts disease outbreaks. Inspects flower and vegetable seed stocks and flowering bulbs, to determine presence of diseases, infections, and insect infestation. Identifies and classifies plants or fungi based on study and research. Tests disease control measures under laboratory and field conditions for comparative effectiveness, practicality, and economy. Plans and administers environmental research programs for government, research firms, medical industries, or manufacturing firms. Devises methods of destroying or controlling disease-causing agents. Prepares reports and recommendations based upon research outcomes. Develops drugs, medicines, molds, yeasts, or foods from plants or fungi, or develops new types of plants. Develops practices to prevent or reduce deterioration of perishable plant products in transit or storage. Develops improved methods of propagating and growing edible fungi.

Occupational Type

Investigative occupations frequently involve working with ideas, and require an extensive amount of thinking. These occupations can involve searching for facts and figuring out problems mentally.

Skills required of Botanists

Reading Comprehension, Writing, Mathematics, Science, Critical Thinking, Active Learning, Information Gathering, Information Organization, Synthesis/Reorganization, Idea Generation, Programming, Identifying Downstream Consequences, Identification of Key Causes

---

College Majors

Plant Sciences, General: An instructional program that generally describes the scientific theories and principles involved in the production and management of plants for food, feed, fiber, and soil conservation.

Supporting Courses

Chemistry: Knowledge of the composition, structure, and properties of substances and of the chemical processes and transformations that they undergo. This includes uses of chemicals and their interactions, danger signs, production techniques, and disposal methods. **Biology:** Knowledge of plant and animal living tissue, cells, organisms, and entities, including their functions, interdependencies, and interactions with each other and the environment.

Microbiologists

Research or study growth, structure, development, and general characteristics of bacteria and other microorganisms. Studies growth, structure, development, and general characteristics of bacteria and other microorganisms. Examines physiological, morphological, and cultural characteristics, using microscope, to identify microorganisms. Studies growth structure and development of viruses and rickettsiae. Observes action of microorganisms upon living tissues of plants, higher animals, and other microorganisms, and on dead organic matter. Isolates and makes cultures of bacteria or other microorganisms in prescribed media, controlling moisture, aeration, temperature, and nutrition. Conducts chemical analyses of substances, such as acids, alcohols, and enzymes. Researches use of bacteria and microorganisms to develop vitamins, antibiotics, amino acids, grain alcohol, sugars, and polymers. Prepares technical reports and recommendations based upon research outcomes. Plans and administers biological research program for government, private research centers, or medical industry.

 Occupational Type

Investigative occupations frequently involve working with ideas, and require an extensive amount of thinking. These occupations can involve searching for facts and figuring out problems mentally.

 Skills required of Microbiologists

Reading Comprehension, Writing, Mathematics, Science, Active Learning, Problem Identification, Information Gathering, Synthesis/Reorganization, Idea Evaluation, Equipment Selection, Programming

 College Majors

Biochemistry: An instructional program that describes the chemical processes of living organisms. Includes instruction in the chemical mechanisms of genetic information storage and transmission; the chemistry of cell components; blood chemistry; the chemistry of biological systems and biological products; and the chemistry of life processes such as respiration, digestion, and reproduction.

Supporting Courses

Mathematics: Knowledge of numbers, their operations, and interrelationships including arithmetic, algebra, geometry, calculus, statistics, and their applications. **Chemistry:** Knowledge of the composition, structure, and properties of substances and of the chemical processes and transformations that they undergo. This includes uses of chemicals and their interactions, danger signs, production techniques, and disposal methods. **Biology:** Knowledge of plant and animal living tissue, cells, organisms, and entities, including their functions, interdependencies, and interactions with each other and the environment. **English Language:** Knowledge of the structure and content of the English language including the meaning and spelling of words, rules of composition, and grammar.

Geneticists

Research or study inheritance and variation of characteristics on forms of life to determine laws, mechanisms, and environmental factors in origin, transmission, and development of inherited traits. Conducts experiments to determine laws, mechanisms, and environmental factors in origin, transmission, and development of inherited traits. Analyses determinants responsible for specific inherited traits, such as color differences, size, and disease resistance. Studies genetic determinants to understand relationship of heredity to maturity, fertility, or other factors. Devises methods for altering or producing new traits, using chemicals, heat, light, or other means. Prepares technical reports and recommendations based upon research outcomes. Counsels clients in human and medical genetics. Plans and administers genetic research program for government, private research centers, or medical industry.

Occupational Type

Investigative occupations frequently involve working with ideas, and require an extensive amount of thinking. These occupations can involve searching for facts and figuring out problems mentally.

Skills required of Geneticists

Reading Comprehension, Active Listening, Writing, Speaking, Mathematics, Science, Critical Thinking, Active Learning, Learning Strategies, Persuasion, Instructing, Problem Identification, Information Gathering, Information Organization, Synthesis/Reorganization, Idea Generation, Idea Evaluation, Equipment Selection, Programming, Visioning, Systems Perception, Management of Financial Resources, Management of Personnel Resources

College Majors

Biochemistry: An instructional program that describes the chemical processes of living organisms. Includes instruction in the chemical mechanisms of genetic information storage and transmission; the chemistry of cell components; blood chemistry; the chemistry of biological systems and biological products; and the chemistry of life processes such as respiration, digestion, and reproduction.

 Supporting Courses

Administration and Management: Knowledge of principles and processes involved in business and organizational planning, coordination, and execution. This includes strategic planning, resource allocation, manpower modeling, leadership techniques, and production methods. **Mathematics:** Knowledge of numbers, their operations, and interrelationships including arithmetic, algebra, geometry, calculus, statistics, and their applications. **Chemistry:** Knowledge of the composition, structure, and properties of substances and of the chemical processes and transformations that they undergo. This includes uses of chemicals and their interactions, danger signs, production techniques, and disposal methods. **Biology:** Knowledge of plant and animal living tissue, cells, organisms, and entities, including their functions, interdependencies, and interactions with each other and the environment. **Medicine and Dentistry:** Knowledge of the information and techniques needed to diagnose and treat injuries, diseases, and deformities. This includes symptoms, treatment alternatives, drug properties and interactions, and preventive healthcare measures. **Therapy and Counseling:** Knowledge of information and techniques needed to rehabilitate physical and mental ailments and to provide career guidance including alternative treatments, rehabilitation equipment and its proper use, and methods to evaluate treatment effects. **Foreign Language:** Knowledge of the structure and content of a foreign (non-English) language including the meaning and spelling of words, rules of composition and grammar, and pronunciation.

Physiologists and Cytologists

Research or study cellular structure and functions, or organ-system functions, of plants and animals. Studies cells, cellular structure, cell division, and organ-system functions of plants and animals. Studies functions of plants and animals, such as growth, respiration, movement, and reproduction, under normal and abnormal conditions. Conducts experiments to determine effects of internal and external environmental factors on life processes and functions. Studies physiology of plants, animals, or particular human body area, function, organ, or system. Utilizes microscope, X-ray equipment, spectroscope, and other equipment to study cell structure and function and to perform experiments. Studies glands and their relationship to bodily functions. Analyzes reproductive cells and methods by which chromosomes divide or unite. Studies formation of sperm and eggs in animal sex glands, and studies origin of blood and tissue cells. Researches physiology of unicellular organisms, such as protozoa, to ascertain physical and chemical factors of growth. Studies influence of physical and chemical factors on malignant and normal cells. Assesses and evaluates hormonal status and presence of atypical or malignant changes in exfoliated, aspirated, or abraded cells. Selects and sections minute particles of animal or plant tissue for microscopic study, using microtome and other equipment. Stains tissue sample to make cell structures visible or to differentiate parts. Prepares technical reports and recommendations based upon research outcomes. Plans and administers biological research programs for government, private research centers, or medical industry.

Occupational Type

Investigative occupations frequently involve working with ideas, and require an extensive amount of thinking. These occupations can involve searching for facts and figuring out problems mentally.

Skills required of Physiologists and Cytologists

Reading Comprehension, Writing, Mathematics, Science, Critical Thinking, Active Learning, Problem Identification, Information Gathering, Information Organization, Synthesis/Reorganization, Idea Generation, Idea Evaluation, Implementation Planning, Equipment Selection, Programming, Operation Monitoring, Operation and Control, Visioning, Identifying Downstream Consequences, Identification of Key Causes

College Majors

Plant Sciences, General: An instructional program that generally describes the scientific theories and principles involved in the production and management of plants for food, feed, fiber, and soil conservation.

Supporting Courses

Administration and Management: Knowledge of principles and processes involved in business and organizational planning, coordination, and execution. This includes strategic planning, resource allocation, manpower modeling, leadership techniques, and production methods. **Chemistry:** Knowledge of the composition, structure, and properties of substances and of the chemical processes and transformations that they undergo. This includes uses of chemicals and their interactions, danger signs, production techniques, and disposal methods. **Biology:** Knowledge of plant and animal living tissue, cells, organisms, and entities, including their functions, interdependencies, and interactions with each other and the environment.

Zoologists

Research or study origins, interrelationships, classification, habits, life histories, life processes, diseases, relation to environment, growth, development, genetics, and distribution of animals. Studies origins, interrelationships, classification, life histories, diseases, development, genetics, and distribution of animals. Analyzes characteristics of animals to identify and classify animals. Studies animals in their natural habitats, and assesses effects of environment on animals. Collects and dissects animal specimens and examines specimens under microscope. Prepares collections of preserved specimens or microscopic slides for species identification and study of species development or animal disease. Conducts experimental studies, using chemicals and various types of scientific equipment. Raises specimens for study and observation or for use in experiments.

Occupational Type

Investigative occupations frequently involve working with ideas, and require an extensive amount of thinking. These occupations can involve searching for facts and figuring out problems mentally.

Skills required of Zoologists

Reading Comprehension, Writing, Mathematics, Science, Critical Thinking, Active Learning, Learning Strategies, Problem Identification, Information Gathering, Information Organization, Synthesis/Reorganization, Idea Generation, Idea Evaluation, Equipment Selection, Identifying Downstream Consequences

College Majors

Zoology, General: An instructional program that generally describes the scientific study of animals, including their structure, reproduction, growth, heredity, evolution, behavior, and distribution.

Supporting Courses

Chemistry: Knowledge of the composition, structure, and properties of substances and of the chemical processes and transformations that they undergo. This includes uses of chemicals and their interactions, danger signs, production techniques, and disposal methods. **Biology:** Knowledge of plant and animal living tissue, cells, organisms, and entities, including their functions, interdependencies, and interactions with each other and the environment.

Toxicologists

Research or study the effects of toxic substances on physiological functions of humans, animals, and plants. Researches effects of toxic substances on physiological functions of humans, animals, and plants for consumer protection and industrial safety programs. Designs and conducts studies to determine physiological effects of various substances on laboratory animals, plants, and human tissue. Interprets results of studies in terms of toxicological properties of substances and hazards associated with their misuse. Collects and prepares samples of toxic materials for analysis or examination. Dissects dead animals, using surgical instruments, and examines organs for toxic substances. Applies cosmetic or ingredient onto skin, or injects substance into animal, and observes animal for abnormalities, inflammation, or irritation. Analyzes samples of toxic materials to identify compound and develop treatment. Tests and analyzes blood samples for presence of toxic conditions, using microscope and laboratory test equipment. Reviews toxicological data for accuracy, and suggests clarifications or corrections to data. Writes and maintains records and reports of studies and tests for use as toxicological resource material. Informs regulatory agency personnel and industrial firms concerning toxicological properties of products and materials. Advises governmental and industrial personnel on degree of hazard of toxic materials and on precautionary labeling. Testifies as expert witness on toxicology in hearings and court proceedings.

Occupational Type

Investigative occupations frequently involve working with ideas, and require an extensive amount of thinking. These occupations can involve searching for facts and figuring out problems mentally.

Skills required of Toxicologists

Reading Comprehension, Writing, Mathematics, Science, Critical Thinking, Active Learning, Learning Strategies, Problem Identification, Information Gathering, Idea Evaluation, Equipment Selection, Programming, Testing, Identification of Key Causes

College Majors

Biochemistry: An instructional program that describes the chemical processes of living organisms. Includes instruction in the chemical mechanisms of genetic information storage and transmission; the chemistry of cell components; blood chemistry; the chemistry of biological systems and biological products; and the chemistry of life processes such as respiration, digestion, and reproduction.

Supporting Courses

Mathematics: Knowledge of numbers, their operations, and interrelationships including arithmetic, algebra, geometry, calculus, statistics, and their applications. **Chemistry:** Knowledge of the composition, structure, and properties of substances and of the chemical processes and transformations that they undergo. This includes uses of chemicals and their interactions, danger signs, production techniques, and disposal methods. **Biology:** Knowledge of plant and animal living tissue, cells, organisms, and entities, including their functions, interdependencies, and interactions with each other and the environment. **English Language:** Knowledge of the structure and content of the English language including the meaning and spelling of words, rules of composition, and grammar.

LOAN OFFICERS AND COUNSELORS

Loan Officers and Counselors

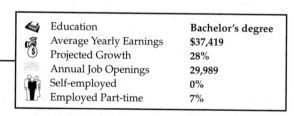

Education	Bachelor's degree
Average Yearly Earnings	$37,419
Projected Growth	28%
Annual Job Openings	29,989
Self-employed	0%
Employed Part-time	7%

Evaluate, authorize, or recommend approval of commercial, real estate, or credit loans. Advise borrowers on financial status and methods of payments. Include mortgage loan officers or agents, collection analysts, and loan servicing officers. Analyzes applicant financial status, credit, and property evaluation to determine feasibility of granting loan. Approves loan within specified limits. Refers loan to loan committee for approval. Evaluates acceptability of loan to corporations that buy real estate loans on secondary mortgage markets. Interviews applicant and requests specified information for loan application. Contacts applicant or creditors to resolve questions regarding application information. Ensures loan agreements are complete and accurate according to policy. Computes payment schedule. Submits application to credit analyst for verification and recommendation. Petitions court to transfer title and deeds of collateral to bank. Confers with underwriters to aid in resolving mortgage application problems. Analyzes potential loan markets to develop prospects for loans. Arranges for maintenance and liquidation of delinquent property. Contacts customers to arrange payment of delinquent loan balances. Supervises loan personnel.

Occupational Type

Enterprising occupations frequently involve starting up and carrying out projects. These occupations can involve leading people and making many decisions. Sometimes they involve risk taking and often deal with business.

Skills required of Loan Officers and Counselors

Active Listening, Speaking, Information Gathering, Judgment and Decision Making, Management of Personnel Resources

College Majors

Financial Services Marketing Operations: An instructional program that prepares individuals to perform marketing tasks specifically applicable to banks, credit unions, and other financial institutions.

Supporting Courses

Clerical: Knowledge of administrative and clerical procedures and systems such as word processing systems, filing and records management systems, stenography and transcription, forms design principles, and other office procedures and terminology. **Economics and Accounting:** Knowledge of economic and accounting principles and practices, the financial markets, banking, and the analysis and reporting of financial data. **Sales and Marketing:** Knowledge of principles and methods involved in showing, promoting, and selling products or services. This includes marketing strategies and tactics, product demonstration and sales techniques, and sales control systems. **Customer and Personal Service:** Knowledge of principles and processes for providing customer and personal services including needs assessment techniques, quality service standards, alternative delivery systems, and customer satisfaction evaluation techniques. **Personnel and Human Resources:** Knowledge of policies and practices involved in personnel/human resource functions. This includes recruitment, selection, training, and promotion regulations and procedures; compensation and benefits packages; labor relations and negotiation strategies; and personnel information systems. **Mathematics:** Knowledge of numbers, their operations, and interrelationships including arithmetic, algebra, geometry, calculus, statistics, and their applications. **Law, Government, and Jurisprudence:** Knowledge of laws, legal codes, court procedures, precedents, government regulations, executive orders, agency rules, and the democratic political process. **Communications and Media:** Knowledge of media production, communication, and dissemination techniques and methods including alternative ways to inform and entertain via written, oral, and visual media.

MANAGEMENT ANALYSTS

Education	Master's degree
Average Yearly Earnings	$48,194
Projected Growth	21%
Annual Job Openings	46,026
Self-employed	45%
Employed Part-time	20%

Management Analysts

Review, analyze, and suggest improvements to business and organizational systems to assist management in operating more efficiently and effectively. Conduct organizational studies and evaluations, design systems and procedures, conduct work simplification and measurement studies, and prepare operations and procedures manuals. (Excludes computer systems analysts.) Reviews forms and reports, and confers with management and users about format, distribution, and purpose to identify problems and improvements. Develops and implements records management program for filing, protection, and retrieval of records, and assures compliance with program. Reviews records retention schedules and recordkeeping requirements to plan transfer of active records to inactive or archival storage or destruction. Reports findings and prepares recommendations for new systems, procedures, or organizational changes. Interviews personnel and conducts on-site observation to ascertain unit functions, work performed, and methods, equipment, and personnel used. Prepares manuals and trains workers in use of new forms, reports, procedures, or equipment, according to organizational policy. Designs, evaluates, recommends, and approves changes of forms and reports. Implements new systems, trains personnel in use, and reviews operations to ensure that systems are applied and functioning as designed. Recommends purchase of storage equipment, and designs area layout to locate equipment in space available. Directs records management personnel and supporting technical, micrographics, and printing workers.

 Occupational Type

Enterprising occupations frequently involve starting up and carrying out projects. These occupations can involve leading people and making many decisions. Sometimes they involve risk taking and often deal with business.

 Skills required of Management Analysts

Reading Comprehension, Active Listening, Writing, Speaking, Critical Thinking, Active Learning, Learning Strategies, Monitoring, Social Perceptiveness, Coordination, Persuasion,

Negotiation, Instructing, Problem Identification, Information Gathering, Information Organization, Synthesis/Reorganization, Idea Generation, Idea Evaluation, Implementation Planning, Operations Analysis, Equipment Selection, Visioning, Systems Perception, Identifying Downstream Consequences, Identification of Key Causes, Judgment and Decision Making, Systems Evaluation, Time Management, Management of Material Resources, Management of Personnel Resources

College Majors

Business Administration and Management, General: An instructional program that generally prepares individuals to plan, organize, direct, and control the functions and processes of a firm or organization. Includes instruction in management theory, human resources management and behavior, accounting and other quantitative methods, purchasing and logistics, organization and production, marketing, and business decision making.

Supporting Courses

Administration and Management: Knowledge of principles and processes involved in business and organizational planning, coordination, and execution. This includes strategic planning, resource allocation, manpower modeling, leadership techniques, and production methods. **Clerical:** Knowledge of administrative and clerical procedures and systems such as word processing systems, filing and records management systems, stenography and transcription, forms design principles, and other office procedures and terminology. **Economics and Accounting:** Knowledge of economic and accounting principles and practices, the financial markets, banking, and the analysis and reporting of financial data. **Personnel and Human Resources:** Knowledge of policies and practices involved in personnel/human resource functions. This includes recruitment, selection, training, and promotion regulations and procedures; compensation and benefits packages; labor relations and negotiation strategies; and personnel information systems. **Production and Processing:** Knowledge of inputs, outputs, raw materials, waste, quality control, costs, and techniques for maximizing the manufacture and distribution of goods. **Mathematics:** Knowledge of numbers, their operations, and interrelationships including arithmetic, algebra, geometry, calculus, statistics, and their applications. **Psychology:** Knowledge of human behavior and performance, mental processes, psychological research methods, and the assessment and treatment of behavioral and affective disorders. **Education and Training:** Knowledge of instructional methods and training techniques including curriculum design principles, learning theory, group and individual teaching techniques, design of individual development plans, and test design principles. **English Language:** Knowledge of the structure and content of the English language including the meaning and spelling of words, rules of composition, and grammar. **Law, Government, and Jurisprudence:** Knowledge of laws, legal codes, court procedures, precedents, government regulations, executive orders, agency rules, and the democratic political process.

MANAGEMENT SUPPORT SPECIALISTS

Purchasing Agents and Buyers, Farm Products

Education	Bachelor's degree
Average Yearly Earnings	$38,251
Projected Growth	20%
Annual Job Openings	124,342
Self-employed	6%
Employed Part-time	8%

Arrange or contract for the purchase of farm products for further processing or resale. Negotiates contracts with farmers for production or purchase of agricultural products such as milk, grains, and Christmas trees. Arranges sales, loans, or financing for supplies, such as equipment, seed, feed, fertilizer, and chemicals. Reviews orders and determines product types and quantities required to meet demand. Plans and arranges for transportation for crops, milk, or other products to dairy or processing facility. Inspects and tests crops or other farm products to determine quality and to detect evidence of disease or insect damage. Estimates production possibilities by surveying property and studying factors such as history of crop rotation, soil fertility, and irrigation facilities. Maintains records of business transactions. Advises farm groups and growers on land preparation and livestock care to maximize quantity and quality of production. Coordinates and directs activities of workers engaged in cutting, transporting, storing, or milling products, and in maintaining records. Writes articles for publication.

Occupational Type

Enterprising occupations frequently involve starting up and carrying out projects. These occupations can involve leading people and making many decisions. Sometimes they involve risk taking and often deal with business.

Skills required of Purchasing Agents and Buyers, Farm Products

Writing, Speaking, Mathematics, Coordination, Persuasion, Negotiation, Management of Financial Resources, Management of Material Resources

College Majors

Agricultural Production Workers and Managers, General: An instructional program that generally prepares individuals to plan and economically use facilities, natural resources, labor, and capital in the production of plant and animal products.

Supporting Courses

Administration and Management: Knowledge of principles and processes involved in business and organizational planning, coordination, and execution. This includes strategic planning, resource allocation, manpower modeling, leadership techniques, and production methods. **Clerical:** Knowledge of administrative and clerical procedures and systems such as word processing systems, filing and records management systems, stenography and transcription, forms design principles, and other office procedures and terminology.

Economics and Accounting: Knowledge of economic and accounting principles and practices, the financial markets, banking, and the analysis and reporting of financial data. **Sales and Marketing:** Knowledge of principles and methods involved in showing, promoting, and selling products or services. This includes marketing strategies and tactics, product demonstration and sales techniques, and sales control systems. **Production and Processing:** Knowledge of inputs, outputs, raw materials, waste, quality control, costs, and techniques for maximizing the manufacture and distribution of goods. **Food Production:** Knowledge of techniques and equipment for planting, growing, and harvesting of food for consumption including crop rotation methods, animal husbandry, and food storage/handling techniques. **Mathematics:** Knowledge of numbers, their operations, and interrelationships including arithmetic, algebra, geometry, calculus, statistics, and their applications. **Biology:** Knowledge of plant and animal living tissue, cells, organisms, and entities, including their functions, interdependencies, and interactions with each other and the environment. **English Language:** Knowledge of the structure and content of the English language including the meaning and spelling of words, rules of composition, and grammar. **Communications and Media:** Knowledge of media production, communication, and dissemination techniques and methods including alternative ways to inform and entertain via written, oral, and visual media. **Transportation:** Knowledge of principles and methods for moving people or goods by air, rail, sea, or road, including their relative costs, advantages, and limitations.

Legislative Assistants

Perform research into governmental laws and procedures to resolve problems or complaints of constituents or to assist legislator in preparation of proposed legislation. Conducts research in such areas as laws, procedures, and systems of government and subject matter of proposed legislation. Analyzes voting records, existing and pending legislation, political activity, or constituent problems to determine action to take. Confers with personnel, such as constituents, representatives of Federal agencies, and members of press to gather and provide information. Attends committee meetings to obtain information on proposed legislation. Briefs legislator on issues and recommends action to be taken. Prepares correspondence, reports, and preliminary drafts of bills and speeches. Assists in campaign activities.

 Occupational Type

Enterprising occupations frequently involve starting up and carrying out projects. These occupations can involve leading people and making many decisions. Sometimes they involve risk taking and often deal with business.

 Skills required of Legislative Assistants

Reading Comprehension, Active Listening, Writing, Critical Thinking, Active Learning, Coordination, Persuasion, Negotiation, Problem Identification, Information Gathering, Synthesis/Reorganization, Idea Generation, Idea Evaluation, Implementation Planning, Visioning, Systems Perception, Identifying Downstream Consequences, Identification of Key Causes, Judgment and Decision Making, Systems Evaluation

College Majors

Paralegal/Legal Assistant: An instructional program that prepares individuals to perform research, drafting, investigatory, recordkeeping and related administrative functions under the supervision of an attorney. Includes instruction in legal research, drafting legal documents, appraising, pleading, courthouse procedures and legal specializations.

Supporting Courses

English Language: Knowledge of the structure and content of the English language including the meaning and spelling of words, rules of composition, and grammar. **Law, Government, and Jurisprudence:** Knowledge of laws, legal codes, court procedures, precedents, government regulations, executive orders, agency rules, and the democratic political process.

Executive Secretaries and Administrative Assistants

Aid executive by coordinating office services, such as personnel, budget preparation and control, housekeeping, records control, and special management studies. Coordinates and directs office services, such as records and budget preparation, personnel, and housekeeping, to aid executives. Prepares records and reports, such as recommendations for solutions of administrative problems and annual reports. Files and retrieves corporation documents, records, and reports. Analyzes operating practices and procedures to create new or to revise existing methods. Interprets administrative and operating policies and procedures for employees. Studies management methods to improve workflow, simplify reporting procedures, or implement cost reductions. Plans conferences. Reads and answers correspondence.

Occupational Type

Conventional occupations frequently involve following set procedures and routines. These occupations can include working with data and details more than with ideas. Usually there is a clear line of authority to follow.

Skills required of Executive Secretaries and Administrative Assistants

Coordination, Synthesis/Reorganization, Programming, Time Management, Management of Financial Resources, Management of Material Resources, Management of Personnel Resources

College Majors

Business Administration and Management, General: An instructional program that generally prepares individuals to plan, organize, direct, and control the functions and processes of a firm or organization. Includes instruction in management theory, human resources management and behavior, accounting and other quantitative methods, purchasing and logistics, organization and production, marketing, and business decision making.

Supporting Courses

Administration and Management: Knowledge of principles and processes involved in business and organizational planning, coordination, and execution. This includes strategic planning, resource allocation, manpower modeling, leadership techniques, and production methods. **Clerical:** Knowledge of administrative and clerical procedures and systems such as word processing systems, filing and records management systems, stenography and transcription, forms design principles, and other office procedures and terminology. **Economics and Accounting:** Knowledge of economic and accounting principles and practices, the financial markets, banking, and the analysis and reporting of financial data.

Land Leasing and Permit Agents

Arrange for property leases or permits for special use, such as mineral prospecting or movie production. Negotiates agreements, such as leases, options, and royalty payments, with property representatives. Draws up agreements according to negotiated terms, applying knowledge of company policies and local, state, and Federal laws. Confers with others regarding characteristics of location desired and lease and use of property. Obtains signatures on documents from company and property representatives. Seeks new locations for prospecting or production activities. Consults with authorities and landowners, and researches company policies and local, state, and Federal laws to obtain regulatory information. Searches public records to determine legal ownership of land and mineral rights for property. Writes purchase orders and bank checks as specified by leases, agreements, and contracts. Draws sketches of locations and terrain to be traversed. Posts markers on property to indicate locations.

 Occupational Type

Enterprising occupations frequently involve starting up and carrying out projects. These occupations can involve leading people and making many decisions. Sometimes they involve risk taking and often deal with business.

 Skills required of Land Leasing and Permit Agents

Writing, Negotiation, Management of Material Resources

 College Majors

Real Estate: An instructional program that prepares individuals to develop, buy, sell, appraise, and manage real property. Includes instruction in land use development policy, real estate law, real estate marketing procedures, agency management, brokerage, property inspection and appraisal, real estate investing, leased and rental properties, commercial real estate, and property management.

Supporting Courses

Economics and Accounting: Knowledge of economic and accounting principles and practices, the financial markets, banking, and the analysis and reporting of financial data. **Geography:** Knowledge of various methods for describing the location and distribution of land, sea, and air masses including their physical locations, relationships, and characteristics. **Law, Government, and Jurisprudence:** Knowledge of laws, legal codes, court procedures, precedents, government regulations, executive orders, agency rules, and the democratic political process.

Meeting and Convention Planners

Coordinate activities of staff and convention personnel to make arrangements for group meetings and conventions. Directs and coordinates activities of staff and convention personnel to make arrangements, prepare facilities, and provide services for events. Consults with customer to determine objectives and requirements for events, such as meetings, conferences, and conventions. Plans and develops programs, budgets, and services, such as lodging, catering, and entertainment, according to customer requirements. Evaluates and selects providers of services, such as meeting facilities, speakers, and transportation, according to customer requirements. Negotiates contracts with such providers as hotels, convention centers, and speakers. Inspects rooms and displays for conformance to customer requirements, and conducts post-meeting evaluations to improve future events. Speaks with attendees and resolves complaints to maintain goodwill. Obtains permits from fire and health departments to erect displays and exhibits and to serve food at events. Reviews bills for accuracy and approves payment. Maintains records of events. Reads trade publications, attends seminars, and consults with other meeting professionals to keep abreast of meeting management standards and trends.

Occupational Type

Enterprising occupations frequently involve starting up and carrying out projects. These occupations can involve leading people and making many decisions. Sometimes they involve risk taking and often deal with business.

Skills required of Meeting and Convention Planners

Speaking, Monitoring, Social Perceptiveness, Coordination, Persuasion, Negotiation, Service Orientation, Implementation Planning, Time Management, Management of Financial Resources, Management of Material Resources, Management of Personnel Resources

College Majors

Foods and Nutrition Studies, General: An instructional program that generally describes the study of the role of food and nutrition in individual and family health and wellness, and in the study of food production, preparation and service operations. Includes instruction in food product consumption, nutritional care and education, and the organization and administration of food systems.

Supporting Courses

Administration and Management: Knowledge of principles and processes involved in business and organizational planning, coordination, and execution. This includes strategic planning, resource allocation, manpower modeling, leadership techniques, and production methods. **Economics and Accounting:** Knowledge of economic and accounting principles and practices, the financial markets, banking, and the analysis and reporting of financial data. **Sales and Marketing:** Knowledge of principles and methods involved in showing, promoting, and selling products or services. This includes marketing strategies and tactics, product demonstration and sales techniques, and sales control systems. **Customer and Personal Service:** Knowledge of principles and processes for providing customer and personal services including needs assessment techniques, quality service standards, alternative delivery systems, and customer satisfaction evaluation techniques. **Sociology and Anthropology:** Knowledge of group behavior and dynamics, societal trends and influences, cultures, their history, migrations, ethnicity, and origins. **Foreign Language:** Knowledge of the structure and content of a foreign (non-English) language including the meaning and spelling of words, rules of composition and grammar, and pronunciation. **Public Safety and Security:** Knowledge of weaponry, public safety, and security operations, rules, regulations, precautions, prevention, and the protection of people, data, and property. **Law, Government, and Jurisprudence:** Knowledge of laws, legal codes, court procedures, precedents, government regulations, executive orders, agency rules, and the democratic political process. **Telecommunications:** Knowledge of transmission, broadcasting, switching, control, and operation of telecommunications systems. **Communications and Media:** Knowledge of media production, communication, and dissemination techniques and methods including alternative ways to inform and entertain via written, oral, and visual media.

Customs Brokers

Prepare and compile documents required by Federal government for discharge of foreign cargo at domestic port to serve as intermediary between importers, merchant shipping companies, airlines, railroads, trucking companies, pipeline operators, and the United States Customs Service. Completes entry papers from shipper's invoice, in accordance with Federal regulations, for discharge of foreign cargo at domestic port. Submits entry papers to U.S. Customs Service, according to Federal regulations. Prepares papers for shipper to appeal duty charges imposed by Customs Service. Quotes duty rates on goods to be imported, based on knowledge of Federal tariffs and excise taxes. Arranges for payment of duties as specified by law. Registers foreign ships with U.S. Coast Guard. Provides storage and transportation of imported goods from port to final destination.

Occupational Type

Conventional occupations frequently involve following set procedures and routines. These occupations can include working with data and details more than with ideas. Usually there is a clear line of authority to follow.

Skills required of Customs Brokers

Information on specific skills required is not available.

 ### College Majors

International Business: An instructional program that prepares individuals to manage international businesses and/or business operations. Includes instruction in the principles and processes of export sales, trade controls, foreign operations and related problems, monetary issues, international business policy, and applications to doing business in specific countries and markets.

 ### Supporting Courses

Economics and Accounting: Knowledge of economic and accounting principles and practices, the financial markets, banking, and the analysis and reporting of financial data. **Geography:** Knowledge of various methods for describing the location and distribution of land, sea, and air masses including their physical locations, relationships, and characteristics. **Foreign Language:** Knowledge of the structure and content of a foreign (non-English) language including the meaning and spelling of words, rules of composition and grammar, and pronunciation. **Law, Government, and Jurisprudence:** Knowledge of laws, legal codes, court procedures, precedents, government regulations, executive orders, agency rules, and the democratic political process. **Transportation:** Knowledge of principles and methods for moving people or goods by air, rail, sea, or road, including their relative costs, advantages, and limitations.

All Other Management Support Workers

All other management support workers not classified separately above.

 ### Occupational Type

Specific information is not available.

 ### Skills required of All Other Management Support Workers

Information on specific skills required is not available.

 ### College Majors

General Selling Skills and Sales Operations: An instructional program that prepares individuals to perform the techniques of direct consumer persuasion, involving planned, personalized communications, as agents for a wide variety of industries and product types.

Supporting Courses

Specific information is not available.

MANAGEMENT SUPPORT WORKERS

✏️	Education	Bachelor's degree
💰	Average Yearly Earnings	$35,339
	Projected Growth	26%
	Annual Job Openings	154,129
👥	Self-employed	2%
	Employed Part-time	21%

Interpreters and Translators

Translate and interpret written or spoken communications from one language to another or from spoken to manual sign language used by hearing-impaired. Translates approximate or exact message of speaker into specified language, orally or by using hand signs for hearing-impaired. Translates responses from second language to first. Reads written material, such as legal documents, scientific works, or news reports, and rewrites material into specified language, according to established rules of grammar. Listens to statements of speaker to ascertain meaning and to remember what is said, using electronic audio system. Receives information on subject to be discussed prior to interpreting session.

 ## Occupational Type

Artistic occupations frequently involve working with forms, designs, and patterns. They often require self-expression and the work can be done without following a clear set of rules.

 ## Skills required of Interpreters and Translators

Reading Comprehension, Active Listening, Writing, Speaking, Service Orientation

 ## College Majors

Foreign Languages and Literatures, General: An instructional program that describes an undifferentiated program in foreign languages and literatures.

 ## Supporting Courses

Sociology and Anthropology: Knowledge of group behavior and dynamics, societal trends and influences, cultures, their history, migrations, ethnicity, and origins. **English Language:** Knowledge of the structure and content of the English language including the meaning and spelling of words, rules of composition, and grammar. **Foreign Language:** Knowledge of the structure and content of a foreign (non-English) language including the meaning and spelling of words, rules of composition and grammar, and pronunciation. **History and Archeology:** Knowledge of past historical events and their causes, indicators, and impact on particular civilizations and cultures. **Communications and Media:** Knowledge of media production, communication, and dissemination techniques and methods including alternative ways to inform and entertain via written, oral, and visual media.

City Planning Aides

Compile data from various sources, such as maps, reports, and field and file investigations, for use by city planner in making planning studies. Summarizes information from maps, reports, investigations, and books. Prepares reports, using statistics, charts, and graphs, to illustrate planning studies in areas such as population, land use, or zoning. Prepares and updates files and records. Conducts interviews and surveys and observes conditions which affect land usage. Answers public inquiries.

Occupational Type

Conventional occupations frequently involve following set procedures and routines. These occupations can include working with data and details more than with ideas. Usually there is a clear line of authority to follow.

Skills required of City Planning Aides

Writing, Mathematics

College Majors

Civil Engineering/Civil Technology/Technician: An instructional program that prepares individuals to apply basic engineering principles and technical skills in support of civil engineers engaged in designing and executing public works projects such as highways, dams, bridges, tunnels and other facilities. Includes instruction in site analysis, structural testing procedures, field and laboratory testing procedures, plan and specification preparation, test equipment operation and maintenance, and report preparation.

Supporting Courses

Clerical: Knowledge of administrative and clerical procedures and systems such as word processing systems, filing and records management systems, stenography and transcription, forms design principles, and other office procedures and terminology. **Mathematics:** Knowledge of numbers, their operations, and interrelationships including arithmetic, algebra, geometry, calculus, statistics, and their applications. **Geography:** Knowledge of various methods for describing the location and distribution of land, sea, and air masses including their physical locations, relationships, and characteristics.

MARKETING, ADVERTISING, AND PUBLIC RELATIONS MANAGERS

Advertising and Promotions Managers

Education	Work experience, plus degree	
Average Yearly Earnings	$53,602	
Projected Growth	29%	
Annual Job Openings	54,601	
Self-employed	2%	
Employed Part-time	3%	

Plan and direct advertising policies and programs or produce collateral materials, such as posters, contests, coupons, or giveaways, to create extra interest in the purchase of a product or service for a department, an entire organization, or on an account basis. Directs activities of workers engaged in developing and producing advertisements. Plans and executes advertising policies of organization. Plans and prepares advertising and promotional material. Confers with department heads and/or staff to discuss topics such as contracts, selection of advertising media, or product to be advertised. Formulates plans to extend business with established accounts and transacts business as agent for advertising accounts. Coordinates activities of departments, such as sales, graphic arts, media, finance, and research. Confers with clients to provide marketing or technical advice. Monitors and analyzes sales promotion results to determine cost effectiveness of promotion campaign. Inspects layouts and advertising copy and edits scripts, audio and video tapes, and other promotional material for adherence to specifications. Supervises and trains service representatives. Reads trade journals and professional literature to stay informed on trends, innovations, and changes that affect media planning. Consults publications to learn about conventions and social functions, and organizes prospect files for promotional purposes. Represents company at trade association meetings to promote products. Directs product research and development. Contacts organizations to explain services and facilities offered or to secure props, audiovisual materials, and sound effects. Adjusts broadcasting schedules due to program cancellation. Directs conversion of products from USA to foreign standards. Inspects premises of assigned stores for adequate security and compliance with safety codes and ordinances.

Occupational Type

Artistic occupations frequently involve working with forms, designs, and patterns. They often require self-expression and the work can be done without following a clear set of rules.

Skills required of Advertising and Promotions Managers

Reading Comprehension, Active Listening, Writing, Speaking, Critical Thinking, Active Learning, Learning Strategies, Monitoring, Social Perceptiveness, Coordination, Persuasion, Negotiation, Instructing, Service Orientation, Problem Identification, Information Gathering, Information Organization, Synthesis/Reorganization, Idea Generation, Idea Evaluation, Implementation Planning, Operations Analysis, Product Inspection, Visioning, Systems Perception, Identifying Downstream Consequences, Identification of Key Causes, Judgment and Decision Making, Systems Evaluation, Time Management, Management of Financial Resources, Management of Material Resources, Management of Personnel Resources

College Majors

Hospitality and Recreation Marketing Operations, General: An instructional program that generally prepares individuals to perform marketing tasks applicable to a wide variety of hospitality and leisure industry settings.

Supporting Courses

Administration and Management: Knowledge of principles and processes involved in business and organizational planning, coordination, and execution. This includes strategic

planning, resource allocation, manpower modeling, leadership techniques, and production methods. **Economics and Accounting:** Knowledge of economic and accounting principles and practices, the financial markets, banking, and the analysis and reporting of financial data. **Sales and Marketing:** Knowledge of principles and methods involved in showing, promoting, and selling products or services. This includes marketing strategies and tactics, product demonstration and sales techniques, and sales control systems. **Customer and Personal Service:** Knowledge of principles and processes for providing customer and personal services including needs assessment techniques, quality service standards, alternative delivery systems, and customer satisfaction evaluation techniques. **Personnel and Human Resources:** Knowledge of policies and practices involved in personnel/human resource functions. This includes recruitment, selection, training, and promotion regulations and procedures; compensation and benefits packages; labor relations and negotiation strategies; and personnel information systems. **Mathematics:** Knowledge of numbers, their operations, and interrelationships including arithmetic, algebra, geometry, calculus, statistics, and their applications. **Psychology:** Knowledge of human behavior and performance, mental processes, psychological research methods, and the assessment and treatment of behavioral and affective disorders. **Sociology and Anthropology:** Knowledge of group behavior and dynamics, societal trends and influences, cultures, their history, migrations, ethnicity, and origins. **Geography:** Knowledge of various methods for describing the location and distribution of land, sea, and air masses including their physical locations, relationships, and characteristics. **Education and Training:** Knowledge of instructional methods and training techniques including curriculum design principles, learning theory, group and individual teaching techniques, design of individual development plans, and test design principles. **English Language:** Knowledge of the structure and content of the English language including the meaning and spelling of words, rules of composition, and grammar. **Foreign Language:** Knowledge of the structure and content of a foreign (non-English) language including the meaning and spelling of words, rules of composition and grammar, and pronunciation. **Fine Arts:** Knowledge of theory and techniques required to produce, compose, and perform works of music, dance, visual arts, drama, and sculpture. **History and Archeology:** Knowledge of past historical events and their causes, indicators, and impact on particular civilizations and cultures. **Philosophy and Theology:** Knowledge of different philosophical systems and religions, including their basic principles, values, ethics, ways of thinking, customs, and practices, and their impact on human culture. **Public Safety and Security:** Knowledge of weaponry, public safety, and security operations, rules, regulations, precautions, prevention, and the protection of people, data, and property. **Law, Government, and Jurisprudence:** Knowledge of laws, legal codes, court procedures, precedents, government regulations, executive orders, agency rules, and the democratic political process. **Telecommunications:** Knowledge of transmission, broadcasting, switching, control, and operation of telecommunications systems. **Communications and Media:** Knowledge of media production, communication, and dissemination techniques and methods including alternative ways to inform and entertain via written, oral, and visual media.

Sales Managers

Direct the actual distribution or movement of a product or service to customers. Coordinate sales distribution by establishing sales territories, quotas, and goals, and establish training programs for sales representatives. Analyze sales statistics gathered by staff to determine sales potential and inventory requirements, and monitor the preferences of customers. Directs and coordinates activities involving sales of manufactured goods, service outlets, technical services, operating retail chain, and advertising services for publication. Plans and directs staffing, training, and performance evaluations to develop and control sales and service programs. Directs, coordinates, and reviews activities in sales and service accounting and recordkeeping, and receiving and shipping operations. Analyzes marketing potential of new and existing store locations, sales statistics, and expenditures to formulate policy. Confers or consults with department heads to plan advertising services, secure information on appliances and equipment, and customer-required specifications. Reviews operational records and reports to project sales and determine profitability. Advises dealers and distributors on policies and operating procedures to ensure functional effectiveness of business. Directs foreign sales and service outlets of organization. Visits franchised dealers to stimulate interest in establishment or expansion of leasing programs. Directs clerical staff to maintain export correspondence, bid requests, and credit collections, and current information on tariffs, licenses, and restrictions. Confers with potential customers regarding equipment needs and advises customers on types of equipment to purchase. Resolves customer complaints regarding sales and service. Represents company at trade association meetings to promote products. Directs product research and development. Inspects premises of assigned stores for adequate security exits and compliance with safety codes and ordinances. Direct conversion of products from USA to foreign standards.

 ## Occupational Type

Enterprising occupations frequently involve starting up and carrying out projects. These occupations can involve leading people and making many decisions. Sometimes they involve risk taking and often deal with business.

 ## Skills required of Sales Managers

Active Listening, Speaking, Critical Thinking, Active Learning, Learning Strategies, Monitoring, Social Perceptiveness, Coordination, Persuasion, Negotiation, Instructing, Service Orientation, Problem Identification, Information Gathering, Synthesis/Reorganization, Idea Generation, Idea Evaluation, Implementation Planning, Operations Analysis, Visioning, Systems Perception, Identifying Downstream Consequences, Identification of Key Causes, Judgment and Decision Making, Systems Evaluation, Time Management, Management of Financial Resources, Management of Material Resources, Management of Personnel Resources

 ## College Majors

General Retailing Operations: An instructional program that prepares individuals to perform marketing tasks specifically applicable to retail operations in a wide variety of settings.

 ## Supporting Courses

Administration and Management: Knowledge of principles and processes involved in business and organizational planning, coordination, and execution. This includes strategic

planning, resource allocation, manpower modeling, leadership techniques, and production methods. **Clerical:** Knowledge of administrative and clerical procedures and systems such as word processing systems, filing and records management systems, stenography and transcription, forms design principles, and other office procedures and terminology. **Economics and Accounting:** Knowledge of economic and accounting principles and practices, the financial markets, banking, and the analysis and reporting of financial data. **Sales and Marketing:** Knowledge of principles and methods involved in showing, promoting, and selling products or services. This includes marketing strategies and tactics, product demonstration and sales techniques, and sales control systems. **Customer and Personal Service:** Knowledge of principles and processes for providing customer and personal services including needs assessment techniques, quality service standards, alternative delivery systems, and customer satisfaction evaluation techniques. **Personnel and Human Resources:** Knowledge of policies and practices involved in personnel/human resource functions. This includes recruitment, selection, training, and promotion regulations and procedures; compensation and benefits packages; labor relations and negotiation strategies; and personnel information systems. **Mathematics:** Knowledge of numbers, their operations, and interrelationships including arithmetic, algebra, geometry, calculus, statistics, and their applications. **Psychology:** Knowledge of human behavior and performance, mental processes, psychological research methods, and the assessment and treatment of behavioral and affective disorders. **Sociology and Anthropology:** Knowledge of group behavior and dynamics, societal trends and influences, cultures, their history, migrations, ethnicity, and origins. **Geography:** Knowledge of various methods for describing the location and distribution of land, sea, and air masses including their physical locations, relationships, and characteristics. **Education and Training:** Knowledge of instructional methods and training techniques including curriculum design principles, learning theory, group and individual teaching techniques, design of individual development plans, and test design principles. **English Language:** Knowledge of the structure and content of the English language including the meaning and spelling of words, rules of composition, and grammar. **Foreign Language:** Knowledge of the structure and content of a foreign (non-English) language including the meaning and spelling of words, rules of composition and grammar, and pronunciation. **History and Archeology:** Knowledge of past historical events and their causes, indicators, and impact on particular civilizations and cultures. **Philosophy and Theology:** Knowledge of different philosophical systems and religions, including their basic principles, values, ethics, ways of thinking, customs, and practices, and their impact on human culture. **Public Safety and Security:** Knowledge of weaponry, public safety, and security operations, rules, regulations, precautions, prevention, and the protection of people, data, and property. **Law, Government, and Jurisprudence:** Knowledge of laws, legal codes, court procedures, precedents, government regulations, executive orders, agency rules, and the democratic political process. **Communications and Media:** Knowledge of media production, communication, and dissemination techniques and methods including alternative ways to inform and entertain via written, oral, and visual media. **Transportation:** Knowledge of principles and methods for moving people or goods by air, rail, sea, or road, including their relative costs, advantages, and limitations.

Marketing Managers

Determine the demand for products and services offered by a firm and its competitors and identify potential customers. Develop pricing strategies with the goal of maximizing the firm's profits or share of the market while ensuring the firm's customers are satisfied. Oversee product development or monitor trends that indicate the need for new products and services. Plans and administers marketing and distribution of broadcasting television programs and negotiates agreements for ancillary properties. Develops marketing strategy, based on knowledge of establishment policy, nature of market, and cost and mark-up factors. Coordinates and publicizes product marketing activities. Directs activities of world trade department in chamber of commerce to assist business concerns in developing and utilizing foreign markets. Conducts economic and commercial surveys in foreign countries to locate markets for products and services. Analyzes foreign business developments and fashion and trade journals regarding fashion trends and opportunities for selling and buying products. Promotes new fashions and coordinates promotional activities, such as fashion shows, to induce consumer acceptance. Reviews inventory of television programs and films produced and distribution rights to determine potential markets for broadcasting station. Consults with buying personnel to gain advice regarding type of fashions store will purchase and feature for season. Advises exporters and importers on documentation procedures and certifies commercial documents that are required by foreign countries. Confers with legal staff to resolve problems, such as copyrights and royalty sharing with outside producers and distributors. Advises business and other groups on local, national, and international legislation affecting world trade. Negotiates with media agents to secure agreements for translation of materials into other media. Entertains foreign governmental officials and business representatives to promote trade relations. Prepare report of marketing activities for state and Federal agencies. Contracts with models, musicians, caterers, and other personnel to manage staging of fashion shows. Selects garments and accessories to be shown at fashion shows. Arranges for reproduction of visual materials and edits materials according to specific market or customer requirements. Promotes travel to other countries. Compiles catalog of audiovisual offerings and sets prices and rental fees. Provides information on current fashion, style trends, and use of accessories.

Occupational Type

Enterprising occupations frequently involve starting up and carrying out projects. These occupations can involve leading people and making many decisions. Sometimes they involve risk taking and often deal with business.

Skills required of Marketing Managers

Reading Comprehension, Active Listening, Writing, Speaking, Critical Thinking, Active Learning, Learning Strategies, Monitoring, Social Perceptiveness, Coordination, Persuasion, Negotiation, Service Orientation, Problem Identification, Information Gathering, Information Organization, Synthesis/Reorganization, Idea Generation, Idea Evaluation,

Implementation Planning, Operations Analysis, Visioning, Systems Perception, Identifying Downstream Consequences, Identification of Key Causes, Judgment and Decision Making, Systems Evaluation, Time Management, Management of Financial Resources, Management of Material Resources, Management of Personnel Resources

College Majors

Apparel and Accessories Marketing Operations, General: An instructional program that generally prepares individuals to perform marketing tasks specifically applicable to all segments of the apparel and fashion industry.

Supporting Courses

Administration and Management: Knowledge of principles and processes involved in business and organizational planning, coordination, and execution. This includes strategic planning, resource allocation, manpower modeling, leadership techniques, and production methods. **Economics and Accounting:** Knowledge of economic and accounting principles and practices, the financial markets, banking, and the analysis and reporting of financial data. **Sales and Marketing:** Knowledge of principles and methods involved in showing, promoting, and selling products or services. This includes marketing strategies and tactics, product demonstration and sales techniques, and sales control systems. **Customer and Personal Service:** Knowledge of principles and processes for providing customer and personal services including needs assessment techniques, quality service standards, alternative delivery systems, and customer satisfaction evaluation techniques. **Personnel and Human Resources:** Knowledge of policies and practices involved in personnel/human resource functions. This includes recruitment, selection, training, and promotion regulations and procedures; compensation and benefits packages; labor relations and negotiation strategies; and personnel information systems. **Mathematics:** Knowledge of numbers, their operations, and interrelationships including arithmetic, algebra, geometry, calculus, statistics, and their applications. **Psychology:** Knowledge of human behavior and performance, mental processes, psychological research methods, and the assessment and treatment of behavioral and affective disorders. **Sociology and Anthropology:** Knowledge of group behavior and dynamics, societal trends and influences, cultures, their history, migrations, ethnicity, and origins. **Geography:** Knowledge of various methods for describing the location and distribution of land, sea, and air masses including their physical locations, relationships, and characteristics. **Education and Training:** Knowledge of instructional methods and training techniques including curriculum design principles, learning theory, group and individual teaching techniques, design of individual development plans, and test design principles. **English Language:** Knowledge of the structure and content of the English language including the meaning and spelling of words, rules of composition, and grammar. **Foreign Language:** Knowledge of the structure and content of a foreign (non-English) language including the meaning and spelling of words, rules of composition and grammar, and pronunciation. **Fine Arts:** Knowledge of theory and techniques required to produce, compose, and perform works of music, dance, visual arts, drama, and sculpture. **History and Archeology:** Knowledge of past historical events and their causes, indicators, and impact on particular civilizations and cultures. **Philosophy and Theology:** Knowledge of different philosophical systems and religions, including their basic principles, values, ethics, ways of thinking, customs, and practices, and their impact on human culture. **Law, Government, and Jurisprudence:** Knowledge of laws, legal codes, court procedures, precedents, government regulations, executive orders, agency rules, and the democratic political process. **Communications and Media:** Knowledge of media production, communication, and dissemination techniques and methods including alternative ways to inform and entertain via written, oral, and visual media. **Transportation:** Knowledge of principles and methods for moving people or goods by air, rail, sea, or road, including their relative costs, advantages, and limitations.

Fundraising Directors

Plan and direct activities to solicit and maintain funds for special projects and nonprofit organizations,such as charities, universities, museums, and other organizations dependent upon voluntary financial contributions. Plan and directs solicitation of funds for broadcasting stations and institutions such as zoos and museums. Establishes fundraising goals. Assigns responsibilities for personal solicitation efforts. Plans and coordinates benefit events. Develops schedule for disbursing solicited funds. Develops public relations materials to enhance institution image and promote fundraising program. Organizes direct mail campaign to reach potential contributors. Researches public and private grant agencies and foundations to identify sources of funding. Supervises and coordinates activities of workers engaged in maintaining records of contributors and grants and preparing letters of appreciation. Purchases mailing list of potential donors or negotiates agreements with other organizations for exchange of mailing lists. Specializes in solicitation of funding from government, foundation, or corporation sources. Serves as liaison between broadcast departmental staff and funding establishment personnel to provide project information and to solve problems.

Occupational Type

Enterprising occupations frequently involve starting up and carrying out projects. These occupations can involve leading people and making many decisions. Sometimes they involve risk taking and often deal with business.

Skills required of Fundraising Directors

Active Listening, Speaking, Monitoring, Social Perceptiveness, Coordination, Persuasion, Negotiation, Service Orientation, Information Gathering, Information Organization, Synthesis/Reorganization, Idea Generation, Idea Evaluation, Implementation Planning, Visioning, Systems Perception, Identifying Downstream Consequences, Identification of Key Causes, Judgment and Decision Making, Systems Evaluation, Time Management, Management of Financial Resources, Management of Material Resources, Management of Personnel Resources

College Majors

Public Relations and Organizational Communications: A instructional program that describes the methods and techniques for communicating image-oriented corporate and sponsor messages to various audiences, for promoting client interests, and for managing client-media relations, and that prepares individuals to perform public relations and related services.

 Supporting Courses

Administration and Management: Knowledge of principles and processes involved in business and organizational planning, coordination, and execution. This includes strategic planning, resource allocation, manpower modeling, leadership techniques, and production methods. **Economics and Accounting:** Knowledge of economic and accounting principles and practices, the financial markets, banking, and the analysis and reporting of financial data. **Sales and Marketing:** Knowledge of principles and methods involved in showing, promoting, and selling products or services. This includes marketing strategies and tactics, product demonstration and sales techniques, and sales control systems. **Psychology:** Knowledge of human behavior and performance, mental processes, psychological research methods, and the assessment and treatment of behavioral and affective disorders. **Sociology and Anthropology:** Knowledge of group behavior and dynamics, societal trends and influences, cultures, their history, migrations, ethnicity, and origins. **Geography:** Knowledge of various methods for describing the location and distribution of land, sea, and air masses including their physical locations, relationships, and characteristics. **English Language:** Knowledge of the structure and content of the English language including the meaning and spelling of words, rules of composition, and grammar. **Foreign Language:** Knowledge of the structure and content of a foreign (non-English) language including the meaning and spelling of words, rules of composition and grammar, and pronunciation. **Fine Arts:** Knowledge of theory and techniques required to produce, compose, and perform works of music, dance, visual arts, drama, and sculpture. **Philosophy and Theology:** Knowledge of different philosophical systems and religions, including their basic principles, values, ethics, ways of thinking, customs, and practices, and their impact on human culture. **Law, Government, and Jurisprudence:** Knowledge of laws, legal codes, court procedures, precedents, government regulations, executive orders, agency rules, and the democratic political process. **Telecommunications:** Knowledge of transmission, broadcasting, switching, control, and operation of telecommunications systems. **Communications and Media:** Knowledge of media production, communication, and dissemination techniques and methods including alternative ways to inform and entertain via written, oral, and visual media.

Grant Coordinators

Research, develop, and coordinate development of proposals for funding and funding sources to establish or maintain grant-funded programs in public or private organizations. Prepares proposal narrative justifying budgetary expenditures for approval by organization officials. Writes and submits grant proposal application to funding agency or foundation. Directs and coordinates evaluation and monitoring of grant-funded programs. Consults with personnel to determine goals, objectives, and budgetary requirements of organizations, such as nonprofit agencies, institutions, or school systems. Researches availability of grant funds from public and private agencies to determine feasibility of developing programs to supplement budget allocations. Completes reports as specified by grant. Confers with representatives of funding sources to complete details of proposal. Maintains files on grants.

Occupational Type

Enterprising occupations frequently involve starting up and carrying out projects. These occupations can involve leading people and making many decisions. Sometimes they involve risk taking and often deal with business.

Skills required of Grant Coordinators

Writing, Coordination, Persuasion, Negotiation, Information Gathering, Information Organization, Idea Evaluation, Systems Perception, Identifying Downstream Consequences, Management of Financial Resources, Management of Material Resources, Management of Personnel Resources

College Majors

Public Administration: An instructional program that prepares individuals to serve as managers in the executive arm of local, state, and Federal government; and that describes the systematic study of executive organization and management. Includes instruction in the roles, development, and principles of public administration; the management of public policy; executive-legislative relations; public budgetary processes and financial management; administrative law; public personnel management; professional ethics; and research methods.

Supporting Courses

Administration and Management: Knowledge of principles and processes involved in business and organizational planning, coordination, and execution. This includes strategic planning, resource allocation, manpower modeling, leadership techniques, and production methods. **Economics and Accounting:** Knowledge of economic and accounting principles and practices, the financial markets, banking, and the analysis and reporting of financial data. **English Language:** Knowledge of the structure and content of the English language including the meaning and spelling of words, rules of composition, and grammar. **Law, Government, and Jurisprudence:** Knowledge of laws, legal codes, court procedures, precedents, government regulations, executive orders, agency rules, and the democratic political process.

Agents/Business Managers of Artists, Performers, and Athletes

Represent and promote artists, performers, and athletes to prospective employers. May handle contract negotiations and other business matters for clients. Negotiates with management, promoters, union officials, and other persons, to obtain contracts for clients such as entertainers, artists, and athletes. Manages business affairs for clients, such as obtaining travel and lodging accommodations, selling tickets, marketing and advertising, and paying expenses. Schedules promotional or performance engagements for clients. Advises clients on financial and legal matters, such as investments and taxes. Collects fees, commission, or other payment, according to contract terms. Obtains information and inspects facilities, equipment, and accommodations of potential performance venue. Hires trainer or coach to advise client on performance matters, such as training techniques or presentation of act. Prepares periodic accounting statements for clients concerning financial affairs. Conducts auditions or interviews new clients.

Occupational Type

Enterprising occupations frequently involve starting up and carrying out projects. These occupations can involve leading people and making many decisions. Sometimes they involve risk taking and often deal with business.

Skills required of Agents/Business Managers of Artists, Performers, and Athletes

Speaking, Coordination, Persuasion, Negotiation, Service Orientation, Implementation Planning, Time Management, Management of Financial Resources, Management of Personnel Resources

College Majors

Business and Personal Services Marketing Operations, Other: Any instructional program in business or personal services marketing operations not described above.

Supporting Courses

Administration and Management: Knowledge of principles and processes involved in business and organizational planning, coordination, and execution. This includes strategic planning, resource allocation, manpower modeling, leadership techniques, and production methods. **Economics and Accounting:** Knowledge of economic and accounting principles and practices, the financial markets, banking, and the analysis and reporting of financial data. **Sales and Marketing:** Knowledge of principles and methods involved in showing, promoting, and selling products or services. This includes marketing strategies and tactics, product demonstration and sales techniques, and sales control systems. **Personnel and Human Resources:** Knowledge of policies and practices involved in personnel/human resource functions. This includes recruitment, selection, training, and promotion regulations and procedures; compensation and benefits packages; labor relations and negotiation strategies; and personnel information systems. **Fine Arts:** Knowledge of theory and techniques required to produce, compose, and perform works of music, dance, visual arts, drama, and sculpture. **Law, Government, and Jurisprudence:** Knowledge of laws, legal codes, court procedures, precedents, government regulations, executive orders, agency rules, and the democratic political process.

MATERIALS ENGINEERS

Education		Bachelor's degree
Average Yearly Earnings		$49,566
Projected Growth		7%
Annual Job Openings		933
Self-employed		0%
Employed Part-time		3%

Ceramic Engineers

Conduct research, design machinery, and develop processing techniques related to the manufacturing of ceramic products. Conducts research into methods of processing, forming, and firing of clays to develop new ceramic products. Designs machinery, equipment, and apparatus for forming, firing, and handling products. Develops processing techniques and directs technical work concerned with manufacture of ceramic products. Directs testing of physical, chemical, and heat-resisting properties of materials. Analyzes results of tests to determine combinations of materials that will improve quality of products. Coordinates testing activities of finished products for such characteristics as texture, color, durability, glazing, and refractory properties. Directs and coordinates manufacturing of prototype ceramic product. Designs and directs others in fabrication of testing and test-control apparatus and equipment. Directs and coordinates activities concerned with development, procurement, installation, and calibration of test and recording instruments, equipment, and control devices. Prepares or directs preparation of product layout and detailed drawings. Prepares technical reports for use by engineering and management personnel.

Occupational Type

Investigative occupations frequently involve working with ideas, and require an extensive amount of thinking. These occupations can involve searching for facts and figuring out problems mentally.

Skills required of Ceramic Engineers

Reading Comprehension, Active Listening, Writing, Speaking, Mathematics, Science, Critical Thinking, Active Learning, Coordination, Problem Identification, Information Gathering, Information Organization, Synthesis/Reorganization, Idea Generation, Idea Evaluation, Implementation Planning, Operations Analysis, Technology Design, Equipment Selection, Installation, Programming, Testing, Product Inspection, Visioning, Systems Perception, Identifying Downstream Consequences, Identification of Key Causes, Judgment and Decision Making, Systems Evaluation, Time Management, Management of Material Resources, Management of Personnel Resources

College Majors

Ceramic Sciences and Engineering: An instructional program that prepares individuals to apply mathematical and scientific principles to the design, development, and operational evaluation of inorganic nonmetallic materials, such as porcelains, cements, industrial ceramics, ceramic superconductors, abrasive, and related materials and systems.

Supporting Courses

Administration and Management: Knowledge of principles and processes involved in business and organizational planning, coordination, and execution. This includes strategic planning, resource allocation, manpower modeling, leadership techniques, and production methods. **Production and Processing:** Knowledge of inputs, outputs, raw materials, waste, quality control, costs, and techniques for maximizing the manufacture and distribution of goods. **Computers and Electronics:** Knowledge of electric circuit boards, processors, chips, and computer hardware and software, including applications and programming. **Engineering and Technology:** Knowledge of equipment, tools, mechanical devices, and their uses to produce motion, light, power, technology, and other applications. **Design:** Knowledge of design techniques, principles, tools and instruments involved in the production and use of precision technical plans, blueprints, drawings, and models. **Mathematics:** Knowledge of numbers, their operations, and interrelationships including arithmetic, algebra, geometry, calculus, statistics, and their applications. **Physics:** Knowledge and prediction of physical principles, laws, and applications including air, water, material dynamics, light, atomic principles, heat, electric theory, earth formations, and meteorological and related natural phenomena. **Chemistry:** Knowledge of the composition, structure, and properties of substances and of the chemical processes and transformations that they undergo. This includes uses of chemicals and their interactions, danger signs, production techniques, and disposal methods. **English Language:** Knowledge of the structure and content of the English language including the meaning and spelling of words, rules of composition, and grammar.

Metallurgists

Investigate properties of metals and develop methods to produce new alloys, applications, and processes of extracting metals from their ores, and to commercially fabricate products from metals. Conducts microscopic and macroscopic studies of metals and alloys to determine their physical characteristics, properties, and reactions to processing techniques. Tests and investigates alloys to develop new or improved grades or production methods, and to determine compliance with manufacturing standards. Develops and improves processes for melting, hot-working, cold-working, heat-treating, molding, and pouring metals. Originates, controls, and develops processes used in extracting metals from their ores. Studies ore reduction problems to determine most efficient methods of producing metals commercially. Consults with engineers to develop methods of manufacturing alloys at minimum costs. Interprets findings and prepares drawings, charts, and graphs for reference or instructional purposes. Makes experimental sand molds, and tests sand for permeability, strength, and chemical composition. Writes reports referencing findings, conclusions, and recommendations. Directs laboratory personnel in preparing samples, and designates area of samples for microscopic or macroscopic examinations. Controls temperature adjustments, charge mixtures, and other variables on blast and steel-melting furnaces.

Occupational Type

Investigative occupations frequently involve working with ideas, and require an extensive amount of thinking. These occupations can involve searching for facts and figuring out problems mentally.

Skills required of Metallurgists

Reading Comprehension, Active Listening, Writing, Speaking, Mathematics, Science, Critical Thinking, Active Learning, Instructing, Problem Identification, Information Gathering, Information Organization, Synthesis/Reorganization, Idea Generation, Idea Evaluation, Implementation Planning, Operations Analysis, Technology Design, Testing, Operation Monitoring, Operation and Control, Product Inspection, Visioning, Systems Perception, Identifying Downstream Consequences, Judgment and Decision Making

 College Majors

Metallurgical Engineering: An instructional program that prepares individuals to apply mathematical and metallurgical principles to the design, development and operational evaluation of metal components of structural, load-bearing, power, transmission, and moving systems; and the analysis of engineering problems such as stress, creep, failure, alloy behavior, environmental fluctuations, stability, electromagnetic and thermodynamic characteristics, optimal manufacturing processes, and related design considerations.

 Supporting Courses

Administration and Management: Knowledge of principles and processes involved in business and organizational planning, coordination, and execution. This includes strategic planning, resource allocation, manpower modeling, leadership techniques, and production methods. **Production and Processing:** Knowledge of inputs, outputs, raw materials, waste, quality control, costs, and techniques for maximizing the manufacture and distribution of goods. **Engineering and Technology:** Knowledge of equipment, tools, mechanical devices, and their uses to produce motion, light, power, technology, and other applications. **Design:** Knowledge of design techniques, principles, tools and instruments involved in the production and use of precision technical plans, blueprints, drawings, and models. **Physics:** Knowledge and prediction of physical principles, laws, and applications including air, water, material dynamics, light, atomic principles, heat, electric theory, earth formations, and meteorological and related natural phenomena. **Chemistry:** Knowledge of the composition, structure, and properties of substances and of the chemical processes and transformations that they undergo. This includes uses of chemicals and their interactions, danger signs, production techniques, and disposal methods. **Geography:** Knowledge of various methods for describing the location and distribution of land, sea, and air masses including their physical locations, relationships, and characteristics. **English Language:** Knowledge of the structure and content of the English language including the meaning and spelling of words, rules of composition, and grammar.

Welding Engineers

Develop welding techniques, procedures, and applications of welding equipment to problems involving fabrication of metals. Conducts research and development investigations to improve existing or to develop new welding equipment. Conducts research and development investigations to develop new or to modify current welding techniques and procedures. Conducts research and development investigations to develop and test new fabrication processes and procedures. Establishes welding procedures for production and welding personnel, to ensure compliance with specifications, processes, and heating requirements. Evaluates new equipment, techniques, and materials in welding field for possible application to current welding problems or production processes. Prepares technical reports identifying results of research and development and preventive maintenance investigations. Directs and coordinates technical inspections to ensure compliance with established welding procedures and standards. Contacts other agencies, engineering personnel, or clients to exchange ideas, information, or technical advice.

Occupational Type

Realistic occupations frequently involve work activities that include practical, hands-on problems and solutions. They often deal with plants, animals, and real-world materials like wood, tools, and machinery. Many of the occupations require working outside, and do not involve a lot of paperwork or working closely with others.

Skills required of Welding Engineers

Active Listening, Writing, Speaking, Mathematics, Science, Critical Thinking, Active Learning, Coordination, Problem Identification, Information Gathering, Information Organization, Synthesis/Reorganization, Idea Generation, Idea Evaluation, Implementation Planning, Operations Analysis, Technology Design, Equipment Selection, Testing, Product Inspection, Troubleshooting, Visioning, Systems Perception, Identifying Downstream Consequences, Identification of Key Causes, Judgment and Decision Making, Systems Evaluation, Management of Material Resources

College Majors

Metallurgical Engineering: An instructional program that prepares individuals to apply mathematical and metallurgical principles to the design, development and operational evaluation of metal components of structural, load-bearing, power, transmission, and moving systems; and the analysis of engineering problems such as stress, creep, failure, alloy behavior, environmental fluctuations, stability, electromagnetic and thermodynamic characteristics, optimal manufacturing processes, and related design considerations.

Supporting Courses

Engineering and Technology: Knowledge of equipment, tools, mechanical devices, and their uses to produce motion, light, power, technology, and other applications. **Design:** Knowledge of design techniques, principles, tools and instruments involved in the production and use of precision technical plans, blueprints, drawings, and models. **Building and Construction:** Knowledge of materials, methods, and the appropriate tools to construct objects, structures, and buildings. **Mathematics:** Knowledge of numbers, their operations, and interrelationships including arithmetic, algebra, geometry, calculus, statistics, and their applications. **Physics:** Knowledge and prediction of physical principles, laws, and applications including air, water, material dynamics, light, atomic principles, heat, electric theory, earth formations, and meteorological and related natural phenomena.

Materials Engineers

Evaluate materials and develop machinery and processes to manufacture materials for use in products that must meet specialized design and performance specifications. Develop new uses for known materials. Include those working with composite materials or specializing in one type of material, such as graphite, metal and metal alloys, ceramics and glass, plastics and polymers, and naturally occurring materials. Include metallurgists and metallurgical engineers, ceramic engineers, and welding engineers. Reviews new product plans and makes recommendations for material selection based on design objectives and cost. Plans and implements laboratory operations to develop material and fabrication procedures that maintain cost and performance standards. Evaluates technical and economic factors relating to process or product design objectives. Reviews product failure data and interprets laboratory test results to determine material or process causes. Confers with producers of material during investigation and evaluation of material for product applications.

Occupational Type

Investigative occupations frequently involve working with ideas, and require an extensive amount of thinking. These occupations can involve searching for facts and figuring out problems mentally.

Skills required of Materials Engineers

Reading Comprehension, Active Listening, Writing, Speaking, Mathematics, Science, Critical Thinking, Active Learning, Coordination, Problem Identification, Information Gathering, Information Organization, Synthesis/Reorganization, Idea Generation, Idea Evaluation, Implementation Planning, Operations Analysis, Technology Design, Equipment Selection, Product Inspection, Troubleshooting, Visioning, Systems Perception, Identifying Downstream Consequences, Identification of Key Causes, Judgment and Decision Making, Systems Evaluation

College Majors

Materials Science: An instructional program that generally describes the application of mathematical and scientific principles to the analysis and evaluation of the characteristics and behavior of solids, including internal structure, chemical properties, transport and energy flow properties, thermodynamics of solids, stress and failure factors, chemical transformation states and processes, compound materials, and research on industrial applications of specific materials.

Supporting Courses

Economics and Accounting: Knowledge of economic and accounting principles and practices, the financial markets, banking, and the analysis and reporting of financial data. **Production and Processing:** Knowledge of inputs, outputs, raw materials, waste, quality control, costs, and techniques for maximizing the manufacture and distribution of goods. **Engineering and Technology:** Knowledge of equipment, tools, mechanical devices, and their uses to produce motion, light, power, technology, and other applications. **Design:** Knowledge of design techniques, principles, tools and instruments involved in the production and use of precision technical plans, blueprints, drawings, and models. **Mathematics:** Knowledge of numbers, their operations, and interrelationships including arithmetic, algebra, geometry, calculus, statistics, and their applications. **Physics:** Knowledge and prediction of physical principles, laws, and applications including air, water, material dynamics, light, atomic principles, heat, electric theory, earth formations, and meteorological and related natural phenomena. **Chemistry:** Knowledge of the composition, structure, and properties of substances and of the chemical processes and transformations that they undergo. This includes uses of chemicals and their interactions, danger signs, production techniques, and disposal methods. **English Language:** Knowledge of the structure and content of the English language including the meaning and spelling of words, rules of composition, and grammar.

MATHEMATICIANS

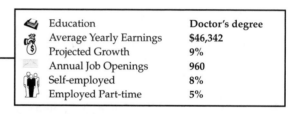

Education		Doctor's degree
Average Yearly Earnings		$46,342
Projected Growth		9%
Annual Job Openings		960
Self-employed		8%
Employed Part-time		5%

Mathematicians

Conduct research in fundamental mathematics or in application of mathematical techniques to science, management, and other fields. Solve or direct solutions to problems in various fields by mathematical methods. Conducts research in fundamental mathematics and in application of mathematical techniques to science, management, and other fields. Conceives or directs ideas for application of mathematics to wide variety of fields, including science, engineering, military planning, electronic data processing, and management. Conducts research in such branches of mathematics as algebra, geometry, number theory, logic, and topology. Performs computations and applies methods of numerical analysis. Studies and tests hypotheses and alternative theories. Applies mathematics or mathematical methods of numerical analysis, and operates or directs operation of desk calculators and mechanical and other functional areas. Utilizes knowledge of such subjects or fields as physics, engineering, astronomy, biology, economics, business and industrial management, or cryptography. Operates or directs operation of desk calculators and mechanical and electronic computation machines, analyzers, and plotters in problem solving support of mathematical, scientific, or industrial research. Acts as advisor or consultant to research personnel concerning mathematical methods and applications.

Occupational Type

Investigative occupations frequently involve working with ideas, and require an extensive amount of thinking. These occupations can involve searching for facts and figuring out problems mentally.

Skills required of Mathematicians

Mathematics, Critical Thinking, Active Learning, Learning Strategies, Information Gathering, Information Organization, Synthesis/Reorganization, Idea Generation, Programming

College Majors

Mathematics: An instructional program that describes the rigorous analysis of quantities, magnitudes, forms, and their relationships, using symbolic logic and language. Includes instruction in algebra, calculus, functional analysis, geometry, number theory, logic, topology, and other mathematical specializations.

Supporting Courses

Administration and Management: Knowledge of principles and processes involved in business and organizational planning, coordination, and execution. This includes strategic planning, resource allocation, manpower modeling, leadership techniques, and production methods. **Economics and Accounting:** Knowledge of economic and accounting principles and practices, the financial markets, banking, and the analysis and reporting of financial data. **Computers and Electronics:** Knowledge of electric circuit boards, processors, chips, and computer hardware and software, including applications and programming. **Engineering and Technology:** Knowledge of equipment, tools, mechanical devices, and their uses to produce motion, light, power, technology, and other applications. **Mathematics:** Knowledge of numbers, their operations, and interrelationships including arithmetic, algebra, geometry, calculus, statistics, and their applications. **Physics:** Knowledge and prediction of physical principles, laws, and applications including air, water, material dynamics, light, atomic principles, heat, electric theory, earth formations, and meteorological and related natural phenomena.

Weight Analysts

Analyze and calculate weight data of structural assemblies, components, and loads for purposes of weight, balance, loading, and operational functions of ships, aircraft, space vehicles, missiles, research instrumentation, and commercial and industrial products and systems. Studies weight factors involved in new designs or modifications, utilizing computer techniques for analysis and simulation. Analyzes data and prepares reports of weight distribution estimates for use in design studies. Weighs parts, assemblies, or completed products; estimates weight of parts from engineering drawings; and calculates weight distribution to determine balance. Confers with design engineering personnel to ensure coordination of weight, balance, and load specification with other phases of product development. May analyze various systems, structures, and support equipment designs to obtain information on most efficient compromise between weight, operations, and cost. May prepare cargo and equipment loading sequences to maintain balance of aircraft or space vehicle within specified load limits. Prepares reports or graphic data for designers when weight and balance require engineering changes. Prepares technical reports on inertia, static and dynamic balance, dead weight distribution, cargo and fuselage compartments, and fuel center of gravity travel. May conduct research and analysis to develop new techniques for weight-estimating criteria.

 Occupational Type

Investigative occupations frequently involve working with ideas, and require an extensive amount of thinking. These occupations can involve searching for facts and figuring out problems mentally.

 Skills required of Weight Analysts

Mathematics, Science, Information Gathering, Operations Analysis

 College Majors

Applied Mathematics, General: An instructional program that describes the application of mathematical principles to the solution of functional area problems, using the knowledge base of the subject or field for which the analytical procedures are being developed. Includes instruction in computer-assisted mathematical analysis and the development of tailored algorithms for solving specific research problems.

 Supporting Courses

Production and Processing: Knowledge of inputs, outputs, raw materials, waste, quality control, costs, and techniques for maximizing the manufacture and distribution of goods. **Computers and Electronics:** Knowledge of electric circuit boards, processors, chips, and computer hardware and software, including applications and programming. **Engineering and Technology:** Knowledge of equipment, tools, mechanical devices, and their uses to produce motion, light, power, technology, and other applications. **Design:** Knowledge of design techniques, principles, tools and instruments involved in the production and use of precision technical plans, blueprints, drawings, and models. **Mathematics:** Knowledge of numbers, their operations, and interrelationships including arithmetic, algebra, geometry, calculus, statistics, and their applications. **Physics:** Knowledge and prediction of physical principles, laws, and applications including air, water, material dynamics, light, atomic principles, heat, electric theory, earth formations, and meteorological and related natural phenomena. **Transportation:** Knowledge of principles and methods for moving people or goods by air, rail, sea, or road, including their relative costs, advantages, and limitations.

All Other Mathematical Scientists

All other mathematical scientists not classified separately above.

 Occupational Type

Specific information is not available.

 Skills required of All Other Mathematical Scientists

Information on specific skills required is not available.

 College Majors

Mathematics: An instructional program that describes the rigorous analysis of quantities, magnitudes, forms, and their relationships, using symbolic logic and language. Includes instruction in algebra, calculus, functional analysis, geometry, number theory, logic, topology, and other mathematical specializations.

 Supporting Courses

Specific information is not available.

MECHANICAL ENGINEERS

Mechanical Engineers

Education	Bachelor's degree
Average Yearly Earnings	$48,901
Projected Growth	16%
Annual Job Openings	14,290
Self-employed	1%
Employed Part-time	2%

Perform engineering duties in planning and designing tools, engines, machines, and other mechanically functioning equipment. Oversee installation, operation, maintenance, and repair of such equipment as centralized heat, gas, water, and steam systems. Designs products and systems to meet process requirements, applying knowledge of engineering principles. Oversees installation to ensure machines and equipment are installed and functioning according to specifications. Coordinates building, fabrication, and installation of product design and operation, maintenance, and repair activities to utilize machines and equipment. Specifies system components or directs modification of products to ensure conformance with engineering design and performance specifications. Inspects, evaluates, and arranges field installations, and recommends design modifications to eliminate machine or system malfunctions. Alters or modifies design to obtain specified functional and operational performance. Investigates equipment failures and difficulties, diagnoses faulty operation, and makes recommendations to maintenance crew. Examines gas-powered equipment after installation to ensure proper functioning, and solves problems concerned with equipment. Studies industrial processes to determine where and how application of gas fuel consuming equipment can be made. Researches and analyzes data, such as customer design proposal, specifications, and manuals, to determine feasibility of design or application. Plans and directs engineering personnel in fabrication of test control apparatus and equipment, and develops procedures for testing products. Confers with establishment personnel and engineers to implement operating procedures and resolve system malfunctions, and to provide technical information. Develops models of alternate processing methods to test feasibility or new applications of system components, and recommends implementation of procedures. Tests ability of machines, such as robot, to perform tasks, using teach pendant and precision measuring instruments and following specifications. Selects or designs robot tools to meet specifications, using robot manuals and either drafting tools or computer and software programs. Assists drafter in developing structural design of product, using drafting tools or computer-assisted design/drafting equipment and software. Conducts experiments to test and analyze existing designs and equipment to obtain data on performance of product, and prepares reports. Determines parts supply, maintenance tasks, safety procedures, and service schedules required to maintain machines and equipment in prescribed condition. Writes operating programs, using existing computer program, or writes own computer programs, applying knowledge of programming language and computer. Participates in meetings, seminars, and training sessions to stay apprised of new developments in field.

Occupational Type

Realistic occupations frequently involve work activities that include practical, hands-on problems and solutions. They often deal with plants, animals, and real-world materials like wood, tools, and machinery. Many of the occupations require working outside, and do not involve a lot of paperwork or working closely with others.

Skills required of Mechanical Engineers

Reading Comprehension, Mathematics, Science, Critical Thinking, Active Learning, Monitoring, Problem Identification, Information Gathering, Information Organization, Synthesis/Reorganization, Idea Generation, Idea Evaluation, Operations Analysis, Technology Design, Equipment Selection, Programming, Testing, Product Inspection, Troubleshooting, Visioning, Systems Perception, Judgment and Decision Making, Management of Material Resources

College Majors

Mechanical Engineering: An instructional program that prepares individuals to apply mathematical and scientific principles to the design, development and operational evaluation of physical systems used in manufacturing and end-product systems used for specific uses, including machine tools, jigs and other manufacturing equipment; stationary power units and appliances; engines; self-propelled vehicles; housings and containers; hydraulic and electric systems for controlling movement; and the integration of computers and remote control with operating systems.

Supporting Courses

Production and Processing: Knowledge of inputs, outputs, raw materials, waste, quality control, costs, and techniques for maximizing the manufacture and distribution of goods. **Computers and Electronics:** Knowledge of electric circuit boards, processors, chips, and computer hardware and software, including applications and programming. **Engineering and Technology:** Knowledge of equipment, tools, mechanical devices, and their uses to produce motion, light, power, technology, and other applications. **Design:** Knowledge of design techniques, principles, tools and instruments involved in the production and use of precision technical plans, blueprints, drawings, and models. **Building and Construction:** Knowledge of materials, methods, and the appropriate tools to construct objects, structures, and buildings. **Mechanical:** Knowledge of machines and tools, including their designs, uses, benefits, repair, and maintenance. **Mathematics:** Knowledge of numbers, their operations, and interrelationships including arithmetic, algebra, geometry, calculus, statistics, and their applications. **Physics:** Knowledge and prediction of physical principles, laws, and applications including air, water, material dynamics, light, atomic principles, heat, electric theory, earth formations, and meteorological and related natural phenomena.

MEDICAL RECORDS TECHNICIANS

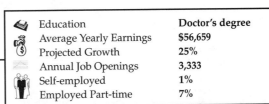

Education		Associate degree
Average Yearly Earnings		$20,488
Projected Growth		51%
Annual Job Openings		13,258
Self-employed		0%
Employed Part-time		23%

MEDICAL SCIENTISTS

Education		Doctor's degree
Average Yearly Earnings		$56,659
Projected Growth		25%
Annual Job Openings		3,333
Self-employed		1%
Employed Part-time		7%

Medical Scientists

Conduct research dealing with the understanding of human diseases and the improvement of human health. Engage in clinical investigation or other research, production, technical writing, or related activities. Include medical scientists such as physicians, dentists, public health specialists, pharmacologists, and medical pathologists. (Excludes practitioners who provide medical care or dispense drugs.) Plans and directs studies to investigate human or animal disease, preventive methods, and treatments for disease. Analyzes data, applying statistical techniques and scientific knowledge, prepares reports, and presents findings. Investigates cause, progress, life cycle, or mode of transmission of diseases or parasites. Studies effects of drugs, gases, pesticides, parasites, or microorganisms, or health and physiological processes of animals and humans. Conducts research to develop methodologies, instrumentation, or identification, diagnosing, and treatment procedures for medical application. Plans methodological design of research study and arranges for data collection. Examines organs, tissues, cell structures, or microorganisms by systematic observation or using microscope. Consults with and advises physicians, educators, researchers, and others regarding medical applications of sciences, such as physics, biology, and chemistry. Prepares and analyzes samples for toxicity, bacteria, or microorganisms or to study cell structure and properties. Confers with health department, industry personnel, physicians, and others to develop health safety standards and programs to improve public health. Standardizes drug dosages, methods of immunization, and procedures for manufacture of drugs and medicinal compounds. Teaches principles of medicine and medical and laboratory procedures to physicians, residents, students, and technicians. Supervises activities of clerical and statistical or laboratory personnel.

Occupational Type

Investigative occupations frequently involve working with ideas, and require an extensive amount of thinking. These occupations can involve searching for facts and figuring out problems mentally.

Skills required of Medical Scientists

Reading Comprehension, Active Listening, Writing, Speaking, Mathematics, Science, Critical Thinking, Active Learning, Learning Strategies, Monitoring, Social Perceptiveness, Coordination, Persuasion, Negotiation, Instructing, Service Orientation, Problem Identification, Information Gathering, Information Organization, Synthesis/Reorganization, Idea Generation, Idea Evaluation, Implementation Planning, Operations Analysis, Equipment Selection, Programming, Testing, Visioning, Systems Perception, Identifying Downstream Consequences, Identification of Key Causes, Judgment and Decision Making, Systems Evaluation, Time Management, Management of Financial Resources, Management of Material Resources, Management of Personnel Resources

College Majors

Biochemistry: An instructional program that describes the chemical processes of living organisms. Includes instruction in the chemical mechanisms of genetic information storage and transmission; the chemistry of cell components; blood chemistry; the chemistry of biological systems and biological products; and the chemistry of life processes such as respiration, digestion, and reproduction.

Supporting Courses

Food Production: Knowledge of techniques and equipment for planting, growing, and harvesting of food for consumption including crop rotation methods, animal husbandry, and food storage/handling techniques. **Mathematics:** Knowledge of numbers, their operations, and interrelationships including arithmetic, algebra, geometry, calculus, statistics, and their applications. **Physics:** Knowledge and prediction of physical principles, laws, and applications including air, water, material dynamics, light, atomic principles, heat, electric theory, earth formations, and meteorological and related natural phenomena. **Chemistry:** Knowledge of the composition, structure, and properties of substances and of the chemical processes and transformations that they undergo. This includes uses of chemicals and their interactions, danger signs, production techniques, and disposal methods. **Biology:** Knowledge of plant and animal living tissue, cells, organisms, and entities, including their functions, interdependencies, and interactions with each other and the environment. **Psychology:** Knowledge of human behavior and performance, mental processes, psychological research methods, and the assessment and treatment of behavioral and affective disorders. **Medicine and Dentistry:** Knowledge of the information and techniques needed to diagnose and treat injuries, diseases, and deformities. This includes symptoms, treatment alternatives, drug properties and interactions, and preventive healthcare measures. **Therapy and Counseling:** Knowledge of information and techniques needed to rehabilitate physical and mental ailments and to provide career guidance including alternative treatments, rehabilitation equipment and its proper use, and methods to evaluate treatment effects. **Education and Training:** Knowledge of instructional methods and training techniques including curriculum design principles, learning theory, group and individual teaching techniques, design of individual development plans, and test design principles. **Foreign Language:** Knowledge of the structure and content of a foreign (non-English) language including the meaning and spelling of words, rules of composition and grammar, and pronunciation. **History and Archeology:** Knowledge of past historical events and their causes, indicators, and impact on particular civilizations and cultures. **Public Safety and Security:** Knowledge of weaponry, public safety, and security operations, rules, regulations, precautions, prevention, and the protection of people, data, and property. **Law, Government, and Jurisprudence:** Knowledge of laws, legal codes, court procedures, precedents, government regulations, executive orders, agency rules, and the democratic political process. **Telecommunications:** Knowledge of transmission, broadcasting, switching, control, and operation of telecommunications systems. **Communications and Media:** Knowledge of media production, communication, and dissemination techniques and methods including alternative ways to inform and entertain via written, oral, and visual media. **Transportation:** Knowledge of principles and methods for moving people or goods by air, rail, sea, or road, including their relative costs, advantages, and limitations.

MINING ENGINEERS

Mining Engineers, Including Mine Safety

Education		Bachelor's degree
Average Yearly Earnings		$49,837
Projected Growth		-13%
Annual Job Openings		130
Self-employed		0%
Employed Part-time		3%

Determine the location and plan the extraction of coal, metallic ores, nonmetallic minerals, and building materials, such as stone and gravel. Work involves conducting preliminary surveys of deposits or undeveloped mines and planning their development; examining deposits or mines to determine whether they can be worked at a profit; making geological and topographical surveys; evolving methods of mining best suited to character, type, and size of deposits; and supervising mining operations. Lays out and directs mine construction operations. Plans and coordinates mining processes and labor utilization. Plans, conducts, or directs others in performing mining experiments to test or prove research findings. Evaluates data to develop new mining products, equipment, or processes. Devises methods to solve environmental problems and reclaim mine sites. Analyzes labor requirements, equipment needs, and operational costs to prepare budget. Plans and supervises construction of access roads, power supplies, and water, communication, ventilation, and drainage systems. Directs and coordinates manufacturing or building of prototype mining product or system. Inspects mining areas for unsafe equipment and working conditions, tests air, and recommends installation or alteration of air-circulation equipment. Prepares technical reports for use by mining, engineering, and management personnel. Prepares or directs preparation of product or system layout and detailed drawings and schematics. Determines conditions under which tests are to be conducted and sequences and phases of test operations. Designs and maintains protective and rescue equipment and safety devices. Instructs mine personnel in safe working practices, first aid, and compliance with mining laws and practices, and promotes safety. Leads rescue activities, investigates accidents, reports causes, and recommends remedial actions. Confers with others to clarify or resolve problems. Designs and directs other personnel in fabrication of testing and test-control apparatus and equipment. Directs and coordinates activities concerned with development, procurement, installation, and calibration of test and recording instruments, equipment, and control devices.

Occupational Type

Investigative occupations frequently involve working with ideas, and require an extensive amount of thinking. These occupations can involve searching for facts and figuring out problems mentally.

Skills required of Mining Engineers, Including Mine Safety

Reading Comprehension, Active Listening, Writing, Speaking, Mathematics, Science, Critical Thinking, Active Learning, Learning Strategies, Monitoring, Coordination, Persuasion, Negotiation, Instructing, Problem Identification, Information Gathering, Information Organization, Synthesis/Reorganization, Idea Generation, Idea Evaluation, Implementation Planning, Operations Analysis, Technology Design, Equipment Selection, Installation, Programming, Testing, Product Inspection, Troubleshooting, Visioning, Systems Perception, Identifying Downstream Consequences, Identification of Key Causes, Judgment and Decision Making, Systems Evaluation, Time Management, Management of Financial Resources, Management of Material Resources, Management of Personnel Resources

College Majors

Mining and Mineral Engineering: An instructional program that prepares individuals to apply mathematical and scientific principles to the design, development and operational evaluation of mineral extraction, processing and refining systems, including open pit and shaft mines, prospecting and site analysis equipment and instruments, environmental and safety systems, mine equipment and facilities, mineral processing and refining methods and systems, and logistics and communications systems.

Supporting Courses

Administration and Management: Knowledge of principles and processes involved in business and organizational planning, coordination, and execution. This includes strategic planning, resource allocation, manpower modeling, leadership techniques, and production methods. **Economics and Accounting:** Knowledge of economic and accounting principles and practices, the financial markets, banking, and the analysis and reporting of financial data. **Personnel and Human Resources:** Knowledge of policies and practices involved in personnel/human resource functions. This includes recruitment, selection, training, and promotion regulations and procedures; compensation and benefits packages; labor relations and negotiation strategies; and personnel information systems. **Production and Processing:** Knowledge of inputs, outputs, raw materials, waste, quality control, costs, and techniques for maximizing the manufacture and distribution of goods. **Engineering and Technology:** Knowledge of equipment, tools, mechanical devices, and their uses to produce motion, light, power, technology, and other applications. **Design:** Knowledge of design techniques, principles, tools and instruments involved in the production and use of precision technical plans, blueprints, drawings, and models. **Building and Construction:** Knowledge of materials, methods, and the appropriate tools to construct objects, structures, and buildings. **Mechanical:** Knowledge of machines and tools, including their designs, uses, benefits, repair, and maintenance. **Mathematics:** Knowledge of numbers, their operations, and interrelationships including arithmetic, algebra, geometry, calculus, statistics, and their applications. **Physics:** Knowledge and prediction of physical principles, laws, and applications including air, water, material dynamics, light, atomic principles, heat, electric theory, earth formations, and meteorological and related natural phenomena. **Chemistry:** Knowledge of the composition, structure, and properties of substances and of the chemical processes and transformations that they undergo. This includes uses of chemicals and their interactions, danger signs, production techniques, and disposal methods. **Geography:** Knowledge of various methods for describing the location and distribution of land, sea, and air masses including their physical locations, relationships, and characteristics. **Education and Training:** Knowledge of instructional methods and training techniques including curriculum design principles, learning theory, group and individual teaching techniques, design of individual development plans, and test design principles. **English Language:** Knowledge of the structure and content of the English language including the meaning and spelling of words, rules of composition, and grammar. **Public Safety and Security:** Knowledge of weaponry, public safety, and security operations, rules, regulations, precautions, prevention, and the protection of people, data, and property. **Law, Government, and Jurisprudence:** Knowledge of laws, legal codes, court procedures, precedents, government regulations, executive orders, agency rules, and the democratic political process. **Transportation:** Knowledge of principles and methods for moving people or goods by air, rail, sea, or road, including their relative costs, advantages, and limitations.

NUCLEAR ENGINEERS

Nuclear Engineers

	Education	Bachelor's degree
	Average Yearly Earnings	$57,741
	Projected Growth	5%
	Annual Job Openings	714
	Self-employed	0%
	Employed Part-time	3%

Conduct research on nuclear engineering problems or apply principles and theory of nuclear science to problems concerned with release, control, and utilization of nuclear energy. Determines potential hazard and accident conditions that may exist in fuel handling and storage and recommends preventive measures. Performs experiments to determine acceptable methods of nuclear material usage, nuclear fuel reclamation, and waste disposal. Formulates equations that describe phenomena occurring during fission of nuclear fuels, and develops analytical models for research. Analyzes available data and consults with other scientists to determine parameters of experimentation and suitability of analytical models. Plans and designs nuclear research to discover facts or to test, prove, or modify known nuclear theories. Conducts tests to research nuclear fuel behavior and nuclear machinery and equipment performance. Examines accidents and obtains data to formulate preventive measures. Evaluates research findings to develop new concepts of thermonuclear analysis and new uses of radioactive models. Synthesizes analyses of tests results and prepares technical reports of findings and recommendations. Inspects nuclear fuels, waste, equipment, test-reactor vessel and related systems, and control instrumentation to identify potential problems or hazards. Monitors nuclear operations to identify potential or inherent design, construction, or operational problems to ensure safe operations. Designs and develops nuclear machinery and equipment, such as reactor cores, radiation shielding, and associated instrumentation and control mechanisms. Designs and oversees construction and operation of nuclear fuels reprocessing systems and reclamation systems. Computes cost estimates of construction projects, prepares project proposals, and discusses projects with vendors, contractors, and nuclear facility's review board. Formulates and initiates corrective actions and orders plant shutdown in emergency situations. Maintains reports to summarize work and document plant operations. Writes operational instructions relative to nuclear plant operation and nuclear fuel and waste handling and disposal. Directs operating and maintenance activities of operational nuclear facility.

Occupational Type

Investigative occupations frequently involve working with ideas, and require an extensive amount of thinking. These occupations can involve searching for facts and figuring out problems mentally.

Skills required of Nuclear Engineers

Reading Comprehension, Active Listening, Writing, Speaking, Mathematics, Science, Critical Thinking, Active Learning, Learning Strategies, Monitoring, Coordination, Persuasion, Instructing, Problem Identification, Information Gathering, Information Organization, Synthesis/Reorganization, Idea Generation, Idea Evaluation, Implementation Planning, Operations Analysis, Technology Design, Equipment Selection, Installation, Programming, Testing, Operation Monitoring, Operation and Control, Product Inspection, Equipment Maintenance, Troubleshooting, Repairing, Visioning, Systems Perception, Identifying Downstream Consequences, Identification of Key Causes, Judgment and Decision Making, Systems Evaluation, Time Management, Management of Financial Resources, Management of Material Resources, Management of Personnel Resources

College Majors

Civil Engineering, General: An instructional program that generally prepares individuals to apply mathematical and scientific principles to the design, development and operational evaluation of structural, loadbearing, material moving, transportation, water resource, and material control systems; and related equipment and environmental safety measures.

Supporting Courses

Administration and Management: Knowledge of principles and processes involved in business and organizational planning, coordination, and execution. This includes strategic

planning, resource allocation, manpower modeling, leadership techniques, and production methods. **Economics and Accounting:** Knowledge of economic and accounting principles and practices, the financial markets, banking, and the analysis and reporting of financial data. **Computers and Electronics:** Knowledge of electric circuit boards, processors, chips, and computer hardware and software, including applications and programming. **Engineering and Technology:** Knowledge of equipment, tools, mechanical devices, and their uses to produce motion, light, power, technology, and other applications. **Design:** Knowledge of design techniques, principles, tools and instruments involved in the production and use of precision technical plans, blueprints, drawings, and models. **Building and Construction:** Knowledge of materials, methods, and the appropriate tools to construct objects, structures, and buildings. **Mathematics:** Knowledge of numbers, their operations, and interrelationships including arithmetic, algebra, geometry, calculus, statistics, and their applications. **Physics:** Knowledge and prediction of physical principles, laws, and applications including air, water, material dynamics, light, atomic principles, heat, electric theory, earth formations, and meteorological and related natural phenomena. **Chemistry:** Knowledge of the composition, structure, and properties of substances and of the chemical processes and transformations that they undergo. This includes uses of chemicals and their interactions, danger signs, production techniques, and disposal methods. **Education and Training:** Knowledge of instructional methods and training techniques including curriculum design principles, learning theory, group and individual teaching techniques, design of individual development plans, and test design principles. **English Language:** Knowledge of the structure and content of the English language including the meaning and spelling of words, rules of composition, and grammar. **Public Safety and Security:** Knowledge of weaponry, public safety, and security operations, rules, regulations, precautions, prevention, and the protection of people, data, and property.

Nuclear medicine technologists

	Education	**Associate degree**
	Average Yearly Earnings	$38,605
	Projected Growth	13%
	Annual Job Openings	865
	Self-employed	0%
	Employed Part-time	18%

Occupational therapists

Occupational Therapists

	Education	**Bachelor's degree**
	Average Yearly Earnings	$46,779
	Projected Growth	66%
	Annual Job Openings	9,543
	Self-employed	4%
	Employed Part-time	21%

Plan, organize, and participate in medically oriented occupational programs in hospital or similar institution to rehabilitate patients who are physically or mentally ill. Plans, organizes, and conducts occupational therapy program in hospital,

institutional, or community setting. Plans programs and social activities to help patients learn work skills and adjust to handicaps. Selects activities that will help individual learn work skills within limits of individual's mental and physical capabilities. Teaches individual skills and techniques required for participation in activities, and evaluates individual's progress. Recommends changes in individual's work or living environment, consistent with needs and capabilities. Consults with rehabilitation team to select activity programs and coordinate occupational therapy with other therapeutic activities. Arranges salaried employment for mentally ill patients within hospital environment. Lays out materials for individual's use, and cleans and repairs tools after therapy sessions. Requisitions supplies and equipment, and designs and constructs special equipment, such as splints and braces. Trains nurses and other medical staff in therapy techniques and objectives. Processes payroll, distributes salaries, and completes and maintains necessary records.

Occupational Type

Social occupations frequently involve working with, communicating with, and teaching people. These occupations often involve helping or providing service to others.

Skills required of Occupational Therapists

Active Listening, Speaking, Learning Strategies, Social Perceptiveness, Coordination, Instructing, Service Orientation, Idea Generation, Implementation Planning, Technology Design, Equipment Selection, Time Management, Management of Material Resources

College Majors

Occupational Therapy: An instructional program that prepares individuals to employ self-care, work and play activities as therapeutic regimes for patients in order to increase independent functioning, enhance development and assist recovery from disability. Includes instruction in adapting therapeutic tasks or environments to achieve maximum independence and enhance the quality of life for each patient.

Supporting Courses

Administration and Management: Knowledge of principles and processes involved in business and organizational planning, coordination, and execution. This includes strategic planning, resource allocation, manpower modeling, leadership techniques, and production methods. **Clerical:** Knowledge of administrative and clerical procedures and systems such as word processing systems, filing and records management systems, stenography and transcription, forms design principles, and other office procedures and terminology. **Economics and Accounting:** Knowledge of economic and accounting principles and practices, the financial markets, banking, and the analysis and reporting of financial data. **Customer and Personal Service:** Knowledge of principles and processes for providing customer and personal services including needs assessment techniques, quality service standards, alternative delivery systems, and customer satisfaction evaluation techniques. **Personnel and Human Resources:** Knowledge of policies and practices involved in personnel/

human resource functions. This includes recruitment, selection, training, and promotion regulations and procedures; compensation and benefits packages; labor relations and negotiation strategies; and personnel information systems. **Biology:** Knowledge of plant and animal living tissue, cells, organisms, and entities, including their functions, interdependencies, and interactions with each other and the environment. **Psychology:** Knowledge of human behavior and performance, mental processes, psychological research methods, and the assessment and treatment of behavioral and affective disorders. **Sociology and Anthropology:** Knowledge of group behavior and dynamics, societal trends and influences, cultures, their history, migrations, ethnicity, and origins. **Medicine and Dentistry:** Knowledge of the information and techniques needed to diagnose and treat injuries, diseases, and deformities. This includes symptoms, treatment alternatives, drug properties and interactions, and preventive healthcare measures. **Therapy and Counseling:** Knowledge of information and techniques needed to rehabilitate physical and mental ailments and to provide career guidance including alternative treatments, rehabilitation equipment and its proper use, and methods to evaluate treatment effects. **Education and Training:** Knowledge of instructional methods and training techniques including curriculum design principles, learning theory, group and individual teaching techniques, design of individual development plans, and test design principles. **Foreign Language:** Knowledge of the structure and content of a foreign (non-English) language including the meaning and spelling of words, rules of composition and grammar, and pronunciation.

Manual Arts Therapists

Instruct patients in prescribed manual arts activities, such as woodworking, photography, or graphic arts, to prevent anatomical and physiological deconditioning and to assist in maintaining, improving, or developing work skills. Teaches patient manual arts activities, such as woodworking, graphic arts, or photography. Observes and interacts with patient to evaluate progress of patient in meeting physical and mental demands of employment. Confers with other rehabilitation team members to develop treatment plan to prevent physical deconditioning and enhance work skills of patient. Plans and organizes work activities according to patients' capabilities and disabilities. Prepares reports showing development of patient's work tolerance and emotional and social adjustment.

 Occupational Type

Social occupations frequently involve working with, communicating with, and teaching people. These occupations often involve helping or providing service to others.

 Skills required of Manual Arts Therapists

Social Perceptiveness, Instructing, Service Orientation

⚓ College Majors

Occupational Therapy: An instructional program that prepares individuals to employ self-care, work and play activities as therapeutic regimes for patients in order to increase

---

independent functioning, enhance development and assist recovery from disability. Includes instruction in adapting therapeutic tasks or environments to achieve maximum independence and enhance the quality of life for each patient.

 Supporting Courses

Customer and Personal Service: Knowledge of principles and processes for providing customer and personal services including needs assessment techniques, quality service standards, alternative delivery systems, and customer satisfaction evaluation techniques. **Psychology:** Knowledge of human behavior and performance, mental processes, psychological research methods, and the assessment and treatment of behavioral and affective disorders. **Therapy and Counseling:** Knowledge of information and techniques needed to rehabilitate physical and mental ailments and to provide career guidance including alternative treatments, rehabilitation equipment and its proper use, and methods to evaluate treatment effects. **Education and Training:** Knowledge of instructional methods and training techniques including curriculum design principles, learning theory, group and individual teaching techniques, design of individual development plans, and test design principles. **Fine Arts:** Knowledge of theory and techniques required to produce, compose, and perform works of music, dance, visual arts, drama, and sculpture.

OPERATIONS RESEARCH ANALYSTS

Operations and Systems Researchers and Analysts, Except Computer

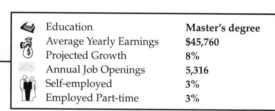

Education	Master's degree
Average Yearly Earnings	$45,760
Projected Growth	8%
Annual Job Openings	5,316
Self-employed	3%
Employed Part-time	3%

Conduct analyses of management and operational problems in terms of management information and concepts. Formulate mathematical or simulation models of the problem for solution by computer or other method. May develop and supply time and cost networks, such as program evaluation and review techniques. Analyzes problem in terms of management information, and conceptualizes and defines problem. Prepares model of problem in form of one or several equations that relate constants and variables, restrictions, alternatives, conflicting objectives, and their numerical parameters. Specifies manipulative or computational methods to be applied to model. Performs validation and testing of model to ensure adequacy, or determines need for reformulation. Evaluates implementation and effectiveness of research. Designs, conducts, and evaluates experimental operational models where insufficient data exists to formulate model. Develops and applies time and cost networks to plan and control large projects. Defines data requirements and gathers and validates information, applying judgment and statistical tests. Studies information and selects plan from competitive proposals that afford maximum probability of profit or effectiveness relating to cost or risk. Prepares for management reports defining problem, evaluation, and possible solution.

Occupational Type

Investigative occupations frequently involve working with ideas, and require an extensive amount of thinking. These occupations can involve searching for facts and figuring out problems mentally.

Skills required of Operations and Systems Researchers and Analysts, Except Computer

Reading Comprehension, Active Listening, Writing, Speaking, Mathematics, Science, Critical Thinking, Active Learning, Learning Strategies, Monitoring, Coordination, Persuasion, Problem Identification, Information Gathering, Information Organization, Synthesis/Reorganization, Idea Generation, Idea Evaluation, Implementation Planning, Operations Analysis, Programming, Visioning, Systems Perception, Identifying Downstream Consequences, Identification of Key Causes, Judgment and Decision Making, Systems Evaluation, Time Management, Management of Financial Resources

College Majors

Applied Mathematics, General: An instructional program that describes the application of mathematical principles to the solution of functional area problems, using the knowledge base of the subject or field for which the analytical procedures are being developed. Includes instruction in computer-assisted mathematical analysis and the development of tailored algorithms for solving specific research problems.

Supporting Courses

Administration and Management: Knowledge of principles and processes involved in business and organizational planning, coordination, and execution. This includes strategic planning, resource allocation, manpower modeling, leadership techniques, and production methods. **Clerical:** Knowledge of administrative and clerical procedures and systems such as word processing systems, filing and records management systems, stenography and transcription, forms design principles, and other office procedures and terminology. **Economics and Accounting:** Knowledge of economic and accounting principles and practices, the financial markets, banking, and the analysis and reporting of financial data. **Sales and Marketing:** Knowledge of principles and methods involved in showing, promoting, and selling products or services. This includes marketing strategies and tactics, product demonstration and sales techniques, and sales control systems. **Personnel and Human Resources:** Knowledge of policies and practices involved in personnel/human resource functions. This includes recruitment, selection, training, and promotion regulations and procedures; compensation and benefits packages; labor relations and negotiation strategies; and personnel information systems. **Production and Processing:** Knowledge of inputs, outputs, raw materials, waste, quality control, costs, and techniques for maximizing the manufacture and distribution of goods. **Computers and Electronics:** Knowledge of electric circuit boards, processors, chips, and computer hardware and software, including applications and programming. **Mathematics:** Knowledge of numbers, their operations, and interrelationships including arithmetic, algebra, geometry, calculus, statistics, and their applications. **Communications and Media:** Knowledge of media production, communication, and dissemination techniques and methods including alternative ways to inform and entertain via written, oral, and visual media.

OPTOMETRISTS

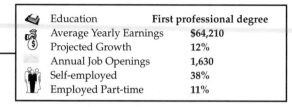

	Education	First professional degree
	Average Yearly Earnings	$64,210
	Projected Growth	12%
	Annual Job Openings	1,630
	Self-employed	38%
	Employed Part-time	11%

Optometrists

Diagnose, manage, and treat conditions and diseases of the human eye and visual system. Examine eyes to determine visual efficiency and performance by use of instruments and observation. Prescribe corrective procedures. Prescribes eyeglasses, contact lenses, and other vision aids or therapeutic procedures to correct or conserve vision. Examines eyes to determine visual acuity and perception and to diagnose diseases and other abnormalities, such as glaucoma and color blindness. Consults with and refers patients to ophthalmologist or other healthcare practitioner if additional medical treatment is determined necessary. Prescribes medications to treat eye diseases if state laws permit. Conducts research, instructs in college or university, acts as consultant, or works in public health field.

Occupational Type

Investigative occupations frequently involve working with ideas, and require an extensive amount of thinking. These occupations can involve searching for facts and figuring out problems mentally.

Skills required of Optometrists

Reading Comprehension, Active Listening, Writing, Speaking, Mathematics, Science, Learning Strategies, Monitoring, Social Perceptiveness, Instructing, Synthesis/Reorganization, Idea Evaluation, Technology Design

College Majors

Optometry (O.D.): An instructional program that prepares individuals for the independent professional practice of optometry and that describes the principles and techniques for examining, diagnosing and treating conditions of the visual system. Includes instruction in prescribing glasses and contact lenses, other optical aids, corrective therapies, patient counseling, physician referral, practice management, and ethics and professional standards.

Supporting Courses

Chemistry: Knowledge of the composition, structure, and properties of substances and of the chemical processes and transformations that they undergo. This includes uses of chemicals and their interactions, danger signs, production techniques, and disposal methods. **Biology:** Knowledge of plant and animal living tissue, cells, organisms, and entities, including their functions, interdependencies, and interactions with each other and the environment. **Medicine and Dentistry:** Knowledge of the information and techniques needed to diagnose and treat injuries, diseases, and deformities. This includes symptoms, treatment alternatives, drug properties and interactions, and preventive healthcare measures. **Therapy and Counseling:** Knowledge of information and techniques needed to rehabilitate physical and mental ailments and to provide career guidance including alternative treatments, rehabilitation equipment and its proper use, and methods to evaluate treatment effects. **Education and Training:** Knowledge of instructional methods and training techniques including curriculum design principles, learning theory, group and individual teaching techniques, design of individual development plans, and test design principles. **Foreign Language:** Knowledge of the structure and content of a foreign (non-English) language including the meaning and spelling of words, rules of composition and grammar, and pronunciation.

PARALEGALS

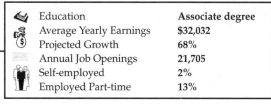

	Education	**Associate degree**
	Average Yearly Earnings	$32,032
	Projected Growth	68%
	Annual Job Openings	21,705
	Self-employed	2%
	Employed Part-time	13%

PERSONNEL, TRAINING, AND LABOR RELATIONS MANAGERS

Human Resources Managers

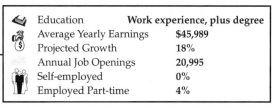

	Education	**Work experience, plus degree**
	Average Yearly Earnings	$45,989
	Projected Growth	18%
	Annual Job Openings	20,995
	Self-employed	0%
	Employed Part-time	4%

Plan, direct, and coordinate human resource management activities of an organization to maximize the strategic use of human resources, and maintain functions such as employee compensation, recruitment, personnel policies, and regulatory compliance. Formulates policies and procedures for recruitment, testing, placement, classification, orientation, benefits, and labor and industrial relations. Plans, directs, supervises, and coordinates work activities of subordinates and staff relating to employment, compensation, labor relations, and employee relations. Directs preparation and distribution of written and verbal information to inform employees of benefits, compensation, and personnel policies. Evaluates and modifies benefits policies to establish competitive programs and to ensure compliance with legal requirements. Analyzes compensation policies, government regulations, and prevailing wage rates to develop competitive compensation plan. Develops methods to improve employment policies, processes, and practices, and recommends changes to management. Prepares personnel forecast to project employment needs. Prepares budget for personnel operations. Prepares and delivers presentations and reports to corporate officers or other management regarding human resource management policies and practices and recommendations for change. Negotiates bargaining agreements and resolves labor disputes. Meets with shop stewards and supervisors to resolve grievances. Conducts exit interviews to identify reasons for employee termination and writes separation notices. Plans and conducts new employee orientation to foster positive attitude toward organizational objectives. Writes directives advising department managers of organization policy in personnel matters such as equal employment opportunity, sexual harassment, and discrimination. Studies legislation, arbitration decisions, and collective bargaining contracts to assess industry trends. Maintains records and compiles statistical reports concerning personnel-related data such as hires, transfers, performance appraisals, and absenteeism rates. Analyzes statistical data and reports to identify and determine causes of personnel problems and develop recommendations for improvement of organization's personnel policies and practices. Represents organization at personnel-related hearings and investigations. Contracts with vendors to provide employee services, such as canteen, transportation, or relocation service. Investigates industrial accidents and prepares reports for insurance carrier.

Occupational Type

Enterprising occupations frequently involve starting up and carrying out projects. These occupations can involve leading people and making many decisions. Sometimes they involve risk taking and often deal with business.

Skills required of Human Resources Managers

Active Listening, Writing, Speaking, Critical Thinking, Active Learning, Learning Strategies, Monitoring, Social Perceptiveness, Coordination, Persuasion, Negotiation, Instructing, Problem Identification, Information Gathering, Synthesis/Reorganization, Idea Generation, Idea Evaluation, Implementation Planning, Programming, Visioning, Systems Perception, Identifying Downstream Consequences, Identification of Key Causes, Judgment and Decision Making, Systems Evaluation, Time Management, Management of Financial Resources, Management of Material Resources, Management of Personnel Resources

College Majors

Human Resources Management: An instructional program that prepares individuals to manage the development of human capital in organizations, and to provide related services to individuals and groups. Includes instruction in personnel and organization policy, human resource dynamics and flows, labor relations, sex roles, civil rights, human resources law and regulations, motivation and compensation systems, work systems, career management, employee testing and assessment, recruitment and selection, managing employee and job training programs, and the management of human resources programs and operations.

Supporting Courses

Administration and Management: Knowledge of principles and processes involved in business and organizational planning, coordination, and execution. This includes strategic planning, resource allocation, manpower modeling, leadership techniques, and production methods. **Economics and Accounting:** Knowledge of economic and accounting principles and practices, the financial markets, banking, and the analysis and reporting of financial data. **Personnel and Human Resources:** Knowledge of policies and practices involved in personnel/human resource functions. This includes recruitment, selection, training, and promotion regulations and procedures; compensation and benefits packages; labor relations and negotiation strategies; and personnel information systems. **Mathematics:** Knowledge of numbers, their operations, and interrelationships including arithmetic, algebra, geometry, calculus, statistics, and their applications. **Psychology:** Knowledge of human behavior and performance, mental processes, psychological research methods, and the assessment and treatment of behavioral and affective disorders. **Education and Training:** Knowledge of instructional methods and training techniques including curriculum design principles, learning theory, group and individual teaching techniques, design of individual development plans, and test design principles. **English Language:** Knowledge of the structure and content of the English language including the meaning and spelling of words, rules of composition, and grammar. **Law, Government, and Jurisprudence:** Knowledge of laws, legal codes, court procedures, precedents, government regulations, executive orders, agency rules, and the democratic political process.

Training and Development Managers

Plan, direct, and coordinate the training activities of an organization. Analyzes training needs to develop new training programs or to modify and improve existing programs. Plans and develops training procedures utilizing knowledge of relative effectiveness of individual training, classroom training, demonstrations, on-the-job training, meetings, conferences, and workshops. Formulates training policies and schedules, utilizing knowledge of identified training needs. Evaluates effectiveness of training programs and instructor performance. Develops and organizes training manuals, multimedia visual aids, and other educational materials. Coordinates established courses with technical and professional courses provided by community schools, and designates training procedures. Develops testing and evaluation procedures. Confers with management and supervisory personnel to identify training needs based on projected production processes, changes, and other factors. Reviews and evaluates training and apprenticeship programs for compliance with government standards. Prepares training budget for department or organization. Trains instructors and supervisors in effective training techniques. Interprets and clarifies regulatory policies governing apprenticeship training programs, and provides information and assistance to trainees and labor and management representatives.

Occupational Type

Enterprising occupations frequently involve starting up and carrying out projects. These occupations can involve leading people and making many decisions. Sometimes they involve risk taking and often deal with business.

Skills required of Training and Development Managers

Speaking, Critical Thinking, Learning Strategies, Instructing, Problem Identification, Information Gathering, Idea Generation, Idea Evaluation, Implementation Planning, Operations Analysis, Visioning, Identifying Downstream Consequences, Identification of Key Causes, Systems Evaluation, Time Management, Management of Financial Resources, Management of Personnel Resources

College Majors

Public Administration: An instructional program that prepares individuals to serve as managers in the executive arm of local, state, and Federal government; and that describes the systematic study of executive organization and management. Includes instruction in the roles, development, and principles of public administration; the management of public policy; executive-legislative relations; public budgetary processes and financial management; administrative law; public personnel management; professional ethics; and research methods.

Supporting Courses

Administration and Management: Knowledge of principles and processes involved in business and organizational planning, coordination, and execution. This includes strategic planning, resource allocation, manpower modeling, leadership techniques, and production methods. **Personnel and Human Resources:** Knowledge of policies and practices involved in personnel/human resource functions. This includes recruitment, selection, training, and promotion regulations and procedures; compensation and benefits packages; labor relations and negotiation strategies; and personnel information systems. **Psychology:** Knowledge of human behavior and performance, mental processes, psychological research methods, and the assessment and treatment of behavioral and affective disorders. **Education and Training:** Knowledge of instructional methods and training techniques including curriculum design principles, learning theory, group and individual teaching techniques, design of individual development plans, and test design principles. **Law, Government, and Jurisprudence:** Knowledge of laws, legal codes, court procedures, precedents, government regulations, executive orders, agency rules, and the democratic political process.

Labor Relations Managers

Plan, direct, and coordinate the labor relations program of an organization. Analyze and interpret collective bargaining agreements and advise management and union officials in development, application, and interpretation of labor relations policies and practices. Represents management in labor contract negotiations to reconcile opposing claims and recommend concessions, or proposes adoption of new procedures. Analyzes collective bargaining agreements to interpret intent, spirit, and terms of contract. Compiles information on disagreement and determines points of issue, according to knowledge of labor, business, and government responsibilities under law. Advises management and union officials on development, application, and interpretation of company labor relations policies and practices. Arranges and schedules meetings between parties in labor dispute to investigate and resolve grievances. Monitors implementation of policies concerning wages, hours, and working conditions to ensure compliance to labor contract terms. Supervises work activities of employees involved in labor relations functions of organization. Completes statistical reports on cases, findings, and resolved issues.

Occupational Type

Enterprising occupations frequently involve starting up and carrying out projects. These occupations can involve leading people and making many decisions. Sometimes they involve risk taking and often deal with business.

Skills required of Labor Relations Managers

Active Listening, Persuasion, Negotiation, Programming, Visioning, Identifying Downstream Consequences, Time Management, Management of Personnel Resources

College Majors

Human Resources Management: An instructional program that prepares individuals to manage the development of human capital in organizations, and to provide related services to individuals and groups. Includes instruction in personnel and organization policy, human resource dynamics and flows, labor relations, sex roles, civil rights, human resources law and regulations, motivation and compensation systems, work systems, career management, employee testing and assessment, recruitment and selection, managing employee and job training programs, and the management of human resources programs and operations.

Supporting Courses

Administration and Management: Knowledge of principles and processes involved in business and organizational planning, coordination, and execution. This includes strategic planning, resource allocation, manpower modeling, leadership techniques, and production methods. **Personnel and Human Resources:** Knowledge of policies and practices involved in personnel/human resource functions. This includes recruitment, selection, training, and promotion regulations and procedures; compensation and benefits packages; labor relations and negotiation strategies; and personnel information systems. **Mathematics:** Knowledge of numbers, their operations, and interrelationships including arithmetic, algebra, geometry, calculus, statistics, and their applications. **English Language:** Knowledge of the structure and content of the English language including the meaning and spelling of words, rules of composition, and grammar. **Law, Government, and Jurisprudence:** Knowledge of laws, legal codes, court procedures, precedents, government regulations, executive orders, agency rules, and the democratic political process.

PERSONNEL, TRAINING, AND LABOR RELATIONS SPECIALISTS

Employee Assistance Specialists

Education	Bachelor's degree
Average Yearly Earnings	$36,566
Projected Growth	18%
Annual Job Openings	36,049
Self-employed	4%
Employed Part-time	7%

Coordinate activities of employers to set up and operate programs to help employees overcome behavioral or medical problems, such as substance abuse, that affect job performance. Develops or leads group to develop employee assistance programs, policies, and procedures. Plans and conducts training sessions for company officials to develop skills to identify and assist with resolving employee behavioral problems. Consults with employer to establish referral network for group or individual counseling of troubled employees. Consults with staff of employee assistance program to monitor progress of program. Consults with employer representatives to develop education and prevention program. Analyzes character and type of business establishments, and compiles list of prospective employers to implement assistance programs. Contacts prospective employers to explain program advantages and fees, and negotiates participation agreement with interested employers. Writes announcements and advertisements for newspapers and other publications to promote employee assistance program within business community.

Occupational Type

Social occupations frequently involve working with, communicating with, and teaching people. These occupations often involve helping or providing service to others.

Skills required of Employee Assistance Specialists

Reading Comprehension, Active Listening, Speaking, Critical Thinking, Active Learning, Learning Strategies, Monitoring, Social Perceptiveness, Coordination, Persuasion, Negotiation, Instructing, Service Orientation, Problem Identification, Information Gathering, Idea Generation, Idea Evaluation, Implementation Planning, Systems Evaluation, Management of Personnel Resources

College Majors

Alcohol/Drug Abuse Counseling: An instructional program that prepares individuals to counsel drug users, addicts, family members, and associates in a wide variety of settings, using various preventive strategies and treatment regimes. Includes instruction in outreach; patient education; therapeutic intervention methods; diagnostic procedures; addiction symptomology; recordkeeping; liaison with community health, social services, law enforcement, and legal services; and applicable regulations.

Supporting Courses

Administration and Management: Knowledge of principles and processes involved in business and organizational planning, coordination, and execution. This includes strategic planning, resource allocation, manpower modeling, leadership techniques, and production methods. **Sales and Marketing:** Knowledge of principles and methods involved in showing, promoting, and selling products or services. This includes marketing strategies and tactics, product demonstration and sales techniques, and sales control systems. **Customer and Personal Service:** Knowledge of principles and processes for providing customer and personal services including needs assessment techniques, quality service standards, alternative delivery systems, and customer satisfaction evaluation techniques. **Personnel and Human Resources:** Knowledge of policies and practices involved in personnel/human resource functions. This includes recruitment, selection, training, and promotion regulations and procedures; compensation and benefits packages; labor relations and negotiation strategies; and personnel information systems. **Psychology:** Knowledge of human behavior and performance, mental processes, psychological research methods, and the assessment and treatment of behavioral and affective disorders. **Sociology and Anthropology:** Knowledge of group behavior and dynamics, societal trends and influences, cultures, their history, migrations, ethnicity, and origins. **Therapy and Counseling:** Knowledge of information and techniques needed to rehabilitate physical and mental ailments and to provide career guidance including alternative treatments, rehabilitation equipment and its proper use, and methods to evaluate treatment effects. **Education and Training:** Knowledge of instructional methods and training techniques including curriculum design principles, learning theory, group and individual teaching techniques, design of individual development plans, and test design principles.

Job and Occupational Analysts

Collect, analyze, and classify occupational data to develop job or occupational descriptions or profiles to facilitate personnel management decision making and to develop career information. Analyzes organizational, occupational, and industrial data to facilitate organizational functions and provide technical information to business, industry, and government. Researches job and worker requirements, structural and functional relationships among jobs and occupations, and occupational trends. Observes and interviews employees to collect job, organizational, and occupational information. Prepares reports, such as job descriptions, organization and flow charts, and career path reports, to summarize job analysis information. Consults with business, industry, government, and union officials to arrange for, plan, and design occupational studies and surveys. Prepares research results for publication in form of journals, books, manuals, and film. Determines need for and develops job analysis instruments and materials. Evaluates and improves methods and techniques for selecting, promoting, evaluating, and training workers. Plans and develops curricula and materials for training programs and conducts training.

Occupational Type

Investigative occupations frequently involve working with ideas, and require an extensive amount of thinking. These occupations can involve searching for facts and figuring out problems mentally.

Skills required of Job and Occupational Analysts

Reading Comprehension, Active Listening, Writing, Speaking, Critical Thinking, Active Learning, Learning Strategies, Monitoring, Social Perceptiveness, Coordination, Persuasion, Negotiation, Instructing, Service Orientation, Information Gathering, Information Organization, Synthesis/Reorganization, Idea Generation, Idea Evaluation, Implementation Planning, Operations Analysis, Programming, Visioning, Systems Perception, Identifying Downstream Consequences, Identification of Key Causes, Systems Evaluation, Management of Personnel Resources

College Majors

Human Resources Management: An instructional program that prepares individuals to manage the development of human capital in organizations, and to provide related services to individuals and groups. Includes instruction in personnel and organization policy, human resource dynamics and flows, labor relations, sex roles, civil rights, human resources law and regulations, motivation and compensation systems, work systems, career management, employee testing and assessment, recruitment and selection, managing employee and job training programs, and the management of human resources programs and operations.

Supporting Courses

Administration and Management: Knowledge of principles and processes involved in business and organizational planning, coordination, and execution. This includes strategic planning, resource allocation, manpower modeling, leadership techniques, and production methods. **Clerical:** Knowledge of administrative and clerical procedures and systems such as word processing systems, filing and records management systems, stenography and transcription, forms design principles, and other office procedures and terminology. **Personnel and Human Resources:** Knowledge of policies and practices involved in personnel/human resource functions. This includes recruitment, selection, training, and promotion regulations and procedures; compensation and benefits packages; labor relations and negotiation strategies; and personnel information systems. **Food Production:** Knowledge of techniques and equipment for planting, growing, and harvesting of food for consumption including crop rotation methods, animal husbandry, and food storage/handling techniques. **Computers and Electronics:** Knowledge of electric circuit boards, processors, chips, and computer hardware and software, including applications and programming. **Mathematics:** Knowledge of numbers, their operations, and interrelationships including arithmetic, algebra, geometry, calculus, statistics, and their applications. **Psychology:** Knowledge of human behavior and performance, mental processes, psychological research methods, and the assessment and treatment of behavioral and affective disorders. **Education and Training:** Knowledge of instructional methods and training techniques including curriculum design principles, learning theory, group and individual teaching techniques, design of individual development plans, and test design principles. **English Language:** Knowledge of the structure and content of the English language including the meaning and spelling of words, rules of composition, and grammar. **History and Archeology:** Knowledge of past historical events and their causes, indicators, and impact on particular civilizations and cultures. **Philosophy and Theology:** Knowledge of different philosophical systems and religions, including their basic principles, values, ethics, ways of thinking, customs, and practices, and their impact on human culture. **Communications and Media:** Knowledge of media production, communication, and dissemination techniques and methods including alternative ways to inform and entertain via written, oral, and visual media.

Employer Relations and Placement Specialists

Develop relationships with employers to facilitate placement of job applicants or students in employment opportunities. Establishes and maintains relationships with employers to determine personnel needs, promote use of service, and monitor progress of placed individuals. Confers with employers to resolve problems relating to employment service effectiveness, employer compliance, and employer recruitment activities. Arranges job interviews for applicants. Receives and records information from employers regarding employment opportunities. Directs and coordinates job placement programs and job analysis services. Conducts surveys of local labor market, and assists employers in revising organizational policies such as job standards and compensation. Promotes, develops, and terminates on-the-job and auxiliary training programs and assists in writing contracts. Instructs applicants in resume writing, job search, and interviewing skills, and conducts in-service training for personnel of placement service. Interviews applicants to determine interests, qualifications, and employment eligibility, and assists in developing employment and curriculum plans. Collects, organizes, and analyzes occupational, educational, and economic information for placement services and to maintain occupational library. Develops placement office procedures, establishes workloads, assigns tasks, and reviews activity reports.

Occupational Type

Social occupations frequently involve working with, communicating with, and teaching people. These occupations often involve helping or providing service to others.

Skills required of Employer Relations and Placement Specialists

Active Listening, Writing, Speaking, Critical Thinking, Active Learning, Learning Strategies, Monitoring, Social Perceptiveness, Coordination, Persuasion, Negotiation, Instructing, Service Orientation, Problem Identification, Information Gathering, Information Organization, Synthesis/Reorganization, Idea Generation, Idea Evaluation, Implementation Planning, Operations Analysis, Programming, Visioning, Systems Perception, Identifying Downstream Consequences, Identification of Key Causes, Judgment and Decision Making, Systems Evaluation, Time Management, Management of Financial Resources, Management of Personnel Resources

College Majors

Human Resources Management: An instructional program that prepares individuals to manage the development of human capital in organizations, and to provide related services to individuals and groups. Includes instruction in personnel and organization policy, human resource dynamics and flows, labor relations, sex roles, civil rights, human resources law and regulations, motivation and compensation systems, work systems, career management, employee testing and assessment, recruitment and selection, managing employee and job training programs, and the management of human resources programs and operations.

 Supporting Courses

Administration and Management: Knowledge of principles and processes involved in business and organizational planning, coordination, and execution. This includes strategic planning, resource allocation, manpower modeling, leadership techniques, and production methods. **Clerical:** Knowledge of administrative and clerical procedures and systems such as word processing systems, filing and records management systems, stenography and transcription, forms design principles, and other office procedures and terminology. **Sales and Marketing:** Knowledge of principles and methods involved in showing, promoting, and selling products or services. This includes marketing strategies and tactics, product demonstration and sales techniques, and sales control systems. **Customer and Personal Service:** Knowledge of principles and processes for providing customer and personal services including needs assessment techniques, quality service standards, alternative delivery systems, and customer satisfaction evaluation techniques. **Personnel and Human Resources:** Knowledge of policies and practices involved in personnel/human resource functions. This includes recruitment, selection, training, and promotion regulations and procedures; compensation and benefits packages; labor relations and negotiation strategies; and personnel information systems. **Computers and Electronics:** Knowledge of electric circuit boards, processors, chips, and computer hardware and software, including applications and programming. **Psychology:** Knowledge of human behavior and performance, mental processes, psychological research methods, and the assessment and treatment of behavioral and affective disorders. **Sociology and Anthropology:** Knowledge of group behavior and dynamics, societal trends and influences, cultures, their history, migrations, ethnicity, and origins. **Geography:** Knowledge of various methods for describing the location and distribution of land, sea, and air masses including their physical locations, relationships, and characteristics. **Therapy and Counseling:** Knowledge of information and techniques needed to rehabilitate physical and mental ailments and to provide career guidance including alternative treatments, rehabilitation equipment and its proper use, and methods to evaluate treatment effects. **Education and Training:** Knowledge of instructional methods and training techniques including curriculum design principles, learning theory, group and individual teaching techniques, design of individual development plans, and test design principles.

Employee Relations Specialists

Perform a variety of duties to promote employee welfare, such as resolving human relations problems and promoting employee health and well-being. Interviews workers and discusses with personnel human relations, and work-related problems that adversely affect morale, health, and productivity. Evaluates and resolves human relations, labor relations, and work-related problems, and meets with management to determine appropriate action. Explains and provides advice to workers about company and governmental rules, regulations, and procedures, and need for compliance. Counsels employees regarding work, family, or personal problems. Explains company compensation and benefit programs, such as medical, insurance, retirement, and savings plans, and enrolls workers in specified programs. Arranges for employee library, lunchroom, recreational facilities, and activities. Develops, schedules, and conducts technical, management, and interpersonal skills training to improve employee performance. Prepares newsletter and other reports to communicate information about employee concerns and comments and organizational actions taken. Attends conferences and meetings, as employee-management liaison, to facilitate communication between parties. Prepares reports and enters and updates medical, insurance, retirement, and other personnel forms and records, using computer. Audits benefit accounts and examines records to ensure compliance with standards and regulations. Arranges for employee physical examinations, first aid, and other medical attention. Inspects facilities to determine if lighting, sanitation, and security are adequate and to ensure compliance to standards. Supervises clerical or administrative personnel.

Occupational Type

Social occupations frequently involve working with, communicating with, and teaching people. These occupations often involve helping or providing service to others.

Skills required of Employee Relations Specialists

Reading Comprehension, Active Listening, Writing, Speaking, Critical Thinking, Active Learning, Learning Strategies, Monitoring, Social Perceptiveness, Coordination, Persuasion, Negotiation, Instructing, Service Orientation, Problem Identification, Information Organization, Idea Generation, Idea Evaluation, Implementation Planning, Operations Analysis, Programming, Visioning, Systems Perception, Identifying Downstream Consequences, Identification of Key Causes, Systems Evaluation, Time Management, Management of Financial Resources, Management of Material Resources, Management of Personnel Resources

College Majors

Human Resources Management: An instructional program that prepares individuals to manage the development of human capital in organizations, and to provide related services to individuals and groups. Includes instruction in personnel and organization policy, human resource dynamics and flows, labor relations, sex roles, civil rights, human resources law and regulations, motivation and compensation systems, work systems, career management, employee testing and assessment, recruitment and selection, managing employee and job training programs, and the management of human resources programs and operations.

Supporting Courses

Administration and Management: Knowledge of principles and processes involved in business and organizational planning, coordination, and execution. This includes strategic

planning, resource allocation, manpower modeling, leadership techniques, and production methods. **Clerical:** Knowledge of administrative and clerical procedures and systems such as word processing systems, filing and records management systems, stenography and transcription, forms design principles, and other office procedures and terminology. **Economics and Accounting:** Knowledge of economic and accounting principles and practices, the financial markets, banking, and the analysis and reporting of financial data. **Customer and Personal Service:** Knowledge of principles and processes for providing customer and personal services including needs assessment techniques, quality service standards, alternative delivery systems, and customer satisfaction evaluation techniques. **Personnel and Human Resources:** Knowledge of policies and practices involved in personnel/ human resource functions. This includes recruitment, selection, training, and promotion regulations and procedures; compensation and benefits packages; labor relations and negotiation strategies; and personnel information systems. **Computers and Electronics:** Knowledge of electric circuit boards, processors, chips, and computer hardware and software, including applications and programming. **Psychology:** Knowledge of human behavior and performance, mental processes, psychological research methods, and the assessment and treatment of behavioral and affective disorders. **Sociology and Anthropology:** Knowledge of group behavior and dynamics, societal trends and influences, cultures, their history, migrations, ethnicity, and origins. **Therapy and Counseling:** Knowledge of information and techniques needed to rehabilitate physical and mental ailments and to provide career guidance including alternative treatments, rehabilitation equipment and its proper use, and methods to evaluate treatment effects. **Education and Training:** Knowledge of instructional methods and training techniques including curriculum design principles, learning theory, group and individual teaching techniques, design of individual development plans, and test design principles. **Law, Government, and Jurisprudence:** Knowledge of laws, legal codes, court procedures, precedents, government regulations, executive orders, agency rules, and the democratic political process. **Communications and Media:** Knowledge of media production, communication, and dissemination techniques and methods including alternative ways to inform and entertain via written, oral, and visual media.

Employee Training Specialists

Coordinate and conduct employee training programs to train new and existing employees how to perform required work, improve work methods, or comply with policies, procedures, or regulations. Develops and conducts orientation and training for employees or customers of industrial or commercial establishment. Confers with managers, instructors, or customer representatives of industrial or commercial establishment to determine training needs. Evaluates training materials, such as outlines, text, and handouts, prepared by instructors. Assigns instructors to conduct training and assists them in obtaining required training materials. Schedules classes based on availability of classrooms, equipment, and instructors. Coordinates recruitment and placement of participants in skill training. Organizes and develops training procedure manuals and guides. Attends meetings and seminars to obtain information useful to train staff and to inform management of training programs and goals. Maintains records and writes reports to monitor and evaluate training activities and program effectiveness. Supervises instructors, monitors and evaluates instructor performance, and refers instructors to classes for skill development. Monitors training costs to ensure budget is not exceeded, and prepares budget report to justify expenditures. Refers trainees with social problems to appropriate service agency. Screens, hires, and assigns workers to positions based on qualifications.

Occupational Type

Social occupations frequently involve working with, communicating with, and teaching people. These occupations often involve helping or providing service to others.

Skills required of Employee Training Specialists

Active Listening, Writing, Speaking, Active Learning, Learning Strategies, Monitoring, Social Perceptiveness, Coordination, Persuasion, Negotiation, Instructing, Service Orientation, Problem Identification, Information Gathering, Information Organization, Idea Generation, Idea Evaluation, Implementation Planning, Operations Analysis, Programming, Visioning, Systems Perception, Identifying Downstream Consequences, Identification of Key Causes, Judgment and Decision Making, Systems Evaluation, Time Management, Management of Financial Resources, Management of Material Resources, Management of Personnel Resources

College Majors

Education Administration and Supervision, General: An instructional program that generally describes the study of the principles and techniques of administering a wide variety of schools and other educational organizations and facilities, supervising educational personnel at the school or staff level, and that may prepare individuals as general administrators and supervisors.

Supporting Courses

Administration and Management: Knowledge of principles and processes involved in business and organizational planning, coordination, and execution. This includes strategic planning, resource allocation, manpower modeling, leadership techniques, and production methods. **Clerical:** Knowledge of administrative and clerical procedures and systems such as word processing systems, filing and records management systems, stenography and transcription, forms design principles, and other office procedures and terminology. **Economics and Accounting:** Knowledge of economic and accounting principles and practices, the financial markets, banking, and the analysis and reporting of financial data. **Sales and Marketing:** Knowledge of principles and methods involved in showing, promoting, and selling products or services. This includes marketing strategies and tactics, product demonstration and sales techniques, and sales control systems. **Customer and Personal Service:** Knowledge of principles and processes for providing customer and personal services including needs assessment techniques, quality service standards, alternative delivery systems, and customer satisfaction evaluation techniques. **Personnel and Human Resources:** Knowledge of policies and practices involved in personnel/human resource functions. This includes recruitment, selection, training, and promotion regulations and procedures; compensation and benefits packages; labor relations and negotiation strategies; and personnel information systems. **Psychology:** Knowledge of human behavior and performance, mental processes, psychological research methods, and the assessment and treatment of behavioral and affective disorders. **Sociology and Anthropology:** Knowledge of group behavior and dynamics, societal trends and influences, cultures, their history, migrations, ethnicity, and origins. **Therapy and Counseling:** Knowledge of information and techniques needed to rehabilitate physical and mental ailments and to provide career guidance including alternative treatments, rehabilitation equipment and its proper use, and methods to evaluate treatment effects. **Education and Training:** Knowledge of instructional methods and training techniques including curriculum design principles, learning theory, group and individual teaching techniques, design of individual development plans, and test design principles. **Foreign Language:** Knowledge of the structure and content of a foreign (non-English) language including the meaning and spelling of words, rules of composition and grammar, and pronunciation. **Communications and Media:** Knowledge of media production, communication, and dissemination techniques and methods including alternative ways to inform and entertain via written, oral, and visual media.

Personnel Recruiters

Seek out, interview, and screen applicants to fill existing and future job openings and promote career opportunities within organization. Interviews applicants to obtain work history, training, education, job skills, and other background information. Provides potential applicants with information regarding facilities, operations, benefits, and job or career opportunities in organization. Conducts reference and background checks on applicants. Contacts college representatives to arrange for and schedule on-campus interviews with students. Reviews and evaluates applicant qualifications or eligibility for specified licensing, according to established guidelines and designated licensing codes. Notifies applicants by mail or telephone to inform them of employment possibilities, consideration, and selection. Hires or refers applicants to other hiring personnel in organization. Arranges for interviews and travel and lodging for selected applicants at company expense. Evaluates recruitment and selection criteria to ensure conformance to professional, statistical, and testing standards, and recommends revision as needed. Assists and advises establishment management in organizing, preparing, and implementing recruiting and retention programs. Speaks to civic, social, and other groups to provide information concerning job possibilities and career opportunities. Prepares and maintains employment records and authorizes paperwork assigning applicant to positions. Corrects and scores portions of examinations used to screen and select applicants. Projects yearly recruitment expenditures for budgetary consideration and control.

 Occupational Type

Enterprising occupations frequently involve starting up and carrying out projects. These occupations can involve leading people and making many decisions. Sometimes they involve risk taking and often deal with business.

Skills required of Personnel Recruiters

Active Listening, Writing, Speaking, Learning Strategies, Monitoring, Social Perceptiveness, Persuasion, Negotiation, Instructing, Service Orientation, Information Organization, Idea Generation, Idea Evaluation, Implementation Planning, Visioning, Identifying Downstream Consequences, Judgment and Decision Making, Systems Evaluation, Management of Financial Resources, Management of Personnel Resources

 ## College Majors

Education, General: An instructional program that generally describes the theory and practice of learning and teaching; the basic principles of educational psychology; the art of teaching; the planning and administration of educational activities; and the social foundations of education.

 ## Supporting Courses

Administration and Management: Knowledge of principles and processes involved in business and organizational planning, coordination, and execution. This includes strategic planning, resource allocation, manpower modeling, leadership techniques, and production methods. **Clerical:** Knowledge of administrative and clerical procedures and systems such as word processing systems, filing and records management systems, stenography and transcription, forms design principles, and other office procedures and terminology. **Sales and Marketing:** Knowledge of principles and methods involved in showing, promoting, and selling products or services. This includes marketing strategies and tactics, product demonstration and sales techniques, and sales control systems. **Personnel and Human Resources:** Knowledge of policies and practices involved in personnel/human resource functions. This includes recruitment, selection, training, and promotion regulations and procedures; compensation and benefits packages; labor relations and negotiation strategies; and personnel information systems. **Computers and Electronics:** Knowledge of electric circuit boards, processors, chips, and computer hardware and software, including applications and programming. **Psychology:** Knowledge of human behavior and performance, mental processes, psychological research methods, and the assessment and treatment of behavioral and affective disorders. **Philosophy and Theology:** Knowledge of different philosophical systems and religions, including their basic principles, values, ethics, ways of thinking, customs, and practices, and their impact on human culture. **Law, Government, and Jurisprudence:** Knowledge of laws, legal codes, court procedures, precedents, government regulations, executive orders, agency rules, and the democratic political process.

Labor Relations Specialists

Mediate, arbitrate, and conciliate disputes over negotiations of labor agreements or labor relations disputes. Conducts arbitration hearings concerning disputes over negotiations of labor contracts and agreements between labor and management. Mediates and assists disagreeing parties to compromise or otherwise negotiate on agreement regarding dispute. Renders decision to settle dispute, protect public interests, prevent employee wage loss, and minimize business interruptions, and issues report concerning settlement. Interrogates parties and clarifies problems to focus discussion on crucial points of disagreement. Investigates labor disputes upon request of bona fide party, following labor laws, industry practices, and labor relations social policies. Analyzes information to evaluate contentions of parties regarding disputed contract provisions. Promotes use of fact-finding, mediation, conciliation, and advisory services to prevent or resolve labor disputes and maintain labor relations. Prepares and issues reports regarding results of arbitration, decisions reached, or outcomes of negotiations. Conducts representation elections and oversees balloting procedures according to written consent agreement of concerned parties in labor dispute.

Occupational Type

Enterprising occupations frequently involve starting up and carrying out projects. These occupations can involve leading people and making many decisions. Sometimes they involve risk taking and often deal with business.

Skills required of Labor Relations Specialists

Active Listening, Writing, Speaking, Critical Thinking, Active Learning, Learning Strategies, Monitoring, Social Perceptiveness, Coordination, Persuasion, Negotiation, Service Orientation, Problem Identification, Information Gathering, Information Organization, Synthesis/Reorganization, Idea Generation, Idea Evaluation, Implementation Planning, Visioning, Systems Perception, Identifying Downstream Consequences, Identification of Key Causes, Judgment and Decision Making, Systems Evaluation, Management of Financial Resources, Management of Personnel Resources

College Majors

Human Resources Management: An instructional program that prepares individuals to manage the development of human capital in organizations, and to provide related services to individuals and groups. Includes instruction in personnel and organization policy, human resource dynamics and flows, labor relations, sex roles, civil rights, human resources law and regulations, motivation and compensation systems, work systems, career management, employee testing and assessment, recruitment and selection, managing employee and job training programs, and the management of human resources programs and operations.

Supporting Courses

Administration and Management: Knowledge of principles and processes involved in business and organizational planning, coordination, and execution. This includes strategic planning, resource allocation, manpower modeling, leadership techniques, and production methods. **Customer and Personal Service:** Knowledge of principles and processes for providing customer and personal services including needs assessment techniques, quality service standards, alternative delivery systems, and customer satisfaction evaluation techniques. **Personnel and Human Resources:** Knowledge of policies and practices involved in personnel/human resource functions. This includes recruitment, selection, training, and promotion regulations and procedures; compensation and benefits packages; labor relations and negotiation strategies; and personnel information systems. **Psychology:** Knowledge of human behavior and performance, mental processes, psychological research methods, and the assessment and treatment of behavioral and affective disorders. **Law, Government, and Jurisprudence:** Knowledge of laws, legal codes, court procedures, precedents, government regulations, executive orders, agency rules, and the democratic political process.

PETROLEUM ENGINEERS

Education		Bachelor's degree
Average Yearly Earnings		$68,224
Projected Growth		-14%
Annual Job Openings		549
Self-employed		5%
Employed Part-time		3%

Petroleum Engineers

Devise methods to improve oil and gas well production and determine the need for new or modified tool designs. Oversee drilling and offer technical advice to achieve economical and satisfactory progress. Designs or modifies mining and oil field machinery and tools, applying engineering principles. Conducts engineering research experiments to improve or modify mining and oil machinery and operations. Develops plans for oil and gas field drilling, and for product recovery and treatment. Confers with scientific, engineering, and technical personnel to resolve design, research, and testing problems. Evaluates findings to develop, design, or test equipment or processes. Monitors production rates, and plans rework processes to improve production. Analyzes data to recommend placement of wells and supplementary processes to enhance production. Assists engineering and other personnel to solve operating problems. Coordinates activities of workers engaged in research, planning, and development. Inspects oil and gas wells to determine that installations are completed. Assigns work to staff to obtain maximum utilization of personnel. Interprets drilling and testing information for personnel. Tests machinery and equipment to ensure conformance to performance specifications and to ensure safety. Writes technical reports for engineering and management personnel.

 Occupational Type

Realistic occupations frequently involve work activities that include practical, hands-on problems and solutions. They often deal with plants, animals, and real-world materials like wood, tools, and machinery. Many of the occupations require working outside, and do not involve a lot of paperwork or working closely with others.

 Skills required of Petroleum Engineers

Reading Comprehension, Writing, Speaking, Mathematics, Science, Critical Thinking, Active Learning, Monitoring, Coordination, Instructing, Problem Identification, Information

Gathering, Information Organization, Synthesis/Reorganization, Idea Generation, Idea Evaluation, Implementation Planning, Operations Analysis, Technology Design, Equipment Selection, Installation, Programming, Testing, Operation Monitoring, Operation and Control, Product Inspection, Troubleshooting, Systems Perception, Identifying Downstream Consequences, Identification of Key Causes, Judgment and Decision Making, Systems Evaluation, Time Management, Management of Financial Resources, Management of Material Resources, Management of Personnel Resources

College Majors

Mining and Mineral Engineering: An instructional program that prepares individuals to apply mathematical and scientific principles to the design, development and operational evaluation of mineral extraction, processing and refining systems, including open pit and shaft mines, prospecting and site analysis equipment and instruments, environmental and safety systems, mine equipment and facilities, mineral processing and refining methods and systems, and logistics and communications systems.

Supporting Courses

Administration and Management: Knowledge of principles and processes involved in business and organizational planning, coordination, and execution. This includes strategic planning, resource allocation, manpower modeling, leadership techniques, and production methods. **Personnel and Human Resources:** Knowledge of policies and practices involved in personnel/human resource functions. This includes recruitment, selection, training, and promotion regulations and procedures; compensation and benefits packages; labor relations and negotiation strategies; and personnel information systems. **Production and Processing:** Knowledge of inputs, outputs, raw materials, waste, quality control, costs, and techniques for maximizing the manufacture and distribution of goods. **Engineering and Technology:** Knowledge of equipment, tools, mechanical devices, and their uses to produce motion, light, power, technology, and other applications. **Design:** Knowledge of design techniques, principles, tools and instruments involved in the production and use of precision technical plans, blueprints, drawings, and models. **Mechanical:** Knowledge of machines and tools, including their designs, uses, benefits, repair, and maintenance. **Mathematics:** Knowledge of numbers, their operations, and interrelationships including arithmetic, algebra, geometry, calculus, statistics, and their applications. **Physics:** Knowledge and prediction of physical principles, laws, and applications including air, water, material dynamics, light, atomic principles, heat, electric theory, earth formations, and meteorological and related natural phenomena. **English Language:** Knowledge of the structure and content of the English language including the meaning and spelling of words, rules of composition, and grammar.

PHARMACISTS

Education		Bachelor's degree
Average Yearly Earnings		$55,328
Projected Growth		13%
Annual Job Openings		13,827
Self-employed		4%
Employed Part-time		25%

Pharmacists

Compound and dispense medications following prescriptions issued by physicians, dentists, or other authorized medical practitioners. Compounds medications, using standard formulas and processes, such as weighing, measuring, and mixing ingredients. Compounds radioactive substances and reagents to prepare radiopharmaceuticals, following radiopharmacy laboratory procedures. Plans and implements procedures in pharmacy, such as mixing, packaging, and labeling pharmaceuticals according to policies and legal requirements. Reviews prescription to assure accuracy and determine ingredients needed and suitability of radiopharmaceutical prescriptions. Answers questions and provides information to pharmacy customers on drug interactions, side effects, dosage, and storage of pharmaceuticals. Assays prepared radiopharmaceutical, using instruments and equipment to verify rate of drug disintegration and to ensure patient receives required dose. Calculates volume of radioactive pharmaceutical required to provide patient with desired level of radioactivity at prescribed time. Consults medical staff to advise on drug applications and characteristics and to review and evaluate quality and effectiveness of radiopharmaceuticals. Maintains established procedures concerning quality assurance, security of controlled substances, and disposal of hazardous waste. Maintains records, such as pharmacy files, charge system, inventory, and control records for radioactive nuclei. Oversees preparation and dispensation of experimental drugs. Verifies that specified radioactive substance and reagent will give desired results in examination or treatment procedures. Analyzes records to indicate prescribing trends and excessive usage. Directs and coordinates, through subordinate supervisory personnel, activities and functions of pharmacy. Directs pharmacy personnel programs, such as hiring, training, and intern programs. Prepares pharmacy budget. Observes pharmacy personnel at work to develop quality assurance techniques to ensure safe, legal, and ethical practices. Participates in development of computer programs for pharmacy information-management systems, patient and department charge systems, and inventory control. Conducts research to develop or improve radiopharmaceuticals. Instructs students, interns, and other medical personnel on matters pertaining to pharmacy or concerning radiopharmacy use, characteristics, and compounding procedures.

Occupational Type

Investigative occupations frequently involve working with ideas, and require an extensive amount of thinking. These occupations can involve searching for facts and figuring out problems mentally.

Skills required of Pharmacists

Reading Comprehension, Active Listening, Writing, Speaking, Mathematics, Science, Critical Thinking, Active Learning, Learning Strategies, Monitoring, Instructing, Service Orientation, Problem Identification, Operations Analysis, Programming, Product Inspection, Visioning, Identifying Downstream Consequences, Identification of Key Causes, Judgment and Decision Making, Systems Evaluation, Time Management, Management of Financial Resources, Management of Material Resources, Management of Personnel Resources

College Majors

Pharmacy (B.Pharm., Pharm.D.): An instructional program that prepares individuals for the independent professional practice of pharmacy. Includes instruction in principles of medicinal chemistry, drug behavior, and drug metabolism; mixing, preparing, and dispensing prescription medications; pharmacy practice management; patient advising; ethical and professional standards; and applicable laws and regulations.

Supporting Courses

Administration and Management: Knowledge of principles and processes involved in business and organizational planning, coordination, and execution. This includes strategic planning, resource allocation, manpower modeling, leadership techniques, and production methods. **Clerical:** Knowledge of administrative and clerical procedures and systems such as word processing systems, filing and records management systems, stenography and transcription, forms design principles, and other office procedures and terminology. **Economics and Accounting:** Knowledge of economic and accounting principles and practices, the financial markets, banking, and the analysis and reporting of financial data. **Personnel and Human Resources:** Knowledge of policies and practices involved in personnel/human resource functions. This includes recruitment, selection, training, and promotion regulations and procedures; compensation and benefits packages; labor relations and negotiation strategies; and personnel information systems. **Computers and Electronics:** Knowledge of electric circuit boards, processors, chips, and computer hardware and software, including applications and programming. **Chemistry:** Knowledge of the composition, structure, and properties of substances and of the chemical processes and transformations that they undergo. This includes uses of chemicals and their interactions, danger signs, production techniques, and disposal methods. **Biology:** Knowledge of plant and animal living tissue, cells, organisms, and entities, including their functions, interdependencies, and interactions with each other and the environment. **Medicine and Dentistry:** Knowledge of the information and techniques needed to diagnose and treat injuries, diseases, and deformities. This includes symptoms, treatment alternatives, drug properties and interactions, and preventive healthcare measures. **Therapy and Counseling:** Knowledge of information and techniques needed to rehabilitate physical and mental ailments and to provide career guidance including alternative treatments, rehabilitation equipment and its proper use, and methods to evaluate treatment effects. **Education and Training:** Knowledge of instructional methods and training techniques including curriculum design principles, learning theory, group and individual teaching techniques, design of individual development plans, and test design principles. **English Language:** Knowledge of the structure and content of the English language including the meaning and spelling of words, rules of composition, and grammar. **Foreign Language:** Knowledge of the structure and content of a foreign (non-English) language including the meaning and spelling of words, rules of composition and grammar, and pronunciation. **Law, Government, and Jurisprudence:** Knowledge of laws, legal codes, court procedures, precedents, government regulations, executive orders, agency rules, and the democratic political process.

PHYSICAL SCIENTISTS

Education		Bachelor's degree
Average Yearly Earnings		$47,632
Projected Growth		28%
Annual Job Openings		4,131
Self-employed		7%
Employed Part-time		7%

Materials Scientists

Research and study the structures and chemical properties of various natural and manmade materials, including metals, alloys, rubber, ceramics, semiconductors, polymers, and glass. Determine ways to strengthen or combine materials, or develop new materials with new or specific properties for use in a variety of products and applications. Include glass scientists, ceramic scientists, metallurgical scientists, and polymer scientists. Plans laboratory experiments to confirm feasibility of processes and techniques to produce materials having special characteristics. Studies structures and properties of materials, such as metals, alloys, polymers, and ceramics, to obtain research data. Reports materials study findings for other scientists and requesters. Guides technical staff engaged in developing materials for specific use in projected product or device.

Occupational Type

Investigative occupations frequently involve working with ideas, and require an extensive amount of thinking. These occupations can involve searching for facts and figuring out problems mentally.

Skills required of Materials Scientists

Reading Comprehension, Writing, Mathematics, Science, Active Learning, Operations Analysis, Testing, Product Inspection

College Majors

Materials Science: An instructional program that generally describes the application of mathematical and scientific principles to the analysis and evaluation of the characteristics and behavior of solids, including internal structure, chemical properties, transport and energy flow properties, thermodynamics of solids, stress and failure factors, chemical transformation states and processes, compound materials, and research on industrial applications of specific materials.

Supporting Courses

Administration and Management: Knowledge of principles and processes involved in business and organizational planning, coordination, and execution. This includes strategic planning, resource allocation, manpower modeling, leadership techniques, and production methods. **Engineering and Technology:** Knowledge of equipment, tools, mechanical devices, and their uses to produce motion, light, power, technology, and other applications. **Mathematics:** Knowledge of numbers, their operations, and interrelationships including arithmetic, algebra, geometry, calculus, statistics, and their applications. **Physics:** Knowledge and prediction of physical principles, laws, and applications including air, water, material dynamics, light, atomic principles, heat, electric theory, earth formations, and meteorological and related natural phenomena. **Chemistry:** Knowledge of the composition, structure, and properties of substances and of the chemical processes and transformations that they undergo. This includes uses of chemicals and their interactions, danger signs, production techniques, and disposal methods. **English Language:** Knowledge of the structure and content of the English language including the meaning and spelling of words, rules of composition, and grammar. **Foreign Language:** Knowledge of the structure and content of a foreign (non-English) language including the meaning and spelling of words, rules of composition and grammar, and pronunciation. **Communications and Media:**

Knowledge of media production, communication, and dissemination techniques and methods including alternative ways to inform and entertain via written, oral, and visual media.

PHYSICAL THERAPISTS

	Education	Bachelor's degree
	Average Yearly Earnings	$52,811
	Projected Growth	71%
	Annual Job Openings	19,122
	Self-employed	6%
	Employed Part-time	21%

Physical Therapists

Apply techniques and treatments that help relieve pain, increase the patient's strength, and decrease or prevent deformity and crippling. Administers manual exercises to improve and maintain function. Administers treatment involving application of physical agents, using equipment, moist packs, ultraviolet and infrared lamps, and ultrasound machines. Administers massage, applying knowledge of massage techniques and body physiology. Administers traction to relieve pain, using traction equipment. Instructs, motivates, and assists patient to perform various physical activities and use supportive devices, such as crutches, canes, and prostheses. Evaluates effects of treatment at various stages and adjusts treatment to achieve maximum benefit. Tests and measures patient's strength, motor development, sensory perception, functional capacity, and respiratory and circulatory efficiency, and records data. Reviews physician's referral and patient's condition and medical records to determine physical therapy treatment required. Plans and prepares written treatment program based on evaluation of patient data. Instructs patient and family in treatment procedures to be continued at home. Evaluates, fits, and adjusts prosthetic and orthotic devices and recommends modification to orthotist. Confers with medical practitioners to obtain additional information, suggest revisions in treatment, and integrate physical therapy into patient's care. Records treatment, response, and progress in patient's chart, or enters information into computer. Plans, directs, and coordinates physical therapy program. Orients, instructs, and directs work activities of assistants, aides, and students. Plans and develops physical therapy research programs and participates in conducting research. Writes technical articles and reports for publications. Plans and conducts lectures and training programs on physical therapy and related topics for medical staff, students, and community groups.

Occupational Type

Social occupations frequently involve working with, communicating with, and teaching people. These occupations often involve helping or providing service to others.

Skills required of Physical Therapists

Reading Comprehension, Active Listening, Writing, Speaking, Science, Critical Thinking, Active Learning, Learning Strategies, Monitoring, Social Perceptiveness, Instructing, Service Orientation, Problem Identification, Information Gathering, Synthesis/ Reorganization, Idea Generation, Idea Evaluation, Implementation Planning, Technology

Design, Equipment Selection, Identification of Key Causes, Judgment and Decision Making, Management of Financial Resources, Management of Material Resources

College Majors

Health and Physical Education, General: An instructional program that generally describes the study and practice of activities and principles that promote physical fitness, achieve and maintain athletic prowess, and accomplish related research and service goals. Includes instruction in human movement studies, motivation studies, rules and practice of specific sports, exercise and fitness principles and techniques, basic athletic injury prevention and treatment, and organizing and leading fitness and sports programs.

Supporting Courses

Administration and Management: Knowledge of principles and processes involved in business and organizational planning, coordination, and execution. This includes strategic planning, resource allocation, manpower modeling, leadership techniques, and production methods. **Customer and Personal Service:** Knowledge of principles and processes for providing customer and personal services including needs assessment techniques, quality service standards, alternative delivery systems, and customer satisfaction evaluation techniques. **Biology:** Knowledge of plant and animal living tissue, cells, organisms, and entities, including their functions, interdependencies, and interactions with each other and the environment. **Psychology:** Knowledge of human behavior and performance, mental processes, psychological research methods, and the assessment and treatment of behavioral and affective disorders. **Medicine and Dentistry:** Knowledge of the information and techniques needed to diagnose and treat injuries, diseases, and deformities. This includes symptoms, treatment alternatives, drug properties and interactions, and preventive healthcare measures. **Therapy and Counseling:** Knowledge of information and techniques needed to rehabilitate physical and mental ailments and to provide career guidance including alternative treatments, rehabilitation equipment and its proper use, and methods to evaluate treatment effects. **Education and Training:** Knowledge of instructional methods and training techniques including curriculum design principles, learning theory, group and individual teaching techniques, design of individual development plans, and test design principles. **English Language:** Knowledge of the structure and content of the English language including the meaning and spelling of words, rules of composition, and grammar.

Corrective Therapists

Apply techniques and treatments designed to prevent muscular deconditioning resulting from long convalescence or inactivity due to chronic illness. Applies skin lubricant and massages client's body to relax muscles, stimulate nerves, promote range of motion, and release tissue. Plans and organizes program treatment procedures with client, or in collaboration with others on rehabilitation team. Demonstrates and directs client to participate in body movements designed to improve muscular function and flexibility and to reduce tension. Teaches client spatial and body awareness, new movement skills, and effective and expressive body habits. Instructs patient in use of prostheses, devices such as canes, crutches, and braces, and walking skills for sightless patients. Observes and/or photographs client's arm and leg movements, posture, and flexibility to evaluate client in relation to established norms. Observes and evaluates client's progress during treatment program and modifies treatment as required. Teaches client stress management, relaxation, and hygiene techniques to compensate for disabilities. Interviews patient or consults client's questionnaire to determine client's medical history and physical condition. Prepares reports describing client's treatment, progress, emotional reactions, and response to treatment. Consults with client to establish rapport, discuss program goals, and motivate patient.

Occupational Type

Social occupations frequently involve working with, communicating with, and teaching people. These occupations often involve helping or providing service to others.

Skills required of Corrective Therapists

Active Listening, Writing, Speaking, Monitoring, Social Perceptiveness, Service Orientation, Problem Identification, Judgment and Decision Making

College Majors

Health and Physical Education, General: An instructional program that generally describes the study and practice of activities and principles that promote physical fitness, achieve and maintain athletic prowess, and accomplish related research and service goals. Includes instruction in human movement studies, motivation studies, rules and practice of specific sports, exercise and fitness principles and techniques, basic athletic injury prevention and treatment, and organizing and leading fitness and sports programs.

Supporting Courses

Customer and Personal Service: Knowledge of principles and processes for providing customer and personal services including needs assessment techniques, quality service standards, alternative delivery systems, and customer satisfaction evaluation techniques. **Biology:** Knowledge of plant and animal living tissue, cells, organisms, and entities, including their functions, interdependencies, and interactions with each other and the environment. **Psychology:** Knowledge of human behavior and performance, mental processes, psychological research methods, and the assessment and treatment of behavioral and affective disorders. **Medicine and Dentistry:** Knowledge of the information and techniques needed to diagnose and treat injuries, diseases, and deformities. This includes symptoms, treatment alternatives, drug properties and interactions, and preventive healthcare measures. **Therapy and Counseling:** Knowledge of information and techniques needed to rehabilitate physical and mental ailments and to provide career guidance including alternative treatments, rehabilitation equipment and its proper use, and methods to evaluate treatment effects. **Education and Training:** Knowledge of instructional methods and training techniques including curriculum design principles, learning theory, group and individual teaching techniques, design of individual development plans, and test design principles. **Communications and Media:** Knowledge of media production, communication, and dissemination techniques and methods including alternative ways to inform and entertain via written, oral, and visual media.

PHYSICIAN'S ASSISTANTS

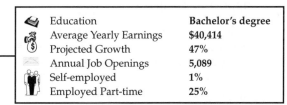

Education	Bachelor's degree
Average Yearly Earnings	$40,414
Projected Growth	47%
Annual Job Openings	5,089
Self-employed	1%
Employed Part-time	25%

Physician's Assistants

Provide patient services under direct supervision and responsibility of doctor of medicine or osteopathy. Elicit detailed patient histories and make complete physical examinations. Reach tentative diagnoses and order appropriate laboratory tests. Require substantial educational preparation, usually at junior or four-year colleges. Most physician's assistants complete two years of formal training, but training may vary from one to five years depending on the nature of the training and previous education and experience. May require certification. (Excludes nurses and ambulance attendants, whose training is limited to the application of first aid.) Examines patient. Administers or orders diagnostic tests, such as X-ray, electrocardiogram, and laboratory tests. Compiles patient medical data, including health history and results of physical examination. Interprets diagnostic test results for deviations from normal. Performs therapeutic procedures, such as injections, immunizations, suturing and wound care, and managing infection. Counsels patients regarding prescribed therapeutic regimens, normal growth and development, family planning, emotional problems of daily living, and health maintenance. Develops and implements patient management plans, records progress notes, and assists in provision of continuity of care.

Occupational Type

Investigative occupations frequently involve working with ideas, and require an extensive amount of thinking. These occupations can involve searching for facts and figuring out problems mentally.

Skills required of Physician's Assistants

Reading Comprehension, Active Listening, Writing, Speaking, Science, Critical Thinking, Active Learning, Learning Strategies, Monitoring, Social Perceptiveness, Persuasion, Service Orientation, Problem Identification, Information Gathering, Synthesis/Reorganization, Idea Generation, Judgment and Decision Making

College Majors

Physician Assistant: An instructional program that prepares individuals to manage the treatment of patients with routine or chronic health problems, in consultation with a physician or under indirect supervision. Includes instruction in patient interviewing and history-taking, counseling, laboratory testing and analysis, administration of medication, minor surgery, prescribing routine drugs, preparing medical reports and referrals to physicians and other specialists.

Supporting Courses

Chemistry: Knowledge of the composition, structure, and properties of substances and of the chemical processes and transformations that they undergo. This includes uses of chemicals and their interactions, danger signs, production techniques, and disposal methods. **Biology:** Knowledge of plant and animal living tissue, cells, organisms, and entities, including their functions, interdependencies, and interactions with each other and the environment. **Psychology:** Knowledge of human behavior and performance, mental processes, psychological research methods, and the assessment and treatment of behavioral and affective disorders. **Medicine and Dentistry:** Knowledge of the information and techniques needed to diagnose and treat injuries, diseases, and deformities. This includes symptoms, treatment alternatives, drug properties and interactions, and preventive healthcare measures. **Therapy and Counseling:** Knowledge of information and techniques needed to rehabilitate physical and mental ailments and to provide career guidance including alternative treatments, rehabilitation equipment and its proper use, and methods to evaluate treatment effects.

PHYSICIANS

Doctors of Medicine (M.D.)

Education	**First professional degree**	
Average Yearly Earnings	$96,637	
Projected Growth	21%	
Annual Job Openings	29,681	
Self-employed	16%	
Employed Part-time	7%	

Diagnose illness and prescribe and administer treatment for injury and disease. (Excludes doctors of osteopathy, psychiatrists, anesthesiologists, surgeons, and pathologists.) Examines or conducts tests on patient to provide information on medical condition. Analyzes records, reports, test results, or examination information to diagnose medical condition of patient. Prescribes or administers treatment, therapy, medication, vaccination, and other specialized medical care to treat or prevent illness, disease, or injury. Monitors patient's condition and progress and reevaluates treatments as necessary. Explains procedures and discusses test results on prescribed treatments with patients. Operates on patients to remove, repair, or improve functioning of diseased or injured body parts and systems, and delivers babies. Collects, records, and maintains patient information, such as medical history, reports, and examination results. Refers patients to medical specialist or other practitioner when necessary. Advises patients and community concerning diet, activity, hygiene, and disease prevention. Plans, implements, or administers health programs or standards in hospital, business, or community for information, prevention, or treatment of injury or illness. Directs and coordinates activities of nurses, students, assistants, specialists, therapists, and other medical staff. Prepares reports for government or management of birth, death, and disease statistics, workforce evaluations, or medical status of individuals. Conducts research to study anatomy and develop or test medications, treatments, or procedures to prevent or control disease or injury.

Occupational Type

Investigative occupations frequently involve working with ideas, and require an extensive amount of thinking. These occupations can involve searching for facts and figuring out problems mentally.

Skills required of Doctors of Medicine (M.D.)

Reading Comprehension, Active Listening, Writing, Speaking, Mathematics, Science, Critical Thinking, Active Learning, Learning Strategies, Monitoring, Social Perceptiveness, Coordination, Persuasion, Negotiation, Instructing, Service Orientation, Problem Identification, Information Gathering, Information Organization, Synthesis/Reorganization, Idea Generation, Idea Evaluation, Implementation Planning, Equipment Selection, Programming, Testing, Product Inspection, Troubleshooting, Systems Perception, Identifying Downstream Consequences, Identification of Key Causes, Judgment and Decision Making, Systems Evaluation, Time Management, Management of Personnel Resources

College Majors

Medicine (M.D.): An instructional program that prepares individuals for the independent professional practice of allopathic medicine. Includes instruction in the principles and procedures used in the observation, diagnosis, care and treatment of illness, disease, injury, deformity, or other anomalies in humans; ethics and professional standards; and supervised clinical practice.

Supporting Courses

Administration and Management: Knowledge of principles and processes involved in business and organizational planning, coordination, and execution. This includes strategic planning, resource allocation, manpower modeling, leadership techniques, and production methods. **Personnel and Human Resources:** Knowledge of policies and practices involved in personnel/human resource functions. This includes recruitment, selection, training, and promotion regulations and procedures; compensation and benefits packages; labor relations and negotiation strategies; and personnel information systems. **Mathematics:** Knowledge of numbers, their operations, and interrelationships including arithmetic, algebra, geometry, calculus, statistics, and their applications. **Physics:** Knowledge and prediction of physical principles, laws, and applications including air, water, material dynamics, light, atomic principles, heat, electric theory, earth formations, and meteorological and related natural phenomena. **Chemistry:** Knowledge of the composition, structure, and properties of substances and of the chemical processes and transformations that they undergo. This includes uses of chemicals and their interactions, danger signs, production techniques, and disposal methods. **Biology:** Knowledge of plant and animal living tissue, cells, organisms, and entities, including their functions, interdependencies, and interactions with each other and the environment. **Psychology:** Knowledge of human behavior and performance, mental processes, psychological research methods, and the assessment and treatment of behavioral and affective disorders. **Sociology and Anthropology:** Knowledge of group behavior and dynamics, societal trends and influences, cultures, their history, migrations, ethnicity, and origins. **Medicine and Dentistry:** Knowledge of the information and techniques needed to diagnose and treat injuries, diseases, and deformities. This includes symptoms, treatment alternatives, drug properties and interactions, and preventive healthcare measures. **Therapy and Counseling:** Knowledge of information and techniques needed to rehabilitate physical and mental ailments and to provide career guidance including alternative treatments, rehabilitation equipment and its proper use, and methods to evaluate treatment effects. **Education and Training:** Knowledge of instructional methods and training techniques including curriculum design principles, learning theory, group and individual teaching techniques, design of individual development plans, and test design principles. **English Language:** Knowledge of the structure and content of the English language including the meaning and spelling of words, rules of composition, and grammar. **Foreign Language:** Knowledge of the structure and content of a foreign (non-English) language including the meaning and spelling of words, rules of composition and grammar, and pronunciation. **Law, Government, and Jurisprudence:** Knowledge of laws, legal codes, court procedures, precedents, government regulations, executive orders, agency rules, and the democratic political process.

Doctors of Osteopathy (D.O.)

Diagnose illness and prescribe and administer treatment for injury and disease with emphasis on body's musculoskeletal system. Prescribes and administers medical, surgical, or manipulative therapy treatments to correct disorders or injuries of bones, muscles, or nerves. Examines or conducts test on patient to provide information on musculoskeletal system, using diagnostic images, drugs, and other aids. Analyzes reports and test or examination findings to diagnose musculoskeletal system impairment. Operates on patient to repair injuries or improve functions of musculoskeletal system. Advises patient and community of prevention and treatment of injury of musculoskeletal system. Conducts research to develop and test medications or medical techniques to cure or control disease or injury of musculoskeletal system. Directs and coordinates activities of nurses, assistants, and other medical staff.

Occupational Type

Investigative occupations frequently involve working with ideas, and require an extensive amount of thinking. These occupations can involve searching for facts and figuring out problems mentally.

Skills required of Doctors of Osteopathy (D.O.)

Reading Comprehension, Active Listening, Writing, Speaking, Science, Critical Thinking, Active Learning, Learning Strategies, Monitoring, Coordination, Persuasion, Service Orientation, Problem Identification, Information Gathering, Information Organization, Synthesis/Reorganization, Idea Generation, Idea Evaluation, Implementation Planning, Equipment Selection, Visioning, Systems Perception, Identifying Downstream Consequences, Identification of Key Causes, Judgment and Decision Making, Systems Evaluation, Time Management, Management of Material Resources, Management of Personnel Resources

College Majors

Osteopathic Medicine (D.O.): An instructional program that prepares individuals for the independent professional practice of osteopathy, a system of holistic diagnosis and treatment of health problems. Includes instruction in all accepted allopathic medical diagnostic and treatment methods, plus spinal manipulation; musculoskeletal and nervous system influence on body health; promoting natural defense mechanisms; and the interrelation of the various body systems.

Supporting Courses

Customer and Personal Service: Knowledge of principles and processes for providing customer and personal services including needs assessment techniques, quality service standards, alternative delivery systems, and customer satisfaction evaluation techniques. **Mathematics:** Knowledge of numbers, their operations, and interrelationships including arithmetic, algebra, geometry, calculus, statistics, and their applications. **Chemistry:** Knowledge of the composition, structure, and properties of substances and of the chemical processes and transformations that they undergo. This includes uses of chemicals and their interactions, danger signs, production techniques, and disposal methods. **Biology:** Knowledge of plant and animal living tissue, cells, organisms, and entities, including their functions, interdependencies, and interactions with each other and the environment. **Psychology:** Knowledge of human behavior and performance, mental processes, psychological research methods, and the assessment and treatment of behavioral and affective disorders. **Sociology and Anthropology:** Knowledge of group behavior and dynamics, societal trends and influences, cultures, their history, migrations, ethnicity, and origins. **Medicine and Dentistry:** Knowledge of the information and techniques needed to diagnose and treat injuries, diseases, and deformities. This includes symptoms, treatment alternatives, drug properties and interactions, and preventive healthcare measures. **Therapy and Counseling:** Knowledge of information and techniques needed to rehabilitate physical and mental ailments and to provide career guidance including alternative treatments, rehabilitation equipment and its proper use, and methods to evaluate treatment effects. **English Language:** Knowledge of the structure and content of the English language including the meaning and spelling of words, rules of composition, and grammar.

Psychiatrists

Diagnose mental, emotional, and behavioral disorders and prescribe medication or administer psychotherapeutic treatments to treat disorders. Analyzes and evaluates patient data and test or examination findings to diagnose nature and extent of mental disorder. Prescribes, directs, and administers psychotherapeutic treatments or medications to treat mental, emotional, or behavioral disorders. Examines or conducts laboratory or diagnostic tests on patient to provide information on general physical condition and mental disorder. Gathers and maintains patient information and records, including social and medical history obtained from patient, relatives, and other professionals. Reviews and evaluates treatment procedures and outcomes of other psychiatrists and medical professionals. Advises and informs guardians, relatives, and significant others of patient's condition and treatment.

Prepares case reports and summaries for government agencies. Teaches, conducts research, and publishes findings to increase understanding of mental, emotional, and behavioral states and disorders.

Occupational Type

Investigative occupations frequently involve working with ideas, and require an extensive amount of thinking. These occupations can involve searching for facts and figuring out problems mentally.

Skills required of Psychiatrists

Reading Comprehension, Active Listening, Writing, Speaking, Science, Critical Thinking, Active Learning, Learning Strategies, Monitoring, Social Perceptiveness, Coordination, Persuasion, Negotiation, Instructing, Service Orientation, Problem Identification, Information Gathering, Information Organization, Synthesis/Reorganization, Idea Generation, Idea Evaluation, Implementation Planning, Programming, Visioning, Systems Perception, Identifying Downstream Consequences, Identification of Key Causes, Judgment and Decision Making, Systems Evaluation

College Majors

Psychoanalysis: An instructional program that prepares individuals to provide psychotherapy to individuals and groups, based on the psychodynamic theory evolved from the work of Freud, Adler and Jung. Includes instruction in personality theory, dream analysis, free association and transference theory and techniques, psychodynamic theory, developmental processes, applications to specific clinical conditions, practice standards and management, and client relations.

Supporting Courses

Customer and Personal Service: Knowledge of principles and processes for providing customer and personal services including needs assessment techniques, quality service standards, alternative delivery systems, and customer satisfaction evaluation techniques. **Chemistry:** Knowledge of the composition, structure, and properties of substances and of the chemical processes and transformations that they undergo. This includes uses of chemicals and their interactions, danger signs, production techniques, and disposal methods. **Biology:** Knowledge of plant and animal living tissue, cells, organisms, and entities, including their functions, interdependencies, and interactions with each other and the environment. **Psychology:** Knowledge of human behavior and performance, mental processes, psychological research methods, and the assessment and treatment of behavioral and affective disorders. **Sociology and Anthropology:** Knowledge of group behavior and dynamics, societal trends and influences, cultures, their history, migrations, ethnicity, and origins. **Medicine and Dentistry:** Knowledge of the information and techniques needed to diagnose and treat injuries, diseases, and deformities. This includes symptoms, treatment alternatives, drug properties and interactions, and preventive healthcare measures. **Therapy and Counseling:** Knowledge of information and techniques needed to rehabilitate physical and mental ailments and to provide career guidance including alternative treatments, rehabilitation equipment and its proper use, and methods to evaluate treatment effects. **Education and Training:** Knowledge of instructional methods and training techniques including curriculum design principles, learning theory, group and individual teaching techniques, design of individual development plans, and test design principles. **English Language:** Knowledge of the structure and content of the English language including the meaning and spelling of words, rules of composition, and grammar. **Philosophy and Theology:** Knowledge of different philosophical systems and religions, including their basic principles, values, ethics, ways of thinking, customs, and practices, and their impact on human culture. **Law, Government, and Jurisprudence:** Knowledge of laws, legal codes, court procedures, precedents, government regulations, executive orders, agency rules, and the democratic political process. **Communications and Media:** Knowledge of media production, communication, and dissemination techniques and methods including alternative ways to inform and entertain via written, oral, and visual media.

Anesthesiologists

Administer anesthetic during surgery or other medical procedures. Administers anesthetic or sedation during medical procedures, using local, intravenous, spinal, or caudal methods. Monitors patient before, during, and after anesthesia and counteracts adverse reactions or complications. Examines patient to determine risk during surgical, obstetrical, and other medical procedures. Confers with medical professional to determine type and method of anesthetic or sedation to render patient insensible to pain. Records type and amount of anesthesia and patient condition throughout procedure. Positions patient on operating table to maximize patient comfort and surgical accessibility. Informs students and staff of types and methods of anesthesia administration, signs of complications, and emergency methods to counteract reactions.

 Occupational Type

Investigative occupations frequently involve working with ideas, and require an extensive amount of thinking. These occupations can involve searching for facts and figuring out problems mentally.

 Skills required of Anesthesiologists

Reading Comprehension, Active Listening, Speaking, Science, Critical Thinking, Active Learning, Monitoring, Coordination, Instructing, Problem Identification, Information Gathering, Information Organization, Idea Generation, Idea Evaluation, Implementation Planning, Equipment Selection, Testing, Operation Monitoring, Operation and Control, Troubleshooting, Visioning, Systems Perception, Identification of Key Causes, Judgment and Decision Making, Systems Evaluation

College Majors

Medical Clinical Sciences (M.S., Ph.D.): An instructional program that describes the scientific study, by medical residents and other medical doctors, of specialized medical practice arts and related clinical research. Includes instruction in fields such as pediatrics, anesthesiology, obstetrics, gynecology, oncology, surgery, radiology, internal medicine, neurology, clinical pathology, psychiatry, and others.

Supporting Courses

Chemistry: Knowledge of the composition, structure, and properties of substances and of the chemical processes and transformations that they undergo. This includes uses of chemicals and their interactions, danger signs, production techniques, and disposal methods. **Biology:** Knowledge of plant and animal living tissue, cells, organisms, and entities, including their functions, interdependencies, and interactions with each other and the environment. **Medicine and Dentistry:** Knowledge of the information and techniques needed to diagnose and treat injuries, diseases, and deformities. This includes symptoms, treatment alternatives, drug properties and interactions, and preventive healthcare measures. **English Language:** Knowledge of the structure and content of the English language including the meaning and spelling of words, rules of composition, and grammar.

Surgeons

Perform surgery to repair injuries; remove or repair diseased organs, bones, or tissue; correct deformities; or improve function in patients. Operates on patient to correct deformities, repair injuries, prevent diseases, or improve or restore patient's functions. Analyzes patient's medical history, medication allergies, physical condition, and examination results to verify operation's necessity and to determine best procedure. Examines patient to provide information on medical condition and patient's surgical risk. Refers patient to medical specialist or other practitioners when necessary. Conducts research to develop and test surgical techniques to improve operating procedures and outcomes. Examines instruments, equipment, and operating room to ensure sterility. Directs and coordinates activities of nurses, assistants, specialists, and other medical staff.

Occupational Type

Investigative occupations frequently involve working with ideas, and require an extensive amount of thinking. These occupations can involve searching for facts and figuring out problems mentally.

Skills required of Surgeons

Reading Comprehension, Active Listening, Writing, Speaking, Science, Critical Thinking, Active Learning, Monitoring, Social Perceptiveness, Coordination, Persuasion, Negotiation, Instructing, Service Orientation, Problem Identification, Information Gathering, Synthesis/Reorganization, Idea Generation, Idea Evaluation, Implementation Planning, Operations Analysis, Equipment Selection, Testing, Operation and Control, Product Inspection, Troubleshooting, Visioning, Systems Perception, Identifying Downstream Consequences, Identification of Key Causes, Judgment and Decision Making, Systems Evaluation, Time Management, Management of Personnel Resources

College Majors

Critical Care Surgery Residency: A residency training program that prepares physicians in surgical procedures for patients with multiple trauma, critical illness, patients on life support and elderly or very young patients with disease complications. Requires full or partial prior completion of a program in general surgery or another surgical specialty.

Supporting Courses

Administration and Management: Knowledge of principles and processes involved in business and organizational planning, coordination, and execution. This includes strategic planning, resource allocation, manpower modeling, leadership techniques, and production methods. **Physics:** Knowledge and prediction of physical principles, laws, and applications including air, water, material dynamics, light, atomic principles, heat, electric theory, earth formations, and meteorological and related natural phenomena. **Chemistry:** Knowledge of the composition, structure, and properties of substances and of the chemical processes and transformations that they undergo. This includes uses of chemicals and their interactions, danger signs, production techniques, and disposal methods. **Biology:** Knowledge of plant and animal living tissue, cells, organisms, and entities, including their functions, interdependencies, and interactions with each other and the environment. **Psychology:** Knowledge of human behavior and performance, mental processes, psychological research methods, and the assessment and treatment of behavioral and affective disorders. **Medicine and Dentistry:** Knowledge of the information and techniques needed to diagnose and treat injuries, diseases, and deformities. This includes symptoms, treatment alternatives, drug properties and interactions, and preventive healthcare measures. **Therapy and Counseling:** Knowledge of information and techniques needed to rehabilitate physical and mental ailments and to provide career guidance including alternative treatments, rehabilitation equipment and its proper use, and methods to evaluate treatment effects. **English Language:** Knowledge of the structure and content of the English language including the meaning and spelling of words, rules of composition, and grammar.

Pathologists

Research or study the nature, cause, effects, and development of diseases; and determine presence and extent of disease in body tissue, fluids, secretions, and other specimens. Conducts research to gain knowledge of nature, cause, and development of diseases, and resulting structural and functional body changes. Examines, collects tissue or fluid samples, and conducts tests on patient to provide information on patient's disease. Diagnoses nature, cause, and development of disease and resulting changes of patient's body, using results of sample analyses and tests. Performs autopsies to determine nature and extent of disease, cause of death, and effects of treatment. Advises other medical practitioners on nature, cause, and development of diseases. Directs and coordinates activities of nurses, students, and other staff in medical school, hospital, medical examiner's office, or research institute.

Occupational Type

Investigative occupations frequently involve working with ideas, and require an extensive amount of thinking. These occupations can involve searching for facts and figuring out problems mentally.

Skills required of Pathologists

Reading Comprehension, Writing, Speaking, Mathematics, Science, Critical Thinking, Active Learning, Monitoring, Coordination, Problem Identification, Information Gathering, Information Organization, Synthesis/Reorganization, Idea Generation, Idea Evaluation, Implementation Planning, Visioning, Systems Perception, Identifying Downstream Consequences, Identification of Key Causes, Judgment and Decision Making, Systems Evaluation, Time Management, Management of Personnel Resources

College Majors

Medical Pathology: An instructional program that describes advanced research, by medical graduates and others, on the causes and effects of diseases and disease mechanisms in human beings. Includes instruction in renal, cardiovascular, neuro-, pulmonary, bone, liver and gastrointestinal, surgical, autopsy, cellular, biochemical and immunopathology.

Supporting Courses

Administration and Management: Knowledge of principles and processes involved in business and organizational planning, coordination, and execution. This includes strategic planning, resource allocation, manpower modeling, leadership techniques, and production methods. **Mathematics:** Knowledge of numbers, their operations, and interrelationships including arithmetic, algebra, geometry, calculus, statistics, and their applications. **Chemistry:** Knowledge of the composition, structure, and properties of substances and of the chemical processes and transformations that they undergo. This includes uses of chemicals and their interactions, danger signs, production techniques, and disposal methods. **Biology:** Knowledge of plant and animal living tissue, cells, organisms, and entities, including their functions, interdependencies, and interactions with each other and the environment. **Medicine and Dentistry:** Knowledge of the information and techniques needed to diagnose and treat injuries, diseases, and deformities. This includes symptoms, treatment alternatives, drug properties and interactions, and preventive healthcare measures. **Therapy and Counseling:** Knowledge of information and techniques needed to rehabilitate physical and mental ailments and to provide career guidance including alternative treatments, rehabilitation equipment and its proper use, and methods to evaluate treatment effects. **Education and Training:** Knowledge of instructional methods and training techniques including curriculum design principles, learning theory, group and individual teaching techniques, design of individual development plans, and test design principles. **English Language:** Knowledge of the structure and content of the English language including the meaning and spelling of words, rules of composition, and grammar.

PHYSICISTS AND ASTRONOMERS

	Education	Doctor's degree
	Average Yearly Earnings	$62,774
	Projected Growth	-2%
	Annual Job Openings	1,073
	Self-employed	0%
	Employed Part-time	7%

Physicists

Conduct research into the phases of physical phenomena, develop theories and laws on the basis of observation and experiments, and devise methods to apply laws and theories to industry and other fields. Observes structure and properties of matter and transformation and propagation of energy, using masers, lasers, telescopes, and other equipment. Analyzes results of experiments designed to detect and measure previously unobserved physical phenomena. Conducts instrumental analyses to determine physical properties of materials. Describes and expresses observations and conclusions in mathematical terms. Conducts application analysis to determine commercial, industrial, scientific, medical, military, or other uses for electro-optical devices. Assists in developing standards of permissible concentrations of radioisotopes in liquids and gases. Designs electronic circuitry and optical components with scientific characteristics to fit within specified mechanical limits and perform according to specifications. Assists with development of manufacturing, assembly, and fabrication processes of lasers, masers, infrared, and other light-emitting and light-sensitive devices. Conducts research pertaining to potential environmental impact of proposed atomic energy–related industrial development to determine qualifications for licensing. Directs testing and monitoring of contamination of radioactive equipment and recording of personnel and plant area radiation exposure data. Consults other scientists regarding innovations to ensure equipment or plant design conforms to health physics standards for protection of personnel. Incorporates methods for maintenance and repair of components and designs, and develops test instrumentation and test procedures. Advises authorities in procedures to be followed in radiation incidents or hazards, and assists in civil defense planning. Supervises subordinate personnel, including graduate students, in scientific activities or research. Writes for or serves as consultant for professional journals or other media. Trains technicians to assist in scientific experimentation and research.

Occupational Type

Investigative occupations frequently involve working with ideas, and require an extensive amount of thinking. These occupations can involve searching for facts and figuring out problems mentally.

Skills required of Physicists

Reading Comprehension, Writing, Speaking, Mathematics, Science, Critical Thinking, Active Learning, Learning Strategies, Monitoring, Coordination, Instructing, Problem Identification, Information Gathering, Information Organization, Synthesis/Reorganization, Idea

Generation, Idea Evaluation, Implementation Planning, Operations Analysis, Technology Design, Equipment Selection, Programming, Testing, Operation Monitoring, Visioning, Systems Perception, Identifying Downstream Consequences, Identification of Key Causes, Judgment and Decision Making, Systems Evaluation, Time Management, Management of Personnel Resources

 ## College Majors

Astronomy: An instructional program that describes the scientific study of matter and energy in the universe, using observational techniques such as spectroscopy, photometry, interferometry, radio astronomy and optical astronomy. Includes instruction in celestial mechanics, cosmology, and stellar physics; and applications to research on lunar, planetary, solar, stellar, and galactic phenomena.

Supporting Courses

Personnel and Human Resources: Knowledge of policies and practices involved in personnel/human resource functions. This includes recruitment, selection, training, and promotion regulations and procedures; compensation and benefits packages; labor relations and negotiation strategies; and personnel information systems. **Production and Processing:** Knowledge of inputs, outputs, raw materials, waste, quality control, costs, and techniques for maximizing the manufacture and distribution of goods. **Computers and Electronics:** Knowledge of electric circuit boards, processors, chips, and computer hardware and software, including applications and programming. **Engineering and Technology:** Knowledge of equipment, tools, mechanical devices, and their uses to produce motion, light, power, technology, and other applications. **Design:** Knowledge of design techniques, principles, tools and instruments involved in the production and use of precision technical plans, blueprints, drawings, and models. **Mathematics:** Knowledge of numbers, their operations, and interrelationships including arithmetic, algebra, geometry, calculus, statistics, and their applications. **Physics:** Knowledge and prediction of physical principles, laws, and applications including air, water, material dynamics, light, atomic principles, heat, electric theory, earth formations, and meteorological and related natural phenomena. **Chemistry:** Knowledge of the composition, structure, and properties of substances and of the chemical processes and transformations that they undergo. This includes uses of chemicals and their interactions, danger signs, production techniques, and disposal methods. **Education and Training:** Knowledge of instructional methods and training techniques including curriculum design principles, learning theory, group and individual teaching techniques, design of individual development plans, and test design principles. **English Language:** Knowledge of the structure and content of the English language including the meaning and spelling of words, rules of composition, and grammar. **Foreign Language:** Knowledge of the structure and content of a foreign (non-English) language including the meaning and spelling of words, rules of composition and grammar, and pronunciation. **History and Archeology:** Knowledge of past historical events and their causes, indicators, and impact on particular civilizations and cultures. **Communications and Media:** Knowledge of media production, communication, and dissemination techniques and methods including alternative ways to inform and entertain via written, oral, and visual media.

Astronomers

Observe, research, and interpret celestial and astronomical phenomena to increase basic knowledge; and apply such information to practical problems. Studies celestial phenomena from ground or above atmosphere, using various optical devices such as telescopes situated on ground or attached to satellites. Studies history, structure, extent, and evolution of stars, stellar systems, and universe. Calculates orbits and determines sizes, shapes, brightness, and motions of different celestial bodies. Computes positions of sun, moon, planets, stars, nebulae, and galaxies. Determines exact time by celestial observations, and conducts research into relationships between time and space. Analyzes wavelengths of radiation from celestial bodies, as observed in all ranges of spectrum. Develops mathematical tables giving positions of sun, moon, planets, and stars at given times for use by air and sea navigators. Designs optical, mechanical, and electronic instruments for astronomical research.

Occupational Type

Investigative occupations frequently involve working with ideas, and require an extensive amount of thinking. These occupations can involve searching for facts and figuring out problems mentally.

Skills required of Astronomers

Reading Comprehension, Writing, Mathematics, Science, Critical Thinking, Active Learning, Information Gathering, Information Organization, Synthesis/Reorganization, Idea Generation, Idea Evaluation, Operations Analysis, Technology Design, Equipment Selection, Programming, Systems Perception, Identifying Downstream Consequences

College Majors

Astronomy: An instructional program that describes the scientific study of matter and energy in the universe, using observational techniques such as spectroscopy, photometry, interferometry, radio astronomy, and optical astronomy. Includes instruction in celestial mechanics, cosmology, and stellar physics; and applications to research on lunar, planetary, solar, stellar, and galactic phenomena.

Supporting Courses

Computers and Electronics: Knowledge of electric circuit boards, processors, chips, and computer hardware and software, including applications and programming. **Engineering and Technology:** Knowledge of equipment, tools, mechanical devices, and their uses to produce motion, light, power, technology, and other applications. **Design:** Knowledge of design techniques, principles, tools and instruments involved in the production and use of precision technical plans, blueprints, drawings, and models. **Mathematics:** Knowledge of numbers, their operations, and interrelationships including arithmetic, algebra, geometry, calculus, statistics, and their applications. **Physics:** Knowledge and prediction of physical principles, laws, and applications including air, water, material dynamics, light, atomic principles, heat, electric theory, earth formations, and meteorological and related natural phenomena. **Geography:** Knowledge of various methods for describing the location and distribution of land, sea, and air masses including their physical locations, relationships, and characteristics. **English Language:** Knowledge of the structure and content of the English language including the meaning and spelling of words, rules of composition, and grammar. **History and Archeology:** Knowledge of past historical events and their causes, indicators, and impact on particular civilizations and cultures.

PODIATRISTS

Podiatrists

Education	First professional degree	
Average Yearly Earnings	$85,134	
Projected Growth	10%	
Annual Job Openings	617	
Self-employed	33%	
Employed Part-time	11%	

Diagnose and treat diseases and deformities of the human foot. Diagnoses ailments, such as tumors, ulcers, fractures, skin or nail diseases, and deformities, utilizing urinalysis, blood tests, and X-rays. Treats conditions such as corns, calluses, ingrown nails, tumors, shortened tendons, bunions, cysts, and abscesses by surgical methods. Corrects deformities by means of plaster casts and strapping. Treats bone, muscle, and joint disorders. Treats deformities by mechanical and electrical methods, such as whirlpool or paraffin baths and short-wave and low-voltage currents. Prescribes corrective footwear. Prescribes drugs. Makes and fits prosthetic appliances. Performs surgery. Treats children's foot diseases. Advises patients concerning continued treatment of disorders and foot care to prevent recurrence of disorders. Refers patients to physician when symptoms indicative of systemic disorders, such as arthritis or diabetes, are observed in feet and legs.

 Occupational Type

Social occupations frequently involve working with, communicating with, and teaching people. These occupations often involve helping or providing service to others.

Skills required of Podiatrists

Reading Comprehension, Active Listening, Speaking, Science, Critical Thinking, Active Learning, Learning Strategies, Monitoring, Social Perceptiveness, Persuasion, Instructing, Service Orientation, Problem Identification, Information Gathering, Information Organization, Synthesis/Reorganization, Idea Generation, Idea Evaluation, Implementation Planning, Technology Design, Equipment Selection, Visioning, Systems Perception, Identifying Downstream Consequences, Identification of Key Causes, Judgment and Decision Making, Systems Evaluation, Time Management, Management of Personnel Resources

 College Majors

Podiatry (D.P.M., D.P., Pod.D.): An instructional program that prepares individuals for the independent professional practice of podiatric medicine. Includes instruction in the

principles and procedures used in the observation, diagnosis, care and treatment of disease, injury, deformity, or other anomalies of the human foot; ethics and professional standards; and supervised clinical practice.

Supporting Courses

Customer and Personal Service: Knowledge of principles and processes for providing customer and personal services including needs assessment techniques, quality service standards, alternative delivery systems, and customer satisfaction evaluation techniques. **Physics:** Knowledge and prediction of physical principles, laws, and applications including air, water, material dynamics, light, atomic principles, heat, electric theory, earth formations, and meteorological and related natural phenomena. **Chemistry:** Knowledge of the composition, structure, and properties of substances and of the chemical processes and transformations that they undergo. This includes uses of chemicals and their interactions, danger signs, production techniques, and disposal methods. **Biology:** Knowledge of plant and animal living tissue, cells, organisms, and entities, including their functions, interdependencies, and interactions with each other and the environment. **Psychology:** Knowledge of human behavior and performance, mental processes, psychological research methods, and the assessment and treatment of behavioral and affective disorders. **Sociology and Anthropology:** Knowledge of group behavior and dynamics, societal trends and influences, cultures, their history, migrations, ethnicity, and origins. **Medicine and Dentistry:** Knowledge of the information and techniques needed to diagnose and treat injuries, diseases, and deformities. This includes symptoms, treatment alternatives, drug properties and interactions, and preventive healthcare measures. **Therapy and Counseling:** Knowledge of information and techniques needed to rehabilitate physical and mental ailments and to provide career guidance including alternative treatments, rehabilitation equipment and its proper use, and methods to evaluate treatment effects. **English Language:** Knowledge of the structure and content of the English language including the meaning and spelling of words, rules of composition, and grammar. **Philosophy and Theology:** Knowledge of different philosophical systems and religions, including their basic principles, values, ethics, ways of thinking, customs, and practices, and their impact on human culture.

PRESCHOOL AND KINDERGARTEN TEACHERS

✍	Education	Bachelor's degree
💰	Average Yearly Earnings	$30,181
	Projected Growth	20%
	Annual Job Openings	77,151
👥	Self-employed	1%
	Employed Part-time	32%

Teachers: Preschool

Instruct children (normally up to 5 years of age) in activities designed to promote social, physical, and intellectual growth needed for primary school in preschool, daycare center, or other child development facility. May be required to hold state certification. Instructs children in activities designed to promote social, physical, and intellectual growth in a facility such as preschool or daycare center. Plans

P

individual and group activities for children, such as learning to listen to instructions, playing with others, and using play equipment. Demonstrates activity. Structures play activities to instill concepts of respect and concern for others. Monitors individual and/or group activities to prevent accidents and promote social skills. Reads books to entire class or to small groups. Confers with parents to explain preschool program and to discuss ways they can develop their child's interest. Plans instructional activities for teacher aide. Administers tests to determine each child's level of development according to design of test. Attends staff meetings.

Occupational Type

Social occupations frequently involve working with, communicating with, and teaching people. These occupations often involve helping or providing service to others.

Skills required of Teachers: Preschool

Learning Strategies, Monitoring, Social Perceptiveness, Instructing

College Majors

Education, General: An instructional program that generally describes the theory and practice of learning and teaching; the basic principles of educational psychology; the art of teaching; the planning and administration of educational activities; and the social foundations of education.

Supporting Courses

Customer and Personal Service: Knowledge of principles and processes for providing customer and personal services including needs assessment techniques, quality service standards, alternative delivery systems, and customer satisfaction evaluation techniques. **Psychology:** Knowledge of human behavior and performance, mental processes, psychological research methods, and the assessment and treatment of behavioral and affective disorders. **Sociology and Anthropology:** Knowledge of group behavior and dynamics, societal trends and influences, cultures, their history, migrations, ethnicity, and origins. **Therapy and Counseling:** Knowledge of information and techniques needed to rehabilitate physical and mental ailments and to provide career guidance including alternative treatments, rehabilitation equipment and its proper use, and methods to evaluate treatment effects. **Education and Training:** Knowledge of instructional methods and training techniques including curriculum design principles, learning theory, group and individual teaching techniques, design of individual development plans, and test design principles. **Foreign Language:** Knowledge of the structure and content of a foreign (non-English) language including the meaning and spelling of words, rules of composition and grammar, and pronunciation. **Fine Arts:** Knowledge of theory and techniques required to produce, compose, and perform works of music, dance, visual arts, drama, and sculpture. **History and Archeology:** Knowledge of past historical events and their causes, indicators, and impact on particular civilizations and cultures. **Philosophy and Theology:** Knowledge of different philosophical systems and religions, including their basic principles, values, ethics, ways of thinking, customs, and practices, and their impact on human culture.

Teachers: Kindergarten

Teach elemental natural and social science, personal hygiene, music, art, and literature to children from 4 to 6 years old. Promote physical, mental, and social development. May be required to hold state certification. Teaches elemental science, personal hygiene, and humanities to children to promote physical, mental, and social development. Supervises student activities, such as field visits, to stimulate student interest and broaden understanding of physical and social environment. Organizes and conducts games and group projects to develop cooperative behavior and assist children in forming satisfying relationships. Encourages students in activities, such as singing, dancing, and rhythmic activities, to promote self-expression and appreciation of aesthetic experience. Instructs children in practices of personal cleanliness and self-care. Observes children to detect signs of ill health or emotional disturbance, and to evaluate progress. Discusses student problems and progress with parents. Alternates periods of strenuous activity with periods of rest or light activity to avoid overstimulation and fatigue.

Occupational Type

Social occupations frequently involve working with, communicating with, and teaching people. These occupations often involve helping or providing service to others.

Skills required of Teachers: Kindergarten

Learning Strategies, Monitoring, Social Perceptiveness, Instructing, Service Orientation

College Majors

Education, General: An instructional program that generally describes the theory and practice of learning and teaching; the basic principles of educational psychology; the art of teaching; the planning and administration of educational activities; and the social foundations of education.

Supporting Courses

Customer and Personal Service: Knowledge of principles and processes for providing customer and personal services including needs assessment techniques, quality service standards, alternative delivery systems, and customer satisfaction evaluation techniques. **Psychology:** Knowledge of human behavior and performance, mental processes, psychological research methods, and the assessment and treatment of behavioral and affective disorders. **Sociology and Anthropology:** Knowledge of group behavior and dynamics, societal trends and influences, cultures, their history, migrations, ethnicity, and origins. **Geography:** Knowledge of various methods for describing the location and distribution of land, sea, and air masses including their physical locations, relationships, and characteristics.

Medicine and Dentistry: Knowledge of the information and techniques needed to diagnose and treat injuries, diseases, and deformities. This includes symptoms, treatment alternatives, drug properties and interactions, and preventive healthcare measures. **Therapy and Counseling:** Knowledge of information and techniques needed to rehabilitate physical and mental ailments and to provide career guidance including alternative treatments, rehabilitation equipment and its proper use, and methods to evaluate treatment effects. **Education and Training:** Knowledge of instructional methods and training techniques including curriculum design principles, learning theory, group and individual teaching techniques, design of individual development plans, and test design principles. **English Language:** Knowledge of the structure and content of the English language including the meaning and spelling of words, rules of composition, and grammar. **Foreign Language:** Knowledge of the structure and content of a foreign (non-English) language including the meaning and spelling of words, rules of composition and grammar, and pronunciation. **Fine Arts:** Knowledge of theory and techniques required to produce, compose, and perform works of music, dance, visual arts, drama, and sculpture. **History and Archeology:** Knowledge of past historical events and their causes, indicators, and impact on particular civilizations and cultures. **Philosophy and Theology:** Knowledge of different philosophical systems and religions, including their basic principles, values, ethics, ways of thinking, customs, and practices, and their impact on human culture. **Law, Government, and Jurisprudence:** Knowledge of laws, legal codes, court procedures, precedents, government regulations, executive orders, agency rules, and the democratic political process. **Communications and Media:** Knowledge of media production, communication, and dissemination techniques and methods including alternative ways to inform and entertain via written, oral, and visual media.

PRODUCTION ENGINEERS

Education	Bachelor's degree
Average Yearly Earnings	$54,330
Projected Growth	14%
Annual Job Openings	19,706
Self-employed	3%
Employed Part-time	5%

Agricultural Engineers

Apply knowledge of engineering technology and biological science to agricultural problems concerned with power and machinery, electrification, structures, soil and water conservation, and processing of agricultural products. Designs and directs manufacture of equipment for land tillage and fertilization, plant and animal disease and insect control, and for harvesting or moving commodities. Designs and supervises erection of crop storage, animal shelter, and residential structures and heating, lighting, cooling, plumbing, and waste disposal systems. Designs and supervises installation of equipment and instruments used to evaluate and process farm products, and to automate agricultural operations. Develops criteria for design, manufacture, or construction of equipment, structures, and facilities. Plans and directs construction of rural electric-power distribution systems, and irrigation, drainage, and flood control systems for soil and water conservation. Designs sensing, measuring, and recording devices and instrumentation used to study plant or animal life. Studies such problems as effect of temperature, humidity, and light on plants and animals and effectiveness of different insecticides. Conducts research to develop agricultural machinery and equipment. Designs agricultural machinery and equipment. Conducts tests on agricultural machinery and equipment. Conducts radio and television educational programs to provide assistance to farmers, local groups, and related farm cooperatives.

Occupational Type

Investigative occupations frequently involve working with ideas, and require an extensive amount of thinking. These occupations can involve searching for facts and figuring out problems mentally.

Skills required of Agricultural Engineers

Reading Comprehension, Active Listening, Writing, Speaking, Mathematics, Science, Critical Thinking, Active Learning, Learning Strategies, Monitoring, Coordination, Persuasion, Negotiation, Instructing, Problem Identification, Information Gathering, Information Organization, Synthesis/Reorganization, Idea Generation, Idea Evaluation, Implementation Planning, Operations Analysis, Technology Design, Equipment Selection, Installation, Programming, Testing, Product Inspection, Troubleshooting, Visioning, Systems Perception, Identifying Downstream Consequences, Identification of Key Causes, Judgment and Decision Making, Systems Evaluation, Time Management, Management of Personnel Resources

College Majors

Engineering, General: An instructional program that generally prepares individuals to apply mathematical and scientific principles to solve a wide variety of practical problems in industry, social organization, public works, and commerce.

Supporting Courses

Administration and Management: Knowledge of principles and processes involved in business and organizational planning, coordination, and execution. This includes strategic planning, resource allocation, manpower modeling, leadership techniques, and production methods. **Economics and Accounting:** Knowledge of economic and accounting principles and practices, the financial markets, banking, and the analysis and reporting of financial data. **Production and Processing:** Knowledge of inputs, outputs, raw materials, waste, quality control, costs, and techniques for maximizing the manufacture and distribution of goods. **Food Production:** Knowledge of techniques and equipment for planting, growing, and harvesting of food for consumption including crop rotation methods, animal husbandry, and food storage/handling techniques. **Computers and Electronics:** Knowledge of electric circuit boards, processors, chips, and computer hardware and software, including applications and programming. **Engineering and Technology:** Knowledge of equipment, tools, mechanical devices, and their uses to produce motion, light, power, technology, and other applications. **Design:** Knowledge of design techniques, principles, tools and instruments involved in the production and use of precision technical plans, blueprints, drawings, and models. **Building and Construction:** Knowledge of materials, methods, and the appropriate tools to construct objects, structures, and buildings. **Mechanical:** Knowledge of machines and tools, including their designs, uses, benefits, repair, and maintenance. **Mathematics:** Knowledge of numbers, their operations, and interrelationships including arithmetic, algebra, geometry, calculus, statistics, and their applications. **Physics:** Knowledge and prediction of physical principles, laws, and applications including air, water, material dynamics, light, atomic principles, heat, electric theory, earth formations, and meteorological and related natural phenomena. **Chemistry:** Knowledge of the composition, structure, and properties of substances and of the chemical processes and transformations that they undergo. This includes uses of chemicals and their interactions, danger signs, production techniques, and disposal methods. **Biology:** Knowledge of plant and animal living tissue, cells, organisms, and entities, including their functions, interdependencies, and interactions with each other and the environment. **Sociology and Anthropology:** Knowledge of group behavior and dynamics, societal trends and influences, cultures, their history, migrations, ethnicity, and origins. **Geography:** Knowledge of various methods for describing the location and distribution of land, sea, and air masses including their physical locations, relationships, and characteristics. **Education and Training:** Knowledge of instructional methods and training techniques including curriculum design principles, learning theory, group and individual teaching techniques, design of individual development plans, and test design principles. **English Language:** Knowledge of the structure and content of the English language including the meaning and spelling of words, rules of composition, and grammar. **Philosophy and Theology:** Knowledge of different philosophical systems and religions, including their basic principles, values, ethics, ways of thinking, customs, and practices, and their impact on human culture. **Law, Government, and Jurisprudence:** Knowledge of laws, legal codes, court procedures, precedents, government regulations, executive orders, agency rules, and the democratic political process. **Communications and Media:** Knowledge of media production, communication, and dissemination techniques and methods including alternative ways to inform and entertain via written, oral, and visual media. **Transportation:** Knowledge of principles and methods for moving people or goods by air, rail, sea, or road, including their relative costs, advantages, and limitations.

Industrial Safety and Health Engineers

Plan, implement, and coordinate safety programs to prevent or correct unsafe environmental working conditions. Devises and implements safety or industrial health program to prevent, correct, or control unsafe environmental conditions. Examines plans and specifications for new machinery or equipment to determine if all safety requirements have been included. Conducts or coordinates training of workers concerning safety laws and regulations; use of safety equipment, devices, and clothing; and first aid. Inspects facilities, machinery, and safety equipment to identify and correct potential hazards, and to ensure compliance with safety regulations. Conducts or directs testing of air quality, noise, temperature, or radiation to verify compliance with health and safety regulations. Provides technical guidance to organizations regarding how to handle health-related problems, such as water and air pollution. Compiles, analyzes, and interprets statistical data related to exposure factors concerning occupational illnesses and accidents. Installs or directs installation of safety devices on machinery. Investigates causes of industrial accidents or injuries to develop solutions to minimize or prevent recurrence. Conducts plant or area surveys to determine safety levels for exposure to materials and conditions. Checks floors of plant to ensure they are strong enough to support heavy machinery. Designs and builds safety devices for machinery or safety clothing. Prepares reports of findings from investigation of accidents, inspection of facilities, or testing of environment. Maintains liaison with outside organizations, such as fire departments, mutual aid societies, and rescue teams.

 ## Occupational Type

Investigative occupations frequently involve working with ideas, and require an extensive amount of thinking. These occupations can involve searching for facts and figuring out problems mentally.

 ## Skills required of Industrial Safety and Health Engineers

Writing, Speaking, Mathematics, Science, Critical Thinking, Active Learning, Learning Strategies, Monitoring, Coordination, Persuasion, Instructing, Problem Identification, Information Organization, Synthesis/Reorganization, Idea Generation, Idea Evaluation, Implementation Planning, Operations Analysis, Technology Design, Equipment Selection, Installation, Programming, Testing, Product Inspection, Visioning, Systems Perception, Identifying Downstream Consequences, Identification of Key Causes, Judgment and Decision Making, Systems Evaluation

 ## College Majors

Engineering, General: An instructional program that generally prepares individuals to apply mathematical and scientific principles to solve a wide variety of practical problems in industry, social organization, public works, and commerce.

 ## Supporting Courses

Administration and Management: Knowledge of principles and processes involved in business and organizational planning, coordination, and execution. This includes strategic planning, resource allocation, manpower modeling, leadership techniques, and production methods. **Engineering and Technology:** Knowledge of equipment, tools, mechanical devices, and their uses to produce motion, light, power, technology, and other applications. **Design:** Knowledge of design techniques, principles, tools and instruments involved in the production and use of precision technical plans, blueprints, drawings, and models. **Building and Construction:** Knowledge of materials, methods, and the appropriate tools to construct objects, structures, and buildings. **Mathematics:** Knowledge of numbers, their operations, and interrelationships including arithmetic, algebra, geometry, calculus, statistics, and their applications. **Physics:** Knowledge and prediction of physical principles, laws, and applications including air, water, material dynamics, light, atomic principles, heat, electric theory, earth formations, and meteorological and related natural phenomena. **Chemistry:** Knowledge of the composition, structure, and properties of substances and of the chemical processes and transformations that they undergo. This includes uses of chemicals and their interactions, danger signs, production techniques, and disposal methods. **Biology:** Knowledge of plant and animal living tissue, cells, organisms, and entities, including their functions, interdependencies, and interactions with each other and the environment. **Education and Training:** Knowledge of instructional methods and training techniques including curriculum design principles, learning theory, group and individual teaching techniques, design of individual development plans, and test design principles. **Public Safety and Security:** Knowledge of weaponry, public safety, and security operations, rules, regulations, precautions, prevention, and the protection of people, data, and property. **Law, Government, and Jurisprudence:** Knowledge of laws, legal codes, court procedures, precedents, government regulations, executive orders, agency rules, and the democratic political process.

Fire-Prevention and Protection Engineers

Research causes of fires; determine fire-protection methods; and design or recommend materials or equipment, such as structural components or fire-detection equipment, to assist organizations in safeguarding life and property against fire, explosion, and related hazards. Determines fire causes and methods of fire prevention. Studies properties concerning fire-prevention factors, such as fire-resistance of construction, contents, water supply and delivery, and exits. Recommends and advises on use of fire-detection equipment, extinguishing devices, or methods to alleviate conditions conducive to fire. Conducts research on fire retardants and fire safety of materials and devices to determine cause and methods of fire prevention. Advises and plans for prevention of destruction by fire, wind, water, or other causes of damage. Evaluates fire departments and laws and regulations affecting fire prevention or fire safety. Organizes and trains personnel to carry out fire-protection programs. Designs fire-detection equipment, alarm systems, fire-extinguishing devices and systems, or structural components protection. Teaches courses on fire prevention and protection.

 Occupational Type

Investigative occupations frequently involve working with ideas, and require an extensive amount of thinking. These occupations can involve searching for facts and figuring out problems mentally.

 Skills required of Fire-Prevention and Protection Engineers

Speaking, Science, Active Learning, Instructing, Information Gathering, Idea Generation, Implementation Planning, Operations Analysis, Technology Design, Equipment Selection, Testing, Product Inspection, Identifying Downstream Consequences, Judgment and Decision Making, Systems Evaluation

 College Majors

Engineering, General: An instructional program that generally prepares individuals to apply mathematical and scientific principles to solve a wide variety of practical problems in industry, social organization, public works, and commerce.

Supporting Courses

Sales and Marketing: Knowledge of principles and methods involved in showing, promoting, and selling products or services. This includes marketing strategies and tactics, product demonstration and sales techniques, and sales control systems. **Engineering and Technology:** Knowledge of equipment, tools, mechanical devices, and their uses to produce motion, light, power, technology, and other applications. **Design:** Knowledge of design techniques, principles, tools and instruments involved in the production and use of precision technical plans, blueprints, drawings, and models. **Building and Construction:** Knowledge of materials, methods, and the appropriate tools to construct objects, structures, and buildings. **Physics:** Knowledge and prediction of physical principles, laws, and applications including air, water, material dynamics, light, atomic principles, heat, electric theory, earth formations, and meteorological and related natural phenomena. **Chemistry:** Knowledge of the composition, structure, and properties of substances and of the chemical processes and transformations that they undergo. This includes uses of chemicals and their interactions, danger signs, production techniques, and disposal methods. **Geography:** Knowledge of various methods for describing the location and distribution of land, sea, and air masses including their physical locations, relationships, and characteristics. **Education and Training:** Knowledge of instructional methods and training techniques including curriculum design principles, learning theory, group and individual teaching techniques, design of individual development plans, and test design principles. **Public Safety and Security:** Knowledge of weaponry, public safety, and security operations, rules, regulations, precautions, prevention, and the protection of people, data, and property. **Law, Government, and Jurisprudence:** Knowledge of laws, legal codes, court procedures, precedents, government regulations, executive orders, agency rules, and the democratic political process. **Telecommunications:** Knowledge of transmission, broadcasting, switching, control, and operation of telecommunications systems. **Communications and Media:** Knowledge of media production, communication, and dissemination techniques and methods including alternative ways to inform and entertain via written, oral, and visual media.

Product Safety Engineers

Develop and conduct tests to evaluate product safety levels, and recommend measures to reduce or eliminate hazards. Conducts research to evaluate safety levels for products. Evaluates potential health hazards or damage that could occur from misuse of product, and engineers solutions to improve safety. Investigates causes of accidents, injuries, or illnesses from product usage to develop solutions to minimize or prevent recurrence. Advises and recommends procedures for detection, prevention, and elimination of physical, chemical, or other product hazards. Participates in preparation of product usage and precautionary label instructions. Prepares reports of findings from investigation of accidents.

Occupational Type

Investigative occupations frequently involve working with ideas, and require an extensive amount of thinking. These occupations can involve searching for facts and figuring out problems mentally.

Skills required of Product Safety Engineers

Writing, Mathematics, Science, Critical Thinking, Active Learning, Monitoring, Problem Identification, Information Gathering, Information Organization, Synthesis/Reorganization, Idea Generation, Idea Evaluation, Implementation Planning, Operations Analysis, Technology Design, Testing, Product Inspection, Troubleshooting, Identifying Downstream Consequences, Identification of Key Causes, Judgment and Decision Making

College Majors

Engineering, General: An instructional program that generally prepares individuals to apply mathematical and scientific principles to solve a wide variety of practical problems in industry, social organization, public works, and commerce.

Supporting Courses

Production and Processing: Knowledge of inputs, outputs, raw materials, waste, quality control, costs, and techniques for maximizing the manufacture and distribution of goods. **Engineering and Technology:** Knowledge of equipment, tools, mechanical devices, and their uses to produce motion, light, power, technology, and other applications. **Physics:** Knowledge and prediction of physical principles, laws, and applications including air, water, material dynamics, light, atomic principles, heat, electric theory, earth formations, and meteorological and related natural phenomena. **Chemistry:** Knowledge of the composition, structure, and properties of substances and of the chemical processes and transformations that they undergo. This includes uses of chemicals and their interactions, danger signs, production techniques, and disposal methods. **Biology:** Knowledge of plant and animal living tissue, cells, organisms, and entities, including their functions, interdependencies, and interactions with each other and the environment. **English Language:** Knowledge of the structure and content of the English language including the meaning and spelling of words, rules of composition, and grammar. **Public Safety and Security:** Knowledge of weaponry, public safety, and security operations, rules, regulations, precautions, prevention, and the protection of people, data, and property.

Marine Engineers

Design, develop, and take responsibility for the installation of ship machinery and related equipment, including propulsion machines and power supply systems. (Excludes marine architects.) Designs and oversees testing, installation, and repair of marine apparatus and equipment. Conducts analytical, environmental, operational, or performance studies to develop design for products, such as marine engines, equipment, and structures. Prepares or directs preparation of product or system layout and detailed drawings and schematics. Evaluates operation of marine equipment during acceptance testing and shakedown cruises. Analyzes data to determine feasibility of product proposal. Directs and coordinates manufacturing or building of prototype marine product or system. Confers with research personnel to clarify or resolve problems and develop or modify design. Investigates and observes tests on machinery and equipment for compliance with standards. Conducts environmental, operational, or performance tests on marine machinery and equipment. Plans, conducts, or directs personnel in performing engineering experiments to test or prove theories and principles. Determines conditions under which tests are to be conducted and sequences and phases of test operations. Maintains and coordinates repair of marine machinery and equipment for installation on vessels. Inspects marine equipment and machinery to draw up work requests and job specifications. Reviews work requests and compares them with previous work completed on ship to ensure costs are economically sound. Prepares technical reports on types of testing conducted, completed repairs, and cost of repairs for engineering, management, or sales personnel. Prepares technical reports for use by engineering, management, or sales personnel. Maintains contact and formulates reports for contractors and clients to ensure completion of work at minimum cost. Coordinates activities with those of regulatory bodies to ensure repairs and alterations are at minimum cost, consistent with safety. Obtains readings on tail shaft and tail shaft bearings, using measuring devices. Procures materials needed to repair marine equipment and machinery.

Occupational Type

Realistic occupations frequently involve work activities that include practical, hands-on problems and solutions. They often deal with plants, animals, and real-world materials like wood, tools, and machinery. Many of the occupations require working outside, and do not involve a lot of paperwork or working closely with others.

Skills required of Marine Engineers

Reading Comprehension, Active Listening, Writing, Speaking, Mathematics, Science, Critical Thinking, Active Learning, Monitoring, Coordination, Negotiation, Problem Identification, Information Gathering, Information Organization, Synthesis/Reorganization, Idea Generation, Idea Evaluation, Implementation Planning, Operations Analysis, Technology Design, Equipment Selection, Installation, Testing, Operation Monitoring, Product Inspection, Equipment Maintenance, Troubleshooting, Visioning, Systems Perception, Identifying Downstream Consequences, Identification of Key Causes, Judgment and Decision Making, Systems Evaluation, Time Management, Management of Material Resources, Management of Personnel Resources

College Majors

Engineering, General: An instructional program that generally prepares individuals to apply mathematical and scientific principles to solve a wide variety of practical problems in industry, social organization, public works, and commerce.

Supporting Courses

Administration and Management: Knowledge of principles and processes involved in business and organizational planning, coordination, and execution. This includes strategic planning, resource allocation, manpower modeling, leadership techniques, and production methods. **Economics and Accounting:** Knowledge of economic and accounting principles and practices, the financial markets, banking, and the analysis and reporting of financial data. **Engineering and Technology:** Knowledge of equipment, tools, mechanical devices, and their uses to produce motion, light, power, technology, and other applications. **Design:** Knowledge of design techniques, principles, tools and instruments involved in the production and use of precision technical plans, blueprints, drawings, and models. **Building and Construction:** Knowledge of materials, methods, and the appropriate tools to construct objects, structures, and buildings. **Mechanical:** Knowledge of machines and tools, including their designs, uses, benefits, repair, and maintenance. **Mathematics:** Knowledge of numbers, their operations, and interrelationships including arithmetic, algebra, geometry, calculus, statistics, and their applications. **Physics:** Knowledge and prediction of physical principles, laws, and applications including air, water, material dynamics, light, atomic principles, heat, electric theory, earth formations, and meteorological and related natural phenomena. **Chemistry:** Knowledge of the composition, structure, and properties of substances and of the chemical processes and transformations that they undergo. This includes uses of chemicals and their interactions, danger signs, production techniques, and disposal methods. **Geography:** Knowledge of various methods for describing the location and distribution of land, sea, and air masses including their physical locations, relationships, and characteristics. **English Language:** Knowledge of the structure and content of the English language including the meaning and spelling of words, rules of composition, and grammar. **Public Safety and Security:** Knowledge of weaponry, public safety, and security operations, rules, regulations, precautions, prevention, and the protection of people, data, and property. **Law, Government, and Jurisprudence:** Knowledge of laws, legal codes, court procedures, precedents, government regulations, executive orders, agency rules, and the democratic political process. **Transportation:** Knowledge of principles and methods for moving people or goods by air, rail, sea, or road, including their relative costs, advantages, and limitations.

Production Engineers

Develop, advance, and improve products, processes, or materials, and build or supervise the building of prototypes. May operate machinery, equipment, or hand tools to produce their prototypes. Conducts research and analytical studies to develop design or specifications for products. Directs and coordinates manufacturing of building of prototype or system. Confers with research and other engineering personnel to clarify and resolve problems, and prepares design modifications as needed. Prepares or directs preparation of product or system layout and detailed drawings and schematics. Analyzes data to determine feasibility of product proposal. Plans and develops experimental test programs. Analyzes test data and reports to determine if design meets functional and performance specifications. Evaluates engineering test results for possible application to development of systems or other uses.

 Occupational Type

Investigative occupations frequently involve working with ideas, and require an extensive amount of thinking. These occupations can involve searching for facts and figuring out problems mentally.

Skills required of Production Engineers

Reading Comprehension, Active Listening, Writing, Speaking, Mathematics, Science, Critical Thinking, Active Learning, Learning Strategies, Monitoring, Coordination, Problem Identification, Information Gathering, Information Organization, Synthesis/Reorganization, Idea Generation, Idea Evaluation, Implementation Planning, Operations Analysis, Technology Design, Equipment Selection, Programming, Testing, Operation Monitoring, Operation and Control, Product Inspection, Troubleshooting, Visioning, Systems Perception, Identifying Downstream Consequences, Identification of Key Causes, Judgment and Decision Making, Systems Evaluation, Time Management, Management of Material Resources, Management of Personnel Resources

 ## College Majors

Engineering, General: An instructional program that generally prepares individuals to apply mathematical and scientific principles to solve a wide variety of practical problems in industry, social organization, public works, and commerce.

 ## Supporting Courses

Administration and Management: Knowledge of principles and processes involved in business and organizational planning, coordination, and execution. This includes strategic planning, resource allocation, manpower modeling, leadership techniques, and production methods. **Production and Processing:** Knowledge of inputs, outputs, raw materials, waste, quality control, costs, and techniques for maximizing the manufacture and distribution of goods. **Computers and Electronics:** Knowledge of electric circuit boards, processors, chips, and computer hardware and software, including applications and programming. **Engineering and Technology:** Knowledge of equipment, tools, mechanical devices, and their uses to produce motion, light, power, technology, and other applications. **Design:** Knowledge of design techniques, principles, tools and instruments involved in the production and use of precision technical plans, blueprints, drawings, and models. **Mechanical:** Knowledge of machines and tools, including their designs, uses, benefits, repair, and maintenance. **Mathematics:** Knowledge of numbers, their operations, and interrelationships including arithmetic, algebra, geometry, calculus, statistics, and their applications. **Physics:** Knowledge and prediction of physical principles, laws, and applications including air, water, material dynamics, light, atomic principles, heat, electric theory, earth formations, and meteorological and related natural phenomena. **English Language:** Knowledge of the structure and content of the English language including the meaning and spelling of words, rules of composition, and grammar.

All Other Engineers

All other engineers not classified separately above.

Occupational Type

Specific information is not available.

Skills required of All Other Engineers

Information on specific skills required is not available.

College Majors

Engineering, General: An instructional program that generally prepares individuals to apply mathematical and scientific principles to solve a wide variety of practical problems in industry, social organization, public works, and commerce.

Supporting Courses

Specific information is not available.

PROPERTY AND REAL ESTATE MANAGERS

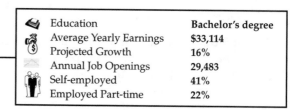

Education	Bachelor's degree
Average Yearly Earnings	$33,114
Projected Growth	16%
Annual Job Openings	29,483
Self-employed	41%
Employed Part-time	22%

Land Leasing and Development Managers

Plan, direct, and coordinate the acquisition or disposition of land, rights-of-way, or property rights for development, mineral, oil, or gas rights, or other special use through options, purchase, or lease agreements. Makes final decisions regarding sales, leases, and purchases of real property based on evaluation of costs, available resources, and organizational interests. Negotiates terms and conditions of agreements with property owners, public officials, and community representatives, and signs contracts to finalize transactions. Directs and coordinates collection and auditing of funds from sales, purchases, and leases. Directs staff activities, such as preparing appraisal reports and feasibility studies, identifying availability and quality of land, and ascertaining ownership. Administers and interprets general policies made by company officials and ensures conformance to established standards. Studies financial transactions of competing companies or brokers to determine expenditure necessary to obtain leases and other contracts. Prepares statistical abstracts to reveal trends in tax rates and proportion of workforce having specified skills in a given community. Evaluates and promotes industrial-development potential of company properties. Plans and directs field staff activities such as mineral sampling, surveying, and water testing to determine optimal land usage. Coordinates research activities with public utilities, universities, and other groups. Authorizes or requests authorization for maintenance of noncontrolled company properties such as dwellings, hotels, or commissaries. Determines roads, bridges, and utility systems that must be maintained during construction. Settles claims for property or crop damage.

Occupational Type

Enterprising occupations frequently involve starting up and carrying out projects. These occupations can involve leading people and making many decisions. Sometimes they involve risk taking and often deal with business.

Skills required of Land Leasing and Development Managers

Reading Comprehension, Active Listening, Writing, Speaking, Critical Thinking, Active Learning, Social Perceptiveness, Coordination, Persuasion, Negotiation, Service Orientation, Problem Identification, Information Gathering, Information Organization, Synthesis/Reorganization, Idea Generation, Idea Evaluation, Implementation Planning, Programming, Systems Perception, Identifying Downstream Consequences, Identification of Key Causes, Judgment and Decision Making, Systems Evaluation, Time Management, Management of Financial Resources, Management of Material Resources, Management of Personnel Resources

College Majors

Real Estate: An instructional program that prepares individuals to develop, buy, sell, appraise, and manage real property. Includes instruction in land use development policy, real estate law, real estate marketing procedures, agency management, brokerage, property inspection and appraisal, real estate investing, leased and rental properties, commercial real estate, and property management.

Supporting Courses

Administration and Management: Knowledge of principles and processes involved in business and organizational planning, coordination, and execution. This includes strategic planning, resource allocation, manpower modeling, leadership techniques, and production methods. **Economics and Accounting:** Knowledge of economic and accounting principles and practices, the financial markets, banking, and the analysis and reporting of financial data. **Sales and Marketing:** Knowledge of principles and methods involved in showing, promoting, and selling products or services. This includes marketing strategies and tactics, product demonstration and sales techniques, and sales control systems. **Mathematics:** Knowledge of numbers, their operations, and interrelationships including arithmetic, algebra, geometry, calculus, statistics, and their applications. **Geography:** Knowledge of various methods for describing the location and distribution of land, sea, and air masses including their physical locations, relationships, and characteristics. **English Language:** Knowledge of the structure and content of the English language including the meaning and spelling of words, rules of composition, and grammar. **Law, Government, and Jurisprudence:** Knowledge of laws, legal codes, court procedures, precedents, government regulations, executive orders, agency rules, and the democratic political process.

Property, Real Estate, and Community Association Managers

Plan, direct, and coordinate selling, buying, leasing, or governance activities of commercial, industrial, or residential real estate properties. Include managers of homeowner and condominium associations, rented or leased housing units, buildings, or land—including rights-of-way. (Excludes workers whose duties are not primarily managerial. Workers who are engaged primarily in direct buying, selling, or renting of real estate are reported as sales workers.) Manages and oversees operations, maintenance, and administrative functions for commercial, industrial, or residential properties. Directs collection of monthly assessments, rental fees and deposits, and payment of insurance premiums, mortgage, taxes, and incurred operating expenses. Meets with clients to negotiate management and service contracts, determine priorities, and discuss financial and operational status of property. Plans, schedules, and coordinates general maintenance, major repairs, and remodeling or construction projects for commercial or residential property. Investigates complaints, disturbances, and violations, and resolves problems following management rules and regulations. Recruits, hires, and trains managerial, clerical, and maintenance staff, or contracts with vendors for security, maintenance, extermination, or groundskeeping personnel. Directs and coordinates the activities of staff and contract personnel and evaluates performance. Maintains records of sales, rental or usage activity, special permits issued, maintenance and operating costs, or property availability. Purchases building and maintenance supplies, equipment, or furniture. Develops and administers annual operating budget. Negotiates for sale, lease, or development of property, and completes or reviews appropriate documents and forms. Inspects facilities and equipment, and inventories building contents to document damage and determine repair needs. Assembles and analyzes construction and vendor service contract bids. Confers with legal authority to ensure transactions and terminations of contracts and agreements are in accordance with court orders, laws, and regulations. Maintains contact with insurance carrier, fire and police departments, and other agencies to ensure protection and compliance with codes and regulations. Prepares reports summarizing financial and operational status of property or facility. Meets with prospective leasers to show property, explain terms of occupancy, and provide information about local area.

Occupational Type

Enterprising occupations frequently involve starting up and carrying out projects. These occupations can involve leading people and making many decisions. Sometimes they involve risk taking and often deal with business.

Skills required of Property, Real Estate, and Community Association Managers

Reading Comprehension, Active Listening, Writing, Speaking, Social Perceptiveness, Coordination, Persuasion, Negotiation, Service Orientation, Problem Identification, Information Gathering, Idea Generation, Idea Evaluation, Implementation Planning, Visioning, Systems Perception, Identifying Downstream Consequences, Identification of Key Causes, Judgment and Decision Making, Systems Evaluation, Time Management, Management of Financial Resources, Management of Material Resources, Management of Personnel Resources

College Majors

Real Estate: An instructional program that prepares individuals to develop, buy, sell, appraise, and manage real property. Includes instruction in land use development policy, real estate law, real estate marketing procedures, agency management, brokerage, property inspection and appraisal, real estate investing, leased and rental properties, commercial real estate, and property management.

 Supporting Courses

Administration and Management: Knowledge of principles and processes involved in business and organizational planning, coordination, and execution. This includes strategic planning, resource allocation, manpower modeling, leadership techniques, and production methods. **Economics and Accounting:** Knowledge of economic and accounting principles and practices, the financial markets, banking, and the analysis and reporting of financial data. **Sales and Marketing:** Knowledge of principles and methods involved in showing, promoting, and selling products or services. This includes marketing strategies and tactics, product demonstration and sales techniques, and sales control systems. **Personnel and Human Resources:** Knowledge of policies and practices involved in personnel/human resource functions. This includes recruitment, selection, training, and promotion regulations and procedures; compensation and benefits packages; labor relations and negotiation strategies; and personnel information systems. **Building and Construction:** Knowledge of materials, methods, and the appropriate tools to construct objects, structures, and buildings. **Law, Government, and Jurisprudence:** Knowledge of laws, legal codes, court procedures, precedents, government regulations, executive orders, agency rules, and the democratic political process.

Property Records Managers

Direct and coordinate activities in an organization relating to searching, examining, and recording information for property-related documents to determine status of property titles or property rights. Directs and coordinates researching and recordkeeping activities concerning ownership, contractual terms and conditions, and expiration dates of land documents. Prepares work schedules, and assigns projects to prioritize activities for title search staff. Monitors status of pending research assignments, and confers with staff to resolve production and quality problems. Confers with employees and other managers to establish and modify policies and procedures. Conducts performance appraisals and makes recommendations for personnel actions such as promotions, remedial training, transfers, and terminations. Authorizes royalty payments, bonuses, and other compensation as specified by terms and conditions of legal documents. Oversees the signing of real estate closing documents to verify transfer of title and proper disbursement of documents and escrow funds. Develops and conducts training programs for new hires, and provides continuing in-service training for current employees. Oversees preparation of timesheets, and reviews payroll information. Recruits, interviews, and hires title department personnel. Performs difficult and involved title searches. Reviews accuracy and completeness of legal documents, such as title reports, deeds, affidavits, and other data, to ensure the legality of business transactions. Discusses search delays and title defects, such as outstanding liens or judgments, with legal counsel. Prepares reports to summarize terms and conditions of existing contracts, leases, and agreements, and to provide information for renegotiations. Completes purchase orders for equipment and supplies.

Occupational Type

Enterprising occupations frequently involve starting up and carrying out projects. These occupations can involve leading people and making many decisions. Sometimes they involve risk taking and often deal with business.

Skills required of Property Records Managers

Reading Comprehension, Active Listening, Writing, Speaking, Active Learning, Learning Strategies, Social Perceptiveness, Coordination, Persuasion, Negotiation, Instructing, Information Gathering, Information Organization, Idea Generation, Idea Evaluation, Implementation Planning, Systems Perception, Identifying Downstream Consequences, Identification of Key Causes, Judgment and Decision Making, Systems Evaluation, Time Management, Management of Financial Resources, Management of Material Resources, Management of Personnel Resources

College Majors

Paralegal/Legal Assistant: An instructional program that prepares individuals to perform research, drafting, investigatory, recordkeeping and related administrative functions under the supervision of an attorney. Includes instruction in legal research, drafting legal documents, appraising, pleading, courthouse procedures and legal specializations.

Supporting Courses

Administration and Management: Knowledge of principles and processes involved in business and organizational planning, coordination, and execution. This includes strategic planning, resource allocation, manpower modeling, leadership techniques, and production methods. **Economics and Accounting:** Knowledge of economic and accounting principles and practices, the financial markets, banking, and the analysis and reporting of financial data. **Personnel and Human Resources:** Knowledge of policies and practices involved in personnel/human resource functions. This includes recruitment, selection, training, and promotion regulations and procedures; compensation and benefits packages; labor relations and negotiation strategies; and personnel information systems. **Education and Training:** Knowledge of instructional methods and training techniques including curriculum design principles, learning theory, group and individual teaching techniques, design of individual development plans, and test design principles. **English Language:** Knowledge of the structure and content of the English language including the meaning and spelling of words, rules of composition, and grammar. **Law, Government, and Jurisprudence:** Knowledge of laws, legal codes, court procedures, precedents, government regulations, executive orders, agency rules, and the democratic political process.

PSYCHIATRIC TECHNICIANS

Education		Associate degree
Average Yearly Earnings		$20,218
Projected Growth		9%
Annual Job Openings		14,819
Self-employed		0%
Employed Part-time		26%

PSYCHOLOGISTS

Education		Master's degree
Average Yearly Earnings		$48,090
Projected Growth		8%
Annual Job Openings		10,913
Self-employed		40%
Employed Part-Time		23%

Developmental Psychologists

Study and research the emotional, mental, physical, and social growth and development of individuals, from birth to death, to increase understanding of human behavior and processes of human growth and decline. Formulates hypothesis or researches problem regarding growth, development, and decline of emotional, mental, physical, and social processes in individuals. Selects or develops method of investigation to test hypothesis. Studies behavior of children to analyze processes of learning, language development, and parental influence on children's behavior. Analyzes growth or change of social values and attitudes, using information obtained from observation, questionnaires, and interviews. Administers intelligence and performance tests to establish and measure human patterns of intellectual and psychological growth, development, and decline. Observes and records behavior of infants to establish patterns of social, motor, and sensory development. Formulates theories based on research findings for application in such fields as juvenile delinquency, education, parenting, and gerontology. Experiments with animals to conduct cross-species comparative studies to contribute to understanding of human behavior.

 ## Occupational Type

Investigative occupations frequently involve working with ideas, and require an extensive amount of thinking. These occupations can involve searching for facts and figuring out problems mentally.

 ## Skills required of Developmental Psychologists

Reading Comprehension, Active Listening, Writing, Speaking, Mathematics, Science, Critical Thinking, Active Learning, Learning Strategies, Monitoring, Social Perceptiveness, Service Orientation, Problem Identification, Information Gathering, Information Organization,

Synthesis/Reorganization, Idea Generation, Idea Evaluation, Implementation Planning, Programming, Visioning, Systems Perception, Identifying Downstream Consequences, Identification of Key Causes, Judgment and Decision Making, Systems Evaluation

 College Majors

Psychology, General: An instructional program that generally describes the scientific study of individual and collective behavior, the physical and environmental bases of behavior, and the analysis and treatment of behavior problems and disorders. Includes instruction in the principles of the various subfields of psychology, research methods, and psychological assessment and testing methods.

Supporting Courses

Mathematics: Knowledge of numbers, their operations, and interrelationships including arithmetic, algebra, geometry, calculus, statistics, and their applications. **Biology:** Knowledge of plant and animal living tissue, cells, organisms, and entities, including their functions, interdependencies, and interactions with each other and the environment. **Psychology:** Knowledge of human behavior and performance, mental processes, psychological research methods, and the assessment and treatment of behavioral and affective disorders. **Sociology and Anthropology:** Knowledge of group behavior and dynamics, societal trends and influences, cultures, their history, migrations, ethnicity, and origins. **Therapy and Counseling:** Knowledge of information and techniques needed to rehabilitate physical and mental ailments and to provide career guidance including alternative treatments, rehabilitation equipment and its proper use, and methods to evaluate treatment effects. **Education and Training:** Knowledge of instructional methods and training techniques including curriculum design principles, learning theory, group and individual teaching techniques, design of individual development plans, and test design principles. **English Language:** Knowledge of the structure and content of the English language including the meaning and spelling of words, rules of composition, and grammar. **Philosophy and Theology:** Knowledge of different philosophical systems and religions, including their basic principles, values, ethics, ways of thinking, customs, and practices, and their impact on human culture.

Experimental Psychologists

Plan, design, and conduct, laboratory experiments to investigate animal or human physiology, perception, memory, learning, personality, and cognitive processes. Conduct interdisciplinary studies with scientists in such fields as physiology, biology, and sociology. Formulates hypotheses and experimental designs to investigate problems of perception, memory, learning, personality, and cognitive processes. Selects, controls, and modifies variables in human or animal laboratory experiments, and observes and records behavior in relation to variables. Analyzes test results, using statistical techniques, and evaluates significance of data in relation to original hypotheses. Conducts research in areas such as aesthetics, learning, emotion, motivation, electroencephalography, motor skills, autonomic functions, and the relationship of behavior to physiology. Designs and constructs equipment and apparatus for laboratory study. Writes scientific papers describing experiments and interpreting research results for publication or presentation. Studies animal behavior to develop theories on comparison of animal and human behavior. Collaborates with scientists in such fields as physiology, biology, and sociology to conduct interdisciplinary studies and formulate theories of behavior.

Occupational Type

Investigative occupations frequently involve working with ideas, and require an extensive amount of thinking. These occupations can involve searching for facts and figuring out problems mentally.

Skills required of Experimental Psychologists

Reading Comprehension, Active Listening, Writing, Speaking, Mathematics, Science, Critical Thinking, Active Learning, Monitoring, Social Perceptiveness, Problem Identification, Information Gathering, Information Organization, Synthesis/Reorganization, Idea Generation, Idea Evaluation, Implementation Planning, Operations Analysis, Technology Design, Programming, Systems Perception, Judgment and Decision Making, Systems Evaluation

College Majors

Psychology, General: An instructional program that generally describes the scientific study of individual and collective behavior, the physical and environmental bases of behavior, and the analysis and treatment of behavior problems and disorders. Includes instruction in the principles of the various subfields of psychology, research methods, and psychological assessment and testing methods.

Supporting Courses

Mathematics: Knowledge of numbers, their operations, and interrelationships including arithmetic, algebra, geometry, calculus, statistics, and their applications. **Biology:** Knowledge of plant and animal living tissue, cells, organisms, and entities, including their functions, interdependencies, and interactions with each other and the environment. **Psychology:** Knowledge of human behavior and performance, mental processes, psychological research methods, and the assessment and treatment of behavioral and affective disorders. **Sociology and Anthropology:** Knowledge of group behavior and dynamics, societal trends and influences, cultures, their history, migrations, ethnicity, and origins. **English Language:** Knowledge of the structure and content of the English language including the meaning and spelling of words, rules of composition, and grammar.

Educational Psychologists

Investigate processes of learning and teaching, and develop psychological principles and techniques applicable to educational problems. Conducts experiments to study educational problems, such as motivation, adjustment, teacher training, and individual differences in mental abilities. Conducts research to aid introduction of programs in schools to meet current psychological, educational, and sociological needs of children. Investigates traits, attitudes, and feelings of teachers to predict conditions that affect teachers' mental health and success with students. Formulates achievement, diagnostic, and predictive tests to aid teachers in planning methods and content of instruction. Interprets and explains test results, in terms of norms, reliability, and validity to teachers, counselors, students, and other entitled parties. Plans remedial classes and testing programs designed to meet needs of special students. Advises teachers and other school personnel on methods to enhance school and classroom atmosphere to maximize student learning and motivation. Analyzes characteristics and adjustment needs of students having various mental abilities, and recommends educational program to promote maximum adjustment. Evaluates needs, limitations, and potentials of child, through observation, review of school records, and consultation with parents and school personnel. Administers standardized tests to evaluate intelligence, achievement, and personality, and to diagnose disabilities and difficulties among students. Collaborates with education specialists in developing curriculum content and methods of organizing and conducting classroom work. Recommends placement of students in classes and treatment programs based on individual needs. Counsels pupils individually and in groups to assist pupils to achieve personal, social, and emotional adjustment. Advises school board, superintendent, administrative committees, and parent-teacher groups regarding provision of psychological services within educational system or school. Refers individuals to community agencies to obtain medical, vocational, or social services for child or family.

Occupational Type

Investigative occupations frequently involve working with ideas, and require an extensive amount of thinking. These occupations can involve searching for facts and figuring out problems mentally.

Skills required of Educational Psychologists

Reading Comprehension, Active Listening, Writing, Speaking, Mathematics, Science, Critical Thinking, Active Learning, Learning Strategies, Monitoring, Social Perceptiveness, Coordination, Persuasion, Negotiation, Instructing, Service Orientation, Problem Identification, Information Gathering, Information Organization, Synthesis/Reorganization, Idea Generation, Idea Evaluation, Implementation Planning, Operations Analysis, Programming, Visioning, Systems Perception, Identifying Downstream Consequences, Identification of Key Causes, Judgment and Decision Making, Systems Evaluation

College Majors

Educational Assessment, Testing and Measurement: An instructional program that describes the principles and procedures for designing, developing, implementing and evaluating tests and other mechanisms used to measure learning, evaluate student progress, and assess the performance of specific teaching tools, strategies and curricula. Includes instruction in psychometric measurement, instrument design, test implementation techniques, research evaluation, data reporting requirements, and data analysis and interpretation.

Supporting Courses

Administration and Management: Knowledge of principles and processes involved in business and organizational planning, coordination, and execution. This includes strategic planning, resource allocation, manpower modeling, leadership techniques, and production methods. **Mathematics:** Knowledge of numbers, their operations, and interrelationships including arithmetic, algebra, geometry, calculus, statistics, and their applications. **Psychology:** Knowledge of human behavior and performance, mental processes, psychological research methods, and the assessment and treatment of behavioral and affective disorders. **Sociology and Anthropology:** Knowledge of group behavior and dynamics, societal trends and influences, cultures, their history, migrations, ethnicity, and origins. **Therapy and Counseling:** Knowledge of information and techniques needed to rehabilitate physical and mental ailments and to provide career guidance including alternative treatments, rehabilitation equipment and its proper use, and methods to evaluate treatment effects. **Education and Training:** Knowledge of instructional methods and training techniques including curriculum design principles, learning theory, group and individual teaching techniques, design of individual development plans, and test design principles. **English Language:** Knowledge of the structure and content of the English language including the meaning and spelling of words, rules of composition, and grammar.

Social Psychologists

Investigate psychological aspects of human interrelationships to gain understanding of individual and group thought, feeling, and behavior. Conduct research to analyze attitude, motivation, opinion, and group behavior, using behavioral observation, experimentation, or survey techniques. Observes and analyzes individual relationships, behavior, and attitudes within and toward religious, racial, political, occupational, and other groups. Researches variables, such as prejudice, values transmission, motivation, morals, leadership, and the contribution of social factors to behavior. Conducts surveys and polls, using statistical sampling techniques, to measure and analyze attitudes and opinions. Utilizes research findings to predict economic, political, and other behavior of groups. Develops techniques, such as rating scales and sampling methods, to collect and measure behavioral data. Prepares reports documenting research methods and findings.

Occupational Type

Investigative occupations frequently involve working with ideas, and require an extensive amount of thinking. These occupations can involve searching for facts and figuring out problems mentally.

Skills required of Social Psychologists

Reading Comprehension, Active Listening, Writing, Speaking, Mathematics, Science, Critical Thinking, Active Learning, Social Perceptiveness, Information Gathering, Information Organization, Synthesis/Reorganization, Implementation Planning, Programming, Systems Perception, Identifying Downstream Consequences, Systems Evaluation

College Majors

Psychology, General: An instructional program that generally describes the scientific study of individual and collective behavior, the physical and environmental bases of behavior, and the analysis and treatment of behavior problems and disorders. Includes instruction in the principles of the various subfields of psychology, research methods, and psychological assessment and testing methods.

 Supporting Courses

Administration and Management: Knowledge of principles and processes involved in business and organizational planning, coordination, and execution. This includes strategic planning, resource allocation, manpower modeling, leadership techniques, and production methods. **Mathematics:** Knowledge of numbers, their operations, and interrelationships including arithmetic, algebra, geometry, calculus, statistics, and their applications. **Psychology:** Knowledge of human behavior and performance, mental processes, psychological research methods, and the assessment and treatment of behavioral and affective disorders. **Sociology and Anthropology:** Knowledge of group behavior and dynamics, societal trends and influences, cultures, their history, migrations, ethnicity, and origins. **English Language:** Knowledge of the structure and content of the English language including the meaning and spelling of words, rules of composition, and grammar. **Philosophy and Theology:** Knowledge of different philosophical systems and religions, including their basic principles, values, ethics, ways of thinking, customs, and practices, and their impact on human culture.

Clinical Psychologists

Diagnose or evaluate mental and emotional disorders of individuals through observation, interview, and psychological tests; formulate and administer programs of treatment. Observes individual at play, in group interactions, or other situations to detect indications of mental deficiency, abnormal behavior, or maladjustment. Develops treatment plan, including type, frequency, intensity, and duration of therapy, in collaboration with psychiatrists and other specialists. Analyzes information to assess client problems, determine advisability of counseling, and refer client to other specialists, institutions, or support services. Conducts individual and group counseling sessions regarding psychological or emotional problems, such as stress, substance abuse, and family situations. Responds to client reactions, evaluates effectiveness of counseling or treatment, and modifies plan as needed. Interviews individuals, couples, or families, and reviews records to obtain information on medical, psychological, emotional, relationship, or other problems. Selects, administers, scores, and interprets psychological tests to obtain information on individual's intelligence, achievement, interest, and personality. Utilizes treatment methods, such as psychotherapy, hypnosis, behavior modification, stress reduction therapy, psychodrama, and play therapy. Plans and develops accredited psychological service programs in psychiatric center or hospital, in collaboration with psychiatrists and other professional staff. Consults reference material, such as textbooks, manuals, and journals, to identify symptoms, make diagnoses, and develop approach to treatment. Assists clients to gain insight, define goals, and plan action to achieve effective personal, social, educational, and vocational development and adjustment. Provides occupational, educational, and other information to enable individual to formulate realistic educational and vocational plans. Plans, supervises, and conducts psychological research in fields such as personality development and diagnosis, treatment, and prevention of mental disorders. Directs, coordinates, and evaluates activities of psychological staff and student interns engaged in patient evaluation and treatment in psychiatric facility. Provides psychological services and advice to private firms and community agencies on individual cases or mental health programs. Develops, directs, and participates in staff training programs.

 ## Occupational Type

Investigative occupations frequently involve working with ideas, and require an extensive amount of thinking. These occupations can involve searching for facts and figuring out problems mentally.

 ## Skills required of Clinical Psychologists

Reading Comprehension, Active Listening, Writing, Speaking, Science, Critical Thinking, Active Learning, Learning Strategies, Monitoring, Social Perceptiveness, Coordination, Persuasion, Negotiation, Instructing, Service Orientation, Problem Identification, Information Gathering, Information Organization, Synthesis/Reorganization, Idea Generation, Idea Evaluation, Implementation Planning, Visioning, Systems Perception, Identifying Downstream Consequences, Identification of Key Causes, Judgment and Decision Making, Systems Evaluation, Time Management, Management of Personnel Resources

 ## College Majors

Psychology, General: An instructional program that generally describes the scientific study of individual and collective behavior, the physical and environmental bases of behavior, and the analysis and treatment of behavior problems and disorders. Includes instruction in the principles of the various subfields of psychology, research methods, and psychological assessment and testing methods.

 ## Supporting Courses

Administration and Management: Knowledge of principles and processes involved in business and organizational planning, coordination, and execution. This includes strategic planning, resource allocation, manpower modeling, leadership techniques, and production methods. **Customer and Personal Service:** Knowledge of principles and processes for providing customer and personal services including needs assessment techniques, quality service standards, alternative delivery systems, and customer satisfaction evaluation techniques. **Personnel and Human Resources:** Knowledge of policies and practices involved in personnel/human resource functions. This includes recruitment, selection, training, and promotion regulations and procedures; compensation and benefits packages; labor relations and negotiation strategies; and personnel information systems. **Biology:** Knowledge

P

of plant and animal living tissue, cells, organisms, and entities, including their functions, interdependencies, and interactions with each other and the environment. **Psychology:** Knowledge of human behavior and performance, mental processes, psychological research methods, and the assessment and treatment of behavioral and affective disorders. **Sociology and Anthropology:** Knowledge of group behavior and dynamics, societal trends and influences, cultures, their history, migrations, ethnicity, and origins. **Medicine and Dentistry:** Knowledge of the information and techniques needed to diagnose and treat injuries, diseases, and deformities. This includes symptoms, treatment alternatives, drug properties and interactions, and preventive healthcare measures. **Therapy and Counseling:** Knowledge of information and techniques needed to rehabilitate physical and mental ailments and to provide career guidance including alternative treatments, rehabilitation equipment and its proper use, and methods to evaluate treatment effects. **Education and Training:** Knowledge of instructional methods and training techniques including curriculum design principles, learning theory, group and individual teaching techniques, design of individual development plans, and test design principles. **English Language:** Knowledge of the structure and content of the English language including the meaning and spelling of words, rules of composition, and grammar.

Counseling Psychologists

Assess and evaluate individuals' problems through the use of case histories, interviews, and observation, and provide individual or group counseling services to assist individuals in achieving more effective personal, social, educational, and vocational development and adjustment. Counsels clients to assist them in understanding personal or interactive problems, defining goals, and developing realistic action plans. Collects information about individuals or clients, using interviews, case histories, observational techniques, and other assessment methods. Develops therapeutic and treatment plans based on individual interests, abilities, or needs of clients. Selects, administers, or interprets psychological tests to assess intelligence, aptitude, ability, or interests. Advises clients on the potential benefits of counseling, or makes referrals to specialists or other institutions for noncounseling problems. Analyzes data, such as interview notes, test results, and reference manuals and texts to identify symptoms and diagnose the nature of client's problems. Evaluates results of counseling methods to determine the reliability and validity of treatments. Consults with other professionals to discuss therapy or treatment, counseling resources or techniques, and to share occupational information. Conducts research to develop or improve diagnostic or therapeutic counseling techniques.

Occupational Type

Social occupations frequently involve working with, communicating with, and teaching people. These occupations often involve helping or providing service to others.

Skills required of Counseling Psychologists

Reading Comprehension, Active Listening, Writing, Speaking, Science, Critical Thinking, Active Learning, Learning Strategies, Monitoring, Social Perceptiveness, Persuasion,

Negotiation, Instructing, Service Orientation, Problem Identification, Information Gathering, Information Organization, Synthesis/Reorganization, Idea Generation, Idea Evaluation, Implementation Planning, Visioning, Identifying Downstream Consequences, Identification of Key Causes, Judgment and Decision Making

College Majors

Counselor Education/Student Counseling and Guidance Services: An instructional program that prepares individuals to apply the theory and principles of guidance and counseling to the provision of support for the personal, social, educational, and vocational development of students, and the organizing of guidance services within elementary, middle and secondary educational institutions. Includes instruction in legal and professional requirements, therapeutic counselor intervention, vocational counseling, and related sociological and psychological foundations.

Supporting Courses

Psychology: Knowledge of human behavior and performance, mental processes, psychological research methods, and the assessment and treatment of behavioral and affective disorders. **Sociology and Anthropology:** Knowledge of group behavior and dynamics, societal trends and influences, cultures, their history, migrations, ethnicity, and origins. **Therapy and Counseling:** Knowledge of information and techniques needed to rehabilitate physical and mental ailments and to provide career guidance including alternative treatments, rehabilitation equipment and its proper use, and methods to evaluate treatment effects. **Education and Training:** Knowledge of instructional methods and training techniques including curriculum design principles, learning theory, group and individual teaching techniques, design of individual development plans, and test design principles. **Philosophy and Theology:** Knowledge of different philosophical systems and religions, including their basic principles, values, ethics, ways of thinking, customs, and practices, and their impact on human culture.

Industrial-Organizational Psychologists

Apply principles of psychology and human behavior to personnel, administration, management, sales, and marketing problems. Develop personnel policies, instruments, and programs for the selection, placement, training and development, and evaluation of employees. Conduct organizational analysis and programs for organizational development. Conduct research studies of leadership, supervision, morale, motivation, and worker productivity. Develops interview techniques, rating scales, and psychological tests to assess skills, abilities, and interests as aids in selection, placement, and promotion. Conducts research studies of physical work environments, organizational structure, communication systems, group interaction, morale, and motivation to assess organizational functioning. Analyzes data, using statistical methods and applications, to evaluate and measure the effectiveness of program implementation or training. Advises management in strategic changes to personnel, managerial, and marketing policies and practices to improve organizational effectiveness and efficiency. Studies consumer reaction to new products and package designs, using surveys and tests, and measures the effectiveness of advertising media. Plans, develops, and organizes training programs, applying principles of learning and individual differences. Analyzes job requirements to establish criteria for classification, selection, training, and other related personnel functions. Observes and interviews workers to identify the physical, mutual, and educational requirements of job.

Occupational Type

Investigative occupations frequently involve working with ideas, and require an extensive amount of thinking. These occupations can involve searching for facts and figuring out problems mentally.

Skills required of Industrial-Organizational Psychologists

Reading Comprehension, Active Listening, Writing, Speaking, Mathematics, Science, Critical Thinking, Active Learning, Learning Strategies, Monitoring, Social Perceptiveness, Coordination, Persuasion, Negotiation, Instructing, Problem Identification, Information Gathering, Information Organization, Synthesis/Reorganization, Idea Generation, Idea Evaluation, Implementation Planning, Operations Analysis, Visioning, Systems Perception, Identifying Downstream Consequences, Identification of Key Causes, Judgment and Decision Making, Systems Evaluation, Management of Personnel Resources

College Majors

Psychology, General: An instructional program that generally describes the scientific study of individual and collective behavior, the physical and environmental bases of behavior, and the analysis and treatment of behavior problems and disorders. Includes instruction in the principles of the various subfields of psychology, research methods, and psychological assessment and testing methods.

Supporting Courses

Administration and Management: Knowledge of principles and processes involved in business and organizational planning, coordination, and execution. This includes strategic planning, resource allocation, manpower modeling, leadership techniques, and production methods. **Sales and Marketing:** Knowledge of principles and methods involved in showing, promoting, and selling products or services. This includes marketing strategies and tactics, product demonstration and sales techniques, and sales control systems. **Personnel and Human Resources:** Knowledge of policies and practices involved in personnel/human resource functions. This includes recruitment, selection, training, and promotion regulations and procedures; compensation and benefits packages; labor relations and negotiation strategies; and personnel information systems. **Mathematics:** Knowledge of numbers, their operations, and interrelationships including arithmetic, algebra, geometry, calculus, statistics, and their applications. **Psychology:** Knowledge of human behavior and performance, mental processes, psychological research methods, and the assessment and treatment of behavioral and affective disorders. **Sociology and Anthropology:** Knowledge of group behavior and dynamics, societal trends and influences, cultures, their history, migrations, ethnicity, and origins. **Therapy and Counseling:** Knowledge of information and techniques needed to rehabilitate physical and mental ailments and to provide career guidance including alternative treatments, rehabilitation equipment and its proper use, and methods to evaluate treatment effects. **Education and Training:** Knowledge of instructional methods and training techniques including curriculum design principles, learning theory, group and individual teaching techniques, design of individual development plans, and test design principles. **Philosophy and Theology:** Knowledge of different philosophical systems and religions, including their basic principles, values, ethics, ways of thinking, customs, and practices, and their impact on human culture.

PUBLIC RELATIONS SPECIALISTS AND PUBLICITY WRITERS

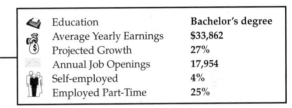

Education		Bachelor's degree
Average Yearly Earnings		$33,862
Projected Growth		27%
Annual Job Openings		17,954
Self-employed		4%
Employed Part-Time		25%

Public Relations Specialists and Publicity Writers

Engage in promoting or creating goodwill for individuals, groups, or organizations by writing or selecting favorable publicity material and releasing it through various communications media. Prepare and arrange displays, make speeches, and perform related publicity efforts. Plans and directs development and communication of informational programs designed to keep public informed of client's products, accomplishments, or agenda. Prepares and distributes fact sheets, news releases, photographs, scripts, motion pictures, or tape recordings to media representatives and others. Promotes sales and/or creates goodwill for client's products, services, or persona by coordinating exhibits, lectures, contests, or public appearances. Prepares or edits organizational publications, such as newsletters to employees or public or stockholders' reports, to favorably present client's viewpoint. Studies needs, objectives, and policies of organization or individual seeking to influence public opinion or promote specific products. Conducts market and public opinion research to introduce or test specific products or measure public opinion. Counsels clients in effective ways of communicating with public. Consults with advertising agencies or staff to arrange promotional campaigns in all types of media for products, organizations, or individuals. Purchases advertising space and time as required to promote client's product or agenda. Arranges for and conducts public-contact programs designed to meet client's objectives. Confers with production and support personnel to coordinate production of advertisements and promotions. Represents client during community projects and at public, social, and business gatherings.

Occupational Type

Enterprising occupations frequently involve starting up and carrying out projects. These occupations can involve leading people and making many decisions. Sometimes they involve risk taking and often deal with business.

Skills required of Public Relations Specialists and Publicity Writers

Active Listening, Writing, Speaking, Critical Thinking, Active Learning, Learning Strategies, Monitoring, Social Perceptiveness, Coordination, Persuasion, Negotiation, Instructing, Service Orientation, Problem Identification, Information Gathering, Information Organization, Synthesis/Reorganization, Idea Generation, Idea Evaluation, Implementation Planning, Programming, Visioning, Systems Perception, Identifying Downstream Consequences, Identification of Key Causes, Systems Evaluation, Time Management, Management of Financial Resources, Management of Material Resources, Management of Personnel Resources

College Majors

Business Services Marketing Operations: An instructional program that prepares individuals to perform marketing tasks specifically applicable to business community services.

Supporting Courses

Clerical: Knowledge of administrative and clerical procedures and systems such as word processing systems, filing and records management systems, stenography and transcription, forms design principles, and other office procedures and terminology. **Sales and Marketing:** Knowledge of principles and methods involved in showing, promoting, and selling products or services. This includes marketing strategies and tactics, product demonstration and sales techniques, and sales control systems. **Personnel and Human Resources:** Knowledge of policies and practices involved in personnel/human resource functions. This includes recruitment, selection, training, and promotion regulations and procedures; compensation and benefits packages; labor relations and negotiation strategies; and personnel information systems. **Computers and Electronics:** Knowledge of electric circuit boards, processors, chips, and computer hardware and software, including applications and programming. **Psychology:** Knowledge of human behavior and performance, mental processes, psychological research methods, and the assessment and treatment of behavioral and affective disorders. **Sociology and Anthropology:** Knowledge of group behavior and dynamics, societal trends and influences, cultures, their history, migrations, ethnicity, and origins. **Therapy and Counseling:** Knowledge of information and techniques needed to rehabilitate physical and mental ailments and to provide career guidance including alternative treatments, rehabilitation equipment and its proper use, and methods to evaluate treatment effects. **Education and Training:** Knowledge of instructional methods and training techniques including curriculum design principles, learning theory, group and individual teaching techniques, design of individual development plans, and test design principles. **Communications and Media:** Knowledge of media production, communication, and dissemination techniques and methods including alternative ways to inform and entertain via written, oral, and visual media.

PURCHASING MANAGERS

Education	Work experience, plus degree	
Average Yearly Earnings	$40,934	
Projected Growth	8%	
Annual Job Openings	10,746	
Self-employed	0%	
Employed Part-Time	3%	

Purchasing Managers

Plan, direct, and coordinate the activities of buyers, purchasing officers, and related workers involved in purchasing materials, products, or services. Include wholesale or retail trade merchandising managers. Directs and coordinates activities of personnel engaged in buying, selling, and distributing materials, equipment, machinery, and supplies. Develops and implements office, operations, and systems instructions, policies, and procedures. Conducts inventory and directs buyers in purchase of products, materials, and supplies. Determines merchandise costs and formulates and coordinates merchandising policies and activities to ensure profit. Represents company in formulating policies and negotiating contracts with suppliers and unions. Prepares, reviews, and processes requisitions and purchase orders for supplies and equipment. Analyzes market and delivery systems to determine present and future material availability. Prepares report regarding market conditions and merchandise costs. Consults with department personnel to develop and plan sales promotion programs. Studies work flow, sequence of operations, and office arrangement to determine need for new or improved office machines.

Occupational Type

Enterprising occupations frequently involve starting up and carrying out projects. These occupations can involve leading people and making many decisions. Sometimes they involve risk taking and often deal with business.

Skills required of Purchasing Managers

Active Listening, Writing, Speaking, Social Perceptiveness, Coordination, Persuasion, Negotiation, Problem Identification, Information Gathering, Information Organization, Idea Generation, Idea Evaluation, Implementation Planning, Systems Perception, Identifying Downstream Consequences, Identification of Key Causes, Judgment and Decision Making, Systems Evaluation, Time Management, Management of Financial Resources, Management of Material Resources, Management of Personnel Resources

College Majors

General Retailing Operations: An instructional program that prepares individuals to perform marketing tasks specifically applicable to retail operations in a wide variety of settings.

Supporting Courses

Administration and Management: Knowledge of principles and processes involved in business and organizational planning, coordination, and execution. This includes strategic planning, resource allocation, manpower modeling, leadership techniques, and production methods. **Economics and Accounting:** Knowledge of economic and accounting principles and practices, the financial markets, banking, and the analysis and reporting of financial data. **Sales and Marketing:** Knowledge of principles and methods involved in showing, promoting, and selling products or services. This includes marketing strategies and tactics, product demonstration and sales techniques, and sales control systems. **Personnel and Human Resources:** Knowledge of policies and practices involved in personnel/human resource functions. This includes recruitment, selection, training, and promotion regulations and procedures; compensation and benefits packages; labor relations and negotiation strategies; and personnel information systems. **Production and Processing:** Knowledge of inputs, outputs, raw materials, waste, quality control, costs, and techniques for maximizing the manufacture and distribution of goods. **Mathematics:** Knowledge of numbers, their operations, and interrelationships including arithmetic, algebra, geometry, calculus, statistics, and their applications. **Sociology and Anthropology:** Knowledge of group behavior and dynamics, societal trends and influences, cultures, their history, migrations, ethnicity, and origins.

RADIOLOGIC TECHNOLOGISTS

Education	Associate degree
Average Yearly Earnings	$31,970
Projected Growth	29%
Annual Job Openings	12,865
Self-employed	0%
Employed Part-Time	18%

RECREATION WORKERS

Education	Bachelor's degree
Average Yearly Earnings	$17,139
Projected Growth	22%
Annual Job Openings	29,880
Self-employed	0%
Employed Part-Time	14%

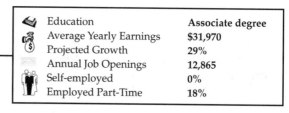

Recreation Workers

Conduct recreation activities with groups in public, private, or volunteer agencies or recreation facilities. Organize and promote activities such as arts and crafts, sports, games, music, dramatics, social recreation, camping, and hobbies, taking into account needs and interests of individual members. Organizes, leads, and promotes interest in facility activities, such as arts, crafts, sports, games, camping, and hobbies. Conducts recreational activities and instructs participants to develop skills in provided activities. Arranges for activity requirements, such as entertainment and setting up equipment and decorations. Schedules facility activities and maintains record of programs. Explains principles, techniques, and safety procedures of facility activities to participants, and demonstrates use of material and equipment. Ascertains and interprets group interests, evaluates equipment and facilities, and adapts activities to meet participant needs. Meets and collaborates with agency personnel, community organizations, and other professional personnel to plan balanced recreational programs for participants. Enforces rules and regulations of facility, maintains discipline, and ensures safety. Greets and introduces new arrivals to other guests, acquaints arrivals with facilities, and encourages group participation. Tests and documents content of swimming pool water, and schedules maintenance and use of facilities. Supervises and coordinates work activities of personnel, trains staff, and assigns duties. Schedules maintenance and use of facilities. Evaluates staff performance and records reflective information on performance evaluation forms. Completes and maintains time and attendance forms and inventory lists. Meets with staff to discuss rules, regulations, and work-related problems. Administers first aid, according to prescribed procedures, or notifies emergency medical personnel when necessary. Assists management to resolve complaints.

Occupational Type

Social occupations frequently involve working with, communicating with, and teaching people. These occupations often involve helping or providing service to others.

Skills required of Recreation Workers

Learning Strategies, Social Perceptiveness, Coordination, Instructing, Service Orientation, Implementation Planning, Time Management, Management of Material Resources, Management of Personnel Resources

College Majors

Childcare and Guidance Workers and Managers, General: An instructional program that generally prepares individuals for occupations in childcare and guidance in institutional and residential family settings, often under the supervision of professional personnel. Includes instruction in child growth and development; nutrition; recreation, play and learning activities planning and supervision; child abuse and neglect prevention; parent-child relationships; and applicable legal and administrative requirements.

Supporting Courses

Administration and Management: Knowledge of principles and processes involved in business and organizational planning, coordination, and execution. This includes strategic planning, resource allocation, manpower modeling, leadership techniques, and production methods. **Customer and Personal Service:** Knowledge of principles and processes for providing customer and personal services including needs assessment techniques, quality service standards, alternative delivery systems, and customer satisfaction evaluation techniques. **Personnel and Human Resources:** Knowledge of policies and practices involved in personnel/human resource functions. This includes recruitment, selection, training, and promotion regulations and procedures; compensation and benefits packages; labor relations and negotiation strategies; and personnel information systems. **Psychology:** Knowledge of human behavior and performance, mental processes, psychological research methods, and the assessment and treatment of behavioral and affective disorders. **Sociology and Anthropology:** Knowledge of group behavior and dynamics, societal trends and influences, cultures, their history, migrations, ethnicity, and origins. **Medicine and Dentistry:** Knowledge of the information and techniques needed to diagnose and treat injuries, diseases, and deformities. This includes symptoms, treatment alternatives, drug properties and interactions, and preventive healthcare measures. **Therapy and Counseling:** Knowledge of information and techniques needed to rehabilitate physical and mental ailments and to provide career guidance including alternative treatments, rehabilitation equipment and its proper use, and methods to evaluate treatment effects. **Education and Training:** Knowledge of instructional methods and training techniques including curriculum design principles, learning theory, group and individual teaching techniques, design of individual development plans, and test design principles. **Foreign Language:** Knowledge of the structure and content of a foreign (non-English) language including the meaning and spelling of words, rules of composition and grammar, and pronunciation. **Fine Arts:** Knowledge of theory and techniques required to produce, compose, and perform works of music, dance, visual arts, drama, and sculpture. **Public Safety and Security:** Knowledge of weaponry, public safety, and security operations, rules, regulations, precautions, prevention, and the protection of people, data, and property. **Law, Government, and Jurisprudence:** Knowledge of laws, legal codes, court procedures, precedents, government regulations, executive orders, agency rules, and the democratic political process. **Communications and Media:** Knowledge of media production, communication, and dissemination techniques and methods including alternative ways to inform and entertain via written, oral, and visual media.

RECREATIONAL THERAPISTS

✍	Education	Bachelor's degree
💰	Average Yearly Earnings	$26,770
	Projected Growth	21%
	Annual Job Openings	3,414
👥	Self-employed	26%
	Employed Part-Time	21%

Recreational Therapists

Plan, organize, and direct medically approved recreation programs for patients in hospitals, nursing homes, or other institutions. Activities include sports, trips, dramatics, social activities, and arts and crafts. Organizes and participates in activities to assist patient in developing needed skills and to make patient aware of available recreational resources. Instructs patient in activities and techniques, such as sports, dance, gardening, music, or art, designed to meet specific physical or psychological needs. Observes and confers with patient to assess patient's needs, capabilities, and interests and to devise treatment plan. Develops treatment plan to meet needs of patient, based on needs assessment and objectives of therapy. Analyzes patient's reactions to treatment experiences to assess progress and effectiveness of treatment plan. Modifies content of patient's treatment program based on observation and evaluation of progress. Confers with members of treatment team to determine patient's needs, capabilities, and interests, and to determine objectives of therapy. Counsels and encourages patient to develop leisure activities. Prepares and submits reports and charts to treatment team to reflect patients' reactions and evidence of progress or regression. Attends and participates in professional conferences and workshops to enhance efficiency and knowledge. Maintains and repairs art materials and equipment.

Occupational Type

Social occupations frequently involve working with, communicating with, and teaching people. These occupations often involve helping or providing service to others.

Skills required of Recreational Therapists

Active Listening, Writing, Speaking, Critical Thinking, Active Learning, Learning Strategies, Monitoring, Social Perceptiveness, Coordination, Persuasion, Instructing, Service Orientation, Problem Identification, Information Gathering, Synthesis/Reorganization, Idea Generation, Idea Evaluation, Implementation Planning, Visioning, Systems Perception, Identification of Key Causes, Judgment and Decision Making, Time Management, Management of Material Resources

College Majors

Health and Physical Education, General: An instructional program that generally describes the study and practice of activities and principles that promote physical fitness, achieve and maintain athletic prowess, and accomplish related research and service goals. Includes instruction in human movement studies, motivation studies, rules and practice of specific sports, exercise and fitness principles and techniques, basic athletic injury prevention and treatment, and organizing and leading fitness and sports programs.

Supporting Courses

Administration and Management: Knowledge of principles and processes involved in business and organizational planning, coordination, and execution. This includes strategic planning, resource allocation, manpower modeling, leadership techniques, and production methods. **Customer and Personal Service:** Knowledge of principles and processes for providing customer and personal services including needs assessment techniques, quality service standards, alternative delivery systems, and customer satisfaction evaluation techniques. **Biology:** Knowledge of plant and animal living tissue, cells, organisms, and entities, including their functions, interdependencies, and interactions with each other and the environment. **Psychology:** Knowledge of human behavior and performance, mental processes, psychological research methods, and the assessment and treatment of behavioral and affective disorders. **Sociology and Anthropology:** Knowledge of group behavior and dynamics, societal trends and influences, cultures, their history, migrations, ethnicity, and origins. **Medicine and Dentistry:** Knowledge of the information and techniques needed to diagnose and treat injuries, diseases, and deformities. This includes symptoms, treatment alternatives, drug properties and interactions, and preventive healthcare measures. **Therapy and Counseling:** Knowledge of information and techniques needed to rehabilitate physical and mental ailments and to provide career guidance including alternative treatments, rehabilitation equipment and its proper use, and methods to evaluate treatment effects. **Education and Training:** Knowledge of instructional methods and training techniques including curriculum design principles, learning theory, group and individual teaching techniques, design of individual development plans, and test design principles. **English Language:** Knowledge of the structure and content of the English language including the meaning and spelling of words, rules of composition, and grammar. **Philosophy and Theology:** Knowledge of different philosophical systems and religions, including their basic principles, values, ethics, ways of thinking, customs, and practices, and their impact on human culture.

REGISTERED NURSES

Education		Associate degree
Average Yearly Earnings		$40,310
Projected Growth		21%
Annual Job Openings		165,362
Self-employed		0%
Employed Part-Time		26%

REPORTERS AND CORRESPONDENTS

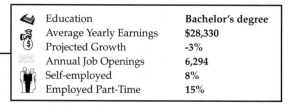

Education		Bachelor's degree
Average Yearly Earnings		$28,330
Projected Growth		-3%
Annual Job Openings		6,294
Self-employed		8%
Employed Part-Time		15%

Reporters and Correspondents

Collect and analyze facts about newsworthy events by interview, investigation, or observation. Report and write stories for newspaper, newsmagazine, radio, or television. (Excludes correspondents who broadcast news for radio and television.) Gathers and verifies factual information regarding story through interview, observation, and research. Organizes material and determines slant or emphasis. Writes news stories for publication or broadcast from written or recorded notes provided by reporting staff, following prescribed editorial style and format standards. Reviews and evaluates notes to isolate pertinent facts and details. Monitors police and fire department radio communications to obtain story leads. Conducts taped or filmed interviews or narratives. Receives assignment or evaluates news leads and news tips to develop story idea. Reports live from site of event or mobile broadcast unit. Transmits information to writing staff to write story. Edits or assists in editing videos for broadcast. Takes photographs or shoots video to illustrate stories.

Occupational Type

Artistic occupations frequently involve working with forms, designs, and patterns. They often require self-expression and the work can be done without following a clear set of rules.

Skills required of Reporters and Correspondents

Reading Comprehension, Active Listening, Writing, Speaking, Critical Thinking, Active Learning, Social Perceptiveness, Persuasion, Information Gathering, Information Organization, Synthesis/Reorganization, Idea Generation

 College Majors

Journalism: An instructional program that describes the methods and techniques for gathering, processing and delivering news, and that prepares individuals to be professional print journalists. Includes instruction in news writing and editing, reporting, journalism law and policy, professional standards and ethics, and journalism history and research.

 Supporting Courses

Computers and Electronics: Knowledge of electric circuit boards, processors, chips, and computer hardware and software, including applications and programming. **Sociology and Anthropology:** Knowledge of group behavior and dynamics, societal trends and influences, cultures, their history, migrations, ethnicity, and origins. **Geography:** Knowledge of various methods for describing the location and distribution of land, sea, and air masses including their physical locations, relationships, and characteristics. **English Language:** Knowledge of the structure and content of the English language including the meaning and spelling of words, rules of composition, and grammar. **Telecommunications:** Knowledge of transmission, broadcasting, switching, control, and operation of telecommunications systems. **Communications and Media:** Knowledge of media production, communication, and dissemination techniques and methods including alternative ways to inform and entertain via written, oral, and visual media.

RESIDENTIAL COUNSELORS

Residential Counselors

Education	Bachelor's degree
Average Yearly Earnings	$19,261
Projected Growth	41%
Annual Job Openings	38,515
Self-employed	0%
Employed Part-Time	18%

Coordinate activities for residents of care and treatment institutions, boarding schools, college fraternities or sororities, children's homes, or similar establishments. Work includes developing or assisting in the development of program plans for individuals, maintaining household records, and assigning rooms. Counsel residents in identifying and resolving social or other problems. Order supplies and determine need for maintenance, repairs, and furnishings. Assigns room, assists in planning recreational activities, and supervises work and study programs. Counsels residents in identifying and resolving social and other problems. Orders supplies and determines need for maintenance, repairs, and furnishings. Compiles records of daily activities of residents. Ascertains need for and secures service of physician. Escorts individuals on trips outside establishment for shopping or to obtain medical or dental services. Chaperons group-sponsored trips and social functions. Hires and supervises activities of housekeeping personnel. Plans menus of meals for residents of establishment. Answers telephone. Sorts and distributes mail.

Occupational Type

Social occupations frequently involve working with, communicating with, and teaching people. These occupations often involve helping or providing service to others.

Skills required of Residential Counselors

Active Listening, Speaking, Learning Strategies, Social Perceptiveness, Coordination, Persuasion, Negotiation, Service Orientation, Idea Generation, Implementation Planning, Time Management, Management of Financial Resources, Management of Material Resources, Management of Personnel Resources

College Majors

Childcare and Guidance Workers and Managers, General: An instructional program that generally prepares individuals for occupations in childcare and guidance in institutional and residential family settings, often under the supervision of professional personnel. Includes instruction in child growth and development; nutrition; recreation, play and learning activities planning and supervision; child abuse and neglect prevention; parent-child relationships; and applicable legal and administrative requirements.

Supporting Courses

Administration and Management: Knowledge of principles and processes involved in business and organizational planning, coordination, and execution. This includes strategic planning, resource allocation, manpower modeling, leadership techniques, and production methods. **Customer and Personal Service:** Knowledge of principles and processes for providing customer and personal services including needs assessment techniques, quality service standards, alternative delivery systems, and customer satisfaction evaluation techniques. **Personnel and Human Resources:** Knowledge of policies and practices involved in personnel/human resource functions. This includes recruitment, selection, training, and promotion regulations and procedures; compensation and benefits packages; labor relations and negotiation strategies; and personnel information systems. **Psychology:** Knowledge of human behavior and performance, mental processes, psychological research methods, and the assessment and treatment of behavioral and affective disorders. **Sociology and Anthropology:** Knowledge of group behavior and dynamics, societal trends and influences, cultures, their history, migrations, ethnicity, and origins. **Medicine and Dentistry:** Knowledge of the information and techniques needed to diagnose and treat injuries, diseases, and deformities. This includes symptoms, treatment alternatives, drug properties and interactions, and preventive healthcare measures. **Therapy and Counseling:** Knowledge of information and techniques needed to rehabilitate physical and mental ailments and to provide career guidance including alternative treatments, rehabilitation equipment and its proper use, and methods to evaluate treatment effects. **Philosophy and Theology:** Knowledge of different philosophical systems and religions, including their basic principles, values, ethics, ways of thinking, customs, and practices, and their impact on human culture. **Transportation:** Knowledge of principles and methods for moving people or goods by air, rail, sea, or road, including their relative costs, advantages, and limitations.

RESPIRATORY THERAPISTS

Education		Associate degree
Average Yearly Earnings		$32,781
Projected Growth		46%
Annual Job Openings		9,452
Self-employed		0%
Employed Part-Time		21%

SCIENCE AND MATHEMATICS TECHNICIANS

Education		Associate degree
Average Yearly Earnings		$34,466
Projected Growth		13%
Annual Job Openings		23,271
Self-employed		0%
Employed Part-Time		12%

SECONDARY SCHOOL TEACHERS

Teachers: Secondary School

Education		Bachelor's degree
Average Yearly Earnings		$36,784
Projected Growth		22%
Annual Job Openings		168,392
Self-employed		0%
Employed Part-Time		11%

Instruct students in public or private schools in one or more subjects, such as English, mathematics, or social studies. May be designated according to subject matter specialty, such as typing instructors, commercial teachers, or English teachers. Include vocational high school teachers. Instructs students, using various teaching methods, such as lecture and demonstration. Assigns lessons and corrects homework. Develops and administers tests. Prepares course outlines and objectives according to curriculum guidelines or state and local requirements. Uses audiovisual aids and other materials to supplement presentations. Evaluates, records, and reports student progress. Confers with students, parents, and school counselors to resolve behavioral and academic problems. Maintains discipline in classroom. Participates in faculty and professional meetings, educational conferences, and teacher training workshops. Selects, stores, orders, issues, and inventories classroom equipment, materials, and supplies. Keeps attendance records. Performs advisory duties, such as sponsoring student organizations or clubs, helping students select courses, and counseling students with problems.

Occupational Type

Social occupations frequently involve working with, communicating with, and teaching people. These occupations often involve helping or providing service to others.

 Skills required of Teachers: Secondary School

Reading Comprehension, Active Listening, Writing, Speaking, Mathematics, Active Learning, Learning Strategies, Monitoring, Social Perceptiveness, Instructing, Service Orientation, Information Organization, Synthesis/Reorganization, Implementation Planning, Operations Analysis, Time Management

 College Majors

Education, General: An instructional program that generally describes the theory and practice of learning and teaching; the basic principles of educational psychology; the art of teaching; the planning and administration of educational activities; and the social foundations of education.

 Supporting Courses

Administration and Management: Knowledge of principles and processes involved in business and organizational planning, coordination, and execution. This includes strategic planning, resource allocation, manpower modeling, leadership techniques, and production methods. **Clerical:** Knowledge of administrative and clerical procedures and systems such as word processing systems, filing and records management systems, stenography and transcription, forms design principles, and other office procedures and terminology. **Psychology:** Knowledge of human behavior and performance, mental processes, psychological research methods, and the assessment and treatment of behavioral and affective disorders. **Sociology and Anthropology:** Knowledge of group behavior and dynamics, societal trends and influences, cultures, their history, migrations, ethnicity, and origins. **Geography:** Knowledge of various methods for describing the location and distribution of land, sea, and air masses including their physical locations, relationships, and characteristics. **Therapy and Counseling:** Knowledge of information and techniques needed to rehabilitate physical and mental ailments and to provide career guidance including alternative treatments, rehabilitation equipment and its proper use, and methods to evaluate treatment effects. **Education and Training:** Knowledge of instructional methods and training techniques including curriculum design principles, learning theory, group and individual teaching techniques, design of individual development plans, and test design principles. **English Language:** Knowledge of the structure and content of the English language including the meaning and spelling of words, rules of composition, and grammar. **Foreign Language:** Knowledge of the structure and content of a foreign (non-English) language including the meaning and spelling of words, rules of composition and grammar, and pronunciation. **History and Archeology:** Knowledge of past historical events and their causes, indicators, and impact on particular civilizations and cultures. **Philosophy and Theology:** Knowledge of different philosophical systems and religions, including their basic principles, values, ethics, ways of thinking, customs, and practices, and their impact on human culture.

SERVICE MANAGERS

Nursing Directors

Education	Work experience, plus degree	
Average Yearly Earnings	$48,339	
Projected Growth	21%	
Annual Job Openings	171,229	
Self-employed	52%	
Employed Part-Time	7%	

Plan, direct, and coordinate facilities or programs providing nursing care. Include directors of schools of nursing. Plans curricula and schedules health education instruction training and counseling for nursing school, in-service, and community programs. Plans, directs, and administers nursing services or educational programs in healthcare facilities. Establishes and revises policies and procedures, such as selection, performance, and compensation standards, organizational objectives, and medical and maintenance procedures. Prepares budget and administers healthcare programs and services within budgetary limitations. Recruits, interviews, selects, and assigns nursing and health services staff, faculty, and students. Conducts studies and site visits to assess program needs and evaluate the cost-effectiveness and efficiency of existing services. Prepares, maintains, and updates nursing policy and procedure manuals. Establishes records of management systems for health services, patients, staff, and nursing students. Consults with legal counsel, community groups, medical staff, and administrators regarding the application of nursing principles to industrial and social welfare problems. Directs collection, analysis, and interpretation of health service and utilization statistics. Acts as liaison between healthcare institution or facility and community to promote cooperative relationships and plan integrated programming.

Occupational Type

Social occupations frequently involve working with, communicating with, and teaching people. These occupations often involve helping or providing service to others.

Skills required of Nursing Directors

Reading Comprehension, Active Listening, Writing, Speaking, Mathematics, Critical Thinking, Active Learning, Learning Strategies, Monitoring, Social Perceptiveness, Coordination, Persuasion, Negotiation, Instructing, Problem Identification, Information Gathering, Idea Generation, Idea Evaluation, Implementation Planning, Visioning, Systems Perception, Identifying Downstream Consequences, Identification of Key Causes, Judgment and Decision Making, Systems Evaluation, Time Management, Management of Financial Resources, Management of Material Resources, Management of Personnel Resources

College Majors

Communication Disorders Sciences and Services, Other: Any instructional program in communication disorders sciences and services not described above.

Supporting Courses

Administration and Management: Knowledge of principles and processes involved in business and organizational planning, coordination, and execution. This includes strategic

planning, resource allocation, manpower modeling, leadership techniques, and production methods. **Clerical:** Knowledge of administrative and clerical procedures and systems such as word processing systems, filing and records management systems, stenography and transcription, forms design principles, and other office procedures and terminology. **Economics and Accounting:** Knowledge of economic and accounting principles and practices, the financial markets, banking, and the analysis and reporting of financial data. **Sales and Marketing:** Knowledge of principles and methods involved in showing, promoting, and selling products or services. This includes marketing strategies and tactics, product demonstration and sales techniques, and sales control systems. **Customer and Personal Service:** Knowledge of principles and processes for providing customer and personal services including needs assessment techniques, quality service standards, alternative delivery systems, and customer satisfaction evaluation techniques. **Personnel and Human Resources:** Knowledge of policies and practices involved in personnel/human resource functions. This includes recruitment, selection, training, and promotion regulations and procedures; compensation and benefits packages; labor relations and negotiation strategies; and personnel information systems. **Mathematics:** Knowledge of numbers, their operations, and interrelationships including arithmetic, algebra, geometry, calculus, statistics, and their applications. **Biology:** Knowledge of plant and animal living tissue, cells, organisms, and entities, including their functions, interdependencies, and interactions with each other and the environment. **Psychology:** Knowledge of human behavior and performance, mental processes, psychological research methods, and the assessment and treatment of behavioral and affective disorders. **Sociology and Anthropology:** Knowledge of group behavior and dynamics, societal trends and influences, cultures, their history, migrations, ethnicity, and origins. **Medicine and Dentistry:** Knowledge of the information and techniques needed to diagnose and treat injuries, diseases, and deformities. This includes symptoms, treatment alternatives, drug properties and interactions, and preventive healthcare measures. **Therapy and Counseling:** Knowledge of information and techniques needed to rehabilitate physical and mental ailments and to provide career guidance including alternative treatments, rehabilitation equipment and its proper use, and methods to evaluate treatment effects. **Education and Training:** Knowledge of instructional methods and training techniques including curriculum design principles, learning theory, group and individual teaching techniques, design of individual development plans, and test design principles.

Medical and Health Services Managers

Plan, direct, and coordinate medicine and health services in hospitals, clinics, managed care organizations, public health agencies, or similar organizations. Include hospital administrators, long-term care administrators, and other healthcare facility administrators. Administers fiscal operations, such as planning budgets, authorizing expenditures, and coordinating financial reporting. Directs and coordinates activities of medical, nursing, technical, clerical, service, and maintenance personnel of healthcare facility or mobile unit. Develops or expands medical programs or health services for research, rehabilitation, and community health promotion. Develops organizational policies and procedures, and establishes evaluative or operational criteria for facility or medical unit. Implements and administers programs and services for healthcare or medical facility. Establishes work schedules and assignments for staff, according to workload, space, and equipment availability. Prepares activity reports to inform management of the status and implementation plans of programs, services, and quality initiatives. Recruits, hires, and evaluates the performance of medical staff and auxiliary personnel. Reviews and analyzes facility activities and data to aid planning and cash- and risk-management and to improve service utilization. Consults with medical, business, and community groups to discuss service problems, coordinate activities and plans, and promote health programs. Develops instructional materials and conducts in-service and community-based educational programs. Inspects facilities for emergency readiness and compliance of access, safety, and sanitation regulations, and recommends building or equipment modifications. Develops and maintains computerized records management system to store or process personnel or activity data.

Occupational Type

Enterprising occupations frequently involve starting up and carrying out projects. These occupations can involve leading people and making many decisions. Sometimes they involve risk taking and often deal with business.

Skills required of Medical and Health Services Managers

Reading Comprehension, Active Listening, Writing, Speaking, Learning Strategies, Monitoring, Social Perceptiveness, Coordination, Instructing, Problem Identification, Idea Generation, Idea Evaluation, Implementation Planning, Operations Analysis, Visioning, Systems Perception, Identifying Downstream Consequences, Identification of Key Causes, Judgment and Decision Making, Systems Evaluation, Time Management, Management of Financial Resources, Management of Material Resources, Management of Personnel Resources

College Majors

Communication Disorders Sciences and Services, Other: Any instructional program in communication disorders sciences and services not described above.

Supporting Courses

Administration and Management: Knowledge of principles and processes involved in business and organizational planning, coordination, and execution. This includes strategic planning, resource allocation, manpower modeling, leadership techniques, and production methods. **Clerical:** Knowledge of administrative and clerical procedures and systems such as word processing systems, filing and records management systems, stenography and transcription, forms design principles, and other office procedures and terminology. **Economics and Accounting:** Knowledge of economic and accounting principles and practices, the financial markets, banking, and the analysis and reporting of financial data. **Sales and Marketing:** Knowledge of principles and methods involved in showing, promoting, and selling products or services. This includes marketing strategies and tactics, product demonstration and sales techniques, and sales control systems. **Customer and Personal**

Service: Knowledge of principles and processes for providing customer and personal services including needs assessment techniques, quality service standards, alternative delivery systems, and customer satisfaction evaluation techniques. **Personnel and Human Resources:** Knowledge of policies and practices involved in personnel/human resource functions. This includes recruitment, selection, training, and promotion regulations and procedures; compensation and benefits packages; labor relations and negotiation strategies; and personnel information systems. **Mathematics:** Knowledge of numbers, their operations, and interrelationships including arithmetic, algebra, geometry, calculus, statistics, and their applications. **Psychology:** Knowledge of human behavior and performance, mental processes, psychological research methods, and the assessment and treatment of behavioral and affective disorders. **Medicine and Dentistry:** Knowledge of the information and techniques needed to diagnose and treat injuries, diseases, and deformities. This includes symptoms, treatment alternatives, drug properties and interactions, and preventive healthcare measures. **Therapy and Counseling:** Knowledge of information and techniques needed to rehabilitate physical and mental ailments and to provide career guidance including alternative treatments, rehabilitation equipment and its proper use, and methods to evaluate treatment effects. **Education and Training:** Knowledge of instructional methods and training techniques including curriculum design principles, learning theory, group and individual teaching techniques, design of individual development plans, and test design principles. **Public Safety and Security:** Knowledge of weaponry, public safety, and security operations, rules, regulations, precautions, prevention, and the protection of people, data, and property. **Communications and Media:** Knowledge of media production, communication, and dissemination techniques and methods including alternative ways to inform and entertain via written, oral, and visual media.

Amusement and Recreation Establishment Managers

Plan, direct, and coordinate the activities of organizations that provide amusement or recreational facilities or services to the public. Plans, organizes, and coordinates programs of recreational activities, entertainment, or instructional classes. Formulates and establishes operational policies, such as hours of operation, fee amounts, and accounting procedures. Determines work activities necessary to operate facility, and assigns duties to staff accordingly. Prepares, compiles, and maintains budgets, schedules of activities or personnel, and inventory or accounting records. Hires, promotes, and discharges workers. Enforces laws, safety regulations, and establishment rules concerning personnel or patron behavior. Purchases or orders supplies and equipment. Confers with patrons or employees to resolve grievances or work problems. Trains staff or instructs patrons in recreational activities, such as swimming, skating, dancing, riding animals, or shooting firearms. Inspects facilities for cleanliness, maintenance needs, or compliance with health and safety regulations. Plans and initiates promotional projects and writes materials to publicize and advertise recreational facilities and activities. Advises patrons of available facilities and activities and registers them for rental of facility or equipment, or for particular activity. Collects fees and issues receipts to patrons for use of facilities or participation in activities. Sells recreational supplies and equipment or lessons to patrons.

Occupational Type

Enterprising occupations frequently involve starting up and carrying out projects. These occupations can involve leading people and making many decisions. Sometimes they involve risk taking and often deal with business.

Skills required of Amusement and Recreation Establishment Managers

Social Perceptiveness, Negotiation, Instructing, Problem Identification, Idea Generation, Equipment Selection, Time Management, Management of Financial Resources, Management of Material Resources, Management of Personnel Resources

College Majors

General Retailing Operations: An instructional program that prepares individuals to perform marketing tasks specifically applicable to retail operations in a wide variety of settings.

Supporting Courses

Administration and Management: Knowledge of principles and processes involved in business and organizational planning, coordination, and execution. This includes strategic planning, resource allocation, manpower modeling, leadership techniques, and production methods. **Economics and Accounting:** Knowledge of economic and accounting principles and practices, the financial markets, banking, and the analysis and reporting of financial data. **Sales and Marketing:** Knowledge of principles and methods involved in showing, promoting, and selling products or services. This includes marketing strategies and tactics, product demonstration and sales techniques, and sales control systems. **Customer and Personal Service:** Knowledge of principles and processes for providing customer and personal services including needs assessment techniques, quality service standards, alternative delivery systems, and customer satisfaction evaluation techniques. **Personnel and Human Resources:** Knowledge of policies and practices involved in personnel/human resource functions. This includes recruitment, selection, training, and promotion regulations and procedures; compensation and benefits packages; labor relations and negotiation strategies; and personnel information systems. **Education and Training:** Knowledge of instructional methods and training techniques including curriculum design principles, learning theory, group and individual teaching techniques, design of individual development plans, and test design principles. **Public Safety and Security:** Knowledge of weaponry, public safety, and security operations, rules, regulations, precautions, prevention, and the protection of people, data, and property. **Law, Government, and Jurisprudence:** Knowledge of laws, legal codes, court procedures, precedents, government regulations, executive orders, agency rules, and the democratic political process.

Social and Community Service Managers

Plan, organize, and coordinate the activities of a social service program or community outreach organization. Oversee the program or organization's budget and policies regarding participant involvement, program requirements, and benefits. Work may involve directing social workers, counselors, or probation officers. Confers and consults with individuals, groups, and committees to determine needs and to plan, implement, and extend organization's programs and services. Determines organizational policies and defines scope of services offered and administration of procedures. Establishes and maintains relationships with other agencies and organizations in community to meet and not duplicate community needs and services. Assigns duties to staff or volunteers. Plans, directs, and prepares fundraising activities and public relations materials. Researches and analyzes member or community needs as basis for community development. Participates in program activities to serve clients of agency. Prepares, distributes, and maintains records and reports, such as budgets, personnel records, or training manuals. Coordinates volunteer service programs, such as Red Cross, hospital volunteers, or vocational training for disabled individuals. Speaks to community groups to explain and interpret agency purpose, programs, and policies. Advises volunteers and volunteer leaders to ensure quality of programs and effective use of resources. Instructs and trains agency staff or volunteers in skills required to provide services. Interviews, recruits, or hires volunteers and staff. Observes workers to evaluate performance and ensure that work meets established standards.

Occupational Type

Social occupations frequently involve working with, communicating with, and teaching people. These occupations often involve helping or providing service to others.

Skills required of Social and Community Service Managers

Speaking, Learning Strategies, Social Perceptiveness, Coordination, Persuasion, Negotiation, Instructing, Service Orientation, Problem Identification, Idea Generation, Implementation Planning, Visioning, Identification of Key Causes, Time Management, Management of Financial Resources, Management of Material Resources, Management of Personnel Resources

College Majors

Community Organization, Resources and Services: An instructional program that describes the theories, principles, and practice of providing services to communities, organizing communities and neighborhoods for social action, serving as community liaisons to public agencies, and using community resources to furnish information, instruction, and assistance to all members of a community. May prepare individuals to apply such knowledge and skills in community service positions.

Supporting Courses

Administration and Management: Knowledge of principles and processes involved in business and organizational planning, coordination, and execution. This includes strategic planning, resource allocation, manpower modeling, leadership techniques, and production methods. **Economics and Accounting:** Knowledge of economic and accounting principles and practices, the financial markets, banking, and the analysis and reporting of financial data. **Customer and Personal Service:** Knowledge of principles and processes for providing customer and personal services including needs assessment techniques, quality service standards, alternative delivery systems, and customer satisfaction evaluation techniques. **Personnel and Human Resources:** Knowledge of policies and practices involved in personnel/human resource functions. This includes recruitment, selection, training, and promotion regulations and procedures; compensation and benefits packages; labor relations and negotiation strategies; and personnel information systems. **Sociology and Anthropology:** Knowledge of group behavior and dynamics, societal trends and influences, cultures, their history, migrations, ethnicity, and origins. **Education and Training:** Knowledge of instructional methods and training techniques including curriculum design principles, learning theory, group and individual teaching techniques, design of individual development plans, and test design principles. **English Language:** Knowledge of the structure and content of the English language including the meaning and spelling of words, rules of composition, and grammar. **Communications and Media:** Knowledge of media production, communication, and dissemination techniques and methods including alternative ways to inform and entertain via written, oral, and visual media.

Association Managers and Administrators

Direct and coordinate activities of professional, trade, or business associations to achieve goals, objectives, and standards of association. Coordinates committees or board of directors of association to evaluate services, recommend new programs, or promote association. Plans, directs, or participates in preparation and presentation of educational material to membership or public using various media. Plans, develops, and implements new programs and ideas based on evaluation of current programs. Directs and coordinates association functions, such as conventions, exhibits, and local or regional workshops or meetings. Directs surveys and compilation of membership data, such as average income, benefits, standards, or common problems. Advises chapters, members, or businesses of association regarding financial, organizational, growth, or membership problems. Analyzes factors affecting association, members, or member organizations, such as legislation and taxation or economic conditions and trends. Prepares monthly or annual budget reports and oversees finances of association. Represents association at public, social, or business receptions, or in negotiations with representatives of government, business, or labor organizations. Visits members or chapters of association to ensure association standards are being met and to promote goodwill.

 ### Occupational Type

Enterprising occupations frequently involve starting up and carrying out projects. These occupations can involve leading people and making many decisions. Sometimes they involve risk taking and often deal with business.

 ### Skills required of Association Managers and Administrators

Writing, Speaking, Mathematics, Critical Thinking, Learning Strategies, Monitoring, Social Perceptiveness, Coordination, Persuasion, Negotiation, Instructing, Problem Identification,

Information Gathering, Idea Generation, Idea Evaluation, Implementation Planning, Programming, Visioning, Systems Perception, Identifying Downstream Consequences, Identification of Key Causes, Judgment and Decision Making, Systems Evaluation, Management of Financial Resources, Management of Personnel Resources

 College Majors

Nursing Administration (Post-R.N.): An instructional program that prepares registered nurses (R.N.) to manage nursing personnel and services in hospitals and other healthcare delivery agencies.

 Supporting Courses

Administration and Management: Knowledge of principles and processes involved in business and organizational planning, coordination, and execution. This includes strategic planning, resource allocation, manpower modeling, leadership techniques, and production methods. **Economics and Accounting:** Knowledge of economic and accounting principles and practices, the financial markets, banking, and the analysis and reporting of financial data. **Mathematics:** Knowledge of numbers, their operations, and interrelationships including arithmetic, algebra, geometry, calculus, statistics, and their applications. **Education and Training:** Knowledge of instructional methods and training techniques including curriculum design principles, learning theory, group and individual teaching techniques, design of individual development plans, and test design principles.

Service Establishment Managers

Manage service establishment or direct and coordinate service activities within an establishment. Plan, direct, and coordinate service operations within an organization, or the activities of organizations that provide services. Directs worker activities in service establishments, such as travel agencies, health clubs, or beauty salons, or in customer service departments. Plans and adjusts work schedule and assigns duties to meet customer demands. Coordinates sales promotion activities and sells services to clients. Communicates with customer to ascertain needs, advise on services, adjust complaints, or negotiate contracts. Keeps records of work hours, labor costs, expenditures, receipts, and materials used, to analyze and prepare operation reports or budget. Observes worker performance and reviews employees' work to ensure accuracy or quality of work. Interviews and hires personnel. Orients and trains new personnel in job duties, safety and health rules, company policies, and performance requirements. Confers with employees to give performance feedback, assist with providing services, and solve problems. Transfers or discharges employees, according to work performance. Requisitions or purchases equipment or supplies to enable establishment to provide services.

Occupational Type

Enterprising occupations frequently involve starting up and carrying out projects. These occupations can involve leading people and making many decisions. Sometimes they involve risk taking and often deal with business.

Skills required of Service Establishment Managers

Speaking, Social Perceptiveness, Persuasion, Negotiation, Instructing, Service Orientation, Idea Generation, Implementation Planning, Systems Perception, Identification of Key Causes, Time Management, Management of Financial Resources, Management of Material Resources, Management of Personnel Resources

 College Majors

Agricultural Mechanization, General: An instructional program that prepares individuals in a general way to sell, select and service agriculture or agribusiness technical equipment and facilities, including computers, specialized software, power units, machinery, equipment, structures and utilities. Includes instruction in agricultural power units; the planning and selection of materials for the construction of agricultural facilities; the mechanical practices associated with irrigation and water conservation; erosion control; and data processing systems.

 Supporting Courses

Administration and Management: Knowledge of principles and processes involved in business and organizational planning, coordination, and execution. This includes strategic planning, resource allocation, manpower modeling, leadership techniques, and production methods. **Economics and Accounting:** Knowledge of economic and accounting principles and practices, the financial markets, banking, and the analysis and reporting of financial data. **Sales and Marketing:** Knowledge of principles and methods involved in showing, promoting, and selling products or services. This includes marketing strategies and tactics, product demonstration and sales techniques, and sales control systems. **Customer and Personal Service:** Knowledge of principles and processes for providing customer and personal services including needs assessment techniques, quality service standards, alternative delivery systems, and customer satisfaction evaluation techniques. **Personnel and Human Resources:** Knowledge of policies and practices involved in personnel/human resource functions. This includes recruitment, selection, training, and promotion regulations and procedures; compensation and benefits packages; labor relations and negotiation strategies; and personnel information systems. **Education and Training:** Knowledge of instructional methods and training techniques including curriculum design principles, learning theory, group and individual teaching techniques, design of individual development plans, and test design principles.

Gambling Establishment Managers

Plan, direct, and coordinate the activities of organizations or establishments—such as casinos, cardrooms, and racetracks—that provide gambling or games-of-chance activities to the public. Review operational expenses, budget estimates, betting accounts, and collection reports for accuracy. Observes and supervises operation to ensure that employees render prompt and courteous service to patrons. Establishes policies on types of gambling offered, odds, extension of credit, and serving food and beverages. Directs workers compiling summary sheets for each race or event to show amount wagered and amount to be paid to

---

winners. Prepares work schedules, assigns work stations, and keeps attendance records. Resolves customer complaints regarding service. Interviews and hires workers. Trains new workers and evaluates their performance. Explains and interprets house rules, such as game rules and betting limits, to patrons. Records, issues receipts for, and pays off bets.

 ## Occupational Type

Enterprising occupations frequently involve starting up and carrying out projects. These occupations can involve leading people and making many decisions. Sometimes they involve risk taking and often deal with business.

 ## Skills required of Gambling Establishment Managers

Speaking, Critical Thinking, Monitoring, Social Perceptiveness, Negotiation, Instructing, Service Orientation, Idea Generation, Identifying Downstream Consequences, Identification of Key Causes, Time Management, Management of Financial Resources, Management of Material Resources, Management of Personnel Resources

 ## College Majors

Business Administration and Management, General: An instructional program that generally prepares individuals to plan, organize, direct, and control the functions and processes of a firm or organization. Includes instruction in management theory, human resources management and behavior, accounting and other quantitative methods, purchasing and logistics, organization and production, marketing, and business decision making.

 ## Supporting Courses

Administration and Management: Knowledge of principles and processes involved in business and organizational planning, coordination, and execution. This includes strategic planning, resource allocation, manpower modeling, leadership techniques, and production methods. **Economics and Accounting:** Knowledge of economic and accounting principles and practices, the financial markets, banking, and the analysis and reporting of financial data. **Customer and Personal Service:** Knowledge of principles and processes for providing customer and personal services including needs assessment techniques, quality service standards, alternative delivery systems, and customer satisfaction evaluation techniques. **Personnel and Human Resources:** Knowledge of policies and practices involved in personnel/human resource functions. This includes recruitment, selection, training, and promotion regulations and procedures; compensation and benefits packages; labor relations and negotiation strategies; and personnel information systems. **Mathematics:** Knowledge of numbers, their operations, and interrelationships including arithmetic, algebra, geometry, calculus, statistics, and their applications.

Security Managers

Plan, direct, and coordinate implementation of security procedures, systems, and personnel to protect private or public property and personnel from theft, fire, and personal injury.

Inspects premises to determine security needs, test alarm systems and safety equipment, or detect safety hazards. Analyzes security needs; plans and directs implementation of security measures, such as security or safety systems; and estimates costs of operation. Develops and establishes security procedures for establishment or for protection of individual, group, or property. Confers with management to determine need for programs and to formulate and coordinate security programs with establishment activities. Directs activities of personnel in developing, revising, or updating company security measures, to comply with Federal regulations. Confers with client regarding security needs, evaluation of services, or problems with security systems. Assigns workers to shifts, posts, or patrol, according to protection requirements or size and nature of establishment. Interviews and hires security workers. Observes workers' performance of duties to evaluate efficiency and to detect and correct inefficient or improper work practices. Trains workers in security operations, such as first aid, fire safety, and detecting and apprehending intruders or shoplifters. Conducts background investigations of job applicants or employees to obtain information such as personal histories, character references, or wage garnishments. Monitors or supervises monitoring of alarm system controls and investigation of alarm signals. Conducts or directs surveillance of premises or suspects. Interprets company policies and procedures for workers. Studies Federal security regulations, and consults with Federal representatives for interpretation or application of particular regulations to company operations. Responds to calls from subordinates to direct activities during fires, storms, riots, and other emergencies. Prepares reports concerning investigations, security needs and recommendations, or security manual of procedures. Investigates crimes committed against client or establishment, such as fraud, robbery, arson, or patent infringement. Confers and cooperates with police, fire, and civil defense authorities to coordinate activities during emergency. Contacts business establishments to promote sales of security services.

Occupational Type

Enterprising occupations frequently involve starting up and carrying out projects. These occupations can involve leading people and making many decisions. Sometimes they involve risk taking and often deal with business.

Skills required of Security Managers

Critical Thinking, Active Learning, Learning Strategies, Coordination, Persuasion, Negotiation, Instructing, Problem Identification, Information Gathering, Idea Generation, Idea Evaluation, Implementation Planning, Operations Analysis, Equipment Selection, Visioning, Identifying Downstream Consequences, Identification of Key Causes, Systems Evaluation, Time Management, Management of Financial Resources, Management of Material Resources, Management of Personnel Resources

College Majors

Security and Loss Prevention Services: An instructional program that prepares individuals to perform routine inspection, patrol, and crime prevention services for private clients. Includes instruction in the provision of personal protection as well as property security.

Supporting Courses

Administration and Management: Knowledge of principles and processes involved in business and organizational planning, coordination, and execution. This includes strategic planning, resource allocation, manpower modeling, leadership techniques, and production methods. **Sales and Marketing:** Knowledge of principles and methods involved in showing, promoting, and selling products or services. This includes marketing strategies and tactics, product demonstration and sales techniques, and sales control systems. **Customer and Personal Service:** Knowledge of principles and processes for providing customer and personal services including needs assessment techniques, quality service standards, alternative delivery systems, and customer satisfaction evaluation techniques. **Personnel and Human Resources:** Knowledge of policies and practices involved in personnel/human resource functions. This includes recruitment, selection, training, and promotion regulations and procedures; compensation and benefits packages; labor relations and negotiation strategies; and personnel information systems. **Education and Training:** Knowledge of instructional methods and training techniques including curriculum design principles, learning theory, group and individual teaching techniques, design of individual development plans, and test design principles. **Public Safety and Security:** Knowledge of weaponry, public safety, and security operations, rules, regulations, precautions, prevention, and the protection of people, data, and property. **Law, Government, and Jurisprudence:** Knowledge of laws, legal codes, court procedures, precedents, government regulations, executive orders, agency rules, and the democratic political process.

All Other Managers and Administrators

All other managers and administrators not classified separately above.

 Occupational Type

Specific information is not available.

 Skills required of All Other Managers and Administrators

Information on specific skills required is not available.

 College Majors

General Retailing Operations: An instructional program that prepares individuals to perform marketing tasks specifically applicable to retail operations in a wide variety of settings.

 Supporting Courses

Specific information is not available.

SOCIAL SCIENTISTS

	Education	**Master's degree**
	Average Yearly Earnings	**$36,296**
	Projected Growth	**5%**
	Annual Job Openings	**4,907**
	Self-employed	**5%**
	Employed Part-Time	**18%**

Geographers

Study nature and use of areas of earth's surface, relating and interpreting interactions of physical and cultural phenomena. Conduct research on physical aspects of a region, including land forms, climates, soils, plants, and animals; and conduct research on the spatial implications of human activities within a given area, including social characteristics, economic activities, and political organization, as well as researching interdependence between regions at scales ranging from local to global. Collects data on physical characteristics of specified area, such as geological formation, climate, and vegetation, using surveying or meteorological equipment. Studies population characteristics within area, such as ethnic distribution and economic activity. Constructs and interprets maps, graphs, and diagrams. Uses surveying equipment to assess geology, physics, and biology within given area. Prepares environmental impact reports based on results of study. Advises governments and organizations on ethnic and natural boundaries between nation or administrative areas.

Occupational Type

Investigative occupations frequently involve working with ideas, and require an extensive amount of thinking. These occupations can involve searching for facts and figuring out problems mentally.

Skills required of Geographers

Reading Comprehension, Writing, Mathematics, Critical Thinking, Information Gathering, Information Organization

College Majors

Geography: An instructional program that describes the systematic study of the spatial distribution and interrelationships of people, natural resources, plant and animal life. Includes instruction in historical and political geography, cultural geography, economic and physical geography, regional science, cartographic methods, remote sensing, spatial analysis, and applications to areas such as land-use planning, development studies, and analyses of specific countries, regions, and resources.

Supporting Courses

Physics: Knowledge and prediction of physical principles, laws, and applications including air, water, material dynamics, light, atomic principles, heat, electric theory, earth formations, and meteorological and related natural phenomena. **Biology:** Knowledge of plant and animal living tissue, cells, organisms, and entities, including their functions, interdependencies, and interactions with each other and the environment. **Sociology and Anthropology:** Knowledge of group behavior and dynamics, societal trends and influences, cultures, their history, migrations, ethnicity, and origins. **Geography:** Knowledge of various methods for describing the location and distribution of land, sea, and air masses including their physical locations, relationships, and characteristics. **Foreign Language:** Knowledge of the structure and content of a foreign (non-English) language including the meaning and spelling of words, rules of composition and grammar, and pronunciation. **History and Archeology:** Knowledge of past historical events and their causes, indicators, and impact on particular civilizations and cultures.

Political Scientists

Study the origin, development, and operation of political systems. Research a wide range of subjects, such as relations between the United States and foreign countries, the beliefs and institutions of foreign nations, or the politics of small towns or a major metropolis. May study topics such as public opinion, political decision making, and ideology. May analyze the structure and operation of governments as well as various political entities. May conduct public opinion surveys, analyze election results, or analyze public documents. Conducts research into political philosophy and theories of political systems, such as governmental institutions, public laws, and international law. Analyzes and interprets results of studies, and prepares reports detailing findings, recommendations, or conclusions. Consults with government officials, civic bodies, research agencies, and political parties. Organizes and conducts public opinion surveys, and interprets results. Recommends programs and policies to institutions and organizations. Prepares reports detailing findings and conclusions.

Occupational Type

Investigative occupations frequently involve working with ideas, and require an extensive amount of thinking. These occupations can involve searching for facts and figuring out problems mentally.

Skills required of Political Scientists

Reading Comprehension, Active Listening, Writing, Speaking, Mathematics, Critical Thinking, Active Learning, Social Perceptiveness, Information Gathering, Information Organization, Synthesis/Reorganization, Idea Generation, Idea Evaluation, Implementation Planning, Operations Analysis, Programming, Visioning, Systems Perception, Identifying Downstream Consequences, Identification of Key Causes, Judgment and Decision Making

College Majors

International Relations and Affairs: An instructional program that describes the systematic study of international politics and institutions, and the conduct of diplomacy and foreign policy. Includes instruction in international relations theory, foreign policy analysis, national security and strategic studies, international law and organization, the comparative study of specific countries and regions, and the theory and practice of diplomacy.

 ## Supporting Courses

Psychology: Knowledge of human behavior and performance, mental processes, psychological research methods, and the assessment and treatment of behavioral and affective disorders. **Sociology and Anthropology:** Knowledge of group behavior and dynamics, societal trends and influences, cultures, their history, migrations, ethnicity, and origins. **Geography:** Knowledge of various methods for describing the location and distribution of land, sea, and air masses including their physical locations, relationships, and characteristics. **English Language:** Knowledge of the structure and content of the English language including the meaning and spelling of words, rules of composition, and grammar. **Foreign Language:** Knowledge of the structure and content of a foreign (non-English) language including the meaning and spelling of words, rules of composition and grammar, and pronunciation. **History and Archeology:** Knowledge of past historical events and their causes, indicators, and impact on particular civilizations and cultures. **Philosophy and Theology:** Knowledge of different philosophical systems and religions, including their basic principles, values, ethics, ways of thinking, customs, and practices, and their impact on human culture. **Law, Government, and Jurisprudence:** Knowledge of laws, legal codes, court procedures, precedents, government regulations, executive orders, agency rules, and the democratic political process. **Communications and Media:** Knowledge of media production, communication, and dissemination techniques and methods including alternative ways to inform and entertain via written, oral, and visual media.

Sociologists

Conduct research into the development, structure, and behavior of groups of human beings and patterns of culture and social organization. Collects and analyzes scientific data concerning social phenomena, such as community, associations, social institutions, ethnic minorities, and social change. Plans and directs research on crime and prevention, group relations in industrial organization, urban communities, and physical environment and technology. Observes group interaction, and interviews group members to identify problems and collect data related to factors such as group organization and authority relationships. Develops research designs on basis of existing knowledge and evolving theory. Develops approaches to solution of group's problems, based on findings and incorporating sociological research and study in related disciplines. Constructs and tests methods of data collection. Collects information and makes judgments through observation, interview, and review of documents. Analyzes and evaluates data. Develops intervention procedures, utilizing techniques such as interviews, consultations, role-playing, and participant observation of group interaction, to facilitate solution. Monitors group interaction and role affiliations to evaluate progress and to determine need for additional change. Consults with lawmakers, administrators, and other officials who deal with problems of social change. Interprets methods employed and findings to individuals within agency and community.

Prepares publications and reports on subjects (such as social factors) that affect health, demographic characteristics, and social and racial discrimination in society. Collaborates with research workers in other disciplines. Directs work of statistical clerks, statisticians, and others.

Occupational Type

Investigative occupations frequently involve working with ideas, and require an extensive amount of thinking. These occupations can involve searching for facts and figuring out problems mentally.

Skills required of Sociologists

Reading Comprehension, Active Listening, Writing, Speaking, Mathematics, Critical Thinking, Active Learning, Learning Strategies, Social Perceptiveness, Coordination, Instructing, Problem Identification, Information Gathering, Information Organization, Synthesis/Reorganization, Idea Generation, Idea Evaluation, Implementation Planning, Operations Analysis, Programming, Visioning, Systems Perception, Identifying Downstream Consequences, Identification of Key Causes, Judgment and Decision Making, Systems Evaluation, Time Management, Management of Personnel Resources

College Majors

Criminal Justice Studies: An instructional program that describes the study of the criminal justice system, its organizational components and processes, and its legal and public policy contexts. Includes instruction in criminal law and policy, police and correctional systems organization, the administration of justice and the judiciary, and public attitudes regarding criminal justice issues.

Supporting Courses

Administration and Management: Knowledge of principles and processes involved in business and organizational planning, coordination, and execution. This includes strategic planning, resource allocation, manpower modeling, leadership techniques, and production methods. **Psychology:** Knowledge of human behavior and performance, mental processes, psychological research methods, and the assessment and treatment of behavioral and affective disorders. **Sociology and Anthropology:** Knowledge of group behavior and dynamics, societal trends and influences, cultures, their history, migrations, ethnicity, and origins. **Geography:** Knowledge of various methods for describing the location and distribution of land, sea, and air masses including their physical locations, relationships, and characteristics. **Education and Training:** Knowledge of instructional methods and training techniques including curriculum design principles, learning theory, group and individual teaching techniques, design of individual development plans, and test design principles. **English Language:** Knowledge of the structure and content of the English language including the meaning and spelling of words, rules of composition, and grammar. **Foreign Language:** Knowledge of the structure and content of a foreign (non-English) language including the meaning and spelling of words, rules of composition and grammar, and pronunciation. **History and Archeology:** Knowledge of past historical events and their causes, indicators, and impact on particular civilizations and cultures. **Philosophy and Theology:** Knowledge of different philosophical systems and religions, including their basic principles, values, ethics, ways of thinking, customs, and practices, and their impact on human culture. **Law, Government, and Jurisprudence:** Knowledge of laws, legal codes, court procedures, precedents, government regulations, executive orders, agency rules, and the democratic political process. **Communications and Media:** Knowledge of media production, communication, and dissemination techniques and methods including alternative ways to inform and entertain via written, oral, and visual media.

Anthropologists

Research or study the origins and physical, social, and cultural development and behavior of humans, and the cultures and organizations they have created. Gathers, analyzes, and reports data on human physique, social customs, and artifacts, such as weapons, tools, pottery, and clothing. Studies museum collections of skeletal remains and human fossils to determine their meaning in terms of long-range human evolution. Studies physical and physiological adaptations to differing environments and hereditary characteristics of living populations. Studies growth patterns, sexual differences, and aging phenomena of human groups, current and past. Studies cultures, particularly preindustrial and non-Western societies, including religion, economics, mythology and traditions, and intellectual and artistic life. Observes and measures bodily variations and physical attributes of existing human types. Studies relationships between language and culture and sociolinguistic studies, relationship between individual personality and culture, or complex industrialized societies. Formulates general laws of cultural development, general rules of social and cultural behavior, or general value orientations. Applies anthropological data and techniques to solution of problems in human relations. Applies anthropological concepts to current problems. Writes for professional journals and other publications. Supervises field research projects and student study programs.

Occupational Type

Investigative occupations frequently involve working with ideas, and require an extensive amount of thinking. These occupations can involve searching for facts and figuring out problems mentally.

Skills required of Anthropologists

Reading Comprehension, Writing, Speaking, Mathematics, Science, Critical Thinking, Active Learning, Learning Strategies, Monitoring, Social Perceptiveness, Coordination, Instructing, Problem Identification, Information Gathering, Information Organization, Synthesis/Reorganization, Idea Generation, Idea Evaluation, Implementation Planning, Programming, Visioning, Management of Personnel Resources

College Majors

Anthropology: An instructional program that describes the systematic study of human beings, their antecedents and related primates, and their cultural behavior and institutions, in comparative perspective. Includes instruction in biological/physical anthropology, primatology, human paleontology and prehistoric archeology, hominid evolution, anthropological linguistics, ethnography, ethnology, ethnohistory, socio-cultural anthropology, psychological anthropology, research methods, and applications to areas such as medicine, forensic pathology, museum studies, and international affairs.

 ## Supporting Courses

Administration and Management: Knowledge of principles and processes involved in business and organizational planning, coordination, and execution. This includes strategic planning, resource allocation, manpower modeling, leadership techniques, and production methods. **Biology:** Knowledge of plant and animal living tissue, cells, organisms, and entities, including their functions, interdependencies, and interactions with each other and the environment. **Psychology:** Knowledge of human behavior and performance, mental processes, psychological research methods, and the assessment and treatment of behavioral and affective disorders. **Sociology and Anthropology:** Knowledge of group behavior and dynamics, societal trends and influences, cultures, their history, migrations, ethnicity, and origins. **Geography:** Knowledge of various methods for describing the location and distribution of land, sea, and air masses including their physical locations, relationships, and characteristics. **Education and Training:** Knowledge of instructional methods and training techniques including curriculum design principles, learning theory, group and individual teaching techniques, design of individual development plans, and test design principles. **English Language:** Knowledge of the structure and content of the English language including the meaning and spelling of words, rules of composition, and grammar. **Foreign Language:** Knowledge of the structure and content of a foreign (non-English) language including the meaning and spelling of words, rules of composition and grammar, and pronunciation. **Fine Arts:** Knowledge of theory and techniques required to produce, compose, and perform works of music, dance, visual arts, drama, and sculpture. **History and Archeology:** Knowledge of past historical events and their causes, indicators, and impact on particular civilizations and cultures. **Philosophy and Theology:** Knowledge of different philosophical systems and religions, including their basic principles, values, ethics, ways of thinking, customs, and practices, and their impact on human culture. **Communications and Media:** Knowledge of media production, communication, and dissemination techniques and methods including alternative ways to inform and entertain via written, oral, and visual media.

Linguistic Scientists

Study the structure and development of a specific language or language group. Traces origin and evolution of words and syntax through comparative analysis of ancient parent languages and modern language groups. Studies words and structural characteristics, such as morphology, semantics, phonology, accent, grammar, and literature. Identifies and classifies obscure languages, both ancient and modern, according to family and origin. Reconstructs and deciphers ancient languages from examples found in archeological remains of past civilizations. Prepares description of sounds, forms, and vocabulary of language. Develops improved methods in translation, including computerization. Reduces previously unwritten languages to standardized written form. Prepares descriptions of comparative languages to facilitate improvement of teaching and translation. Contributes to development of linguistic theory. Prepares tests for language-learning aptitudes and language proficiency. Prepares language-teaching materials, such as dictionaries and handbooks. Prepares literacy materials. Teaches language to other than native speakers. Consults with government agencies regarding language programs.

Occupational Type

Investigative occupations frequently involve working with ideas, and require an extensive amount of thinking. These occupations can involve searching for facts and figuring out problems mentally.

Skills required of Linguistic Scientists

Reading Comprehension, Active Listening, Writing, Speaking, Critical Thinking, Active Learning, Learning Strategies, Social Perceptiveness, Instructing, Information Gathering, Information Organization, Synthesis/Reorganization, Idea Generation, Idea Evaluation, Implementation Planning, Visioning

College Majors

Foreign Languages and Literatures, General: An instructional program that describes an undifferentiated program in foreign languages and literatures.

Supporting Courses

Sociology and Anthropology: Knowledge of group behavior and dynamics, societal trends and influences, cultures, their history, migrations, ethnicity, and origins. **Geography:** Knowledge of various methods for describing the location and distribution of land, sea, and air masses including their physical locations, relationships, and characteristics. **Education and Training:** Knowledge of instructional methods and training techniques including curriculum design principles, learning theory, group and individual teaching techniques, design of individual development plans, and test design principles. **English Language:** Knowledge of the structure and content of the English language including the meaning and spelling of words, rules of composition, and grammar. **Foreign Language:** Knowledge of the structure and content of a foreign (non-English) language including the meaning and spelling of words, rules of composition and grammar, and pronunciation. **History and Archeology:** Knowledge of past historical events and their causes, indicators, and impact on particular civilizations and cultures. **Philosophy and Theology:** Knowledge of different philosophical systems and religions, including their basic principles, values, ethics, ways of thinking, customs, and practices, and their impact on human culture.

Historians

Research, analyze, record, and interpret the past as recorded in sources such as government and institutional records, newspapers and other periodicals, photographs, interviews, films, and unpublished manuscripts, such as personal diaries and letters. Conducts historical research on subjects of import to society, and presents finding and theories in textbooks, journals, and other publications. Assembles historical data by consulting sources, such as archives, court records, diaries, news files, and miscellaneous published and unpublished materials. Traces historical development within restricted field of research, such as economics, sociology, or philosophy. Organizes and evaluates data on basis of authenticity and relative significance. Reviews and collects data, such as books, pamphlets, periodicals, and rare newspapers, to provide source material for research. Consults experts or witnesses of historical events. Consults with or advises other individuals on historical authenticity of various materials. Reviews publications and exhibits prepared by staff prior to public release in order to ensure historical accuracy of presentations. Advises or consults with individuals, institutions, and commercial organizations on technological evolution or customs peculiar to certain historical period. Approves or recommends purchase of library reference materials for department. Translates or requests translation of reference materials. Directs and coordinates activities of research staff. Speaks before various groups, organizations, and clubs to promote societal aims and activities. Performs administrative duties, such as budget preparation, employee evaluation, and program planning. Edits society publications. Coordinates activities of workers engaged in cataloging and filing materials. Conducts campaigns to raise funds for society programs and projects.

Occupational Type

Investigative occupations frequently involve working with ideas, and require an extensive amount of thinking. These occupations can involve searching for facts and figuring out problems mentally.

Skills required of Historians

Reading Comprehension, Writing, Speaking, Critical Thinking, Active Learning, Coordination, Information Gathering, Information Organization, Synthesis/Reorganization, Idea Generation, Idea Evaluation, Implementation Planning, Time Management, Management of Financial Resources, Management of Material Resources, Management of Personnel Resources

College Majors

History, General: An instructional program that generally describes the study and interpretation of the past, including the gathering, recording, synthesizing and criticizing of evidence and theories about past events. Includes instruction in historiography; historical research methods; studies of specific periods, issues and cultures; and applications to areas such as historic preservation, public policy, and records administration.

Supporting Courses

Administration and Management: Knowledge of principles and processes involved in business and organizational planning, coordination, and execution. This includes strategic planning, resource allocation, manpower modeling, leadership techniques, and production methods. **Economics and Accounting:** Knowledge of economic and accounting principles and practices, the financial markets, banking, and the analysis and reporting of financial data. **Sales and Marketing:** Knowledge of principles and methods involved in showing, promoting, and selling products or services. This includes marketing strategies and tactics, product demonstration and sales techniques, and sales control systems. **Personnel and Human Resources:** Knowledge of policies and practices involved in personnel/human resource functions. This includes recruitment, selection, training, and promotion regulations and procedures; compensation and benefits packages; labor relations and negotiation strategies; and personnel information systems. **Sociology and Anthropology:** Knowledge of group behavior and dynamics, societal trends and influences, cultures, their history, migrations, ethnicity, and origins. **Geography:** Knowledge of various methods for describing the location and distribution of land, sea, and air masses including their physical locations, relationships, and characteristics. **Education and Training:** Knowledge of instructional methods and training techniques including curriculum design principles, learning theory, group and individual teaching techniques, design of individual development plans, and test design principles. **English Language:** Knowledge of the structure and content of the English language including the meaning and spelling of words, rules of composition, and grammar. **Foreign Language:** Knowledge of the structure and content of a foreign (non-English) language including the meaning and spelling of words, rules of composition and grammar, and pronunciation. **Fine Arts:** Knowledge of theory and techniques required to produce, compose, and perform works of music, dance, visual arts, drama, and sculpture. **History and Archeology:** Knowledge of past historical events and their causes, indicators, and impact on particular civilizations and cultures. **Philosophy and Theology:** Knowledge of different philosophical systems and religions, including their basic principles, values, ethics, ways of thinking, customs, and practices, and their impact on human culture. **Communications and Media:** Knowledge of media production, communication, and dissemination techniques and methods including alternative ways to inform and entertain via written, oral, and visual media.

Intelligence Specialists

Collect, record, analyze, and disseminate tactical, political, strategic, or technical intelligence information to facilitate development of military or political strategies. Evaluates results of research and prepares recommendations for implementing or rejecting proposed solution to plans. Segregates and records incoming intelligence data according to type of data to facilitate comparison, study, and accessibility. Prepares and analyzes information concerning strength, equipment, location, disposition, organization, and movement of enemy forces. Compiles intelligence information to be used in preparing situation maps, charts, visual aids, briefing papers, reports, and publications. Examines intelligence source materials. Compiles terrain intelligence, such as condition of land routes, port facilities, and sources of water, sand, gravel, rock, and timbers. Evaluates data concerning subversive activities, enemy propaganda, and military or political conditions in foreign countries to facilitate counteraction. Briefs and debriefs ground or aviation personnel prior to and after missions. Confers with military leaders and supporting personnel to determine dimensions of problem and to discuss proposals for solution. Develops plans for predicting factors, such as cost and probable success of solutions, according to research techniques and computer formulations. Maintains familiarity with geography; cultural traditions; and social, political, and economic structure of countries from which subversive data originates. Maintains intelligence libraries, including maps, charts, documents, and other items. Assists intelligence officers in analysis and selection of aerial bombardment targets. Plans or assists superiors in planning and supervising intelligence activities of unit assigned.

 ## Occupational Type

Investigative occupations frequently involve working with ideas, and require an extensive amount of thinking. These occupations can involve searching for facts and figuring out problems mentally.

 ## Skills required of Intelligence Specialists

Reading Comprehension, Active Listening, Writing, Speaking, Critical Thinking, Active Learning, Learning Strategies, Monitoring, Social Perceptiveness, Coordination, Persuasion, Negotiation, Problem Identification, Information Gathering, Information Organization, Synthesis/Reorganization, Idea Generation, Idea Evaluation, Implementation Planning, Operations Analysis, Systems Perception, Identifying Downstream Consequences, Identification of Key Causes, Judgment and Decision Making, Time Management

 ## College Majors

International Relations and Affairs: An instructional program that describes the systematic study of international politics and institutions, and the conduct of diplomacy and foreign policy. Includes instruction in international relations theory, foreign policy analysis, national security and strategic studies, international law and organization, the comparative study of specific countries and regions, and the theory and practice of diplomacy.

 ## Supporting Courses

Administration and Management: Knowledge of principles and processes involved in business and organizational planning, coordination, and execution. This includes strategic planning, resource allocation, manpower modeling, leadership techniques, and production methods. **Clerical:** Knowledge of administrative and clerical procedures and systems such as word processing systems, filing and records management systems, stenography and transcription, forms design principles, and other office procedures and terminology. **Economics and Accounting:** Knowledge of economic and accounting principles and practices, the financial markets, banking, and the analysis and reporting of financial data. **Psychology:** Knowledge of human behavior and performance, mental processes, psychological research methods, and the assessment and treatment of behavioral and affective disorders. **Sociology and Anthropology:** Knowledge of group behavior and dynamics, societal trends and influences, cultures, their history, migrations, ethnicity, and origins. **Geography:** Knowledge of various methods for describing the location and distribution of land, sea, and air masses including their physical locations, relationships, and characteristics. **Education and Training:** Knowledge of instructional methods and training techniques including curriculum design principles, learning theory, group and individual teaching techniques, design of individual development plans, and test design principles. **Foreign Language:** Knowledge of the structure and content of a foreign (non-English) language including the meaning and spelling of words, rules of composition and grammar, and pronunciation. **History and Archeology:** Knowledge of past historical events and their causes, indicators, and impact on particular civilizations and cultures. **Philosophy and Theology:** Knowledge of different philosophical systems and religions, including their basic principles, values, ethics, ways of thinking, customs, and practices, and their impact on human culture. **Public Safety and Security:** Knowledge of weaponry, public safety, and security operations, rules, regulations, precautions, prevention, and the protection of people, data, and property. **Law, Government, and Jurisprudence:** Knowledge of laws, legal codes, court procedures, precedents, government regulations, executive orders, agency rules, and the democratic political process. **Telecommunications:** Knowledge of transmission, broadcasting, switching, control, and operation of telecommunications systems. **Communications and Media:** Knowledge of media production, communication, and dissemination techniques and methods including alternative ways to inform and entertain via written, oral, and visual media. **Transportation:** Knowledge of principles and methods for moving people or goods by air, rail, sea, or road, including their relative costs, advantages, and limitations.

Genealogists

Research genealogical background of individual or family to establish descent from specific ancestor or to identify forebears of individual or family. Consults American and foreign genealogical tables, publications, and documents to trace lines of descent or succession. References materials, such as church and county records, for evidence of births, baptisms, marriages, deaths, and legacies. Organizes and evaluates data on basis of significance and authenticity. Gathers and appraises available physical evidence, such as drawings and photographs. Constructs chart showing lines of descent and family relationships. Prepares history of family in narrative form, or writes brief sketches emphasizing points of interest in family background.

 ## Occupational Type

Investigative occupations frequently involve working with ideas, and require an extensive amount of thinking. These occupations can involve searching for facts and figuring out problems mentally.

 ## Skills required of Genealogists

Information Gathering, Information Organization

College Majors

History, General: An instructional program that generally describes the study and interpretation of the past, including the gathering, recording, synthesizing and criticizing of evidence and theories about past events. Includes instruction in historiography; historical research methods; studies of specific periods, issues and cultures; and applications to areas such as historic preservation, public policy, and records administration.

Supporting Courses

Sociology and Anthropology: Knowledge of group behavior and dynamics, societal trends and influences, cultures, their history, migrations, ethnicity, and origins. **Geography:** Knowledge of various methods for describing the location and distribution of land, sea, and air masses including their physical locations, relationships, and characteristics. **English Language:** Knowledge of the structure and content of the English language including the meaning and spelling of words, rules of composition, and grammar. **Foreign Language:** Knowledge of the structure and content of a foreign (non-English) language including the meaning and spelling of words, rules of composition and grammar, and pronunciation. **History and Archeology:** Knowledge of past historical events and their causes, indicators, and impact on particular civilizations and cultures.

Archeologists

Conduct research to reconstruct record of past human life and culture from human remains, artifacts, architectural features, and structures recovered through excavation, underwater recovery, or other means of discovery. Studies artifacts, architectural features, and types of structures recovered by excavation in order to determine age and cultural identity. Classifies and interprets artifacts, architectural features, and types of structures recovered by excavation to determine age and cultural identity. Establishes chronological sequence of development of each culture from simpler to more advanced levels.

Occupational Type

Investigative occupations frequently involve working with ideas, and require an extensive amount of thinking. These occupations can involve searching for facts and figuring out problems mentally.

Skills required of Archeologists

Reading Comprehension, Writing, Science, Critical Thinking, Active Learning, Information Gathering, Information Organization, Synthesis/Reorganization, Idea Generation, Idea Evaluation

College Majors

Anthropology: An instructional program that describes the systematic study of human beings, their antecedents and related primates, and their cultural behavior and institutions, in comparative perspective. Includes instruction in biological/physical anthropology, primatology, human paleontology and prehistoric archeology, hominid evolution, anthropological linguistics, ethnography, ethnology, ethnohistory, socio-cultural anthropology, psychological anthropology, research methods, and applications to areas such as medicine, forensic pathology, museum studies, and international affairs.

Supporting Courses

Sociology and Anthropology: Knowledge of group behavior and dynamics, societal trends and influences, cultures, their history, migrations, ethnicity, and origins. **Geography:** Knowledge of various methods for describing the location and distribution of land, sea, and air masses including their physical locations, relationships, and characteristics. **Foreign Language:** Knowledge of the structure and content of a foreign (non-English) language including the meaning and spelling of words, rules of composition and grammar, and pronunciation. **History and Archeology:** Knowledge of past historical events and their causes, indicators, and impact on particular civilizations and cultures. **Philosophy and Theology:** Knowledge of different philosophical systems and religions, including their basic principles, values, ethics, ways of thinking, customs, and practices, and their impact on human culture.

SOCIAL WORKERS

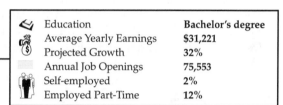

Education	Bachelor's degree
Average Yearly Earnings	$31,221
Projected Growth	32%
Annual Job Openings	75,553
Self-employed	2%
Employed Part-Time	12%

Community Organization Social Workers

Plan, organize, and work with community groups to help solve social problems and deliver specialized social services. Organizes projects, such as discussion groups, and conducts consumer problem surveys to stimulate civic responsibility and promote group work concepts. Investigates problems of assigned community and individuals disadvantaged because of income, age, or economic or personal handicaps, to determine needs. Develops, organizes, and directs customized programs, such as physical, educational, recreational, or cultural activities, for individuals and groups. Reviews and evaluates available resources and services from local agencies to provide social assistance for clients. Secures and coordinates community social service assistance, such as health, welfare, and education for individuals and families. Assists communities in establishing new local affiliates or programs. Initiates and maintains liaison between housing authority and local agencies to promote development and management of public housing. Speaks before groups to explain supportive services and resources available to persons needing special assistance. Facilitates establishment of constructive relationships between tenants and housing management, and among tenants. Interprets standards and program goals of national or state agencies to assist local organizations in establishing goals and standards. Coordinates work activities of individuals to improve vocational skills. Writes proposals to obtain government or private funding for projects designed to meet needs of community. Maintains records and prepares reports on community topics, such as work activities, local conditions, and developing trends. Assesses complexity level of individual's capacity to perform work activities. Identifies individual's behavior deviations and assists individual to resolve work-related difficulties. Demonstrates and instructs participants in activities, such as sports, dances, games, arts, crafts, and dramatics. Demonstrates job duties to individuals, oversees and monitors work performance, and examines workpiece to verify adherence to specifications. Recruits, trains, and supervises paid staff and volunteers in specific assignments. Prepares and presents budgets.

Occupational Type

Social occupations frequently involve working with, communicating with, and teaching people. These occupations often involve helping or providing service to others.

Skills required of Community Organization Social Workers

Reading Comprehension, Active Listening, Writing, Speaking, Critical Thinking, Learning Strategies, Monitoring, Social Perceptiveness, Coordination, Persuasion, Negotiation, Instructing, Service Orientation, Problem Identification, Information Gathering, Synthesis/Reorganization, Idea Generation, Idea Evaluation, Implementation Planning, Visioning, Systems Perception, Identification of Key Causes, Judgment and Decision Making, Time Management, Management of Financial Resources, Management of Material Resources, Management of Personnel Resources

College Majors

Education, General: An instructional program that generally describes the theory and practice of learning and teaching; the basic principles of educational psychology; the art of teaching; the planning and administration of educational activities; and the social foundations of education.

Supporting Courses

Administration and Management: Knowledge of principles and processes involved in business and organizational planning, coordination, and execution. This includes strategic planning, resource allocation, manpower modeling, leadership techniques, and production methods. **Sales and Marketing:** Knowledge of principles and methods involved in showing, promoting, and selling products or services. This includes marketing strategies and tactics, product demonstration and sales techniques, and sales control systems. **Customer and Personal Service:** Knowledge of principles and processes for providing customer and personal services including needs assessment techniques, quality service standards, alternative delivery systems, and customer satisfaction evaluation techniques. **Personnel and Human Resources:** Knowledge of policies and practices involved in personnel/human resource functions. This includes recruitment, selection, training, and promotion regulations and procedures; compensation and benefits packages; labor relations and negotiation strategies; and personnel information systems. **Psychology:** Knowledge of human behavior and performance, mental processes, psychological research methods, and the assessment and treatment of behavioral and affective disorders. **Sociology and Anthropology:** Knowledge of group behavior and dynamics, societal trends and influences, cultures, their history, migrations, ethnicity, and origins. **Therapy and Counseling:** Knowledge of information and techniques needed to rehabilitate physical and mental ailments and to provide career guidance including alternative treatments, rehabilitation equipment and its proper use, and methods to evaluate treatment effects. **Education and Training:** Knowledge of instructional methods and training techniques including curriculum design principles, learning theory, group and individual teaching techniques, design of individual development plans, and test design principles. **English Language:** Knowledge of the structure and content of the English language including the meaning and spelling of words, rules of composition, and grammar. **Communications and Media:** Knowledge of media production, communication, and dissemination techniques and methods including alternative ways to inform and entertain via written, oral, and visual media.

Social Workers

Counsel and aid individuals and families with problems relating to personal and family adjustments, finances, employment, food, clothing, housing, or other human needs and conditions. Counsels individuals or family members regarding behavior modifications, rehabilitation, social adjustments, financial assistance, vocational training, childcare, or medical care. Counsels parents with child-rearing problems and children and youth with difficulties in social adjustments. Interviews individuals to assess social and emotional capabilities, physical and mental impairments, and financial needs. Refers client to community resources for needed assistance. Arranges for daycare, homemaker service, prenatal care, and child planning programs for clients in need of such services. Leads group counseling sessions to provide support in such areas as grief, stress, or chemical dependency. Counsels students whose behavior, school progress, or mental or physical impairment indicates need for assistance. Arranges for medical, psychiatric, and other tests that may disclose cause of difficulties and indicate remedial measures. Consults with parents, teachers, and other school personnel to determine causes of problems and effect solutions. Serves as liaison between student, home, school, family service agencies, child guidance clinics, courts, protective services, doctors, and clergy members. Investigates home conditions to determine suitability of foster or adoptive home, or to protect children from harmful environment. Develops program content and organizes and leads activities planned to enhance social development of individual members and accomplishment of group goals. Determines client's eligibility for financial assistance. Reviews service plan and performs follow-up to determine quantity and quality of service provided to client. Places children in foster or adoptive homes, institutions, or medical treatment centers. Evaluates personal characteristics of foster home or adoption applicants. Maintains case history records and prepares reports. Collects supplementary information, such as employment, medical records, or school reports. Assists travelers, including runaways, migrants, transients, refugees, repatriated Americans, and problem families.

Occupational Type

Social occupations frequently involve working with, communicating with, and teaching people. These occupations often involve helping or providing service to others.

Skills required of Social Workers

Reading Comprehension, Active Listening, Writing, Speaking, Critical Thinking, Active Learning, Learning Strategies, Monitoring, Social Perceptiveness, Coordination, Persuasion, Negotiation, Instructing, Service Orientation, Problem Identification, Information Gathering, Information Organization, Synthesis/Reorganization, Idea Generation, Idea Evaluation, Implementation Planning, Visioning, Identification of Key Causes, Judgment and Decision Making, Time Management

College Majors

Clinical Psychology: An instructional program that prepares individuals for the independent professional practice of clinical psychology, involving the analysis, diagnosis, and clinical treatment of psychological disorders and behavioral pathologies. Includes instruction in clinical assessment and diagnosis, personality appraisal, psychopathology, clinical psychopharmacology, behavior modification, therapeutic intervention skills, patient interviewing, personalized and group therapy, child and adolescent therapy, cognitive and behavioral therapy, supervised clinical practice, ethical standards, and applicable regulations.

Supporting Courses

Administration and Management: Knowledge of principles and processes involved in business and organizational planning, coordination, and execution. This includes strategic planning, resource allocation, manpower modeling, leadership techniques, and production methods. **Clerical:** Knowledge of administrative and clerical procedures and systems such as word processing systems, filing and records management systems, stenography and transcription, forms design principles, and other office procedures and terminology. **Customer and Personal Service:** Knowledge of principles and processes for providing customer and personal services including needs assessment techniques, quality service standards, alternative delivery systems, and customer satisfaction evaluation techniques. **Psychology:** Knowledge of human behavior and performance, mental processes, psychological research methods, and the assessment and treatment of behavioral and affective disorders. **Sociology and Anthropology:** Knowledge of group behavior and dynamics, societal trends and influences, cultures, their history, migrations, ethnicity, and origins. **Therapy and Counseling:** Knowledge of information and techniques needed to rehabilitate physical and mental ailments and to provide career guidance including alternative treatments, rehabilitation equipment and its proper use, and methods to evaluate treatment effects. **Foreign Language:** Knowledge of the structure and content of a foreign (non-English) language including the meaning and spelling of words, rules of composition and grammar, and pronunciation. **Philosophy and Theology:** Knowledge of different philosophical systems and religions, including their basic principles, values, ethics, ways of thinking, customs, and practices, and their impact on human culture. **Law, Government, and Jurisprudence:** Knowledge of laws, legal codes, court procedures, precedents, government regulations, executive orders, agency rules, and the democratic political process.

Probation and Correctional Treatment Specialists

Provide social services to assist in rehabilitation of law offenders in custody or on probation. Include probation and parole officers. Counsels offender and refers offender to social resources of community for assistance. Provides guidance to inmates or offenders, such as development of vocational and educational plans and available social services. Formulates rehabilitation plan for each assigned offender or inmate. Interviews offender or inmate to determine social progress and individual problems, needs, interests, and attitude. Consults with attorneys, judges, and institution personnel to evaluate inmate's social progress. Conducts follow-up interview with offender or inmate to ascertain progress made. Determines nature and extent of inmate's or offender's criminal record and current and prospective social problems. Reviews and evaluates legal and social history and progress of offender or inmate. Informs offender or inmate of requirements of conditional release, such as office visits, restitution payments, or educational and employment stipulations. Confers with inmate's or offender's family to identify needs and problems, and to ensure that family and business are attended to. Makes recommendations concerning conditional release or institutionalization of offender or inmate. Assists offender or inmate with matters concerning detainers, sentences in other jurisdictions, writs, and applications for social assistance. Develops and prepares informational packets of social agencies and assistance organizations and programs for inmate or offender. Prepares and maintains case folder for each assigned inmate or offender. Conducts prehearing or presentencing investigations, and testifies in court.

Occupational Type

Social occupations frequently involve working with, communicating with, and teaching people. These occupations often involve helping or providing service to others.

Skills required of Probation and Correctional Treatment Specialists

Active Listening, Speaking, Social Perceptiveness, Persuasion, Negotiation, Service Orientation, Problem Identification, Idea Evaluation, Implementation Planning, Identifying Downstream Consequences, Identification of Key Causes, Judgment and Decision Making, Systems Evaluation

College Majors

Social Work: An instructional program that prepares individuals for the professional practice of social welfare administration and counseling, and that describes the study of organized means of providing basic support services for vulnerable individuals and groups. Includes instruction in social welfare policy; case work planning; social counseling and intervention strategies; administrative procedures and regulations; and specific applications in areas such as child welfare and family services, probation, employment services, and disability counseling.

Supporting Courses

Psychology: Knowledge of human behavior and performance, mental processes, psychological research methods, and the assessment and treatment of behavioral and affective disorders. **Sociology and Anthropology:** Knowledge of group behavior and dynamics, societal trends and influences, cultures, their history, migrations, ethnicity, and origins. **Therapy and Counseling:** Knowledge of information and techniques needed to rehabilitate physical and mental ailments and to provide career guidance including alternative treatments, rehabilitation equipment and its proper use, and methods to evaluate treatment effects. **Public Safety and Security:** Knowledge of weaponry, public safety, and security operations, rules, regulations, precautions, prevention, and the protection of people, data, and property. **Law, Government, and Jurisprudence:** Knowledge of laws, legal codes, court procedures, precedents, government regulations, executive orders, agency rules, and the democratic political process.

SPECIAL EDUCATION TEACHERS

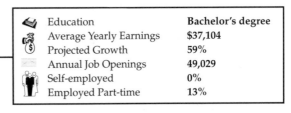

Education		Bachelor's degree
Average Yearly Earnings		$37,104
Projected Growth		59%
Annual Job Openings		49,029
Self-employed		0%
Employed Part-time		13%

Special Education Vocational Training Teachers

Plan and conduct special education work and study programs or teach vocational skills to handicapped students. Counsels and instructs students in matters such as vocational choices, job readiness, and job retention skills and behaviors. Instructs students in areas such as personal-social skills and work-related attitudes and behaviors. Confers with students, parents, school personnel, and other individuals to plan vocational training that meets needs, interests, and abilities of students. Develops work opportunities that allow students to experience success in performing tasks of increasing difficulty and that teach work values. Confers with potential employers to obtain cooperation, adapting work situations to special needs of students. Confers with employers and visits worksite to monitor progress of students. Establishes contacts with employers and employment agencies and surveys newspapers and other sources to locate work opportunities for students. Evaluates and selects program participants according to specified criteria. Determines support needed to meet employer requirements and fulfill program goals. Assists students in applying for jobs and accompanies students to employment interviews. Conducts field trips to enable students to learn about job activities and to explore work environments.

Occupational Type

Social occupations frequently involve working with, communicating with, and teaching people. These occupations often involve helping or providing service to others.

Skills required of Special Education Vocational Training Teachers

Speaking, Learning Strategies, Social Perceptiveness, Coordination, Persuasion, Instructing, Service Orientation, Idea Generation, Implementation Planning, Management of Personnel Resources

 College Majors

Education, General: An instructional program that generally describes the theory and practice of learning and teaching; the basic principles of educational psychology; the art of teaching; the planning and administration of educational activities; and the social foundations of education.

 Supporting Courses

Administration and Management: Knowledge of principles and processes involved in business and organizational planning, coordination, and execution. This includes strategic planning, resource allocation, manpower modeling, leadership techniques, and production methods. **Sales and Marketing:** Knowledge of principles and methods involved in showing, promoting, and selling products or services. This includes marketing strategies and tactics, product demonstration and sales techniques, and sales control systems. **Customer and Personal Service:** Knowledge of principles and processes for providing customer and personal services including needs assessment techniques, quality service standards, alternative delivery systems, and customer satisfaction evaluation techniques. **Personnel and Human Resources:** Knowledge of policies and practices involved in personnel/human resource functions. This includes recruitment, selection, training, and promotion regulations and procedures; compensation and benefits packages; labor relations and negotiation strategies; and personnel information systems. **Psychology:** Knowledge of human behavior and performance, mental processes, psychological research methods, and the assessment and treatment of behavioral and affective disorders. **Sociology and Anthropology:** Knowledge of group behavior and dynamics, societal trends and influences, cultures, their history, migrations, ethnicity, and origins. **Therapy and Counseling:** Knowledge of information and techniques needed to rehabilitate physical and mental ailments and to provide career guidance including alternative treatments, rehabilitation equipment and its proper use, and methods to evaluate treatment effects. **Education and Training:** Knowledge of instructional methods and training techniques including curriculum design principles, learning theory, group and individual teaching techniques, design of individual development plans, and test design principles. **Philosophy and Theology:** Knowledge of different philosophical systems and religions, including their basic principles, values, ethics, ways of thinking, customs, and practices, and their impact on human culture.

Teachers: Emotionally Impaired, Mentally Impaired, and Learning Disabled

Teach basic academic and living skills to students with emotional or mental impairments or learning disabilities. Teaches socially acceptable behavior, employing techniques such as behavior modification and positive reinforcement. Instructs students, using special educational strategies and techniques to improve sensory-motor and perceptual-motor development, memory, language, and cognition. Instructs students in academic subjects, utilizing various teaching techniques, such as phonetics, multisensory learning, and repetition, to reinforce learning. Instructs students in daily living skills required for independent maintenance and economic self-sufficiency, such as hygiene, safety, and food preparation. Plans curriculum and other instructional materials to meet student's needs, considering such factors as physical, emotional, and educational abilities. Selects and teaches reading material and math problems related to everyday life of individual student. Administers and interprets results of ability and achievement tests. Confers with parents, administrators, testing specialists, social workers, and others to develop individual educational plan for student. Confers with other staff members to plan programs designed to promote educational, physical, and social development of students. Works with students to increase motivation. Provides consistent reinforcement to learning, and continuous feedback to students. Observes, evaluates, and prepares reports on progress of students. Meets with parents to provide support, guidance in using community resources, and skills in dealing with students' learning impairments.

Occupational Type

Social occupations frequently involve working with, communicating with, and teaching people. These occupations often involve helping or providing service to others.

Skills required of Teachers: Emotionally Impaired, Mentally Impaired, and Learning Disabled

Active Listening, Writing, Speaking, Learning Strategies, Monitoring, Social Perceptiveness, Persuasion, Instructing, Service Orientation, Idea Generation, Idea Evaluation, Implementation Planning, Identification of Key Causes

College Majors

Education, General: An instructional program that generally describes the theory and practice of learning and teaching; the basic principles of educational psychology; the art of teaching; the planning and administration of educational activities; and the social foundations of education.

Supporting Courses

Customer and Personal Service: Knowledge of principles and processes for providing customer and personal services including needs assessment techniques, quality service standards, alternative delivery systems, and customer satisfaction evaluation techniques. **Psychology:** Knowledge of human behavior and performance, mental processes, psychological research methods, and the assessment and treatment of behavioral and affective disorders. **Sociology and Anthropology:** Knowledge of group behavior and dynamics, societal trends and influences, cultures, their history, migrations, ethnicity, and origins. **Medicine and Dentistry:** Knowledge of the information and techniques needed to diagnose and treat injuries, diseases, and deformities. This includes symptoms, treatment alternatives, drug properties and interactions, and preventive healthcare measures. **Therapy and Counseling:** Knowledge of information and techniques needed to rehabilitate physical and mental ailments and to provide career guidance including alternative treatments, rehabilitation equipment and its proper use, and methods to evaluate treatment effects. **Education and Training:** Knowledge of instructional methods and training techniques including curriculum design principles, learning theory, group and individual teaching techniques, design of individual development plans, and test design principles. **English Language:** Knowledge of the structure and content of the English language including the meaning and spelling of words, rules of composition, and grammar. **Foreign Language:** Knowledge of the structure and content of a foreign (non-English) language including the meaning and spelling of words, rules of composition and grammar, and pronunciation.

Teachers: Physically, Visually, and Hearing Impaired

Teach elementary and secondary school subjects to physically, visually, and hearing impaired students. Teaches academic subjects, daily living skills, and vocational skills to students, adapting teaching techniques to meet individual needs of students. Plans curriculum and prepares lessons and other materials, considering such factors as individual needs and learning levels and physical limitations of students. Instructs students in various forms of communication, such as gestures, sign language, finger spelling, and cues. Instructs students in reading and writing, using magnification equipment and large-print material or Braille system. Confers with parents, administrators, testing specialists, social workers, and others to develop individual educational program. Encourages students' participation in verbal and sensory classroom experiences to ensure comprehension of subject matter and development of social and communication skills. Attends and interprets lectures and instructions for students enrolled in regular classes, using sign language. Transcribes lessons and other materials into Braille for blind students or large print for low-vision students. Arranges for and conducts field trips designed to promote experiential learning. Discusses with parents how parents can encourage students' independence and well-being and to provide guidance in using community resources. Tests students' hearing aids to ensure hearing aids are functioning. Arranges and adjusts tools, work aids, and equipment utilized by students in classroom, such as specially equipped work tables, computers, and typewriters. Devises special teaching tools, techniques, and equipment.

 Occupational Type

Social occupations frequently involve working with, communicating with, and teaching people. These occupations often involve helping or providing service to others.

 Skills required of Teachers: Physically, Visually, and Hearing Impaired

Reading Comprehension, Active Listening, Writing, Speaking, Learning Strategies, Monitoring, Social Perceptiveness, Instructing, Service Orientation, Idea Generation, Implementation Planning, Operations Analysis, Technology Design, Identification of Key Causes, Time Management

College Majors

Education, General: An instructional program that generally describes the theory and practice of learning and teaching; the basic principles of educational psychology; the art of teaching; the planning and administration of educational activities; and the social foundations of education.

 Supporting Courses

Administration and Management: Knowledge of principles and processes involved in business and organizational planning, coordination, and execution. This includes strategic planning, resource allocation, manpower modeling, leadership techniques, and production methods. **Clerical:** Knowledge of administrative and clerical procedures and systems such as word processing systems, filing and records management systems, stenography and transcription, forms design principles, and other office procedures and terminology. **Customer and Personal Service:** Knowledge of principles and processes for providing customer and personal services including needs assessment techniques, quality service standards, alternative delivery systems, and customer satisfaction evaluation techniques. **Biology:** Knowledge of plant and animal living tissue, cells, organisms, and entities, including their functions, interdependencies, and interactions with each other and the environment. **Psychology:** Knowledge of human behavior and performance, mental processes, psychological research methods, and the assessment and treatment of behavioral and affective disorders. **Sociology and Anthropology:** Knowledge of group behavior and dynamics, societal trends and influences, cultures, their history, migrations, ethnicity, and origins. **Therapy and Counseling:** Knowledge of information and techniques needed to rehabilitate physical and mental ailments and to provide career guidance including alternative treatments, rehabilitation equipment and its proper use, and methods to evaluate treatment effects. **Education and Training:** Knowledge of instructional methods and training techniques including curriculum design principles, learning theory, group and individual teaching techniques, design of individual development plans, and test design principles. **English Language:** Knowledge of the structure and content of the English language including the meaning and spelling of words, rules of composition, and grammar. **Foreign Language:** Knowledge of the structure and content of a foreign (non-English) language including the meaning and spelling of words, rules of composition and grammar, and pronunciation. **History and Archeology:** Knowledge of past historical events and their causes, indicators, and impact on particular civilizations and cultures. **Philosophy and Theology:** Knowledge of different philosophical systems and religions, including their basic principles, values, ethics, ways of thinking, customs, and practices, and their impact on human culture.

Special Education Evaluators

Assess type and degree of disability of handicapped children to aid in determining special programs and services required to meet educational needs. Observes student behavior and rates strength and weakness of factors, such as motivation, cooperativeness, aggression, and task completion. Tests children to detect learning limitations, and recommends follow-up activities, consultation, or services. Selects, administers, and scores tests to measure individual's aptitudes, educational achievements, perceptual motor skills, vision, and hearing. Evaluates student's readiness to transfer from special classes to regular classroom. Determines evaluation procedures for children having or suspected of having learning disabilities, mental retardation, behavior disorders, or physical handicaps. Confers with school or other personnel and studies records to obtain additional information on nature and severity of disability. Administers work-related tests and reviews records and other data to assess student vocational interests and abilities. Reports findings for staff consideration in placement of children in educational programs. Provides supportive services to regular classroom teacher.

Occupational Type

Social occupations frequently involve working with, communicating with, and teaching people. These occupations often involve helping or providing service to others.

Skills required of Special Education Evaluators

Reading Comprehension, Active Listening, Writing, Speaking, Critical Thinking, Learning Strategies, Monitoring, Social Perceptiveness, Service Orientation, Problem Identification, Synthesis/Reorganization, Idea Generation, Idea Evaluation, Implementation Planning, Identification of Key Causes, Judgment and Decision Making

College Majors

Education, General: An instructional program that generally describes the theory and practice of learning and teaching; the basic principles of educational psychology; the art of teaching; the planning and administration of educational activities; and the social foundations of education.

Supporting Courses

Customer and Personal Service: Knowledge of principles and processes for providing customer and personal services including needs assessment techniques, quality service standards, alternative delivery systems, and customer satisfaction evaluation techniques. **Psychology:** Knowledge of human behavior and performance, mental processes, psychological research methods, and the assessment and treatment of behavioral and affective disorders. **Sociology and Anthropology:** Knowledge of group behavior and dynamics, societal trends and influences, cultures, their history, migrations, ethnicity, and origins. **Therapy and Counseling:** Knowledge of information and techniques needed to rehabilitate physical and mental ailments and to provide career guidance including alternative treatments, rehabilitation equipment and its proper use, and methods to evaluate treatment effects. **Education and Training:** Knowledge of instructional methods and training techniques including curriculum design principles, learning theory, group and individual teaching techniques, design of individual development plans, and test design principles.

Parent Instructors: Child Development and Rehabilitation

Instruct parents of mentally and physically handicapped children in therapy techniques and behavior modification. Instructs parents in behavior modification, physical development, language development, and conceptual learning exercises and activities. Develops individual teaching plan covering self-help, motor, social, cognitive, and language skills development for parents to implement in home. Evaluates child's responses to determine level of physical and mental development. Determines parent's ability to comprehend and apply therapeutic and behavior modification techniques. Revises teaching plan to correspond with child's rate of development. Counsels parents and organizes groups of parents in similar situations to provide social and emotional support to parents. Consults and coordinates plans with other professionals. Teaches preschool subjects, such as limited-vocabulary sign language and color recognition, to children capable of learning such subjects. Refers parents and children to social services agencies for additional services and financial assistance.

Occupational Type

Social occupations frequently involve working with, communicating with, and teaching people. These occupations often involve helping or providing service to others.

Skills required of Parent Instructors: Child Development and Rehabilitation

Reading Comprehension, Active Listening, Speaking, Critical Thinking, Active Learning, Learning Strategies, Monitoring, Social Perceptiveness, Coordination, Persuasion, Instructing, Service Orientation, Problem Identification, Synthesis/Reorganization, Idea Generation, Idea Evaluation, Implementation Planning, Identification of Key Causes, Judgment and Decision Making, Time Management

College Majors

Education, General: An instructional program that generally describes the theory and practice of learning and teaching; the basic principles of educational psychology; the art of teaching; the planning and administration of educational activities; and the social foundations of education.

Supporting Courses

Customer and Personal Service: Knowledge of principles and processes for providing customer and personal services including needs assessment techniques, quality service standards, alternative delivery systems, and customer satisfaction evaluation techniques. **Psychology:** Knowledge of human behavior and performance, mental processes, psychological research methods, and the assessment and treatment of behavioral and affective disorders. **Sociology and Anthropology:** Knowledge of group behavior and dynamics, societal trends and influences, cultures, their history, migrations, ethnicity, and origins. **Medicine and Dentistry:** Knowledge of the information and techniques needed to diagnose and treat injuries, diseases, and deformities. This includes symptoms, treatment alternatives, drug properties and interactions, and preventive healthcare measures. **Therapy and Counseling:** Knowledge of information and techniques needed to rehabilitate physical and mental ailments and to provide career guidance including alternative treatments, rehabilitation equipment and its proper use, and methods to evaluate treatment effects. **Education and Training:** Knowledge of instructional methods and training techniques including curriculum design principles, learning theory, group and individual teaching techniques, design of individual development plans, and test design principles.

SPEECH: LANGUAGE PATHOLOGISTS AND AUDIOLOGISTS

Speech: Language Pathologists and Audiologists

Education		Master's degree
Average Yearly Earnings		$42,702
Projected Growth		51%
Annual Job Openings		12,203
Self-employed		6%
Employed Part-time		21%

Examine and provide remedial services for persons with speech and hearing disorders. Perform research related to speech and language problems. Administers hearing or speech/language evaluations, tests, or examinations to patients to collect information on type and degree of impairment. Conducts or directs research and reports findings on speech or hearing topics to develop procedures, technology, or treatments. Evaluates hearing and speech/language test results and medical or background information to determine hearing or speech impairment and treatment. Counsels and instructs clients in techniques to improve speech or hearing impairment, including sign language or lip-reading. Plans and conducts prevention and treatment programs for clients' hearing or speech problems. Records and maintains reports of speech or hearing research or treatments. Refers clients to additional medical or educational services if needed. Advises educators or other medical staff on speech or hearing topics. Participates in conferences or training to update or share knowledge of new hearing or speech disorder treatment methods or technology. Teaches staff or students about hearing or speech disorders, including explaining new treatments or equipment. Directs and coordinates staff activities of speech or hearing clinic, and hires, trains, and evaluates personnel. Prepares budget requesting funding for specific projects, including equipment, supplies, and staff.

Occupational Type

Social occupations frequently involve working with, communicating with, and teaching people. These occupations often involve helping or providing service to others.

Skills required of Speech: Language Pathologists and Audiologists

Reading Comprehension, Active Listening, Writing, Speaking, Science, Critical Thinking, Active Learning, Learning Strategies, Monitoring, Social Perceptiveness, Coordination, Instructing, Service Orientation, Problem Identification, Information Gathering, Information

Organization, Synthesis/Reorganization, Idea Generation, Idea Evaluation, Implementation Planning, Operations Analysis, Technology Design, Visioning, Identifying Downstream Consequences, Identification of Key Causes, Systems Evaluation, Time Management, Management of Financial Resources, Management of Material Resources, Management of Personnel Resources

 ## College Majors

Communication Disorders, General: An instructional program that generally describes the principles and practice of identifying and treating disorders of human speech and hearing, and related problems of social communication and health. Includes instruction in developmental and acquired disorders, basic research and clinical methods, and prevention and treatment modalities.

 ## Supporting Courses

Administration and Management: Knowledge of principles and processes involved in business and organizational planning, coordination, and execution. This includes strategic planning, resource allocation, manpower modeling, leadership techniques, and production methods. **Economics and Accounting:** Knowledge of economic and accounting principles and practices, the financial markets, banking, and the analysis and reporting of financial data. **Customer and Personal Service:** Knowledge of principles and processes for providing customer and personal services including needs assessment techniques, quality service standards, alternative delivery systems, and customer satisfaction evaluation techniques. **Personnel and Human Resources:** Knowledge of policies and practices involved in personnel/human resource functions. This includes recruitment, selection, training, and promotion regulations and procedures; compensation and benefits packages; labor relations and negotiation strategies; and personnel information systems. **Biology:** Knowledge of plant and animal living tissue, cells, organisms, and entities, including their functions, interdependencies, and interactions with each other and the environment. **Psychology:** Knowledge of human behavior and performance, mental processes, psychological research methods, and the assessment and treatment of behavioral and affective disorders. **Medicine and Dentistry:** Knowledge of the information and techniques needed to diagnose and treat injuries, diseases, and deformities. This includes symptoms, treatment alternatives, drug properties and interactions, and preventive healthcare measures. **Therapy and Counseling:** Knowledge of information and techniques needed to rehabilitate physical and mental ailments and to provide career guidance including alternative treatments, rehabilitation equipment and its proper use, and methods to evaluate treatment effects. **Education and Training:** Knowledge of instructional methods and training techniques including curriculum design principles, learning theory, group and individual teaching techniques, design of individual development plans, and test design principles. **English Language:** Knowledge of the structure and content of the English language including the meaning and spelling of words, rules of composition, and grammar. **Foreign Language:** Knowledge of the structure and content of a foreign (non-English) language including the meaning and spelling of words, rules of composition and grammar, and pronunciation. **Telecommunications:** Knowledge of transmission, broadcasting, switching, control, and operation of telecommunications systems.

STATISTICIANS

Education		Bachelor's degree
Average Yearly Earnings		$47,507
Projected Growth		1%
Annual Job Openings		936
Self-employed		0%
Employed Part-time		5%

Statisticians

Plan surveys and collect, organize, interpret, summarize, and analyze numerical data, applying statistical theory and methods to provide usable information in scientific, business, economic, and other fields. Data derived from surveys may represent either complete enumeration or statistical samples. Include mathematical statisticians who are engaged in the development of mathematical theory associated with the application of statistical techniques. Conducts research into mathematical theories and proofs that form basis of science of statistics. Plans data collection, and analyzes and interprets numerical data from experiments, studies, surveys, and other sources. Applies statistical methodology to provide information for scientific research and statistical analysis. Plans methods to collect information and develops questionnaire techniques according to survey design. Conducts surveys utilizing sampling techniques or complete enumeration bases. Analyzes and interprets statistics to point up significant differences in relationships among sources of information, and prepares conclusions and forecasts. Develops and tests experimental designs, sampling techniques, and analytical methods, and prepares recommendations concerning their use. Investigates, evaluates, and reports on applicability, efficiency, and accuracy of statistical methods used to obtain and evaluate data. Evaluates reliability of source information, adjusts and weighs raw data, and organizes results into form compatible with analysis by computers or other methods. Develops statistical methodology. Examines theories, such as those of probability and inference, to discover mathematical bases for new or improved methods of obtaining and evaluating numerical data. Presents numerical information by computer readouts, graphs, charts, tables, written reports, or other methods. Describes sources of information, and limitations on reliability and usability.

Occupational Type

Investigative occupations frequently involve working with ideas, and require an extensive amount of thinking. These occupations can involve searching for facts and figuring out problems mentally.

Skills required of Statisticians

Reading Comprehension, Active Listening, Writing, Speaking, Mathematics, Science, Critical Thinking, Active Learning, Learning Strategies, Monitoring, Problem Identification, Information Gathering, Information Organization, Synthesis/Reorganization, Idea Generation, Idea Evaluation, Implementation Planning, Operations Analysis, Programming, Testing, Visioning, Systems Perception, Identifying Downstream Consequences, Identification of Key Causes, Judgment and Decision Making, Systems Evaluation

College Majors

Biostatistics: An instructional program that describes the application of statistical methods and techniques to the study of living organisms and biological systems. Includes instruction in experimental design and data analysis, projection methods, descriptive statistics, and specific applications to biological subdisciplines.

 Supporting Courses

Administration and Management: Knowledge of principles and processes involved in business and organizational planning, coordination, and execution. This includes strategic planning, resource allocation, manpower modeling, leadership techniques, and production methods. **Economics and Accounting:** Knowledge of economic and accounting principles and practices, the financial markets, banking, and the analysis and reporting of financial data. **Computers and Electronics:** Knowledge of electric circuit boards, processors, chips, and computer hardware and software, including applications and programming. **Mathematics:** Knowledge of numbers, their operations, and interrelationships including arithmetic, algebra, geometry, calculus, statistics, and their applications. **English Language:** Knowledge of the structure and content of the English language including the meaning and spelling of words, rules of composition, and grammar. **Philosophy and Theology:** Knowledge of different philosophical systems and religions, including their basic principles, values, ethics, ways of thinking, customs, and practices, and their impact on human culture.

Financial Analysts, Statistical

Conduct statistical analyses of information affecting investment programs of public or private institutions and private individuals. Analyzes financial information to forecast business, industry, and economic conditions, for use in making investment decisions. Interprets data concerning price, yield, stability, and future trends in investment risks and economic influences pertinent to investments. Gathers information such as industry, regulatory, and economic information, company financial statements, financial periodicals, and newspapers. Recommends investment timing and buy-and-orders to company or to staff of investment establishment of advising clients. Draws charts and graphs to illustrate reports, using computer. Calls brokers and purchases investments for company, according to company policy.

 Occupational Type

Investigative occupations frequently involve working with ideas, and require an extensive amount of thinking. These occupations can involve searching for facts and figuring out problems mentally.

Skills required of Financial Analysts, Statistical

Reading Comprehension, Writing, Speaking, Mathematics, Critical Thinking, Active Learning, Monitoring, Information Gathering, Information Organization, Synthesis/

Reorganization, Idea Evaluation, Programming, Visioning, Systems Perception, Identifying Downstream Consequences, Identification of Key Causes, Judgment and Decision Making, Systems Evaluation, Management of Financial Resources

College Majors

Finance, General: An instructional program that generally prepares individuals to plan, manage, and analyze the financial and monetary aspects and performance of business enterprises, banking institutions, or other organizations. Includes instruction in principles of accounting; financial instruments; capital planning; funds acquisition; asset and debt management; budgeting; financial analysis; and investments and portfolio management.

Supporting Courses

Economics and Accounting: Knowledge of economic and accounting principles and practices, the financial markets, banking, and the analysis and reporting of financial data. **Sales and Marketing:** Knowledge of principles and methods involved in showing, promoting, and selling products or services. This includes marketing strategies and tactics, product demonstration and sales techniques, and sales control systems. **Computers and Electronics:** Knowledge of electric circuit boards, processors, chips, and computer hardware and software, including applications and programming. **Mathematics:** Knowledge of numbers, their operations, and interrelationships including arithmetic, algebra, geometry, calculus, statistics, and their applications. **Foreign Language:** Knowledge of the structure and content of a foreign (non-English) language including the meaning and spelling of words, rules of composition and grammar, and pronunciation. **History and Archeology:** Knowledge of past historical events and their causes, indicators, and impact on particular civilizations and cultures. **Law, Government, and Jurisprudence:** Knowledge of laws, legal codes, court procedures, precedents, government regulations, executive orders, agency rules, and the democratic political process.

SYSTEMS ANALYSTS

Computer Security Specialists

Education		Bachelor's degree
Average Yearly Earnings		$48,360
Projected Growth		103%
Annual Job Openings		87,318
Self-employed		7%
Employed Part-time		6%

Plan, coordinate, and implement
security measures for information systems to regulate access to computer data files and prevent unauthorized modification, destruction, or disclosure of information. Develops plans to safeguard computer files against accidental or unauthorized modification, destruction, or disclosure and to meet emergency data processing needs. Coordinates implementation of computer system plan with establishment personnel and outside vendors. Tests data processing system to ensure functioning of data processing activities and security measures. Modifies computer security files to incorporate new software, correct errors, or change

individual access status. Confers with personnel to discuss issues such as computer data access needs, security violations, and programming changes. Monitors use of data files and regulates access to safeguard information in computer files. Writes reports to document computer security and emergency measures policies, procedures, and test results.

Occupational Type

Investigative occupations frequently involve working with ideas, and require an extensive amount of thinking. These occupations can involve searching for facts and figuring out problems mentally.

Skills required of Computer Security Specialists

Synthesis/Reorganization, Idea Generation, Implementation Planning, Operations Analysis, Technology Design, Installation, Programming, Testing, Management of Material Resources

College Majors

Computer and Information Sciences, General: An instructional program that generally describes the study of data and information storage and processing systems, including hardware, software, basic design principles, user requirements analysis, and related economic and policy issues.

Supporting Courses

Administration and Management: Knowledge of principles and processes involved in business and organizational planning, coordination, and execution. This includes strategic planning, resource allocation, manpower modeling, leadership techniques, and production methods. **Computers and Electronics:** Knowledge of electric circuit boards, processors, chips, and computer hardware and software, including applications and programming. **Philosophy and Theology:** Knowledge of different philosophical systems and religions, including their basic principles, values, ethics, ways of thinking, customs, and practices, and their impact on human culture. **Public Safety and Security:** Knowledge of weaponry, public safety, and security operations, rules, regulations, precautions, prevention, and the protection of people, data, and property.

Systems Analysts, Electronic Data Processing

Analyze business, scientific, and technical problems for application to electronic data processing systems. (Excludes persons working primarily as engineers, mathematicians, or scientists.) Analyzes, plans, and tests computer programs, using programming and system techniques. Consults with staff and users to identify operating procedure problems. Formulates and reviews plans outlining steps required to develop programs to meet staff and user requirements. Devises flowcharts and diagrams to illustrate steps and to describe logical operational steps of program. Writes documentation to describe and develop installation and operating procedures of programs. Coordinates installation of computer programs and operating systems, and tests, maintains, and monitors computer system. Reads manuals, periodicals, and technical reports to learn how to develop programs to meet staff and user requirements. Sets up computer test to find and correct program or system errors. Writes and revises quality standards and test procedures, and modifies existing procedures for program and system design for evaluation. Reviews and analyzes computer printouts and performance indications to locate code problems. Modifies program to correct errors by correcting computer codes. Enters instructions into computer to test program or system for conformance to standards. Assists staff and users to solve computer-related problems, such as malfunctions and program problems. Trains staff and users to use computer system and its programs.

Occupational Type

Investigative occupations frequently involve working with ideas, and require an extensive amount of thinking. These occupations can involve searching for facts and figuring out problems mentally.

Skills required of Systems Analysts, Electronic Data Processing

Reading Comprehension, Active Listening, Writing, Speaking, Mathematics, Science, Critical Thinking, Active Learning, Learning Strategies, Monitoring, Instructing, Service Orientation, Problem Identification, Information Gathering, Information Organization, Synthesis/Reorganization, Idea Generation, Idea Evaluation, Implementation Planning, Operations Analysis, Technology Design, Equipment Selection, Installation, Programming, Testing, Operation Monitoring, Operation and Control, Product Inspection, Equipment Maintenance, Troubleshooting, Visioning, Systems Perception, Identifying Downstream Consequences, Identification of Key Causes, Systems Evaluation, Time Management, Management of Material Resources

College Majors

Computer and Information Sciences, General: An instructional program that generally describes the study of data and information storage and processing systems, including hardware, software, basic design principles, user requirements analysis, and related economic and policy issues.

Supporting Courses

Clerical: Knowledge of administrative and clerical procedures and systems such as word processing systems, filing and records management systems, stenography and transcription, forms design principles, and other office procedures and terminology. **Customer and Personal Service:** Knowledge of principles and processes for providing customer and personal services including needs assessment techniques, quality service standards, alternative delivery systems, and customer satisfaction evaluation techniques. **Computers and Electronics:** Knowledge of electric circuit boards, processors, chips, and computer hardware and software, including applications and programming. **Mathematics:** Knowledge of numbers, their operations, and interrelationships including arithmetic, algebra, geometry, calculus, statistics, and their applications. **Education and Training:** Knowledge of instructional methods and training techniques including curriculum design principles, learning theory, group and individual teaching techniques, design of individual development plans, and test design principles. **English Language:** Knowledge of the structure and content of the English language including the meaning and spelling of words, rules of composition, and grammar. **Telecommunications:** Knowledge of transmission, broadcasting, switching, control, and operation of telecommunications systems. **Communications and Media:** Knowledge of media production, communication, and dissemination techniques and methods including alternative ways to inform and entertain via written, oral, and visual media.

Geographic Information System Specialists

Design and coordinate development of integrated geographical information system database of spatial and nonspatial data; develop analyses and presentation of this data, applying knowledge of geographic information system. Designs database and coordinates physical changes to database, applying additional knowledge of spatial feature representations. Chooses and applies analysis procedures for spatial and nonspatial data. Determines how to analyze spatial relationships, including adjacency, containment, and proximity. Decides effective presentation of information, and selects cartographic and additional elements. Determines information to be queried, such as location, characteristics of location, trend, pattern, routing, and modeling various series of events. Meets with users to develop system or project requirements. Creates maps and graphs, using computer and geographic information system software and related equipment. Reviews existing and incoming data for currency, accuracy, usefulness, quality, and documentation. Selects or verifies designations of cartographic symbols. Presents information to users and answers questions. Oversees entry of data into database, including applications, keyboard entry, manual digitizing, scanning, and automatic conversion. Recommends procedures to increase data accessibility and ease of use. Discusses problems in development of transportation planning and modeling, marketing and demographic mapping, or assessment of geologic and environmental factors.

Occupational Type

Investigative occupations frequently involve working with ideas, and require an extensive amount of thinking. These occupations can involve searching for facts and figuring out problems mentally.

Skills required of Geographic Information System Specialists

Active Listening, Speaking, Mathematics, Critical Thinking, Active Learning, Monitoring, Information Organization, Synthesis/Reorganization, Idea Generation, Implementation Planning, Operations Analysis, Technology Design, Installation, Programming, Troubleshooting, Systems Perception, Identification of Key Causes, Systems Evaluation

College Majors

Various: Many bachelor studies contribute to expertise in this field.

Supporting Courses

Administration and Management: Knowledge of principles and processes involved in business and organizational planning, coordination, and execution. This includes strategic planning, resource allocation, manpower modeling, leadership techniques, and production methods. **Sales and Marketing:** Knowledge of principles and methods involved in showing, promoting, and selling products or services. This includes marketing strategies and tactics, product demonstration and sales techniques, and sales control systems. **Computers and Electronics:** Knowledge of electric circuit boards, processors, chips, and computer hardware and software, including applications and programming. **Design:** Knowledge of design techniques, principles, tools and instruments involved in the production and use of precision technical plans, blueprints, drawings, and models. **Mathematics:** Knowledge of numbers, their operations, and interrelationships including arithmetic, algebra, geometry, calculus, statistics, and their applications. **Physics:** Knowledge and prediction of physical principles, laws, and applications including air, water, material dynamics, light, atomic principles, heat, electric theory, earth formations, and meteorological and related natural phenomena. **Sociology and Anthropology:** Knowledge of group behavior and dynamics, societal trends and influences, cultures, their history, migrations, ethnicity, and origins. **Geography:** Knowledge of various methods for describing the location and distribution of land, sea, and air masses including their physical locations, relationships, and characteristics. **English Language:** Knowledge of the structure and content of the English language including the meaning and spelling of words, rules of composition, and grammar. **Transportation:** Knowledge of principles and methods for moving people or goods by air, rail, sea, or road, including their relative costs, advantages, and limitations.

Data Communications Analysts

Research, test, evaluate, and recommend data communications hardware and software. Analyzes test data and recommends hardware or software for purchase. Identifies areas of operation which need upgraded equipment, such as modems, fiber-optic cables, and telephone wires. Tests and evaluates hardware and software to determine efficiency, reliability, and compatibility with existing system. Reads technical manuals and brochures to determine equipment which meets establishment requirements. Monitors system performance. Conducts survey to determine user needs. Develops and writes procedures for installation, use, and solving problems of communications hardware and software. Visits vendors to learn about available products or services. Assists users to identify and solve data communication problems. Trains users in use of equipment.

Occupational Type

Investigative occupations frequently involve working with ideas, and require an extensive amount of thinking. These occupations can involve searching for facts and figuring out problems mentally.

Skills required of Data Communications Analysts

Reading Comprehension, Active Listening, Writing, Speaking, Science, Critical Thinking, Active Learning, Learning Strategies, Monitoring, Persuasion, Negotiation, Instructing, Service Orientation, Problem Identification, Information Organization, Synthesis/ Reorganization, Idea Generation, Idea Evaluation, Implementation Planning, Operations Analysis, Technology Design, Equipment Selection, Installation, Programming, Testing, Troubleshooting, Visioning, Systems Perception, Identifying Downstream Consequences, Judgment and Decision Making, Systems Evaluation, Management of Financial Resources, Management of Material Resources

College Majors

Data Processing Technology/Technician: An instructional program that prepares individuals to use and operate computers and associated software packages to perform a variety of tasks, including text processing, number processing, graphics, and database management.

Supporting Courses

Sales and Marketing: Knowledge of principles and methods involved in showing, promoting, and selling products or services. This includes marketing strategies and tactics, product demonstration and sales techniques, and sales control systems. **Customer and Personal Service:** Knowledge of principles and processes for providing customer and personal services including needs assessment techniques, quality service standards, alternative delivery systems, and customer satisfaction evaluation techniques. **Computers and Electronics:** Knowledge of electric circuit boards, processors, chips, and computer hardware and software, including applications and programming. **Mathematics:** Knowledge of numbers, their operations, and interrelationships including arithmetic, algebra, geometry, calculus, statistics, and their applications. **Psychology:** Knowledge of human behavior and performance, mental processes, psychological research methods, and the assessment and treatment of behavioral and affective disorders. **Education and Training:** Knowledge of instructional methods and training techniques including curriculum design principles, learning theory, group and individual teaching techniques, design of individual development plans, and test design principles. **Telecommunications:** Knowledge of transmission, broadcasting, switching, control, and operation of telecommunications systems. **Communications and Media:** Knowledge of media production, communication, and dissemination techniques and methods including alternative ways to inform and entertain via written, oral, and visual media.

TAX EXAMINERS AND REVENUE AGENTS

Tax Examiners, Collectors, and Revenue Agents

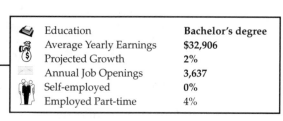

Education		Bachelor's degree
Average Yearly Earnings		$32,906
Projected Growth		2%
Annual Job Openings		3,637
Self-employed		0%
Employed Part-time		4%

Determine tax liability or collect taxes from individuals or business firms, according to prescribed laws and regulations. Examines and analyzes tax assets and liabilities to determine resolution of delinquent tax problems. Investigates legal instruments, other documents, financial transactions, operation methods, and industry practices to assess inclusiveness of accounting records and tax returns. Conducts independent field audits and investigations of Federal income tax returns to verify or amend tax liabilities. Examines selected tax returns to determine nature and extent of audits to be performed. Selects appropriate remedy, such as partial-payment agreement, offer of compromise, or seizure and sale of property. Analyzes accounting books and records to determine appropriateness of accounting methods employed and compliance with statutory provisions. Secures taxpayer's agreement to discharge tax assessment, or submits contested determination to other administrative or judicial conferees for appeals hearings. Directs service of legal documents, such as subpoenas, warrants, notices of assessment, and garnishments. Confers with taxpayer or representative to explain issues involved and applicability of pertinent tax laws and regulations. Participates in informal appeals hearings on contested cases from other agents. Serves as member of regional appeals board to reexamine unresolved issues in terms of relevant laws and regulations. Recommends criminal prosecutions and civil penalties.

Occupational Type

Conventional occupations frequently involve following set procedures and routines. These occupations can include working with data and details more than with ideas. Usually there is a clear line of authority to follow.

Skills required of Tax Examiners, Collectors, and Revenue Agents

Reading Comprehension, Active Listening, Writing, Speaking, Mathematics, Critical Thinking, Active Learning, Monitoring, Persuasion, Negotiation, Problem Identification, Information Gathering, Information Organization, Synthesis/Reorganization, Idea Evaluation, Judgment and Decision Making, Systems Evaluation, Management of Financial Resources

College Majors

Accounting: An instructional program that prepares individuals to practice the profession of accounting, and to perform related business functions. Includes instruction in accounting principles and theory, financial accounting, managerial accounting, cost accounting, budget control, tax accounting, legal aspects of accounting, auditing, reporting procedures, statement analysis, planning and consulting, business information systems, accounting research methods, professional standards and ethics, and applications to specific for-profit, public, and non-profit organizations.

Supporting Courses

Economics and Accounting: Knowledge of economic and accounting principles and practices, the financial markets, banking, and the analysis and reporting of financial data. **Mathematics:** Knowledge of numbers, their operations, and interrelationships including arithmetic, algebra, geometry, calculus, statistics, and their applications. **Law, Government, and Jurisprudence:** Knowledge of laws, legal codes, court procedures, precedents, government regulations, executive orders, agency rules, and the democratic political process.

THERAPEUTIC SERVICES AND ADMINSTRATION

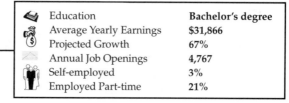

Education	Bachelor's degree
Average Yearly Earnings	$31,866
Projected Growth	67%
Annual Job Openings	4,767
Self-employed	3%
Employed Part-time	21%

Social Workers, Medical and Psychiatric

Counsel and aid individuals and families with problems that may arise during or following the recovery from physical or mental illness, by providing supportive services designed to help the persons understand, accept, and follow medical recommendations. Include chemical dependency counselors. Counsels clients and patients, individually and in group sessions, to assist in overcoming dependencies, adjusting to life, and making changes. Counsels family members to assist in understanding, dealing with, and supporting client or patient. Interviews client, reviews records, and confers with other professionals to evaluate mental or physical condition of client or patient. Formulates or coordinates program plan for treatment, care, and rehabilitation of client or patient, based on social work experience and knowledge. Monitors, evaluates, and records client progress according to measurable goals described in treatment and care plan. Modifies treatment plan to comply with changes in client's status. Refers patient, client, or family to community resources to assist in recovery from mental or physical illness. Intervenes as advocate for client or patient to resolve emergency problems in crisis situation. Plans and conducts programs to prevent substance abuse or improve health and counseling services in community. Develops and monitors budgetary expenditures for program. Supervises and directs other workers providing services to client or patient.

Occupational Type

Social occupations frequently involve working with, communicating with, and teaching people. These occupations often involve helping or providing service to others.

Skills required of Social Workers, Medical and Psychiatric

Reading Comprehension, Active Listening, Writing, Speaking, Critical Thinking, Active Learning, Learning Strategies, Monitoring, Social Perceptiveness, Coordination, Persuasion, Negotiation, Instructing, Service Orientation, Problem Identification, Idea Generation, Idea Evaluation, Implementation Planning, Visioning, Systems Perception, Identifying Downstream Consequences, Identification of Key Causes, Judgment and Decision Making, Systems Evaluation, Time Management, Management of Financial Resources, Management of Personnel Resources

College Majors

Clinical Psychology: An instructional program that prepares individuals for the independent professional practice of clinical psychology, involving the analysis, diagnosis, and clinical treatment of psychological disorders and behavioral pathologies. Includes instruction in clinical assessment and diagnosis, personality appraisal, psychopathology, clinical psychopharmacology, behavior modification, therapeutic intervention skills, patient interviewing, personalized and group therapy, child and adolescent therapy, cognitive and behavioral therapy, supervised clinical practice, ethical standards, and applicable regulations.

Supporting Courses

Customer and Personal Service: Knowledge of principles and processes for providing customer and personal services including needs assessment techniques, quality service standards, alternative delivery systems, and customer satisfaction evaluation techniques. **Personnel and Human Resources:** Knowledge of policies and practices involved in personnel/human resource functions. This includes recruitment, selection, training, and promotion regulations and procedures; compensation and benefits packages; labor relations and negotiation strategies; and personnel information systems. **Psychology:** Knowledge of human behavior and performance, mental processes, psychological research methods, and the assessment and treatment of behavioral and affective disorders. **Sociology and Anthropology:** Knowledge of group behavior and dynamics, societal trends and influences, cultures, their history, migrations, ethnicity, and origins. **Medicine and Dentistry:** Knowledge of the information and techniques needed to diagnose and treat injuries, diseases, and deformities. This includes symptoms, treatment alternatives, drug properties and interactions, and preventive healthcare measures. **Therapy and Counseling:** Knowledge of information and techniques needed to rehabilitate physical and mental ailments and to provide career guidance including alternative treatments, rehabilitation equipment and its proper use, and methods to evaluate treatment effects. **Education and Training:** Knowledge of instructional methods and training techniques including curriculum design principles, learning theory, group and individual teaching techniques, design of individual development plans, and test design principles. **Philosophy and Theology:** Knowledge of different philosophical systems and religions, including their basic principles, values, ethics, ways of thinking, customs, and practices, and their impact on human culture. **Communications and Media:** Knowledge of media production, communication, and dissemination techniques and methods including alternative ways to inform and entertain via written, oral, and visual media.

Exercise Physiologists

Develop, implement, and coordinate exercise programs and administer medical tests, under physician's supervision, to program participants to promote physical fitness. Records heart activity, using electrocardiograph (EKG) machine, while participant undergoes stress test on treadmill, under physician's supervision. Measures oxygen consumption and lung functioning, using spirometer. Measures amount of fat in body, using hydrostatic scale, skinfold calipers, and tape measure to assess body composition. Performs routine laboratory tests of blood samples for cholesterol level and glucose tolerance. Conducts individual and group aerobic, strength, and flexibility exercises. Writes initial and follow-up exercise prescriptions for participants, following physician's recommendation, specifying equipment, such as treadmill, track, or bike. Demonstrates correct use of exercise equipment and exercise routines. Interprets test results. Observes participants during exercise for signs of stress. Teaches behavior modification classes, such as stress management, weight control, and related subjects. Interviews participants to obtain vital statistics and medical history and records information. Explains program and test procedures to participants. Schedules other examinations and tests, such as physical examination, chest X-ray, and urinalysis. Records test data in participant's record. Orders material and supplies. Adjusts and calibrates exercise equipment, using hand tools.

 Occupational Type

Social occupations frequently involve working with, communicating with, and teaching people. These occupations often involve helping or providing service to others.

 Skills required of Exercise Physiologists

Active Listening, Speaking, Learning Strategies, Social Perceptiveness, Instructing, Service Orientation, Implementation Planning

 College Majors

Health and Physical Education, General: An instructional program that generally describes the study and practice of activities and principles that promote physical fitness, achieve and maintain athletic prowess, and accomplish related research and service goals. Includes instruction in human movement studies, motivation studies, rules and practice of specific sports, exercise and fitness principles and techniques, basic athletic injury prevention and treatment, and organizing and leading fitness and sports programs.

 Supporting Courses

Customer and Personal Service: Knowledge of principles and processes for providing customer and personal services including needs assessment techniques, quality service standards, alternative delivery systems, and customer satisfaction evaluation techniques. **Chemistry:** Knowledge of the composition, structure, and properties of substances and of the chemical processes and transformations that they undergo. This includes uses of chemicals and their interactions, danger signs, production techniques, and disposal methods. **Biology:** Knowledge of plant and animal living tissue, cells, organisms, and entities, including their functions, interdependencies, and interactions with each other and the environment. **Psychology:** Knowledge of human behavior and performance, mental processes, psychological research methods, and the assessment and treatment of behavioral and affective disorders. **Medicine and Dentistry:** Knowledge of the information and techniques needed to diagnose and treat injuries, diseases, and deformities. This includes symptoms, treatment alternatives, drug properties and interactions, and preventive healthcare measures. **Therapy and Counseling:** Knowledge of information and techniques needed to rehabilitate physical and mental ailments and to provide career guidance including alternative treatments, rehabilitation equipment and its proper use, and methods to evaluate treatment effects. **Education and Training:** Knowledge of instructional methods and training techniques including curriculum design principles, learning theory, group and individual teaching techniques, design of individual development plans, and test design principles. **Foreign Language:** Knowledge of the structure and content of a foreign (non-English)

language including the meaning and spelling of words, rules of composition and grammar, and pronunciation.

Orientation and Mobility Therapists

Train blind and visually impaired clients in the techniques of daily living to maximize independence and personal adjustment. Trains clients in awareness of physical environment through sense of smell, hearing, and touch. Teaches clients personal skills, such as eating, grooming, dressing, and use of bathroom facilities. Teaches clients home management skills, such as cooking and coin and money identification. Teaches clients communication skills, such as use of telephone. Teaches clients to protect body, using hands and arms to detect obstacles. Teaches clients to read and write Braille. Trains clients to travel alone, with or without cane, through use of variety of actual or simulated travel situations and exercises. Instructs clients in use of reading machines and common electrical devices, and in development of effective listening techniques. Administers assessment tests to clients to determine present and required or desired orientation and mobility skills. Instructs clients in arts, crafts, and recreational skills, such as macrame, leatherworking, sewing, ceramics, and piano playing. Interviews clients to obtain information concerning medical history, lifestyle, or other pertinent information. Instructs clients in group activities, such as swimming, dancing, or playing modified sports activities. Prepares progress report for use of rehabilitation team to evaluate clients' ability to perform varied activities essential to daily living.

 ## Occupational Type

Social occupations frequently involve working with, communicating with, and teaching people. These occupations often involve helping or providing service to others.

 ## Skills required of Orientation and Mobility Therapists

Active Listening, Speaking, Learning Strategies, Monitoring, Social Perceptiveness, Persuasion, Instructing, Service Orientation, Synthesis/Reorganization, Implementation Planning

 ## College Majors

Special Education, General: An instructional program that generally describes the design and provision of teaching and other educational services to children or adults with special learning needs or disabilities, and that may prepare individuals to function as special education teachers. Includes instruction in diagnosing learning disabilities, developing individual education plans, teaching and supervising special education students, special education counseling, and applicable laws and policies.

 ## Supporting Courses

Customer and Personal Service: Knowledge of principles and processes for providing customer and personal services including needs assessment techniques, quality service standards, alternative delivery systems, and customer satisfaction evaluation techniques.

Psychology: Knowledge of human behavior and performance, mental processes, psychological research methods, and the assessment and treatment of behavioral and affective disorders. **Medicine and Dentistry:** Knowledge of the information and techniques needed to diagnose and treat injuries, diseases, and deformities. This includes symptoms, treatment alternatives, drug properties and interactions, and preventive healthcare measures. **Therapy and Counseling:** Knowledge of information and techniques needed to rehabilitate physical and mental ailments and to provide career guidance including alternative treatments, rehabilitation equipment and its proper use, and methods to evaluate treatment effects. **Education and Training:** Knowledge of instructional methods and training techniques including curriculum design principles, learning theory, group and individual teaching techniques, design of individual development plans, and test design principles. **Foreign Language:** Knowledge of the structure and content of a foreign (non-English) language including the meaning and spelling of words, rules of composition and grammar, and pronunciation. **Fine Arts:** Knowledge of theory and techniques required to produce, compose, and perform works of music, dance, visual arts, drama, and sculpture. **Telecommunications:** Knowledge of transmission, broadcasting, switching, control, and operation of telecommunications systems.

TUTORS AND INSTRUCTORS

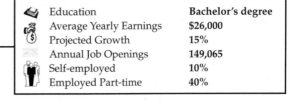

Education	Bachelor's degree
Average Yearly Earnings	$26,000
Projected Growth	15%
Annual Job Openings	149,065
Self-employed	10%
Employed Part-time	40%

Public Health Educators

Plan, organize, and direct health education programs for group and community needs. Plans and provides educational opportunities for health personnel. Collaborates with health specialists and civic groups to ascertain community health needs, determine availability of services, and develop goals. Promotes health discussions in schools, industry, and community agencies. Conducts community surveys to ascertain health needs, develop desirable health goals, and determine availability of professional health services. Prepares and disseminates educational and informational materials. Develops and maintains cooperation between public, civic, professional, and voluntary agencies.

Occupational Type

Social occupations frequently involve working with, communicating with, and teaching people. These occupations often involve helping or providing service to others.

Skills required of Public Health Educators

Active Listening, Writing, Speaking, Active Learning, Learning Strategies, Social Perceptiveness, Coordination, Persuasion, Instructing, Service Orientation, Information

Gathering, Information Organization, Synthesis/Reorganization, Idea Generation, Idea Evaluation, Implementation Planning, Visioning, Systems Perception, Systems Evaluation

College Majors

Curriculum and Instruction: An instructional program that describes the study of the curriculum and related instructional processes and tools, and that may prepare individuals to serve as professional curriculum specialists. Includes instruction in curriculum theory, curriculum design and planning, instructional material design and evaluation, curriculum evaluation, and applications to specific subject matter, programs or educational levels.

Supporting Courses

Administration and Management: Knowledge of principles and processes involved in business and organizational planning, coordination, and execution. This includes strategic planning, resource allocation, manpower modeling, leadership techniques, and production methods. **Sales and Marketing:** Knowledge of principles and methods involved in showing, promoting, and selling products or services. This includes marketing strategies and tactics, product demonstration and sales techniques, and sales control systems. **Customer and Personal Service:** Knowledge of principles and processes for providing customer and personal services including needs assessment techniques, quality service standards, alternative delivery systems, and customer satisfaction evaluation techniques. **Biology:** Knowledge of plant and animal living tissue, cells, organisms, and entities, including their functions, interdependencies, and interactions with each other and the environment. **Psychology:** Knowledge of human behavior and performance, mental processes, psychological research methods, and the assessment and treatment of behavioral and affective disorders. **Sociology and Anthropology:** Knowledge of group behavior and dynamics, societal trends and influences, cultures, their history, migrations, ethnicity, and origins. **Medicine and Dentistry:** Knowledge of the information and techniques needed to diagnose and treat injuries, diseases, and deformities. This includes symptoms, treatment alternatives, drug properties and interactions, and preventive healthcare measures. **Therapy and Counseling:** Knowledge of information and techniques needed to rehabilitate physical and mental ailments and to provide career guidance including alternative treatments, rehabilitation equipment and its proper use, and methods to evaluate treatment effects. **Education and Training:** Knowledge of instructional methods and training techniques including curriculum design principles, learning theory, group and individual teaching techniques, design of individual development plans, and test design principles. **English Language:** Knowledge of the structure and content of the English language including the meaning and spelling of words, rules of composition, and grammar. **Philosophy and Theology:** Knowledge of different philosophical systems and religions, including their basic principles, values, ethics, ways of thinking, customs, and practices, and their impact on human culture. **Communications and Media:** Knowledge of media production, communication, and dissemination techniques and methods including alternative ways to inform and entertain via written, oral, and visual media.

UNDERWRITERS

	Education	Bachelor's degree
	Average Yearly Earnings	$38,792
	Projected Growth	6%
	Annual Job Openings	10,918
	Self-employed	0%
	Employed Part-time	8%

Underwriters

Review individual applications for insurance to evaluate degree of risk involved and determine acceptance of applications. Examines documents to determine degree of risk from such factors as applicant financial standing and value and condition of property. Evaluates possibility of losses due to catastrophe or excessive insurance. Declines excessive risks. Authorizes reinsurance of policy when risk is high. Decreases value of policy when risk is substandard, and specifies applicable endorsements or applies rating to ensure safe, profitable distribution of risks, using reference materials. Reviews company records to determine amount of insurance in force on single risk or group of closely related risks. Writes to field representatives, medical personnel, and others to obtain further information, quote rates, or explain company underwriting policies.

Occupational Type

Conventional occupations frequently involve following set procedures and routines. These occupations can include working with data and details more than with ideas. Usually there is a clear line of authority to follow.

Skills required of Underwriters

Mathematics, Critical Thinking, Information Gathering, Judgment and Decision Making, Systems Evaluation

College Majors

Finance, General: An instructional program that generally prepares individuals to plan, manage, and analyze the financial and monetary aspects and performance of business enterprises, banking institutions, or other organizations. Includes instruction in principles of accounting; financial instruments; capital planning; funds acquisition; asset and debt management; budgeting; financial analysis; and investments and portfolio management.

Supporting Courses

Clerical: Knowledge of administrative and clerical procedures and systems such as word processing systems, filing and records management systems, stenography and transcription, forms design principles, and other office procedures and terminology. **Economics and Accounting:** Knowledge of economic and accounting principles and practices, the financial markets, banking, and the analysis and reporting of financial data. **Mathematics:** Knowledge of numbers, their operations, and interrelationships including arithmetic, algebra, geometry, calculus, statistics, and their applications.

URBAN AND REGIONAL PLANNERS

Education	Master's degree
Average Yearly Earnings	$40,934
Projected Growth	5%
Annual Job Openings	3,856
Self-employed	3%
Employed Part-time	18%

Urban and Regional Planners

Develop comprehensive plans and programs for use of land and physical facilities of cities, counties, and metropolitan areas. Develops alternative plans with recommendations for program or project. Compiles, organizes, and analyzes data on economic, social, and physical factors affecting land use, using statistical methods. Reviews and evaluates environmental impact reports applying to specific private and public planning projects and programs. Evaluates information to determine feasibility of proposals or to identify factors requiring amendment. Recommends governmental measures affecting land use, public utilities, community facilities, housing, and transportation. Discusses purpose of land use projects, such as transportation, conservation, residential, commercial, industrial, and community use, with planning officials. Prepares or requisitions graphic and narrative report on land use data. Determines regulatory limitations on project. Conducts field investigations, economic or public opinion surveys, demographic studies, or other research to gather required information. Advises planning officials on feasibility, cost effectiveness, regulatory conformance, and alternative recommendations for project. Maintains collection of socioeconomic, environmental, and regulatory data related to land use for governmental and private sectors.

Occupational Type

Investigative occupations frequently involve working with ideas, and require an extensive amount of thinking. These occupations can involve searching for facts and figuring out problems mentally.

Skills required of Urban and Regional Planners

Reading Comprehension, Active Listening, Writing, Speaking, Mathematics, Critical Thinking, Active Learning, Learning Strategies, Monitoring, Social Perceptiveness, Coordination, Persuasion, Negotiation, Problem Identification, Information Gathering, Information Organization, Synthesis/Reorganization, Idea Generation, Idea Evaluation, Implementation Planning, Operations Analysis, Visioning, Systems Perception, Identifying Downstream Consequences, Identification of Key Causes, Judgment and Decision Making, Systems Evaluation, Time Management, Management of Financial Resources, Management of Material Resources

College Majors

City/Urban, Community, and Regional Planning: An instructional program that prepares individuals to apply principles of planning and analysis to the development and improvement of urban areas or surrounding regions, including the development of master plans, the design of urban services systems, and the economic and policy issues related to planning and plan implementation.

Supporting Courses

Administration and Management: Knowledge of principles and processes involved in business and organizational planning, coordination, and execution. This includes strategic planning, resource allocation, manpower modeling, leadership techniques, and production methods. **Clerical:** Knowledge of administrative and clerical procedures and systems such as word processing systems, filing and records management systems, stenography and transcription, forms design principles, and other office procedures and terminology. **Economics and Accounting:** Knowledge of economic and accounting principles and practices, the financial markets, banking, and the analysis and reporting of financial data. **Sales and Marketing:** Knowledge of principles and methods involved in showing, promoting, and selling products or services. This includes marketing strategies and tactics, product demonstration and sales techniques, and sales control systems. **Computers and Electronics:** Knowledge of electric circuit boards, processors, chips, and computer hardware and software, including applications and programming. **Engineering and Technology:** Knowledge of equipment, tools, mechanical devices, and their uses to produce motion, light, power, technology, and other applications. **Design:** Knowledge of design techniques, principles, tools and instruments involved in the production and use of precision technical plans, blueprints, drawings, and models. **Building and Construction:** Knowledge of materials, methods, and the appropriate tools to construct objects, structures, and buildings. **Mathematics:** Knowledge of numbers, their operations, and interrelationships including arithmetic, algebra, geometry, calculus, statistics, and their applications. **Biology:** Knowledge of plant and animal living tissue, cells, organisms, and entities, including their functions, interdependencies, and interactions with each other and the environment. **Sociology and Anthropology:** Knowledge of group behavior and dynamics, societal trends and influences, cultures, their history, migrations, ethnicity, and origins. **Geography:** Knowledge of various methods for describing the location and distribution of land, sea, and air masses including their physical locations, relationships, and characteristics. **Education and Training:** Knowledge of instructional methods and training techniques including curriculum design principles, learning theory, group and individual teaching techniques, design of individual development plans, and test design principles. **English Language:** Knowledge of the structure and content of the English language including the meaning and spelling of words, rules of composition, and grammar. **History and Archeology:** Knowledge of past historical events and their causes, indicators, and impact on particular civilizations and cultures. **Philosophy and Theology:** Knowledge of different philosophical systems and religions, including their basic principles, values, ethics, ways of thinking, customs, and practices, and their impact on human culture. **Public Safety and Security:** Knowledge of weaponry, public safety, and security operations, rules, regulations, precautions, prevention, and the protection of people, data, and property. **Law, Government, and Jurisprudence:** Knowledge of laws, legal codes, court procedures, precedents, government regulations, executive orders, agency rules, and the democratic political process. **Communications and Media:** Knowledge of media production, communication, and dissemination techniques and methods including alternative ways to inform and entertain via written, oral, and visual media. **Transportation:** Knowledge of principles and methods for moving people or goods by air, rail, sea, or road, including their relative costs, advantages, and limitations.

VETERINARIANS AND VETERINARY INSPECTORS

Veterinary Pathologists

Education		First professional degree
Average Yearly Earnings		$52,936
Projected Growth		23%
Annual Job Openings		2,381
Self-employed		35%
Employed Part-time		11%

Study nature, cause, and development of animal diseases; form and structure of animals; or drugs related to veterinary medicine. Performs biopsies, and tests and analyzes body tissue and fluids to diagnose presence, source, and stage of disease in animals. Investigates efficiency of vaccines, antigens, antibiotics, and other materials in prevention, diagnosis, and cure of animal diseases. Studies drugs, including material medical and therapeutics, as related to veterinary medicine. Conducts research on animal parasites in domestic animals to determine control and preventive measures, utilizing chemicals, heat, electricity, and methods. Studies factors influencing existence and spread of diseases among humans and animals, particularly those diseases transmissible from animals to humans. Conducts further research to expand scope of findings, or recommends treatment to consulting veterinary personnel. Identifies laboratory cultures of microorganisms taken from diseased animals by microscopic examination and bacteriological tests. Tests virulence of pathogenic organisms by observing effects of inoculations on laboratory and other animals. Studies form and structure of animals, both gross and microscopic. Studies function and mechanism of systems and organs in healthy and diseased animals. Prepares laboratory cultures of microorganisms taken from body fluids and tissues of diseased animals for additional study. Directs activities of veterinary pathology department in educational institution or industrial establishment.

Occupational Type

Investigative occupations frequently involve working with ideas, and require an extensive amount of thinking. These occupations can involve searching for facts and figuring out problems mentally.

Skills required of Veterinary Pathologists

Reading Comprehension, Active Listening, Writing, Speaking, Mathematics, Science, Critical Thinking, Active Learning, Learning Strategies, Monitoring, Coordination, Persuasion, Instructing, Problem Identification, Information Gathering, Information Organization, Synthesis/Reorganization, Idea Generation, Idea Evaluation, Implementation Planning,

Equipment Selection, Programming, Testing, Product Inspection, Visioning, Systems Perception, Identifying Downstream Consequences, Identification of Key Causes, Judgment and Decision Making, Systems Evaluation, Time Management, Management of Material Resources, Management of Personnel Resources

College Majors

Veterinary Medicine (D.V.M.): An instructional program that prepares individuals for the independent professional practice of veterinary medicine. Includes instruction in the principles and procedures used in the observation, diagnosis, care and treatment of illness, disease, injury, deformity, or other anomalies in animals; ethics and professional standards; and supervised clinical practice.

Supporting Courses

Administration and Management: Knowledge of principles and processes involved in business and organizational planning, coordination, and execution. This includes strategic planning, resource allocation, manpower modeling, leadership techniques, and production methods. **Food Production:** Knowledge of techniques and equipment for planting, growing, and harvesting of food for consumption including crop rotation methods, animal husbandry, and food storage/handling techniques. **Mathematics:** Knowledge of numbers, their operations, and interrelationships including arithmetic, algebra, geometry, calculus, statistics, and their applications. **Chemistry:** Knowledge of the composition, structure, and properties of substances and of the chemical processes and transformations that they undergo. This includes uses of chemicals and their interactions, danger signs, production techniques, and disposal methods. **Biology:** Knowledge of plant and animal living tissue, cells, organisms, and entities, including their functions, interdependencies, and interactions with each other and the environment. **Medicine and Dentistry:** Knowledge of the information and techniques needed to diagnose and treat injuries, diseases, and deformities. This includes symptoms, treatment alternatives, drug properties and interactions, and preventive healthcare measures. **Therapy and Counseling:** Knowledge of information and techniques needed to rehabilitate physical and mental ailments and to provide career guidance including alternative treatments, rehabilitation equipment and its proper use, and methods to evaluate treatment effects. **Education and Training:** Knowledge of instructional methods and training techniques including curriculum design principles, learning theory, group and individual teaching techniques, design of individual development plans, and test design principles. **English Language:** Knowledge of the structure and content of the English language including the meaning and spelling of words, rules of composition, and grammar. **Philosophy and Theology:** Knowledge of different philosophical systems and religions, including their basic principles, values, ethics, ways of thinking, customs, and practices, and their impact on human culture. **Public Safety and Security:** Knowledge of weaponry, public safety, and security operations, rules, regulations, precautions, prevention, and the protection of people, data, and property.

Veterinarians

Diagnose and treat medical problems in animals. (Excludes veterinary inspectors and veterinary pathologists.) Examines animal to determine nature of disease or injury, and treats animal surgically or medically. Inspects and tests horses, sheep, poultry flocks, and other animals for diseases, and inoculates animals against various diseases, including rabies. Examines laboratory animals to detect indications of disease or injury, and treats animals to prevent spread of disease. Conducts postmortem studies and analyzes results to determine cause of death. Establishes and conducts quarantine and testing procedures for incoming animals to prevent spread of disease and compliance with governmental regulations. Inspects housing and advises animal owners regarding sanitary measures, feeding, and general care to promote health of animals. Consults with veterinarians in general practice seeking advice in treatment of exotic animals. Participates in research projects, plans procedures, and selects animals for scientific research based on knowledge of species and research principles. Ensures compliance with regulations governing humane and ethical treatment of animals used in scientific research. Oversees activities concerned with feeding, care, and maintenance of animal quarters to ensure compliance with laboratory regulations. Participates in planning and executing nutrition and reproduction programs for animals, particularly animals on endangered species list. Trains zoo personnel in handling and care of animals. Exchanges information with zoos and aquariums concerning care, transfer, sale, or trade of animals to maintain all-species nationwide inventory. Teaches or conducts research in universities or in commercial setting.

Occupational Type

Investigative occupations frequently involve working with ideas, and require an extensive amount of thinking. These occupations can involve searching for facts and figuring out problems mentally.

Skills required of Veterinarians

Reading Comprehension, Active Listening, Writing, Speaking, Mathematics, Science, Critical Thinking, Active Learning, Learning Strategies, Monitoring, Social Perceptiveness, Coordination, Persuasion, Negotiation, Instructing, Problem Identification, Information Gathering, Information Organization, Synthesis/Reorganization, Idea Generation, Idea Evaluation, Implementation Planning, Operations Analysis, Equipment Selection, Testing, Visioning, Systems Perception, Identifying Downstream Consequences, Identification of Key Causes, Judgment and Decision Making, Systems Evaluation, Time Management, Management of Material Resources, Management of Personnel Resources

College Majors

Veterinary Medicine (D.V.M.): An instructional program that prepares individuals for the independent professional practice of veterinary medicine. Includes instruction in the principles and procedures used in the observation, diagnosis, care and treatment of illness, disease, injury, deformity, or other anomalies in animals; ethics and professional standards; and supervised clinical practice.

Supporting Courses

Mathematics: Knowledge of numbers, their operations, and interrelationships including arithmetic, algebra, geometry, calculus, statistics, and their applications. **Chemistry:** Knowledge of the composition, structure, and properties of substances and of the chemical processes and transformations that they undergo. This includes uses of chemicals and their interactions, danger signs, production techniques, and disposal methods. **Biology:** Knowledge of plant and animal living tissue, cells, organisms, and entities, including their functions, interdependencies, and interactions with each other and the environment. **Psychology:** Knowledge of human behavior and performance, mental processes, psychological research methods, and the assessment and treatment of behavioral and affective disorders. **Medicine and Dentistry:** Knowledge of the information and techniques needed to diagnose and treat injuries, diseases, and deformities. This includes symptoms, treatment alternatives, drug properties and interactions, and preventive healthcare measures. **Therapy and Counseling:** Knowledge of information and techniques needed to rehabilitate physical and mental ailments and to provide career guidance including alternative treatments, rehabilitation equipment and its proper use, and methods to evaluate treatment effects. **Education and Training:** Knowledge of instructional methods and training techniques including curriculum design principles, learning theory, group and individual teaching techniques, design of individual development plans, and test design principles. **English Language:** Knowledge of the structure and content of the English language including the meaning and spelling of words, rules of composition, and grammar. **Philosophy and Theology:** Knowledge of different philosophical systems and religions, including their basic principles, values, ethics, ways of thinking, customs, and practices, and their impact on human culture. **Public Safety and Security:** Knowledge of weaponry, public safety, and security operations, rules, regulations, precautions, prevention, and the protection of people, data, and property.

Veterinary Inspectors

Inspect animals for presence of disease in facilities such as laboratories, livestock sites, and livestock slaughter or meat-processing facilities. Examines animals used in production process to determine presence of disease. Examines animal and carcass before and after slaughtering to detect evidence of disease or other abnormal conditions. Tests animals and submits specimens of tissue and other parts for laboratory analysis. Inspects processing areas where livestock and poultry are slaughtered and processed to ensure compliance with governmental standards. Reports existence of disease conditions to state and Federal authorities. Inspects facilities engaged in processing milk and milk products to ensure compliance with governmental standards. Inspects facilities where serums and other products used in treatment of animals are manufactured to ensure governmental standards are maintained. Institutes and enforces quarantine or other regulations governing import, export, and interstate movement of livestock. Determines that ingredients used in processing and marketing meat and meat products comply with governmental standards of purity and grading. Advises livestock owners of economic aspects of disease eradication. Advises consumers and public health officials of implications of diseases transmissible from animals to humans.

Occupational Type

Investigative occupations frequently involve working with ideas, and require an extensive amount of thinking. These occupations can involve searching for facts and figuring out problems mentally.

Skills required of Veterinary Inspectors

Reading Comprehension, Active Listening, Writing, Speaking, Science, Critical Thinking, Active Learning, Learning Strategies, Monitoring, Persuasion, Problem Identification, Information Gathering, Information Organization, Synthesis/Reorganization, Idea Generation, Idea Evaluation, Implementation Planning, Testing, Product Inspection, Visioning, Systems Perception, Identifying Downstream Consequences, Identification of Key Causes, Judgment and Decision Making, Systems Evaluation, Time Management

College Majors

Veterinary Medicine (D.V.M.): An instructional program that prepares individuals for the independent professional practice of veterinary medicine. Includes instruction in the principles and procedures used in the observation, diagnosis, care and treatment of illness, disease, injury, deformity, or other anomalies in animals; ethics and professional standards; and supervised clinical practice.

Supporting Courses

Economics and Accounting: Knowledge of economic and accounting principles and practices, the financial markets, banking, and the analysis and reporting of financial data. **Production and Processing:** Knowledge of inputs, outputs, raw materials, waste, quality control, costs, and techniques for maximizing the manufacture and distribution of goods. **Food Production:** Knowledge of techniques and equipment for planting, growing, and harvesting of food for consumption including crop rotation methods, animal husbandry, and food storage/handling techniques. **Chemistry:** Knowledge of the composition, structure, and properties of substances and of the chemical processes and transformations that they undergo. This includes uses of chemicals and their interactions, danger signs, production techniques, and disposal methods. **Biology:** Knowledge of plant and animal living tissue, cells, organisms, and entities, including their functions, interdependencies, and interactions with each other and the environment. **Geography:** Knowledge of various methods for describing the location and distribution of land, sea, and air masses including their physical locations, relationships, and characteristics. **Medicine and Dentistry:** Knowledge of the information and techniques needed to diagnose and treat injuries, diseases, and deformities. This includes symptoms, treatment alternatives, drug properties and interactions, and preventive healthcare measures. **English Language:** Knowledge of the structure and content of the English language including the meaning and spelling of words, rules of composition, and grammar. **Philosophy and Theology:** Knowledge of different philosophical systems and religions, including their basic principles, values, ethics, ways of thinking, customs, and practices, and their impact on human culture. **Public Safety and Security:** Knowledge of weaponry, public safety, and security operations, rules, regulations, precautions, prevention, and the protection of people, data, and property. **Law, Government, and Jurisprudence:** Knowledge of laws, legal codes, court procedures, precedents, government regulations, executive orders, agency rules, and the democratic political process.

WHOLESALE AND RETAIL BUYERS

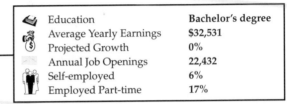

	Education	Bachelor's degree
	Average Yearly Earnings	$32,531
	Projected Growth	0%
	Annual Job Openings	22,432
	Self-employed	6%
	Employed Part-time	17%

Wholesale and Retail Buyers, Except Farm Products

Buy merchandise or commodities (other than farm products) for resale to consumers at the wholesale or retail level, including both durable and nondurable goods. Analyze past buying trends, sales records, price, and quality of merchandise to determine value and yield. Select, order, and authorize payment for merchandise according to contractual agreements. May conduct meetings with sales personnel and introduce new products. Include assistant buyers. Selects and orders merchandise from suppliers, or purchases merchandise from other merchants. Obtains and analyzes information about customer needs and preferences. Consults with store or merchandise managers about budget and goods to be purchased. Confers with assistant buyers and sales clerks to determine likes and dislikes of customers. Analyzes sales records to determine what goods are in demand. Examines and selects merchandise at local and remote sites. Inspects, grades, or approves merchandise or products to determine value or yield. Conducts staff meetings with sales personnel to introduce new merchandise. Authorizes payment of invoices or return of merchandise. Sets or recommends mark-up rates and selling prices. Arranges for transportation of purchases. Determines mark-downs on slow-selling merchandise. Trains sales personnel and/or assistant buyers. Provides clerks with information, such as price, mark-ups or mark-downs, manufacturer number, season code, and style number, to print on price tags. Approves advertising materials.

Occupational Type

Enterprising occupations frequently involve starting up and carrying out projects. These occupations can involve leading people and making many decisions. Sometimes they involve risk taking and often deal with business.

Skills required of Wholesale and Retail Buyers, Except Farm Products

Active Listening, Speaking, Active Learning, Monitoring, Social Perceptiveness, Persuasion, Negotiation, Instructing, Service Orientation, Information Gathering, Idea

Evaluation, Implementation Planning, Operations Analysis, Product Inspection, Systems Perception, Identification of Key Causes, Management of Financial Resources, Management of Material Resources, Management of Personnel Resources

College Majors

Agricultural Supplies Retailing and Wholesaling: An instructional program that generally prepares individuals to sell supplies for agricultural production, provide agricultural services and purchase and market agricultural products.

Supporting Courses

Administration and Management: Knowledge of principles and processes involved in business and organizational planning, coordination, and execution. This includes strategic planning, resource allocation, manpower modeling, leadership techniques, and production methods. **Economics and Accounting:** Knowledge of economic and accounting principles and practices, the financial markets, banking, and the analysis and reporting of financial data. **Sales and Marketing:** Knowledge of principles and methods involved in showing, promoting, and selling products or services. This includes marketing strategies and tactics, product demonstration and sales techniques, and sales control systems. **Customer and Personal Service:** Knowledge of principles and processes for providing customer and personal services including needs assessment techniques, quality service standards, alternative delivery systems, and customer satisfaction evaluation techniques. **Personnel and Human Resources:** Knowledge of policies and practices involved in personnel/human resource functions. This includes recruitment, selection, training, and promotion regulations and procedures; compensation and benefits packages; labor relations and negotiation strategies; and personnel information systems. **Mathematics:** Knowledge of numbers, their operations, and interrelationships including arithmetic, algebra, geometry, calculus, statistics, and their applications. **Psychology:** Knowledge of human behavior and performance, mental processes, psychological research methods, and the assessment and treatment of behavioral and affective disorders. **Sociology and Anthropology:** Knowledge of group behavior and dynamics, societal trends and influences, cultures, their history, migrations, ethnicity, and origins. **Geography:** Knowledge of various methods for describing the location and distribution of land, sea, and air masses including their physical locations, relationships, and characteristics. **Education and Training:** Knowledge of instructional methods and training techniques including curriculum design principles, learning theory, group and individual teaching techniques, design of individual development plans, and test design principles. **Foreign Language:** Knowledge of the structure and content of a foreign (non-English) language including the meaning and spelling of words, rules of composition and grammar, and pronunciation. **Philosophy and Theology:** Knowledge of different philosophical systems and religions, including their basic principles, values, ethics, ways of thinking, customs, and practices, and their impact on human culture. **Communications and Media:** Knowledge of media production, communication, and dissemination techniques and methods including alternative ways to inform and entertain via written, oral, and visual media. **Transportation:** Knowledge of principles and methods for moving people or goods by air, rail, sea, or road, including their relative costs, advantages, and limitations.

WRITERS AND EDITORS

📎	Education	Bachelor's degree
💰	Average Yearly Earnings	$38,355
💲	Projected Growth	21%
📈	Annual Job Openings	41,449
👥	Self-employed	31%
🧍	Employed Part-time	19%

Columnists, Critics, and Commentators

Write commentaries or critical reviews based on analysis of news items or literary, musical, or artistic works and performances. Analyzes and interprets news, current issues, and personal experiences to formulate ideas and other materials for column or commentary. Analyzes factors such as theme, expression, and technique, and forms critical opinions of literary, musical, dramatic, or visual art works and performances. Writes column, editorial, commentary, or review to stimulate or influence public opinion. Gathers information and develops perspective through research, interview, experience, and attendance at political, news, sports, artistic, social, and other functions. Revises text to meet editorial approval or to fit time or space requirements. Selects and organizes material pertinent to presentation into appropriate media form and format. Enters information into computer to prepare commentary or review. Discusses issues with editor of publication or broadcast facility editorial board to establish priorities and positions. Presents commentary live or in recorded form when working in broadcast medium.

Occupational Type

Artistic occupations frequently involve working with forms, designs, and patterns. They often require self-expression and the work can be done without following a clear set of rules.

Skills required of Columnists, Critics, and Commentators

Reading Comprehension, Writing, Speaking, Critical Thinking, Active Learning, Persuasion, Information Gathering, Synthesis/Reorganization, Idea Generation, Idea Evaluation, Visioning

College Majors

Journalism: An instructional program that describes the methods and techniques for gathering, processing and delivering news, and that prepares individuals to be professional print journalists. Includes instruction in news writing and editing, reporting, journalism law and policy, professional standards and ethics, and journalism history and research.

Supporting Courses

Computers and Electronics: Knowledge of electric circuit boards, processors, chips, and computer hardware and software, including applications and programming. **English Language:** Knowledge of the structure and content of the English language including the meaning and spelling of words, rules of composition, and grammar. **Fine Arts:** Knowledge of theory and techniques required to produce, compose, and perform works of music, dance, visual arts, drama, and sculpture. **Communications and Media:** Knowledge of media production, communication, and dissemination techniques and methods including alternative ways to inform and entertain via written, oral, and visual media.

Poets and Lyricists

Write poetry or song lyrics for publication or performance. Writes words to fit musical compositions, including lyrics for operas, musical plays, and choral works. Writes narrative, dramatic, lyric, or other types of poetry for publication. Adapts text to accommodate musical requirements of composer and singer. Chooses subject matter and suitable form to express personal feeling and experience or ideas or to narrate story or event.

 ### Occupational Type

Artistic occupations frequently involve working with forms, designs, and patterns. They often require self-expression and the work can be done without following a clear set of rules.

 ### Skills required of Poets and Lyricists

Writing

 ### College Majors

English Creative Writing: An instructional program that describes the process and techniques of original composition in various literary forms such as the short story, poetry, the novel, and others. Includes instruction in technical and editorial skills, criticism, and the marketing of finished manuscripts.

 ### Supporting Courses

English Language: Knowledge of the structure and content of the English language including the meaning and spelling of words, rules of composition, and grammar. **Fine Arts:** Knowledge of theory and techniques required to produce, compose, and perform works of music, dance, visual arts, drama, and sculpture. **Communications and Media:** Knowledge of media production, communication, and dissemination techniques and methods including alternative ways to inform and entertain via written, oral, and visual media.

Creative Writers

Create original written works, such as plays or prose, for publication or performance. Writes fiction or nonfiction prose work, such as short story, novel, biography, article, descriptive or critical analysis, or essay. Writes play or script for moving pictures or television, based on original ideas or adapted from fictional, historical, or narrative sources. Writes humorous material for publication or performance, such as comedy routines, gags, comedy shows, or scripts for entertainers. Organizes material for project, plans arrangement or outline, and writes synopsis. Develops factors, such as theme, plot, characterization, psychological analysis, historical environment, action, and dialogue, to create material. Selects subject or theme for writing project based on personal interest and writing specialty, or on assignment from publisher, client, producer, or director. Reviews, submits for approval, and revises written material to meet personal standards and satisfy needs of client, publisher, director, or producer. Conducts research to obtain factual information and authentic detail, utilizing sources such as newspaper accounts, diaries, and interviews. Confers with client, publisher, or producer to discuss development changes or revisions. Collaborates with other writers on specific projects.

Occupational Type

Artistic occupations frequently involve working with forms, designs, and patterns. They often require self-expression and the work can be done without following a clear set of rules.

Skills required of Creative Writers

Reading Comprehension, Writing, Critical Thinking, Coordination, Idea Generation, Idea Evaluation

College Majors

Journalism: An instructional program that describes the methods and techniques for gathering, processing and delivering news, and that prepares individuals to be professional print journalists. Includes instruction in news writing and editing, reporting, journalism law and policy, professional standards and ethics, and journalism history and research.

Supporting Courses

Sociology and Anthropology: Knowledge of group behavior and dynamics, societal trends and influences, cultures, their history, migrations, ethnicity, and origins. **English Language:** Knowledge of the structure and content of the English language including the meaning and spelling of words, rules of composition, and grammar. **Fine Arts:** Knowledge of theory and techniques required to produce, compose, and perform works of music, dance, visual arts, drama, and sculpture. **Communications and Media:** Knowledge of media production, communication, and dissemination techniques and methods including alternative ways to inform and entertain via written, oral, and visual media.

Editors

Perform variety of editorial duties, such as laying out, indexing, and revising content of written materials in preparation for final publication. (Excludes managing editors, programming and script editors, book editors, and film editors.) Plans and prepares page layouts to position and space articles and photographs or illustrations. Reads and evaluates manuscripts or other materials submitted for publication, and confers with authors regarding changes or publication. Writes and rewrites headlines, captions, columns, articles, and stories to conform to publication's style, editorial policy, and publishing requirements. Determines placement of stories based on relative significance, available space, and knowledge of layout principles. Confers with management and editorial staff members regarding placement of developing news stories. Reads copy or proof to detect and correct errors in spelling, punctuation, and syntax, and indicates corrections, using standard proofreading and typesetting symbols. Selects and crops photographs and illustrative materials to conform to space and subject matter requirements. Reviews and approves proofs submitted by composing room. Reads material to determine items to be included in index of book or other publication. Arranges topical or alphabetical list of index items, according to page or chapter, indicating location of item in text. Verifies facts, dates, and statistics, using standard reference sources. Compiles index cross-references and related items, such as glossaries, bibliographies, and footnotes. Selects local, state, national, and international news items received by wire from press associations.

Occupational Type

Artistic occupations frequently involve working with forms, designs, and patterns. They often require self-expression and the work can be done without following a clear set of rules.

Skills required of Editors

Reading Comprehension, Writing, Persuasion, Product Inspection

College Majors

Journalism: An instructional program that describes the methods and techniques for gathering, processing and delivering news, and that prepares individuals to be professional print journalists. Includes instruction in news writing and editing, reporting, journalism law and policy, professional standards and ethics, and journalism history and research.

Supporting Courses

English Language: Knowledge of the structure and content of the English language including the meaning and spelling of words, rules of composition, and grammar. **Communications and Media:** Knowledge of media production, communication, and dissemination techniques and methods including alternative ways to inform and entertain via written, oral, and visual media.

Managing Editors

Direct and coordinate editorial operations of newspaper, newspaper department, or magazine. Include workers who formulate editorial policy. Formulates editorial and publication policies in consultation and negotiation with owner's representative, executives, editorial policy committee, and department heads. Directs and coordinates editorial departments and activities of personnel engaged in selecting, gathering, and editing news and photography for radio, television station, or print. Assigns research, writing, and editorial duties to staff members and reviews work products. Confers with management and staff to relay information, develop operating procedures and schedules, allocate space or time, and solve problems. Originates or approves story ideas or themes, sets priorities, and assigns coverage to members of reporting and photography staff. Directs page make-up of publication, organizes material, plans page layouts, and selects type. Edits copy or reviews edited copy to ensure that writing meets establishment standards and slanderous, libelous, and profane statements are avoided. Reviews final proofs, approves or makes changes, and performs other editorial duties. Coordinates and tracks assignments, using computer and two-way radio. Writes leading or policy editorials, headlines, articles, and other materials. Reads and selects submitted material, such as letters and articles, for publication. Secures graphic material from picture sources and assigns artists and photographers to produce pictures, illustrations, and cartoons. Interviews individuals and attends gatherings to obtain items for publication, verify facts, and clarify information. Represents organization at professional and community functions and maintains contact with outside agencies. Performs personnel-related activities, such as hiring, reviewing work, and terminating employment.

Occupational Type

Enterprising occupations frequently involve starting up and carrying out projects. These occupations can involve leading people and making many decisions. Sometimes they involve risk taking and often deal with business.

Skills required of Managing Editors

Reading Comprehension, Active Listening, Writing, Speaking, Critical Thinking, Active Learning, Learning Strategies, Monitoring, Social Perceptiveness, Coordination, Negotiation, Instructing, Problem Identification, Information Gathering, Information Organization, Synthesis/Reorganization, Idea Evaluation, Programming, Visioning, Judgment and Decision Making, Systems Evaluation, Time Management, Management of Material Resources, Management of Personnel Resources

College Majors

Journalism: An instructional program that describes the methods and techniques for gathering, processing and delivering news, and that prepares individuals to be professional print journalists. Includes instruction in news writing and editing, reporting, journalism law and policy, professional standards and ethics, and journalism history and research.

Supporting Courses

Administration and Management: Knowledge of principles and processes involved in business and organizational planning, coordination, and execution. This includes strategic planning, resource allocation, manpower modeling, leadership techniques, and production methods. **Personnel and Human Resources:** Knowledge of policies and practices involved in personnel/human resource functions. This includes recruitment, selection, training, and promotion regulations and procedures; compensation and benefits packages; labor relations and negotiation strategies; and personnel information systems. **Computers and Electronics:** Knowledge of electric circuit boards, processors, chips, and computer hardware and software, including applications and programming. **English Language:** Knowledge of the structure and content of the English language including the meaning and spelling of words, rules of composition, and grammar. **Communications and Media:** Knowledge of media production, communication, and dissemination techniques and methods including alternative ways to inform and entertain via written, oral, and visual media.

Programming and Script Editors and Coordinators

Direct and coordinate activities of workers who prepare scripts for radio, television, or motion picture productions. Include workers who develop, write, and edit proposals for new radio or television programs. Reviews writers' work and gives instruction and direction regarding changes, additions, and corrections. Hires, assigns work to, and supervises staff and freelance writers or other employees. Writes or edits proposals for original program concepts, and submits proposals for review by programming, financial, and other departmental personnel. Evaluates stories, proposals, or other materials to determine potential and feasibility of development into scripts or programs. Reads and evaluates written material to select writers and stories for radio, television, or motion picture production. Edits material to ensure conformance with company policy and standards, copyright laws, and Federal regulations. Rewrites, combines, and polishes draft scripts, as necessary, to prepare scripts for production. Participates in selection of researchers, consultants, producers, and on-air personalities to facilitate development of program ideas. Maintains liaison between program production department and proposal originators to ensure timely exchange of information regarding project. Recommends purchasing material for use in developing scripts, in consultation with production head. Authorizes budget preparation for final proposals.

 ## Occupational Type

Artistic occupations frequently involve working with forms, designs, and patterns. They often require self-expression and the work can be done without following a clear set of rules.

 ## Skills required of Programming and Script Editors and Coordinators

Reading Comprehension, Writing, Critical Thinking, Active Learning, Learning Strategies, Coordination, Persuasion, Negotiation, Idea Generation, Idea Evaluation, Management of Financial Resources, Management of Personnel Resources

College Majors

Broadcast Journalism: An instructional program that describes the methods and techniques by which radio and television news programs are produced and delivered, and that prepares individuals to be professional broadcast journalists. Includes instruction in principles of broadcast technology; program design and production; broadcast editing; on- and off-camera procedures and techniques; and broadcast media law and policy.

Supporting Courses

Administration and Management: Knowledge of principles and processes involved in business and organizational planning, coordination, and execution. This includes strategic planning, resource allocation, manpower modeling, leadership techniques, and production methods. **Economics and Accounting:** Knowledge of economic and accounting principles and practices, the financial markets, banking, and the analysis and reporting of financial data. **Personnel and Human Resources:** Knowledge of policies and practices involved in personnel/human resource functions. This includes recruitment, selection, training, and promotion regulations and procedures; compensation and benefits packages; labor relations and negotiation strategies; and personnel information systems. **English Language:** Knowledge of the structure and content of the English language including the meaning and spelling of words, rules of composition, and grammar. **Fine Arts:** Knowledge of theory and techniques required to produce, compose, and perform works of music, dance, visual arts, drama, and sculpture. **Communications and Media:** Knowledge of media production, communication, and dissemination techniques and methods including alternative ways to inform and entertain via written, oral, and visual media.

Book Editors

Secure, select, and coordinate publication of manuscripts in book form. Confers with author and publisher to arrange purchase and details such as publication date, royalties, and quantity to be printed. Coordinates book design and production activities. Makes recommendations regarding procurement and revision of manuscript. Contracts design and production or personally designs and produces book. Reviews submitted book manuscript and determines market demand based on consumer trends and personal knowledge. Assigns and supervises editorial staff work activities.

Occupational Type

Artistic occupations frequently involve working with forms, designs, and patterns. They often require self-expression and the work can be done without following a clear set of rules.

Skills required of Book Editors

Reading Comprehension, Writing, Coordination, Persuasion, Negotiation, Idea Evaluation, Operations Analysis, Judgment and Decision Making, Management of Personnel Resources

College Majors

English Creative Writing: An instructional program that describes the process and techniques of original composition in various literary forms such as the short story, poetry, the novel, and others. Includes instruction in technical and editorial skills, criticism, and the marketing of finished manuscripts.

Supporting Courses

Administration and Management: Knowledge of principles and processes involved in business and organizational planning, coordination, and execution. This includes strategic planning, resource allocation, manpower modeling, leadership techniques, and production methods. **Sales and Marketing:** Knowledge of principles and methods involved in showing, promoting, and selling products or services. This includes marketing strategies and tactics, product demonstration and sales techniques, and sales control systems. **English Language:** Knowledge of the structure and content of the English language including the meaning and spelling of words, rules of composition, and grammar. **Communications and Media:** Knowledge of media production, communication, and dissemination techniques and methods including alternative ways to inform and entertain via written, oral, and visual media.

Readers

Read books, plays, or scripts to prepare synopses for review by editorial staff or to recommend content revisions. Reads novels, stories, and plays and prepares synopses for review by editorial department or film, radio, or television producer. Recommends revisions to or disallows broadcast of materials violating Federal regulations or station standards. Reads and listens to material to be broadcast on radio or television to detect vulgar, libelous, or misleading statements. Prepares recommended editorial revisions in script, using computer or typewriter. Suggests possible treatment of selected materials in film or program. Confers with sales or advertising agency personnel to report on revised or disallowed commercials.

 Occupational Type

Artistic occupations frequently involve working with forms, designs, and patterns. They often require self-expression and the work can be done without following a clear set of rules.

 Skills required of Readers

Reading Comprehension, Writing, Critical Thinking, Active Learning, Idea Evaluation

 College Majors

Broadcast Journalism: An instructional program that describes the methods and techniques by which radio and television news programs are produced and delivered, and that prepares individuals to be professional broadcast journalists. Includes instruction in principles of broadcast technology; program design and production; broadcast editing; on- and off-camera procedures and techniques; and broadcast media law and policy.

 Supporting Courses

English Language: Knowledge of the structure and content of the English language including the meaning and spelling of words, rules of composition, and grammar. **Communications and Media:** Knowledge of media production, communication, and dissemination techniques and methods including alternative ways to inform and entertain via written, oral, and visual media.

Caption Writers

Write caption phrases of dialogue for hearing-impaired and foreign-language-speaking viewers of movie or television productions. Writes captions to describe music and background noises. Watches production and reviews captions simultaneously to determine which caption phrases require editing. Translates foreign-language dialogue into English-language captions or English dialogue into foreign-language captions. Enters commands to synchronize captions with dialogue and place on the screen. Operates computerized captioning system for movies or television productions for hearing-impaired and foreign-language speaking viewers. Edits translations for correctness of grammar, punctuation, and clarity of expression. Oversees encoding of captions to master tape of television production. Discusses captions with directors or producers of movie and television productions.

Occupational Type

Artistic occupations frequently involve working with forms, designs, and patterns. They often require self-expression and the work can be done without following a clear set of rules.

Skills required of Caption Writers

Writing

College Majors

Foreign Languages and Literatures, General: An instructional program that describes an undifferentiated program in foreign languages and literatures.

Supporting Courses

Computers and Electronics: Knowledge of electric circuit boards, processors, chips, and computer hardware and software, including applications and programming. **English Language:** Knowledge of the structure and content of the English language including the meaning and spelling of words, rules of composition, and grammar. **Foreign Language:** Knowledge of the structure and content of a foreign (non-English) language including the meaning and spelling of words, rules of composition and grammar, and pronunciation. **Communications and Media:** Knowledge of media production, communication, and dissemination techniques and methods including alternative ways to inform and entertain via written, oral, and visual media.

Copy Writers

Write advertising copy for use by publication or broadcast media to promote sale of goods and services. Writes advertising copy for use by publication or broadcast media and revises copy according to supervisor's instructions. Writes articles, bulletins, sales letters, speeches, and other related informative and promotional material. Prepares advertising copy, using computer. Consults with sales media and marketing representatives to obtain information on product or service and discuss style and length of advertising copy. Obtains additional background and current development information through research and interviews. Reviews advertising trends, consumer surveys, and other data regarding marketing of goods and services to formulate approach.

Occupational Type

Artistic occupations frequently involve working with forms, designs, and patterns. They often require self-expression and the work can be done without following a clear set of rules.

Skills required of Copy Writers

Reading Comprehension, Writing, Active Learning, Social Perceptiveness, Persuasion, Idea Generation, Idea Evaluation, Programming

College Majors

Advertising: An instructional program that describes the creation, execution, transmission, and evaluation of commercial messages concerned with the promotion and sale of products and services, and that prepares individuals to function as advertising assistants, technicians, managers and executives. Includes instruction in advertising theory; marketing strategy; advertising copy/art, layout and production methods; and media relations.

Supporting Courses

Sales and Marketing: Knowledge of principles and methods involved in showing, promoting, and selling products or services. This includes marketing strategies and tactics, product demonstration and sales techniques, and sales control systems. **Computers and Electronics:** Knowledge of electric circuit boards, processors, chips, and computer hardware and software, including applications and programming. **English Language:** Knowledge of the structure and content of the English language including the meaning and spelling of words, rules of composition, and grammar. **Communications and Media:** Knowledge of media production, communication, and dissemination techniques and methods including alternative ways to inform and entertain via written, oral, and visual media.

Dictionary Editors

Research information about words, and write and review definitions for publication in dictionary. Conducts or directs research to discover origin, spelling, syllabication, pronunciation, meaning, and usage of words. Organizes research material and writes definitions for general or specialized dictionary. Studies frequency of use for specific words and other factors to select words for inclusion in dictionary. Edits and reviews definitions written by other staff prior to publication. Selects drawings or other graphic material to illustrate word meaning.

Occupational Type

Investigative occupations frequently involve working with ideas, and require an extensive amount of thinking. These occupations can involve searching for facts and figuring out problems mentally.

Skills required of Dictionary Editors

Reading Comprehension, Writing, Information Gathering, Information Organization, Synthesis/Reorganization

College Majors

English Creative Writing: An instructional program that describes the process and techniques of original composition in various literary forms such as the short story, poetry, the novel, and others. Includes instruction in technical and editorial skills, criticism, and the marketing of finished manuscripts.

Supporting Courses

English Language: Knowledge of the structure and content of the English language including the meaning and spelling of words, rules of composition, and grammar.

Technical Writers

Write or edit technical materials, such as equipment manuals, appendices, and operating and maintenance instructions. May oversee preparation of illustrations, photographs, diagrams, and charts; and assist in layout work. Organizes material and completes writing assignment according to set standards regarding order, clarity, conciseness, style, and terminology. Writes speeches, articles, and public or employee relations releases. Studies drawings, specifications, mock-ups, and product samples to integrate and delineate technology, operating procedure, and production sequence and detail. Reviews published materials and recommends revisions or changes in scope, format, content, and methods of reproduction and binding. Assists in laying out material for publication. Interviews production and engineering personnel and reads journals and other material to become familiar with product technologies and production methods. Reviews manufacturer's and trade catalogs, drawings, and other data relative to operation, maintenance, and service of equipment. Edits, standardizes, or makes changes to material prepared by other writers or establishment personnel. Analyzes developments in specific field to determine need for revisions in previously published materials and development of new material. Observes production, developmental, and experimental activities to determine operating procedure and detail. Selects photographs, drawings, sketches, diagrams, and charts to illustrate material. Maintains records and files of work and revisions. Draws sketches to illustrate specified materials or assembly sequence. Arranges for typing, duplication, and distribution of material. Assigns work to other writers and oversees and edits their work.

Occupational Type

Artistic occupations frequently involve working with forms, designs, and patterns. They often require self-expression and the work can be done without following a clear set of rules.

 Skills required of Technical Writers

Reading Comprehension, Active Listening, Writing, Speaking, Critical Thinking, Active Learning, Learning Strategies, Monitoring, Coordination, Instructing, Information Gathering, Information Organization, Synthesis/Reorganization, Idea Generation, Idea Evaluation, Implementation Planning, Operations Analysis, Product Inspection, Visioning, Systems Perception, Identification of Key Causes, Judgment and Decision Making, Time Management, Management of Personnel Resources

 College Majors

English Creative Writing: An instructional program that describes the process and techniques of original composition in various literary forms such as the short story, poetry, the novel, and others. Includes instruction in technical and editorial skills, criticism, and the marketing of finished manuscripts.

 Supporting Courses

Administration and Management: Knowledge of principles and processes involved in business and organizational planning, coordination, and execution. This includes strategic planning, resource allocation, manpower modeling, leadership techniques, and production methods. **Clerical:** Knowledge of administrative and clerical procedures and systems such as word processing systems, filing and records management systems, stenography and transcription, forms design principles, and other office procedures and terminology. **Computers and Electronics:** Knowledge of electric circuit boards, processors, chips, and computer hardware and software, including applications and programming. **Engineering and Technology:** Knowledge of equipment, tools, mechanical devices, and their uses to produce motion, light, power, technology, and other applications. **Design:** Knowledge of design techniques, principles, tools and instruments involved in the production and use of precision technical plans, blueprints, drawings, and models. **Sociology and Anthropology:** Knowledge of group behavior and dynamics, societal trends and influences, cultures, their history, migrations, ethnicity, and origins. **Education and Training:** Knowledge of instructional methods and training techniques including curriculum design principles, learning theory, group and individual teaching techniques, design of individual development plans, and test design principles. **English Language:** Knowledge of the structure and content of the English language including the meaning and spelling of words, rules of composition, and grammar. **Telecommunications:** Knowledge of transmission, broadcasting, switching, control, and operation of telecommunications systems. **Communications and Media:** Knowledge of media production, communication, and dissemination techniques and methods including alternative ways to inform and entertain via written, oral, and visual media.

Appendix

In each of the descriptions for the best jobs found in Section 2, we've included a listing of skills required for each job. In this table you'll find specific definitions of each skill. Use it as a key to gathering more information about the jobs that interest you.

Skill	Definition
Basic Skills	**Developed capacities that facilitate learning or the more rapid acquisition of knowledge**
Reading Comprehension	Understanding written sentences and paragraphs in work related documents
Active Listening	Listening to what other people are saying and asking questions as appropriate
Writing	Communicating effectively with others in writing as indicated by the needs of the audience
Speaking	Talking to others to effectively convey information
Mathematics	Using mathematics to solve problems
Science	Using scientific methods to solve problems
Process	Procedures that contribute to the more rapid acquisition of knowledge and skill across a variety of domains
Critical Thinking	Using logic and analysis to identify the strengths and weaknesses of different approaches
Active Learning	Working with new material or information to grasp its implications
Learning Strategies	Using multiple approaches when learning or teaching new things
Monitoring	Assessing how well one is doing when learning or doing something
Social Skills	**Developed capacities used to work with people to achieve goals**
Social Perceptiveness	Being aware of others' reactions and understanding why they react the way they do
Coordination	Adjusting actions in relation to others' actions
Persuasion	Persuading others to approach things differently
Negotiation	Bringing others together and trying to reconcile differences
Instructing	Teaching others how to do something
Service Orientation	Actively looking for ways to help people

continued

EXPLANATION OF SKILLS

Skill	Definition
Complex Problem Solving Skills	**Developed capacities used to solve novel, ill-defined problems in complex, real-world settings**
Problem Identification	Identifying the nature of problems
Information Gathering	Knowing how to find information and identifying essential information
Information Organization	Finding ways to structure or classify multiple pieces of information
Synthesis/Reorganization	Reorganizing information to get a better approach to problems or tasks
Idea Generation	Generating a number of different approaches to problems
Idea Evaluation	Evaluating the likely success of an idea in relation to the demands of the situation
Implementation Planning	Developing approaches for implementing an idea
Solution Appraisal	Observing and evaluating the outcomes of a problem solution to identify lessons learned or redirect efforts
Technical Skills	**Developed capacities used to design, set-up, operate, and correct malfunctions involving application of machines or technological systems**
Operations Analysis	Analyzing needs and product requirements to create a design
Technology Design	Generating or adapting equipment and technology to serve user needs
Equipment Selection	Determining the kind of tools and equipment needed to do a job
Installation	Installing equipment, machines, wiring, or programs to meet specifications
Programming	Writing computer programs for various purposes
Testing	Conducting tests to determine whether equipment, software, or procedures are operating as expected
Operation Monitoring	Watching gauges, dials, or other indicators to make sure a machine is working properly
Operation and Control	Controlling operations of equipment or systems
Product Inspection	Inspecting and evaluating the quality of products
Equipment Maintenance	Performing routine maintenance and determining when and what kind of maintenance is needed
Troubleshooting	Determining what is causing an operating error and deciding what to do about it
Repairing	Repairing machines or systems using the needed tools

Skill	Definition
Systems Skills	**Developed capacities used to understand, monitor, and improve socio-technical systems**
Visioning	Developing an image of how a system should work under ideal conditions
Systems Perception	Determining when important changes have occurred in a system or are likely to occur
Identifying Downstream Consequences	Determining the long-term outcomes of a change in operations
Identification of Key Causes	Identifying the things that must be changed to achieve a goal
Judgment and Decision Making	Weighing the relative costs and benefits of a potential action
Systems Evaluation	Looking at many indicators of system performance, taking into account their accuracy
Resource Management Skills	**Developed capacities used to allocate resources efficiently**
Time Management	Managing one's own time and the time of others
Management of Financial Resources	Determining how money will be spent to get the work done, and accounting for these expenditures
Management of Material Resources	Obtaining and seeing to the appropriate use of equipment, facilities, and materials needed to do certain work
Management of Personnel Resources	Motivating, developing, and directing people as they work, identifying the best people for the job

Here Are Just Some of Our Products!

JIST publishes hundreds of books, videos, software products, and other items. Some of our best-selling career and educational reference books and software are presented here, followed by an order form. You can also order these books through any bookstore or Internet bookseller's site.

Check out JIST's Web site at www.jist.com for tables of contents and free chapters on these and other products.

Occupational Outlook Handbook, 2000-2001 Edition

U.S. Department of Labor

We will meet or beat ANY price on the OOH!

The *Occupational Outlook Handbook* is the most widely used career exploration re-source. This is a quality reprint of the government's *OOH,* only at a less-expensive price. It describes 250 jobs–jobs held by almost 90 percent of the U.S. workforce–making it ideal for students, counselors, teachers, librarians, and job seekers. Job descriptions cover the nature of the work, working conditions, training, job outlook, and earnings. Well-written narrative with many charts and photos. New edition every two years.

ISBN 1-56370-676-8 / Order Code LP-J6768 / **$18.95** Softcover
ISBN 1-56370-677-6 / Order Code LP-J6776 / **$22.95** Hardcover

*O*NET Dictionary of Occupational Titles,* Second Edition

Based on data from the U.S. Department of Labor
Compiled by J. Michael Farr and LaVerne L. Ludden, Ed.D.,
with database work by Laurence Shatkin, Ph.D.

JIST was the first publisher to use the Department of Labor's new O*NET data, which was developed to replace the *Dictionary of Occupational Titles.* This updated reference includes descriptions of all 1,000 jobs in the O*NET database and is the only printed source of this information!

ISBN 1-56370-845-0 /Order Code LP-J8450 / **$39.95** Softcover
ISBN 1-56370-846-9 / Order Code LP-J8469 / **$49.95** Hardcover

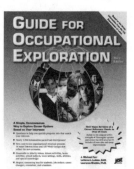

The Quick Resume & Cover Letter Book,

Second Edition

Write and Use an Effective Resume in Only One Day

J. Michael Farr

This unique book will help you write a solid resume in just a few hours and improve it later, in stages, as you have time. This edition features over 90 sample resumes from professional resume writers, plus notes on the resumes highlighting easy-to-imitate techniques. Special sections cover career planning, other correspondence, and the most effective job search techniques.

ISBN 1-56370-634-2 / Order Code LP-J6342
$14.95

America's Top Resumes for America's Top Jobs®

J. Michael Farr

The only book with sample resumes for all major occupations covering 85 percent of the workforce. Here you'll find nearly 400 of the best resumes submitted by professional resume writers, grouped by occupation, and annotated by the author to highlight their best features. Also includes career planning and job search advice.

ISBN 1-56370-288-6 / Order Code LP-J2886
$19.95

Gallery of Best Resumes, Second Edition

A Collection of Quality Resumes by Professional Resume Writers

David F. Noble, Ph.D.

Sample more than 200 great resumes with an expansive range of styles, formats, occupations, and situations—all arranged in easy-to-find groups and written by professional resume writers. You also get the author's 101 best resume tips on design, layout, writing style, and mistakes to avoid.

ISBN 1-56370-809-4 / Order Code LP-J8094
$18.95

Gallery of Best Cover Letters

A Collection of Quality Cover Letters by Professional Resume Writers

David F. Noble, Ph.D.

This new Gallery showcases 292 superior cover letters for a wide range of job seekers—from entry-level workers to senior staff members—in 38 occupational fields. Instructive comments point out distinctive situations, features, and strategies to help you focus your thinking about your own cover letters.

ISBN 1-56370-551-6 / Order Code LP-J5516
$18.95

Young Person's Occupational Outlook Handbook, Third Edition

Compiled by JIST Editors from U.S. government data

Based on the *Occupational Outlook Handbook,* this text is ideal for helping young people explore careers. This book covers almost 250 jobs—each on one page—held by 85 percent of the workforce. It clusters job descriptions, making it easy to explore job options based on interest. It also makes direct connections between school subjects and the skills needed for jobs.

ISBN 1-56370-731-4 / Order Code LP-J7314
$19.95

The College Majors Handbook

The Actual Jobs, Earnings, and Trends for Graduates of 60 College Majors

Neeta P. Fogg, Paul E. Harrington, and Thomas F. Harrington

Faced with the college decision? This book details what actually happened to more than 15,000 undergraduates from 60 college majors. This is the only college planning guide with the perspective of what actually happened to college undergraduates. It identifies jobs in which the graduates now work and their earnings on those jobs.

ISBN 1-56370-518-4 / Order Code LP-J5184
$24.95

The Kids' College Almanac, Second Edition

A First Look at College

Barbara C. Greenfield and Robert A. Weinstein

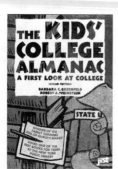

Selected by the New York Public Library as one of the best books for teens and preteens, it provides helpful information about going to college and encourages career and educational planning.

ISBN 1-56370-730-6 / Order Code LP-J7306
$16.95

Cover Letter Magic

Trade Secrets of Professional Resume Writers

Wendy S. Enelow and Louise Kursmark

Over 150 winning cover letters for every professional and situation, from blue-collar to senior management, as well as "before-and-after" transformations. Follow the steps to write, format, and distribute cover letters for maximum impact.

ISBN 1-56370-732-2 / Order Code LP-J7322
$16.95

America's Top White-Collar Jobs®, Fifth Edition

J. Michael Farr

Pinpoint top office, management, sales, and professional jobs with this up-to-date reference based on data from the *Occupational Outlook Handbook.* Job descriptions cover job responsibilities, working conditions, salary ranges, education and training needed, growth outlook, and more. Ideal for students and anyone considering white-collar fields. A special section helps you find a job fast!

ISBN 1-56370-719-5 / Order Code LP-J7195
$16.95

America's Top Military Careers, Third Edition

Based on information from the Department of Defense

This accurate, up-to-date reference helps people make the transition into and out of the armed forces. It describes military occupations, including information on working conditions, physical demands, advancement opportunities, duty locations, pay, benefits, and more. It also shows how military experience relates to civilian jobs. Ideal for those considering military careers; active military personnel developing long-term goals; former military personnel seeking civilian jobs; career counselors; and others.

ISBN 1-56370-706-3 / Order Code LP-J7063
$19.95

America's Top Medical, Education & Human Services Jobs®, Fifth Edition

J. Michael Farr

This is an indispensable reference for anyone interested in three large, fast-growing fields. It describes major medical, education, and human services jobs and includes details on skills needed, education and training required, growth opportunities, salary ranges, and more. Descriptions are based on the latest data from the *Occupational Outlook Handbook.* Extra sections cover the most effective job search techniques and industry trends.

ISBN 1-56370-721-7 / Order Code LP-J7217
$16.95

Health-Care Careers for the 21st Century

Dr. Saul Wischnitzer and Edith Wischnitzer

This three-in-one book is a career guidance manual, job description overview, and training program directory. It provides detailed descriptions of over 80 health-care careers, organized into five groups. It lists thousands of training programs with complete contact information. And it offers career guidance on everything from self-assessment to the interview process. Sample resumes and cover letters are included.

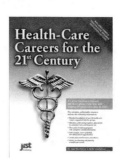

ISBN 1-56370-667-9 / Order Code LP-J6679
$24.95

JIST Ordering Information

JIST specializes in publishing the very best results-oriented career and self-directed job search material. Since 1981 we have been a leading publisher in career assessment devices, books, videos, and software. We continue to strive to make our materials the best there are, so that people can stay abreast of what's happening in the labor market, and so they can clarify and articulate their skills and experiences for themselves as well as for prospective employers. **Our products are widely available through your local bookstores, wholesalers, and distributors.**

The World Wide Web

For more occupational or book information, get online and see our Web site at **www.jist.com**. Advance information about new products, services, and training events is continually updated.

Quantity Discounts Available!

Quantity discounts are available for businesses, schools, and other organizations.

The JIST Guarantee

We want you to be happy with everything you buy from JIST. If you aren't satisfied with a product, return it to us within 30 days of purchase along with the reason for the return. Please include a copy of the packing list or invoice to guarantee quick credit to your order.

How to Order

For your convenience, the last page of this book contains an order form.

24-Hour Consumer Order Line:
Call toll free 1-800-648-JIST
Please have your credit card (VISA, MC, or AMEX) information ready!

Mail your order to:

JIST Publishing, Inc.
8902 Otis Avenue
Indianapolis, IN 46216-1033
Fax: Toll free 1-800-JIST-FAX

⸝ Order and Catalog Request Form

⸝ase Order #: _____ (Required by some organizations)

Billing Information

Organization Name: _____

Accounting Contact: _____

Street Address: _____

_____

_____

City, State, Zip: _____

Phone Number: ( ) _____

Shipping Information with Street Address (If Different from Above)

Organization Name: _____

Contact: _____

Street Address: (We *cannot* ship to P.O. boxes) _____

_____

_____

City, State, Zip: _____

Phone Number: ( ) _____

> Please copy this form if you
> need more lines for your order.

Phone: 1-800-648-JIST
Fax: 1-800-JIST-FAX
World Wide Web Address:
http://www.jist.com

Credit Card Purchases: VISA____ MC____ AMEX____

Card Number: _____

Exp. Date: _____

Name As on Card: _____

Signature: _____

Quantity	Order Code	Product Title	Unit Price	Total
	———	Free JIST Catalog	Free	———

jist Publishing

8902 Otis Avenue
Indianapolis, IN 46216

Shipping / Handling / Insurance Fees

In the continental U.S. add 7% of subtotal:
• Minimum amount charged = $4.00
• Maximum amount charged = $100.00
• FREE shipping and handling on any prepaid orders over $40.00
Above pricing is for regular ground shipment only. For rush or special delivery, call JIST Customer Service at 1-800-648-JIST for the correct shipping fee.

Outside the continental U.S. call JIST Customer Service at 1-800-648-JIST for an estimate of these fees.

Payment in U.S. funds only!

Subtotal	
+5% Sales Tax *Indiana Residents*	
+Shipping / Handling / Ins. (See left)	
TOTAL	

JIST thanks you for your order!